Alessandro Cipriani • Maurizio Giri

ELECTRONIC MUSIC AND SOUND DESIGN

Theory and Practice with Max and MSP - Volume 2

Cipriani, Alessandro. Giri, Maurizio.
Electronic Music and Sound Design : theory and practice with Max and MSP. Vol. 2.
/ Alessandro Cipriani, Maurizio Giri.
Includes bibliographical references and index.
ISBN 978-88-905484-4-4
1. Computer Music - Instruction and study. 2. Computer composition.

Original Title: Musica Elettronica e Sound Design - Teoria e Pratica con Max e MSP
Copyright © 2013 Contemponet s.a.s. Rome - Italy

Translation by Richard Dudas

Copyright © 2013 - 2014 - ConTempoNet s.a.s., Rome - Italy
First edition 2014

Audio and Interactive Examples: Vincenzo Core
Index: Salvatore Mudanò

ConTempoNet s.a.s., Rome (Italy)
e-mail   **posta@contemponet.com**
             posta@virtual-sound.com
URL: **www.contemponet.com**
             www.virtual-sound.com
facebook www.facebook.com/electronic.music.and.sound.design

CONTENTS

III

FOREWORD TO THE SECOND VOLUME
by Richard Boulanger

With their *Electronic Music and Sound Design: Theory and Practice with Max and MSP* the master teachers and composers – Alessandro Cipriani and Maurizio Giri have produced a series of "interactive and enhanced books" that present the student of computer music with the finest and most comprehensive electroacoustic curriculum in the world. By "illustrating" the text with a wealth of figures and clearly explained equations, they take the reader "under the hood" and reveal the algorithms that make our computing machines "sing". By using David Zicarelli's incredibly powerful and intuitive media-toolkit – *Max* to create hundreds of synthesis, signal processing, algorithmic composition, interactive performance, and audio analysis software examples, Cipriani and Giri have provided the means for students to learn by hearing, by touching, by modifying, by designing, by creating, and by composing. On page after page, and with Max patch after Max patch, they brilliantly guide the student to a deeper knowledge and understanding that is guaranteed to release their musical creativity in new and profound ways.

As we all know, digital cameras are so "smart" today that it is virtually impossible to take a bad picture. But how to frame and freeze a moment in time, and then to have that frozen moment "speak" through time – no camera can do that. A "photographer" does that. And it takes a great teacher, a great mentor to help a student "see" what is right before their eyes. How does a great teacher do this? They practice what they preach, and they teach by example. This is exactly what Cipriani and Giri do in this series. *Electronic Music and Sound Design* is filled to overflowing with working and teaching examples, models, and code. It is a treasure chest of riches that will enlighten and inspire the 21st century musician, audio artist, and designer to make the most of their "instrument" – the computer itself. They are teaching the next generation how to play it!

Today, brilliant design provides us with intuitive tools and systems that "anyone" can make work; but understanding how they actually work, and understanding how one might actually work with them – that is the challenge. Innovation doesn't spring from accidents and good luck. For sure, turning knobs can produce some crazy sounds, but a collection of crazy sounds is far from musical. As Varese would say, "music is organized sound". I would humbly expand this by saying that "music is structured sound", "music is sculpted sound"; music is the manifestation and articulation of "thought forms" that we resonate with and share, "mind models" that spring fourth from "sound understanding". The masterpieces of tomorrow's Audio Art will reveal a vision that comes into focus as today's students grow in their appreciation and understanding of how things work and how to work with them, and Cipriani and Giri are paving the way for an age of audio enlightenment.

I firmly believe that this series by Cipriani and Giri, these "interactive and enhanced books", in which definition and design, in which theory and practice, in which compositional advice supported by an analysis of historical masterworks are all so tightly coupled with audio examples and editable and working Max and Max for Live patches, set the stage for the next generation of innovators. This book is essential for young and creative computer musician who have the tools and want to know how they work and how to work with them. In *Electronic Music and Sound Design*, Cipriani and Giri feed the hands, they feed the ears, and they feed the minds of the students in ways and to a degree that no computer music textbook has ever done.

Volume 1 moved from basic audio to software synthesis, filtering, spatialization, and some MIDI, with a great introduction to Max and a good assortment of Max tricks. Along the way, they introduced and covered a lot of synthesis and signal processing theory. The book is structured with a "theoretical and practical" chapter to be studied in parallel. A unique collection of Max patches is provided, in "presentation" mode, so that the theoretical concepts can be "explored". There is audio ear training, chapter tests, activities, suggested projects and modifications, and a unique glossary of terms, at the end of each chapter. In fact, each chapter begins with a set of "learning objectives" and "competencies", and a list of prerequisites (usually the contents of the previous chapters). The chapters are filled with exercises, activities, assignments and end with a quiz. It is a great curricular model. I am a particular fan of Chapter 3 on Noise, Filters, and Subtractive Synthesis as it is a great balance of practical, mathematical and theoretical. The "practical" chapters feature full Max Patches ready to be modified, repaired, expanded, and explored. In addition to the theoretical and practical chapters, there are two "Interludes" that focus on Max programming. In addition to all the patches featured in the "text", Cipriani and Giri provide a huge library of abstractions (they call them "macros") that make programming and design even more efficient. There are many solutions, optimizations, and tricks revealed in this collection too, and it is worth some serious study as well. It is truly amazing how much computer music you are learning and how much Max you are learning – at the same time!

Volume 2 is structured much like Volume 1 – starting each with chapter objectives and outcomes and ending with a quiz and a chapter-specific glossary of terms. In fact, it picks up where the first volume left off – starting with chapter 5! In general it features a more in depth coverage of topics and builds on what was learned in Volume 1. By this point, the student is more advanced in their understanding and skills and so more depth is presented and more difficult challenges are assigned. As might be expected, in this volume three "Interludes" take the reader even deeper into Max with a focus on time and sequencing, advanced preset, data, time, polyphony, and score management and the idiosyncrasies of working with bpatchers, concluding with a major interlude focusing on Max for Live and the Live API that helps the reader to move all their studies into a rich and robust production and performance environment. As in Volume 1, the chapters are again organized in pairs with a theoretical chapter supporting a practical chapter.

Chapter 5 focuses on Digital Audio and Sampling and features some really exciting "sample-cutters" and "scrubbers". Chapter 6 focuses on Delay Lines and associated effects such as comb-filtering and pitch shifting and culminating in delay-line based synthesis – the famous Karplus-Strong plucked string algorithm. Lots of great sounds here. Chapter 7 focuses on Dynamic Processors, Envelope Followers, Compressors, Limiters, and their creative use – such as side-chaining. There are a lot of practical and useful performance tools here.

The game changer in the series, and the masterpiece of this book is what is covered in Chapter 8. Here Cipriani and Giri begin to teach the reader about the world of computer music and how to "speak" the language with some fluency – how to compose Audio Art. It is titled: "The Art of Organizing Sound: Motion Processes". In it Cipriani and Giri present and analyze a number of masterworks, link to them on their website, and showcase some of the processes that define their uniqueness. Further, the compositional approach, and the aesthetic ideas of a number of innovative composers is cited. This chapter is not only filled with musical models, but also filled with some wonderful role models – including the inspiring compositions of Cipriani and Giri themselves. This chapter is so important at this point in the "course" because it establishes context and sets the stage for more expanded compositional work with the techniques that have been learned and the systems that have been built. This is where Cipriani and Giri teach the student to "see".

Finally, Chapter 9 focuses on MIDI and gives us a deeper and more complete review of the MIDI spec and shows the ways that this knowledge and these messages can be applied in Max. This chapter sets the stage for the final Interlude that focuses on the incredibly important Max for Live application of the work thus far.

And so…

Volume 1 was fantastic. Volume 2 raises the bar and brings insights into the compositional process, new ideas on working with "time-forms", and new ways to integrate signal processing and synthesis algorithms into a powerful performance and production tool via Max For Live. I can't wait for Volume 3! Until then, I will close by saying that I am deeply honored to be associated with this great pedagogical milestone and to write the foreword for Volume 2. Moreover, I am so happy for all the students around the world who will learn so much from working their way through the text, the examples, the music, the quizzes, the projects – all under the guidance of these great teachers – Alessandro Cipriani and Maurizio Giri.

Max is the brilliant and inspired artistic creation of David Zicarelli and Miller Puckette. This software has revolutionized the field of computer music and made it possible for "musicians" to write software; for "musicians" to develop their own custom interactive systems. As such Max has liberated the artist, and revolutionized the field of computer music, and made possible the most incredible, diverse, and profound musical creations and performances.
For many years now, the international community of Max users, developers, and teachers has grown. Their numbers are vast, and the work that they have

created and shared has been so inspiring; but to date, there has never been a full synthesis, signal processing, composition and production curriculum built on top of Max – not until now. The series of "interactive and enhanced books" under the title *Electronic Music and Sound Design: Theory and Practice with Max and MSP* clearly establishes Alessandro Cipriani and Maurizio Giri as two of the greatest and most important teachers of computer music in the world.

Dr. Richard Boulanger
Professor of Electronic Production and Design, Berklee College of Music
Author and Editor of The Csound Book & The Audio Programming Book
– MIT Press

TRANSLATOR'S NOTE
by Richard Dudas

Back in the days when Max had just a few dozen objects and a relatively restricted range of what it was capable of doing compared with the program today, it nonetheless still seemed like a limitless environment. Its basic object set could be employed, arranged and rearranged in countless ways to build whatever one's imagination desired. It was an ideal tinkerer's toolkit – much like the popular crystal radio sets and erector sets of the 50s and 60s, the more modern construction sets made of interlocking plastic pieces which first appeared in the 60s and 70s, or the basic microcomputer systems from the 80s. When Max came along at the dawn of 1990s, its "do it yourself" paradigm was perfectly suited to the creative and eager musician in the MIDI-based home studio in an era when much of the available commercial software had highly limited functionality. Max offered musicians and sound artists the ability to create their own software to "go outside the box" without needing to learn the intricacies of a textual programming language nor the mundane specifics of interfacing with the computer's operating system.

Since that time, the Max environment has continued to grow and evolve from a program geared toward interacting with MIDI and simple media to one that encompasses audio and video processing and connections to external software and hardware. But in getting bigger, the sheer magnitude of features available within it has caused it to become rather daunting for many musicians, even though they may actually be keen to discover what it has to offer. Furthermore, the instruments and audio effects that have become prevalent since digital audio workstations moved from the studio to the home studio have become increasingly more complex, so understanding their inner workings has consequently also oftentimes become mystifying. That is where this series of books by Alessandro Cipriani and Maurizio Giri comes to the rescue.

This series of books provides a straightforward, musically-oriented framework to help new users get into the program and at the same time effortlessly learn the theory behind each of the topics they are studying. It also helps intermediate and advanced level students and professionals better grasp concepts they may already be acquainted with. In addition to presenting a progressive series of compelling musical tools and explaining their theoretical underpinning, it also supplies useful pre-fabricated high-level modules in instances where none readily exist in Max. Since these modules are provided as patches, they can be taken apart, analyzed, modified and learned from, or simply used as-is, depending on the user's level of familiarity with the program. Most importantly, the books in this series do not attempt to teach every esoteric detail and object that is available in the environment – that is a good thing! – they concentrate on shedding light on those fundamental notions and tools (and some more advanced ones, too) that are immediately necessary to help users understand what they are doing and get started using the program creatively and practically.

I have been a devoted and passionate user of Max nearly since its inception, was fortunate enough to be a beta-tester of early versions of the program, and later also worked as one of the developers of the software at Cycling '74. Max has been an important part of my personal creative musical output (and sometimes also my free time on the weekends!), and has additionally been central to my work as educator in the field of computer music. Now, while working in the rôle of translator for this second volume, I have discovered (via both Cipriani and Giri's admirable text as well as the Max program itself) that there are still new ideas to contemplate, new information to absorb, new techniques to amass and many alternate ways to design and improve commonly used algorithms for sound processing and synthesis. For me, this is one of the most amazing aspects of Max, and indeed of music and the arts, in general. From my perspective as an educator, this book is everything I would hope for, and more – its very strength is that it offers the reader technical knowledge alongside compelling artistic and creative motivations for using open-ended software such as Max instead of encouraging blind reliance on commonplace off-the-shelf tools, however seductive their sound may initially seem. Thus, I am both happy and proud to have been able to play a part in bringing this excellent series of books, written from a decidedly *musical* perspective, to a wider audience.

Richard Dudas
Assistant Professor of Composition and Computer Music, Hanyang University School of Music

INTRODUCTION TO THE SECOND VOLUME

This book is the second in a series of three volumes dedicated to digital synthesis and sound processing. The first volume of the series covers a variety of topics including additive synthesis, noise generators, filters, subtractive synthesis and control signals. The third volume will cover reverberation and spatialization, various techniques for non-linear synthesis (such as AM, FM, waveshaping and sound distortion techniques), granular synthesis, analysis and resynthesis, physical models, procedural sound design and a second chapter dedicated to the organization of sound.

PREREQUISITES
All three volumes consist of chapters containing theoretical background material interleaved with chapters that help guide the user's practice of that theory via practical computing techniques. Each pair of chapters (theory and practice) work together as a unit and therefore should be studied alongside one another. This second volume has been designed for users with various levels of knowledge and experience, although they should already fully understand the concepts and use of Max which have been outlined in the first volume. The contents of this volume have been designed to be studied either by oneself or under the guidance of an instructor.

SOUND EXAMPLES AND INTERACTIVE EXAMPLES
The theoretical chapters of this book are meant to be accompanied throughout by numerous sound examples and interactive examples that can be downloaded from the Virtual Sound website at: **www.virtual-sound.com/mat2**. By referring to these examples, the user can immediately listen to the sound being discussed (in the case of sound examples), or discover and experiment with sound creation and processing techniques (with the interactive examples), without having to spend intervening time on the practical task of programming. In this way, the study of theory is always concretely connected to our experience and perception of both the sounds themselves, and the many possible ways they can be processed and modified.

MAX
The practical chapters of this book are based on the software Max 6, although Max 5 users can still use this text. We have made sure that all the patches and activities that are presented here can be realized with both versions. The sole object specific to Max 6 that we have used is scale~. For Max 5 users, we have included an abstraction that reproduces the functionality of scale~ on our support page at: **www.virtual-sound.com/mat2**. The patches, sound files, library extensions and other supporting material for this volume's practical activities can also be found on that page.

MAX FOR LIVE
The final chapter, or rather "interlude," of this book deals with Max for Live – an application that lets users create plug-ins for Ableton Live using Max. This is decidedly substantial chapter, in which all the knowledge learned over the

course of the first two volumes will be put to use to create devices (the term used for plug-ins in the Live environment). Special emphasis has been given to the discussion and study of the "Live API" which allows users to create devices which can be used to control other plug-ins or even the Live application itself.

TEACHING APPROACH AND METHOD OF THIS BOOK

As with the first volume, this second volume should be studied by reading each theory chapter in alternation with its corresponding practice chapter, in addition to carrying out the recommended computer-based activities. Nonetheless, one major difference, compared to the first volume, is in the type of practice activities which are suggested: the final activities of correcting, analyzing and completing algorithms, as well as substituting parts of algorithms for one another, are no longer present in this volume. Here, throughout each practice chapter, a copious selection of activities is presented to help the reader both test and deepen the various skills and knowledge that he has acquired thus far, in addition to suggesting ways of using them creatively. Throughout this volume the analysis of algorithms and patches is still carried out in detail (as it was in the first volume) when new techniques are being illustrated. However, where older, familiar processes and techniques are concerned, analysis is now left up to the reader. In other words, we have catered the second volume to a different type of reader. When writing the first volume, we were aware that our target reader was someone who, although thoroughly interested in the subject matter, could have been completely devoid of prior experience within the realm of electronic music. In this volume we can now presume that the reader is at an "intermediate" level – someone who has already made sounds with Max and/or with other software, and who knows the basics of synthesis and sound processing: in short, a reader who has already "digested" the material presented in the previous volume. Even those who have not yet read the first volume but possess the aforementioned skills will still be able to greatly benefit from this book, although we should point out that many of the concepts, objects and algorithms presented in the first volume will be referred to throughout the course of this text.

We would also like to point out the presence of a chapter in this volume titled "The Art of Organizing Sound: Motion Processes" (chapter 8 in both theory and practice). This chapter was designed to give the reader an opportunity to develop his own individual versions of the proposed activities in a more complex and creative way than in the first volume. This means that the reader will be encouraged to use his perception, analysis and critical thinking, in addition to his own experience and ingenuity. The importance of such a section dedicated to the creative use of one's knowledge and skills should neither be overlooked nor underestimated. Even though the software that we use may continue to evolve and change over time, the skills that we obtain through active personal practice and creation act as a flexible tool which can be applied in different technological contexts. It is our firm belief that a passive and "bookish" approach to learning is sterile and devoid of meaning, therefore our aim is to enable the reader to associate and interconnect his knowledge, skills, perception, analytic ability, ability to ask the right questions and to solve problems, and ability to create original musical forms with sound, in a natural, inventive and personal way. The goal of this section is thus to impart how to work within one's own area of competence.

In order to be able to say one is competent in the field of electronic and computer music it is not enough simply to know how to create an LFO, for example, but more importantly how to use it and what to do with it in specific creative contexts. Indeed, simply knowing how to follow a series of steps is not an indication of competence; the expert also needs to know how to interpret those steps. Essentially, knowing how to provide the proper settings for a patch, or how to modify an object's parameters, not simply as an abstract task, but with the aim of achieving a certain goal for a sound's motion or evolution over time (or within in the listening space) is an essential ability for sound artists, sound designers and composers.

The reverse-engineering exercises in the first volume hinted at the possibility that the starting point for being able to use any given synthesis and sound processing system is not so much the theory behind it, as the actual context for which it will be used. In the case of the reverse-engineering exercises, the starting point was a pre-existing sound, specifically selected for the exercise at hand, whose properties and characteristics needed to be recognized in order to be able to simulate its spectrum, envelope, etc....

In chapter 8 of this second volume, however, the theoretical knowledge and practical abilities that we have thus far developed will be put to use and further strengthened by focusing on the reader's own original sound processing skills and ability to construct motion processes. Nonetheless, the basic compositional activities that we propose in this chapter should be limited to sound forms not exceeding one minute in duration, and should be designed outside the bounds of a wider formal scope and context, such as that of a larger compositional project. That having been said, exactly what kind of sound creation is being proposed, here?

The scope of sound creation practices is both immense and diverse. It ranges from algorithmic composition to "laptop orchestras", from live electronics with human-machine interaction to acousmatic compositions. There are also soundscape compositions, sound installations, audio-visual installations, sound art, sound design work – the list is seemingly endless.
Not surprisingly, an infinite number of schools of thought have emerged, each with its own unique formal approach, ranging from narrative to abstract, or even in other directions such as forms of an ambient nature, etc.... It is therefore our desire to supply just a few pertinent tools to allow the reader to sharpen his own personal skills. We will also try to avoid providing rules and regulations as much as possible, but rather to try to propose a personalized experience for sonic discovery. Consequently, we have decided to reinterpret and adapt some ideas about spectromorphology, as proposed by Denis Smalley in some of his articles, for creative endeavors. Thus we are introducing the categories of simple motion, complex motion and compound motion. For the interaction between theory and practice, we suggest that each student interpret the type of motion being described, based on both the technical

information provided and the specific purpose for which it will be used, in order to be able to make use of it within his personal sounds.

SUPPORTING MATERIAL
All the material referenced throughout the course of this book can be downloaded from the Virtual Sound website's support page:
www.virtual-sound.com/mat2.
In order to begin working with this text, you will first need to download all of the Sound Examples and Interactive Examples located on the support page. Bear in mind that you should constantly refer to these examples while reading through the theory chapters.

In order to work interactively with the practice chapters of this book, you will first need to install the Max program, which can be obtained at the site: www.cycling74.com. Once Max has been installed, you will also need to download and install the Virtual Sound Macros library from the support page mentioned above. The support page includes detailed instructions concerning the correct installation procedure for the library. Last but not least, the support page also includes the necessary patches (Max programs) related to the practice chapters of this book.

BIBLIOGRAPHY
As in the previous volume, the final pages of this book include a list of the most absolutely essential reference works, in addition to the bibliographical references cited throughout the course of the text itself.

COMMENTS AND CORRECTIONS
Corrections and comments are always welcome. Please contact the authors by e-mail at: a.cipriani@edisonstudio.it and maurizio@giri.it

ACKNOWLEDGEMENTS
The authors would like to thank Vincenzo Core and Salvatore Mudanò for their patience and long hours of work, Lorenzo Seno for his advice about digital audio, and Richard Boulanger, Marco Massimi and David Zicarelli for their generosity.
We particularly wish to thank Richard Dudas, whose invaluable work on this book went far beyond simply translating it. His constant feedback provided us with some very useful insights.

DEDICATIONS
This volume is dedicated to Arianna Giri, Sara Mascherpa and Gian Marco Sandri.

5T
DIGITAL AUDIO AND SAMPLED SOUNDS

LEARNING AGENDA

PREREQUISITES FOR THE CHAPTER
• THE CONTENTS OF VOLUME 1 (THEORY AND PRACTICE)

OBJECTIVES
KNOWLEDGE
• TO KNOW THE UNDERLYING PRINCIPLES OF ANALOG-TO-DIGITAL AND DIGITAL-TO-ANALOG SOUND CONVERSION
• TO KNOW THE MEASURABLE CHARACTERISTICS OF AUDIO INTERFACES AND SOUND CONVERSION
• TO KNOW THE FUNDAMENTALS OF DATA COMPRESSION
• TO KNOW THE CAUSES AND EFFECTS OF FOLDOVER AND QUANTIZATION NOISE
• TO KNOW VARIOUS TECHNIQUES FOR EDITING AND ORGANIZING SOUNDS INSIDE A SAMPLER
• TO KNOW SEVERAL METHODS OF SEGMENTATION AND PITCH MANIPULATION OF SAMPLED SOUNDS

SKILLS
• TO BE ABLE TO AURALLY DISTINGUISH AND CLEARLY DESCRIBE THE KEY DIFFERENCES BETWEEN DECIMATION AND SAMPLE RATE REDUCTION
• TO BE ABLE TO AURALLY DISTINGUISH AND CLEARLY DESCRIBE THE DIFFERENCES BETWEEN A GIVEN SOUND AND THE SAME SOUND PLAYED IN REVERSE
• TO BE ABLE TO AURALLY DISTINGUISH THE MAIN DIFFERENCES BETWEEN A SOUND PROCESSED WITH THE BLOCKS TECHNIQUE AND ONE PROCESSED VIA SLICING

CONTENTS
• AUDIO INTERFACES AND A-TO-D / D-TO-A SOUND CONVERSION
• THE NYQUIST THEOREM AND FOLDOVER
• QUANTIZATION NOISE AND DITHERING
• THE ORGANIZATION OF SOUNDS IN A SAMPLER
• SEGMENTATION OF SAMPLED SOUNDS: THE BLOCKS TECHNIQUE AND SLICING
• PITCH MODULATION IN SAMPLED SOUNDS
• AUDIO DATA COMPRESSION
• AUDIO DATA TRANSMISSION AND JITTER

ACTIVITIES
• SOUND EXAMPLES - INTERACTIVE EXAMPLES

TESTING
• QUESTIONS WITH SHORT ANSWERS
• LISTENING AND ANALYSIS

SUPPORTING MATERIALS
GLOSSARY

5.1 DIGITAL SOUND

In section 1.2T we already established that (a) sound is a mechanical phenom- enon coming from a disturbance through a medium of transmission (generally the air) that has characteristics that can be perceived by the human ear. An acoustic sound can be amplified, reproduced and modified; but in order to do so, it must first be transformed into a signal capable of being measured, record- ed, reproduced and modified in simple ways. Let's suppose we have a flautist friend who is playing; to transform his acoustic sound we can use a microphone. The microphone will operate as an electro-acoustic transducer, simply meaning that it acts as a constant gauge of variations in air pressure. At the same time the microphone will generate an electrical signal corresponding to the original, in the sense that its outgoing flow of electric tension corresponds to – in other words is analogous to – that of the input sound wave. For this reason the signal coming from the microphone is called an *analog signal*. However, be aware that the analog signal is never exactly identical to the original, but contains a certain amount of distortion (however minimal it may be) in addition to the introduc- tion of noise (see figure 5.1).

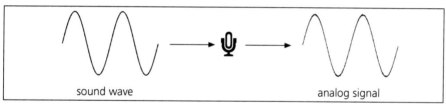

sound wave   analog signal

Fig. 5.1 An analog signal

In digital signals, however, the signal is represented by a series of numbers (remember that a digit is a base component of a numerical value). Each of the numbers in a digital signal represents the value of the instantaneous pressure, that is to say the value of the sound pressure at a given instant.

In order to generate a digital signal, the amplitude of the sound is measured at regular intervals (figure 5.2). This process is called sampling and is entirely analog.[1]

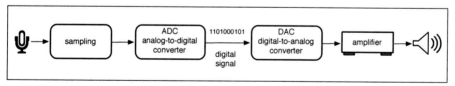

Fig. 5.2 Sampling and conversion

---

[1] The sampling system that is most often used is Pulse Code Modulation (PCM), based on the acquisition of the analog signal at regular time intervals. This sampling process is achieved by product modulation, which consists of multiplying the signal by a series of impulses. The result of this multiplication is a spectrum containing frequencies equal to the sums and differences of the two multiplied signals. In other words, this produces ring modulation – a technique which we will cover in more detail in the section of the third volume dedicated to non-linear synthesis.

Once the individual analog samples are arranged in time so each one assumes the amplitude value of the signal at that particular instant, they become subsequently converted into a flow of (binary) numerical data. This process is called *analog-to-digital* conversion. In order to be able to listen to the digitally converted signal again, a process of *digital-to-analog conversion* is necessary. This is the process by which the digital signal becomes converted into an analog signal once again, so it can be sent to an amplifier and subsequently to the speakers.

The audio interfaces in our computers (or the external audio interfaces attached to them) generally include both an analog-to-digital converter (or ADC) and a digital-to-analog converter (or DAC).

ANALOG TO DIGITAL CONVERSION

As we just stated, analog to digital conversion entails "translating" a signal composed of variations in electric tension into a numerical signal by defining its electric tension in (binary) numerical terms at regular intervals. In reality, however, transforming a sound from an analog signal to a digital one requires several different steps, as we will see at the end of this section where the subject is covered in more detail. For now it is enough for you to simply understand that the ADC contains both analog sampling and digital conversion.

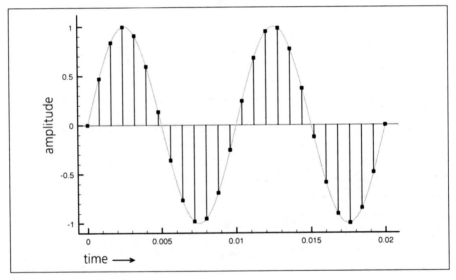

Fig. 5.3 A sampled signal

In figure 5.3, the continuous line represents the flow of an analog signal (i.e., voltage or electric tension), while the superimposed points represent the value of the sampled signal after being converted into numerical values. The sampling and the conversion of the signal's first amplitude value (the value 0) takes place at time 0. After a given amount of time (at time 0.001) a second sampling and a conversion takes place. In the interval between the two sampling times, the analog signal has evolved in its instantaneous amplitude value, and now has an amplitude value equal to about 0.5. The next sampling takes place at time 0.002, and the converted amplitude value is a little above 0.8. As you can see, the process of sampling records only a few out of an infinite number of values which make up the analog signal over time, so you might therefore think that the resulting digital signal contains errors, or is otherwise not faithful to the original signal. However, we will soon discover that as long as the analog signal contains only frequencies which are less than half the sampling rate, it is possible to reconstruct the original signal from the digital samples without any ambiguity.

The time interval that passes between one sample and the next is called the *sampling period*, and is measured in seconds or in a subdivision thereof (milliseconds or microseconds). In figure 5.4 it is indicated with the label *sp*.

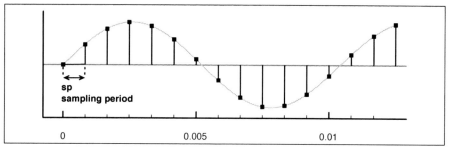

Fig. 5.4 The sampling period

The inverse of the sampling period is known as the *sampling rate* (it is also referred to as the *sampling frequency*, or *sample rate*), which was briefly described in section 1.5 of the first volume of this series. It is commonly abbreviated *sr*, as it is throughout this text, and is measured in Hertz (Hz). For example, if we use a sampling rate of 48000 Hz to sample a sound, it means that in one second of time its amplitude will be measured 48000 times.

We can therefore define the following relationships:

sr = 1/ sp

sp = 1/sr

In other words, the sampling rate (the number of samples per second) is equal to the inverse of the sampling period, and vice-versa.

To find out how to calculate a sampling rate *sr* that will allow a sound to be correctly sampled, we need to refer to the *Nyquist theorem* (also called the *sampling theorem*), which states that the sampling rate must be greater than twice the maximum frequency contained in the signal. Therefore, if *fmax* is the maximum frequency contained in a given signal, the minumum sampling rate *sr* that we would need to use to faithfully reproduce it would be:

sr >= 2 · fmax

This naturally implies that the maximum representable frequency will be less than half the sampling rate. The frequency equal to half the sampling rate is called the *Nyquist frequency*.

Before carrying out the process of sampling on a sound, any frequencies above the Nyquist frequency that are contained in the analog signal must first be eliminated, otherwise they would create an undesirable effect known as foldover, which we will discuss shortly. For this reason, conversion systems incorporate some important measures, including the application of an analog lowpass filter before sampling (called an *anti-aliasing filter*), in order to eliminate frequencies above the Nyquist.

Bear in mind, however, that it is impossible to create an ideal analog filter with an infinitely steep slope at its cutoff frequency, and it is even technically extraordinarily difficult to design one with a very sharp slope. Consequently, there is always a risk that some frequencies above the Nyquist frequency will remain in the sound after filtering. To resolve this problem, sampling systems use a technique of *oversampling* after the analog filtering step (using a filter whose slope is not steep). When using oversampling, the sound is sampled at a higher sampling rate than the one that was initially chosen, in order to create a new Nyquist frequency far above the cutoff frequency of the analog filter. Subsequently, a digital lowpass filter, with a steep slope, is applied to the oversampled signal. This eliminates any frequencies above our original (higher) Nyquist frequency (the one before the oversampling). The sound can now finally be resampled at the chosen sampling rate, using a process of *downsampling*. By using this method we can be certain that there will be no undesired effects resulting from foldover when sounds are sampled.

The best results (above and beyond the stated techniques) can be obtained using sampling rates above 44.1 kHz, in order to move undesired spectral images to higher frequencies. It is precisely for this reason that higher sampling rates are generally used. So, which sampling rates are more frequently used for audio? In the case of compact discs, a *sr* of 44.1 kHz was adopted (permitting reproduction of sounds up to 22050 Hz), whereas, the *sr* of DVD and Blu-ray Discs can go up to 192 KHz (therefore permitting reproduction of frequencies up to 96000 Hz, well above the maximum audible frequency).

FOLDOVER IN DIGITALLY GENERATED SOUNDS

What would happen if the sampling system did not include an anti-aliasing filter, and thus allowed frequencies above the Nyquist to pass through to the sampling stage? Or what would happen if, instead of sampling a sound, we digitally generated a signal inside the computer whose frequency was above the Nyquist frequency? In both of these scenarios, we would obtain an effect known as foldover. Foldover is the phenomenon by which frequency components that exceed half the *sr* become *reflected* back under it. For example, a frequency component of 11000 Hz converted using a sampling rate of 20000 Hz, will produce a foldover component of 9000 Hz, as we will see in detail shortly.

Let's imagine that we want to generate a sine wave with a frequency of 12000 Hz. If we use a sampling rate of 18000 Hz, we will have a Nyquist frequency equal to 9000 Hz. The sound that we want to generate will thus *exceed* the Nyquist frequency by 3000 Hz. Consequently, that sound will not have its original frequency (in this case defined as 12000 Hz), but instead will appear 3000 Hz *below* the Nyquist frequency with its sign inverted[2] (in other words 6000 Hz, but with a negative sign).

Therefore, in the case where an oscillator's frequency is set above the Nyquist, the actual output frequency due to foldover can be calculated with the following formula, where *sr* is the sampling rate, f_c is the frequency to convert and f_o is the output frequency:

$$f_o = f_c - sr$$

Let's now apply that formula to our previous example:

12000 - 18000 = -6000

Note that this formula is only valid in the case where frequency f_c is between half the sampling rate (i.e., the Nyquist frequency) and 1.5 times the sampling rate *sr*. In the section dedicated to *aliasing* we will learn a general formula that works for all frequencies.

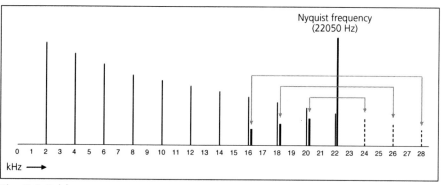

Fig. 5.5 Foldover

Naturally, this phenomenon occurs not only in relation to sinusoidal signals but for any component of a complex signal. Let's take a look at figure 5.5, which shows a signal made up of various harmonic partials whose fundamental frequency is equal to 2000 Hz. The solid lines represent components actually present in the signal after conversion, whereas the dashed lines represent the original components of the analog signal that are no longer present in the converted

---

[2] The behavior of each partial, when its sign is inverted from positive to negative (or from negative to positive), will depend on its waveform and phase. For example, when the sign of the frequency of a sinusoid is inverted, its phase is inverted, but when we invert the sign of the frequency of a cosine it remains the same. From this perspective, we can see that it not easy to calculate the effect of foldover upon the output spectrum.

signal. The bold solid lines represent these latter components which have become "reflected" back under the Nyquist frequency (which in this example is equal to 22050 Hz). Let's now take a closer look at the frequency at 24000 Hz (that is, the 12th harmonic of the 2000 Hz fundamental in this example): since it is above the Nyquist frequency, it is subject to foldover, and therefore becomes:

frequency to convert - sampling rate = output frequency
24000 - 44100 = -20100

Similarly, the frequency at 28000 Hz (the 14th harmonic of the 2000 Hz fundamental) becomes:

28000 - 44100 = 16100

In the interactive examples which follow, we can hear three different sound events, each based on a sampling rate of 22050 Hz and therefore having a Nyquist at 11025 Hz. From this we can conclude that any sound above 11025 Hz will be subjected to the effect of foldover.

- in the first example we will sweep the frequency of a sinusoidal sound from 20 to 10000 Hz; there is no foldover in this scenario so we will therefore hear a simple ascending glissando

- in the second example the glissando will extend from 20 to 20000 Hz. At the moment the sound passes above 11025 Hz, we will hear the phenomenon of foldover. Once it goes above the threshold of the Nyquist frequency, the upward glissando will become a descending one, since the more the frequency ascends, the more the reflected frequency will descend due to foldover. The sound will continue to sweep downward until it stops at 2050 Hz. According to the above formula we can calculate:

f_c - sr = f_o
20000 Hz - 22050 = -2050 Hz

- In the third example the sound will sweep from 20 to 30000 Hz. In this case we can audibly discern a double foldover. Let's take a look at it in detail:

1) in the initial stage from 20 to 11025 Hz, the output frequency corresponds to the frequency we have specified.
2) at the moment it exceeds 11025 Hz the first foldover occurs, making the resulting frequency glissando downward until it arrives at the 0 (in other words, it does this as the frequency goes upward from 11025 to 22050 Hz).

f_c - sr = f_o
22050 Hz - 22050 - 0

3) our generated frequency now continues beyond 22050 until it arrives at 30000 Hz. At the instant when the reflected sound goes below the threshold at 0 (into the negative), the frequency will once again begin to ascend, thereby creating another foldover taking place when the frequency of the signal is less than zero. In general, frequencies less than zero reappear with their sign inverted, in other words mirrored into the positive (-200 Hz becomes 200 Hz, -300 Hz becomes 300 Hz, etc.).

As a result of this second foldover, the output frequency rises again until 7950 Hz. So, how do we obtain this final frequency? 7950 Hz is equal to 30000 Hz (the final destination frequency of the signal we are converting) minus 22050 Hz (the sampling rate). Note that because it is caused by a second foldover, the final frequency has a second inversion of its sign, back into the positive.

To summarize what has happened, when the frequency we specify exceeds the Nyquist Frequency (in this case 11025 Hz), a first foldover occurs. When the specified frequency goes beyond the sampling rate (in this case 22050 Hz) a second foldover takes place (see figure 5.6, below).

$$f_c - sr = f_o$$
$$30000 - 22050 = 7950$$

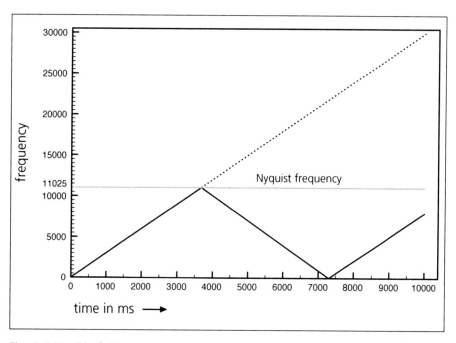

Fig. 5.6 Double foldover

SOUND EXAMPLES 5A • Foldover

5A.1 Simple ascending glissando from 20 Hz to 10000 Hz; *sr* = 22050
5A.2 Ascending glissando from 20 Hz to 20000 Hz with foldover; *sr* = 22050
5A.3 Ascending glissando from 20 Hz to 30000 Hz with double foldover; *sr* = 22050

. . . .

ALIASING: THE CAUSES

Although we have already explained the effects resulting from foldover, if we want to better understand its causes we will need to explain the Nyquist theorem in more detail. In order to have a more precise notion of the limitations imposed by the Nyquist theorem, let's imagine a hypothetical sampling system without anti-aliasing filters that uses a given sampling rate, **sr**, to sample a sinusoidal waveform whose frequency, **f**, is less than the Nyquist frequency. With this system we obtain is a series of samples that numerically represent the sine wave. Now, if with the same sampling rate sr we sample a sine wave whose frequency is (**f + sr**) – in other words, a sine wave whose frequency is equal to the sum of the previous sine wave's frequency and the sampling rate (and therefore greater than the Nyquist frequency) – we obtain exactly the same series of samples as we do when sampling the sine wave with frequency f. Furthermore, we would also obtain the exact same series of values when sampling sine waves with frequencies (**f + 2 · sr**), (**f + 3 · sr**), (**f + 4 · sr**), etc., ad infinitum. We can therefore generalize that given a sampling rate sr, all of the sine waves at frequencies of f + an integer multiple of the sampling rate will be converted into the same series of samples.

To provide a more concrete example, if our sampling rate sr is 5000 Hz, and we sample a sine wave whose frequency f is 1000 Hz, we will obtain a series of sampled values. If we then sample a sine wave whose frequency is 6000 Hz – i.e., a frequency equal to f (1000 Hz) plus sr (5000 Hz) – we will get an identical series of values.

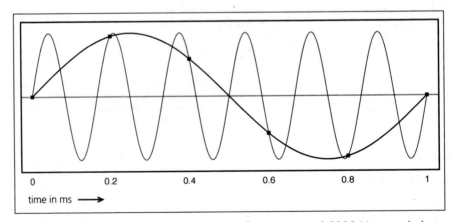

Fig. 5.7 Two sine waves with frequencies of 1000 Hz and 6000 Hz sampled at a rate of 5000 Hz.

Figure 5.7 illustrates how two sine waves with different frequencies – 1000 Hz and 6000 Hz, respectively – sampled at the same sampling rate of 5000 Hz, yield identical sample values (identified by the square-shaped points in the graph). This same series of values also can be obtained by sampling sinusoids at 11000 Hz (**f + 2 · sr**), 16000 Hz (**f + 3 · sr**), etc.

This mathematical equivalence also holds true when using *negative integer multiples* of the sampling rate; sampled sine waves with frequencies of (**f - sr**), (**f - 2 · sr**), (**f - 3 · sr**), (**f - 4 · sr**), etc., will all produce the same series of samples. To continue from our previous example, a sine wave with frequency -4000 Hz – the sum of the frequency 1000 Hz (**f**) and sampling rate -5000 Hz (-sr) – will generate the same amplitude values as the sine wave with frequency 1000 Hz. Note that a sine wave of -4000 Hz is equal to a 4000 Hz sine wave with its sign inverted (see figure 5.8).

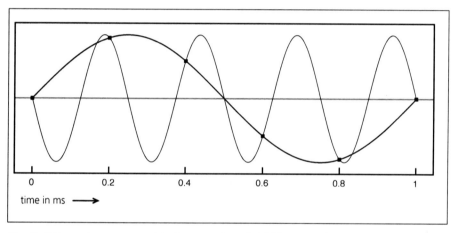

0   0.2   0.4   0.6   0.8   1

time in ms ⟶

Fig. 5.8 Two sine waves with frequencies of 1000 Hz and -4000 Hz sampled at a rate of 5000 Hz.

To summarize, we can say that: *given a sampling rate sr and any integer k, positive or negative, we can not distinguish between the sampled values of a sine wave of frequency f Hz and that of a sine wave with the frequency (**f + k · sr**) Hz.*

Returning to our previous example, here are the frequencies of the sine waves that we find inside the audio spectrum, and which generate identical sample values:

frequency (f+k · sr)
1000 Hz = 1000 + (0 · 5000)
6000 Hz = 1000 + (1 · 5000)
11000 Hz = 1000 + (2 · 5000)
16000 Hz = 1000 + (3 · 5000)
-4000 Hz = 1000 + (-1 · 5000)
-9000 Hz = 1000 + (-2 · 5000)
-14000 Hz = 1000 + (-3 · 5000)

This situation also holds true when converting a sound that is more complex than a sine wave: the mathematical relation ($f + k \cdot sr$), in fact, is valid for any and all spectral components in a sampled sound.
From this relationship we can derive a formula that will allow us to calculate the output frequency of any arbitrary frequency to be sampled. We will indicate the frequency that we are sampling with f_c, the sampling rate with the usual sr, the output frequency with f_o, and the whole number multiple of sr that is closest to f_c using N, in order to obtain the formula:

$$f_o = f_c - N \cdot sr$$

As we can see, this formula is very similar to the simplified one that we used earlier in the section dedicated to foldover.

Here are some examples:

1) f_c = 6000, sr = 10000, N = 6000/10000 = 0.6 = 1 (closest whole number value)

therefore: **6000 - 1 · 10000 = -4000**

2) f_c = 13000, sr = 10000, N = 13000/10000 = 1.3 = 1 (closest whole number value)

therefore: **13000 - 1 · 10000 = 3000**

3) f_c = 21000, sr = 10000, N = 21000/10000 = 2.1 = 2 (closest whole number value)

therefore: **21000 - 2 · 10000 = 1000**

4) f_c = 2500, sr = 10000, N = 2500/10000 = 0.25 = 0 (closest whole number value)

therefore: **2500 - 0 · 10000 = 2500** (in this case there is no foldover because f_c < sr/2)

Let's now take a look at what happens in the frequency domain:

In a hypothetical sampling system without *antialiasing* filters, the components (due to the foldover effects we have just described) will make more images of the same spectrum called *aliases*, replicated periodically around multiples of the sampling rate. More precisely, we will obtain a periodic spectrum that, in an ideal sampling system, will repeat along the frequency axis to infinity. In figure 5.9 we see how the various copies are positioned in the frequency domain in the case of a sine wave of 1000 Hz sampled with sr = 5000. The frequencies shown in the image are the same as in the preceding table 1000, 6000, 11000, 16000, -4000, -9000 and -14000.

As we have already learned, the negative frequencies reflect into the positive frequency range, therefore in the image components are shown at 1000 (the sampled frequency, which we will call f), 4000 (**sr-f**, which is 5000-1000), 6000 (**sr+f**), 9000 (**sr · 2-f**), 11000 (**sr · 2+f**), 14000 (**sr · 3-f**), 16000 (**sr · 3+f**), etc. In figure 5.9, the spectrum is represented as symmetrical around 0, and the successive copies are mathematically translated so they also appear symmetrical around integer multiples of the sampling rate.

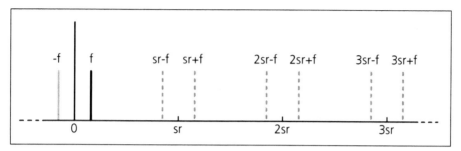

Fig. 5.9 *Aliasing*

Naturally, in real-world sampling systems frequencies above the Nyquist are eliminated before sampling precisely in order to cancel out the phenomena that we have been discussing. As we will see later, in the case of decimation, when undersampling a digital signal, frequencies resulting from *aliasing* will become present and therefore audible and should be filtered beforehand with an appropriate lowpass digital filter.

So, what happens if instead of sampling a sine wave we sample a sound composed of several partials? In this case, each and every one of the sound's components will be replicated in this same way. Consequently the aliased sonic image will contain copies of the complex spectrum, as shown in figure 5.10.

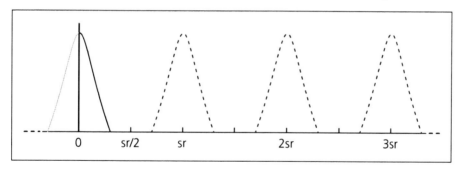

Fig. 5.10 Aliasing of a complex sound.

DIGITAL-TO-ANALOG CONVERSION

Let's now take a look at the reverse process: *digital-to-analog conversion*. When converting from a digital signal to an analog one, it becomes a piecewise (or stepped) signal in which, after each sample and until the next, a *sample-and-hold* mechanism (see section 4.7T and footnote 14, chapter 3.4P) is applied in order to sustain the electric tension value (i.e., voltage) of the analog output until the subsequent sample (remember that each sample represents a single point and there are no other values in-between samples). Using this method, a signal composed of discrete samples can be converted into a continuous (albeit slightly jagged) analog signal. Since this process introduces angular steps not present in the original (smooth) analog signal, we have inevitably modified the signal by altering its waveform, creating components not present in the original. These components, called *aliases*, form other images of the original spectrum (basically, harmonics of it) around the oversampling frequency, each one decreasing in amplitude as frequency increases.

In figure 5.11 we can see how the *sample-and-hold* mechanism reduces the components at high frequencies. More precisely, in the upper part of figure (a) we can see an ideal sampling system made with impulses of an infinitesimal duration: the resulting spectrum extends to infinity without losing the amplitudes of the components. In the lower part (b) we can see a sampling system realized by means of *sample-and-hold* which as we previously stated, is comprised of progressively quieter copies of the spectrum.[3]

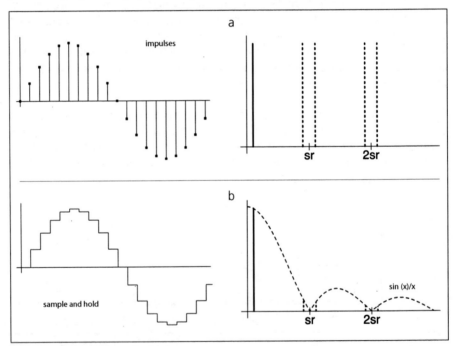

Fig. 5.11 Sampling and aliasing

Naturally, if the spectrum in this case is composed of several partials we will also have copies of the spectrum decreasing in amplitude as the frequency increases.

---

[3] The copies of the spectrum in a sample and hold -based sampling system will decrease according to the function sin(x)/x (see the image in the lower right hand corner of figure 5.11)

FOLDOVER: THE CAUSES

We will now take a look at the relationship between *aliasing* and foldover, and more closely explain their causes. When we try to digitally generate a sound whose spectrum has a bandwidth greater than the Nyquist frequency (as in figure 5.12a), a part of the image becomes superimposed upon the original spectrum, thereby changing it. In other words, if the sampling rate is too low, the frequencies appearing virtually above the Nyquist frequency cannot be reproduced and will appear below it.

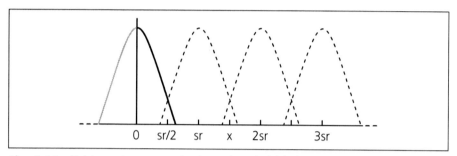

Fig. 5.12a Foldover in a sound whose bandwidth is greater than the Nyquist frequency.

This does not happen when we generate a sound that has a bandwidth less than the Nyquist frequency (as shown in figure 5.12b).

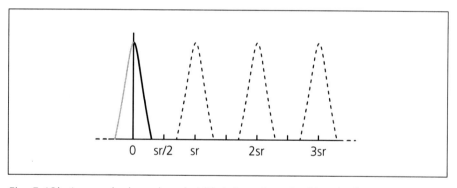

Fig. 5.12b A sound whose bandwidth is less than the Nyquist frequency.

THE CONVERSION PROCESS IN DETAIL

Now that we are at the end of this rather lengthy section, we will summarize, in a more detailed manner and with the aid of some helpful diagrams, the process of going from an analog input sound, converting it from an analog to a digital signal, and once again from digital to analog, in order to produce the final analog output sound.

A) Sampling is done at very high frequencies (oversampling) with respect to the actual desired sampling rate (which might be, for example, 48,000 Hz).

Before sampling, the signal is filtered with an analog lowpass (*anti-aliasing*) filter with a gentle slope, and generally having a cutoff frequency above the maximum audible frequency (e.g., 24,000 Hz). This filter is used to eliminate frequencies above the oversampling frequency's own Nyquist frequency, which would create foldover phenomena. The Nyquist of the oversampling frequency, in fact, is far above the cutoff frequency of the analog filter, and therefore even though its slope is not steep it succeeds in eliminating any undesirable frequencies. As we can see in figure 5.13a, the analog filter has eliminated the high frequencies above half of the oversampling frequency.

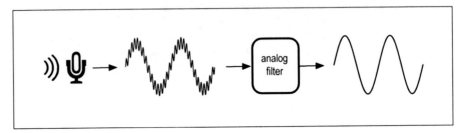

Fig. 5.13a Analog anti-aliasing filtering

B) The analog-filtered sound enters into the sampling system. In figure 5.13b we can see the analog-filtered signal at the input of the sampling system, and the oversampled sound at the output. In other words this is now a signal consisting of single analog samples positioned in time, each one of which assumes the amplitude value of the signal at that instant. The subsequent conversion transforms the amplitude values of the oversampled signal into numerical (i.e., digital) data. The digital signal is then filtered with a lowpass filter (needless to say, a digital one!) with a steep slope at a cutoff frequency equal to that of the desired Nyquist, and subsequently *downsampled* to the desired sampling rate (*sr*).
The process described here is included in an integrated circuit, the audio ADC chip.

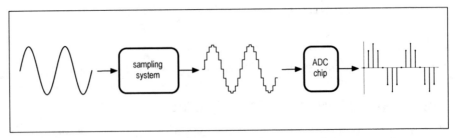

Fig. 5.13b Sampling, A-D conversion, digital filtering and downsampling

C) The digital signal can be saved to a data storage medium and/or modified through digital sound processing of the sound. In figure 5.13c, for example, we see the sampled sound at the input (of the signal processing unit) and the modified digital signal at the output (the series of samples has, in fact, been changed).

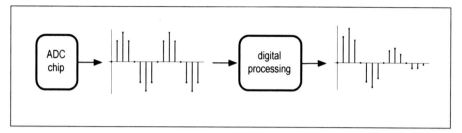

Fig. 5.13c Digital processing of sound

D) The signal output by the processing unit is still a discrete signal. At this point comes the reverse process of that which was used by the audio ADC. The signal undergoes a process of oversampling and digital filtering at the desired Nyquist frequency (**sr**/2), followed by a digital-to-analog conversion. As we can see in figure 5.13d, at the output of the converter we will have a stepped signal, caused by a system of *sample and hold*, that maintains a fixed value of electric tension between one sample and the next.

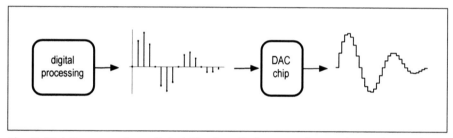

Fig. 5.13d Oversampling, digital filtering, D-A conversion and sample and hold

E) In order to smooth out the steps and eliminate high frequency components, the system uses a second analog filter. This is made up of a lowpass filter (called a *reconstruction filter*) that serves to eliminate frequencies above the oversampling Nyquist frequency. In figure 5.13e we can see a stepped signal at the input, and a signal in which the steps are no longer present, having been smoothed out by the filter, at the output.

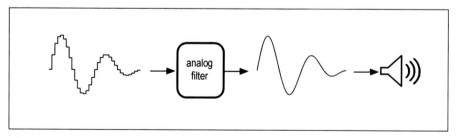

Fig. 5.13e Reconstruction filter (lowpass)

In figure 5.14 we have schematically reunited the various steps into one diagram, beginning with an acoustic sound at input and returning to an acoustic sound at output:

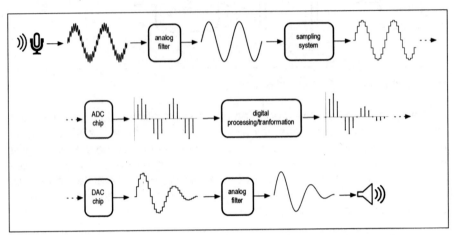

Fig. 5.14 Acoustic sound → modified digital sound → acoustic sound

We start out with a sound wave, the microphone works as an electroacoustic transducer, outputting an analog signal. After the procedure described in the five above examples, the output analog signal enters the amplifier, then into the loudspeaker that effectuates a new electroacoustic transduction and we once again obtain a sound wave.

🔍 TECHNICAL DETAILS • AUDIO INTERFACES, DIGITAL AND ANALOG SIGNALS

Almost every computer has a built-in system for recording and reproducing sound. However, in order to obtain a professional-level sound quality, you need to use audio interfaces that have external conversion units (DAC and ADC). This is because the inner workings of a computer produce an extremely high level of electrical noise due to electromagnetic fields generated by the signal flow, which can add undesirable sounds to our analog signal. An external audio interface, on the other hand, avoids this noise because the audio signal is converted away from these fields.

Naturally, hobbyists, tinkerers and other nonprofessional users will not need such high quality audio, and in these cases the internal audio interface may be used, if it is of decent quality. In general, the following are the essential features to keep an eye on where sound cards are concerned:

the *total harmonic distortion (THD)*, this is a measure of signal degradation due to the presence of sound waves generated by the signal flow – this should be less than 0.03%;

the *signal to noise ratio*, which indicates the ratio between the strength of the input signal and the background noise (analog and digital noise are different) – in theory this should be at least 97.8 dB (presuming you are making a 16 bit conversion);

the *frequency response*, which represents the response of the converter to all the frequencies within the range of 20 Hz to 20 kHz – the closer the graph comes to having 0 dB across the entire frequency range, the better its frequency response is;

the *dynamic range*, which is the ratio between the maximum and minimum amplitudes that can be represented. In theory this should be at least 97.8 dB (when converting to 16 bits);

the amount of *quantization noise*, which we will look at in depth in the next section.

You can use different **systems** or types of **digital data storage media** to listen to music, for example

- *writable or re-writable optical media* (DVD, CD, Blu-Ray Disc, etc.)
- *magnetic tape* (DAT, ADAT, etc.)
- *solid state memory* such as *Flash Memory*, as used in USB flash drives and the MP3 *Flash Player*
- *hard disk drive*, in this category we can include some specialized readers for MP3, WMA, A4C, etc.
- *streaming via wired or wireless IP networks*
- *digital TV* (earthbound, satellite, HDTV, etc.)

In all these cases the signal is, precisely speaking, a *digital* one, represented by a succession of numbers generally expressed in binary as a group of *bits*, which themselves are the *smallest unit of digital information*.

Music can also come from **non-digital data storage media** (for example vinyl discs, analog tape, audio cassettes, analog videocassettes, analog radio or television, etc.) In this case the electric signal is *analog*, in that it consists of a variation in electric tension that precisely describes the movement of sound pressure, as has already been stated. This type of non-digital storage has now become quite rare in our daily lives, because digital systems offer many advantages over analog systems where the storage and transmission of signals is concerned, even though they are not perfect from the point of view of temporal robustness.

However, it is important to consider that what we call a *digital audio signal* is something that must always be converted into an analog signal, and only later transformed, via electroacoustic transduction by speakers, into an acoustic sound that we can listen to. On the other hand no acoustic sound can be converted into the digital domain if it is not first transformed into an analog signal. The domain of analog signals therefore persists as an important step in the electroacoustic signal chain, even where *digital audio* is concerned.

AUDIO DATA COMPRESSION

Warning! The word *compression* can be ambiguous, since it is used both to mean the *reduction of the quantity of data necessary to represent a signal* (this is the definition that will be discussed in this section) as well as to indicate compression intended to *reduce the dynamic range of a sound* (which we will discuss later in this volume, in the chapter dedicated to audio dynamics processing). For this reason we will refer specifically to the reduction of data as *data compression*, leaving the simple term *compression* on its own to indicate a reduction of dynamic range.

Data compression is an operation composed of various steps to reduce the quantity of data in a file. The inverse operation is called data *decompression or data expansion*.

There are two kinds of data compression systems:

Lossless data compression. With this type of compression the original data can be reconstructed exactly as it originally was – it is therefore non-destructive. One of the most well-known examples of this data compression format is called *zip*, which works well on non-audio documents, or *lossless* compression formats designed specifically for audio, such as FLAC (*Free Lossless Audio Codec*), or the *Apple Lossless* format which all reduce the file dimensions by approximately 50%.

Lossy data compression. With this type of data compression the original data cannot be reconstructed *exactly* as it was – it is therefore a destructive operation. It should be noted that the data discarded is generally considered to be more or less insignificant. Some common examples include the data compression formats *MP3*, *WMA* or *AAC* for audio, *JPEG* data compression for images, and *MPEG* data compression for films and video. These destructive systems are based on human *perceptual* models that work on the fact that our ability to perceive information is limited.
In the case of destructive data compression, the user can choose the *compression ratio*, and therefore control the amount of loss in quality.

5.2 QUANTIZATION AND DECIMATION

QUANTIZATION, QUANTIZATION NOISE AND DITHERING

One factor that can greatly affect the quality of the audio conversion is the number of different amplitude values that can be produced by the converter. The instantaneous amplitude of the analog input signal is transformed into a series of discrete values representing the signal's electric tension. This process is called *quantization*.

Generally speaking, at the moment when an analog signal is measured and converted into a numerical value, its amplitude is never exactly equal to one of the available amplitude values. The converter, in fact, is not able to produce an infinite number of numbers. A 16-bit number, for example, can be expressed only by whole number values between -32768 and +32767, therefore a total number of 65536 different amplitude values. This means there are 65536 (or 2^{16}) different configurations of ones and zeros that the 16-bit binary "word" can have: half the numbers are reserved for the positive range and the other half for the negative. In Table A we can see the relationship between the number of bits and its associated numerical range. For example, if we use 8-bit numbers, we only have 256 (or 2^8) different amplitude values, resulting in poor quality audio.

Number of bits	Number of quantization levels	Range of available numbers	Binary representation
2	4	from −2 to +1	positive values: 00, 01 negative values: 10, 11
3	8	from −4 to +3	positive values: 000, 001, 010, 011 negative values: 100, 101, 110, 111
4	16	from −8 to +7	0000, 0001, 0010, 0011, 0100, 0101, 0110, 0111, etc.
8	256	from −128 to +127	00000000, 00000001, 00000010, 00000011, 00000100, 00000101, 00000110, 00000111, 00001000, etc.
16	65536	from −32768 to +32767	0000000000000000, 0000000000000001, 0000000000000010, 0000000000000011, etc.
20	1048576	from −524288 to +524287	00000000000000000000, 00000000000000000001, 00000000000000000010, 00000000000000000011, etc.
24	16777216	from −8388608 to +8388607	000000000000000000000000, 000000000000000000000001, 000000000000000000000010, 000000000000000000000011, etc.
32	4294967296	from −2147483648 to +2147483647	00000000000000000000000000000000, 00000000000000000000000000000001, 00000000000000000000000000000010, 00000000000000000000000000000011, etc.

Table A

The fewer possible amplitude values there are, the greater will be the differ-ence between the actual amplitude value of the analog signal (which is located at any given moment at a point in-between two neighboring numerical values) and the closest digital amplitude value, and therefore the greater will be the *quantization error* and subsequent *harmonic distortion* of the signal.

For good quality audio, we need at least 16-bit binary whole numbers (integers). There exist several *standards* which are of even higher quality. For example, the DVD (*Digital Versatile Disk*) format provides 16, 20 and 24 bit encodings at sampling rates from 44100 Hz to 192000 Hz. With 24 bit numbers the range of values is from -8388608 to + 8388607, providing 16777216 different possible amplitude values for each sample.[4]

We can describe *quantization* in relation to the number of bits, and therefore to the number of possible amplitude values: The higher this number is, the greater will be the *sound's resolution in terms of amplitude*. The *sampling rate*, on the other hand, looks at the number of samples per second: the higher this number is, the greater will be the *resolution of the sound in time*.

Note that the vast majority of programming languages use floating-point binary numbers, whose encoding is slightly more complicated than it is for integers. For floating-point numbers, a group of bits (called the fractional part) is used to represent the number's digits, and another group (called the significand, coef-ficient, or mantissa) is used to define an exponent that serves as a multiplier, or scaling factor, for the fractional part.

To understand the how floating-point encoding works, we can look at a simple example using our base-10 number system. The numbers 3670, 36.7 and 0.00367 all use the same three digits 3, 6 and 7 (apart from some zeros at the beginning or end of the number). These numbers can also be written in scien-tific notation respectively as $3.67 \cdot 10^3$ (or $3.67 \cdot 1000 = 3670$), $3.67 \cdot 10^1$ (or $3.67 \cdot 10 = 36.7$ and $3.67 \cdot 10^{-3}$ (or $3.67 \cdot 0.001 = 0.00367$).[5]

As you can see, the digits that define the different numbers (the fractional part) are always 3, 6 and 7. What changes is the power of 10 (the scaling factor) by which the numbers are multiplied. By using just three digits to define the frac-tional part, and one (signed) digit to represent the scaling factor, we can create values between a maximum of $9.99 \cdot 10^9 = 9990000000$ and a minimum of $0.01 \cdot 10^{-9} = 0.00000000001$. The same scenario exists for the binary repre-sentation of numbers, with the main difference being that the scaling factor indicates a power of 2, not a power of 10 as we have been using in this simple

---

[4] It is worth noting that in "two's compliment" encoding, the first (leftmost) bit indicates the number's sign, negative if 1 and positive if 0, except in the case where the binary number consists entirely of zeros, in which case it is set to 0.

[5] Another method of representing the same three numbers in scientific notation is as follows 3.67e3, 3.67e1 and 3.67e-3.

example. Typically a 32-bit floating-point number uses 1 bit for the sign, 8 bits for the scaling factor (the power of 2 used as a multiplier) and 23 bits for the fractional part: the range of values which can be represented with this encoding are roughly from $\pm 3.4 \cdot 10^{38}$ (the largest positive and negative values) to $\pm 1.18 \cdot 10^{-38}$ (the smallest positive and negative values). It is important to know that the levels of quantization in a floating-point number correspond to the number of bits that define the fractional part plus one. Therefore, a 32-bit floating point number has 2^{24} levels of quantization (remember there are 23 bits in the fractional part: 23+1 = 24).

With this type of encoding, we get small quantization errors for small signal values and large quantization errors for large signal values. The advantage in this is that the amount of quantization error is constant, in terms of percentage, in relation to the number of bits used.

As we have already seen, digital signals are not continuous, but composed of steps, or discrete values (i.e., *quanta* or "quantum values", from which the term quantization is derived). which in the case of 16-bit numbers signifies 65535 possible values. There are as many *quantization regions* as there are discrete numerical binary values that can be used to represent the amplitude. A quantization region is made up of all the values that must be approximated with the same binary amplitude. If the value being sampled falls into a given quantization region it will be converted to the closest available binary amplitude value. In the explanation of figure 5.15, for example, we can see that the quantization region extending from from -0.5 to 0.5 (excluded) can be approximated with a binary amplitude value of 0, the region that extends from 0.5 to 1.5 (excluded) can be approximated with a binary amplitude of 1, the region from 1.5 to 2.5 (excluded) can be approximated with the binary amplitude 2, and so forth. Note that the amplitude of every quantization region (the difference between the maximum and minimum value of each region) is equal to 1.

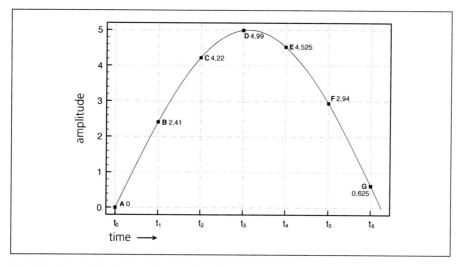

Fig. 5.15 Quantization and quantization error

Let's take a look at figure 5.15 which, for the sake of simplicity, depicts a scenario in which there are only eleven discrete values (from -5 to 5) represented by integers.

The analog signal to which we are referring is the positive half-period of a sine wave. The amplitude value at the peak of this signal is 5, and we have marked the samples, measured at different points in time, with 7 letters (A, B, C, D, E, F and G).

Point A has a value of zero, which does not pose a problem. Point B has a value of 2.41, which is located inside the quantization region corresponding to the value 2, and is thus approximated with that value, with an error of 0.41. In table B we will list the actual measured amplitude values, the quantized values and the corresponding quantization error.

Point	Actual Value	Quantized Value	Error
A	0.0	0	0.0
B	2.41	2	0.41
C	4.22	4	0.22
D	4.99	5	0.01
E	4.525	5	0.475
F	2.94	3	0.06
G	0.625	1	0.375

Table B

The maximum possible error is equivalent to 0.5, equal to half the amplitude of a quantization region.
The larger the number of bits, the less the quantization error will be, and consequently the less noise resulting from this error. Quantization error (also sometimes referred to as round-off error) will actually produce an *audible sound* called *quantization noise* (the use of the term "noise" is not strictly correct, because quantization error is by its very nature not random and related to the sampling rate). This *quantization noise* is added to the original signal and therefore, in turn, has an influence on the overall signal-to-noise ratio.

Don't forget that the adding a bit to a binary number will double its range of values. This corresponds to a 6 dB increase in the dynamic range (see section 1.2T). Actually, in digital systems, the dynamic range corresponds to the distance between the minimum and maximum representable values. Consequently a 16-bit digital signal will have an approximate dynamic range of

16 · 6 = 96 dB

In the table below we can see that the relationship between approximate dynamic range values and binary numbers of different bit-lengths:

Number of bits	8	12	16	18	20	24	32
dB	48	72	96	108	120	144	192

As we have already stated, the maximum quantization error possible can be half the size of the quantization region. Compared to the number of available values, the percentage of error that we will have with a 16-bit number is

(1/2) / 216 = 0.5 / 65536 = 0.000008 · 100 = 0.0008 %

hence producing a negligible amount of error in the audio domain.

However this refers to the only to parts of the signal with the greatest amplitude – those in which we are making use of the entire available 96 dB dynamic range. For the parts of the signal which are at low intensity, the number of decibels of our dynamic range is drastically reduced because we are not using all sixteen bits, but only those which are necessary to express the smaller numbers that approximate the values of the low-level signal (see note 4). For this reason, quantization error will lead to greater problems for low-amplitude parts of the signal.

Let's consider a sine wave with an amplitude of -78 dB, equivalent to 3 bits (see figure 5.16).

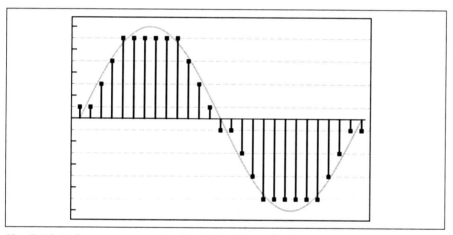

Fig. 5.16 A sine wave quantized to 3 bits (out of 16)

The result, after the conversion, is a waveform that is not at all sinusoidal, but squared-off at its peaks, and therefore having a complex spectrum with many harmonics. This harmonic distortion is due to the fact that only three bits are used for this part of the signal, so it therefore has only 8 different amplitude values (*quantization levels*), resulting in more apparent quantization error within the signal. In order to help mask these undesired harmonics which constitute quantization noise, a small quantity of broadband noise whose amplitude is less than that which can represented by a single bit (i.e the least significant bit) is added to the signal. This is known as *dither*. To calculate the relative amplitude of the least significant bit, you simply divide 1 (the maximum amplitude) by the number of quantization levels. For example, when we use 4 bits, there are 16 quantization levels, so the amplitude of a single level (also known as the *quantization interval*) is equal to 1/16, or 0.0625. Naturally dither adds very slight noise to the signal, but the tradeoff is that by doing so we are able to effectively mask quantization noise. The added *dithering* noise will occupy the low volume levels of the signal, so any quantization errors will be rendered less audible.

The following table summarizes what we have discussed (Table C)

Sampling rate and resolution	Theoretical bandwidth	Theoretical dynamic range	Theoretical signal-to-noise ratio	Bit rate (number of bits per second for each channel)
44100 Hz - 16 bit	22050 Hz	96.32 dB	96.32 dB	705600
48000 Hz - 16 bit	24000 Hz	96.32 dB	96.32 dB	768000
96000 Hz - 24 bit	48000 Hz	144.49 dB	144.49 dB	2304000
192000 Hz - 24 bit	96000 Hz	144.49 dB	144.49 dB	4608000
192000 Hz - 32 bit	96000 Hz	192.66 dB	192.66 dB	6144000

Table C

It is important to note that some of these values are theoretical. For example, the actual dynamic range of a sound could be less than the value stated if the sound being sampled does not fill the maximum available dynamic range, or the signal-to-noise ratio could be altered by additional noise coming from the audio interface, etc. Bit rate is the transfer speed requested by the system in order to be able to transfer sounds to digital media in uncompressed PCM format (this type of data is used by audio files such as WAV, AIFF, SDII and BWF, among others).

Note that in the field of computer music we often used **normalized amplitude**: in other words an amplitude represented by floating-point values that vary between -1 and 1, which is independent of the actual bit resolution of the samples.

DECIMATION, DOWNSAMPLING AND BIT REDUCTION

We have said that the higher the number of bits, the greater will be a sound's definition in terms of amplitude; the higher the sampling frequency, the greater will be a sound's resolution in time. We could purposefully choose to use techniques to reduce a sound's fidelity, either for technical reasons or creative goals: both downsampling and bit-reduction belong to this set of techniques.

Downsampling (sometimes called decimation in signal processing terminology) is a process of resampling a sound at a lower sampling rate. For example if we want to reduce the sampling rate to one quarter of the original rate, we need to use one sample out of 4, throwing away the other three samples. Since the audio interface will keep the original sampling rate, each of the samples we keep will be repeated 4 times (this is a sample and hold operation – see figure 5.17).

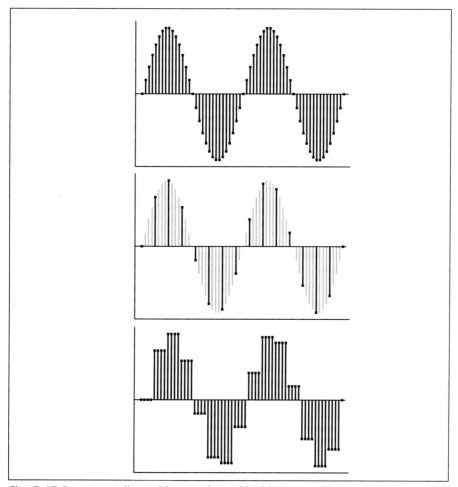

Fig. 5.17 Downsampling with *sample and hold*

Obviously, by reducing the sampling rate, frequencies above the Nyquist of the new sampling rate will create audible aliasing. So, in order to eliminate or reduce this problem, the signal should be filtered with a lowpass filter prior to *downsampling* (since downsampling effectively reduces the sampling rate). The general effect of *downsampling* is very distinctive, especially when used without a lowpass filter, and is often used creatively to obtain a sound with digital distortion, often informally known as "lo-fi".

Downsampling can be used also for technical reasons, such as saving memory or when calculating certain DSP operations whose size is proportional to the sampling rate.

As we have previously learned, *downsampling* is used in sampling systems after oversampling a signal (see section 5.1), in order to return to a standard sampling rate when sampling a sound. This is a good example of *downsampling* being used for technical, as opposed to creative, purposes.

Bit-reduction has a creative use similar to *downsampling* and is often combined with it in order to obtain a more extreme lo-fi effect. It amounts to requantizing a sound using a lower number of bits in order to give the sound less definition in terms of amplitude values and thus a greater amount of quantization noise.

· ·

INTERACTIVE EXAMPLE 5B • *Downsampling* **and bit reduction**

· ·

ⓐⓑⓒ FUNDAMENTAL CONCEPTS

1) A *digital signal* is represented by a series of numbers, each one of which represents an instantaneous pressure value – in other words, the value of the air pressure at any given instant. For example, if we use a sampling rate of 48000 Hz to sample a sound, that means that in one second we will measure its amplitude 48,000 times.

2) The Nyquist theorem states that the sampling rate must be greater than twice the maximum frequency contained in the signal.

3) If we try to generate a digital signal whose *sampling rate* is too low, we get a phenomenon known as foldover: the frequency components that are above half the sr will be reflected under it.

4) The measurable characteristics of an audio interface are: its *total harmonic distortion*, its *signal to noise ratio*, its *frequency response*, its *dynamic range*, its *quantization noise*, its bit depth and the *sampling rates available* to it.

5) Other than the sampling rate, one factor which influences the quality of the conversion is the number of different amplitude values which can be produced by the converter. The fewer the available amplitude values, the greater the probability that, at any given instant, the amplitude of the analog signal will be located midway between one value and the next, thus becoming farther away from their true value when approximated to the nearest available binary value. This creates excessive *quantization error* and pronounced *quantization noise*.

6) *Quantization* relates to the number of bits and therefore to the number of encodable amplitude values: the larger this number the greater the *sound's definition will be in terms of amplitude*. The sampling rate, on the other hand relates to the number of samples per second: the higher this number is, the greater the *temporal definition of the sound*.

7) *Data compression* is a technique used to reduce the amount of data necessary to represent a given signal. The inverse operation is called *data expansion* or *decompression*. The word "compression" can be ambiguous, since it can be used to mean both *data reduction* (as it is here) or compression designed to *reduce the dynamic range of a sound*. These are two entirely different procedures.

5.3 USING SAMPLED SOUNDS: SAMPLERS AND LOOPING TECHNIQUES

THE SAMPLER

We have already talked about sampling sounds, but it is also important to understand how such sounds can be organized, edited, overlapped and modified in simple ways. One of the most often used devices for such operations is known as a sampler, which could be either a dedicated piece of hardware, or could exist simply as stand-alone software, or a software plug-in used by another application. A sampler is designed to capture sounds, and let you organize, edit and play them back via a keyboard or other musical interface that you can play. Traditionally the main purpose of a sampler has been to simulate acoustic and electroacoustic musical instruments, but instead of multiple samples of piano or cello notes you can also use a sampler to arrange groups of sound objects that have nothing to do with the imitation of existing instruments. Here we are more concerned with being able to program a sampler than simply being able to use one, so it is therefore necessary to point out a few of the sampler's basic features.

Unlike a synthesizer, which generates an audio signal on its own (even when using a wavetable containing a single cycle of a waveform), a sampler uses entire sounds. Generally, these are actual recorded sounds which consequently have their own envelope, frequency and spectrum. Obviously, some of these parameters can also be modified by a sampler, for example when transposing a sampled sound to different pitches, associating each of the pitches to different keys of a keyboard. Within synthesizers, on the other hand, we can freely set each internal parameter of the sound, even before generating the sound itself.

Another difference between synthesizers and samplers is the different way a sound's pitch can be transposed. Generally if we record a sound with a sampler, when we transpose that sound an octave higher, its duration will be halved, and the relationship of the amplitudes and frequencies that make up the sound will remain unchanged. As we are well aware, with musical instruments (such as a violin, for example) the relationship of the amplitudes of the various components of a sound are quite different if we play an A at 440 Hz, compared to an A at 880 Hz on the same instrument. This happens because, even though the string may be vibrating at a different frequency, the resonant body of the instrument tends to emphasize a particular group of frequencies (called formants), independently of the note played. The relationship between the note played and the formants will be different depending on the note. In synthesizers we can arbitrarily set a sound's internal parameters, and therefore we are able to simulate these kinds of differences for a virtual instrument that can be played at different pitches. On the contrary, in a sampler we generally do not have this level of control, since the sound itself has already been sampled and therefore its spectrum (and together with it the relationship between fundamental frequency and formants) has already been defined. For this reason, if we want to have a sampler play a realistic piano sound for every note in the instrument's range, we need to have a hundred or so different sounds in order to reproduce the different pitches and different dynamics, especially if we want to avoid the perception of shortening or lengthening sounds when their frequency is adjusted. This technique of creating banks of sounds of similar timbres is used by many samplers and is called **multisampling**.

 SOUND EXAMPLES 5C • *Sampling and Multisampling*

5C.1 Example of a sampled sound played at different pitches.
5C.2 Example of sounds from a multisampler being played at different pitches.

LOOPING TECHNIQUES AND OTHER SAMPLER FUNCTIONS

Another problem that needs to be resolved in order to effectively simulate real sounds has to do with sustained sounds. A sampled sound has its own fixed duration, but often we need to be able to prolong the sound for a greater length of time. To do this, we need to identify appropriate *loop* points to be able to take a sound, such as that of a violin, with duration of 10 seconds, and be able to sustain it for a longer period of time by repeating the part of the sound within the loop. In most cases, simply reading a piece of a sampled sound circularly like this will result in an unnatural, mechanical loop. Indeed, even when locating loop start and end points whose amplitudes are both zero (in order to avoid an unwanted click in the looped sound) it is still highly probable that we will hear a cyclic rhythm in the timbre, with a clear discontinuity at the point where the sound is looped. It is possible to partially avoid this problem by using a *crossfade loop*, which is simply a loop that has a given fade time at the looping point, for example between the end of the sound and the point where the loop begins again.

 SOUND EXAMPLE 5D • *Loops with and without crossfades*

A sampler will also usually include different kinds of filtering, envelopes, LFOs, and the ability to play several sounds simultaneously, either triggered together by a key on a keyboard (with the possibility of controlling the mix between them based on the key pressure, or in other ways which we will look at later), using systems like vector synthesis to create crossfades between different timbres, or to create random loops controlled by an LFO, etc. These days there are many creative ways to use samplers, including the option of using banks of different sounds linked to multiple keys on a keyboard, for example to have a percussion set with completely different or unrelated sounds on each key, such as putting a bass drum on C3, a triangle on C# and a woodblock on the D, and so on.

In reality, the distinction between sampler and synthesizer, which may have made sense at the time when digital audio equipment first appeared, has become increasingly blurry with the introduction of computer-based virtual instruments used as plug-ins: these instruments can easily be hybrids containing a mix of different functions traditionally referred to as either synthesizer or sampler. Consequently, today there exists a continuum of virtual instruments in-between "pure" synthesizers at one end and "pure" samplers on the other, each built with different proportions of the two, so that it is now often difficult to tell the difference between a sampler which also incorporates synthesis, or a synthesizer capable of manipulating samples.

• •

**INTERACTIVE EXAMPLE 5E • *An example of mapping percussion sounds*
*to a keyboard***

• •

Activating a sound with a sampler is generally done by *triggering*: either with a sequencer, MIDI keyboard, or other controller. In addition to this very basic function, let's take a look at five more features that are typically found in samplers:

Looping: a technique which is used to reiterate a sound or portion thereof. A sampler can be configured to play a sound file triggered by a key on a keyboard, and to repeat part of that sound as long as the key remains depressed (*sustain loop*), and/or repeat a different part of the same sound for a given amount of time when the key is released (*release loop*).

• •

**INTERACTIVE EXAMPLE 5F • *Examples of loops, including sustain loop*
*and release loop***

• •

Cue time (or *skiptime*): a sampler can also be configured to skip part of the initial portion of the sound being played, applying a different envelope when starting from this point than the one which would normally be used when starting from the beginning of the sound.

⌐⌐ INTERACTIVE EXAMPLE 5G • *Listening to a sound file at different cue times*

• •

In the next section we will take a closer look at a composite technique, called the blocks technique, based on a progressive, controlled displacement of *cue* points.

Reverse: this term is naturally used to refer to playing a sound backwards from the last sample to the first. A sampler could be configured to play a sound either forward (from the beginning of the sound) or backward (in reverse from the end to the beginning), depending on the pressure of the key being played, for example.

• •

⌐⌐ INTERACTIVE EXAMPLE 5H • *Listening to a sound file both forward and in reverse*

• •

Stereo Panning: a sampler can also be configured to control the distribution of a sound in the stereo listening field. The simplest example would be when simulating a piano on a sampler with multisampling, the low notes are usually *panned* to the left side of the stereo field and the high notes to the right. Some samplers could also be designed to use multichannel output, in order to distribute the sound within a more complex listening space than a simple stereo setup.

Normalizing sampled sounds: this function is designed to scale a sound's amplitude so its peak value has the maximum possible representable value in the sampling system (not to be confused with the concept of *normalized amplitude* which we discussed above in section 5.2). See figure 5.18.

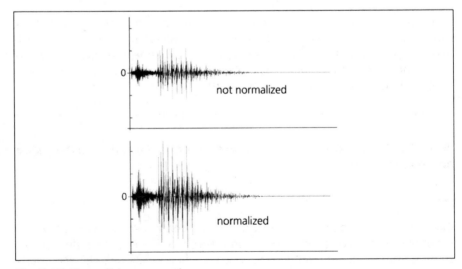

Fig. 5.18 *Normalizing* a sound

DC OFFSET REMOVAL

It is always possible that a recorded or synthesized sound could contain a *DC offset*. This basically means that the waveform's negative and positive areas are not equal. (See figure 5.19)

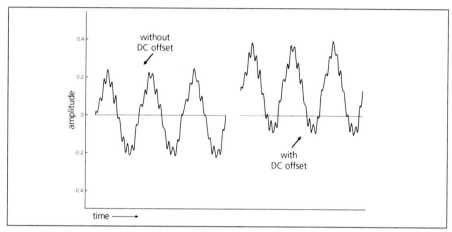

Fig. 5.19 A sound with and without *DC Offset*

In this case the sound is said to have either a positive or negative *DC offset*. A *DC offset* (as already explained in section 4.2) is a signal with a continuous current at a frequency of 0 Hz, or rather a fixed quantity (or value) that is added to a signal. Typically *DC offset* is unwanted: a sound with a positive DC offset will never attain the maximum possible amplitude since the maximum representable amplitude level in a system would be reached sooner in the positive range, preventing the sound from being able to be increased in amplitude without distortion. The same goes for a sound with a negative *DC offset*. A sound with *DC offset* influences (and therefore also offsets) any sound without *DC offset* that is mixed together with it. Furthermore, processing a sound that has a DC offset can create other problems: in the case of a digital delay with feedback (or other algorithms based on feedback-delay), for example, if a sound with DC offset is sent to the input, that offset will continue to accumulate each time that the sound is re-injected into the signal path, as we will see in section 6.2. The solution generally used to eliminate this problem is to apply a highpass filter with a cutoff frequency around 5 to 10 Hz, in other words in a sub-audio area of the sound spectrum, in order to filter out all the components within the lowest frequency range (from 0 Hz to 5-10 Hz). Applying a highpass filter at these low frequencies will not create changes to the perceptible audio range of the sound, but will fix the annoying problem of a sound whose amplitude values are not centered around zero.[6]

---

[6] Note that even a waveform that is centered around 0, but whose positive and negative ranges are different, contains a DC offset (for example a square wave with a duty cycle other than 0.5) and, although it is centered around 0, it will also create the problems which we have been describing.

5.4 SEGMENTATION OF SAMPLED SOUNDS: BLOCKS TECHNIQUE AND SLICING

BLOCKS TECHNIQUE

Strictly speaking, the *blocks technique* is neither a synthesis technique nor a sound processing method. It is a composite technique based on the control of *cues*, or reading points within a sampled sound. The technique was first developed in Vancouver in 1994 by Alessandro Cipriani, using the PODX system, developed by Barry Truax[7], which could be used to control the auto-increment of a *loop*[8]. Subsequently Cipriani has further developed and improved this technique at Edison Studio using Csound and other systems.[9] The blocks technique is a compositional system of fragmentation and reconstruction based on four distinct methods of reading any sampled sound and subsequently constructing a dense polyphony of fragments based on that particular sound.

The main idea is the subdivision of the sound file into *blocks*; these are portions of the sound whose duration can be anywhere between a tenth of a second and three seconds long. The file can be read, or more precisely *performed*, according to a score that indicates which blocks to play, in which order and direction, and when to play them, based on the location of a cue pointer within the file.

Lets take a look at some practical examples using a recording of Gregorian Chant (Angelus Domini) as a sound source.[10] The text of the chant excerpt that we are listening to is: "sicut dixit alleluia."

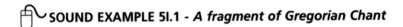

🖱 **SOUND EXAMPLE 5I.1 - *A fragment of Gregorian Chant***

1) O+I - Blocks played in the original (forward) direction, cue pointer incrementing

We can read the file in the "original" mode, in other words from the beginning to the end, reading one 1.3-second block at a time and incrementing the *cue start* with each block ("Sicu-Sicut-Sicut/D- Sicut/Di-icut/Di-icut/Dii-Dii-ii-iix-ixi-xii-iit-itA-Al-All-Alle" etc.). Each fragment will be read in "original" mode (forward from the cue point for 1.3 seconds), and the cue pointer will move

---

[7] The PODX interactive composition system, the first system which implemented real-time granular synthesis, was designed by Barry Truax in 1985 at Simon Fraser University, Burnaby (Vancouver) Canada.
[8] This is a technique of creating a loop whose starting point and/or duration can be incremented or decremented with each successive repetition.
[9] Examples of this technique can be found throughout the following pieces by Cipriani: Recordare, In Memory of a Recorder, Aqua Sapientiae/Angelus Domini, Al Nur (La Luce), Motherless Child, Scène de Naufrage.
[10] This plainchant recording was performed by Giacomo Baroffio.

from the beginning to the end of the file each time advancing by an amount of time less than the duration of an individual block. For this reason each successive fragment will begin with the same sound material that was heard at the end of the preceding block. In this first example, we can see that the blocks are read in the original (forward) playback direction and that the cue is continually incremented.

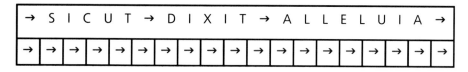

SOUND EXAMPLE 5I.2 - *BLOCKS TECHNIQUE - Original playback direction*
with incrementing cue

2) O+D - Blocks played in the original direction, cue pointer decrementing

Let's now play the cues in reverse order, from the last to the first, reading blocks of one second in length in their original, forward, direction for one second from the cue point ("a-aa-aaa-iaa-uia-uui-luu-elu-eee-Alle-it/a-ii-ixit-Di-ii-Di/cut-Sicut"). In this scenario we are reading the blocks in their original direction, but decrementing the cues – in other words playing them in retrograde.

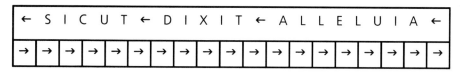

SOUND EXAMPLE 5I.3 - *BLOCKS TECHNIQUE - Original playback direction*
with decrementing cue

3) R+I - Blocks played in reverse (backward), cue pointer incrementing

We can also read one-second blocks of sound, incrementing each of the cues from the beginning of the sound file, as we originally did, but this time reading the blocks themselves backward – from the last sample of the block towards the cue (start) location. ("uciS – tuciS - D/tuciS - iD/tuci - iiD/tuci – iiD – ii – xii – ixi – iix – iii - tii - A/ti – laA – llA – ellA – ell – eel - eee" etc.). For this case we say that the blocks are read in reverse and that the cue increments.

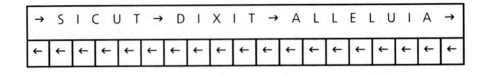

. . . .

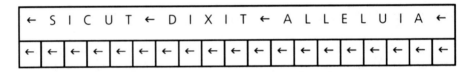

SOUND EXAMPLE 5I.4 - *BLOCKS TECHNIQUE - Reverse playback direction with incrementing cue*

. . . .

4) R+D - Blocks played in reverse, cue pointer decrementing

Finally, we can reverse the order of the cues (from the last to the first) while also playing each block backwards, with a 1.3 second duration. This amounts to reverse block direction with decrementing cues ("eee – eel – ell – ellA - llA – laA - A/ti – tii – iii – iix – ixi – xii – ii – iiD - iiD/tuci - iD/tuci - D/tuciS – tuciS – uciS").

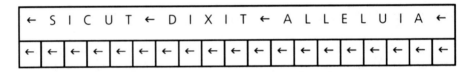

. . . .

SOUND EXAMPLE 5I.5 - *BLOCKS TECHNIQUE - Reverse playback direction with decrementing cue*

. . . .

This technique offers the possibility of exploring the timbre of a sound through the use of rhythm, or better yet, to think about the temporal restructuring of the timbral variations within a single sound object. In a certain sense, the *blocks technique* borders on the broader technique of granulation (which we will take a closer look at in the third volume). Without going into too much detail, it is worth briefly pointing out that the "grains" which are the basic building blocks of granular synthesis have characteristics that are similar to those of the blocks that we have been describing, but generally have a much shorter duration ("grains" typically have a durations shorter than 100 ms, whereas blocks generally have longer durations). The purpose of using "grains" is generally to create complex sounds by overlapping, mixing and varying the speed of a multitude of grains in order to blend them into an entirely new sound. Similarly, when blocks follow one another without pause and their duration is set below a certain threshold, we no longer perceive a steady rhythmic pulse but rather a new sound with a sensation of roughness, due to the fact that the pulse of the blocks within the sound is so quick that we no longer hear it as a steady rhythm. There are no precise boundaries, but generally a "granulated" sound ceases to be granular when we can clearly perceive (and are able to manually imitate) its internal rhythm being generated. In the next example we will listen to a repeated block of sound whose duration becomes increasingly shorter until its repetition no longer produces a sensation of rhythm, but rather transforms into a timbral profile of the original sound.[11]

As we can hear in the sound, there is an indistinct border zone when the block duration is around 80-100 ms., where the sounds lose their separation and begin to be heard as a single sound with rough, "granular" features. It is in this zone when blocks become "grains." However, we should likewise remember that the loss of rhythmic perception can also occur when using the *blocks technique*. For this to happen, even while keeping the block duration above 100 ms., the scan rate (or re-triggering) of the blocks can be set so high that a large number of blocks will be overlapped at the same time, presuming the delay between each successive block is very short. The effect we obtain is somewhat different from that produced by granulation, as we will see in section 5.4P. The main feature of the *blocks technique* is the progression of the cue position in the sound file for each block or rather the manner in which the cue is incremented or decremented to read each successive fragment of sound. In cases where the cue is in a fixed location or moves in a random pattern, we are no longer following the model based on the above 4 playback modes (combinations of original and reverse), so therefore we are using techniques bordering on the blocks technique, rather than actually using the *blocks technique* itself.

· ·

**INTERACTIVE EXAMPLE 5I.6 - *Blocks with progressively decreasing*
*duration***

· ·

The blocks technique has several parameters (which we will also see again when we look at granulation):

Duration = the duration of each block in milliseconds..

· ·

SOUND EXAMPLE 5I.7 - *Different block durations*

· ·

Envelope = each sound fragment should have an envelope (either symmetrical or asymmetrical) superimposed on it in such a way that it does not cause unwanted sounds resulting from attack or decay times that are too short.

---

[11] Already in 1961, Stockhausen spoke extensively about this transformation of rhythm into timbre, and tested out the ideas in Kontakte (cfr. Stockhausen, K., 1963).

Cue Pointer = The progression of the cue pointer position within the file, or the mode in which the cue start location is incremented or decremented in order to read each fragment of sound. In the examples we have listened to so far, the displacement of the cue is *less* than the duration of each block, and due to this the end of one block is repeated at the beginning of the following one. If the cue displacement is greater than the duration of each block it will create jumps in the reading of the sound file, skipping some sections of sound entirely. If the pointer is stationary, it will create a typical *loop* whose duration is equal to that of the block. The *blocks technique*, however, is defined as having a controlled and progressive displacement of the cue pointer position.

Delay = the distance in milliseconds between the playback of one fragment and the next. If the delay is 0 the playback of fragments is continuous. If it is less than 0 successive fragments will be overlapped, and if it is greater than 0 there will be a pause between one fragment and the next. This parameter can also be expressed as a rate for the generation of blocks. In this case, if the scan rate is equal to the block duration the fragments are played back continuously. If the scan rate is less than the block duration successive fragments will be over-lapped, and if is greater there will be a pause between fragments.

· ·

INTERACTIVE EXAMPLE 5I.8 - *Different delay values: positive, 0 and negative*

· ·

Random Variation of Duration = It is possible to randomly vary the duration of each block between a value of 0 (no variation) and a given maximum deviation from the base value, expressed in milliseconds. If we set the maximum deviation (either positive or negative) to 100, and we have a given block duration of 500 ms., the duration of each block will randomly vary between 400 and 600 ms. In order to randomly set the values of a parameter to fall within a range that we have pre-determined, we could use a pseudo-random generator as a low frequency oscillator (LFO, see chapter 4). The amplitude of this oscillator will randomly fluctuate between a minimum of -1 and a maximum of 1, and will therefore output different values at a given rate. It is up to us, as the user to determine an appropriate multiplication factor for these values (in the previous example, we would multiply by 100).

· ·

INTERACTIVE EXAMPLE 5I.9 - *Different random variations in block duration*

· ·

Random Variation of Delay = It is also possible to randomly vary the temporal distance (in milliseconds) between one fragment and the next by providing a maximum deviation from the base value. If we use a multiplication factor of 10 with the output of our pseudo-random generator, the maximum variance from the base value will be exactly 10 (either positive or negative). If our blocks have a base delay of -30 ms, the delay of each block will randomly change between -20 and -40 ms., resulting in an irregular rate. Naturally, if the delay is alternately expressed as a rate for reading each block we could apply the random variation to the rate parameter.

• •

INTERACTIVE EXAMPLE 5I.10 - *Random variation for the delay values*

• •

BEYOND THE BLOCKS TECHNIQUE:
RANDOM OR STATIC CUE POSITION

Random Variation of Cue Position = Just as we did for the Duration and Delay parameters, it is possible to randomly vary the progression of the cue pointer's position when reading blocks from the file. For example, if we are using one of the two modes with an incrementing *cue* pointer (and using a 200 ms. increment between cue read pointers) adding random variation will result in advancing irregularly through the file. If the random cue position variation in this example is 20 milliseconds, the cue will be incremented anywhere from 180 to 220 ms., and result in reading through the sound in an irregular manner. Obviously, this is also possible to do when reading the cues in reverse. This example is near the boundary between granulation and the blocks technique, due to the very short duration of the blocks themselves.

• •

INTERACTIVE EXAMPLE 5I.11 - *Different random variation values for the* *increment/decrement of the cue*

• •

One particularly interesting use of the blocks technique results from being able to easily switch between it and straightforward looping by stopping (or "freezing") the cue pointer for a few moments at a specific point in the file, later moving it to another part of the file, and stopping the pointer again, and so on.

• •

SOUND EXAMPLE 5I.12 - *Interaction between the looping and the blocks* *technique*

39

Naturally, the rhythmic and timbral aspects of the compositional work should take into account the interactions between all of these parameters and their simultaneous use. Essentially, even when starting with very few source sounds, or just a single sound file, it is possible to compose an entire piece of music, exploring a sound and its internal character via a dialog between repetition and variations of rhythm and timbre.

One special example, in which the cue pointer no longer progresses in any definite direction, can be achieved by placing a static cue in the middle of the sound file. If the sound file is 6 seconds long, the cue should be set at the 3-second point and randomly vary the position between +3 and -3 seconds, in order to make the pointer position for each successive block jump to any point in the file[12]. In this way, a control oscillator can be used to continually and randomly displace the read point (or cue) within the sampled sound.

· ·

INTERACTIVE EXAMPLE 5I.13 - *Random variation of values with a fixed cue*

SOUND EXAMPLE 5I.14 - *Excerpt from Cipriani, A. "Scène de Naufrage" - Vocal sounds processed with the Blocks Technique*

· ·

SLICING

Slicing (which we will describe shortly) is a technique constantly used in *dance music* and other musical forms heavily based on rhythm. Although several different techniques called "slicing" have been developed, we can divide them into two basic categories: beat slicing and live slicing.

BEAT SLICING

The first is known as *beat slicing*. With a *beat slicer* you can cut a pre-recorded sound file (generally a percussive or rhythmic sound) into different segments (generally an even number of equal length) and change their order, the delay between one block and another (arranging them in different ways and thereby slowing down or speeding up the rhythm), their playback direction, their pitch and the filtering of individual segments. The result of this is the ability to create variations on the original rhythm by completely re-arranging it.

---

[12] In reality, as we will see in the practice section, you need to take the maximum block length into consideration and subtract this value from the total duration of the sound file, otherwise it would be possible that, while reading a block, the pointer could move beyond the end of the file.

When talking about beat slicing, it is easy to imagine that only of certain types of sound material (percussive sounds) are well-suited to this technique. In reality, though, it can be interesting to use this technique in unorthodox ways and with unconventional source material in order to discover new sonic territory. Of course, one traditional use can be to apply a beat slicer to an easily segmented drum sequence.

· ·

INTERACTIVE EXAMPLE 5J.1 - *Beat sliced drum sequence using reverse* *playback, filters, different block order, etc.*

· ·

The same effect can also be used on material that is not intrinsically based on rhythm.

· ·

INTERACTIVE EXAMPLE 5J.2 - *Beat sliced Gregorian Chant using reverse* *playback, filters, different block order, etc.*

· ·

As we have heard, it is also possible to repeat the same fragment several times: this effect is known as *stuttering*. We will take a look at a different type of *stuttering* in the following section on *live slicing*.

In the examples shown, the segmentation of the files into blocks was done simply by mathematically dividing the audio file into 8 equal fragments. However, *beat slicers* normally provide the option of using a *beat detection* algorithm based on amplitude thresholds which can be adjusted to alter the algorithm's sensitivity. This way, the program can differentiate between important amplitude peaks, such as those of drum beat, and those which we do not want to take into consideration. By using such a system of beat detection, a sound file can be subdivided (or segmented) into pieces that are not derived from a simple subdivision of the sound file into equally-sized blocks, but rather sound fragments which follow the temporal variations inherent in the original file. This kind of system is even able to track the small imprecisions in a drummer's performance, in which case the beginning of each relevant beat is taken to be the beginning of a new block of sound. When a sound is segmented in equal parts, there is a chance that a single sound in the original file will be accidentally divided into two parts, one containing the attack and the other the decay, if the sound happens to begin before a point where a subdivision starts.

Needless to say, *beat detection* algorithms would be completely impractical with our Gregorian Chant example sound, but nonetheless there are still a lot of unexplored possibilities for processing sounds with a *beat slicer*.

LIVE SLICING

The second technique is usually simply called *slicing*, but also sometimes called a *gate sequencer*. These vastly different names already suggest that this is a hybrid technique which is not just the product of a simple re-arrangement of sampled sounds. Some hardware manufacturers have even created "slicers" designed to manipulate real-time input signals. Instead of being segmented into blocks, an envelope is applied at a regular rate to the input sound by the *slicer* using an LFO whose frequency can be synchronized to other machines via MIDI. By applying different filters (also synchronized) to the individual fragments, rhythmic sequences with accents determined by variations in filtering and pitch can be created.

Because of the complexity of the various elements involved, and due to the specific use of *gating*, we will talk about this technique later in the chapter dedicated to dynamics processing.

5.5 PITCH MANIPULATION IN SAMPLED SOUNDS: AUDIO SCRUBBING

Audio scrubbing consists of dragging the playback pointer across a sound's waveform in order to listen to sections of it, or locate precise points in it. The playback speed is not standard, but generally depends on the speed with which the cursor is moved over the waveform. It is possible to read the chosen part of the sound both forward and backward. One of the most common uses for scrubbing is to precisely locate the beginning and end of a particular region, or a particular point in a sound file, such as locating a click you want to eliminate.

. . . .

INTERACTIVE EXAMPLE 5K.1 - *Traditional use of a scrubber: Find the click in the sound file by dragging the mouse across its waveform.*

. . . .

As with many of the applications that have been described up to now, even a scrubber can be used for creative purposes. One example is provided in Sound Example 5K.2, which contains glissandos resulting from the speed with which the cursor is manually scrolled across the sound.

. . . .

SOUND EXAMPLE 5K.2 - *Creative use of a scrubber (from the piece "Net" by A. Cipriani)*

. . . .

Another, more complex, example is that of the *random scrubber*, described in section 5.5P, in which the starting point and/or duration of sections of the audio file which will be read by the *scrubber* are not manually selected but chosen according to random values between a minimum and maximum set by the user.

• •

TESTING • QUESTIONS WITH SHORT ANSWERS (max. 30 words)

1) How do you define a sound represented by a variation in electric tension (voltage)?
2) In what way can the quantization process lead to errors?
3) What are the important parameters for sound definition, in terms of frequency and amplitude?
4) What happens when the frequency of a sound that we would like to convert is more than half the sampling rate?
5) What circumstances can result in a double foldover?
6) What would happen as a result of timing errors in relation to the clock signal?
7) What are the principal features used to evaluate the quality of an audio interface?
8) For which purposes would we want to use sampling rates above 48,000 Hz.?

• •

TESTING • LISTENING AND ANALYSIS

Sound Example AA5.1
In the sounds presented in Sound Example AA5.1, which of the two sounds has a reduction in its sampling rate and which has undergone bit reduction?

Sound Example AA5.2
Which effect was applied to the sound of the voice in example AA5.2?

Sound Example AA5.3
Which effect was applied to the sound of the voice in example AA5.3?

Sound Example AA5.4
Which effect was applied to the sound of the voice in example AA5.4?

Sound Example AA5.5
Which effect was applied to the sound of the voice in example AA5.5?

GLOSSARY

Aliases
Multiple images of the fundamental spectrum which are contained in the digital signal converted to analog. These are made up of repetitions of the spectrum at higher frequencies.

Anti-Aliasing Filter
A special analog low-pass filter which is used to remove multiple spectral images (*aliases*).

Auto-Increment Loop
A technique for creating a loop whose *cue* position value and/or duration can be incremented with each repetition of the loop.

Bit reduction
Re-quantization of a sound using a lower number of bits.

Data Compression
An operation capable of reducing a given quantity of data in a file. There are two data compression systems: lossless (non-destructive) and lossy (destructive). The MP3 format is a common example of the latter.

Distortion
The alteration of a signal by either changing its waveform, resulting in the introduction of components not present in the original signal (harmonic distortion), or changing its frequency response (spectral distortion).

Dithering
Adding a small amount of wide-band noise (known as *dither*), whose amplitude is equal to that of the least significant bit, to a signal in order to mask quantization noise.

Dynamic Range
The relationship between the maximum and minimum amplitudes that can be represented with a given digital system. In analog systems, the dynamic range is equal to the *Signal to Noise Ratio*, in other words, between the maximum signal and the minimum distinguishable signal (i.e., the noise floor).

Foldover
The effect of mirroring frequencies higher than the Nyquist frequency back under it, as well as mirroring those lower than 0 Hz (i.e., negative frequencies) back into the positive range.

Nyquist Frequency
Half the sampling rate of a digital system. In order to be correctly sampled in a digital system, a signal's maximum frequency must be less than the Nyquist frequency.

Protocol
A set of rules for the transmission and reception of data (MIDI, for example).

Quantization
The process by which the instantaneous amplitude of an analog input signal is transformed into a series of discrete values representing signal tension.

Quantization Error
The approximation of a signal to the nearest discrete amplitude value, which results in the creation of *quantization noise*.

Quantization Noise
Unwanted sound introduced by quantization error, due to the fact

that in any given system there are a finite number of binary numbers that can be used to represent amplitude values, which are therefore subjected to approximation.

Signal to Noise Ratio
The ratio between the amplitude of an input signal and the noise floor of a system.

5P
DIGITAL AUDIO AND SAMPLED SOUNDS

PREREQUISITES FOR THE CHAPTER
• THE CONTENTS OF VOLUME 1 (THEORY AND PRACTICE) + CHAPTER 5T

LEARNING OBJECTIVES
SKILLS
• TO KNOW HOW TO MANAGE THE GLOBAL AUDIO SETTINGS FOR MSP
• TO KNOW HOW TO RECORD A SOUND
• TO KNOW HOW TO USE SAMPLED SOUNDS AND MODIFY THEIR AMPLITUDE, FREQUENCY AND BIT RESOLUTION
• TO KNOW HOW TO CONTROL THE PLAYBACK OF A SOUND IN REVERSE
• TO KNOW HOW TO CREATIVELY CONTROL LOOPING OF SAMPLED SOUNDS
• TO KNOW HOW TO IMPORT A SAMPLED SOUND INTO A BUFFER AND USE THIS TO GENERATE SOUND
• TO KNOW HOW TO ASSEMBLE A SIMPLE SAMPLER
• TO KNOW HOW TO CREATIVELY CONTROL THE DEGRADATION OF A SOUND BY MEANS OF BIT REDUCTION AND DECIMATION

COMPETENCE
• TO BE ABLE TO REALIZE A SHORT ETUDE BASED ON SAMPLED SOUNDS, USING LOOPING, REVERSE PLAYBACK, READING FROM DIFFERENT STARTING AND ENDING POINTS IN THE FILE, ENVELOPES, GLISSANDI, ETC.

CONTENTS
• AUDIO SETTINGS IN MSP
• FOLDOVER
• BIT REDUCTION AND DECIMATION
• QUANTIZATION NOISE AND DITHERING
• SAMPLED SOUND ACQUISITION AND PLAYBACK METHODS
• THE CONSTRUCTION OF A SAMPLER
• THE BLOCKS TECHNIQUE
• SLICING
• AUDIO SCRUBBING AND DESIGNING A RANDOM SCRUBBER

ACTIVITIES
• BUILDING AND MODIFYING ALGORITHMS

SUPPORTING MATERIALS
• LIST OF MAX OBJECTS - LIST OF ATTRIBUTES AND MESSAGES FOR SPECIFIC MAX OBJECTS - GLOSSARY

5.1 DIGITAL SOUND

GLOBAL AUDIO SETTINGS IN MSP

In order to manage the global audio settings and choose the audio interface that MSP will communicate with, you will need to open the Audio Status window[1] which is found in the Options Menu (figure 5.1).

Fig. 5.1 The Audio Status window

We will now take a look at the main features of this important window. It is not necessary to memorize all the information that is described here; you can always refer back to this section each time you need information about the Audio Status window.

The window is divided into five boxed sections, each of which contains a group of related parameters. The first section primarily deals with the audio interface. Let's look at some of its main features:

Audio: this can be used to start or stop the DSP engine (this has the same function as sending the start and stop messages to the object **adc~** or **dac~**).

---

[1] This name was adopted beginning with Max 6, in older versions this window was called DSP Status.

Driver: this chooses the audio driver used by MSP. It can be used either to select the driver for an audio interface connected to the computer (in the figure above, the "CoreAudio" driver of a Macintosh computer is selected), or to send the signal to an application compatible with the ReWire protocol[2], by selecting the "ad_rewire" menu option. The "NonRealTime" option can also be selected to generate a signal out of real-time, which can be very useful if the computation algorithm is too complex to be able to be executed in real-time by the computer. In this case the signal will naturally be saved to disk so you can listen to it when processing is finished. Finally, by selecting the option "Live," users of Max For Live[3] can send the audio directly to the program Ableton Live.

Input Device, Output Device: these two parameters allow us to specify the input and output devices. Their function depends on the type of driver and audio interface used.

The second boxed section allows us to regulate the relationship between efficiency and latency for the audio processing, as well as to regulate the temporal precision of Max messages.

I/O Vector Size: digital audio signals do not pass between MSP and the audio interface one sample at a time, but rather in groups of samples called *vectors*. The size in samples of the input/output vector can be set here. The smaller the vector is, the less latency (i.e., delay) there will be between input and output. On the other hand, processing each vector has a certain computational cost – this means that, when using a very small vector size, more vectors will need to be computed per second than with larger vectors, and this will increase the percentage of CPU needed to compute the signal. What's more, a vector that is too large can create problems, in so much as MSP may not be able to calculate the signal in the time available, and this could create a click in the audio being output. We recommend using a setting no greater than 256 samples, even though the range of possible values for this setting will depend on the audio interface (some interfaces, for example, could have a minimum I/O latency of 512 samples).

Signal Vector Size: this parameter indicates the number of samples that the MSP *patch* itself will process at a time. Also in this case, the larger the vector is, the less the computational cost will be. The difference between this and the former vector setting is that the signal vector size will have no effect on latency, and cannot be set to values larger than that the I/O Vector Size. For certain objects (we will see which ones at the appropriate moment) there can nonetheless be useful minimum values. We recommend using a value between 16 and 128 samples.

Sampling Rate: here we can specify the sampling rate. The list of sampling rates available will vary depending on the audio interface used.

---

[2] For more about the ReWire protocol, see http://www.propellerheads.se.
[3] We will talk about Max For Live at the end of this Volume.

Scheduler in Overdrive: this option can also be set using the Options menu. When Max is in overdrive, it gives priority to timed events (for example, bangs sent by the **metro** object) and MIDI messages that it receives, over other tasks of secondary importance, such as the refreshing the patch's graphics, or responding to mouse or computer keyboard input. This means that Max will be rhythmically more precise, but may run the risk of no longer responding to keyboard or mouse input if there are too many timed events to deal with. Nonetheless, MSP signals always have priority over Max messages.

in Audio Interrupt: this option is available only when Max is in overdrive mode. When this option is set to *yes*, timed events are always processed immediately before calculating each signal vector. This allows us to more precisely synchronize audio with Max messages[4]. However, when using this option we should select a very small Signal Vector size (less than 64 samples) otherwise the Max messages are likely to be sent at times significantly different from those expected. This happens because Max must "wait" for MSP to compute its signal vector before being able to generate its timed message. For example, if the signal vector were 1024 samples long using a sampling rate of 44100 Hz, the vectors would be calculated roughly every 23 milliseconds. This means that a sequence of timed Max events would be reproduced in successive bursts every 23 milliseconds. With a signal vector of 16 samples, on the other hand, the time interval between two vectors would be less than a half a millisecond, and therefore would only create very small delays in the timing of Max events and thus absolutely imperceptible to the listener.

The third boxed section presents information about the current signal processing status:

CPU Utilization: indicates the percentage of the computer's processor that MSP occupies in order to perform the active patch's audio algorithm. Obviously, the same patch will use different percentages on computers with different processing power. When a patch requires a percentage equal to or above 95% the computer will become difficult to control and will respond extremely slowly to commands; it is therefore a parameter to keep an eye on.

CPU Limit: this allows you set limits on the percentage of CPU that MSP is able to use (a value equal to zero means "no limit"). This can be useful to keep the program from "taking over" all of the computer's resources.

Signals Used: represents the number of internal *buffers* used to connect MSP objects in the active patch(es).

---

[4] This option is very useful in patches where the Max messages activate the production of sound in MSP, such as in the patch IB_04_sequence.maxpat which was discussed in Interlude B of the first volume: we recommend that you also keep it activated for the patches which will be described in successive sections of this chapter.

Function Calls: reports how many MSP functions are used in the active signal processing network. An MSP function roughly corresponds to an MSP object, although some objects may have multiple internal functions that get added to the overall signal processing network. In general you could think of this number as an estimate of how many calculations are needed to generate a sample in the active patch. Note that the lower the value of these last two fields, the greater the patch's efficiency will be.

The fourth boxed section (present as of Max version 6) allows users to configure the parameters of the *Mixer Engine*, the system that controls the modification of signals in the Max patch. Before Max 6, all signal processing took place inside a single process or *DSP chain*, even when multiple patches were running simultaneously. This meant, among other things, that the global audio would be interrupted every time a patch was modified, because the DSP chain needed to be reconstructed each time. As of Max 6 there is a distinct DSP chain for every active process, and this permits us to work on a patch without interrupting the audio of the other active patches.

Let's take a look at the parameters for the *Mixer Engine*:

Parallel Processing: this parameter lets us assign each DSP chain to a different processor, when running on multiprocessor systems.

Enable Mixer Crossfade: when an active patch (i.e., one that is producing sound) is modified, it is possible to make a crossfade between the sound produced by the patch before and after making the changes. Of course, during the crossfade, the program uses twice the CPU, because there are, in fact, two active copies of the patch running simultaneously. This parameter can be turned *Off* or *On*, or set to automatic (*Auto*), in which case the latency needed to make the crossfade (see below) is added only when the patch is being edited while the DSP engine is on.

Crossfade Latency: the amount of time defined by this parameter is used to rebuild the new DSP chain after a modification to the patch, and to realize the subsequent crossfade. If the time specified is less than the time necessary to rebuild the DSP chain, or if the crossfade is not activated, the audio of the old patch will fade out and that of the modified patch will fade in afterward.

Ramp Time: this is the actual duration of the crossfade. This parameter should have a value less than the amount of time of the Crossfade Latency, so the crossfade will happen correctly.

In addition to using the *Audio Status* window to set the parameters of the *Mixer Engine*, they can also be set in the Max Preferences window, which can be opened using either the *Max* menu (on Macintosh) or the *Options* menu (on Windows). Furthermore it is possible to set some of the *Mixer Engine* parameters by clicking on the last icon (the Mixer icon) in the *Patcher Window Toolbar* located in the lower part of every *Patcher Window*.

Input Channels, Output Channels: these are the number of input and output channels used by the audio interface.

The four menus provided can be used to set the first two of the audio interface's input and output channels. In order to set other channels you need to click on the lower right-hand button marked "I/O Mappings." The button on the lower left, labeled "Audio Driver Setup" can be used to access the preferences for the audio interface you are using.

FOLDOVER

Referring to section 5.1 of the theory chapter, we can see what happens when we move the frequency of a sine-wave oscillator above the Nyquist frequency. Rebuild the patch shown in figure 5.2.

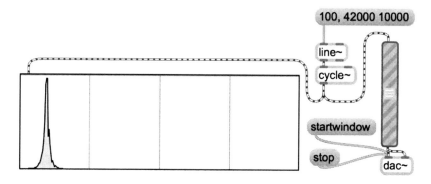

Fig. 5.2 Glissando beyond the Nyquist frequency.

The **cycle~** oscillator object is connected to the **spectroscope~** object which, as we have already seen, can be used to visualize a signal's spectrum. Clicking on the *message box* connected to the **line~** object, triggers a glissando (from 100 to 42000 Hz over 10 seconds) that will go beyond the Nyquist frequency.

The destination frequency indicated in the figure (42000 Hz) assumes that we are using a sampling rate (*sr*) of 44100 Hz. If your audio interface is set to a different sampling rate (you can check this in the *Audio Status* window) you should change it to 44100 Hz, or else use a different destination frequency. The destination frequency should be about 2000 Hz less than the sampling rate being used – for example, for an *sr* of 48000 Hz, the destination frequency of the oscillator should be set to 46000 Hz, whereas for a *sr* of 96000 Hz, the destination should be around 94000 Hz, and so forth. When running the patch, we can see (in the spectroscope) how the sinusoid rises until the Nyquist frequency and then "bounces" back in the opposite direction, stopping at the reflected frequency 2100 Hz (in reality -2100 Hz), which corresponds to the formula that we saw in section 5.2 of the theory chapter:

fc   - sr   =   output frequency
42000 Hz - 44100 Hz =   -2100 Hz

Now let's replace the sine wave with a sawtooth oscillator (figure 5.3).
We will use the **phasor~** object as an oscillator. Although the **phasor~** object outputs a ramp from 0 to 1, by including a few simple math operations, we can convert this into a ramp from - 1 to 1 (as we have already done in the first chapter).

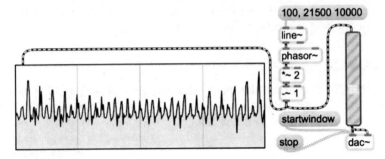

Fig. 5.3 Making a glissando with a non-bandlimited waveform

You will notice that we have lowered the destination frequency to 21500 Hz. This is because we do not need to increase the fundamental beyond the Nyquist since the sawtooth is already rich in harmonics which will pass the Nyquist frequency (as always, you can modify the destination of the ramp in accordance with the sampling rate of your audio interface). If we turn on the patch and trigger the upward glissando, we will hear a shower of harmonics bouncing off the "wall" at the Nyquist frequency. These reflected harmonics quickly descend to 0 Hz, and rebound upward once again, only to be reflected back down, back up, and so forth, creating a constant zigzag throughout the spectrum during the glissando. After 10 seconds, when the ramp is finished, the spectrum will settle into an inharmonic arrangement of partials.

The spectrum of this waveform is extremely rich in harmonics, because it is very close to an ideal sawtooth waveform (which, as we already know, contains an infinite number of harmonic components). This means that it is practically impossible for the **phasor~** object to output a signal without generating foldover[5].

Could the partials that exceed the Nyquist be eliminated by applying a lowpass filter (for example with a cutoff at 20000 Hz) to our non-bandlimited signal generator? Unfortunately, no, because the partials reflected due to foldover inside the reproducible audio band are completely indistinguishable from a sound generated at that frequency, and the filtering would only happen after the reflections. For example, if we use a sampling frequency of 48000 Hz, and we employ the **phasor~** object to generate a non-bandlimited signal with a fundamental of 10000 Hz, we will obtain the following series of harmonics:

---

[5] In reality, when the fundamental frequency is very low, only the very highest harmonics will exceed the Nyquist. As we have seen in section 2.1T, these harmonics are extremely weak, so the foldover is negligible.

Fundamental: 10000 Hz
2nd partial: 20000 Hz
3rd partial: 30000 Hz = 24000 - (30000 - 24000) = 18000 Hz
4th partial: 40000 Hz = 24000 - (40000 - 24000) = 8000 Hz
etc.

Since the third and fourth partials exceed the Nyquist frequency, they are reflected to 18000 and 8000 Hz, respectively. However, these reflected sounds are *actually* already at 18000 and 8000 Hz at the output of the **phasor~** object, so filtering out frequencies above 20000 Hz would have no effect. To filter the unwanted reflections in this scenario, we would need to use a lowpass filter with a cutoff below 8000 Hz, but by doing this we would also eliminate the fundamental and second partial! To fully understand this, try to add the lowpass filter **vs.butterlp~** to the patch shown in figure 5.3, and you will realize that the signal is filtered only *after* the foldover has already taken place.

In chapter 2.1P of the first volume, we have already seen how it is possible to create approximations of ideal waveforms (such as a sawtooth wave) that contain a limited (i.e., not infinite) number of harmonics, using the **vs.buf.gen10** object. Using the method shown in that chapter, we can approximate a sawtooth waveform using only 20 harmonics, and therefore, supposing a sampling frequency of 44100 Hz, we can create an oscillator that can safely go up to about 1102 Hz without incurring foldover (at 1102 Hz, the 20th harmonic will be at 22040 Hz, just slightly under the Nyquist) – above this frequency limit, components within the waveform will begin to be reflected downward.

Fortunately, in MSP there is a group of *bandlimited* oscillators (which we have already seen in section 2.1 of the practice chapter), which generate "classic" waveforms (sawtooth, triangle and square waves), and which allow us to generate the waveform at any frequency under the Nyquist without the effects of foldover. In reality, these waveforms are not written into a predetermined wavetable, but are generated by an algorithm that limits the number of harmonics based on the fundamental frequency of the oscillator: if this is 100 Hz, for example, the waveform will have around 200 harmonics, if it is 1000 Hz it will have only about 20, etc. (assuming we are using a sampling rate of 44100 Hz – for other sampling rates the number of harmonics will vary proportionately). Let's now replace the **phasor~** and math operations in our patch with a **saw~** object, which outputs such a bandlimited sawtooth waveform (see figure 5.4).

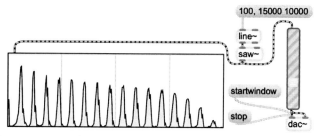

Fig. 5.4 The spectrum of a bandlimited waveform

If we run the patch and trigger the glissando, we can see in the spectroscope that the upper harmonics vanish little by little as they approach the Nyquist frequency. At the end of the ramp, when the fundamental of the oscillator passes 11025 Hz (one quarter of the sampling rate, or half the Nyquist), there is only a single component – the fundamental – left in the spectrum, since at this frequency the second harmonic would create foldover (because it would be greater than 11025 · 2, and thus above the Nyquist frequency).

5.2 QUANTIZATION AND DECIMATION

BIT REDUCTION, QUANTIZATION NOISE AND DITHERING

Within MSP, samples are represented as floating-point numbers that have a length of 64 bits (as of Max version 6). Apart from the bit used for the number's sign, there are 11 bits used for the mantissa and 52 bits for the fractional part of the number. There are therefore 2^{53} levels of quantization (for more on floating-point number theory, scaling factor, etc., see Chapter 5.2T).

Let's look at a practical example of how we can reduce the number of quantization levels of an MSP audio signal. In addition to serving as a pedagogical example, this technique can additionally be used to produce a somewhat clichéd Lo-Fi (low fidelity) sound which has already acquired a musical aesthetic of its own. Recreate the patch shown in figure 5.5.

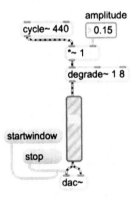

Fig. 5.5 Generating an 8-bit sound

The **degrade~** object can be used to (virtually) reduce both the number of bits used for the samples in a digital signal, as well as its sampling rate. This object has two arguments that can also be changed by using the object's second and third inlets. The first argument indicates the reduction factor of the sampling rate[6] and the second the bit depth of the signal. The example in the above figure therefore shows degradation to an 8-bit signal, which has only 256 levels of quantization.

---

[6] A value of 1 indicates a sampling rate which is unchanged compared to that used by the sound card: further details below.

When the amplitude of the signal (a sine wave oscillator) is at maximum we are using all quantization levels available to us, but even so, quantization noise is still clearly audible. By lowering the value of the number box which controls the sine wave's amplitude to around 0.15 we can hear a much more pronounced effect because the signal uses even fewer degrees of quantization.

Now let's take a look at a patch that will let us apply any desired number of bits and calculate the relative levels of quantization: open the file **05_01_quantize. maxpat** (figure 5.6).

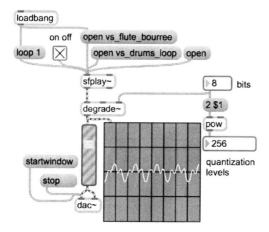

Fig. 5.6 File **05_01_quantize.maxpat**

The right hand part of the patch contains the algorithm that allows us to calculate the number of levels of quantization based on a given number of bits. Since quantization levels are a power of two raised to the number of bits (and therefore always powers of two), we have used the **pow** object to correctly calculate this value. The **pow** object receives a list of 2 values from a message box: the first (the base) is set to 2 and the second (the exponent) is the replaceable argument $1 that can be changed to any value between 1 and 24, thereby allowing us to calculate the number of quantization levels anywhere between 1 and 24 bits.

In this example patch we are also using the **degrade~** object to quantize the input sound to a desired number of bits by sending a bit depth reduction value to the third inlet.
Upon opening the patch, the **loadbang** object triggers two message boxes that tell the **sfplay~** object to open the sound file **vs_flute_bouree.wav**[7] and to

---

[7] This file (and indeed all the other audio files that we will use) is found inside the sound library Virtual Sound Macros, in the folder "soundfiles" Note that in Max it is not strictly necessary to add the file extension to the name of a sound file (in this case .wav). However, if there are multiple sound files in the same folder with the same name but a different extension, Max will load the file whose extension comes first, alphabetically. For example, if there are two files vs_flute_bouree.wav and vs_flute_bouree.aif, Max would load the file with the extension .aif.

activate loop mode for playback. In order to actually trigger the **sfplay~** object to play the sound file, we need to click on the **toggle** connected to it (after having clicked on the "startwindow" message, naturally), and at this point it is possible to hear the result of reducing the number of bits and consequently altering the sound's quantization. You can try to load other sounds and hear how they become degraded by lowering the samples' bit length. Remember that every time you load/open a new sound file you will need to initiate playback once again by reactivating the **toggle** connected to **sfplay~**.

In order to improve the sound quality of our purposely-degraded audio and eliminate as much distortion as possible, we can simulate dithering: open the file **05_02_dither.maxpat** (fig 5.7).

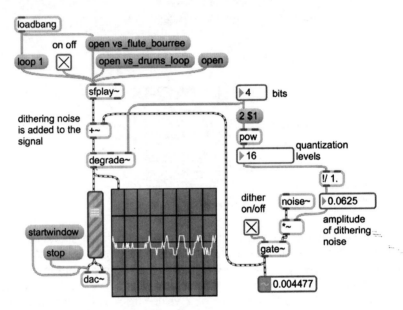

Fig. 5.7 The file **05_02_dither.maxpat**

In the right-hand part of the patch there is a **noise~** object which produces white noise that is scaled down to match the quantization span for the desired bit depth. Using the operator **!/** with an argument of "1." will generate a number representing the amplitude of a single level of quantization: for example if the level of quantization is at 4 bits, as it is in the figure, the amplitude of a single level is equal to 1/16 or 0.0625. This amplitude serves as our multiplication factor for the white noise.

The scaled noise is added to the signal (see the left-hand side of the patch), and the resulting summed signal is sent to the input of the **degrade~** object. The dithering can be turned on and off using the **toggle** in the lower-right side of the patch. This **toggle** is connected to a **gate~** object which lets an input signal in the right inlet pass through to the output if the value sent to the left inlet is 1, or will block the signal if the value sent to the left inlet is 0. When the number of bits is low (under 12) the noise added by the dithering is very apparent, but nevertheless contributes to eliminate harmonics produced because of distortion. Try to use the percussion sound **vs_drums_loop.aif** with a very low number of bits (for example 4): although the result is very noisy, dithering does allow the drum sound to be acceptably reconstructed (especially considering we are only using 4-bit numbers as samples!); when turning off dithering the sound becomes extremely distorted.

To reduce the dithering noise we can use filters: open the file **05_03_dither_filter. maxpat** (figure 5.8).

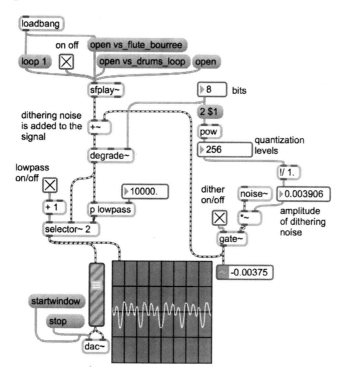

Fig. 5.8 The file **05_03_dither_filter.maxpat**

Here, we have added a lowpass filter with a steep slope (the subpatch [**p** lowpass] actually contains an 8th order *Butterworth* lowpass filter). It is possible to turn the lowpass filtering on and off via the **selector~** object which we have already seen in chapter 1.2P. Try to adjust the cutoff frequency of the filter so it eliminates as much of the dithering noise as possible, without excessively darkening the resulting sound.

DECIMATION

As we already know, decimation is the process by which we reduce the sampling rate of a digital sound, and consequently reduce the band of reproducible frequencies. But what could we possibly use this for? First, we could explore the phenomenon of aliasing which was discussed in section 5.1 in the theory chapter: if we reduce the sampling frequency of a sound to half or a quarter of the sampling rate set on our audio interface, we can hear the aliases generated in the spectrum (as well as see them in the **spectroscope~**), because our interface is able to reproduce them. Second, we can continue to experiment with the degradation of the sound, as explained at the beginning of this chapter, by reducing the levels of quantization of a sampled sound (i.e., bit reduction). Finally, for creative applications of this kind of sound degradation, we could always use these techniques in the realm of *sound design*, for example if we need to imitate the sound of old digital equipment such as early mobile phones or home computers from the 1980s.

To *downsample* a digital signal, i.e., to reduce the number of samples per second, we need to keep some samples and get rid of others. If we wanted to reduce the sampling rate by half we would need to eliminate every other sample from the original sound, or if we wanted to reduce the sampling rate by a quarter of the original rate, we would need to keep one sample out of four, etc.

Downsampling can also be accomplished using the **degrade~** object which we have been using since the beginning of this chapter.

The **degrade~** object can be additionally used to reduce the sampling rate of an input signal via its first argument (or by sending a value to the second inlet). This value, called the *Sampling Rate Ratio*, represents the ratio between the actual sampling rate of the signal and the downsampling performed by the object. If the Sampling Rate Ratio is 0.5, the resampling frequency will be half the sampling rate of the audio interface. If this value is 0.25, then it will be a fourth, and so on.

Now open the file **05_04a_downsample_1.maxpat** (figure 5.9)

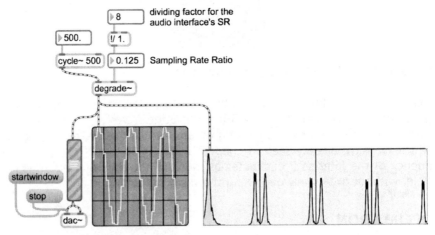

Fig. 5.9 The file **05_04a_downsample_1.maxpat**

In the figure we can see that the value of the Sampling Rate Ratio parameter is set to 0.125: this means that the resampling is equal to 1/8 of the sampling rate of the audio interface. In order to simplify the control of this parameter in the patch, we can add a dividing factor for the sampling rate (which is the Number Box in the upper-central part of the figure) that can be used as a divisor for the value 1 in the object !/ (which we already learned in the first volume). A dividing factor of 2 corresponds to a Sampling Rate Ratio of 0.5 (half the sampling rate), and a dividing factor of 4 corresponds to a Sampling Rate Ratio of 0.25 (a fourth of the sampling rate), etc.

The right hand part of the patch shows us the effect of *aliasing*. The spectroscope display object (appropriately named **spectroscope~**) will in fact show all the frequencies up to 22050 Hz, corresponding to our Nyquist frequency, or half of the 44100 Hz sampling rate set in the audio interface. When the re-sampling frequency of the **degrade~** object is set to 44100/8 = 5512.5 Hz, the resulting Nyquist frequency is 5512.5/2 = 2756.25 Hz. The reproducible audio band therefore corresponds to one eighth of the frequencies shown in the **spectroscope~** object, in other words up until the halfway point of the first of the four rectangles into which the display is divided. The first peak, visible on the left side of the spectroscope display, corresponds to the "real" frequency produced by the sinusoid at 500 Hz, while the peaks visible in other areas of the spectrum are due to the effect of *aliasing*.

Referring to the section on "aliasing and foldover: the causes" in section 5.2 of the theory chapter, we can calculate the precise frequencies produced as a result of aliasing.

f	sr	k	f + ksr	resulting frequency
500 Hz	5512.5 Hz	0	500 + (0 x 5512.5)	500 Hz
500 Hz	5512.5 Hz	1	500 + (1 x 5512.5)	6012.5 Hz
500 Hz	5512.5 Hz	2	500 + (2 x 5512.5)	11525 Hz
500 Hz	5512.5 Hz	3	500 + (3 x 5512.5)	17037.5 Hz
500 Hz	5512.5 Hz	-1	500 + (-1 x 5512.5)	-5012.5 Hz
500 Hz	5512.5 Hz	-2	500 + (-2 x 5512.5)	-10525 Hz
500 Hz	5512.5 Hz	-3	500 + (-3 x 5512.5)	-16037.5 Hz
500 Hz	5512.5 Hz	-4	500 + (-4 x 5512.5)	-21550 Hz

Note that frequency values with an inverted sign are still displayed by the **spectroscope~** object in the positive range (in other words, at the same frequency, without the negative sign). The second peak, visible just to the left of the first vertical line subdividing the display, therefore corresponds to the peak at -5012.5 Hz, the third peak (just to the right of the first subdivision line) corresponds to 6012.5 Hz and so on, until the last peak in the frequency spectrum, which corresponds to -21550 Hz.

We can also see how the copies generated by aliasing gradually decrease in amplitude: this is due to the fact that the **degrade~** object performs a sample and hold between each sample and the next (for more details see section 5.1T "Digital to Analog Conversion")[8]. In the patch shown in figure 5.9 the re-sampling rate is equal to 1/8 of the sampling rate of the audio interface. This means that the **degrade~** object uses only one value in 8 from the signal that it receives, throwing away the other 7. However, the audio interface has not changed its sampling rate, and still needs to process 44100 samples per second. It is therefore necessary to replace the discarded values with alternate ones. For this reason, the **degrade~** object "holds" the first sample value as a replacement for the remaining 7, creating the stepped signal which we can see in the oscilloscope in figure 5.9.

In an ideal sampling system, in which a signal is sampled with impulses of infinitesimal duration, the copies of the spectrum would not have any loss in amplitude across the frequency spectrum. Let's try to simulate an ideal sampling system by setting the discarded sample values to zero. In order to do this, we will use an impulse train – a signal consisting of single-sample impulses of amplitude 1 at a given rate – in place of the **degrade~** object. So, if the sampling rate were 44100 Hz, for example, an impulse train whose frequency is 5512.5 Hz (or one-eighth of the sampling rate) would be a cyclic signal consisting of one sample with an amplitude of 1, followed by 7 with a value of 0. If we were to multiply this impulse train by a digital sound, we would effectively downsample the sound by one eighth of the sampling rate. The multiplication of the two digital signals, in fact, happens sample by sample: when a sample of the sound is multiplied by a peak in the impulse train (a value of 1) the sample will remain unchanged (multiplying by 1 does not change the value), the 7 subsequent samples will conversely be multiplied by 0, and therefore themselves be zeroed, the next sample will be mulitplied by 1 (and therefore will "pass" unchanged) and the next 7 will be zeroes, and so forth (see figure 5.10).

Fig. 5.10 Sampling a waveform

---

[8] The corresponding figure in section 5.1T appears to show a much sharper decrease in amplitude than in the spectroscope display shown here. This is because the MSP **spectroscope~** object by default uses a logarithmic scale on the amplitude axis (the y axis), whereas a linear amplitude scale has been used for the image in section 5.1T.

The object which will allow us to generate an impulse train is **vs.click~** (a non-bandlimited impulse generator that we first saw in section 3.9 of the first volume). This object has two inlets – one for the frequency and the other for the phase – just like the **cycle~** object. Let's make a small patch that allows us listen to the impulse train generated by the **vs.click~** object (see figure 5.11).

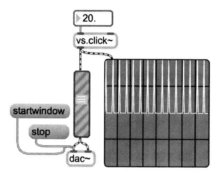

Fig. 5.11 A non-bandlimited impulse generator

In the figure, we can see that the generator has a frequency of 20 Hz, which means that it will generate 20 impulses a second.

The file **05_04b_downsample_2.maxpat** contains a patch that performs downsampling via multiplication with an impulse train (figure 5.12).

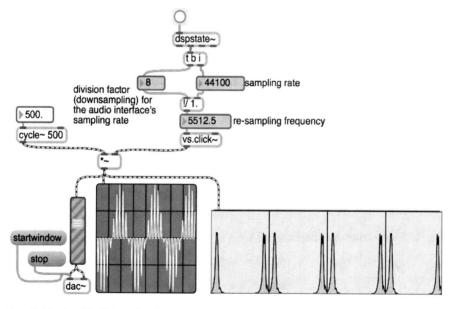

Fig. 5.12 the file **05_04b_downsample_2.maxpat**

Let's first take a look at the top part of the patch: the **dspstate~** object provides us with some information about MSP's audio "engine," namely the

63

information that we can see in the second boxed section of the Audio Status window, which was covered earlier in section 5.1: *Sampling Rate, I/O Vector Size* and *Signal Vector Size*. The object sends the sampling rate out its second outlet each time that audio is started for the patch using by clicking on the "startwindow" message. This frequency value is then divided by a downsampling factor which can be set by the user via the number box, thereby producing a resampling frequency that can be used as an input frequency for the impulse train generator **vs.click~**. This impulse train, multiplied by the audio signal (in this case a sine wave oscillator) essentially resamples it. We can see in the oscilloscope that the waveform is no longer a stepped signal, but appears as a series of impulses whose amplitude follows the waveform of the original sine wave. Moreover, in the spectroscope we can observe that the frequencies generated by aliasing all have the same amplitude.

The main problem with downsampling is that *aliasing* produces frequencies which we generally do not want to hear. The second problem is that of foldover, which occurs when the frequencies present in the signal being resampled are above the new Nyquist frequency. Both problems can be resolved using lowpass filters whose cutoff frequencies are equal to the Nyquist frequency[9]: however, we will need to use a filter with the steepest possible cutoff frequency, in order to completely eliminate the undesired frequencies (and let *only* the useful frequencies through). In order to do this, we will not use any of the filters which we learned about in chapter 3, but instead use a new filter that acts like a "brick wall" at the cutoff frequency: **vs.brickwall~**. Rebuild the patch shown in Figure 5.13.

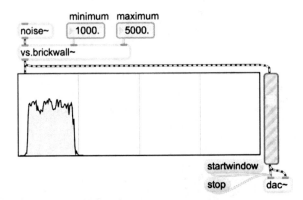

Fig. 5.13 The filter **vs.brickwall~**

---

[9] Naturally, we are talking about the Nyquist frequency relative to the resampling frequency. In this case, the frequencies which could generate foldover need to be filtered before the signal is resampled; filtering them afterward, as we have already learned, is not possible because the frequency components will have already have been reflected inside the Nyquist band. Frequencies generated as a result of aliasing, on the other hand, need to be filtered after resampling (because, obviously, they do not exist before the resampling takes place!)

As can be seen, the object accepts a minimum and a maximum frequency, and does not let any frequencies outside these limits pass through. In reality this object does not use the algorithms that we learned in chapter 3, but operates in the *frequency domain*, by means of the *Fast Fourier Transform* (FFT). We will cover this in a later chapter in the 3rd volume, so don't worry if you don't understand these terms – for the moment this filter should just be accepted as a basic tool that we can use.

Open the file **05_05_downsample_filter.maxpat** (figure 5.14).

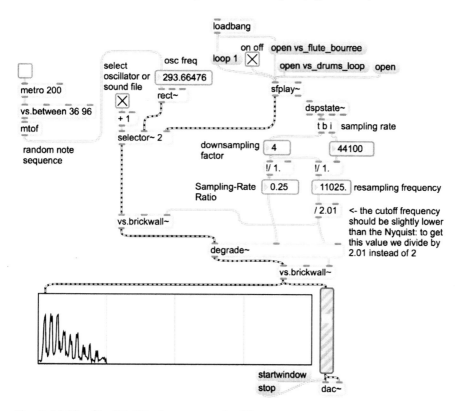

Fig. 5.14 The file **05_05_downsample_filter.maxpat**

This patch uses two **vs.brickwall~** filters: the first is placed immediately after the incoming signal in order to remove frequencies above the Nyquist, and the second immediately after resampling the signal, in order to eliminate aliased copies of the spectrum. The patch gives us a choice between using either a band-limited square-wave oscillator (**rect~**), or a *soundfile* as an input signal (we can select which one to use with the **toggle** connected to the **selector~**). A random note generator (on the left side of the patch) is connected to the oscillator. The cutoff frequency used for both filters should actually be slightly lower than the Nyquist, just to be absolutely certain that all of the unwanted frequencies are eliminated. To do this we simply divide the resampling frequency by 2.01 instead of dividing by 2. Try out the patch for yourself in order to better grasp what a downsampled sound sounds like.

ACTIVITY

Make a patch that allows the user both to change the sampling rate of a signal, as well as to modify the number of bits used for its sample values. The patch should contain the dithering algorithm, with a lowpass filter to attenuate the noise, and a brickwall filter both before and after resampling: in other words this patch should integrate the features of both **05_03_dither_filter.maxpat** and **05_05_downsample_filter.maxpat**. After doing this, you can use the patch to experiment with the effects of signal degradation: feel free to also apply other creative techniques to your patch, such as using an LFO[10] to dynamically vary the different parameters (including number of bits and resampling frequency[11]).

. . . .

SAMPLE AND HOLD

In addition to the **degrade~** object, there is also another object that lets you perform a *sample and hold* operation on an input signal: the **sah~** object. This is a very useful object that we will use throughout this volume and the next. Let's take a look at how it works: reconstruct the simple patch shown in figure 5.14b.

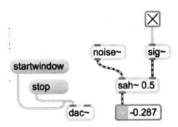

Fig. 5.14b The **sah~** object

First, notice that this patch does not produce any sound; we are using the **dac~** just to turn on the DSP engine. The object's name is simply an abbreviation of *sample and hold* (you may sometimes see this term abbreviated as "S&H" or "S/H") and the object does precisely what its name implies: it samples the input signal and holds the sampled value.

Each time the **toggle** is activated, the **sah~** object will sample the signal output by **noise~** and send it to its own outlet (connected to the **number~** object). This value is sustained until the **toggle** is deactivated and reactivated again. Try it out for yourself.

---

[10] See chapter 4 in the first volume for more details about the LFO.

[11] To vary the 2 parameters of the **degrade~** object you should convert the signal produced by the LFO into Max numerical values using the **snapshot~** object, which we covered in section 2.4P in the first volume.

Let's take a closer look at how this mechanism works. The **sah~** takes two signals: its left inlet receives the signal that will be sampled, and its right inlet receives what is known as a trigger signal. The argument given to **sah~** (0.5 in the patch shown in the figure) represents the threshold that the trigger signal should exceed (i.e., cross in the upward direction) in order for the object to take a new sample of the signal being sampled. Activating and deactivating the **toggle** will cause it to output the values 1 and 0, which are converted into a signal using the **sig~** object and sent to the right inlet of **sah~**. When the trigger is 0, it is under the threshold, but when it changes to 1 it crosses the threshold in an upward direction, causing the left input signal to be sampled.

This object allows us to create a classic sample and hold effect using randomly generated frequencies. Now, rebuild the patch shown in figure 5.14c.

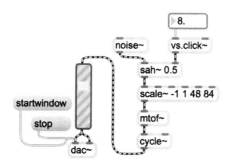

Fig. 5.14c The classic sample and hold effect

In this patch the trigger signal is an impulse train output by **vs.click~** which causes a signal to be sampled with each impulse. There are 8 impulses per second using the settings shown in the figure. This means that the random signal values output by **noise~** will be sampled (and held) 8 times per second. These random values are converted into values between 48 and 84 (corresponding to the MIDI notes C2 and C5) using the **scale~** object, and then converted into frequency values using **mtof~**. Changing the frequency of **vs.click~** allows the speed of random note generation to be varied.

It is also possible to use the **sah~** object to create the same type of downsampling used in the **degrade~** object. Can you figure out how to create a patch that performs this operation? (Hint: you just need to replace one object in the 05_04b_downsample_2.maxpat patch, shown in figure 5.12, with the **sah~** object.)

5.3 USING SAMPLED SOUNDS: THE SAMPLER AND LOOPING

In this section we will both continue and extend some ideas that were already covered in section 1.5 of the first volume: managing and controlling sampled sounds with Max.

SOUND ACQUISITION

Needless to say, it is possible to use Max to acquire (i.e., sample) an external sound sent to the audio input of your audio interface, either from a microphone (in the case of acoustic sounds) or from an audio cable (in case the sound was produced by electronic hardware of some sort). The object that lets us bring these sounds into the Max environment is called **adc~** (Analog to Digital Converter). Connect a microphone or external instrument to the input of your audio interface (or your computer's audio input) and recreate the patch shown in figure 5.15.

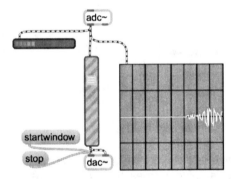

Fig. 5.15 Sound acquisition

By default, the **adc~** object has two outlets corresponding to the first two input channels of the audio interface; these are generally the left and right channels of a stereo setup. This object can also accept numerical arguments to indicate which input channels to use. For instance, if we have an audio interface with 8 inputs we could create an [adc~ 1 3 7] object which would have three outlets corresponding to input channels 1, 3 and 7 of the interface. The comparable **dac~** object can also similarly accept arguments – this has already been covered in section 4.8 in the first volume.

The graphical object to the left of the **adc~** is called **meter~**. It is an audio level indicator similar to the **levelmeter~** object which we looked at in section 1.4. If you activate this patch and send the sound to the interface, you should be able to see the sound in the **scope~** object and the signal level in **meter~**. By cautiously increasing the output volume of the **gain~** slider (avoiding feedback from the microphone) you will be able to hear the sound coming from the speakers that are connected to your audio interface. Obviously, the **gain~** slider does not affect the live input level, but only the listening level. Once the external sound has been acquired and output via the **adc~**, it can be used just like any other audio signal in Max; it could even be recorded to disk. Modify the patch as shown in figure 5.16.

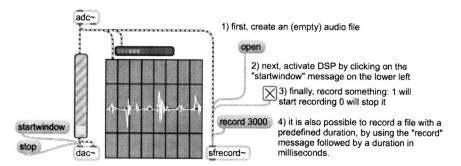

Fig. 5.16 Recording an external sound

Here we have used the **sfrecord~** object, which was already introduced in section 1.5, and which allows us to record a sound file to disk. Remember that each time you want to make a recording, you will need to open a new sound file (it is not possible to add to an existing recording).

READING SOUND FILES FROM DISK

For the following patches we suggest that you activate both the "Scheduler in Overdrive" and "Scheduler in Audio Interrupt" options in the Audio Status window, and set the *Signal Vector Size* to a small value such as 32 samples. (Note that for advanced operations which require high rhythmic precision, you may eventually want to use an even smaller value.)

Once you have recorded a sound file you can listen to it again using **sfplay~**. This object was already briefly shown in section 1.5 of the first volume, but if you need to refresh your memory about its main features, you can open the file **05_06_sfplay_commands.maxpat** (figure 5.17).

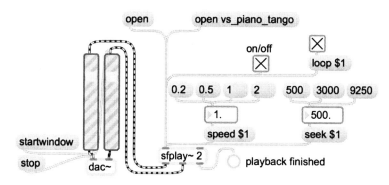

Fig. 5.17 The file **05_06_sfplay_commands.maxpat**

As you can see, this patch shows some new commands alongside those that we previously learned. The **sfplay~** object shown in the figure can play stereo sound files because it has a numerical argument "2" (and consequently also two audio outlets). Without this argument, **sfplay~** would have only one audio outlet. The patch uses two **gain~** sliders: one for each of the two audio channels. Also note that the right outlet of the **gain~** slider on the left is connected to the left inlet of the **gain~** slider on the right.

The right outlet of the **gain~** slider sends the cursor position when the slider is moved: by default the slider position can range from 0 (the lowest value) to 157 (the highest). The left input of the **gain~** object, in addition to taking an audio signal to attenuate, can also accept a numerical value (by default from 0 to 157) which can be used to position its cursor location. The connection between the two **gain~** objects therefore allows us to use the cursor of the left slider to set the output amplitude of both sliders simultaneously when the patch is in performance mode, since every movement of the slider on the left will control that on the right. (On the other hand, if we move the right slider's cursor, the left slider does not change – why?)

As we have already seen, it is possible to open any sound file that is in Max's *search path*[12] simply by using the "open" message followed by the name of the file in question. It is also possible to open any other sound file by simply using the "open" message on its own. Doing this opens a system dialog window that lets us select any file we want. To begin playing the selected sound file, we need to send a numerical value of 1 to **sfplay~**, to stop playback, we can send a 0. The **toggle** object is very useful to for this purpose. Playback of the sound file will naturally stop when the end of the file has been reached, at which point **sfplay~** will send a "bang" message out its rightmost outlet. It is also possible to repeatedly play back the sound file in a loop by sending **sfplay~** a "loop 1" message. Naturally, looping can be turned off by sending a "loop 0" message.

Another interesting feature of **sfplay~** is its ability to change the playback speed of the file, using the "speed" message followed by a number indicating the desired playback speed: 1 indicates normal speed, 2 is used to double the speed, 0.5 is used to halve the speed, etc. In the path in figure 5.17 a float number box is connected to the message "speed $1". There are several message boxes connected to the float number box, each with a different speed to test out; needless to say, you can also manually set the speed directly using the number box itself. The final new message shown in this patch is "seek", which tells **sfplay~** to begin playback from a specific point in the file other than the beginning; the starting point (in milliseconds) is indicated by a numerical value after the message.

In reality, the "seek" message is not very adept at starting from various locations in a sound file in rapid succession, especially in the case of a very

---

[12] See section 2.1 ("Using Wavetables with Oscillators") in the first volume.

long sound file, because the head on the hard disk needs a certain amount of time to physically reposition itself to the desired starting point in the file. In order to be able to more efficiently and quickly start from arbitrary points in a sound file it is necessary to predefine the sections of the sound file that we want to play. These sections (called *cues*) should be defined, using the "preload" message, before actually initiating playback. They tell **sfplay~** to load the beginning part of each cue into memory in order to compensate for the physical limitations of the hard disk head. Figure 5.18 shows how to use this feature.

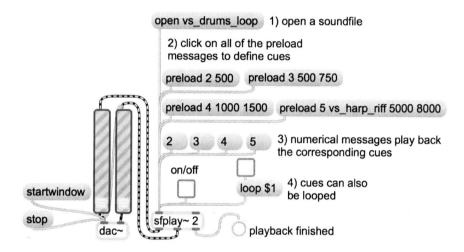

Fig. 5.18 The preload command

In this patch, which we would like you to recreate by modifying the preceding patch, we have defined four different cues. To define a cue, you need to send the "preload" message followed first by the cue number (which can be anything between 2 and 32767)[13], and then by a variable number of items.

For the preload message, if the cue number is followed by a single numerical value, playback of that cue will begin from that point (in milliseconds) until the end of the file. If there are two numerical values after the cue number they represent the starting and ending points of the cue (both values are given in milliseconds). If these numerical messages are preceded by a file name (as in the case of cue 5 in figure 5.18) the fragment of sound will be from the file specified – in other words a preloaded cue can be different from the file that was initially opened. Thus, with a single **sfplay~** object, it is possible to play back fragments of many different sound files.

---

[13] Cue number 1 is reserved for playback of the entire file, and 0 is used to stop playback. In practice, the messages "1" and "0" that we sent to **sfplay~** using the **toggle** object can be used to activate cue 1 (playback of the entire file) and cue 0 (stop playback).

At this point, we could subdivide a single sound file into equal (or unequal) parts by creating cues that could then be played back in any arbitrary order. But before we can do this, we need to know the length of the sound file. This information can be obtained (alongside other useful information) with the **sfinfo~** object. Recreate the patch in figure 5.19.

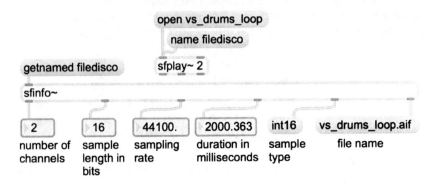

Fig. 5.19 Soundfile information

The **sfinfo~** object, shown in figure 5.19, provides us with useful information about a *sound* file. We can get information about any sound file by sending the "open" message to the **sfinfo~** object; this information is sent out the outlets of the object itself. Alternately, we can obtain information about a file already opened by an **sfplay~** object as follows:

- we provide a name to an **sfplay~** object using the "**name**" message followed by a reference name (any character string)

- then we can "tell" **sfinfo~** to refer to the named **sfplay~** object by using the "**getnamed**" message , followed by the same reference name that was given to the **sfplay~**

As you can see in the figure, **sfinfo~** gives us information about the file opened by the **sfplay~** object, which has been given the name "filedisco". The properties of the relevant linked audio file shown in the figure are sent out the six outlets of the **sfinfo~** object in the following order:

1- number of channels: 2 (a stereo sound file)
2- sample length: 16 bits
3- sampling rate: 44100 Hz
4- duration: 2000.363 milliseconds
5- sample type: 16-bit integer
6- file name: "vs_drums_loop.aif"

Now let's open the file **05_07_cue.maxpat** (Fig. 5.20).

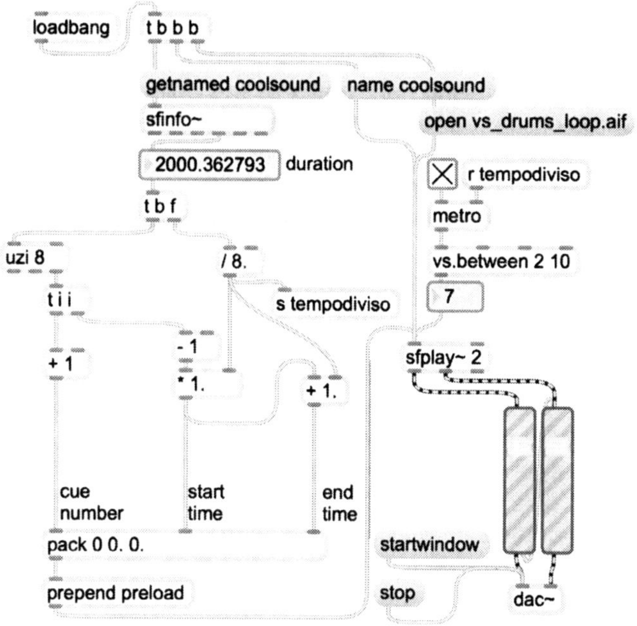

Fig. 5.20 The file **05_07_cue.maxpat**

This is a slightly complex patch that generates 8 cues by dividing an audio file into 8 equally-sized parts, and then playing them back in a random order. Let's analyze it step by step – be sure to have the patch open in front of you while you read this.

As soon as the patch is opened, a **loadbang** and a **trigger** send a bang message to the following places, in the following order:
- first, to a "open vs_drums_loop.aif" message which is connected to the **sfplay~** object that will open the given file
- second, to a "name coolsound" message that is sent to the same **sfplay~** object, so it can be associated with the name "coolsound"
- finally, to a "getnamed coolsound" message which is sent to the **sfinfo~** object, which consequently gives us information about the file which was opened by the **sfplay~** object named "coolsound".

The only bit of information about the sound file which we are actually interested in is its duration in milliseconds (output by the fourth outlet of **sfinfo~**), which we will use to automatically generate cues. This duration value is sent to a **trigger** object with two arguments: "b f" (representing a bang message and a floating point number indicating the duration). First, the **trigger** outputs the value out its right outlet, sending it to a division object which divides it by 8; this will be the duration of each of our cues. The divided duration is then sent to the right inlet of a **metro** object (via a **send/receive** object pair) and to the right inlet of two other math operators: an addition and a multiplication object (later we will take a closer look at what these are used for). Let's return to our **trigger**, which now sends a bang message out its left outlet to an **uzi** with an argument of 8. We will send the numerical index value (a series of numbers from 1 to 8) coming from the right outlet of this object to another **trigger** which is used to construct a series of cues. Before continuing with the analysis of this patch, let's review the information that needs to be put into the cues:

- the cue count (8 cues numbered from 2 to 9)
- the starting point of each cue (8 equidistant values within the soundfile's total duration)
- the ending point of each cue (corresponding to the starting point plus the duration of each cue)

These three values are grouped together into a list using the **pack** object: let's now see what we have to do to generate them. (For the sake of clarity we will analyze the outputs of the **trigger** from left to right, knowing that in reality they will be output from right to left.) The first element of the list (output by the left outlet of **trigger**) is the cue number: this is a value between 2 and 9. Since **uzi** outputs a series of numbers from 1 to 8, we simply add 1 to this series and send the result to the left inlet of the **pack** object. The second element of the list should be the starting point of the cue: by subtracting 1 from the output of the **uzi** we get a series of numbers from 0 to 7. We then multiply each number in the series by the sound file's duration divided by eight: the different starting point will then be 0/8, 1/8, 2/8, etc. up until 7/8 of the total duration of the sound file. To calculate the last element of each list (the ending point of each cue), we will add 1/8 of the soundfile's duration to each of cue starting times. Thus the ending points will be at 1/8, 2/8, 3/8, etc. until 8/8 of the total duration of the file. Once the **pack** object has assembled a list, it sends it to the **prepend** object which attaches the "preload" message to the start of the list and sends it (the complete preload message followed by 3 values) to **sfplay~**. A preload message is sent for each of the 8 cues – cue generation therefore has been completely automated. If we now activate the **toggle** connected to the **metro** (whose tempo is equal to the duration of a cue) it will produce bangs that will be sent to **vs.between** which outputs random numbers between 2 and 9, corresponding to the cue numbers which we generated. In this way, the eight fragments of the drum pattern can be played back in a random order.

If you listen to the sound produced by the patch you will notice that there is a cue that creates a sound similar to a click (cue number 3 to be precise), due to the fact that the following cue (number 4) begins with a drum hit that is slightly ahead of the beat. This leads to two problems: first, the beginning of the attack of cue number 4 is included in the end of cue number 3 (thereby creating an audible click), and second, the attack of cue number 4 is missing its beginning, which was included at the end of the previous cue (even though this is a percussive sound and we can barely notice the difference). The slight anticipation of some beats in a drum loops, in general, often helps provide a heightened rhythmic tension in the music, so this problem therefore could also be present when using other sound files. Let's see how we can resolve these problems: modify the patch as shown in figure 5.21.

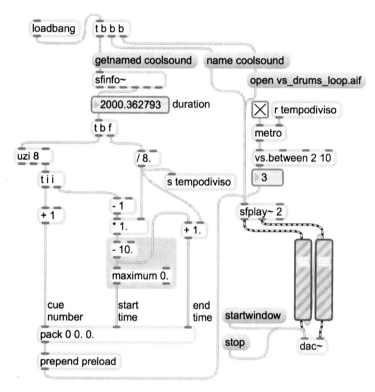

Fig. 5.21 Repositioning cues

We have added two objects to the patch (highlighted by the grey rectangle in the center). The object [- 10.] subtracts 10 milliseconds from the beginning of each cue. Note that we added this object after the number output by **uzi** has already been multiplied by 1/8 the duration of the sound file. We have also moved the connection between the output of the multiplier and the input of the addition that is used to calculate the ending point of the cue: it is now between the output of the operator that subtracts 10 milliseconds and the addition. This causes both the start and the end of each cue to be displaced 10 milliseconds earlier. In order to make sure that the first cue (which normally begins at time 0) is not repositioned early and therefore does not begin with an impossible negative value as a starting time, we have added the **maximum** object with an argument of 0. after the subtraction operator. The **maximum** object takes a value in its left inlet, compares it with the argument, and outputs the higher of the two values[14]. Since the argument is 0., if the input value is positive it will be sent out the outlet (because a positive value is always, by definition, greater

---

[14] As with most of the basic Max objects, the argument provides a default value which can be can be changed by sending a value to the object's right inlet.

than zero). But if the input value is negative, the value 0 will be output, instead (because 0 is greater than any negative value). There also exists a corresponding **minimum** object in the Max environment, which compares an input value with its argument and outputs the lower of the two values.

After modifying the patch you will need to double-click on the **loadbang** object (in performance mode) in order to generate new cues (or alternately you could save, close and re-open the patch).

If you listen to the modified patch, you will notice that the click has disappeared. When using other sound files, you may find that you need to use a different anticipation time for the attack of the cues. In this case you could always add a floating-point number box at the right inlet of the subtraction to be able to change the anticipation time for each sound file, as necessary.

. . . .

⌇ ACTIVITY

Starting from patch 05_07_cue.maxpat, try to eliminate the objects that are used to synchronize the **metro** to the length of the cues, using different tempos for the **metro** object equal to 125, 100 or 200 milliseconds (or other values), listening carefully to the different resulting rhythms.

. . . .

PLAYBACK OF SOUND LOADED INTO MEMORY

When we have to read short sound files, it can be convenient to load them into memory in order to be able to control them more flexibly without putting your computer's hard disk to work unnecessarily[15].

A sound file can be loaded into memory using the **buffer~** object, which we first learned about in chapter 1.5 and put to practical use in chapter 2.1, where we were using it to hold a single cycle of a waveform. Once a sound has been loaded into a **buffer~** it can be read using a variety of MSP objects. Let's now take a look at two of these objects (although we will cover others later, as they become necessary for our musical tasks).

The first is the **wave~** object, which we widely used in the first volume. This object is usually used to periodically read a single cycle of a waveform, but there is nothing stopping us from using it to read longer sounds.

---

[15] The concept of what constitutes a "short sound file" that can be loaded into the computer's internal memory changes with time: in the second half of the 1990's, when MSP was born, this meant up to a few dozen seconds. At the time of writing, at the beginning of the 2010's, an audio file of a few dozen minutes can easily be loaded into memory.

As we already learned, when the **wave~** object receives an input signal consisting of a ramp from 0 to 1, it will read the entire contents of the **buffer~** that it is associated with (see section 2.1 and IB.9 of the first volume). In the previous volume we used a **phasor~** to generate a ramp from 0 to 1 at a given frequency which could be sent to the **wave~** object in order to cause it to read the contents of a **buffer~** associated with it. Here we saw that, as long as the buffer contained a single cycle of a waveform, the resulting sound would be a periodic waveform.

However, we now would like to read an entire sound from beginning to end without repeating it periodically. To do this we will use the **line~** object, instead of the **phasor~**. Recreate the patch shown in figure 5.22.

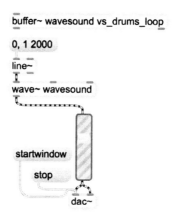

Fig. 5.22 Using **line~** with **wave~**

We have created a **buffer~** named "wavesound" (the first argument), and have loaded the sound vs_drums_loop.aif into the buffer (the second argument). Since we already know that the duration of the sound file **vs_drums_loop.aif** is about 2 seconds (we learned this in the preceding patch), we can use **line~** to generate a ramp from 0 to 1 in 2000 milliseconds and send the resulting signal to the **wave~** object (which has the name of the **buffer~** as an argument). Every time we click on the message box connected to **line~** the entire sound file is played once by the **wave~** object over a duration of 2000 milliseconds, in other words, with a duration equal to the length of the sound file.

• •

ACTIVITY

Answer the following questions and realize them in the form of Max patches – this way you can deepen your knowledge of how to use **wave~**.

1 - What modifications would we need to make to the patch in figure 5.22 in order to play the sound file at twice the speed?

2 - What about playing it at half speed?

3 - How could we play only the first half of the sound?

4 - What about playing only the last half?

5 - What if we wanted to listen to the sound in reverse, starting at the end of the buffer and playing it to the beginning (like playing a tape backwards)?

6 - Substitute the `line~` object with the **curve~** object (which we learned about in section 1.3P of the first volume), and add a curve factor in the message box (for example 0.5 or -0.5). What happens to the sound, and why?

· ·

In example 5.22 we already knew the duration of the file loaded into the buffer. However, if we do not have any information on the sound's duration, we can always use the `info~` object, which provides information about the sound loaded into a **buffer~** object.

Modify the preceding patch as shown in figure 5.23

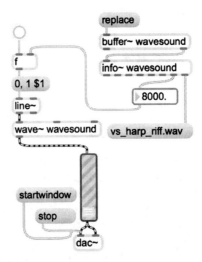

Fig. 5.23 Buffer with variable length

First, we have removed the second argument from the **buffer~** object, because we do not want to load a default sound file. Next, we have connected the right outlet of the **buffer** to an `info~` object that has been given the argument "wavesound" (the name of the **buffer~**). Each time we load a new file into the **buffer~** using the "replace" message, it will output a bang out its right outlet (after the new file has been loaded). The bang is then sent to the `info~` object, which outputs information about the **buffer~**'s contents out its outlets. For the moment, let's skip over the first few outlets of the `info~` object and just take a close look at the last two: the penultimate and last outlets provide us with information about the length and name of the sound file that has been loaded, respectively. In figure 5.23 we can see that when the "replace" message was last used, the file **vs_harp_riff.wav**[16], was loaded into the **buffer~**, and this file's durations is 8 seconds. The duration of the file is sent to the right inlet of a **float** (**f**) object, where it is stored for future use. A bang to the left inlet of the **float** object causes this value to be sent to the message box underneath it, which, in turn, sends **line~** the instructions to generate a ramp from 0 to 1 for the duration of the entire audio file – try clicking on the button to see this in action!

The **wave~** object does not necessarily have to refer to the entire contents of a **buffer~**. The second and third inlets let you define a starting and ending time (in milliseconds) for the playback of the audio buffer. If we send values to these two inlets, the ramp from 0 to 1 that is sent to the object's left inlet will no longer cause it to output the entire file, but rather the portion of the sound between the two specified points. To try this out, connect two number boxes to the second and third inlets, and set their values to 1000 and 4000, respectively. Now click on the **button** again and you will hear only a portion of the sound file **vs_harp_riff.wav** – more precisely the section of the sound beginning at 1000 and ending at 4000 milliseconds.

However, we also notice that there is a problem with the playback: the sound is both slower and lower in pitch than the original sound file. Why? What do we need to modify in the patch to make the sound fragment play back at the correct speed and pitch?

To play our sound file in a loop, all we have to do is replace **line~** with a **phasor~** object, which, as we have already learned, outputs a ramp from 0 to 1 at a given frequency. In figure 5.24 we can see some modifications have been made to the preceding patch.

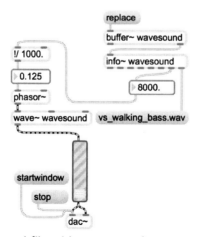

Fig. 5.24 Looping a sound file with **wave~** and **phasor~**

---

[16] Remember that, unless otherwise stated, the audio files that we are using in this book can be found in the "soundfiles" folder inside the Virtual Sound Macros library.

To play the sound file at the correct speed, we need to give the **phasor~** object a frequency equal to the inverse of the sound file's duration in seconds. If, for example, the file is 2 seconds long, the frequency for the **phasor~** should be 1/3 = 0.5 Hz. If the file is 4 seconds long, the frequency should be 1/4 = 0.25 Hz, etc.[17]

In figure 5.24 we have loaded the file **vs_walking_bass.wav** which has a duration of 8 seconds (8000 milliseconds), the frequency of the **phasor~** is therefore equal to 1/8 = 0.125 Hz. Note that because the duration is expressed in milliseconds, and not in seconds, we use the **!/** operator to calculate the ratio 1000/8000, which is the same as 1/8 and gives us the value 0.125.

By changing the frequency of the **phasor~** we can loop the sound file at different speeds, and if we use negative values (try using -0.125) we can play the file in reverse, because negative frequency values cause **phasor~** to output a ramp going from 1 to 0 instead of 0 to 1.

. . . .

⌂ACTIVITIES

- In the patch in figure 5.24, change the frequency of the **phasor** using a **line~** object. For instance, try to raise the frequency from 0 to 1 in 10 seconds, and then have it go back down to -0.125 in 5 seconds. Also try using other values of your choice – you could also draw a more complex trajectory using a **function** object whose total duration (represented on the x axis) and output value range (the y axis) have been set using the *inspector* or the "setdomain" and "setrange" messages.[18]

- Now use an LFO to vary the frequency of the **phasor~**. Create a sine wave oscillator with a very low frequency (for example 0.025 Hz, corresponding to a period of 40 seconds), and use the **scale~** object so that the sine wave's value range goes between -0.125 and 0.5. Change the frequency and the amplitude of the LFO to obtain different variations in the sample playback. Also try using use the drum loop sound **vs_drums_loop.aif**.

- Switch the sine wave LFO with a square wave LFO. Change the frequency and amplitude of the LFO to make some different variations in the sample playback. You could also use the drum loop **vs_drums_loop.aif** for this activity.

- Substitute the sine wave LFO with the random generators **rand~** and **vs.rand3~**. As with the previous activities, will also need to change the frequency and range of the random oscillation.

---

[17] If you are asking "why?" we suggest you re-read about the relationship between frequency and period in section 1.2T of the first volume.
[18] For more about the "setdomain" message, see section IA.8, for "setrange" see section 2.4 (in the practice part), both in the first volume.

- Add a sine wave LFO to the second inlet and another to the third inlet of the **wave~** object, using the same scaling system from activity 2, in order to dynamically change the part of the **buffer~** which is being read. Be sure to set appropriate range values for the **scale~** object. Most importantly, make sure that the values sent to the second inlet of the **wave~** object are not greater than the values sent to the third inlet.

- Replace the two sine wave LFOs in activity 5 with two random generators (**rand~** or **vs.rand3~**).

· ·

Now let's move on to the **groove~** object. This object allows us somewhat more flexible control over the playback of a sound loaded in to a **buffer~**. We already discussed this object in section 1.5P of the first volume. Let's briefly review its features which we already know in addition to introducing some new ones. Open the file **05_08_groove_commands.maxpat** (figure 5.25).

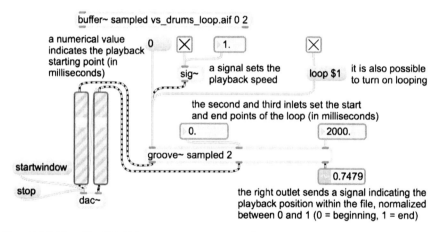

Fig. 5.25 The file **05_08_groove_commands.maxpat**

On the upper left side of the patch there is a **buffer~** object with 4 arguments. The first argument is the name "sampled" which we can use to refer to this buffer, whereas the second is the name of the file which will be loaded by default. This file must be somewhere in Max's search path in order to be automatically loaded (in this example, as before, we have used "vs_drums_loop. aif"). The third argument is the length of the buffer (which is set to 0 for the moment; the buffer will be re-sized when the sound file is loaded) and the fourth is the number of channels (set to 2 here because the file is stereo)[19].

---

[19] This is the first time we have loaded both channels of a stereo file into a **buffer~** object. If the number of channels is not specified, only the sound file's left channel will be loaded into the single-channel buffer.

Double-click on the **groove~** object (in performance mode) in order to see the waveform of the loaded sound file.

The **groove~** object reads the contents of a **buffer~** with the same name and number of channels (not unlike the **wave** object, but the similarities between the two end there). First, notice that **groove~** interprets numerical values in its inlet differently, depending on whether they are audio signals or Max messages: a signal indicates playback speed (1 = normal speed[20], 2 = double speed, etc.), whereas Max messages indicate the starting point in the file (in milliseconds) used for playback. In the figure there is a message box containing a 0 connected to the **groove~** object. This is used to trigger playback from the beginning of the sound. There is also a **toggle** connected to a **sig~** object, which converts a Max message into a signal – this means that by clicking on the **toggle** we can alternately send a signal with a value of 1 or 0 to **groove~**. Consequently, **groove~** will either play the sound at normal speed (speed of 1) or will stop (speed of 0 meaning it will play 0 samples per second).

At first, it can be easy to mix up the command syntax for **groove~**, with the various commands for **sfplay~**. After all, the latter can also be started and stopped using a **toggle**, or alternately by sending a 1 or 0 (see figure 5.17). However, there is one major difference that, if not completely grasped, can tend to cause confusion. For **sfplay~** the messages 1 and 0 sent by the **toggle** are used to recall cue 1 (playback of the entire file from the beginning) and 0 (stop the playback). Conversely, in the example illustrated in figure 5.25 the messages sent by the **toggle** are transformed into a signal by the **sig~** object before reaching **groove~**, and this signal sets the playback speed for the sound (1 meaning normal speed and 0 meaning "zero velocity" or no speed). Try turning the **toggle** "on" and "off" in both the patches in figures 5.17 and 5.25, and you will immediately notice that in the case of **sfplay~**, the file begins playing back again from the beginning each time the **toggle** sends a 1 (in other words it re-triggers playback of cue 1). On the other hand, in the case of the **groove~** object, each time the **toggle** sends a 1, the playback will resume from the point where it was last stopped. To start playback from the beginning, we need to send **groove~** the value 0 as a *Max message* (not a signal) – this numerical value is interpreted as a position in milliseconds within the buffer (and thus 0 denotes the beginning of the file). This is probably the most difficult concept to "digest" when first learning to use these objects – the Max numerical value "0" means "stop" to **sfplay~**, but to **groove~** it means "go back to the beginning." Once you have properly understood this difference in syntax between these two objects, it should not be very difficult to use them correctly.

---

[20] Playback at "normal" speed requires playing back the sound at the sampling rate of the original sound file. If, for example, our sound file was recorded at a sampling rate of 44100 Hz, the normal playback speed will correspond to playback at 44100 samples per second (even if the sr of our audio interface is set to a different sampling rate).

Let's return to the patch in figure 5.25. Next to the **toggle**, there is also a float number box connected to the **sig~** object; this allows us to change the playback speed continuously. Try changing the value to 0.5, 1.5, 2, etc. Remember that these values are interpreted as playback speed values (and not millisecond locations), because the **sig~** object converts them into a signal. If we sent these numerical values to **groove~** as plain Max messages, they would be interpreted as starting points for playback of the sound.

Now try to set the playback speed to a value of -1, and you will notice that the sound is played in reverse. In effect, a value of -1 designates a "negative" speed, which implies that the sound file will be read backwards, from the end to the beginning. Naturally, it is also possible to vary the playback speed when playing in reverse – try setting the playback speed to -0.5, -2, etc., and listen to what happens.

If we are not in loop mode the sound will be played back only once. To play the sound again we do not need to turn the left-hand **toggle** on and off, as we might initially imagine, because this **toggle** controls the playback speed via the **sig~** object. To re-trigger playback we just need to click on the message box containing the 0, which "tells" **groove~** to start again from the begin-ning. When we are using loop mode, we can set the beginning and end of the loop by sending two numerical values (representing locations in milliseconds) to the **groove~** object's second and third inlets. Try changing these values in order to modify the looped portion of the sound. Finally, the rightmost outlet of **groove~** sends a signal that indicates the playback position within the file, or within the loop if loop mode is activated. As with **wave~**, this signal is normalized between 0 and 1, so when the playback is at the beginning of the file this signal is 0, when playback reaches the middle of the file this signal is 0.5 and when it reaches the end, the value is 1. In practice, this outlet sends a ramp signal (similar to the signal generated by **phasor~**) whose period is equal to the duration of the audio file or of the loop.

Let's now try to change the start and end times for the loop – we can do this "by hand" simply by changing the values in the number boxes connected to the **groove~** object's second and third inlets. Alternately, we could create a random loop using two random number generators, as we did with **wave~**.

Try modifying the patch in figure 5.25 as illustrated in figure 5.26.

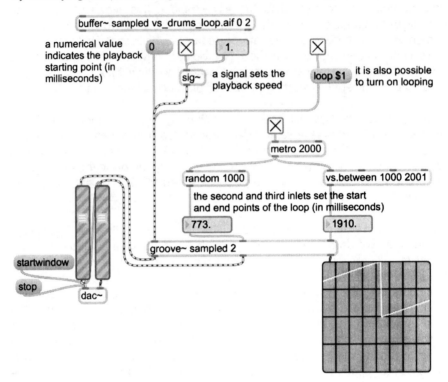

Fig. 5.26 Random loops

Here we have added two random number generators: the first, [**random 1000**], lets us change the start time of the loop between 0 and 999 milliseconds, and the second, [**vs.between** 1000 2001], lets us change the end time of the loop between 1000 and 2000 milliseconds. The **metro** object connected to the two random number generators modifies the loop every two seconds. We have also replaced the **number~** object, which was connected to the last outlet of **groove~**, with an oscilloscope (**scope~**), so we can more easily see that the ramp output by **groove~** is virtually identical to the signal produced by **phasor~**.

Each of the random loops generated in this modified patch has its own duration because the start and end times of the loop are controlled by two independent random generators. If we wanted to have random loops with a fixed duration (for example always 500 milliseconds long) we would need to randomly generate only the start time of the loop and add 500 to that value to obtain the proper end time. In figure 5.27 we can see this simple modification to the patch.

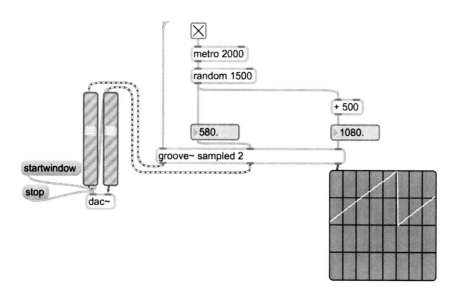

Fig. 5.27 Random loops of equal length

This time, there is only one random generator outputting values between 0 and 1499 – these values represent the start point of the loop. The end point of the loop is calculated by adding 500 to the start point (for example, in the figure, the start point of the loop is at 580 milliseconds, while the end point is at 1080, in other words 580 + 500). This way, all the loops have a fixed duration of 500 milliseconds, and will be repeated exactly 4 times (because the metro currently has a tempo of 2000 milliseconds).

When a portion of a soundfile is looped this way, it will almost certainly create a discontinuity between the end of the loop and the beginning of the next repetition (meaning that the values of the last sample of the loop and the first are almost certainly not adjacent to one another), and this discontinuity in the sound will create an audible click. When using a drum sound, the click is not very disturbing, but when playing a sound with a definite pitch (such as a flute sound) this can become a problem. Since we are using variable loops, one solution would be to add an amplitude envelope to create a fade-in and fade-out at the beginning and end of each loop repetition. To make this envelope, we can use the right outlet of **groove~** which, as has already been stated, outputs a ramp from 0 to 1 with each repetition of the loop. This ramp could be used to control an object like **trapezoid~**, for instance. This object works like **triangle~**[21], with the main difference being that instead of a triangle-shaped signal, it outputs a trapezoidal-shaped signal.

---

[21] see section 1.2P of the first volume

First, let's look at how it works; rebuild the patch shown in figure 5.28.

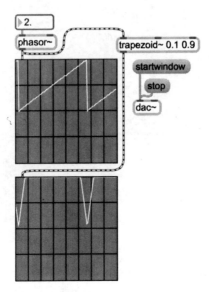

Fig. 5.28 The **trapezoid~** object

In this patch, the **phasor~** object outputs a ramp that goes from 0 to 1 and **trapezoid~** creates a trapezoidal signal with the same duration. The two arguments to **trapezoid~** define the point in which the trapezoidal signal goes from 0 to 1 and the point at which it returns from 1 to 0. In the figure the arguments are 0.1 and 0.9: this means that the signal output by **trapezoid~** reaches the value 1 when the **phasor~** arrives at 0.1, and stays there until the value of the **phasor~** reaches 0.9, at which point it begins to ramp down to 0, which it reaches when the **phasor~** has completed its cycle, and so on.

Let's now look at an application of this trapezoidal envelope technique – open the file **05_09_groove_loops.maxpat** (shown in figure 5.29).

In this patch, loops are created from a sound file containing a flute sound. The start point and duration of the loop are chosen randomly, and each loop repeats exactly 4 times. Activate the patch and listen to the sound it produces.

Let's now analyze the patch. The **loadbang** lets us automatically load the sound file **vs_flute_bouree.wav** into the **buffer~** named "looped", and simultaneously activates the loop mode for the **groove~** object. The **info~** object at the upper right side of the patch lets us retrieve the duration of the sound file loaded into the **buffer~**. We subtract 500 from this duration (we will see why in a moment) and use the resulting length as a parameter for the random number generator. This generator sets the start point of the loop, which can vary between 0 and a value that is 500 milliseconds before the end of the audio file (hence why we initially subtracted 500 from the total duration of the file). Another random number generator, vs.between, will create random values between 50 and 500.

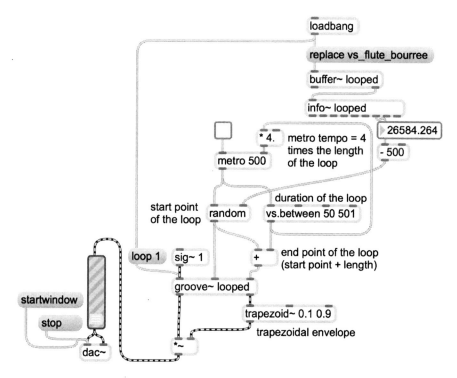

Fig. 5.29 the file **05_09_groove_loops.maxpat**

These represent the duration of the loop and will be added to the start point in order to obtain the correct end point of the loop. Furthermore, the duration of the loop generated by **vs.between** will be multiplied by 4 and sent to the right inlet of the **metro** object. The metronome tempo will therefore change with each new loop and thus corresponds to exactly 4 times the duration of the current loop.

As we have already seen, the right outlet of the **groove~** object will output a ramp going from 0 to 1 which is synchronized with the loop playback. We use this ramp to drive the **trapezoid~** generator, whose signal will be used as an amplitude envelope which is applied to the sound output by the left outlet of **groove~**.

ACTIVITIES

- Try changing the playback speed of **groove~** in the patch in figure 5.29, by setting it to 0.5, for instance (you will need to connect a float number box to the **sig~** object). Now, the loop will be repeated only twice – why? Conversely, what happens when we set the playback speed to 2?

- Now set the playback speed to 1.1 – with each new loop you probably hear a click. This happens because the last repetition of the loop is incomplete, and the trapezoidal envelope is interrupted creating a discontinuity in the signal. What can you do to always create 4 repetitions of the loop, regardless of the speed being used? (Hint: this can be done by adding just one math operator.)

- Return to the activities for the **wave~** object that immediately followed figure 5.24, and add a trapezoidal envelope to exercises 4 and 5 so that they also avoid discontinuities between the segments of sound played by the LFO.

BUILDING A SAMPLER

Now let's try using **buffer~** and **groove~** to build a simple monophonic sampler, which can recognize MIDI notes and that is able to play a sound file at different speeds, transposing it to the pitch which corresponds to the MIDI note received.

We have seen that **groove~** does not modify the pitch of a sound based on a given frequency, let alone based on a MIDI note value. This is logical, since we do not necessarily know the fundamental frequency of a sound file loaded into a **buffer~** (presuming there even is one). We know that **groove~** modifies the pitch of a sound based on the playback speed of that sound, and will interpret 1 as the "normal" speed, 2 as double speed, etc. Presuming we have a sound with a fundamental of 440 Hz, this means that if we play it at double speed we will hear a fundamental of 880 Hz (that is $440 \cdot 2$, or an octave higher), if we play back the sound at a speed of 1.5, we will have a fundamental of 660 Hz ($440 \cdot 1.5 = 660$), and so forth[22].

Therefore, we can transpose the sound file to any arbitrary frequency by dividing this frequency by the fundamental frequency of the original sound. This will give us the appropriate playback speed for the file (figure 5.30).

Let's imagine that we want to take a sound file with a sound at 440 Hz (the A on the second space of the treble clef), and use it to play the note D on the 4th line of the treble clef (this has a frequency of 587.33 Hz).

---

[22] Remember that the change in duration will be inversely proportional to the multiplication factor used.

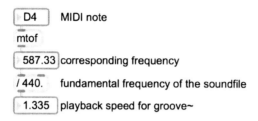

Fig. 5.30 Calculating the transposition of a sampled sound

First we need to convert the MIDI note value into a frequency value using the **mtof** object, and then divide this value by 440, as shown in the figure. The result (1.335) is the playback speed we need to send to **groove~** in order to play the sound as a D (presuming our sampled sound is indeed an A).

Open the file **05_10_monosampler.maxpat** (figure 5.31).

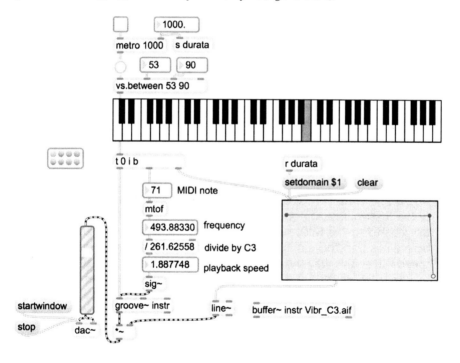

Fig. 5.31 the file **05_10_monosampler.maxpat**

In the patch there is a **buffer~** that loads a vibraphone note whose frequency is middle C (261.62 Hz). This sound is located in the samples folder inside the *Virtual Sound library*. The algorithm that transforms MIDI note values into speed ratios is located at the center of the window. MIDI note values are generated by the **vs.between** object (in the upper part of the window) and are sent first to a **kslider** (for display) and then to a **trigger** which first sends a bang to the **function** object on the right, which contains the amplitude envelope, then it sends the note value to our conversion algorithm (similar to the one in figure 5.30), and finally sends a 0 to the **groove~** object to begin playing back the sound from the beginning. The value used to set the rate of the **metro** object which triggers note generation, at the top left part of the patch, is also sent to the "setdomain $1" message via the [s duration] object. This message is connected to the **function** object in order to set its duration so it matches that of the metronome's beat.

Try out the various different envelope configurations stored in the preset and notice how modifying the envelope greatly influences the timbre of the resulting sound. Try to create several new presets, and also try loading different sounds into the **buffer~**.

· ·

ACTIVITIES

- Add a lowpass filter to the patch in figure 5.31, making sure there is a relationship between the cutoff frequency and the pitch of the note played (key follow: see section 3.5 of the first volume)

- Make the filter's cutoff frequency relate to the amplitude envelope, using the same technique we saw in section 3.5 of the first volume ("Anatomy of a subtractive synthesizer")

- Add a sine wave LFO to make a tremolo, referring to section 4.4 of the first volume if necessary.

- Add a sine wave LFO to add vibrato to the sound, referring to section 4.3 of the first volume, if necessary. In this scenario, we would like you to add the vibrato to the MIDI note produced by the random number generator before it is transformed into a frequency and subsequently into a playback speed value. This way the pitch change will be identical for all notes (i.e., a relative pitch deviation). Note that the algorithm that converts MIDI notes into playback speed values will need to be modified so that it processes MSP signals, otherwise it will be impossible to add an LFO (in practice this means that you will need to replace the **mtof** and / with the equivalent MSP objects **mtof~** and **/~**, and, naturally, also remove the number box and **sig~** object).

- Create a hybrid instrument by mixing the patch from figure 5.31 (and the modifications you made to it in activities 1-4, above) with the subtractive synthesizer shown in section 3.5 of the first volume. Be sure to use different envelopes for the sampled sounds and synthesized sounds, in order to create an intricate fade between the two types of sounds.

· ·

DC OFFSET REMOVAL

Let's take a look at a practical example that shows why it is always good to remove DC offset from a sound. Open the file **05_11_DC_offset.maxpat** (figure 5.32).

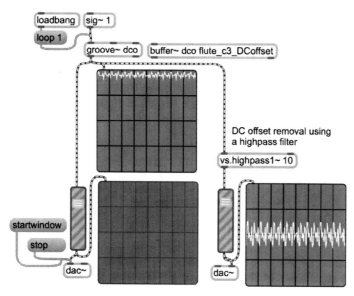

Fig. 5.32 The file **05_11_DC_offset.maxpat**

We have loaded a flute sound with an extreme DC offset into our `buffer~` named "dco," as can be seen in the oscilloscope on the upper left. After clicking on "startwindow," begin raising the cursor of the `gain~` slider on the left, and you will see the signal in the oscilloscope move upwards, until it disappears from the oscilloscope altogether. At this point we can no longer hear any sound. This happens because the DC offset is amplified by `gain~`, and this increase in amplitude "pushes" the flute sound's signal upward until it completely goes over the the maximum value allowed by the digital-to-analog conversion (i.e., it exceeds 1). The signal on the right, however, goes through a first order high-pass filter before being sent to the `gain~`. This filter attenuates or removes all frequencies below 10 Hz, including the DC offset which, being a constant signal at 0 Hz, is removed completely. As can be seen in the oscilloscope on the right, a signal without DC offset can be amplified without distortion.

• •

INTEGRATED CROSS-FUNCTIONAL PROJECT - CREATING A BRIEF SOUND STUDY

Create a brief composition based on the use of sampled sounds, using looping, reverse playback, different starting points for sound file playback, amplitude enve-lopes and glissandos of the sampled sounds, overlapping sounds, multi-pole filters with changing Q factors and center/cutoff frequencies, sound decimation, etc.

5.4 THE SEGMENTATION OF SAMPLED SOUNDS: THE BLOCKS TECHNIQUE AND SLICING

For the patches in this section, we suggest you turn on both the "Scheduler in Overdrive" and "in Audio Interrupt" options in the Audio Status window, and set the Signal Vector Size between 16 and 64 samples (preferably 16).

THE BLOCKS TECHNIQUE

First, we will introduce some new features of the **counter** object, which, as we have already learned, "counts" the bang that it receives (see section IB.6 in the first volume). Rebuild the patch shown in figure 5.33.

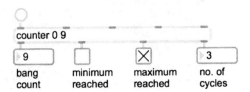

Fig. 5.33 The **counter** object

The left outlet of the **counter** returns the number of bangs it has received: if the two arguments of the **counter** are 0 and 9, the object will count from 0 to 9 and then begin counting again from 0, in a cyclic fashion. The right-most (fourth) outlet will return the number of completed cycles the object has counted: the patch in the figure shows that the object has counted three cycles from 0 to 9. The third outlet is a *flag* (an indicator), whose value is 1 when the **counter** reaches its maximum count value (in this case 9), and 0 for all other values. Notice that to display the flag, we have used a **toggle** object, which is set to the "on" position when it receives a 1 (or other non-zero value), and set to the "off" position when it receives a 0.

The second outlet also outputs a *flag*, but for this outlet the value is 1 when the count reaches (or is reset to) its minimum count value, and 0 for other count values. Obviously, this flag will only output 1 when the count cycles back to its beginning – in this case when it goes from 9 back to 0. The **counter** object is actually able to output consecutive values according to three directions: incrementing (the default), decrementing, or an alternating combination of increment/decrement. To modify the direction of the **counter**, you can send the values 0 (increment), 1 (decrement) or 2 (increment/decrement) to the object's second inlet. Otherwise you can give the object 3 arguments, in which case the first of the three represents the direction. For example if we replaced the "0 9" arguments with "1 0 9" in the patch in figure 5.33, we would have a descending count from 9 to 0, and the minimum flag would activate once the count hits 0. Try doing this.

Lets now take a look at one way to implement the blocks technique with Max: open the file **05_12_blocks_technique.maxpat** (figure. 5.34).

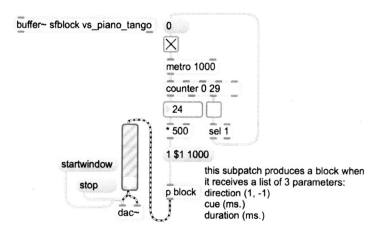

Fig. 5.34 The file **05_12_blocks_technique.maxpat**

For the moment let's take a look at how the main patch generates the parameters used to define the blocks; later we will look at contents of the subpatch in detail.

The **metro** at the top of the patch beats the time at a rate of one bang per second. The **counter** underneath it generates a numerical series from 1 to 29. When the **counter** reaches the end of the series, the flag from its third outlet sends the value 1 to the [**sel 1**] object which, in turn, sends a bang to a message box (with the value 0) which is used to stop the metronome. The numerical series produced by the counter is therefore executed just once. Each value of the series is multiplied by 500, so the numbers in the series 0, 1, 2, 3 etc. become the values 0, 500, 1000, 1500, etc. These values, which represent the cues of the blocks we are going to generate, are sent to the message box directly below the multiply object, which creates the list "1 *cue* 1000". This list, when sent to the subpatch [**p block**], will generate a block in the original (forward) direction, starting from the cue time, each time it is calculated (at 0, 500, 100, etc.), and lasting 1 second (1000 milliseconds).

Let's run the patch. As we can see (and hear), the audio file **vs_piano_tango** is divided into one-second blocks which advance through the sound file 500 milliseconds at a time.

Now let's look at the contents of [p block], opening the subpatch by double-clicking on it (figure 5.35).

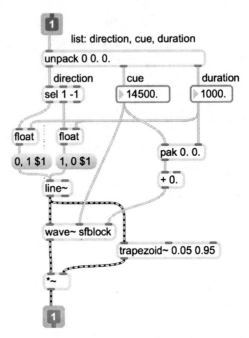

Fig. 5.35 the subpatch [p block]

The list that is send to the inlet of [p block] is split into its three individual elements by the **unpack** object. The middle outlet of **unpack** will send the cue time to the second inlet of the **wave~** object, thereby setting the playback start location (see section 5.3, above, in the subsection titled "Playback of Sounds Loaded into Memory"). The duration value of 1000 coming from the third outlet of **unpack** is added to the cue value and sent to the third inlet of **wave~**. This sets the playback end point. Finally, the direction (coming from the leftmost outlet of **unpack**) is sent to a **sel** object whose arguments are "-1 1". If the direction is -1 (reverse), a bang will be sent form the left outlet of sel to a float whose internal value has been set to the block duration. The subsequent message box and **line~** object create a ramp going from 1 to 0 in the amount of time corresponding to the block duration. If the direction is 1 (forward) a bang is sent out the second outlet of **sel**, to a similar message box connected to the **line~**, in order to create a ramp from 0 to 1 (also corresponding to the block duration). In both cases the ramp, sent to the **wave~** object, will cause a block of sound to be output (either in the original forward direction, or backwards). Note that the same ramp is also sent to the **trapezoid~** object, in order to generate an envelope used to eliminate any discontinuities in the signal at the start and end of each block.

If we would like to generate blocks in a retrograde direction with respect to the sound file (starting from the end and working backwards toward the beginning), but still reading the blocks in a forward direction, and not in reverse, we need to modify the patch as shown in figure 5.36.

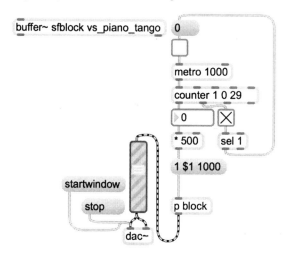

Fig. 5.36 Retrograde block displacement with forward playback direction.

We have modified just two things in the patch. First, we have added an additional argument 1 to the **counter**, to indicate that the numerical series produced by the object will begin from the maximum value (29) and decrement to the minimum value (0). Next, we are using the flag from the second outlet of **counter** to stop the metronome when the series arrives at its minimum value. Try running the patch with these modifications.

. . . .

ACTIVITIES

• Modify the patch in figure 5.34 so it produces blocks whose cues traverse the file in the original (forward) direction, but which, themselves, are read in reverse (just one modification is necessary).

• Modify the patch in figure 5.34 so it produces blocks that traverse the file in a retrograde (backward) direction, and are additionally read in reverse (three modifications are necessary)

. . . .

Now let's go to a patch that uses the blocks technique to create an accelerando: open the file **05_13_blocks_tech_accel.maxpat** (figure 5.37).

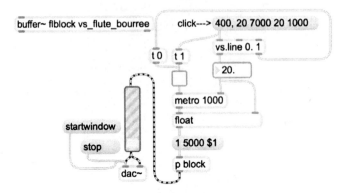

Fig. 5.37 File **05_13_blocks_tech_accel.maxpat**

For this example let's use a flute recording, and create a series of blocks beginning with the cue positioned at 5 seconds into the audio file. The cue's duration will change from 400 to 20 milliseconds. Try to run the patch by clicking on the message box on the upper right. At first, you will clearly hear the recurring blocks, but as the tempo slowly increases it will change into a "rough" sound in which single blocks can no longer be individually distinguished, and the flute's timbre is thereby modified. Note that in the [p block] subpatch the rise and fall of the **trapezoid~** object's envelope has been softened, so as to eliminate excessive "roughness" in the sound.

Are you able to analyze how the patch works? Be aware the **vs.line** object will generate a bang out its right outlet when it has finished.

In section 5.4 of the theory chapter of this book, we said that the rate of block generation can also be less than their duration; in other words the blocks can overlap. However, the patches we have been looking at thus far do not allow this kind of overlap, because objects like **wave~**, **groove~**, etc. can play only one sound file at a time. This means they are not polyphonic. Polyphony management in Max is sufficiently complex that we are dedicating an entire section of this book to discuss it in detail in Interlude C, just after this chapter.

In the *Virtual Sound Macros* library, however, there is an object called **vs.block~**, which allows you to overlap as many blocks as you like. This object is polyphonic and the number of voices it outputs can easily be defined using an argument.

We will not analyze the internal workings of this object just yet, because to do so we would need some additional knowledge about how to deal with polyphony in Max. Nonetheless, for the time being, it is fairly simple to use it without knowing the precise details of how it works. Let's take a look at an example, by opening the file **05_14_poly_blocks.maxpat** (Figure 5.38).

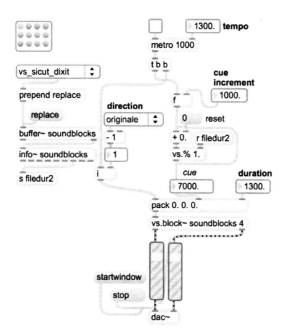

Fig. 5.38 File **05_14_poly_blocks.maxpat**

Before looking at the patch, we may need to clarify one potential error. If you see error messages like "vs.%: no such object" in the Max window when you open the file, this means that you have not installed the *Virtual Sound Macros* library correctly. In this case, please refer to the file "- README (ENG) - Installation.pdf" found in the "Virtual Sound Macros" folder, and make sure you have followed all the instructions carefully, especially **item 3** (transferring a file from the library to the "init" folder of Max). After doing this you will need to quit and relaunch Max.

Returning to the patch, let's first take a look at the **vs.block~** object found in the lower part of the patcher window.

This object requires 2 arguments. The first indicates the buffer from which blocks of sound will be read (in this case, the buffer's name is "soundblocks"). You will also notice that there is a **buffer~** object with the same name on the left side of the patch, in addition to a **umenu** object which can be used to load audio files into it. The second argument to **vs.block~** defines the maximum number of voices of polyphony that the object will use. With this patch we can therefore overlap up to 4 blocks at a time.

The **vs.block~** object in this patch receives a list of three parameters, identical to those in the preceding patches: read direction (1 = forward, -1 = backward), cue (initial read point) and duration. The rate of the **metro** object is set with an additional parameter in the patch, so that bang from the **metro** causes a list of parameters to be sent to **vs.block~**. When the tempo of the **metro** object is less than the duration of a block, the blocks will overlap.

Regarding the cues, we don't directly set this parameter in the patch, but use an increment factor (or decrement if we want to play the cues in retrograde order) which is visible on the upper right. The increment indicates how many milliseconds along the audio file a block's cue will be located, in relation to the previous cue position.

Before continuing to analyze the patch, locate the four number boxes corresponding the four variable parameters (direction, cue increment, duration and generation rate), and listen to the different presets, paying careful attention to how the above parameters are set. The first 4 presets allow us to listen to the 4 different playback modes of the blocks, as described in the theory and interactive examples of section 5.4T:

O+I   Blocks played in the original (forward) direction, cue point incrementing
O+D   Blocks played in the original direction, cue point decrementing (retrograde)
R+I   Blocks played in reverse, cue point incrementing
R+D   Blocks played in reverse, cue point decrementing (retrograde)

For these first four examples we have used the file **vs_sicut_dixit.aif** (Gregorian chant) and a "classic" configuration of this technique.

As we have already seen in the theory chapter, the classic configuration of the blocks technique requires
    - blocks over 100 ms.
    - incrementing or decrementing the cues
    - forward or reverse playback of the individual blocks
    - a regular rhythm for block generation

By listening to the subsequent examples you can discover some other ways of using this technique – for instance how to use a very slow tempo for the **metro** object or how to create a very slowly advancing cue position. Also notice that there is a pause between blocks in the fifth preset because the scan tempo is greater than the block duration.

Let's now see how the patch itself works. Each bang output by the **metro** object is effectively doubled by the **trigger** object immediately below. The bang out the right outlet of the **trigger** generates the list for **vs.block~**, whereas the bang out the left outlet is used to increment the cue value.

Let's see exactly how this happens. The bang is sent to a **float** (**f**) object which contains the increment value for the cues. This value is sent to the left inlet of an addition object, and from there to the **vs.%** modulo operator (which will be discussed shortly), and then sent to the right inlet of the addition object. The cue increment is therefore created using a recursive programming technique similar to the one we have already seen in section IB.2 of the Interlude B in the first book (refer specifically to the file **IB_03_random_arpeggiator.maxpat** shown in figure IB.15). With each successive bang from the **metro** object, the cue increment is therefore added to the previous cue value.

In order to avoid the cue value being greater than the file length, we have inserted a modulo operator (**vs.%**) into the feedback loop. The modulo value is equal to the duration of the file in milliseconds; this value is sent to **vs.%** from the **info~** object on the left side of the patch via a **send/receive** object pair. The **vs.%** math operator is similar to the standard modulo object (**%**), except in the way it deals with negative numbers: it always returns a positive value. This behavior is important because the cue values (i.e., the read locations in the audio file) can never be negative.

Let's look at an example of how the modulo works. If we have a file whose length is 1000 ms., and the cue increment is 200 ms., the succession of cue times would be the following:

increment	modulo			result
0	%	1000	=	0
200	%	1000	=	200
400	%	1000	=	400
600	%	1000	=	600
800	%	1000	=	800
1000	%	1000	=	0
etc.				

As you can see, the cue value always stays within the length of the file.
In the above case the two objects **%** and **vs.%** would give the same results. However, if the increment were a negative value (in order to decrement the successive cue locations) the output of the two objects would be:

increment	modulo			result with [vs.%]	result with [%]
0	%	1000	=	0	0
-200	%	1000	=	800	-200
-400	%	1000	=	600	-400
-600	%	1000	=	400	-600
-800	%	1000	=	200	-800
-1000	%	1000	=	0	0
etc.					

You have probably already noticed that the **%** object returns the same values as the preceding example, but with a negative sign, whereas the **vs.%** object always returns decrementing positive values. For additional information about **vs.%**, refer to the object's help file.

The rest of the patch is easy to analyze: the **pack** object that receives the cue value in its central inlet creates a list made up of playback direction, cue and duration. This list is sent to the object **vs.block~** which generates the corresponding block of sound.

Listen again to the different presets and try creating some new ones. Also try using different audio files.

It is also possible to add random variation to all the parameters. As long as these variations are relatively small and do not affect the basic idea of this technique – reading through a sound file in blocks whose position is incremented or decremented through a regular (or semi-regular) progression through the file – we can still say that we are using the blocks technique. As we already learned in section 5.4T, and as we will also later see in the 3rd volume of this series when we begin using other types of sound processing techniques , there are often boundary zones between techniques, and it is sometimes possible to smoothly transition from one technique to another through "grey" zones between these techniques.

Slicing (which we will discuss in the next section) and granulation are among the techniques which are closely related to the blocks technique.

In order to add random variation to the parameters of the block generator, we will introduce a new object: **vs.randomizer**. Rebuild the simple patch shown in figure 5.39.

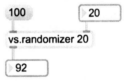

Fig. 5.39 The **vs.randomizer** object

This object randomly modifies any value input to its left inlet by adding or subtracting a random value between 0 and the argument (or between 0 and the value sent to its right inlet). In the figure the input value 100 will be increased or decreased by a random value between 0 and 20. Therefore, with each click on the message box on the left, a random value between 80 and 120 will be generated.

By adding a **vs.randomizer** object to the tempo, cue increment and duration values, we can create interesting variations on the basic blocks technique.

Load the file **05_15_rand_blocks.maxpat** (figure 5.40).

This patch is a variation of the previous one. The bang output by **metro** is connected to a **trigger** which sends three bangs elsewhere in the patch. The first (from the rightmost outlet) is sent to the three parameters that will be slightly varied by **vs.randomizer**: the metronome tempo (at the top), the cue increment (on the center-right) and the duration (on the lower right). Notice that with each bang the **metro** object will even change its own tempo (via the use of **vs.randomizer**). Also, notice that it is possible to set a starting point for the progression of cues through the sound file via the "startpoint" parameter visible on the right side of the patch. The rest of the patch contains nothing new. The audio file that is used by default is a fragment of Gregorian chant. Try listening to the first eight presets – even though these also introduce some random variation for the various parameters, they nonetheless stay within the "classic" implementation of the blocks technique.

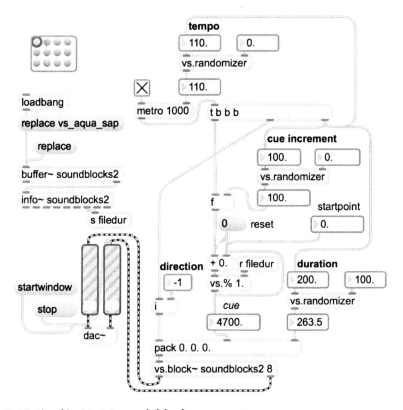

Fig. 5.40 The file **05_15_rand_blocks.maxpat**

The increment (or decrement) of the cue in this example will guarantee a path through the file with a precise direction: either forward or backward.

BEYOND THE BLOCKS TECHNIQUE

Keep the patch in figure 5.40 open and try out the last four presets (no. 9-12). Here, the parameters are set in such as way as to eliminate any specific playback direction through the file. In fact, the cue increment in these presets has been set to zero, so the cue location is incremented or decremented solely by the random parameter. Furthermore, preset number 10 generates very short blocks, bringing us into the domain of granular synthesis (which we will talk about in a later volume). Finally, notice that in the last preset the random choice of either increment or decrement for each cue signifies that each successive block can be chosen from any point in the sound file.

After having listened to all the presets, try to create some new ones.

In order to mix the blocks technique with looping (see sound example 5I-12 in chapter 5T), we need to define a "score" of parameters that change over time. We do not yet have all the necessary pieces in our repertoire to create such a score, but we will return to this topic later, in interlude D.

ACTIVITY

Use the **vs.line** object to control the parameters for the **metro** object, as well as the duration and block parameters, in order to create "duration glissandos" which highlight the transition from the blocks technique to a "rough" sound texture typical of granular synthesis. This can be done using a progressive reduction in both metronome rate and block duration (specifically, refer to the sound example 5I-6, "from blocks to grains" from chapter 5T).

· ·

SLICING

Let's now look at how to realize *slicing* (also known as *beat slicing*) with Max. Open the patch **05_16_beat_slicer.maxpat** (figure 5.41) and start by try out some of the presets in the patch.

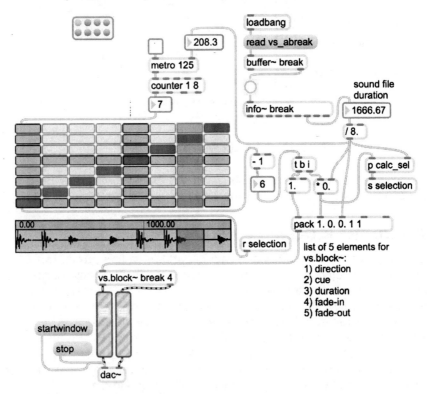

Fig. 5.41 The file **05_16_beat_slicer.maxpat**

This patch shows a very simple example of a beat slicer. Once we have thoroughly understood how it works, we will continue to a more complex version.

The first new thing you will immediately notice is the graphical object in the center of the patch, which is made up of rectangular blocks organized in 8 rows by 8 columns. This object is called `live.grid` and is part of the **Max for Live** library available from Max version 5.1. We will talk more about Max for Live, a separately available extension to Max, at the end of this book. Fortunately, the objects that belong to this extension are available in Max even if you do not own a license to use Max for Live.

The `live.grid` object (we will take a closer look at its main features in a moment) lets us select any one rectangular block per column. The columns, called steps, are numbered from the left, starting with 1.

In the default mode, each step must contain just one single block, placed in any desired row. The position of the block in the row represents the value of the step. The lowest row corresponds to the value 1, the row above it to the value 2, and so forth. Therefore, in the example shown in the figure, step 1 has the value 1, step 2 has the value 2, etc.

When the `live.grid` object receives a numerical value in its left inlet, this value is interpreted as the step number and will cause the value associated with that step to be output. In other words, it outputs the row number where the selected rectangular block is located within that step.

Let's now analyze the patch. When the file is opened, the drum loop **vs_abreak** is loaded into the [`buffer~` break] object (see the upper part of the patch). Once the sound file has been loaded, the `buffer~` object sends a bang to the [`info~` break] object, which, in turn, sends the file's duration to a division object which divides it by 8. This value is used, via the connection on the left, as a tempo for the `metro` object. The bangs generated by the `metro` are sent to a **counter** which creates a sequence of numbers from 1 to 8. This sequence is sent to the left inlet of `live.grid`, which outputs corresponding step values and sends them to the [- 1] object, which lowers the numerical value of each step by one (so the range from 1 to 8 becomes 0 to 7).

Returning to the division object which was used to divide the sound file's duration by 8, we can see that it is also connected to the third inlet of a **pack** object which groups a list of 5 elements together and sends them to the **vs.block~** object. Previously, we had been sending this object a list of three elements to specify playback direction, cue start time and duration. By adding two additional values to this list we can also specify the fade-in and fade-out times that will be applied each sound fragment. By default these values are both set to 20 milliseconds, but in this case we are setting them to 1 millisecond in order to avoid excessively smoothing-out the original envelopes of the percussive sounds.

The divide object sends a value representing 1/8 of the duration of the sound file to the third inlet of **pack**, which corresponds to the duration of the fragment produced by **vs.block~**. The second inlet (corresponding to the start point of the cue) receives the result of multiplying the output of the divide object (the duration of the file divided by 8) by the step value generated by **live.grid** (lowered by 1). Therefore the start time for each cue is located at 0/8 (0 · 1/8 of the duration), 1/8 (1 · 1/8 of the duration), 2/8 (2 · 1/8 of the duration), etc.

The last value sent to the **pack** object is the value 1 sent to its left inlet (the **pack** object's "hot" inlet), which corresponds to the playback direction of the sound fragment. The entire list is subsequently sent to **vs.block~**, which outputs the corresponding sound fragment.

The **waveform~** object located under the **live.grid** object shows the drum loop that we have loaded into the **buffer~**[23]. When running the patch you will notice that the sound fragments generated by **vs.block~** are also highlighted (or more precisely, selected) in **waveform~**. The **waveform~** object is actually able to receive a list of two values in its third inlet, corresponding to the start and end times of the fragment, in order to show that this region of the sound has been selected. This list is sent (via the **send/receive** pair [s selection] and [r selection]) to the [p calc_sel] sub-patch located on the right-hand side of the main patch (figure 5.42).

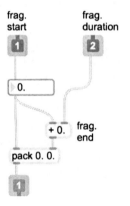

Fig. 5.42 The *subpatch* [p calc_sel]

The subpatch receives the fragment's start time and duration and uses these values to calculate and end time (with a technique similar to that shown in section 5.3, figure 5.20). The start and end values are assembled into a list and sent out the outlet of the subpatch. From here, the list is sent to the third inlet of **waveform~** via the **send/receive** pair [s selection] and [r selection]. Listen once again to the different presets and notice the rela-tionship between the step that is played and the portion of the sound file selected in **waveform~**, then try creating some new presets.

---

[23] If you open the inspector for **waveform~**, you will see that we have set the "**buffer~** Object Name" attribute so it refers to the **buffer~** named "break".

Now let's take a look at the other features of the **live.grid** object. Rebuild the patch shown in figure 5.43.

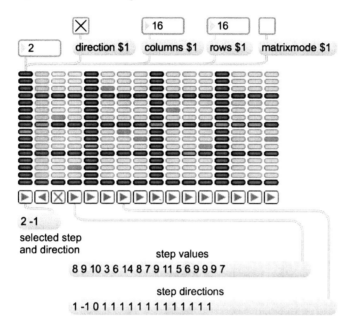

Fig. 5.43 The **live.grid** object

To find the **live.grid** object in the *Max Object Explorer*, select the "UI Objects" tab and go the category "Live". Alternately, you can create an object box and type the name of the object (live.grid) into it.

As you can see, by default **live.grid** displays a grid of 16 rows by 16 columns and has a different color scheme than that which was used in the file **05_16_beat_slicer.maxpat** (the object's colors can be modified in the inspector, as usual).

Also be sure to notice that the lower part of the object has a row of icons representing the playback direction of each step: a triangle pointing right indicates forward, pointing left it indicates backward, and an "x" represents muting (deactivation) of that particular step[24]. To change the icon for a given step you just need to click on it with the mouse. This row of icons is called the *directions panel*.

The *directions panel* can be shown and hidden using the "direction" command – to try this out, change the first **toggle** shown in the upper-left-

---

[24] The **live.grid** object does not produce any sound: it is limited to simply sending numerical values and lists. In order make it work as described, any patch where it is used needs to correctly interpret these messages (as do the patches shown throughout this section).

hand part of the figure. You can also set the appearance of the *directions panel* using the "Display Directions Panel" attribute in the object's inspector.

In order to change the number of rows or columns, you can use the "columns" and "rows" attributes, as shown in the figure (or use the equivalent options in the inspector).

We already know that sending a number to the left inlet causes the corresponding step value to be output. When the directions panel is visible (as it is in Figure 5.43), instead of a single number, the object will output a list consisting of the step value and the indicated direction: 1 indicating forward, -1 indicating reverse, and 0 representing deactivation of this particular step.

Every time the **live.grid** interface is modified with the mouse, two lists representing the series of step values and directions are output from the second and third outlets, respectively.

The "matrixmode" attribute (which can also be accessed via the inspector) activates the matrix mode. This allows us to arbitrarily set multiple values for any or all of the steps (see figure 5.44).

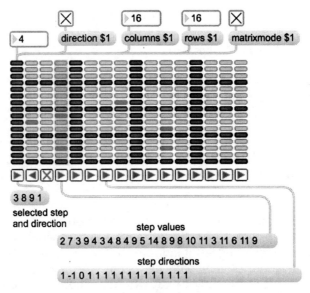

Fig. 5.44 The **live.grid** object in matrix mode

As you can see, when using matrix mode it is also possible to have steps without any selected value, whereas normally each step must have one (and only one) value.

Taking a look at the figure, we can see that the fourth step is selected, so the object has output a list of 4 values – the first three (3, 8, 9) corresponding to the three selected blocks in that step, and the last (1) corresponding to the direction.

The list that was sent out the second outlet in this example can be interpreted as a series of value pairs that indicate the step and its corresponding value, respectively. Therefore, the pairs represent:

step 2, value 7
step 3, value 9
step 4, value 3
step 4, value 8
step 4, value 9 etc.

There are no changes to the list of step directions sent out the third outlet.

At this point, load the file **5_17_beat_slicer2.maxpat** (figure 5.45) to see how to construct a slicer that takes these additional options of **live.grid** into consideration.

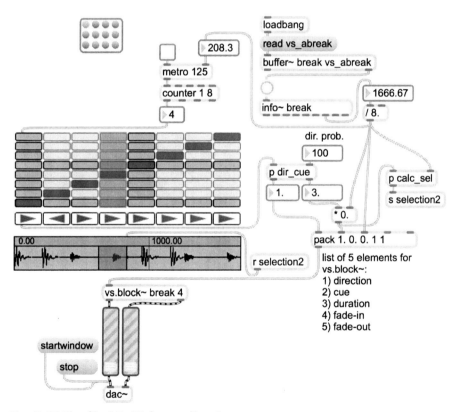

Fig. 5.45 The file **05_17_beat_slicer2.maxpat**

First of all, try out the first 4 presets, paying close attention to the icons displayed in the *directions panel*. Note that when the icon is an arrow pointing to the right, the fragment will be played in the normal (forward) direction, when icon is an arrow pointing to the left, the fragment will be played in reverse, and when the icon is an "x", the fragment will not be played.

107

Now, try out presets 5 through 8 (the second row of the **preset** object). In these presets, we are taking advantage of the matrix mode, allowing us to have several simultaneous values per step. If you listen to these presets long enough, you will realize that each repetition of the 8-step sequence is not always the same, because when there are several values in a given step, that step's fragment is chosen randomly by the algorithm inside the [p dir_cue] subpatch, located just to the right of the **live.grid** object. We will talk about this in a moment.

Finally, try out presets 9 through 12 (the third row of the **preset** object). Here, we have added one final modification: the number box connected to the right input of the [p dir_cue] subpatch indicates the probability (as a percentage) that the fragment will be played in the direction indicated by the directions panel. For example, if the probability value is 20, there is only a 20% chance that the fragment will be played in the direction shown in the directions panel; the remaining 80% of the time, the fragment will be played in the normal (forward) direction.

After you have listened carefully to all of the presets and having understood how the different parameters work, we can analyze the contents of the [p dir_cue] subpatch (figure 5.46).

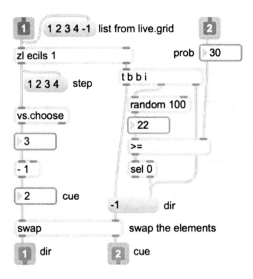

Fig. 5.46 The contents of the [p dir_cue] *subpatch*

The list output by **live.grid** arrives in the left inlet of the subpatch. In the figure this list is [1 2 3 4 -1]. As we already know, the elements in the list correspond to the active blocks for a given step, the last element corresponding to the direction for that step, as set in the directions panel. When there is more than one active block (here there are 4) the object must be in matrix mode. The input list is first sent to the [zl ecils 1] object, whose job it is to divide the list into 2 parts which are sent out the object's two outlets. The numerical argument represents the number of elements that are sent out the right outlet of [z1 ecils][25], in this example 1 element. Therefore, we have separated the step and direction to different outlets: step values on the left and direction on the right.

Because of the right-to-left priority in the Max environment, the first value sent by [z1 ecils] is the direction, sent out the object's right outlet. This value is sent to a **trigger** which has three arguments [b b i], and consequently also three outlets. Here, also, the first message is sent from the right outlet, and connected to the right inlet of a message box on the lower right, in order to store the direction (-1 in this example)[26] for future use. The second outlet of the **trigger** sends a bang that is used to generate a random number between 0 and 99. This number is sent to the >= object[27] whose right inlet has already received the probability value coming from the right input to the [p dir_cue] subpatch (a value of 30, as shown in the figure)[28]. The random number that was generated in the figure is 22. Since this value is less than 30, the conditions of the >= comparison are not satisfied, so the resulting evaluation is false. Consequently the >= object will output a 0 (indicating "false") which is sent to the [sel 0] object which outputs a bang out its left outlet. This bang gets "lost into the void," so to speak, because the left outlet of **sel** is not connected to anything.

The final bang from **trigger**, output from its leftmost outlet, is sent to the message box, underneath, which contains the previously stored direction value. The message box will consequently send its contents to the right inlet of the **swap** object (which we will discuss in a moment) in response to the bang; it is here that this series of messages "stops", since it has arrived at a cold inlet.

So, what would happen if the conditions of the >= comparison were satisfied, resulting in a "true" evaluation (i.e., in the case that the value produced by random were greater or equal than 30)? In this case, the >= object would send a value of 1 ("true") to the **sel** object, and since **sel** does not have an argument of 1, the value will be sent out its right outlet and into the right inlet of the message box where it will replace the existing value of -1 which had previously been stored there. After this, the final bang from the **trigger** object will cause the contents of the message box to be sent to the **swap** object, resulting in the fragment being played in a forward direction.

In summary, using the settings that can be seen in figure 5.46, when the value generated by random is between 0 and 29 (this will happen 30% of the time)

---

[25] As its name suggests this object is the mirror of [z1 slice] which we saw in the first volume in section IA7. The numerical argument of [z1 slice] represents, conversely, the number of elements which will be sent out the left outlet.

[26] Remember that the value of -1 means the fragment will be played in reverse.

[27] If you do not recall how the relational operators and **select** object work, refer to Interlude B, section IB4 of the first volume.

[28] This means that 30% of the time the fragment's direction will be what is indicated in the directions pane, whereas 70% of the time, the fragment will be played in the forward direction.

the fragment will be played in reverse, and when it is between 30 and 99 (70% of the time) it will be played back normally, in a forward direction.

Let's go back to the [zl ecils] object, in the top part of the subpatch, which sends the list of active blocks for the current step. This list is sent to the **vs.choose** object, which will randomly choose one element from the list it receives, as we learned in section 3.7P of the first volume. The chosen element represents the cue which will be played by the **vs.block~** object. As we can see in figure 5.46, the **vs.choose** object has chosen element "3." By subtracting 1 from this value (as we did in the previous patch in figure 5.41) we get cue number 2. This value is sent to the hot inlet of the **swap** object which is used to exchange the numerical values it has received in its two inlets: the value received in its right inlet will be output on the left and vice-versa. After being swapped, the cue number will be output out the right outlet of the [p dir_cue] subpatch and sent to the multiplier in the main patch, just as it was in the preceding patch shown in figure 5.41. The direction, on the other hand, will be sent out the left outlet of the subpatch and sent into the hot inlet of the **pack** object located in the lower right part of the main patch. The **pack** object will, in turn, output a list (whose first element is the playback direction) for **vs.block~**. Note that the **vs.block~** object uses the same convention as **live.grid** to define the playback direction of a block: 1 means normal (forward), -1 means reverse (backward) and 0 means no playback (muting).

Take a moment to think about how the [p dir_cue] subpatch works, and then answer the following question: Why do we need to use the **swap** object? Why can we not simply cross the patch cords, in order to change the output positions for the cue and direction, as shown in figure 5.47?

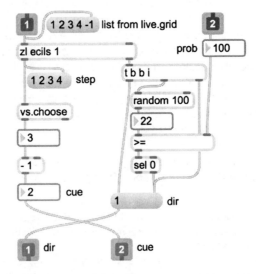

Fig. 5.47 This subpatch is incorrect – why?

Let's now add some additional variations to our slicer. The patch **5_18_beat_slicer3.maxpat** lets us define the pitch, volume and duration of each fragment (see figure 5.48).

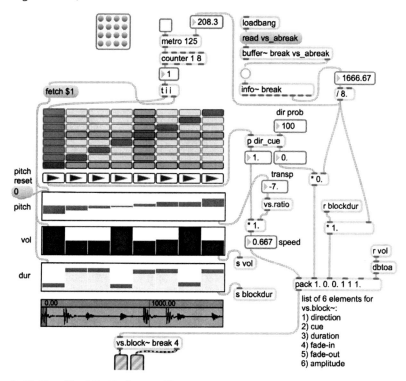

Fig. 5.48 The file **05_18_beat_slicer3.maxpat**

Three `multislider` objects have been added underneath the `live.grid` object in order to control the pitch, volume and duration of each fragment. Each of the three `multisliders` has a different color setting, to help make the three parameters visibly distinguishable from one another.

In this patch, we can see that the series of numbers output by the `counter` object is also sent to the three `multisliders` via the "fetch $1" message (on the left, just above the `live.grid`), in addition to being sent to the `live.grid` object. The "fetch" message, as we learned in section IB.6 of the first volume, can be used to obtain the value of a single slider from `multislider`. Note that the object [t i i] placed under the `counter` means that the "fetch $1" message will be sent to the three `multisliders` before the number is sent to `live.grid`.

Before continuing, let's listen carefully to the different presets.

The first four presets demonstrate variations in pitch. The relevant `multislider`, labelled "pitch," creates values between -12 and 12 (which can be can checked in the object's inspector). These values represent the transposition in semitones, so it is therefore possible to change the fragment's pitch from an octave lower

111

to an octave higher. The transposition value output by **multislider** is sent to the **vs.ratio** object, which converts the semitone transposition value into a corresponding playback speed for the sound file (the same that we would use for the **groove~** object, for example). Figure 5.49 (which we suggest you rebuild for yourself) should help to make the concept clearer.

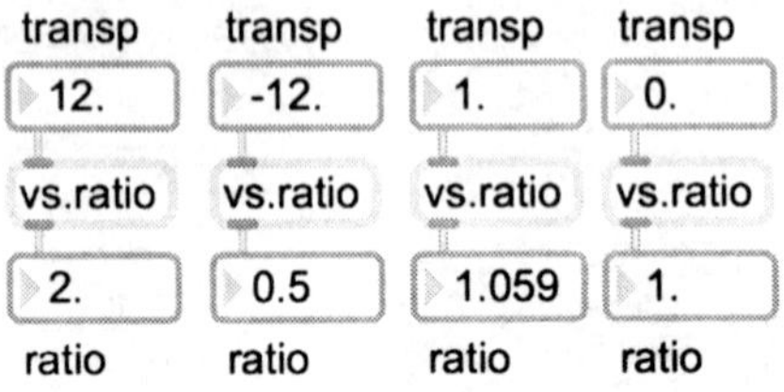

transp	transp	transp	transp
▸12.	▸-12.	▸1.	▸0.
vs.ratio	vs.ratio	vs.ratio	vs.ratio
▸2.	▸0.5	▸1.059	▸1.
ratio	ratio	ratio	ratio

Fig. 5.49 The **vs.ratio** object

As can be seen in the figure, the **vs.ratio** object converts a transposition in semitones into a speed ratio value, so a transposition of 12 semitones (one octave) higher corresponds to a playback speed of 2, a transposition of 12 semitones lower corresponds to a playback speed of 0.5, a transposition of 1 semitone (a half step) higher is equal to a playback speed of about 1.059 and no transposition (0 semitones) means a playback speed of 1, which indicates the normal playback speed.

Until now, we have been using the first parameter to **vs.block~** as a playback direction, but this parameter can actualy also be used to modify the playback speed, in exactly the same way that it does for the **groove~** object. This means that the playback direction also includes transposition when it is set to a value other than 1 or -1.

After being transformed into playback speed by the **vs.ratio** object, the transposition value is multiplied by the playback direction output by the [p dir_cue] subpatch that we have just analyzed. In figure 5.48, for example, the transposition value is -12 which is equal to a playback speed of 0.5. This value is multiplied by the direction (which is -1, indicating playback of the fragment in reverse), so the playback speed therefore becomes -0.5, which indicates an octave lower and in reverse.

Presets 5 through 8 (in the second row) include variations in volume. The **vs.block~** object can receive an amplitude value (which is equal to 1 by default) as the sixth element of the input list. In this patch we therefore send **vs.block~** a list of 6 elements so we can modify the amplitude of the fragments being played back.

The **multslider** labelled "vol" sends values between -30 and 0, representing volume values in dB. Since **vs.block~** object currently works with linear amplitude values, we have to transform the dB into amplitude values using the **dbtoa** object before sending them to the sixth inlet of the **pack** object.

Presets 9 through 12 (the third row) comprise various combinations of all the parameters. Listen carefully once again to all of the presets, trying to understand how each of the parameters contributes to the overall sound modification, and then try creating some new presets of your own.

When comparing the patch in figure 5.45 with that in figure 5.48 you may have noticed that the [**p** calc_sel] subpatch, which had been used to highlight the fragment being played in the **waveform~** object's display, seems to have disappeared entirely. Actually, it has just been made invisible in order to make the patch clearer, by using the menu command Object -> Hide on Lock, which we covered in section 1.1P. If you put the patch into Edit mode, you will see that the subpatch is still there. There are also hidden connections from the third outlet of the preset to various other objects which reappear in edit mode. The objects connected to this outlet are excluded from being stored in the preset[29]. For example, the two **gain~** objects are excluded because we do not want the volume settings of the patch to be stored, since this setting will depend on the audio system we are using. The **toggle** connected to the **metro** has also been excluded since saving the **toggle**'s state (either on or off) in a preset means that we would start or stop the **metro** every time we select that preset.

We will soon take a look at one final modification to our beat slicer: applying a stuttering effect to it. First, however, we need to introduce a new object: **vs.multibang**. This object takes a positive integer in its left inlet and creates several bangs within a given time frame (or tempo). The time interval, in milliseconds, can be given either as an argument or as a value in the right inlet. If, for example, the main tempo is 500 milliseconds, and we send the value 2 into the object's left inlet, it will produce 2 bangs 250 milliseconds apart. If we send the object the number 4, it will output 4 bangs 125 milliseconds apart, and so on.

---

[29] We will look at this and other features of the **preset** object in interlude D later in this volume.

Rebuild the patch shown in figure 5.50.

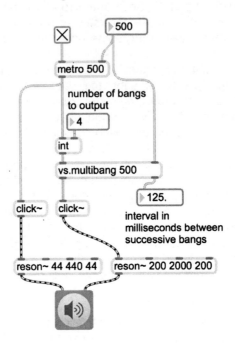

Fig. 5.50 The **vs.multibang** object

At the top of this patch there is a **metro** connected to an **int** object which sends its stored numerical value to the **vs.multibang** object. This, in turn, is connected to the unit impulse generator, **click~** (which we already saw in section 3.9P), whose signal is filtered by a lowpass resonant filter and sent to the right channel of the audio interface. The **metro** object is also connected directly to another impulse generator that is filtered by a second lowpass resonant filter, and the resulting signal is sent to the left channel. Try modifying the numerical value connected to the right inlet of the **int** object and notice how the relationship between the sounds sent to the right and left channels changes. Also try changing the tempo of the **metro**. Note that this tempo value is also sent to **vs.multibang**, so that the bangs it outputs are always synchronized with the tempo of the **metro**, and that the **vs.multibang** object sends the millisecond interval between each of its bangs out its right outlet.

Now open the file **5_19_beat_slicer4.maxpat** (figure 5.51).

First of all, listen carefully to all of the presets, as always, taking special note of both the configuration of the new **multislider** (labelled "stutter") that has been added to the bottom of the patch, and to the number box "stut prob" (probability that stuttering will take place), which is connected to the fourth inlet of the [p dir_cue_stut] subpatch in the lower right hand part of the patch.

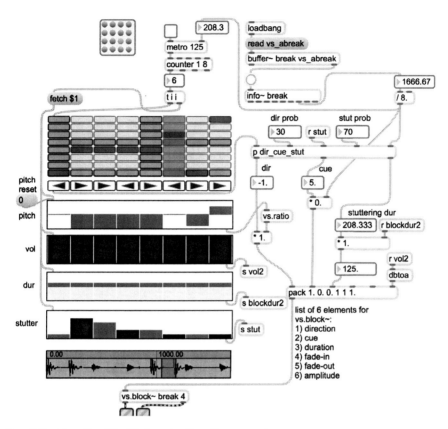

Fig. 5.51 The file **05_19_beat_slicer4.maxpat**

The "stutter" `multislider` outputs whole number values between 1 and 8, representing the number of repetitions of each fragment. For example, if the output value is 2, instead of playing the entire cue, the first half of the cue will be repeated twice; if this value is 3, the first third of the cue will be played three times, and so forth. A value of 1 corresponds to normal playback, without stuttering.

The value output by **multislider** is sent to the third inlet of the [p dir_cue_
stut] subpatch via a pair of **send** and **receive** objects. Let's take a look at the
contents of this subpatch (figure 5.52).

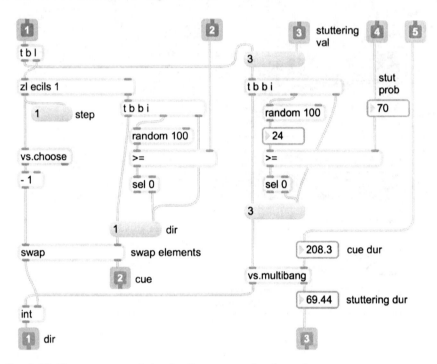

Fig. 5.52 The contents of the [p dir_cue_stut] *subpatch*

This subpatch is an extension of the [p dir_cue] subpatch used in the previous
versions of the slicer, but in addition to the dealing with step and playback
direction it also controls the stuttering mechanism. The stuttering algorithm
is located on the right side of the subpatch and contains a probability-based
selection mechanism similar to the one used by the playback direction, on the
left. The third inlet of the subpatch receives a stuttering value from 1 to 8. This
value is sent from the right outlet of the **trigger** to be stored in the message
box, underneath (with a value of 5, as shown in the figure). The **trigger** then
causes a random value between 0 and 99 to be output by the **random** object
(in the figure the number 24 has been generated), and this value is compared
with the "stut prob" value which was received in the subpatch's fourth inlet (a
probability of 70 in the figure).

The mechanism is the same as the one we used for the direction (see figure 5.46) so we therefore do not need to analyze it again. Needless to say,
the message box will eventually contain either the stuttering value from the
multislider or else a value of 1 (no stuttering), according to whether or not
the random value is greater than or equal to the percentage value set in the
"stut prob" number box in the main patch.

Let's now take a look at the left side of the patch in figure 5.52, noticing that the list coming from the first inlet (step and direction) is sent to a `trigger` that first sends the list to the algorithm that processes the direction and cue number for each step (already described in detail after figure 5.46). Here, however, the direction value is not directly connected to the first outlet, but stored in an `int` object.

Returning to the `trigger`, we can see that the second message it sends is a bang (out its left outlet) connected to the message box on the right which contains the stuttering value. This value is then sent to the `vs.multibang` object which creates a number of bangs equal to the value received, equally spaced within the duration of one cue. The bangs are sent to the hot inlet of the `int` object on the lower-left, which sends the direction value out the subpatch's outlet, arriving at the hot inlet of the `pack` object in the main patch. The list output by the `pack` object is sent to `vs.block~`, which plays the fragment. The `vs.multibang` object additionally sends a value representing the duration of each fragment out its right outlet. This is sent out the third outlet of the subpatch to the main patch, where it is multiplied by the value output by the `multislider` that controls the block duration, before being sent to the third inlet of the `pack` object which assembles the list for `vs.block~`.

Listen once again to the presets in the patch and try creating some new ones.

• •

ACTIVITIES

- When the `vs.block~` object receives a list of 7 elements, the last element in the list is used to control the panning (stereo position) of the block. A value of 0 corresponds to the left channel, whereas a value of 1 corresponds to the right channel. Other values between 0 and 1 denote intermediary positions. Add a fifth `multislider` to the **5_19_beat_slicer4.maxpat** patch in order to control the stereo panning of the blocks generated by `vs.block~`, and naturally also add a 7th argument to the `pack` object.

- Using the modified patch from the previous activity, replace the `multisliders` with different types of LFOs (cyclical or random), in order to control the pitch, volume, duration, stuttering and panning parameters of the blocks. Since we need to use numerical values and not signals for these parameters, you will need to convert the signal generated by each of the LFOs into Max values using the `snapshot~` object, and additionally use the `scale` object to transform the -1 to 1 range of the LFOs into appropriate ranges for each of the parameters.

- Replace the drum loop with the sound file **vs_greg_1666** (which contains a brief fragment of Gregorian chant), and try different presets with this new sound. You will need to find presets that work well with the vocal timbre in this sound file.

• •

5.5 PITCH MANIPULATION OF SAMPLED SOUNDS: AUDIO SCRUBBING

Now let's take a look at how we can "scrub" an audio file with Max. First, we need to learn a new object: **play~**. This object is fairly similar to **wave~**, since it also plays a sound from a **buffer~** object when it receives a ramp signal. However, whereas the **wave~** object plays the entire sound when it receives a ramp from 0 to 1, the **play~** object needs to receive a ramp specifying the position in milliseconds within the sound. So, for example, if the duration of the sound is 2 seconds (2000 milliseconds), the **play~** object needs to receive an input signal that goes from 0 2000 in order to be entirely played. To understand this concept more clearly, take a look at figure 5.53.

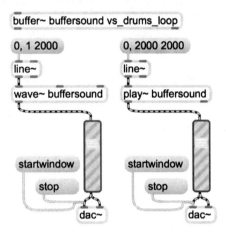

Fig. 5.53 Comparison between **wave~** and **play~**

The patch in the figure (that you are welcome to rebuild for yourself) is an expansion of the patch in figure 5.22, and shows a side-by-side comparison of the **wave~** and **play~** objects.

Both objects play the sound file **vs_drums_loop** (which is 2 seconds long and has been loaded into the **buffer~** named "buffersound") when you click on the message box above the corresponding object. However, the message box used for **wave~** instructs the **line~** object underneath it to create a ramp from 0 to 1 in 2000 milliseconds, whereas the message box for **play~** tells the **line~** to create a ramp from 0 to 2000 in 2000 milliseconds.

In other words, the playback position in the audio file has been normalized between 0 and 1 for **wave~**, whereas the position is expressed in milliseconds for **play~**.

ACTIVITIES

Answer the following questions and create example patches for each of them in order to deepen your knowledge of how to use **play~**.

1- What changes would we need to make to the contents of the message box on the right in the patch shown in figure 5.53 in order to play the sound file at double speed?

2- What about playing back the sound at half speed?

3- How would we play back only the first half of the sound?

4- How would we play back the last half?

5- How could we play back the entire sound in reverse, starting at the end and playing to the beginning of the file (like playing a piece of tape backwards)?

6- Replace the **line~** with the **curve~** object and add a curve factor to the message box (for example 0.5 or -0.5). What happens and why?

7- Rebuild the patch in figure 5.23 (section 5.3) replacing the **wave~** object with the **play~** object (and making any other necessary modifications) and make sure the patch functions correctly with any sound loaded into the **buffer~**.

8- Do the same with the patch in figure 5.24.

· ·

Now open the file **05_20_scrubber.maxpat** (figure 5.54).

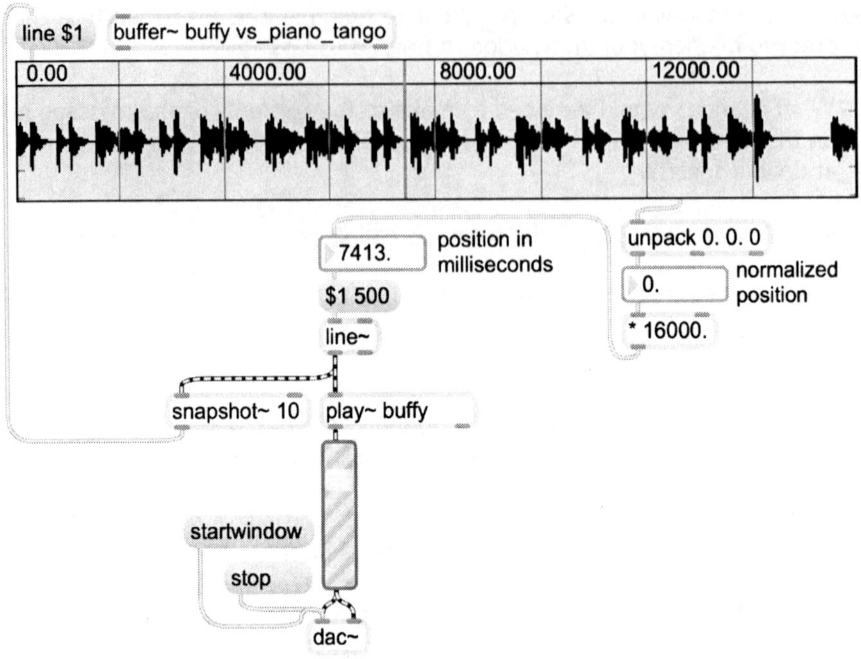

Fig. 5.54 The file **05_20_scrubber.maxpat**

In this patch we will take advantage of the **waveform~** object as an interface for scrubbing.

Activate the DSP engine and try out the scrubbing function by clicking on the **waveform~** object and dragging the mouse. For the time being, this effect is rather primitive, but we will improve it throughout the course of this section.

Let's take a look at how the patch works. When you drag the mouse across the **waveform~** object, its fourth outlet sends a list of 3 elements corresponding to the horizontal position of the mouse, the vertical position and the "state" of the mouse (which we will discuss later). The horizontal and vertical positions are normalized: that is, they each have a minimum value of 0 and a maximum value of 1. Using the **unpack** object we will take just the first element of the list (the horizontal position of the mouse) and multiply it by the duration of the sound file (the file **vs_piano_tango** is 16000 milliseconds long). By using the position values that are creating by dragging the mouse, we can generate a series of ramps using the **line~** object that are 500 milliseconds in duration[30] that can be used

---

[30] The 500 millisecond duration is used in order to be able to listen to the audio fragment for a sufficiently large amount of time while "scrubbing" the sound. We have already used **line~** to interpolate between a stream of values, for example in section 1.4P of the first volume.

to pilot the **play~** object. The output of **line~** is also converted into a constant stream of Max values by the **snapshot~** object[31]. These values are used for the "line" message shown in the message box on the upper left. This has nothing to do at all with the **line~** object, but is used to draw a vertical line inside the **waveform~** display, corresponding to a given millisecond position within the file. In the figure we can see that the line has been drawn about halfway through the file (at 7413 milliseconds from the beginning, to be precise).

One of the problems with the algorithm used in this patch is that when the mouse moves quickly, the sound file playback accelerates, whereas ideally it should not play back faster than the original speed of the sound file (since the main purpose of scrubbing is to locate a specific point in the sound file "by ear"). To correct this problem we will use the **vs.playspeedlim~** object, which lets us put a speed limit on the ramp that is sent to the **play~** object. Modify the patch as shown in figure 5.55.

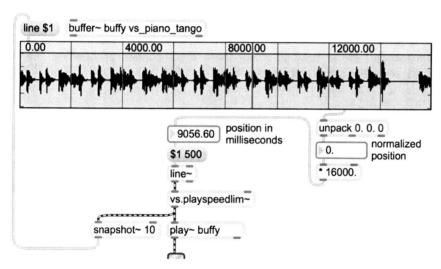

Fig. 5.55 Modified *scrubber*

We have added the **vs.playspeedlim~** object between the **line~** and the **play~** object. By default, **vs.playspeedlim~** modifies the ramp it receives so that when it is sent to **play~** the maximum playback speed of the file relates to the "regular" playback speed of that file. It is possible to modify the maximum playback speed using a numerical value sent to the **vs.playspeedlim~** object's right inlet – 1 corresponds to normal speed (the default value), 2 corresponds to double speed, 0.5 corresponds to half speed, and so forth. Furthermore, a value of 0 can be used to stop the ramp and a value of -1 will entirely eliminate the "speed limit" imposed on the input signal.

---

[31] The **snapshot~** object has already been discussed in section 2.4P of the first volume.

When you try out the modified patch you might notice some other possible improvements that could be made. Once you start dragging the mouse it is not possible to stop playback. If the mouse is dragged from the beginning to the end of the sound displayed in **waveform~** we need to wait 16 seconds before the playback stops. If you have used the scrubbing function in a hard disk recording program, you would probably expect playback to stop when the mouse button is released. It would also be useful if, with every new click of the mouse on the waveform display, the vertical playback position indicator would jump immediately to the mouse click location without playback.

In order to make these modifications, we can take advantage of the "mouse state" – the third element of the list output from the fourth outlet of **waveform~**. This element can have one of the following values:

0 = mouse button released
1 = mouse button pressed
2 = dragging the mouse (with the button depressed)

Let's take a look at how to make these modifications by opening the file **05_21_scrubber2.maxpat** (shown in figure 5.56).

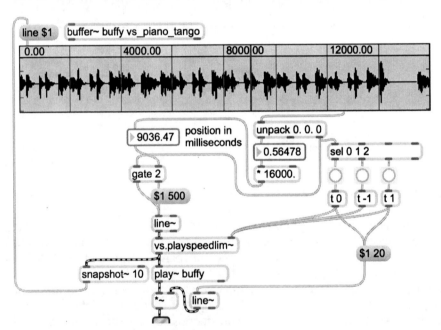

Fig. 5.56 The file **05_21_scrubber2.maxpat**

First, you will notice that the connection from the third outlet of the **unpack** object (which corresponds to the mouse state) is sent to the first inlet of the **gate** object, on the left. The millisecond position in the sound file is connected to the second inlet of the gate. When you drag the mouse along the **waveform~** object, the mouse state value is 2. This value opens the second outlet of the gate and the position is sent to the message box [$1 500], just as it was in the previous patch. When the mouse button is released, the mouse state value is 0; this closes the gate so the position value is not sent to any outlet of the gate. When you click on the **waveform~** (without dragging) the value of the mouse state is 1, so this opens the first outlet of the gate and the position value is therefore sent directly to the **line~** object, without first being sent to the message box. As we have already learned, when a **line~** object receives a single value instead of a list, it will jump immediately to that value.

Now let's see how the behavior of **vs.playspeedlim~** is modified. The **sel** connected to the third outlet of **unpack** uses a **trigger** object to send values to the right inlet of **vs.playspeedlim~** (which controls the "speed limit" of the input ramp), in response to different mouse state values.

When the mouse state is 0 (button released) the value 0 is sent to **vs.playspeedlim~**. This value, as we have already stated, stops the ramp so when the mouse button is released the playback of the sound with **play~** also stops.

When the mouse state is 1 (button pressed), a value of -1 is sent to **vs.playspeedlim~**. This value eliminates any imposed speed limit, so that every time we click on the **waveform~** the position where the mouse is pointing will be sent immediately to the **play~** object, and it will jump to that point in the file (without initiating playback).

When the mouse state is 2 (dragging), the value 1 is sent to **vs.playspeedlim~** to indicate a speed limit corresponding to the sound's "normal" playback speed. When we drag the mouse inside the waveform, the playback will therefore follow the mouse displacement, but playback speed will not go above normal playback speed. Furthermore, the **trigger** connected to the mouse state values 0 and 2 (first and third outlets of the **sel** object) is also sent to the message box [$1 20] (on the right side of the patch) which, in turn, is connected to a **line~** object located underneath **play~**. Can you deduce what this **line~** object is used for, and why it is connected specifically to those two **trigger** objects?

• •

ACTIVITY

Modify the patch **05_21_scrubber2.maxpat** so that it works with a file of any length that is loaded into the **buffer~**.

• •

RANDOM SCRUBBER

Let's now see how we can use the scrubbing technique for creative endeavors, by analyzing a patch that creates automatic scrubbing on a file loaded into memory, based on random number generators.

First, load the file **05_22_auto_scrubber.maxpat** (shown in figure 5.57).

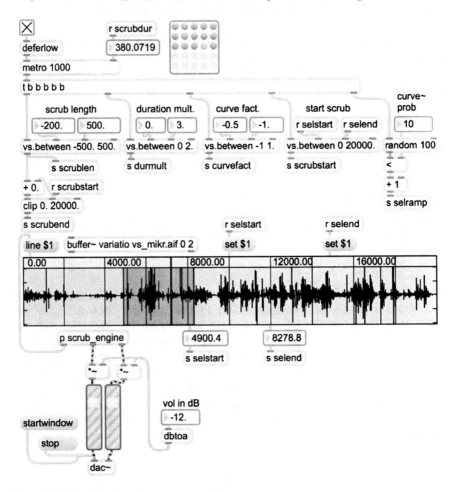

Fig. 5.57 The file **05_22_auto_scrubber.maxpat**

For this patch we will use the sound file **vs_mikr.aif**, which contains processed percussion and electronic sounds. This is a stereo sound file and it is loaded into a `buffer~` named "variatio" located just above the `waveform~` object. Note that the `buffer~` object contains two numerical arguments, 0 and 2 (in addition to the buffer name and the name of the file to load). The first value represents the length of the buffer in milliseconds (which will be changed immediately when the sound file is loaded), and the second value is the number of channels (which is set to 2 because our sound file is stereo). If these values had not been provided to the **buffer~**, it would have loaded only one of the two channels into memory.

Let's begin by listening to the file **vs_mikr.aif** in its entirety by choosing the first preset and turning on the **metro** object in the upper left part of the patch (obviously, after having started the DSP by clicking on the "startwindow" message).

The file is 20 seconds long and presents a series of different timbral configurations, that can be put to good use by the random scrubber in order to generate new sound material. Now listen to the remaining presets in the first row so you can realize just how many different kinds of sonic variations can be achieved using this patch. Also take a look at the values used for the various parameters (which we will obviously describe in a moment), and to both the region selected and the movement of the vertical line inside the **waveform~** object.

Before listening to the remaining presets, let's take a look at the settings of the various parameters. As we previously stated, the scrubbing is automatic and is therefore not made by dragging the mouse, but rather produced directly by the patch itself, using a **play~** object located in the [p scrub_engine] subpatch.

By dragging the mouse inside the **waveform** object, we can select a portion of the sound file from which the patch will randomly select a playback start point. In the upper part of the patch we can see the other adjustable parameters. Under the heading "scrub length" (on the left) we can select a minimum and maximum length for random scrubbing. Once a start point from somewhere within the region of the file selected in **waveform~** has been randomly generated, the ending point is calculated by adding another random value to this number. In the figure we see that the minimum and maximum limits for "scrub length" are between -200 and 500. This means that if our playback start location was randomly chosen to be at 5000 milliseconds, the end location could be anywhere between 4800 (5000 - 200) and 5500 (5000 + 500) milliseconds. Obviously, in the event that the ending location is less than the starting location, the playback would be in reverse. The next parameter (labeled "duration mult.") uses a multiplication factor to change the scrubbing playback speed. In the figure, the minimum and maximum values for this multiplication factor are 0 and 3 – this means that the playback duration of any fragment could be between 0 and 3 times its actual length. Let's imagine an example where the fragment has a starting point of 5000 milliseconds, and a destination point at 5400: its length is therefore 400 milliseconds. If the randomly-generated multiplication factor were 2, the playback would take 800 (400 · 2) milliseconds and the resulting sound would consequently be an octave lower. If the multiplication factor were 0.5, the playback would last 200 (400 · 0.5) milliseconds and the sound would be an octave higher, and so forth.

The next parameter is the curve factor. The **play~** object used for the scrubbing playback can actually be piloted by either the **line~** object or the **curve~** object. In the latter case the curve factor can also be randomly generated. In the figure this parameter can vary between the values -0.5 and -1.

To the right of the "start scrub" parameter, which, as we have said, is set by selecting a region of the sound file in the **waveform~** object with the mouse, we come to the final parameter ("**curve~** prob") which represents the percentage of probability that the scrubbing will be made with **curve~** instead of **line~**. In the figure this is set to 10%. The difference between playback with **line~** and with **curve~** is that the playback speed with **curve~** will change continuously (because of the curvature) and therefore create a glissando.

Now try the different presets, paying close attention the settings of the different parameters and the effect these settings have on the resulting sound. Afterwards, try creating some new presets of your own.

Let's now analyze how the patch works. As we have seen, it is possible to select a portion of the waveform displayed in the **waveform~** object using the mouse. This is made possible by the "Click Mode" attribute (found in the object's inspector), which determines the type of action we can perform with the mouse in the **waveform~** object. Here, the attribute has been set to "Select" which, naturally, lets us select a portion of the sound file[32].

When we make a selection using the mouse, the **waveform~** object sends the start and end times of the selection (shown in the two number boxed underneath the object). These two values are sent to two **send** objects which the arguments "selstart" and "selend," respectively. In the upper part of the patch (under the header "start scrub") we can see two **receive** objects with the same arguments, which send the values they receive to a **vs.between** object.

In the patch, there are two other **receive** objects which get the start and end selection values and which are located above the **waveform~** object. These two **receive** objects are connected to two message boxes, both containing the message "set $1," connected to the third and fourth inlets of **waveform~** (these inlets are used to receive the start and end positions of the selection). This connection is necessary only because the area selected in **waveform~** is not stored by the **preset** object, and therefore recalling different presets would not visually set this region. However, the **preset** object *will* store the values contained in the two number boxes below the **waveform~** object, so each time a new preset is selected these two values will be sent to the **receive** objects connected to **waveform~** and the region will appear selected. The "set $1" message is used so that the numerical values received by **waveform~** are not once again sent to the outputs, or else they would be sent to the **send/receive** object pairs and back into the **waveform~** object's inlets over and over again, provoking a "short circuit" (in the form of an infinite loop) that would stop processing.

---

[32] The other possible modes for the "Click Mode" attribute are "None" (the mouse will have no effect), "Loop" (used to move and modify the selected area), "Move" (allows zooming of the waveform and navigating inside the zoomed region), and "Draw" (allows a waveform to be drawn directly with the mouse). These modes can also be set by sending the object a setmode attribute.

In addition to the uses we have seen in the first volume, the set message can be very useful for setting the internal variables of a lot of Max objects without causing output. As an example, rebuild the simple patch shown in figure 5.58.

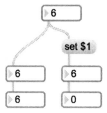

Fig. 5.58 The *set* message

As you can see, the number 6 set in the number box on top is sent to the number box on the left and in turn to the other one below it. The number 6 is also sent to the "set $1" message on the right, which changes the value of the number box below it, however it does not send anything to the number box below it, so its value remains set to 0. In other words we could say that the set message can be used to make a "hot" inlet temporarily "cold."

Let's return to the patch in figure 5.57. In the upper left part of the patch there is a **metro** object that sends bangs to the 5 random number generators (which we have already discussed) via a **trigger**. Proceeding from right to left, the first random value relates to the probability that the **curve~** object will be used. This is a random value between 0 and 99 that is compared with the given parameter (in the figure this is set to 10%). If the random value is less than the parameter value provided, the < object will output 1, otherwise it will output 0. This value is increased by 1, and sent to the [s selramp] object which sends it inside the [p scrub_engine] subpatch (we will soon see how it is used there).

Moving to the left, there is the random value corresponding to the scrubbing start point that is sent to both the [s scrubstart] object inside the [p scrub_engine] subpatch, in addition to a **receive** object on the left side of the patch which we will look at in a moment.

The curve factor is sent from the [s curvefact] object into the [p scrub_engine] subpatch, as is the multiplication factor for the duration (via the [s durmult] object).

The final randomly generated parameter (on the left side of the patch) is the playback length of the fragment. The value of this parameter is sent from [s scrublen] into the [p scrub_engine] subpatch. In addition to this, it is also added to the scrubbing start point (received by [r scrubstart]) and constrained to the range 0 - 20000 (i.e., the duration of the sound file) by the **clip** object. The resulting value is sent into the [p scrub_engine] subpatch from the [s scrubend] object.

Let's now look at the contents of the [p scrub_engine] subpatch (figure 5.59):

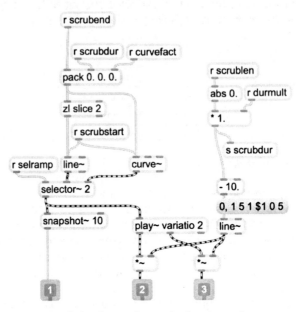

Fig. 5.59 The contents of the [p scrub_engine] *subpatch*

As we have already said, the first value that arrives is used to choose the ramp type (linear or curve). On the left we can see the [r selramp] object connected to a **selector~**. If the value it receives is 1, the signal output by **line~** will be sent to the output of the **selector~** object, if the value it receives is 2, the **curve~** object's output will be sent. This signal is connected to a **play~** object that refers to the buffer named "variatio" in the main patch. Note that the second argument to **play~** is the value 2, representing the number of output channels (since the file we are using is stereo). The signal output by **selector~** is also sent to the **snapshot~** object that is connected to the first outlet of the subpatch.

The second value to arrive to the subpatch is the scrubbing start point. The [r scrubstart] object is connected to both the **line~** and **curve~** objects, but as we already know, only the output of one of them will be sent through the **selector~**.

The third value received is the curve factor ([r curvefact]), which is sent to the third inlet of the **pack** object at the top of the subpatch.
The fourth value is the duration multiplier ([r durmult]), which is sent to the cold inlet of the multiplication object visible on the right.

The fifth parameter outputs two values: the playback fragment length and the end point of the fragment.

The value for the fragment length ([r scrublen]) is first sent to the **abs** object (on the right) which assures it will always be a positive value (even though the length can actually also be negative to indicate playback in reverse). The absolute value of the length is then multiplied by the multiplication factor received from [r durmult]. This way, the duration value can also be used to generate a trapezoidal envelope that is applied to the fragment played back, in order to eliminate clicks. We will leave it to the reader to figure out how this envelope is generated. The duration value is also sent to the [s scrubdur] object. The corresponding [r scrubdur] object is connected to the second inlet of the pack object in the upper part of the subpatch. There is a second [r scrubdur] in the main patch (figure 5.57), connected to the right input of the **metro**. This connection guarantees that the metronome's tempo will always correspond to the duration of the fragment being played.

Finally, the endpoint of the fragment ([r scrubend]) is sent to the hot inlet of the **pack** object which creates a 3-element list (end point, duration, curve factor) for the object **curve**. The first two elements of this list are also sent to the **line~** object (using the [zl slice 2] object to remove the 3rd list element).

Let's now return to the main patch. The left output of the [p scrub_engine] subpatch outputs a stream of Max values (produced by **snapshot~**) that are used to draw the vertical line in the **waveform~** display. The other two outputs are the left and right channel of the fragment being played. Before being sent to the two **gain~** objects, the amplitude of this stereo signal is modified by the parameter labeled "vol in dB" just to the right of the two **gain~** sliders. This way it is possible to individually control the volume for each of the presets (before the general volume set by the **gain~** sliders) in order to avoid excessive amplitude changes between one preset and another.

The last object that we need to explain is the **deferlow** object, located in the upper left part of the patch between the **toggle** and the **metro**. This object guarantees that any message it receives will be sent last, regardless of whether or not it was sent before other messages, irrespectively of its right-to-left position in the patch. This way, when we change from one preset to another we will be sure that the parameters will be set before the **metro** receives the start command from the **toggle**, causing it to output its first bang.

• •

ACTIVITIES

• Add a lowpass and highpass filter to the random scrubber. The cutoff frequencies of the two filters should be generated randomly by two **vs.between** objects each time a fragment is played back. Save some new presets that make use of these modifications.

• Control one or more parameters of the random scrubber using some cyclic or random LFOs and create several new presets taking advantage of these changes.

LIST OF MAX OBJECTS

adc~
Analog to Digital Converter: an object which brings audio signals (even multi-channel ones) from the inputs of the computer's audio interface into the Max environment.

deferlow
Guarantees that any message it receives will be sent last, after all other messages have been sent, regardless of its position within the patch.

degrade~
Used to virtually reduce the sampling rate and number of bits in a signal.

dspstate~
Provides information about the MSP audio engine, particularly its Sampling Rate, I/O Vector Size and Signal Vector Size.

gate~
Sends a signal input into its right inlet to one of its outlets, set with a numerical value to its left inlet (1 = first outlet, 2 = second outlet, etc., the number 0 can be used to ignore the input signal).

groove~
Plays back a sound stored in a table and controls looping. The table is contained in a **buffer~** object. Both **buffer~** and **groove~** should have the same name as an argument.

info~
Provides information about a sound file loaded into a **buffer~** object. The **info~** and **buffer~** should have the same name as an argument.

live.grid
A graphical object that is part of the Max for Live library. It is made up of a grid of rectangular blocks called steps with a default layout of 16 rows by 16 columns.

meter~
A graphical sound level indicator.

play~
Plays back the contents of a **buffer~**

sah~
Performs a *sample and hold* operation on a signal.

sfinfo~
Provides the following information about an audio file on disk: number of channels, sample length in bits, sampling frequency, sound file duration in milliseconds, format of individual samples and file name.

sig~
Transforms a numerical Max message (either integer or floating-point) into a signal.

swap
Exchanges the position of two numerical values.

trapezoid~
A trapezoidal table: it produces one cycle of a trapezoidal waveform each time it receives a ramp from 0 to 1 (a ramp produced by the **phasor~** object, for instance).

vs.block~
Plays back segments of sound from a **buffer~**

vs.brickwall~
A filter with a very steep cutoff based on the Fast Fourier Transform (FFT) analysis/resynthesis technique.

vs.click~
An impulse train generator.

vs.multibang
Outputs a requested number of bangs within a given time frame

vs.playspeedlim~
Transforms the ramps that it receives into output ramps that limit the maximum playback speed for a sound file being played by the **play~** object.

vs.ratio
An object which transforms intervals in semitones (half steps) into frequency ratios.

LIST OF ATTRIBUTES AND MESSAGES FOR SPECIFIC MAX OBJECTS

live.grid
- Directions Panel
Using this graphical element of the **live.grid** object it is possible to show the playback direction for each step.

- Direction or Display Directions Panel (attribute)
Using these attributes you can show and hide the *Directions Panel*.

- Columns (attribute)
With this attribute, also accessible in the inspector, you can change the number of columns.

- Rows (attribute)
With this attribute, also accessible in the inspector, you can change the number of rows.

- Matrixmode (attribute)
This attribute, also accessible via the inspector, will activate the matrix mode that allows any number of values to be set for each step.

sfplay~
- Seek (message)
Using this message, **sfplay~** will play the sound file starting at the millisecond position provided by the number following the message.

- Preload (message)
This message, followed by a cue number, is use to preload a portion of the sound file into memory so it can be read from that point without any initial delay.

- Name (message)
This message, followed by a reference name is used to provide a name for an **sfplay~** object.

sfinfo~
- Getnamed (message)
This message, followed by a name that has already been given to an **sfplay~** object (using the "name" message) allows us to get information about the sound file loaded into the **sfplay~** object with that name.

- Open (message)
This message, sent to the **sfinfo~** object will open a sound file in order to obtain information about its contents.

waveform~

- Buffer~ Object Name (attribute)
This attribute in the object's inspector lets you set the associated **buffer~** name

- Click-Mode (attribute)
This attribute determines the type of action that you can perform with the mouse in the **waveform~** object.
The possible modes are:

"Select" (to select a portion of the sound file with the mouse);
"None"(the mouse will have no effect);
"Loop" (used to move and modify the selected area);
"Move" (allows zooming of the waveform and navigating inside the zoomed region);
"Draw" (allows a waveform to be drawn directly with the mouse);
These modes can also be set by sending the object a *setmode* attribute.

GLOSSARY

Audio Status
This window, accessible from the Options menu, lets you control the global audio settings and choose the audio interface with which MSP will communicate. The window is divided into 5 sections: audio interface selection, buffer length and sampling rate settings, information about CPU usage, global mixer settings (only for Max 6 and later) and I/O channel settings.

Interlude C
MANAGING TIME, POLYPHONY, ATTRIBUTES AND ARGUMENTS

PREREQUISITES FOR THE CHAPTER
• THE CONTENTS OF VOLUME 1 AND CHAPTER 5 (THEORY AND PRACTICE) IN THIS VOLUME.

SKILLS
• TO KNOW HOW TO CONTROL VARIOUS TYPES OF MUSICAL TIME VALUES: DURATION, TEMPO, TIMING, AS WELL AS THE GLOBAL TIME MANAGEMENT SYSTEM IN THE MAX ENVIRONMENT
• TO KNOW HOW TO BUILD AND CONTROL A STEP SEQUENCER
• TO KNOW HOW TO MANAGE POLYPHONY IN MAX
• TO KNOW HOW TO CONTROL ATTRIBUTES AND ARGUMENTS IN ABSTRACTIONS

CONTENTS
• DURATION, METRICAL TEMPOS AND TIMING VALUES IN MAX
• THE GLOBAL TIME MANAGEMENT SYSTEM IN MAX
• ARGUMENTS AND ATTRIBUTES
• ALGORITHMS FOR A STEP SEQUENCER
• POLYPHONIC PATCHES
• ABSTRACTIONS AND ARGUMENTS

TESTING
• ACTIVITES AT THE COMPUTER

SUPPORTING MATERIALS
• LIST OF MAX OBJECTS - LIST OF ATTRIBUTES, MESSAGES AND GRAPHICAL ELEMENTS FOR SPECIFIC MAX OBJECTS - GLOSSARY

IC.1 THE PASSAGE OF TIME (IN MAX)

For this chapter we suggest you activate both the "Scheduler in Overdrive" and "in Audio Interrupt" options in the Audio Status window, and set the Signal Vector Size between 16 and 64 samples (preferably 16).

The units we have been using to measure time until now have either been milliseconds (for instance when indicating the interval between successive bang messages output by the **metro** object) or samples (for example when indicating the delay time of an audio signal input into the **delay~** object)[1]. It is also possible to use other time measurement units within Max, and above all possible to synchronize several objects together using a **_master clock_** (a system of global time management in the Max environment) controlled by the **transport** object, which lets the user, among other things, activate and deactivate the global passage of time.

Rebuild the patch shown in figure IC.1.

Fig. IC.1 The **transport** object

Notice that the argument for the **metro** object is not a value in milliseconds, but a symbol: 4n (we will see what this means shortly). This causes the **metro** object's timing to be linked to the master clock.
First, turn on the **toggle** above the **metro** object. Contrary to what you were probably expecting, the **metro** does not output anything. Now, turn on the **toggle** above the **transport** object and the **metro** will start to produce bangs. The **transport** object has activated the master clock, which, in turn, has activated the **metro** object. In this scenario, the **metro** object will only "run" when the master clock is active. But, what is our metronome's tempo? The symbol 4n that we provided as an argument to **metro** is a _tempo-relative time value_, and more precisely a _note value_ which indicates that our tempo corresponds to one quarter note (crochet). The **metro** object will therefore output a bang every quarter note beat.

However, what is the duration of a quarter note? Its duration depends on the transport object, or more specifically on the object's "**tempo**" attribute. This attribute is used to express the number of beats per minute[2] (abbreviated bpm) and by default its value is set to 120 bpm (120 beats per minute, or one beat every half second).

---

[1] This object has already been discussed in section 3.5P of the first volume.
[2] This is therefore the same tempo that is used for metronome markings.

The metronome's tempo can be changed by sending the **transport** object the "tempo" message followed by a value in bpm. Modify the preceding patch so it resembles the one shown in figure IC.2

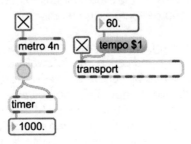

Fig. IC.2 Modifying the metronome tempo

In addition to adding the message to modify the global tempo in bpm, we have also added a **timer** object that lets us calculate the interval between successive bangs (in milliseconds). As you can see, by changing the tempo to 60 bpm, the **metro** will output one bang every second (1000 milliseconds). Try changing the tempo in bpm and see how the millisecond tempo calculated by the **timer** object changes (note that in the patch, the button above the timer is connected to both of its inlets).

The **timer** object is a "stopwatch" that starts when a bang is sent to its left inlet, and outputs the time that has elapsed since it started whenever it receives a bang in its right inlet. You should therefore take note that, unlike the majority of Max objects, the **timer** object's "hot" inlet is its right inlet.

. . . .

ACTIVITY

Create a new patch to try out the **timer** object, sending bangs separately to its left and right inlets, paying careful attention to the values output by **timer**. Afterward, explain why connecting one **button** to both of timer's inlets, as shown in figure IC.2, allows us to calculate the time between successive bangs from a single **button** object.

. . . .

As you may have guessed, there are several different symbols which are used to indicate the main note values. These are furthermore subdivided into minimal units called *ticks*. A quarter note (crochet), as we have already seen, is represented with the symbol 4n, and can be subdivided into 480 ticks. This means that an eighth note (whose symbol is 8n) corresponds to 240 ticks, and a sixteenth note (16n) to 120 ticks, and so on. Obviously the duration of the ticks depends on the metronome tempo of the **transport** object.

Here is a table of symbols and their corresponding fractional note name values, traditional note names, and values in ticks:

1nd   dotted whole note (dotted semibreve) - 2880 *ticks*
1n   whole note (semibreve) - 1920 *ticks*
1nt   whole note triplet (semibreve triplet) - 1280 *ticks*
2nd   dotted half note (dotted minim) - 1440 *ticks*
2n   half note (minim) - 960 *ticks*
2nt   half note triplet (minim triplet) - 640 *ticks*
4nd   dotted quarter note (dotted crochet) - 720 *ticks*
4n   quarter note (crochet) - 480 *ticks*
4nt   quarter note triplet (crochet triplet) - 320 *ticks*
8nd   dotted eighth note (dotted quaver) - 360 *ticks*
8n   eighth note (quaver) - 240 *ticks*
8nt   eighth note triplet (quaver triplet) - 160 *ticks*
16nd   dotted sixteenth note (dotted semiquaver) - 180 *ticks*
16n   sixteenth note (semiquaver) - 120 *ticks*
16nt   sixteenth note triplet (semiquaver triplet) - 80 *ticks*
32nd   dotted thirty-second note (dotted demisemiquaver) - 90 *ticks*
32n   thirty-second note (demisemiquaver) - 60 *ticks*
32nt   thirty-second note triplet (demisemiquaver triplet) - 40 *ticks*
64nd   dotted sixty-fourth note (dotted hemidemisemiquaver) - 45 *ticks*
64n   sixty-fourth note (hemidemisemiquaver) - 30 *ticks*
128n   hundred twenty-eighth note (semihemidemisemiquaver) - 15 *ticks*

In the patch in figure IC.2, change the argument to the **metro** object from 4n to other note values, each time checking the tempo of the resulting beats with the **timer** object.

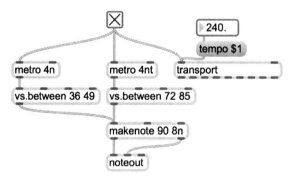

Fig. IC.3 Two against three

We have added a second **metro** object whose beat rate (tempo) is equal to a quarter note triplet (4nt). The two different tempos are used to generate two random MIDI note streams. In the time that it takes for two notes to be generated in the bass voice, three notes are generated in the treble register. Note that the second argument of the **makenote** object, corresponding to the note's duration, is 8n, which indicates an eighth note (quaver) duration – as you can see, the **makenote** object (which we spoke about in section IB.1), can also use tempo-relative time values.

In this patch, a single **toggle** is being used to start the **transport** and two **metro** objects simultaneously – this ensures that the two note streams will start exactly at the same time. If you now change the **transport** object's tempo in bpm you will notice that the two note streams always remain synchronized, in the same 2-against-3 rhythm.
Warning: the tempo in bpm, as well as all the other commands sent to the **transport** are global! This means that they apply to the entire Max environment. If you have two patches open and they both use relative time values, starting and stopping the master clock or modifying the tempo in bpm in one of the two patches will also activate and deactivate the master clock and change the tempo of the other. It is also possible to entirely eliminate the **transport** object from both of the patches and instead use an independent window (known as the **_Global Transport_**) which contains commands for the master clock (this window can be opened at any time by choosing the Global Transport option from the Extras menu). By using this window we can start and stop the master clock, change its tempo in bpm, and see the total elapsed time, among other things.

Let's return to figure IC.3. Try changing the argument of the first **metro** to 8n. Now, for every four notes in the bass we will hear 3 in the upper register, because four eighth notes (quavers) are equal in duration to a quarter note triplet.

. . . .

 ACTIVITY

The metrical rapport of beats between the two random note streams shown in figure IC.3 can be denoted as the ratio 2/3 (i.e., two against three). Try modifying the arguments of the two **metro** objects in order to obtain note streams with the following rhythmic ratios: 3/4, 3/8, 2/6, 4/9 (the latter may not be immediately obvious: you will need to use dotted note values for the numerator).

. . . .

With the available note value symbols you can create only a certain number of metric relationships; they cannot be used to create a 4/5 beat ratio (four against five), just to give one example. In order to obtain these kinds of metric relationships it is necessary to use _ticks_.

In the case of a 4/5 beat ratio, since our quarter note is equal to 480 ticks, a quarter note quintuplet will equal $480 \cdot 4 / 5 = 384$ ticks. This value does not have a corresponding symbol in the list of note values that Max accepts. Unfortunately it is not possible to provide a value in ticks directly as an argument to **metro**, but this can still be done using setting the "**interval**" attribute, either with the object's inspector or by using a message followed by a value and a measurement unit. Modify the patch as shown in figure IC.4.

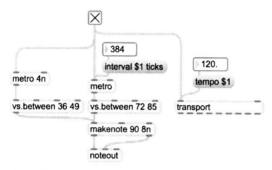

Fig. IC.4 Four against five

Here, the message "interval 384 ticks" is sent to the second **metro** using a message box. As we have already seen above, this corresponds to a quarter note quintuplet.

• •

ACTIVITIES

• Create the following beat ratios, using the "interval" attribute for both metro objects: 3/10, 5/9, 15/8.

• Make Max do the math: modify the preceding patch so that all the user has to do is set the rhythmic ratio in two number boxes (for example the values 4 and 3 to represent 4/3), and let the patch calculate the exact value for the number of ticks. (Hint: you should only need to add one object for each **metro**.)

• •

ARGUMENTS AND ATTRIBUTES

As we already know, almost all Max objects use arguments to set their main internal variables, and these generally also correspond to the object's inlets. For example, the **makenote** object has two arguments corresponding to the velocity and duration of the note. These two values can also be set by sending values to the object's second and third inlets. One important aspect of using arguments is that their order determines their functionality. To continue using **makenote** as an example, the velocity value must be the first argument, and the duration second. This implies that if we *only* need to set the **makenote** object's duration, we must still supply a velocity value, because the second argument (in order to be second) needs to come after a first argument.

In addition to arguments, which are used to set an object's most important variables, we have also seen that objects have attributes, which can be set either using the object's inspector, or with messages. For example, the **metro** object's "interval" attribute can be modified, as we have already seen, via a message (see figure IC.4) or directly in the inspector. You can verify this yourself by opening the **metro** object's inspector – the attribute in question is found in the

141

"**Timing**" category. As you can see, in addition to milliseconds, note values and ticks, the object can work with other time units: we will talk about these later on.

There is a third way to set an object's attribute: by typing it directly into the object box itself. In this case we need to supply the attribute's name preceded by the @ (at) symbol (without a space!), and followed by the appropriate parameters. The "interval" attribute will thus be written @interval. Let's take a look at a practical example: modify the preceding patch as indicated in figure IC.5.

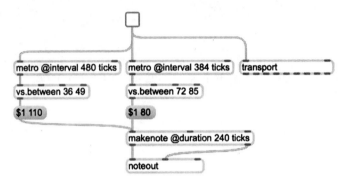

Fig. IC.5 Attributes inside object boxes

In the figure we have created the rhythmic ratio 4/5 using ticks as a temporal measurement unit. As you can see, the attribute that controls the note duration of the notes generated by **makenote** is aptly called "**duration**." Notice that a velocity value does not need to be typed into the **makenote** when the duration is defined as an attribute, as it is here.
Concerning the velocity value, can you tell where this parameter is set, now that we have removed all the arguments from **makenote**? (Hint 1: what are the two message boxes connected to the **vs.between** used for? Hint 2: read section IA.1 in the first volume again, paying particular attention to the text that relates to figure IA.5.) Attributes should be typed into the objet box after any arguments, and their order is unimportant (i.e., if we have 2 or more attributes in an object box, they can be typed in any order). Let's take a look at an example by making the simple patch shown in figure IC.6.

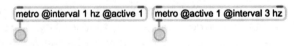

Fig. IC.6 Other attributes for **metro**

First, notice that we do not need a **toggle** object, since the two **metro** objects have already been activated because their "**active**" attribute has been set to 1. This attribute is used to start (1) and stop (0) the **metro** object. In reality, when we use a **toggle** to send a 1 or a 0 to **metro**, this sets the "active" attribute[3].

---
[3] Naturally, the "active" attribute is also included in the **metro** object's inspector in the "Timing" category.

Another interesting point is that the beat is given in Hertz (to see all the available time units open the **metro**'s inspector). For this we do not need a **transport** object because, like milliseconds, Hertz are fixed time units that do not depend on a tempo in bpm generated by the master clock. Finally, notice that the ordering of the attributes in the two objects is different, because, unlike arguments, attributes can be specified in any order.

Let's now clarify what we mean by "attribute name." If we open an object's inspector we will see a descriptive name for each attribute in the "**Setting**" column on the left. For example, in the **multislider** object's inspector, we have an attribute called "Number of Sliders" in the "Sliders" category which, as we have already learned in section IA.7 of the first volume, is used to set the number of slider elements represented by the object. In section IB.6 (also in the first volume) we have seen that it is also possible to modify the number of sliders in a **multislider** by sending a "size" message followed by the number of elements desired. In reality "size" is the *actual name* of the attribute; this is the message name that can be used in a message box connected to **multislider**, whereas "Number of Sliders" (shown in the inspector) is the *descriptive name* of the same attribute, and thus cannot be used as a message to **multislider**.

So, how can we find out the actual name of an attribute, in order to be able to use it in a message? All you have to do is click on the "@" icon in the lower left-hand side of the inspector window, and you will notice that a new column labeled "**Attribute**" appears (just to the left of the "Setting" column). This column contains the actual attribute names. In figure IC.7 we can see the **multislider** inspector with this Attribute column activated. You will notice that the "size" attribute corresponds to the descriptive name "Number of Sliders" (this attribute is listed in the "Sliders" category).

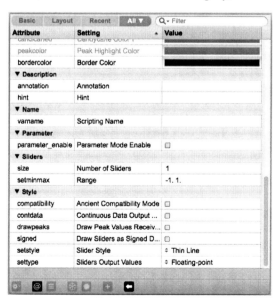

Fig. IC.7 Attributes for **multislider**

TIME VALUES

Let's now take a look at the time values available in Max. Each of the time values can be expressed with one or more numbers and can be followed by a symbol indicating the format.

1) **Fixed Time Values** are time values that do not depend on the master clock.

   Milliseconds are expressed using a single value that can be (optionally) followed by the symbol ms.

   Hours/minutes/seconds (are expressed by three values separated by colons, for example 01:30:11. You can also optionally add a fourth value in milliseconds to this, for example 00:10:37.870. You can also express this using a list followed by the symbol hh:mm:ss (i.e., "0 10 37 hh:mm:ss").

   Samples are expressed as a single value followed by the symbol samples.

   Frequency is expressed as a single value followed by the symbol hz.

2) **Tempo-Relative Time Values** are timing values which depend on the master clock.

   Ticks: represent 1/480 of a quarter note (crochet) beat and are expressed as a single value followed by the symbol ticks.

   Note Values are a collection of symbols (see the list above) that represent different note values. The symbols are made up of numerical values followed (without a space) by the letter n for regular notes, by nd for dotted note values, and by nt for triplet note values.

   Bars/beats/units[4]: are expressed with three values separated by periods, for example 1.3.120. The first value represents the duration in bars (measures), the second represents the duration in beats (divisions of the bar), and the third is the duration in ticks (divisions of the beat). So, if the time signature is 3/4 the beat will be a quarter note (crochet) and each bar will have three beats, if the time signature is 4/8 the beat will be equal to an eighth note (quaver) and each bar will have 4 beats. This time value can also be expressed using a list of three values followed by the symbol bbu (i.e., "1 3 120 bbu").

The number of ticks in a quarter note represents the temporal resolution of the system, and it is expressed in ppq (pulses per quarter note). The master clock, therefore has a resolution of 480 ppq.

---

[4] This is sometimes referred to in Max as bbu.

There are many Max objects that use different time values. We have already seen that this is true of the **metro** and **makenote** objects, but it also applies to signal processing objects like **phasor~** or **delay~**. We will discover this later, at the appropriate time.

In addition to the global master clock, it is possible to create independent beat clocks by providing the **transport** object with a name via the "name" attribute.By using this name with the "transport" attribute in another object (such as a **metro**), that object can be synchronized to the independent transport. Rebuild the patch shown in figure IC.8.

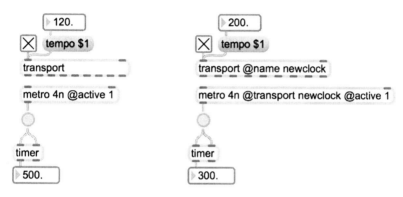

Fig. IC.8 A named **transport** object

As you can see in the figure, the **metro** on the left, whose argument is 4n, uses the global master clock whose tempo has been set to 120 bpm. A quarter note (the symbol 4n) at this tempo has a duration of 500 milliseconds (which we can see in the number box underneath the **timer** object on the left). On the right side of the patch, there is a **transport** object which has been given the name "newclock" by using the @name attribute. This transport has had its tempo set to 200 bpm. The **metro** object on the right has an @transport attribute with the same name ("newclock") and therefore follows the 200 bpm tempo of the **transport**. As you can see in the number box below the timer on the right, a quarter note (4n) at this tempo has a duration of 300 ms.

IC.2 MAKING A STEP SEQUENCER

Let's now take a look at how to build a *step sequencer* – a device that cyclically repeats a sequence of sound events with pre-defined parameters[5].
In order create a step sequencer in Max, we will use the graphical interface object `live.step`, shown in figure IC.9.

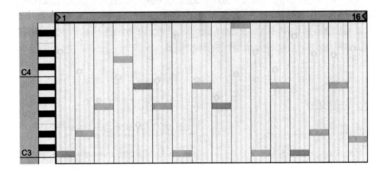

Fig. IC.9 The `live.step` object

Like the `live.grid` object, this object also is part of the Max for Live library. The object looks a little like a `multislider` because it is also divided into a given number of columns (called steps, just as in the `live.grid` object), each one of which can contain values that are graphically displayed in the object itself.

However, unlike `multislider`, each column contains five values by default: the first three are used to represent MIDI note, velocity and duration, respectively, and the last two parameters are extra parameters which can be freely assigned by the user[6]. A small rectangular block inside each step represents the MIDI note value (by its vertical position) and the note's duration (by its horizontal length). The remaining three values are shown by the three lightly-colored vertical lines behind each block.

Along the left side of the object there is a stylized musical keyboard and a gray vertical band with note names. Together these items make up the **Unit Ruler**. Along the top edge of the object is a horizontal gray band called the **Loop Ruler**, which can be used to determine the steps that will be performed (we will cover this in detail shortly).

---

[5] Step sequencers have existed since the days of analog synthesizers, and subsequently re-implemented in many different ways since the advent of digital synthesizers. Within the context of Max programming, we will construct an algorithm that reproduces the functionality of these kinds of sequencers.

[6] In reality, all five of the values are freely assignable, since they are just numerical values whose meaning depends on how they are subsequently used.

When `live.step` receives a numerical value in its inlet, it interprets that number as a step number, and outputs the five values corresponding to the parameters of that step (preceded by the step number itself) via the object's left outlet.

Recreate the patch shown in figure IC.10.

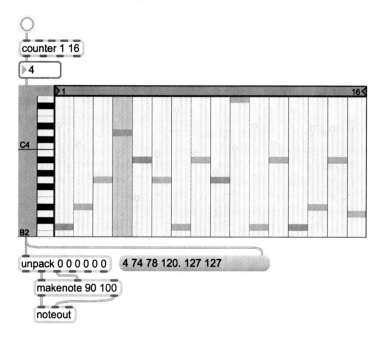

Fig. IC.10 Values generated by `live.step`

In the message box on the lower right we can see the output values of the fourth step. As we have already discussed, the list contains 5 values preceded by the step number, it is therefore a 6-element list. Using the **unpack** object, we can take the second and third element of the list (MIDI note and velocity) and use them to create a note within the computer's internal synthesizer.

The fourth element of the list (120 in the figure) corresponds to the note's duration. This duration is not expressed in milliseconds, but rather in *ticks*. The `live.step` object can, in fact, also work with the relative time format bbu (bars/beats/units, see section IC.1, above).

We can also use tempo-relative time values with `live.step` by taking advantage of the values output by the **transport** object. As we have already seen in the preceding patches, the **transport** object has 9 outlets and some of the messages sent via these outlets can be used to control the tempo of `live.step`.

Rebuild the patch shown in figure IC.11.

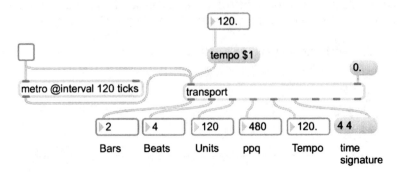

Fig. IC.11 Values generated by **transport**

In the figure we can see the values generated by the first 6 outlets:

outlet 1-3: the three bbu (Bars/Beats/Units) values
outlet 4:   temporal resolution (480 ppq)
outlet 5:   metronomic tempo (120 bpm)
outlet 6:   time signature (a list of 2 values representing the time signature as a fraction – 4/4 as shown in the figure)

These values are output by **transport** (or more precisely are generated by the master clock) each time that the object receives a bang.

Start the **metro** and **transport** objects using the **toggle** and watch the values that are sent out the outlets of the **transport**. Whenever the **metro** object outputs a bang (every 120 ticks, or each sixteenth note), the value of the third outlet is updated with multiples of 120: 0, 120, 240, 360, 0 120, etc. (obviously, the values output are wrapped into the range between 0 and 480)[7].

If we now turn the **toggle** off and then on again, the values output by the third outlet are probably no longer multiples of 120, even though they contin- ue to be incremented by 120 ticks each time (try it out!). This happens because the tempo generated by the master clock stops immediately when the **toggle** is shut off, and it is highly improbable that this will coincide exactly with a multiple of 120 ticks. When the **toggle** is turned on again the master clock's time will start again from the point where it stopped, whereas the **metro** will immediately send the first bang, without waiting for the clock to arrive at a multiple of 120 ticks. Let's imagine we turn off the **toggle** when the time of the master clock has reached 11 ticks. When we turn on the **toggle** again, we will simultaneously start the master clock and the **metro** (which immedi- ately sends a bang when it is started). The output values will therefore start

---

[7] Explain why!

again from the point at which they had been stopped previously, and the third outlet of the transport will therefore output the values 11, 131, 251, 371, 11 131, etc.

One way to realign the **metro**'s beats with the master clock is to set the master clock's bbu counter to 0 by sending a 0 to the right inlet of the **transport** object. This should be done while the master clock is stopped, so you will need to turn off the **toggle** in figure IC.11, first. When you start the **toggle** again the tick values will once again be synchronized with the tempo of the **metro** (try it out for yourself).

Another, decidedly more robust, solution would be to impose a "temporal grid" on the **metro** object's output of beats. We have already seen that the **metro** object will output a bang immediately when it is started, but in some cases (such as the example illustrated in figure IC.11) it is undesirable to have the **metro** start when the master clock is at some subdivision of the beat (for example a fourth or sixteenth of the beat) and not on the first beat of the bar. Fortunately, **metro** has a "**quantize**" attribute that can be used precisely for this purpose: it allows us to specify a value (for example in ticks) that represents a "temporal grid" that will be imposed upon the **metro**'s beats. For example, if the "quantize" value is set to 10 ticks, the **metro** will only produce a bang when the master clock's time is a multiple of 10 ticks. Try adding the "@quantize 10" attribute to the **metro** object in the patch from figure IC.11. By starting and stopping the **toggle** you will immediately notice that the value in ticks generated by the third outlet is now always a multiple of 10 (i.e., the last digit is always 0). This happens because the "quantize" attribute forces the **metro** object to wait for the master clock to reach a multiple of 10 ticks before outputting a bang.

A (very) simple question: what value should we give the "quantize" attribute so that the **metro** will always output its bangs with the sixteenth notes (120 ticks) generated by the master clock? After having figured this out, modify the patch in figure IC.11 accordingly.

Note that the "quantize" attribute only works if the tempo of the **metro** object is specified in tempo-relative time values (ticks, note values or bbu).

To use the **live.step** object with relative time values we have to send the "time" command followed by the position in bbu, the temporal resolution (ppq) and the bar length. These values are sent from outlets 1, 2, 3, 4 and 6 of the **transport** object.

Load the patch **IC_01_step_sequencer.maxpat** (figure IC.12).

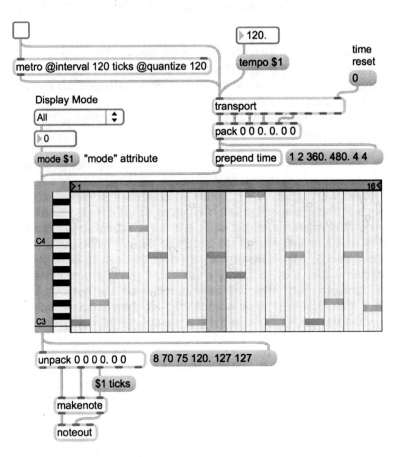

Fig. IC.12 The file **IC_01_step_sequencer.maxpat**

The values output from outlets 1, 2, 3, 4 and 6 of the **transport** are assembled into a list using the **pack** object (in the upper right portion of the patch). Note that the list of two values output from the sixth outlet of the **transport** (corresponding to the time signature) are sent to the fifth inlet of **pack** – this is equivalent to sending the first element to the 5th inlet and the second element to the 6th inlet[8].

In the lower part of the patch we can see that the values corresponding to note duration (fourth outlet of the **unpack** object) are associated with the ticks symbol so that the **makenote** object "understands" (so to speak) that the value is not a millisecond value, but rather a relative time value.

---

[8] Many Max objects will automatically distribute the individual elements of an input list into successive inlets. See also section IA.1, figure IA.5..

The pitch of the notes in each step can be modified by using the mouse within the `live.step` interface (adjusting the height of the rectangular block). If we want to modify the other parameters with the mouse we need to change the object's *Display Mode*. By default, `live.step` shows all five values contained in each step as we have already discussed, above. Using the "mode" attribute we can display each parameter separately and modify it with the mouse. In figure IC.12 you will notice a menu (the `umenu` object) under the `metro` object. This menu can be used to change the display mode. Select some different menu options and notice the changes in the way the interface is displayed, then try changing the velocity values ("mode 2") for some of the steps. Notice that when you modify the velocity with the mouse, you can see the corresponding numerical value displayed in the gray band on the left side of the object[9]. Now try modifying the duration ("mode 3"). Here, when you click on the rectangle and move the mouse vertically for each step, the (horizontal) length of the rectangle representing each note will change. Notice that the values shown in the gray band on the side correspond to note values from 128n to 2n. Finally, try modifying the Loop Ruler (this is the gray band located along the top edge of the object) by dragging the ends of the strip with the mouse. When you change the length of the Loop Ruler it changes the number of steps that will be played. The Loop Ruler can also be changed using the "loop" message, followed by two values representing the starting step and ending step of the loop. For example, the message "loop 1 8" can be used to select just the first half of the sequence, whereas the message "loop 9 16" can be used to select the second half. Try it out for yourself!

. . . .

ACTIVITY

Add a preset object to the patch in figure IC.12 and create different presets with different pitches, velocities, durations for the notes, and different lengths for the Loop Ruler.

. . . .

Before improving our step sequencer further, we need to introduce two new objects. The first of these is called **router**. This object is the Max equivalent to the MSP `matrix~` object that we have already seen in chapter 4 of the first volume. Before continuing, we will recommend that you reread section 4.7P (specifically the part concerning the modulation matrix).

---

[9] Remember that this band and the stylized keyboard next to it are together known as the Unit Ruler.

Now, reconstruct the small patch shown in figure IC.13.

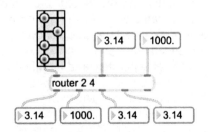

Fig. IC.13 The **router** object

In the upper-left part of the patch you will notice a **matrixctrl** object (also introduced in section 4.7P), which is used to control the inlets and outlets of the **router** in exactly the same way as for the **matrix~** object. The **router** object's arguments are 2 and 4, so the object therefore has 32 inlets and 4 outlets. Consequently **matrixctrl** should have 2 columns (representing the **router**'s inlets) and 4 rows (representing the outlets). To modify **matrixctrl** (which has 8 columns and 4 rows by default) we need to open its inspector and go the "Behavior" category, where we can turn on the "Autosize to Rows and Columns" attribute. This attribute makes the object automatically change its layout when the number of rows or columns is changed in the inspector. Now, set the "Number of Columns" attribute to 2, the "Number of Rows" to 4 and also turn on the "One Non-Zero Cell Per Row" attribute so we can not simultaneously send the values from the two inlets to the same outlet (see figure IC.14).

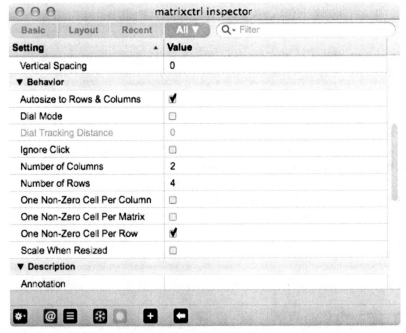

Fig. IC.14 Settings for the **router** object's inspector

Let's now return to figure IC.13. Here the configuration shown in the **matrixctrl** object connects the **router**'s first inlet to outlets 1, 3 and 4 and its second inlet to outlet 2, which you can also verify by looking at the float number boxes connected to the **router**'s inlets and outlets. Try setting some other configurations with the **matrixctrl** and check that the **router** works as you expected.

The second new object we need to learn is the **translate** object. This object lets us convert between the different time units used in Max. Build the simple patch shown in figure IC.15.

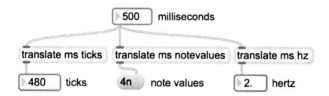

Fig. IC.15 The **translate** object

The two arguments to the object represent the time units of the input values and output values, respectively. The figure shows conversion from milliseconds to ticks, note values and Hertz. The results shown for ticks and note values are tempo-relative time values which depend on the tempo of the master clock in bpm. The values shown in the figure correspond to a tempo of 120 bpm, which is the default tempo for the master clock.

The symbols that you can use as arguments are the following: *ms, ticks, notevalues, hz, bbu, samples* and *hh.mm.ss* (hours, minutes, seconds).

Now open the file **IC_02_subsynth_seq.maxpat**. This patch uses a step sequencer with the subtractive synthesizer that was presented in section 3.5P of the first volume. As always, we strongly suggest you read that section again to refresh your memory. Pay particular attention to the use of the **pvar** object, which can be used to make a "connection without cables" between itself and other objects (such as with number boxes, for example). This object has been provided with a name via the "Scripting Name" attribute.

Now let's take a closer look at the step sequencer (on the right-hand side of the patch), shown in figure IC.16.

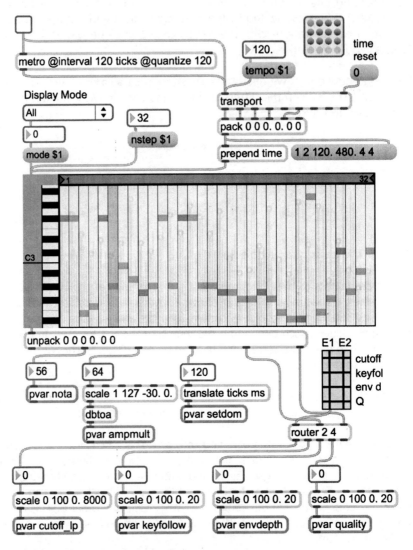

Fig. IC.16 The file **IC_02_subsynth_seq.maxpat**, *step sequencer*

As with the patch shown in figure IC.12, the elements of the list output by `live.step` in this patch are also separated using an **unpack** object. The value corresponding to the note's pitch is sent to a **pvar** object with the argument "nota". This value is sent directly to the **kslider** object (whose scripting name has been set to "nota") located in the control panel for the synthesizer, on the left hand side of the patch (see figure IC.17)[10].

---

[10] If any of this was unclear, read section 3.5P in the first volume once again.

The next value output by `live.step` corresponds to the note's velocity. This value is first scaled from the range 1 to 127 into the range -30 to 0, to represent a decibel value, and then converted from dB into an amplitude value. It is then sent to the [pvar ampmult] object which is sent to the float number box located to the right of the `kslider`. (Obviously, this float number box has the scripting name "ampmult".)

The third value output by `live.step` is the note's duration. This is expressed in ticks, and converted into milliseconds by the `translate` object. The value is then sent from the [pvar setdom] object to the float number box just above the [setdomain $1] message box connected to the `function` object that holds the envelope for the sound (on the right side of the patch shown in figure IC.17).

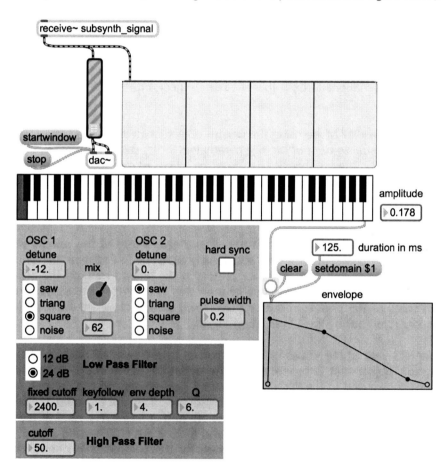

Fig. IC.17 The file **IC_02_subsynth_seq.maxpat**, synthesis parameters

Note that the **pvar** object can both receive and send messages to an object whose scripting name is the same as the name given as an argument to **pvar**. In other words **pvar** acts simultaneously as both send and receive. More precisely, a **pvar** object with the argument "freq", for example sends messages to the object whose scripting name is "freq" and this object then sends the message to all the **pvar** objects with the same argument, "freq", within that same patch. Although there can only be one object per patch with a given scripting name (each object must have a unique scripting name), there can be more than one **pvar** object with the same argument in that patch.

If you now switch the patch over into *edit* mode, you can see the "audio engine" of the synthesizer, which has been hidden using the menu command Object -> Hide on Lock, which was covered in section 1.1P. This part of the patch contains the various **pvar** objects (which were already in the synthesizer patch when it was presented in chapter 3) that receive messages from the corresponding objects in the synthesizer's control panel and/or from the values output by the step sequencer.

Now let's turn on the patch (by clicking on both the **toggle** connected to the **metro** on the upper left, and the "startwindow" message) and listen to the first preset, paying careful attention to the values output by **live.step** and the relative variations in both the **kslider** object and the float number box to its right.

Modify the *Display Mode* using the **umenu** object located above **live.step**, in order to visualize each of the five parameters (note, velocity, duration, extra 1 and extra 2). The number of steps used by **live.step** (in this patch it has 32 steps) can also be changed using the nstep command followed by a numerical value. Try changing the value of the number box connected to the "nstep $1" message just above **live.step**.

The other three presets in the first row illustrate variations of the velocity values of the original sequence (and additionally a change in timbre in the sound played by the synthesizer). The four presets in the second row, on the other hand, illustrate changes in duration of the notes in the sequence. Listen carefully to all of the presets in the first two rows, paying close attention to the sequences output by the **live.step** object.

Now let's look at the values which are output by the two last outputs of the **unpack** object that is connected to the outlet of **live.step**. These two values correspond to the Extra 1 and Extra 2 parameters and can be sent, via the **router** object, to any of the four control parameters of the lowpass filter: cutoff frequency, key follow, envelope depth and Q factor. For each of these four parameters, the values of Extra 1 and Extra 2 are scaled using a **scale** object, naturally) into a range appropriate for the parameter in question[11]. The last four presets (third row) use the values stored in Extra1 and Extra 2; as always listen carefully and observe how the values are routed to the various parameters via the **router** object.

---

[11] As you can see, the values of the Extra 1 and Extra 2 parameters in this patch range between 0 and 100. This range (which by default is 0 - 127) can be set in the inspector (in the "Value" section).

ACTIVITIES

- Create some new presets, modifying the sound's timbre (waveform, envelope, etc.) in addition to the tempo in bpm. Using **live.step**, change the amplitude, duration and lowpass filter parameters, at first changing them separately, then together, for each of the new presets. If you save the patch in a new folder, remember that you will also have to copy the subsynth.filter~.maxpat and subsynth.oscil~.maxpat abstractions into that folder, too. This also applies to the next activity.

- Using the two extra parameters (Extra 1 and Extra 2) in **live.step**, add the ability to be able to control the cutoff frequency of the highpass filter and the detune parameter of the second oscillator. To do this you will need to modify the **matrixctrl** and **router** objects. Create some new presets for these additional controls.

• •

IC.3 POLYPHONY

If, while creating new presets for the patch **IC_02_subsynth_seq.maxpat** in the previous section, you set the note duration to values larger than 1/16 (that is, 120 ticks), you probably noticed that the synthesizer produced audible clicks. This is due to the fact that notes longer than 120 ticks will be interrupted suddenly by the following note, because our synthesizer is monophonic, and thus can only play one note at a time.

It is possible to make a patch polyphonic in Max by loading it inside a **poly~** object. This object generally takes two arguments: the name of the patch to load and the number of notes that can be produced simultaneously.[12]

Let's take a look at a practical example. Open the file **IC_03_polyphony.maxpat** (figure IC.18).

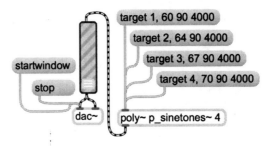

Fig. IC.18 The file **IC_03_polyphony.maxpat**

The patch is very simple and contains a **poly~** object whose arguments are "p_sinetones~" and "4". The first argument indicates that the object has loaded the file **p_sinetones~.maxpat** inside it. (This is a normal Max patch file, created specifically for this chapter, which can be found in the same folder as IC_03_polyphony.maxpat.) The second argument establishes that the object will have 4 "voices" of polyphony, and therefore will also contain 4 "**instances**" (copies) of the patch loaded inside it.

There are 4 message boxes connected to the **poly~** object. Activate the DSP for the patch and click on the 4 message boxes in rapid succession – you should hear 4 superimposed sine waves.

Each message box contains two messages separated by a comma. The first message is made up of the "target" attribute followed by a number progressing from 1 to 4 across the four message boxes. This parameter is used to indicate which "voice" (or instance of the patch) will receive the subsequent messages.

---

[12] In reality, calling this a "note" is rather too simplistic, because patches loaded inside **poly~** can be used to perform any kind of function. For example, a patch containing a filter could be loaded in order to create a polyphonic filter, known as a parallel filter bank (which we will see shortly).

The second of the two messages is a list of 3 values that, as we will soon see, are used to set the frequency (expressed as a MIDI note), amplitude (expressed as a velocity) and duration (in milliseconds) of the sound to be generated. It is important to understand the difference between these two messages: the first ("target n") is sent to the **poly~** object itself, whereas the second (the list of three values) is sent to the patch loaded inside the **poly~** (in this case p_sinetones~.maxpat). As we have already stated, the **poly~** object is a container for a patch, just like the **patcher** (p) object that we have often used to create subpatches. If we double-click on the **poly~** object (in performance mode) it will open the patcher window for the file p_sinetones~.maxpat (figure IC.19).

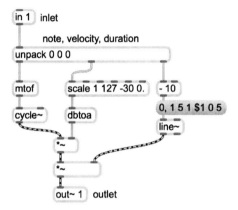

Fig. IC.19 The file **p_sinetones~.maxpat**

This patch is very similar to a subpatch or abstraction, and like them, it also has an inlet and outlet which can be used to transfer messages to and from the "outside" world. The difference is that the inlets and outlets in the patch are not represented with the usual **inlet** and **outlet** objects, but with the **in** and **out** objects (for Max messages) and **in~** and **out~** for MSP signals. These objects have a numerical argument that indicates the inlet or outlet position on the **poly~** object that loaded it – the value 1 indicates the leftmost inlet or outlet, 2 indicates the next outlet to the right, and so forth.

This patch receives the list of three values (note, velocity and duration) sent by each of the message boxes in figure IC.18. We will leave it to you, the reader, to analyze how this very simple algorithm works.

Returning to the patch in figure IC.18, you will notice that every time you click on one of the four message boxes, a list of three values will be sent to one of the four instances of the patch contained inside **poly~**. To demonstrate this, click on the message box with the message [target 1, 60 90 4000], and then immediately double-click on the **poly~** object. A window titled "p_sinetones~ (1)" should open. The number shown in parentheses is the number of the instance of the patch. If you now click on the next message [target 2, 64 90 4000] and immediately double-click on **poly~** another new window will open, this time with the title "p_sinetones~ (2)", and so on. Each time you do this, the window corresponding to the current instance that has been set with the "target" message will be opened.

As we will later discover, the message "target 0" can be used to tell **poly~** to send the subsequent messages to *all* of the instances of the patch that have been loaded inside it.

. . . .

ACTIVITIES

• Click 2 or more times on the same message box before the sound has shut off. What happens and why?

• Change the number of voices of polyphony to 8 and add other message boxes to be able to play the new instances. Modify the velocity and duration inside each of the message boxes. If you save the patch in a new folder, remember that you will also need to copy the file p_sinetones~.maxpat in the same folder. This also applies to subsequent activities.

. . . .

Now let's see how to connect a polyphonic oscillator to a step sequencer. Open the file **IC_04_poly_step_seq.maxpat** (figure IC.20).

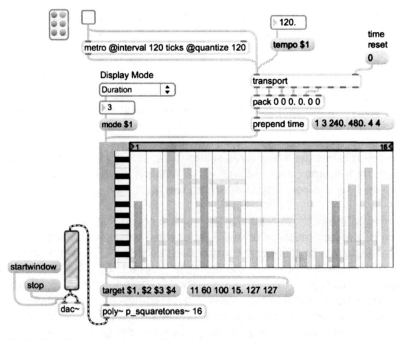

Fig. IC.20 The file **IC_04_poly_step_seq.maxpat**

Before we analyze the patch, try out the first 4 presets.

As we know, for each step the `live.step` object will output a list whose first 4 values are: step number, note, velocity and duration in ticks.

Look carefully at the message box [target $1, $2 $3 $4] located below the `live.step` object. The first message, "target $1", takes the first element of the list output by `live.step` (the step number) and uses it to select an instance of the patch p_squaretones~ loaded inside the `poly~` object (which has 16 voices of polyphony – one for each step). The second message, "$2 $3 $4", then sends the values for note, velocity and duration in ticks.

Now open the patch **p_squaretones~.maxpat** (shown below in figure IC.21) by double-clicking on the `poly~` object[13].

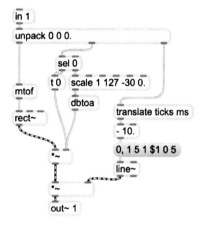

Fig. IC.21 file **p_squaretones~.maxpat**

This patch is very similar to the one shown in figure IC.19, but with a few important differences. One difference is that a band limited square wave oscillator (`rect~`) is used instead of a sine wave. Another difference is the presence of the **translate** object, which converts the duration in ticks output by `live.step` into a duration in milliseconds[14]. Finally, we have also added a system to correctly control the *note-off* messages (MIDI note messages with a velocity of 0)[15]. The [`sel 0`] object connected to the second outlet of **unpack** (corresponding to the velocity) sends only values between 1 and 127 to the **scale** object or conversion, but when it receives a value of 0 (a note-off message) it will send a bang out its left inlet. This bang is then converted back to a 0 by the **trigger** object. When this value is sent to the multiplier it zeroes the oscillator's amplitude, so therefore the note will not be played (actually, to

---

[13] We have given the suffix "p_" to all of the patches designed to be loaded by the `poly~` object as a naming convention.

[14] A small technical note: you will need to turn off the "Listen to Tempo Changes" attribute in the **translate** object's inspector in order to avoid it outputting a new value every time the tempo of the **transport** object changes.

[15] We have already covered the note-off message in section IB.1 in the first volume.

be more precise, the note will still be played, but its volume will be set to zero). The last two presets show how the note off works in this patch.

. . . .

 ACTIVITY

Integrate the note-off management shown in figure IC.21 into the patch IC_02_subsynth_seq.maxpat (figure IC.16).

. . . .

Although the patch in figure IC.21 works perfectly well as-is, it could be somewhat computationally expensive on the CPU (the computer's processor). This is because all 16 oscillators are always active, even though each of them is only used for one single step in the sequence. For today's computers, the workload is negligible, but imagine we have designed a step sequencer with 64 notes – using this technique we would need 64 voices of polyphony, which would therefore require 64 oscillators. If, for example, we wanted to run 8 such step sequencers in parallel, the number of oscillators would total 512. Furthermore, if we wanted to make the sound a little more interesting and we decided to add a pair of filters for each voice, we would have 1024 filters always active in our patch. As you can see, when you add polyphony to a patch it is easy to put a computational strain on even the most powerful of computers, if you do not manage your resources efficiently.

Moreover, if we wanted to play a note with a specific instance (or voice) in this scenario before the previous note played by that instance had finished, we would still get a click, even if we were using 512 voices of polyphony! Needless to say, it is possible to design a more intelligent method to manage polyphony inside Max, and even possible to deactivate the instances of the patch loaded inside `poly~` when they are not being used.

At this point we need to introduce another new object: **thispoly~**. This object is used to activate and deactivate the various instances of the patch loaded inside `poly~`. In figure IC.22 we can see the basic features of this object.

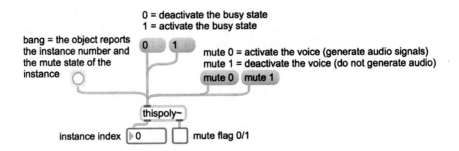

Fig. IC.22 The **thispoly~** object

For once, we will *not* ask you to create this patch, because `thispoly~` *only* works after it has been loaded inside a `poly~` object.

Let's first take a look at the "**mute**" message. This message is used to deactivate the computation of audio signals for a single instance (i.e., it mutes the DSP for that instance). When the `thispoly~` object in a particular instance receives the message "mute 1", the DSP engine stops calculating signals for that instance; this will save on CPU usage. If we have `poly~` object with 512 voices of polyphony (and therefore 512 instances of the patch loaded inside of it) and 510 of these instances have been muted, it will only use the CPU necessary to run the 2 active instances.

By sending the numerical messages "1" and "0" to `thispoly~`, we can activate and deactivate the *busy* state of that instance. When an instance is "busy," generally because it is in the middle of generating a signal, it cannot be "disturbed" by the `poly~` object with a new request until it becomes "free" again (we will shortly take a closer look at how this process works).

Finally, the bang message tells `thispoly~` to output the instance number that it is in (via the left inlet) and the current *mute* state (via the right outlet). Let's now see `thispoly~` in the context of a patch, by taking a look at the file **p_triangletones~.maxpat**, located in the "Interlude C Patches" folder (figure IC.23).

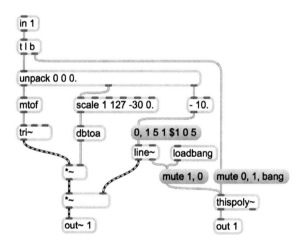

Fig. IC.23 The file **p_triangletones~.maxpat**

This patch, once again quite similar to the preceding patches p_sinetones~ and p_squaretones~, will only work properly once loaded inside a `poly~` object, however, before we try it out in its "natural habitat", let's analyze how it works.

The `thispoly~` object is located in the lower right part of the patch, and receives information from two message boxes. A `loadbang` is connected to the message box on the left so it immediately outputs its two messages ("mute 1" and "0') once the patch is loaded (the messages will be output in all the instances created by the **poly~** object which has loaded the patch). Therefore, when the patch is loaded, all of the instances are set to be inactive (the "mute 1" message) and free (the numerical message "0").

When a message arrives to the [**in** 1] inlet from the main patch (i.e., the patch that has the **poly~** which contains p_triangletones~), the **trigger** object connected to this inlet will first send a bang to the message box which is connected to **thispoly~**, on the right. This message box contains three messages: "mute 0", which activates the instance, "1", which makes the instance busy (so that no other messages from the main patch can arrive to this instance), and a bang which tells **thispoly~** to output the instance number where it is located. The instance number output by **thispoly~** is sent out the [**out** 1] outlet[16].

Now let's return to the **trigger** in the upper part of the patch. The second message it sends is the three-element list which we have already seen in the previous patches, and which is used to generate a sound – note that this time, however, we are using a band limited triangle wave oscillator as a sound source.

Let's take a closer look at the **line~** object that is used to create the envelope for the note. As we have already seen, when the **line** object has finished its ramp it outputs a bang from its right outlet. This message is used to output the two messages from the message box on the left once again, so that when the note is finished the instance will be deactivated ("mute 1") and free ("0"), and thus ready to receive a new message from the main patch.

Let's now look at the main patch. Open the file **IC_05_poly_step_seq2.maxpat** (figure IC.24)

The upper part of this patch, related to the step sequencer, is identical to the preceding patch, so we do not need to analyze it here. What *is* different, however, is the part of the patch located under **live.step**. Here a **trigger** object outputs three copies of the list received from the step sequencer. The rightmost output is simply sent to the right inlet of a message box to be displayed.

The list output by the center outlet is used to manage the note-off messages. Here we are using a different method than in previous examples in order to make our algorithm more efficient. Using the system shown in patch IC_04_poly_step_seq (more specifically in the patch p_squartones~ contained in the **poly~** object) the note will be played even if its amplitude is 0. Using the new system, however, note lists containing a velocity value of 0 will not even be sent to the **poly~** object in the first place.

---

[16] The signal outlets (**out~**) and message outlets (**out**) of the **poly~** object are numbered separately. Signal outlets are always located to the left of message outlets. The **poly~** object that loads this patch, for example, will have 2 outlets: one signal outlet (on the left) and one message outlet (on the right).

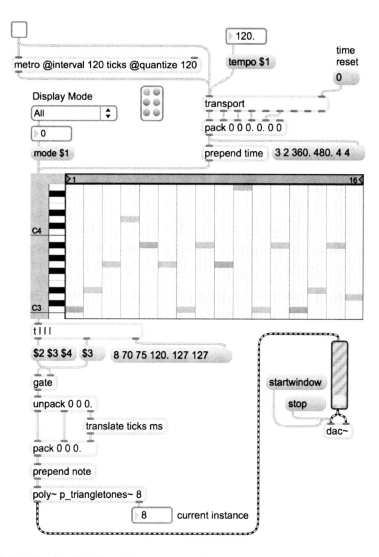

Fig. IC.24 The file **IC_05_poly_step_seq2.maxpat**

Let's take a look at how this works. First, the message box connected to the middle outlet of **trigger** will pick only the third element of the list ($3), corresponding to the velocity. This value is sent to the left inlet of the gate just underneath it. If the velocity value is 0 (note-off) the gate will be closed, and if its value is greater than 0 (note-on) the gate will be opened. Returning to the **trigger**, the list sent out its leftmost outlet is sent to a message box which selects only the second, third and fourth elements ($2 $3 $4) corresponding to the note, velocity and duration values. This list is sent to the right inlet of the gate, and will only be output by the gate if the velocity value (that we already sent to the left inlet) is 0. After the outlet of the gate, an **unpack** object separates the list into its three individual elements. The duration in ticks is then converted into milliseconds and the list is reassembled using the **pack** object.

165

Now comes the most important part of the entire patch. As you can see, we no longer have a "target" message before the **poly~** object to select the instance that will receive the list. Instead, we use the **prepend** object to add the message "note" to the list. This message at the head of a list, tells the **poly~** object to locate the first free voice (the first instance of its subpatch whose busy state is inactive) and to pass that instance the rest of the list (in our case the list of three note values). In practice, the **poly~** object automatically "decides" which instance will receive the list, by searching through the instances and finding a free one. For example, if the first instance is still playing and therefore "busy," the list will be passed to the second instance; if this instance is busy it will passed to the third instance, and so forth.

Remember that when you want to use this type of automatic voice allocation, the patch you load inside the **poly~** object must have a built-in algorithm to make the instance "busy" when it receives a list, and to free the instance when the note has finished playing. This is exactly what we have done for the patch p_triangletones~ shown in figure IC.23. Without including such an algorithm, the **poly~** object will send all "note" messages to the first instance, because this instance will always appear to be available. Try the different presets in the patch and watch the number box connected to the right outlet of the **poly~** object to see the instance number that is being used for each note (you may need to slow down the tempo to be able to see the sequence of numbers more clearly).

· ·

ACTIVITIES

- Make the step sequencer in the file IC_05_poly_step_seq2.maxpat (figure IC.24) generate two simultaneous notes a perfect fifth (7 semitones) apart for each step it plays. You should only need to add one object.

- Implement the new note-off management system (shown in figure IC.24) in the file IC_02_sybsynth_seq.maxpat (figure IC.16).

- Use a **poly~** object with the patch p_triangletones~ in all the arpeggiators that we created in sections IB.2-5 of the first volume. You will need to copy the file p_triangletones~.maxpat into the folder containing the arpeggiators in order for it to be able to be loaded by **poly~**, otherwise, if you want it to be visible to all Max patches, you will need to add it to Max's search path (see section 1.2 and the subsection titled "Abstractions" in section IA.4 of the first volume).

· ·

Now let's make our polyphonic instrument a little more complex by adding an envelope with the **function** object, and a filter whose parameters can be adjusted globally (i.e., one setting for all instances).

Open the file **IC_06_poly_step_seq3.maxpat** (figure IC.25)..

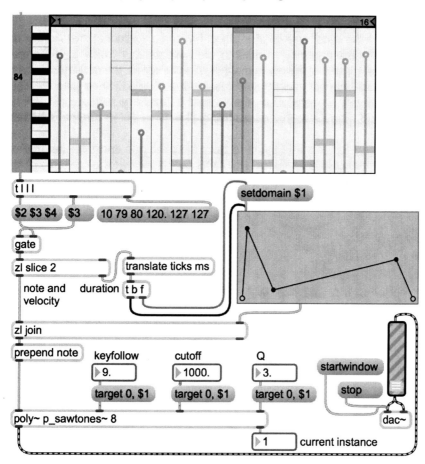

Fig. IC.25 The file **IC_06_poly_step_seq3.maxpat**

In this version of the step sequencer, the `poly~` object uses a new patch, p_sawtones~, which, as we will shortly see, contains a sawtooth waveform generator and a lowpass filter. One problem we need to confront is that the list output by the `function` object can have an arbitrary number of elements, so we cannot use the `pack` object to assemble the list for our polyphonic instrument, because we would need to know the number of elements in the list in advance, and this is not possible.

Let's see how the problem has been solved in the patch. The list of three values (note, velocity and duration) output by `live.step` is divided into 2 parts by the [z1 slice 2] object (for details about `z1` and `slice`, see section IA.7 in the first volume) and the value representing the duration is used, obviously, to specify the duration of the envelope, using the "setdomain" command sent to the `function` object. Immediately thereafter a bang is sent to the `function` object to cause it to output the list of values representing the envelope. This list

167

is appended to the note and velocity list using [z1 join][17]. The "note" message is then inserted at the head of the resulting list which is sent to the **poly~** object[18].

Notice that in this patch the **poly~** object has three additional inlets which are used to send three parameter values to the lowpass filter inside p_sawtones~. These parameters are: keyfollow (a multiplication factor for the oscillator frequency), fixed cutoff frequency (which will be added to keyfollow) and Q factor. Each of these messages is preceded by the "target 0" message because this will tell **poly~** to send the subsequent messages to all instances of its internal subpatch.

Try the different presets and listen to how the envelope and filter parameters affect the timbre of the oscillator. Now let's take a look at the contents of the polyphonic patch p_sawtones~.maxpat (figure IC.26).

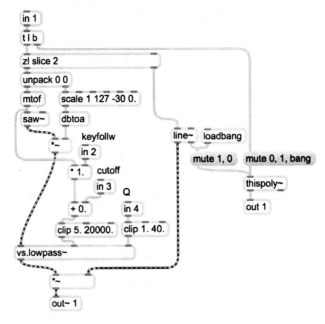

Fig. IC.26 The file **p_sawtones~.maxpat**

---

[17] As we have already seen in section IA.7 of the first volume, the **z1** object with the argument "join" can be used to join two lists together.

[18] Actually, the **function** object outputs two messages by default: the first is a single value that indicates the starting point of the envelope, and the second is a list containing the rest of the envelope's trajectory (see also the patch 01_08_envelopes_2 discussed in section 1.3P of the first volume). When these two messages are sent to the right inlet of [z1 join], the first message will be disregarded, as it will be immediately replaced by the second. This does not cause any problems in our patch because the value of the first message is always 0 (the starting point of the envelope), and the **line~** object in our patch will always be at 0 when we start a new note. It is equally possible to transform the two messages output by **function** into a single list containing the entire trajectory of the envelope, by changing the "Output Mode" attribute to "List" in the object's inspector. This is exactly what we have done in this patch.

As you can see, the list coming from the inlet [in 1] is divided into two separate lists using the [z1 slice 2] object. The first list contains the note and velocity values (which are then separated by the **unpack** object) and the second list contains the envelope which we will send to **line~**. In the lower part of the patch, notice that there are three additional inlets, [in 1], [in 2] and [in 3] which will output the keyfollow, cutoff and Q parameters for the **vs.lowpass~** filter object. The rest of the patch is similar enough to the preceding patches that it should be easy enough for you to analyze by yourself.

• •

ACTIVITIES

• Add a new global parameter to p_sawtones~ in order to control the *env* depth, or the influence the envelope has on the filter's cutoff frequency (see also "Anatomy of a subtractive synthesizer" in section 3.5P of the first volume). Create some new presets for the patch IC_poly_step_seq3.maxpat which make use of this new parameter.

• Change keyfollow and env depth from global parameters to parameters that can be defined for each individual note. Use the Extra 1 and Extra 2 parameters in the step sequencer to set their values.

• Make a polyphonic version of the patch in the file 05_10_monosampler. maxpat, which we looked at in section 5.3P of this volume. In order to do this, you will need to create an abstraction that can be loaded into the **poly~** object, which should either be placed in the same folder as the main patch or somewhere in Max's search path. Play your new sampler using a step sequencer. Additionally, try using your new polyphonic sampler with the arpeggiators shown in sections IB.2-5 of the first volume.

• Make a polyphonic version of the subtractive synthesizer shown in IC_02_ subsynth_seq.maxpat (figure IC.16).

• •

As we have already mentioned, the `poly~` object can be used not only for sound generators, but also for any kind of sound processing or manipulation. As an example, let's see how we can design a bank of resonant filters using `poly~`. Open the file **p_resonbank~.maxpat** located in the "Interlude C Patches" folder (figure IC.27).

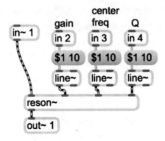

Fig. IC.27 The file **p_resonbank~.maxpat**

This very simple patch contains a second-order resonant bandpass filter (`reson~`), and has 4 inlets[19] – one for each of the `reson~` object's inlets: the input signal to be filtered, and the parameters for gain, cutoff frequency and Q factor, respectively. The three `line~` objects between the inlets and the filter are used to smooth out any abrupt changes in parameter values. Let's now take a look at the main patch; open the file **IC_07_resonant_filters.maxpat** (figure IC.28).

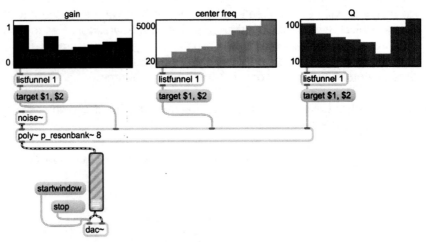

Fig. IC.28 The file **IC_07_filtri_risonanti.maxpat**

---

[19] Note that, unlike the outlets (`out~` and `out`), the numbering for the signal and message inlets (`in~` and `in`) is shared. So if we use the inlet [`in 1`], this would correspond to the leftmost inlet of the `poly~` object, and would therefore be the same inlet as the signal inlet [`in~ 1`]. Although this is perfectly acceptable to do, we prefer separating the signal inlets from the message inlets in order to make the patch clearer.

The **poly~** object shown here has 8 voices of polyphony, and there are three **multislider** objects at the top of the patch (each with 8 sliders) that are used to set the parameters of the resonant filters. The first **multislider** outputs values between 0 and 1 to set the gain of each filter, the second outputs values between 20 and 5000 to set the cutoff frequency, and the third outputs values between 10 and 100 to set the Q factor. The input signal (connected to the first inlet of **poly~**) is a white noise generator.

Each time we modify one of **multislider**'s values with the mouse, the entire list of 8 elements is output and sent to the **listfunnel** object. This object, already introduced in section 2.4P of the first volume, takes an input list and for each element outputs a series of two-element lists made up of the element preceded by a numerical index (if the argument to **listfunnel** is 1, the elements will be numbered starting from 1). These 8 index-element pairs are sent to the message box underneath, which uses the "target" message to send each value to the appropriate instance.

Note that the signal output by **noise~** does not need to be preceded by a "target" message, because, unlike messages, input signals are always sent to all the instances loaded inside **poly~**. Try changing the **multislider** settings in order to create different resonances in the filtered sound.

Now, modify the patch as shown in figure IC.29.

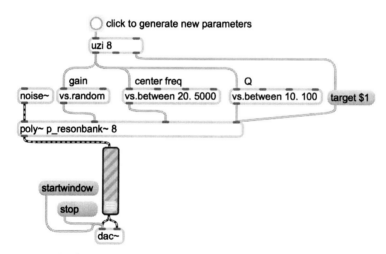

Fig. IC.29 Random resonance generation

In this patch we have removed the **multisliders** (as well as the objects underneath them) and in their place have put a single **uzi** object which outputs a series of values from 1 to 8 out its right outlet and a series of bangs out its left outlet every time it receives a bang in its inlet. Turn on the patch and click several times on the **bang** button connected to the **uzi** object.

ACTIVITIES

- Analyze the patch in figure IC.29 and describe how it works.

- The resonant frequencies in this patch are randomly chosen between 20 and 500 Hz. This favors the selection of high frequencies, because our perception of pitch is not linear with respect to frequency. How could we modify this patch so that the pitches are distributed more uniformly with respect to our pitch perception?

. . . .

As can be seen in figure IC.27, the patch p_resonbank~ does not have a mechanism to mute any of the polyphonic instances, such as we saw in the patch p_sawtones~ (figure IC.26). Nonetheless, it is still possible to mute the various instances contained inside **poly~** by using the "mute" command followed by an instance number and the mute state (0 or 1) that you want to set for it. Take the patch from figure IC.29 and modify it as shown in figure IC.30.

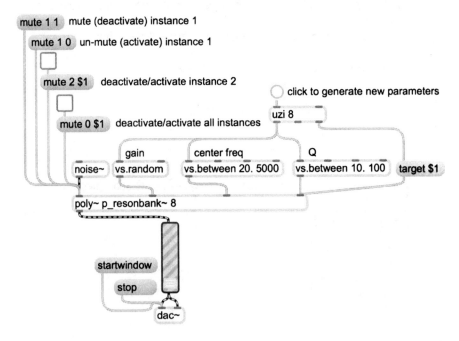

Fig. IC.30 Using the external "mute" message

As you can see in the figure, the first instance can be muted (deactivated) by sending the "mute 1 1" message to the **poly~** object,. The message "mute 1 0" can then be used to reactivate ("unmute") it. The message "mute 2 1" will mute the second instance, and "mute 2 0" will reactivate it. Naturally, messages like "mute 3 1", "mute 3 0", "mute 4 1", "mute 4 0", etc. can be used to mute or reactivate other instances. Additionally, the message "mute 0 1" can be used to mute all instances, and "mute 0 0" can be used to activate them again.[20]

In section 3.9P of the first volume we saw how to build "resonant bodies" using impulses and band pass filters with a very large Q factor. Later, in section IC.7, we saw an algorithm to make resonant bodies that bounce, using the object **fffb~** as a resonant filter bank. Now we can revisit this algorithm and make it more flexible by using the **poly~** object.

Open the file **IC_08_bouncing_bodies.maxpat** (figure IC.31).

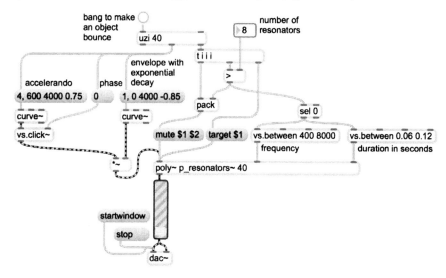

Fig. IC.31 The file **IC_08_bouncing_bodies.maxpat**

This patch is very similar to the patch IB_05_rebounds.maxpat that we saw in section IB.7 in the first volume.[21]

---

[20] The global commands "mute 0 1" and "mute 0 0" do not actually modify the individual states of each instance but work in addition to them. You could think of the global mute commands as a "master switch", such as the main circuit breaker for all the electricity in a house or apartment, whereas the individual mute commands for each instance are like electric switches for individual lights in the house. For example, if the third instance has been muted with the command "mute 3 1" it cannot be reactivated with the global command "mute 0 0", but rather needs to be reactivated with the command "mute 3 0". The converse is also true: if all of the instances have been muted with the global command "mute 0 1", the individual command "mute 3 0" will not reactivate the third voice; the global command "mute 0 0" must be used (in other words, turning the master circuit breaker back on!).

[21] The patch IC_08_bouncing_bodies, as well as the patches which follow it, are inspired by an example ("bouncing lightbulbs, pencils, cans, and other assorted objects") written by James McCartney for his audio programming language SuperCollider (v.2).

First, try out the patch: each time you click on the bang button at the top of the patch, it will generate a simulation of the sound of a small object bouncing on a flat surface. This sound is realized using a series of impulses (output by the **vs.click~** object) filtered by resonators (bandpass resonant filters) located inside the instances of the p_resonators~ patch contained in the **poly~** object. We will look at p_resonators~ after we have finished analyzing the main patch.

The number of resonators used depends on the number box to the right of the bang button in the upper part of the main patch, which can be set between 1 and 40. Note that this number box goes into the "cold" inlet of the comparison operator >. The unused instances inside **poly~** will be muted using the external "mute" command which we saw in figure IC.30, and the other instances will be activated. In the figure, the number of resonators used is 8, and this means that the signal calculation of the first 8 instances will be activated, and the remaining 32 instances will be muted.

Let's take a closer look at how this works. The bang button triggers an **uzi** object which outputs a series of consecutive numbers from 1 to 40 out its right outlet. These values are sent out each of the three outlets of the **trigger** object, below. The values sent out the right outlet of trigger are sent to a message box containing the message "target $1" which is used to select the instance which will receive the subsequent messages. The value sent out the middle outlet of **trigger** is sent to the hot inlet of the > operator which will output either 1 (true) if the value is greater than 8, or 0 (false) if it is less than or equal to 8. The value output by > is first sent to the [**sel** 0] object on the right, which will output a bang when it receives a 0 (i.e., when the value output by **uzi** is less than or equal to 8). In other words, the **sel** object only outputs a bang for the first 8 values output by **uzi**, which correspond to the 8 active instances that we want to use. The bang output by **sel** is sent to two **vs.between** objects which output a value for the resonant frequency (between 400 and 8000) and a value for the duration of the resonance (between 0.06 and 0.12), respectively. The value output by the > object is then also sent to the cold inlet of the **pack** object just below.

Returning to the **trigger** object, the value output out its left outlet is sent to the left inlet (hot inlet) of the **pack** object (whose right inlet has already received the value output by >). The two-element list assembled by **pack** is then sent to the message box with the message "mute $1 $2" – this message will leave instances 1 through 8 active and mute instances 9 through 40. You can verify this yourself by connecting the output of the "mute $1 $2" message box to a **print** object and watching the messages that are printed in the Max window every time you send a bang to the **uzi**.

Finally, at the top of the patch, you will notice that we are using the middle outlet of **uzi** for the first time. This outlet outputs a bang (called the *carry bang*) when the **uzi** has finished outputting both the numerical sequence out its right outlet and the sequence of bangs out its left one. In this patch, the carry bang is connected to three message boxes, two of which are connected to **curve~** objects; let's look at these first. The **curve~** object on the right creates an envelope with exponential decay lasting 4 seconds, whereas the one on the left controls the frequency of the impulse generator (the **vs.click~** object) – this frequency will start at 4 impulses a second and accelerate to 600 over a span of 4 seconds. The remaining message box contains the numerical message "0" which is connected to the right inlet of **vs.click~**. This message is used to reset the phase of the impulse generator, so that its first impulse coincides exactly with the beginning of the exponential envelope.

Try changing the number box in the upper-right part of the patch and listen to how it affects the timbre of the resonant body, depending on the number of resonators used. Now let's look at the patch **p_resonators~** that is loaded inside the **poly~** object (figure IC.32).

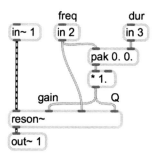

Fig. IC.32 The file **p_resonators~.maxpat**

This is also a very simple patch that takes advantage of the technique discussed in section 3.9P of the first volume (see in particular figure 3.69): by multiplying the frequency and resonance duration together we can easily obtain a value to use for both the gain and Q of the resonant filter (**reson~**).

We can easily modify the characteristics of the resonant body not only by changing the frequency and duration parameters, but by modifying the envelope and rebound speed, as well. Open the file **IC_09_bouncing_bodies2.maxpat** (figure IC.33).

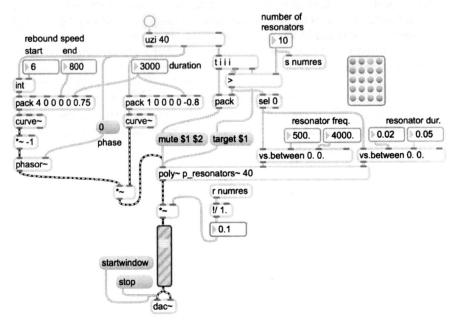

Fig. IC.33 The file **IC_09_bouncing_bodies2.maxpat**

Comparing this to the previous patch, you will notice that we have added the possibility to control the starting and ending rebound velocity, as well as the overall duration of the envelope, via the three number boxes in the left-hand part of the patch. Here, the two message boxes that were connected to the `curve~` object have been replaced with two **pack** objects, so the curve parameters can be easily modified. Note the use of the **int** object on the left, which stores the value for the initial rebound speed, and only sends it to the hot inlet of **pack** when it receives the carry bang from the **uzi** object.

This patch also allows the user to define a minimum and maximum value for both the resonator frequencies and the resonance duration, via the four number boxes connected to the **vs.between** random number generators on the right. Additionally, the number box which determines the number of active resonators (in the upper part of the patch), is sent (via the **send/receive** pair [s numres] and [r numres]) to the mathematical operator !/ in the lower part of the patch. What is this new part of our algorithm used for?

You will notice that the **vs.click~** object which was used to generate impulses in the previous patch has been replaced with a **phasor~** object in this patch. Compared to **vs.click~**, the impulses created by **phasor~** have less energy in the high frequency range, and are much more effective with resonances in the low frequency range. Notice that the frequency value output by **curve~** is multiplied by -1, and therefore becomes a negative value before being sent to **phasor~**. As we already know, a negative frequency value for the **phasor~** object means that it generate a ramp that goes from 1 to 0 instead of one that goes from 0 to 1. So, why did we need to make the frequency negative? Try removing the [*~ -1] multiplier – what difference do you notice? (Do not forget to take into consideration the fact that the **phasor~** object's phase is reset to 0 by the carry bang from **uzi**.) Listen to all of the presets, paying careful attention to the settings of the different parameters, and then try creating some new presets of your own.

• •

ACTIVITIES

• Add a **metro** object to the patch shown in figure IC.33 in order to create successive rebounds at regular intervals.

• Make the **metro** beat at irregular intervals using the technique we saw in 05_15_rand_blocks.maxpat (section 5.4P).

• The resonator frequencies in this patch are also chosen uniformly within a frequency range expressed in Hertz. It therefore tends to favor high frequencies because our perception of pitch is not linear with respect to frequency. How can we modify the patch so the pitches are uniformly distributes with respect to our pitch perception?

• •

In these last few patches we have taken advantage of polyphony to create the components within a complex sound, but the result is still monophonic – we can still only produce one "bouncing object" at a time. Fortunately, there is nothing stopping us from including the entire patch in figure IC.33 (with some necessary modifications) into a `poly~` object, thereby creating a polyphony of bouncing objects. By doing this we will have a `poly~` object that contains instances of a patch which itself contains a `poly~` object! Let's see how this works: open the file **IC_10_poly_bouncing_bodies.maxpat** (figure IC.34).

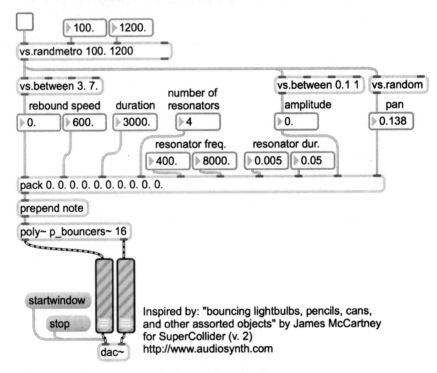

Fig. IC.34 The file **IC_10_poly_bouncing_bodies.maxpat**

First, let's discuss the new object, **vs.randmetro**, in the upper-left part of the patch. This object works like a normal **metro** object, with the difference being that the interval between the bangs that it outputs is not regular, but randomly selected between a given minimum and maximum value. The **vs.randmetro** object shown in the figure will therefore output a series of bangs whose spacing in time randomly varies between 100 and 1200 milliseconds apart.

The bangs output by **vs.randmetro** are sent to three random generators connected, in turn, to other message boxes. These random values, together with other constant values are assembled into a list by the **pack** object at the center of the patch. This list, together with the "note" command, is then sent to the **poly~** object just below. The list contains values for the various parameters that we have already used in the previous patches: the initial number of rebounds per second (between 3 and 7), the final number of rebounds (600), the overall duration of the envelope (3000 milliseconds), the number of resonators (4), the minimum and maximum frequency for each of the resonators (from 400 to 8000 Hz.) and the minimum and maximum duration for each resonator (between 0.005 and 0.05 seconds). There are also two new parameters which we have added to control the global amplitude of each series of bounces (ranging between 0.1 and 1) and the stereo position (panning), which ranges from 0 to 1. This way, each series of rebounds can be placed at any point in the stereo field.

Let's now open the file **p_bouncers~.maxpat** (figure IC.35) to see how this parameter list is used inside the polyphonic patch loaded by `poly~`.

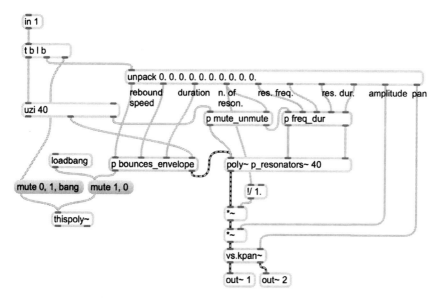

Fig. IC.35 The file **p_bouncers~.maxpat**

This patch contains roughly the same algorithm shown in the patch IC_09_bouncing_bodies2 (figure IC.33), although the different parts of the patch have been encapsulated in three **patcher** (p) objects in order to simplify the various connections from the input list. Note that this patch also contains the dynamic polyphonic voice management mechanism using the **thispoly~** object which we saw for the first time in figure IC.23.

When this patch receives a list from the main patch, the first thing it does is to send a bang to the "mute 0, 1" message box thereby activating the instance and putting it into "busy" mode. After this the input list is disassembled by the **unpack** object and the individual values are sent to various objects in the patch.

The rightmost value is used to define the sound's stereo panning, using **vs.kpan~** which works like the **vs.pan~** object that we have already seen (in section 4.1 in the first volume), except that it only accepts Max messages (not MSP signals) to set the sound to a fixed position in the stereo field. The second value from the right is used to control the overall volume for the sound output by the instance. The next four values (from the right) are sent to the [p freq_dur] subpatch which contains the random number generators that set the frequency and duration for each resonator. The next value ("num reson") is used to set the number of resonators used so it is sent to the [p mute_unmute] subpatch conatining the algorithm to mute or activate the instances of p_resonators~ contained in the **poly~** just below. Finally, the last three values on the left are sent to the [p bounces_envelope] subpatch which contains the part that creates the series of rebounds of the resonant body as well as its overall envelope. When the envelope is finished, this subpatch sends a bang to the "mute 1, 0" message box in order to free the instance and mute it.

Now, activate the main patch so you can listen to the polyphony of bouncing objects. After you have listened to the patch, add a preset object to it in order to save and recall settings of the various parameters.

· ·

 ACTIVITY

Add other random generators to the patch shown in figure IC.35 in order to randomly set the different parameters, such as the number of resonators, duration of each series of rebounds, etc.

· ·

IC.4 ABSTRACTION AND ARGUMENTS

As we have already learned, almost all standard Max objects can accept arguments to set the values for the main variables of that object. In this section we will see how we can also use arguments with abstractions, or patches which can be used like objects.

Open the file **IC_11_abstraction_arguments.maxpat** (figure IC.36).

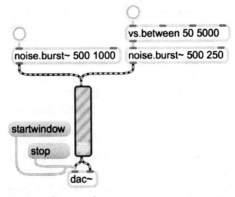

Fig. IC.36 The file **IC_11_abstraction_arguments.maxpat**

In this patch there are two copies (or instances) of the **noise.burst~** object. This object, designed specifically for this example, makes a short noise burst using an envelope with exponential decay that is applied to a variable-band noise generator[22]. The two arguments control the width of the noise band (in Hertz) and the duration of the sound (in milliseconds), respectively. The first instance of **noise.burst~** receives a bang in its left inlet and generates a short burst of noise based on its two arguments (500 Hz and 1000 ms). The second instance, on the other hand, receives a random number between 50 and 5000 (instead of a bang), which it uses as the width of the noise band, while the duration of the burst, specified by the second argument, is always 250 milliseconds. Before continuing, listen to the sounds generated by the two objects. The **noise.burst~** object is actually an abstraction, and therefore you can see its contents by double-clicking on it (figure IC.37a).

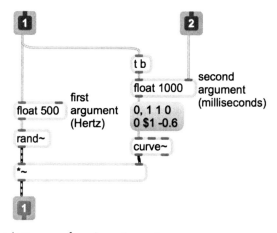

Fig. IC.37a One instance of **noise.burst~**

Look carefully at the patch shown in the figure and analyze how it works.

As you can see, the values that were provided as arguments can also be found inside the two **float** objects. When the **noise.burst~** object receives a bang in its left inlet, it triggers a one-second long exponential envelope (using the value of the second argument) with the **curve~** object. Can you envision the envelope's trajectory by just looking at the values in the message box? The first argument (a value of 500 in the **float** object on the left), on te other hand, is sent to the **rand~** noise generator. If the **noise.burst~** object receives a numeric value in its left inlet (instead of a bang), this value will replace the default value contained in the **float** object and will be sent to **rand~**, while the **float** object on the right will still receive a bang because of the [**t b**] object.

---

[22] We will soon discover that this has been made with the **rand~ object**.

Sending a numerical value to the right inlet of **noise.burst~** will only change the contents of the **float** object on the right, determining the length of sound produced. Connect a number box to the right inlet of the first instance of the **noise.burst~** object in the patch shown in figure IC.36, and use it to modify the length of the envelope. To understand how the arguments to **noise.burst~** ended up inside the two **float** objects, we need to open the original **noise.burst~.maxpat** file located in the "Interlude C Patches" folder (figure IC.37b).[23]

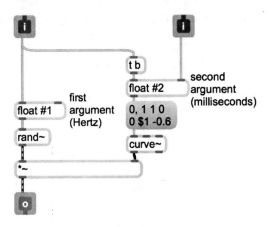

Fig. IC.37b The file **noise.burst~.maxpat**

As you can see, in place of the values corresponding to the first and second arguments, the original file for **noise.burst~** contains the symbols #1 and #2, respectively. These symbols (called *replaceable arguments*) function as placeholders for arguments that will be passed to the abstraction. Naturally, if we needed a third argument, we could use the symbol #3, and so forth, up until #9.

Even abstractions loaded by a **poly~** object can use replaceable arguments, however in order to distinguish these arguments from the arguments to **poly~** itself, it is necessary to precede them with the symbol "args". Open the file **IC_12_poly_arguments.maxpat** (shown in figure IC.38) to see how this works.

---

[23] You can also open an abstraction's original file from an instance of the abstraction itself. You first need to open the abstraction's window and click on the first icon (labeled "Modify Read Only") in the toolbar at the bottom of the window. The icon, which initially looks like a pencil, changes into the lock icon with which the patch can be unlocked. Alternatively, you could also click on the second icon labeled "Patcher Windows." This will open a floating menu where you can choose the "Open Original" option.

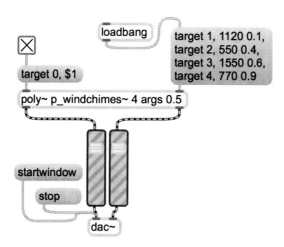

Fig. IC.38 The file **IC_12_poly_arguments.maxpat**

The `poly~` object visible in the figure has 4 arguments. The first two, as we have already learned, represent the name of the abstraction to load and the number of voices of polyphony to use. The third argument is the symbol "args", which is used to indicate that subsequent arguments should be passed to the abstraction contained in `poly~`. The fourth argument (the value 0.5), is therefore actually the first (and only) argument for the p_windchimes~ abstraction loaded by `poly~`.

Turn on the DSP engine and activate the patch by clicking on the `toggle` on its upper left side – the sound it makes is similar to a small set of wind chimes blowing in the wind. Now open the p_windchimes~ abstraction by double-clicking on the `poly~` object that has loaded it (figure IC.39).

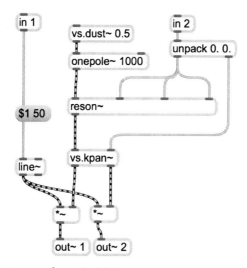

Fig. IC.39 One instance of p_windchimes~

As you can see the argument "0.5" is used by the **vs.dust~** object.[24] If you open the original file you can verify that the **vs.dust~** object actually contains the symbol #1 as an argument.

. . . .

⌖ ACTIVITIES

- Analyze the patches in figure IC.38 and IC.39.

- Why is the first element of the list input into [**in** 2] sent to all three inlets of the **reson~** object? What happens when you set its parameters this way?

- What is the [**onepole~** 1000] object inside **vs.dust~** used for? Try removing it, or changing its argument (in the original patch) – how does this change the resulting sound?

- Modify the p_windchimes~ abstraction so the number of clicks generated by **vs.dust~** can be modified externally by the user (via an inlet). Modify the main patch IC_12_poly_arguments.maxpat (figure IC.38) accordingly.

. . . .

---

[24] Remember that **vs.dust~** is an object that outputs a series of irregular audio clicks; its argument indicates the average number of clicks to generate per second. See section 3.9P.

LIST OF MAX OBJECTS

in
An inlet for Max messages in a patch loaded by **poly~**. This object has a numerical argument indicating the position of the inlet on the **poly~** object itself – 1 represents the leftmost inlet, 2 the next inlet to the right, etc.

in~
An inlet for MSP signals in a patch loaded by **poly~**. This object has a numerical argument indicating the position of the inlet on the **poly~** object itself – 1 represents the leftmost inlet, 2 the next inlet to the right, etc.

live.step
A graphical interface object with the functions of a step sequencer. This is made up of several columns, called steps, each of which contains 5 user-definable values. By default the first three of these represent MIDI note, velocity and duration.

matrixctrl
A graphical interface object that can be used to make connections between the inlets and outlets of the **router** and **matrix~** objects.

out
An outlet for Max messages in a patch loaded by **poly~**. This object has a numerical argument indicating the position of the message outlet on the **poly~** object itself – 1 represents the leftmost inlet, 2 the next inlet to the right, etc. Message outlets appear to the right of the signal outlets.

out~
An outlet for MSP signals in a patch loaded by **poly~**. This object has a numerical argument indicating the position of the signal outlet on the **poly~** object itself – 1 represents the leftmost inlet, 2 the next inlet to the right, etc. Signal outlets appear on the left, before the message outlets.

poly~
This object is used to make a patch polyphonic. This is done by loading the patch inside the **poly~** object. The two main arguments to the object are the name of the patch to load and the number of notes (or voices) that can be played simultaneously.

router
An object with a user-definable number of inlets and outlets that can be used to route Max messages. This is the Max equivalent of the MSP object **matrix~**.

thispoly~
This object is used to activate and deactivate specific instances (voices) of a patch loaded by **poly~**, in addition to providing information about the instance in which it is located. This object only works when it is in a patch that has been loaded inside **poly~**.

timer
An object that lets us calculate the time interval between successive bangs.

translate
Converts any fixed or relative time value into any other fixed or relative time value. For example, ticks to milliseconds.

transport
Allows us to start and stop the global passage of time in Max. If this object has a name as an argument, it can also be used to control time for only those objects which are associated to it using the same name with the "Transport" attribute.

vs.kpan~
This object implements a panning algorithm taking a monophonic input sound in its left inlet and panning it in the stereo field according to the Max messages it receives in its right inlet.

LIST OF ATTRIBUTES, MESSAGES AND GRAPHICAL ELEMENTS FOR SPECIFIC MAX OBJECTS

@ (symbol)
Precedes the attribute name typed into an object.

live.step
-Loop Ruler (graphical element)
Located along the upper edge of the object. By changing the length of the loop ruler you can change the number of steps that will be played.
-Unit Ruler (graphical element)
Located on the left side of the object. This is made up of a stylized musical keyboard and a gray vertical band that displays the note names.

makenote
- Duration (attribute)
Controls the duration of the note in **makenote**.

matrixctrl
- Autosize to Rows & Columns (attribute)
Allows the object to be resized when the number of rows or columns are changed.
- Number of Columns (attribute)
Number of columns in the object.
- Number of Rows (attribute)
Number of rows in the object.
- One Non-Zero Cell Per Row (attribute)
When activated, the object allows only one connection per row. This can be used to avoid having two inlets sent to the same outlet.

metro
- Active (attribute)
Used to start and stop the metro, when followed by a 1 or a 0, respectively.
- Interval (attribute)
Used to set the interval between bangs output by the object. This attribute can use any of the time units available in Max.
- Quantize (attribute)
Allows the user to specify a value that will be used as a "temporal grid" imposed upon the beats of the metro. This attribute can use ticks, bbu or note values as time units.

poly~
- Target (attribute)
Used to indicate which voice (or instance) will receive messages sent to the object.
- Mute (message)
This message, followed by an instance number and mute state (0 or 1), can be used to deactivate (mute) or activate the computation of signals inside the instances contained in **poly~**.
- Note (message)
When added to the beginning of a list, this message tells the **poly~** object to find the first free instance (i.e., the first instance whose busy state is inactive), and to send the rest of the list to that instance. This message is very useful for automatic polyphonic voice allocation. .

thispoly~
- 1 and 0 (messages)
These are used to turn on and off the busy state the instance.
- Bang (message)
Used to tell the thispoly~ object to output the instance number where it is located (left outlet) and the current mute state (right outlet).
- Mute (message)
This message is used to mute (i.e., deactivate) the signal processing inside an instance.

transport
- Tempo (message)
This attribute is used to set the number of beats per minute (bpm). Its default value is 120.

uzi
- Carry bang (message)
This is a bang sent out the middle outlet of the **uzi** object once it has finished outputting the sequence of numbers and bangs out its right and left outlets, respectively.

GLOSSARY

Attribute
The column in an object's inspector that shows the real name of an attribute. This is the name that can be used to set the attribute using an external message.

BBU
A Relative Time format (Bars/Beats/Units) whose duration is not expressed in milliseconds but rather in bars, beats and ticks.

BPM
Beats per minute (generally used to define a musical tempo).

Fixed Time Values
Time values (such as milliseconds) that do not depend on the master clock.

Global Transport
Stand-alone window that contains commands and settings for the master clock. Using this window you can start and stop the master clock, change its tempo in bpm, see the amount of elapsed time, etc.

Instances
Also called "voices" of polyphony - these are copies of a patch loaded inside a `poly~` object.

Master clock
Timing system for the global tempo in Max.

Replaceable Arguments
Symbols made up of the # character followed by a number between 1 and 9 (for example #1, #2, #3, etc.) that can be used inside an abstraction as indicators for the arguments that will be passed to the object.

Setting
The column in an object's inspector that shows the descriptive name for an attribute. Unlike the real name shown in the Attribute column, the descriptive name cannot be used in an external message.

Step sequencer
A device which cyclically repeats a sequence of sound events with predefined parameters.

Tempo-Relative Time Values
Time values (such as ticks) which depend on the master clock.

6T

DELAY LINES: ECHOES, LOOPING, FLANGER, CHORUS, COMB AND ALLPASS FILTERS, PHASER, PITCH SHIFTING, REVERSE, KARPLUS-STRONG ALGORITHM

LEARNING AGENDA

PREREQUISITES FOR THE CHAPTER
- THE CONTENTS OF VOLUME 1, CHAPTER 5 (THEORY AND PRACTICE) AND INTERLUDE C

OBJECTIVES
KNOWLEDGE
- TO KNOW HOW TO USE DELAY LINES FOR VARIOUS PURPOSES
- TO KNOW HOW TO SIMULATE SINGLE AND MULTIPLE ECHOES
- TO KNOW HOW TO USE LOOPS, SLAPBACK, MULTITAP DELAYS AND PING-PONG DELAYS
- TO KNOW THE PARAMETERS AND USE OF FLANGERS, CHORUS AND PHASERS
- TO KNOW THE BASIC THEORY AND SOME POSSIBLE APPLICATIONS OF COMB AND ALLPASS FILTERS
- TO KNOW HOW TO USE PITCH SHIFTING AND REVERSE
- TO KNOW THE BASIC THEORY BEHIND THE KARPLUS-STRONG ALGORITHM
- TO KNOW SEVERAL APPLICATIONS FOR THE SIMULATION OF PLUCKED STRINGS AND PERCUSSION USING THE KARPLUS-STRONG ALGORITHM

SKILLS
- TO BE ABLE TO AURALLY DISTINGUISH AND DESCRIBE THE DIFFERENT TYPES OF ECHOES
- TO BE ABLE TO AURALLY DISTINGUISH AND DESCRIBE THE MAIN DIFFERENCES BETWEEN CHORUS, PHASER AND FLANGER
- TO BE ABLE TO AURALLY DISTINGUISH AND DESCRIBE THE MODIFICATION OF THE MAIN PARAMETERS OF THE KARPLUS-STRONG ALGORITHM

CONTENTS
- DELAY LINES
- DIFFERENT TYPES OF ECHOES
- USING DELAY LINES FOR LOOPING, CHORUS, FLANGER, PHASER, PITCH SHIFTING AND REVERSE
- COMB AND ALLPASS FILTERS
- SYNTHESIS USING THE KARPLUS-STRONG ALGORITHM

ACTIVITIES
- SOUND EXAMPLES AND INTERACTIVE EXAMPLES

TESTING
- QUESTIONS WITH SHORT ANSWERS
- LISTENING AND ANALYSIS

SUPPORTING MATERIALS
FUNDAMENTAL CONCEPTS - GLOSSARY - DISCOGRAPHY

6.1 DELAY TIME: FROM FILTERS TO ECHOES

Delaying a signal is one of the most powerful and versatile tools we have at our disposal in the realm of computer music. A wide variety of synthesis and sound processing techniques, from subtractive synthesis to physical models, from reverb algorithms to the bulk of classic effects (which will be covered in this chapter) all have the use of longer or shorter delay lines in common as the basis of their design.

In section 3.6 we already learned that delay lines are a necessary component of digital filters. In this case the *delay time* between the input and output of the filter is extremely short, and calculated in single samples (for reference, the amount of time that separates one sample and the next, at a sampling rate of 48000 Hz is equal to 1/48000th of a second, or about 0.00002 seconds). Many different types of effects can be created using delays that range from this "microscopic" *delay time* up until a slightly larger span of just a few milliseconds.

In this chapter, in particular, we will take a look at the *flanger* (which has a constantly varying delay time between 1 and 20 ms.), *chorus* (typically using a variable delay time of 20-30 ms.), *slapback delay* – an effect giving a nearly simultaneous doubling of a sound (using a delay somewhere in the range of 10 to 120 ms), and different kinds of *echo* effects (whose delay can range between 100 ms. and several seconds). Furthermore, we will also take a look at the *comb filter* – a handy tool that can be used for different purposes, including the creation of multiple resonances that have a harmonic relationship.

Finally, we will also look at two different implementations of the *allpass filter*: the first can be used alongside a *comb filter* to create reverberation effects (which we will cover in more detail later on, in the third volume), and the second can be used to make a *phaser*. Figure 6.1 shows an illustrative and helpful graph with time values ranges that should give you an approximate idea of the delay times necessary to obtain different effects. The ranges mainly serve as rough guidelines that can be modified as necessary in order to appropriately adapt them to different kinds of input sounds.

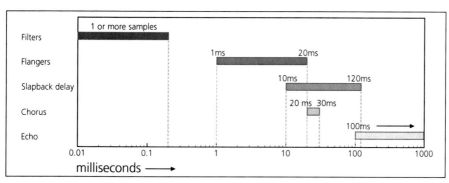

Fig. 6.1 Different delay times from filters to echoes

6.2 ECHOES

The *echo* effect – i.e., the repetition of a sound – can clearly be perceived if the repetition of the sound takes place in a time frame greater than what is known as the *Haas zone* (25-35 ms.). If, on the other hand, the repetition arrives to the listener in a shorter amount of time, the listener will have difficulty perceiving the second sound as a separate one. Moreover, in the case of sounds whose attack is slow, the sound will tend to be perceived not as a separate sound at all, but rather a sound fused together with the first.

To simulate a simple echo effect we need to create an algorithm with a delay, which takes an input audio signal and repeats it at its output after a given amount of time that can vary anywhere between a few milliseconds and several seconds. The delayed sound (defined as the *"wet"* sound) can optionally be added to the original sound (the *"dry"* sound). If we only want to hear the sound of the effect itself (the *wet* sound), we just need to give the *dry* sound an amplitude of zero. The control of the proportion of the dry and the wet sound is known, appropriately enough, as *balance*, and is often defined as a percentage where 100% indicates only the wet sound, 0% indicates only the dry sound, and 50% indicates equal amounts of *wet* and *dry*. Figure 6.2 shows a simple delay example.

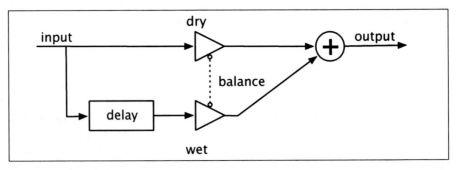

Fig. 6.2 A simple delay example

. . . .

INTERACTIVE EXAMPLE 6A.1 • *Echo effects with delay times inside and outside the Haas zone.*

. . . .

If there is more than one repetition of the input sound we effectively obtain a multiple echo. In order to create multiple echoes, we need to add *feedback* to our algorithm.

Feedback amounts to being able to add the output of a delay back into its input; an example of delay with feedback is shown in figure 6.3.

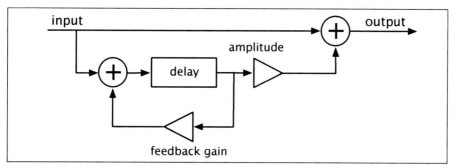

Fig. 6.3 Block diagram for delay with feedback

• •

INTERACTIVE EXAMPLE 6A.2 • *Multiple Echoes*

• •

In this manner, the delay effect can be repeated many times, by adjusting the *feedback* gain. If the gain is zero, there will be no feedback, and therefore the repeated sound will happen just once. By slowly increasing the gain we can get more and more repetitions of the sound.

Technically speaking, the feedback gain is just a multiplication factor for the signal (i.e., a scalar), whose value will typically vary between 0 and 1. With a gain of 50%, for example the feedback signal will be multiplied by 0.5 (in other words its amplitude will be reduced by half with each repetition of the sound). To give an example, if the multiplier is set to 0.5, and the initial amplitude is 1, the various attenuated repetitions will have amplitudes of 0.5, 0.25, 0.125, and so on.

When using a gain of 0% the signal will be multiplied by zero (and therefore silenced), whereas with a gain of 100% it is multiplied by 1 (and is therefore not modified). The percentage of gain actually represents the ratio between the amplitude of the output signal and that of the signal which is sent back to the input. Therefore, if the multiplier value is 0.99 (equal to 99% gain) the output sound will only be reduced by 1% each time the signal is sent back to the input. A multiplier of 1 (equal to 100% gain) is not advisable as it will result in a virtually infinite repetition of the same amplitude, and if other audio signals are meanwhile also sent to the input, distortion is likely to happen once the signal from the feedback loop has been added to it. Obviously, multipliers greater than 1 are also not recommended, for the same reason.

ACCUMULATION OF DC OFFSET

It is possible that a sound's waveform (figure 6.4) might contain a positive or negative *DC offset* (refer to section 5.3).

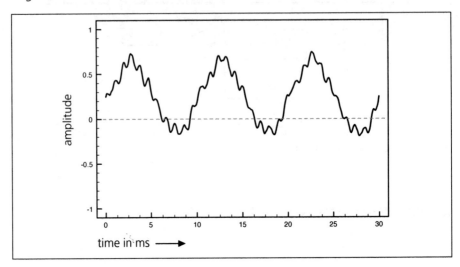

Fig. 6.4 A sampled sound with a significant *DC offset*.

This imbalance might not be problematic when directly playing back the sound. However, you should be aware that when creating a delay with feedback, the DC offset of the various repetitions will accumulate and can easily take the sound out of the amplitude range of the audio interface. To rectify this potential problem, you simply need to add a highpass filter with a very low cutoff frequency (for example 10 Hz) – since DC offset is simply a signal with a frequency of 0 (as already explained in section 5.3), it can be easily filtered out using such a filter.

SIMULATION OF TAPE DELAY AND ANALOG DELAYS

The term **tape delay** refers to old echo systems in which a sound was recorded to tape using one record head, and played back using another playback head, allowing the possibility of feedback. The delay time was dependent on the distance between the two heads and the speed of the tape. This type of echo could have a very long delay time (using two tape recorders placed far from one another), or have multiple echoes via the use of multiple playback heads. Some systems used magnetic discs similar to hard disks instead of tape. The repeated sound in these systems was slightly filtered each time it passed from the playback head to the record head, due to a loss of amplitude in the high frequency range that is typical of analog recording technology. Therefore, in addition to the delay itself, a digital simulation of tape delay requires using filters that will modify the spectral content of the sound each time it passes through the feedback loop. Alongside a lowpass filter, you can also add a highpass filter inside the feedback loop in order to eliminate the accumulation of low frequencies.

Such a system can also be used to simulate another type of analog delay from a later era than tape delay, in which delay lines were no longer recorded to magnetic media but to solid state components (the delay technology used inside analog guitar pedals).

• •

INTERACTIVE EXAMPLE 6A.3 • *Tape Delay - Analog Delay*

• •

SLAPBACK DELAY

Slapback delay is a type of echo with a very short delay time (generally between 10 and 120 milliseconds), usually without feedback (therefore containing just one repetition of the sound), that gives the listener a sense of doubling or bouncing of the original sound. This kind of doubling can be used in mono, but is more often used as a stereo sound spatialization effect, with the input sound on one channel and the output sound on the other. Depending on the delay time, the resulting effect can be that of perceiving two quasi-synchronized "voices", one on the left and one on the right, or one "voice" which responds to the other like a rebound, bouncing from right to left or vice-versa. Naturally, you could imagine (and design!) a more complex sound spatialization effect using these kinds of bouncing sounds if you are working with a multichannel sound system.

• •

INTERACTIVE EXAMPLE 6A.4 • *Slapback Delay with Different Delay*
Times, in Mono or Stereo

• •

MULTITAP DELAY

Multitap delay consists of creating echo effects with irregular delay times and independent amplitude control for each repetition. A *multitap* delay is constructed using a series of different delays in parallel along the same delay line. These delays have adjustable delay times independent of one another (see figure 6.5) and the amplitude of each one can be controlled right down to the point of eliminating it entirely (if its amplitude is zero). It goes without saying that none of the delay times can be larger than the total time of the delay line itself. It is also possible to create a multitap delay using independent delay lines – in other words, a system where each delay uses its own delay line (see figure 6.6). One particular feature of the multitap delay effect, apart from the irregularity of the repetitions in time, is the ability to have an independent feedback loop for each of the delays, whereas the simple delay line described above only has a single feedback loop. In the case where the multitap delay is implemented using a single delay line (see figure 6.5), you need to make sure that the total sum of the feedback gains does not exceed 100%.

In the case where a multitap has a dedicated delay line for each tap (see figure 6.6) each of the individual gains can range between 0% and 100%. Clearly, the resulting effect of each of these two systems is different. The rhythms of the multitap delay (whether regular or not) can be set using a series of delay times that increase logarithmically or exponentially, in order to create a musical accelerando or rallentando effect.

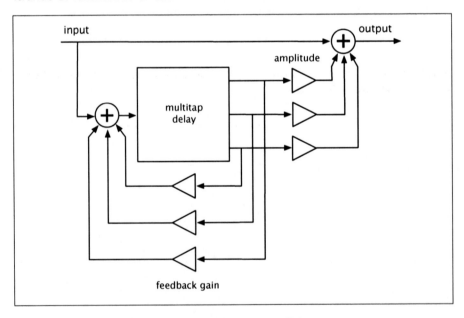

Fig. 6.5 Block diagram showing multitaps in parallel

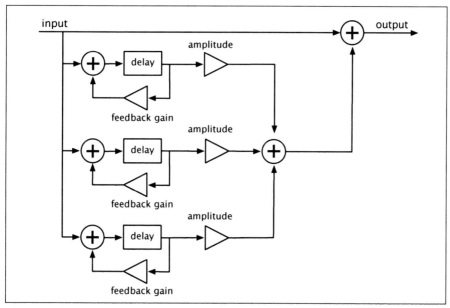

Fig. 6.6 Block diagram showing multitaps in series

Naturally, the delay times can also be varied in time by using an LFO to modulate each delay tap. Modulating a delay line this way, as we will explain in detail in section 6.9, also alters the frequency of the delayed sound. Nonetheless, using a very small amount of modulation can result in interesting beating effects between the original and delayed sounds without an obvious change in pitch.

• •

INTERACTIVE EXAMPLE 6A.5 • *Different Types of Multitap Delays*

• •

MULTIBAND-MULTITAP DELAY

A more complex variation of the multitap delay, the ***multiband-multitap delay***, can be created by dividing the input signal into two or more frequency bands using a crossover filter (a system of separating frequency zones from one another). The different output signals of the crossover filter are then input into different delays, allowing a different delay time and feedback gain to be applied to each frequency band. For example, you could have a 500 millisecond delay for the bass frequencies, and a one second delay for the mid-high range.

• •

INTERACTIVE EXAMPLE 6A.6 • *Different Types of Multiband-Multitap*
Delays

PING-PONG DELAY

The **ping-pong delay** effect, whereby the delayed sound rebounds alternately between the left and right channels, can be created using two separate delay lines. However, instead of returning the feedback to the same delay line, it is sent to the input of the other delay line; crossing the feedback loops in this way forces the sound to bounce from one output to the other. For this effect, you can choose to have one input source or two (one for each delay line, see figure 6.7).

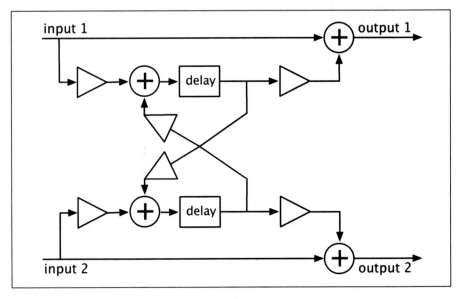

Fig. 6.7 Block diagram for ping-pong delay

. . . .

INTERACTIVE EXAMPLE 6A.7 • *Different Types of Ping-Pong Delays*

. . . .

IMPLEMENTATIONS

In order to implement a digital delay we need a pre-defined amount of memory that will be used to store each successive input sample value. We will use pointers – a **write pointer** and a **read pointer** – to write to and read from this block of memory. Each input sample is written to successive memory locations via the write pointer. In each sampling period (see section 5.1), the read pointer reads one of the previously written sample values. The distance between the write pointer and the read pointer, in terms of memory locations, will depend on the specified delay time. For example, if the sampling rate is 44100 Hz and we want to have a half-second delay, the distance between the two pointers will be 22050 memory locations. When the memory is completely full, the write pointer returns to overwrite the memory starting from the first location. Because of this circularity in writing and reading to memory, this technique is known as a **circular buffer** (see figure 6.8). Naturally, you can use multiple read pointers in a circular buffer to implement more elaborate delay systems, such as that of a multitap delay.

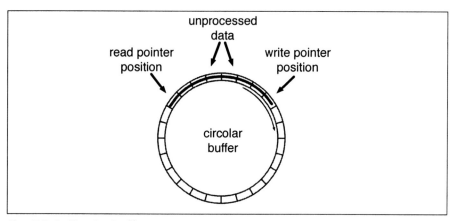

Fig. 6.8 A Circular Buffer

6.3 LOOPING USING DELAY LINES

One technique used frequently in live applications is to employ delay lines to create *loops* – cyclical repetitions of the same sound fragment. This technique consists of sending an input signal (such as the sound of a voice from a micro-phone) into delay line whose delay time is equal to that of the loop we want to create. Once the entire delay buffer has been filled, the amplitude multiplier in the feedback loop is set to 1 (equal to 100% gain) and the input gain is set to 0. This way, the signal in the buffer is cyclically repeated without decreasing in volume, because it continually circulates within the feedback loop without ever changing in amplitude, and it does so without the addition of new input sounds from the microphone (because this is silenced before being input to the delay line). By building several such delay lines, we can create different loops that can be activated or deactivated at will, for example reactivating input on one delay line to create a new loop while the other delays continue to read other looped sound fragments. You can also create different rhythmic relationships between the various loops by setting the delay times of each of their buffers with specifi-cally calculated durations.[1]

---

[1] It is also possible to play a loop in reverse – in other words, from the last sample in the buffer backwards to the first sample – but if we want to put this reversed sound into a loop, it is generally better to first write it into a table (or buffer) not located in a delay line, but rather recorded to memory and subsequently read from that table backwards in a loop. A simple reverse playback (without loop), on the other hand, can be created using a delay line (see section 6.9).

It is important not to forget that we also need to activate a cross-fade or envelope for each loop in order to eliminate sudden changes in amplitude values when we pass from the last sample of the buffer to the first, since these "jumps" in amplitude can produce unwanted clicks, as we have already learned in section 1.3.

. . . .

 INTERACTIVE EXAMPLE 6B.1 • *Single and Multiple Loops*

. . . .

6.4 FLANGER

"The flanging effect is created by summing up two instances of the same sound where one instance is passed through a cyclically varying delay line." (Bianchini, R., Cipriani, A., 2008, p.240).

The ***flanger***, like the *chorus*, which will be covered shortly, is a delay effect with a variable delay time.

The *flanger* was invented in the 1950's as an effect that could be obtained by recording a sound simultaneously on two reel-to-reel tape recorders, and subsequently synchronizing the playback of both recordings, mixing their outputs to a third recording. While playing back both recordings, the studio engineer would slow down one of the recorders at regular intervals by lightly pressing on the flange (the rotating support for the tape) with his finger, hence the term "flanging" meaning produced via the flange of the tape reel. The *flanger* effect can be reproduced digitally using a delay line whose output delay time is modulated slightly, using an LFO (see figure 6.9)

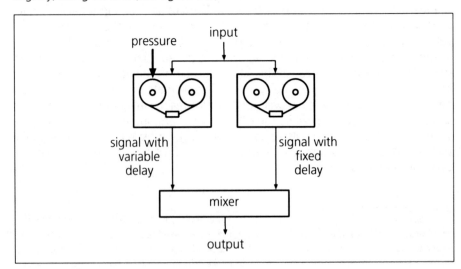

Fig. 6.9 Flanging

The result is the attenuation of several frequency bands due to:
- the use of a delay
- the subsequent mixing of the output of the delay with the input signal.

The distinctiveness of a *flanger*, compared to using a normal delay, is in the use of a constantly changing delay time within a restricted range – between 1 and 10 milliseconds. Using such a small delay time does not produce a delay effect (it is impossible to perceive it as an actual delay when the time between the original sound and repetition is so small), but rather creates a filtering effect due to mixing the delayed sound with the input sound. The frequency components of the delayed sound will have a slightly different phase with respect to those of the original sound as a result of the small delay, and because of this phase difference, mixing the two sounds will create zones of attenuation in the spectrum called *notches*. Additionally, this filtering is dynamic because of the continuous oscillation of the delay time values. Usually the oscillation, between a given minimum and maximum value, is accomplished by using an LFO with a sinusoidal waveform. By mixing the input signal with this dynamically delayed signal, we can obtain different effects, including the attenuation of some parts of the spectrum. When the delay time is increasing, the center frequencies of the attenuated bands glide downward in pitch and when the delay time is decreasing, the center frequencies of each notch glide upward. In section 6.9 we will look at this process in more detail. In a *flanger*, the frequency zones that are attenuated or eliminated have a distinctive trait in that they are all equally spaced, and the spacing of the notches is expanded and contracted in an oscillating manner. Expansion happens as the delay time gets smaller, and contraction happens as it gets larger (see figure 6.10).

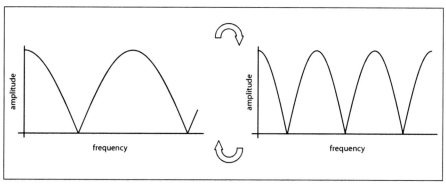

Fig. 6.10 Expansion and contraction of notches in the flanger.

Now let's try to understand how this particular filtering effect is produced. Imagine we have a 5 millisecond delay; in this case, any sound component at 100 Hz would be eliminated because the period of this sound component would be 10 milliseconds.

Therefore a sound delayed by 5 milliseconds would have the opposite phase at this frequency with respect to the original sound (see figure 6.11).

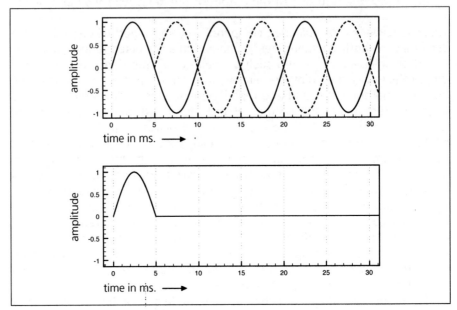

Fig. 6.11 Eliminating components of a sound at 100 Hz.

This component is not the only one to be filtered. A sinusoid at 300 Hz would also be filtered, because the delayed copy would also have the opposite phase of the original signal at this frequency (see figure 6.12).

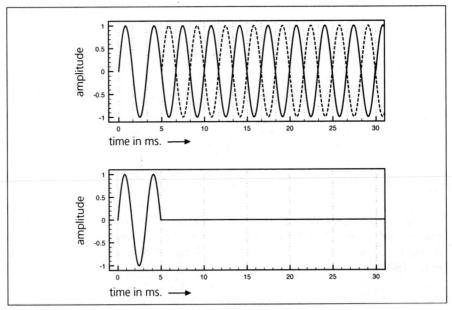

Fig. 6.12 Eliminating components of a sound at 300 Hz.

The same would happen for components at 500 Hz, 700 Hz, 900 Hz, etc. In other words, all odd harmonics of the fundamental frequency 100 Hz would have the opposite phase of the original non-delayed signal. Since the period corresponding to 100 Hz is 10 milliseconds, or half the delay time (5 milliseconds), we can say that the *flanger eliminates all frequencies corresponding to odd harmonics of a fundamental whose period is double that of a given delay time.*

Even harmonics (200 Hz, 400 Hz, 600 Hz, etc.), on the other hand, have the same phase in both the original and delayed signals; they are therefore reinforced. It should be pointed out that the even harmonics of the fundamental frequency 100 Hz are the same as all the harmonics (odd and even) for a fundamental frequency of 200 Hz. The period corresponding to 200 Hz is 5 milliseconds, which corresponds exactly to the delay time we have chosen. Therefore, we can say that the *flanger reinforces frequencies corresponding to all harmonics of a fundamental whose period is equal to that of a given delay time.*

To summarize: given a delay of **d** seconds, a flanger reinforces harmonics of the fundamental 1/r Hz and eliminates odd harmonics of the fundamental 1/(2 · r) Hz.

Note that the flanger is most effective when it is used with full spectrum signals – in other words signals that contain a lot of components to both reinforce and eliminate.

In table 6.A we can see some examples of components that are eliminated and reinforced with different delay settings.

r (delay)	Fundamental at 1/(2·r)	Components eliminated	Fundamentale at 1/r	Components reinforced
10 ms	50 Hz	50 hz, 150 Hz, 250 Hz, 350 Hz...	100 Hz	100 Hz, 200 Hz, 300 Hz, 400 Hz...
5 ms	100 Hz	100 Hz, 300 Hz, 500 Hz, 700 Hz	200 Hz	200 Hz, 400 Hz, 600 Hz, 800 Hz...
2 ms	250 Hz	250 Hz, 750 Hz, 1250 Hz, 1750 Hz...	500 Hz	500 Hz, 1000 Hz, 1500 Hz, 2000 Hz...

Table A

Until now we have been using the input signal (i.e., the dry signal, without processing) and the delayed sound with an oscillating delay time (i.e., the wet signal which has been processed). However, often flanger implementations use a fixed delay on the input sound so that the wet sound is not always delayed with respect to the dry sound, but sometimes comes before it, when the delay time of the wet sound is less than that of the fixed delay applied to the dry sound.

Figure 6.13 shows an algorithm for the flanger.

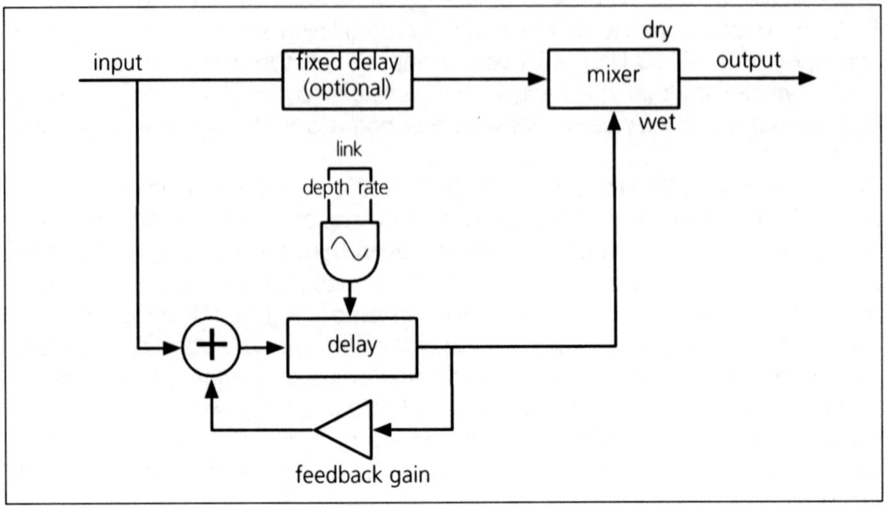

Fig. 6.13 Block diagram for the flanger

• •

INTERACTIVE EXAMPLE 6C.1 • *Flanger Examples*

• •

THE PARAMETERS OF THE FLANGER

As Rocchesso states, "the terminology used for audio effects is not consistent, as terms such as *flanger*, *chorus*, and *phaser* are often associated with a large variety of effects that can be quite different from each other."[2] We are therefore obliged, in the explanations of the parameters for these effects, to find a happy medium between the most commonly used terms (like depth, width, etc.) and the scientific terms used in signal processing (amplitude, frequency, etc.), trying to connect the meanings of both.

DEPTH
In the flanger, it can be useful to be able to determine the amount of filtered sound to mix with the original. Therefore, we can add a parameter that controls the balance between the wet and dry sound, which in flanger applications is called *depth*. The greater the depth (in percentage) the greater will be the attenuation of the frequency bands concerned (100%). In practice, this parameter functions as a multiplier for the amplitude of the filtered sound and the original sound, and is used to control the mix, or *balance* of wet and dry (see figure 6.13).

---
[2] (Rocchesso 2003)

INTERACTIVE EXAMPLE 6C.2 • *Examples of a flanger with variations in depth*

• •

DELAY

This extremely ambiguous and misleading term is used in commercial flanger applications to refer to the minimum delay time to which a certain value (known as *width*) can be added to obtain the maximum delay time. The minimum delay corresponds to the maximum frequency of the first band that will be reinforced, whereas the maximum frequency of the first band to be attenuated has a period corresponding to double this minimum delay (see table 6.A).

• •

INTERACTIVE EXAMPLE 6C.3 • *Examples of a flanger with variations in minimum delay time*

• •

WIDTH

The range of variation in delay time within a flanger is controlled with the width parameter, which therefore represents the amplitude of the LFO used to control this variation. This amplitude, added to the minimum delay, determines the maximum delay which itself corresponds to the minimum frequency of the first reinforced component. Sometimes this parameter is confusingly called *depth* or *sweep depth*. As we have already mentioned, the terminology used for these effects is sometimes conflicting due to their spread in the commercial marketplace. As far as we are concerned, it is important to understand how each parameter functions in order to be able to construct the algorithm clearly. The delay time oscillates between a minimum value determined by the *delay* parameter (discussed above) and a maximum value obtained by adding the *delay* and *width* values (see figure 6.14).

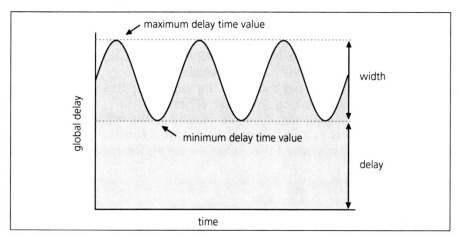

Fig. 6.14 Delay and width in the flanger

205

INTERACTIVE EXAMPLE 6C.4 • *Examples of a flanger with variations in width*

• •

LFO WAVEFORM

You can use a different waveform to control the variations of the flanger (some-times a triangle wave is used because of its linearity), although it can often be preferable to use a sine wave. When using a triangle wave as an LFO, the fil-tered frequencies are diverted to just two fixed values, whereas with a sinusoid, the frequency glides smoothly between a minimum and maximum frequency. This glissando happens when there is an acceleration or deceleration in the variations of the delay. With a sine wave, the increment or decrement of the delay time is variable because the waveform follows a curve, and therefore cre-ates a glissando. With a triangle wave the increment or decrement of the delay time is constant, because the waveform follows a straight line and therefore does not cause a glissando, but rather a sudden pitch shift between a minimum and maximum transposition.[3] You can always experiment with other types of waveforms used as an LFO.

• •

INTERACTIVE EXAMPLE 6C.5 • *Examples of a flanger with variations in the LFO waveform*

• •

FEEDBACK
Feedback, as we already know, consists of adding an output signal back into the input (see figure 6.13). The multiplier used for feedback affects the amplitude of every sound that is re-injected into the feedback loop. For example, if we have a sound with amplitude x and a feedback multiplier of 0.5, each time the sound re-enters the input its amplitude will be halved. The first time it feeds back, its amplitude will be x/2, the second time x/4, the third x/8 and so on.[4]
The multiplier must always be less than one so the amplitude cannot increase with each pass through the feedback loop, otherwise it would result in an unstable system, because the amplitude values would eventually exceed the dynamic range defined by the number of bits used for each sample.
Since we can therefore only use multiplier values less than 1, more and more duplicates of the original sound will be created as the multiplication factor gets closer and closer to 1. A flanger can also have a negative feedback value (thereby subtracting the output signal from the input). This naturally inverts the

---

[3] To learn more about this, see section 6.9.

[4] As we have seen for the echo effect, feedback can also be expressed as a percentage instead of a multiplication factor. In this case, 50% would correspond to a multiplication factor of 0.5, 99% would correspond to 0.99, etc.

distribution of notches and peaks (i.e., reinforcements) in the spectrum, because the phase of the signal that re-enters the feedback loop becomes inverted. The resulting phenomenon is perceived as a lowering of the effect by an octave.

• •

INTERACTIVE EXAMPLE 6C.6 • *Examples of a flanger with variations in*
feedback

• •

SPEED (or RATE)
The speed or rate is the LFO frequency that controls the speed of one cycle of variation in the effect, or more precisely the number of times that the LFO oscillates between the minimum and maximum delay times in one second.

LINK
In order to introduce the concept of *link*, we first need to take into consideration the effects produced by modulating the delay time parameter. If we liken the digital delay in a flanger to the analog delay that can be created using tape (see the earlier section on *tape delay*), we would notice that the playback head would be displaced backward and forward based on the frequency and amplitude of the LFO. In this scenario, the relative velocity of the tape with respect to the position of the playback head would change and result in a change in pitch of the sound being played.[5] This pitch deviation is directly proportional to both the frequency *and* amplitude of the LFO. Therefore, we can increase this pitch deviation either by increasing the frequency and keeping the amplitude constant, or by increasing the amplitude and keeping the frequency constant. If we wanted to vary the frequency of the LFO without modifying the resulting changes in pitch, we would need to make sure that the changes in the frequency and amplitude of the LFO were inversely proportional to one another. In other words if we increased the frequency, the amplitude would decrease proportionally (i.e., if the frequency were doubled, the amplitude would be halved, and so forth). In order to achieve this result, flangers generally have a built-in function that allows these two parameters to always be inversely proportional to one another in order to maintain a constant pitch deviation for the delayed sound, even when increasing its frequency. In this scenario, the frequency of the LFO would also be gradually increased, so its oscillation would be faster, but its pitch deviation would remain constant. Therefore, frequency can be used as a division factor for the amplitude (which therefore ceases to be an absolute amplitude, becoming rather a parameter of "pitch deviation"). With this configuration there are no longer individual user-definable amplitude and frequency values for the LFO, but a pitch deviation parameter whose value depends on the ratio between the frequency and the amplitude of the LFO. In commercial applications there is usually a switch called *link* which can be used to activate and deactivate this operation.

---

[5] For more details see section 6.9.

INTERACTIVE EXAMPLE 6C.7 • *Examples of a flanger with variations in rate and pitch deviation*

. . . .

6.5 CHORUS

"The ***chorus*** is an effect that simulates the presence of many sources that produce more or less the same sound, based on a single sound source: the same difference that there is between a solo voice and a chorus in unison. This effect is created by the superimposition of several copies of a single sound with variable offsets" (Bianchini, R., Cipriani, A., 2003, p.279). The variations in amplitude, frequency and attack time of a group of voices create a particular richness in timbre. A chorus effect can nevertheless be applied to any sound, and is particularly effective with harmonic sounds. To obtain these small differences between one voice and another, a single sound is delayed using a delay line with a variable delay time. The variations in delay time create a slight detuning effect between the input signal and the delayed signal (for a detailed explanation see section 6.9), which are mixed together (figure 6.15).

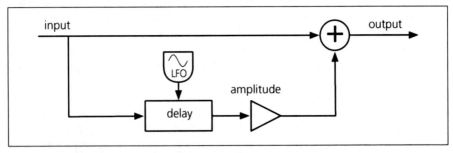

Fig. 6.15 Block diagram for the chorus effect

. . . .

INTERACTIVE EXAMPLE 6D.1 • Examples of *chorus*

. . . .

The delay time in a chorus is greater than that used for a flanger (typical delay values are between 20 and 30 milliseconds). Always remember that some algorithms may have controls that let you set the parameters to the lowest possible values, and therefore reach an effect close to that of the flanger. It is precisely these cases that help us understand that the names used for these effects do not refer to the algorithm as much as they do the effect itself, or better yet, to the way that the effect functions or is used. Where effect design and programming are concerned, the boundaries between these effects are blurred, so it is possible to create seamless transitions from one effect to another simply by varying the parameters of one single algorithm.

Variations in the delay time could be controlled with an LFO (with a frequency of 3 Hz, for example). The waveform of the LFO could be periodic (such as a sine wave), but oftentimes more natural results can be obtained with a pseudo-random waveform or by using another LFO to modify the amplitude and frequency variations of the first LFO over time.

By altering the amplitude, frequency or waveform of the LFO, you can change the amplitude and frequency of the variations in the chorus so that they continually evolve over time.

You can also build a stereo chorus, made up of two mono choruses whose LFOs have different phases.

THE PARAMETERS OF THE CHORUS

DELAY
The delay parameter indicates the minimum delay time to which a variation can be added. This is specified by the amplitude of the LFO (or width).[6]

WIDTH (or SWEEP DEPTH)
This term is often found in plug-ins that simulate this effect, or in hardware expanders. As with the flanger, it simply means the amplitude of the LFO, which expresses how much the delay time will vary over time. The delay time therefore oscillates between a minimum value determined by the delay parameter (above) and a maximum value determined by the sum of the minimum delay and the width (figure 6.14). This variation in delay time affects the frequency of the delayed sound.

• •

INTERACTIVE EXAMPLE 6D.2 • *Examples of chorus with variations in depth*

• •

LFO WAVEFORM
The type of waveform used for the LFO, as previously explained, determines how it will cause the delay time to change over time (for example using a sine or triangle waveform, etc.). Since the frequency of the wet sound depends on the variation in the delay time, the waveform of the LFO determines how the frequency will be varied over time. For example, using a triangle wave causes a constant variation in delay time (both increasing and decreasing), so the detuning of the sound will alternate between two constant values. When using a sine wave, on the other hand, the variations in the delay time are not constant over

---

[6] In some implementations delay can mean the maximum delay time, from which the amplitude of the LFO is subtracted.

time (because they follow the constantly-changing curve of the sine wave), so the detuning therefore continually rises and falls, creating a glissando effect that can be apparent to a greater or lesser extent. As we have already stated, it is also possible to use a pseudo-random generator as a LFO in order to create non-repetitive glissandi.[7]

. . . .

INTERACTIVE EXAMPLE 6D.3 • *Examples of chorus with variations in the LFO waveform*

. . . .

SPEED (or RATE)
This parameter refers to the LFO frequency, which indicates how many times a single cycle of variation in the delay time will happen per second.

. . . .

INTERACTIVE EXAMPLE 6D.4 • *Examples of chorus with variations in rate*

. . . .

NUMBER OF VOICES
A chorus effect can obviously use several copies of the sound, instead of just one. The number of voices refers to the number of copies of the delayed signal, each controlled by a different LFO (resulting in a more natural effect), or using a single LFO with different phases to create different delay times simultaneously.

6.6 COMB FILTERS

The **comb filter** is nothing more than a delay added to the input signal, completely identical to the other kinds of delays have been using up to now. It is precisely this type of filter that can be used to create *echo, flanger* and *chorus* effects like those we have just described. There are many different types of comb filters such as FIR comb filters, which consist of a delay without feedback (using only feedforward, as shown in figure 6.16), and IIR comb filters[8] which are made up of delay with feedback (figure 6.17). There are also more complex configurations of comb filters that feedback and feedforward together, an example of which will be shown in the practice part of this chapter.

---

[7] Be aware that if you use a square wave as an LFO, the variations in delay will alternate between two values; since there any no intermediate values, there will be no detuning effect at all.
[8] For more about FIR and IIR filters refer to section 3.4.

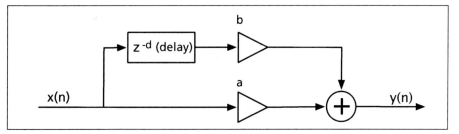

Fig. 6.16 Block diagram for a FIR comb filter with feedforward

As we can see in the IIR comb filter shown in figure 6.17, before feeding the delayed signal back to the input, it is multiplied by a factor (indicated by the letter c) which changes its amplitude.

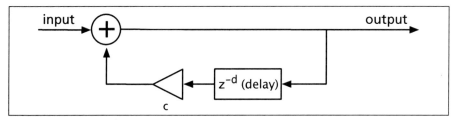

Fig. 6.17 Block diagram for an IIR comb filter with feedback

In figure 6.18 we can see a block diagram of a FIR comb filter that uses both feedforward and feedback. In this diagram, letter *a* represents the gain, letter *b* represents the feedforward multiplier, letter *c* represents the feedback multiplier and *d* represents the delay time expressed in samples. The input sample is labeled *x(n)* and the output sample is labeled *y(n)*. Notice that whereas for filters (see the theory part of section 3.6) we had used the symbol x(n-1) to indicate the previous input sample, here we are using filtering via delays, so the symbol x(n-d) is used instead, referring to the input sample minus d samples. Similarly, for filters we had used the symbol z^{-1} to indicate a one sample delay, while here we see the symbol z^{-d}, that is to say a delay of d samples.

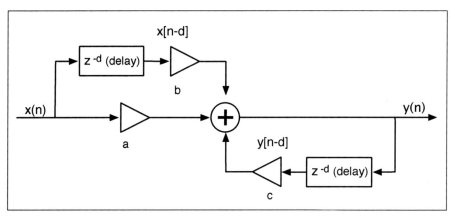

Fig. 6.18 Block diagram for an IIR comb filter with both feedforward and feedback

The comb filter gets its name from the characteristic form of its output spectrum, whose frequencies are reinforced at equidistant intervals, thereby creating a contour resembling the teeth on a comb. This phenomenon is audible when the delay time is very short – generally less than 10 milliseconds – because of the phase cancellation created by adding a slightly delayed signal (and the additional delays produced via feedback) to the input signal.

As the delay time is increased above the 10 millisecond region, individual delays with decreasing amplitude (caused by feedback) begin to be audibly distinguishable.[9] The time it takes for the amplitudes to be attenuated by 60 dB with respect to the input sound is called the *decay time*. In figure 6.19 we can see the impulse response of the comb filter shown in figure 6.17.

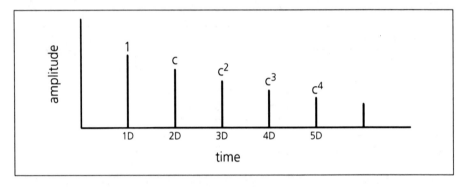

Fig. 6.19 Impulse response of an IIR comb filter

The comb filter can therefore be used to create echoes, but is mainly used to produce complex harmonic resonances, in addition to being used in conjunction with allpass filters to create reverberation, as we will discover in the third volume.

At this point you may be asking what the difference is, exactly, between an IIR comb filter and the flanger with feedback that we covered in section 6.4. Actually, there is no difference whatsoever! As we already mentioned, the terminology used in commercial effects (where the term *flanger* was coined) can often be somewhat vague or imprecise – an effect algorithm may be given different names depending on how it will be put to use (but a term like "IIR comb filter" clearly belongs to the realm of scientific terminology).

The decision to use one term or another depends on how the algorithm will be used and what parameters are given to it. If the delay time is between 1 and 10 milliseconds with a sinusoidal LFO modulating it, and it is added to the original signal on output, we no doubt have a flanger on our hands. The term comb filter would be more appropriate to use in other situations, such as in the construction of reverberation algorithms, where several delay lines are used in parallel, each with its own fixed delay time, typically above 10 milliseconds.

---

[9] This happens because the delay time exceeds the Haas zone. See section 6.2.

One of the most common applications of the comb filter is using it to build tuned resonators. To give an example, putting an impulse into a comb filter with a delay of 1 millisecond will create a resonance at 1000 Hz followed by a series of resonances with a harmonic relationship to this fundamental, resulting precisely in the comb-shaped spectrum typical of this filter. Naturally, it is important to input a sound with a complex spectrum, so that there is ample energy at the resonant frequencies we want to excite. The resonances can be prolonged by introducing feedback, as we will see in the practical section dedicated to comb filters.

· ·

INTERACTIVE EXAMPLE 6E.1 • *Different comb filter effects*

· ·

PARAMETERS OF THE COMB FILTER

DELAY TIME
In an IIR comb filter, the delay time is the amount of time it takes for a signal to make a complete cycle through the feedback loop (from input to output to input again). As a result it is often called *loop time*. The inverse of this value corresponds to the resonant frequency of the filter (also called the natural frequency of the comb). For example, if the loop time is 1 millisecond, the natural frequency would be 1000 Hz (1/0.001 = 1000); if the loop time is 20 milliseconds, the natural frequency would be 50 Hz (1/0.02 = 50), etc.

Remember that in addition to the fundamental frequency, the filter's output will also include other harmonics whose frequencies are multiples of this fundamental.

· ·

INTERACTIVE EXAMPLE 6E.2 • *Different comb filter effects with variations*
in loop time

· ·

FEEDBACK
As with the flanger, the multiplier affects the amplitude of every sound that is re-injected into the feedback loop. As we have already seen in figure 6.17, the amplitude of the delayed copies of the sound is dependent on this multiplier.

Given that only values less than 1 can be used as a multiplier, the closer the multiplier gets to 1, the more it will create additional copies of the delayed sound, and thus the longer the decay of the filtered sound, at the same natural frequency. Obviously, if the natural frequency of the comb is lower, the decay time will be longer, given the longer duration of its delay time, compared to higher frequencies.

· ·

🖱 **INTERACTIVE EXAMPLE 6E.3 • *Different comb filter effects with variations of the feedback multiplier***

· ·

IMPLEMENTATION

The classic comb filter structure is slightly different from the echo effect as described in section 6.2. With the echo effect, additional read pointers can be inserted alongside the main write and read pointers, as is the case for a multitap delay. However, the classic comb filter does not include any additions to the algorithm described above. Naturally, any system can be modified, but the quintessential feedback comb filter is composed of one delay line and one feedback loop. Dodge and Jerse (1997) suggest a formula that can be used to generate a multiplier in order to obtain a specific decay time that defines when the signal has been attenuated by 60 dB. Given a multiplier g and a delay time (or loop time) D, a decay time T, the formula is defined as follows: $g = 0.001^{D/T}$. For example, if we have a loop time equal to 50 milliseconds and we want to have a decay time of 2 seconds, we would have $0.001^{0.05/2}$, which is equal to $0.001^{0.025}$, or 0.841395, which is exactly the feedback multiplier to use.

· ·

🖱 **INTERACTIVE EXAMPLE 6E.4 • *Different comb filter effects with variations of decay time***

· ·

6.7 ALLPASS FILTERS

Allpass filters allow all frequencies in a delayed signal to pass through unchanged in amplitude, although with a modification of their phase. The name allpass already explains its behavior: just as a lowpass filter lets frequencies below the cutoff frequency pass through the filter unchanged, attenuating those above the cutoff, the allpass filter results in an unchanged amplitude response for all frequencies (all frequencies pass through it), even though the phases are modified, depending on the frequency. [10]

---

[10] According to Roads (1996) the allpass filter can actually have an effect when the signal has a sharp or sudden attack or decay, causing a perceptible coloration depending on the phase difference. An allpass filter is therefore only perfectly "transparent" in the case of sustained sounds.

Among the various types of possible allpass filters, there are two that interest us most, due to their filtering properties: allpass filters based on the Schroeder model, and second-order allpass filters.

SCHROEDER ALLPASS MODEL

The **Schroeder allpass filter** exists in several different versions, and has been very frequently used in commercial reverb units. The simplest model can be built by adding a feedforward FIR comb filter component to a IIR comb filter that uses feedback[11] (figure 6.20). For this type of allpass filter it is imperative that the gain of the direct signal (-g in the upper part of figure 6.20) is the negative of the feedback gain (g, in the lower part of the diagram).

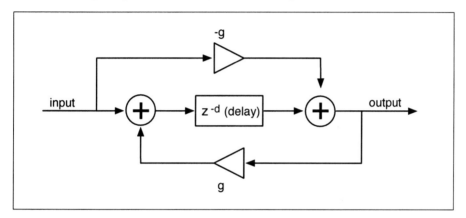

Fig. 6.20 Block diagram for a Schroeder allpass filter (with one delay)

This type of filter is also defined as a universal comb filter.[12]

The gain coefficient (-g) creates phase cancellation so that the comb-shaped effect on the amplitude spectrum (determined by the IIR comb) is eliminated without removing the effect of the delay, itself.

Roads (1996) states that when the delay time is large (more than 5 milliseconds), this allpass model can be used to obtain a series of delays with exponentially decreasing amplitude similar to comb filters with long delay times.

---

[11] For the definition of feedforward see the glossary at the end of this chapter.
[12] A. Uncini, (2006). P. Dutilleux, U. Zolzer, (2002).

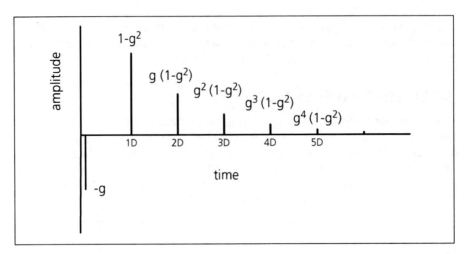

Fig. 6.21 Impulse response of an allpass filter

Figure 6.21 shows the impulse response of the allpass filter from figure 6.20, using a delay time equal to D. Here, we can see that the output amplitude of the impulse at time 0 is equal to -g. The impulse is also scaled by g when it is sent back in the feedback loop. At this point its amplitude is:

-g · g = -g2

This feedback signal is summed to the direct signal (not scaled, in other words multiplied by 1) before entering into the delay line.

The amplitude of the impulse is now:
1+ (-g2), or
1-g2

This signal is delayed and sent to the output at time D.
The subsequent copies of the sound (in this case the impulse) are always multiplied by g before being sent back in the feedback loop, so consequently we always have decreasing amplitudes. At time 2D the amplitude of the impulse will be $g \cdot (1-g^2)$, at time 3D it will be $g^2 \cdot (1-g^2)$, etc. [13]

We can use allpass filters of this type (i.e., with a freely variable delay time) to construct reverbs, as we will see in more detail in the third volume.

---

[13] Since g is less than 1 (as it always is with feedback multipliers), as the exponent increases, the value decreases.

An alternative to this model is shown in figure 6.22.

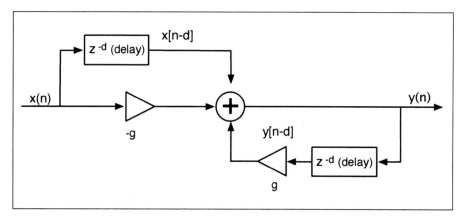

Fig. 6.22 Block diagram for a Schroeder allpass filter (with two delays)

In this configuration, the algorithm uses two delay lines and only one addition (whereas the configuration shown in figure 6.20 has one delay and two additions). The additional delay (on the right in the figure) is the feedback delay line with the g coefficient; the delay on the left implements feedforward that is not scaled.

Let's take a closer look at the signal flow:

- The direct signal (in the central part of the figure) is first inverted in sign (because of the multiplication by -g) and sent to the output.
- Next, the signal delayed by the feedforward delay line (on the upper left) is added to the signal coming from the feedback (which has already been multiplied by the g coefficient).
- Finally, the sum of these two signals is put into the feedback loop, where it is continually scaled by the g coefficient with each pass.

The impulse response of this allpass filter, therefore yields the same results as the one which was described previously.

• •

INTERACTIVE EXAMPLE 6F.1 • *Different effects using the Schroeder allpass filter*

• •

SECOND-ORDER ALLPASS FILTERS

Second-order allpass filters are also IIR filters, but the difference between them and Schroeder allpass filters is that they do not have a variable delay time, but rather take into consideration just the two previous samples[14]. When the delay time is this short, the allpass appears to have no discernible effect on the output, neither in delay nor (obviously) in the modification of the amplitude spectrum however it does still alter the phase spectrum, as explained earlier.[15]

If we add the output signal of the allpass filter to the original signal, we get a clear filtering effect. This happens because one of the frequencies in the output signal of the allpass will have the opposite phase with respect to the original signal, due to the phase modification inherent in this filter, and will thus be cancelled.[16] Frequencies adjacent to this phase-cancelled frequency become progressively more attenuated as they approach it.

If we look at the way any given allpass filter modifies the phases of its input sound, we see that the phases in the output sound gradually vary as they go from low frequency to high, until they reach a point where the phase is completely inverted with respect to that of the input spectrum. This point is called the **turnover frequency**. It is around this point where the phase has been most altered by the filter.

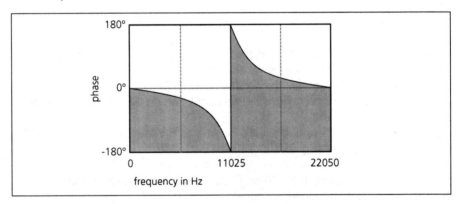

Fig. 6.23 Phase response of a second-order allpass filter

---

[14] This type of filter is actually similar to other types of second-order filters (lowpass, highpass, etc.), and uses the same equation that we saw in section 3.6, although with a different set of coefficients.
[15] At this point we should emphasize the fact that the phase modification of a given frequency is simply a delay to that frequency. Indeed, every filter introduces some kind of temporal delay to the signal (see also section 3.6).
[16] Logically, we should have inserted this section into the chapter on filters, but we prefer to discuss it here because a second-order allpass filter is the basis for the phaser effect, which belongs together with the other effects we are covering in this chapter.

Figure 6.23 shows the phase response of a second-order allpass filter. The x-axis represents the frequencies from 0 to the Nyquist (i.e., 22050 Hz assuming a sampling rate of 44100 Hz), whereas the y-axis represents change in phase. At the center of the y-axis there is deviation of 0° (in other words, phase is unchanged with respect to the input); above this line we have a positive phase deviation (up to 180°), and below it we have a negative deviation (up to -180°). As we can see in the figure, the phases of frequencies near 0 Hz are not altered, but as you go up in frequency little by little, the phase progressively deviates more and more from the center toward the negative part of the graph. At the frequency corresponding to the turnover frequency[17], the phase switches from -180° to 180° and gradually returns to 0°. In a 360° rotation the angles -180° and 180° actually coincide, therefore the allpass filter performs a complete phase rotation from 0 Hz to the Nyquist. The filter's frequency response, on the other hand, is obviously flat, since, by definition it is an allpass filter. If we mix the original sound with the delayed sound, we notice a progressive attenuation of the frequencies from low up to the turnover frequency, at which point there is complete phase cancellation.

As can be seen in figure 6.24, the implementation of a second-order allpass filter is the same as that of the biquadric filters which have already been described in section 3.6. The only difference is the relationship of the five filter coefficients used.

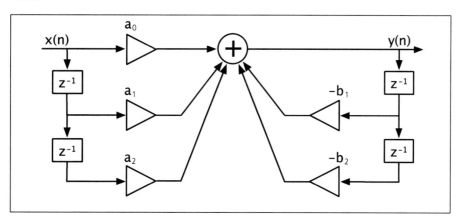

Fig. 6.24 Block diagram showing an implementation of a second-order allpass filter

The effect of this filter, as we have already said, is different from that of the other biquadratic filters in that it does not have a subtractive function per se (as do the lowpass, highpass, bandpass, etc.), but is only used to alter the phase. Nonetheless, a subtractive function can come into play if you add the allpass filter's output sound to the original sound.

---

[17] In the example illustrated, the turnover frequency corresponds to half the nyquist frequency, but naturally any frequency can be set as the turnover frequency.

In the second-order allpass filter you have control over the Q parameter, which in this case represents the slope of the curve defining the phase change.

We can see two examples of Q for a second-order allpass filter in figure 6.25 (a and b). Increasing Q (from 1 to 5) increases the slope of the curve defining the phase. As you can see, when the slope is greater the phase rotation (around the turnover frequency) happens over a smaller part of the spectrum; this means that when adding the output of the filter to the original signal a narrower frequency band will be attenuated.

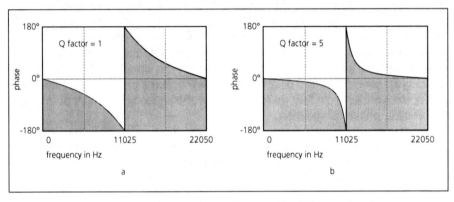

Fig. 6.25 Phase response of two allpass filters with different Q values

Due to its similarity to other second-order filters, we can understand that the turnover frequency of the allpass filter is analogous to both the cutoff frequency of lowpass or highpass filters, and the center frequency of bandpass and notch filters. By cascading several two-pole allpass filters (i.e., connecting them in series), and adding the final output to the original, unfiltered, signal, you can obtain interesting multi-band filtering patterns. Furthermore, modulating the frequency of the allpass filter with one or more LFOs creates the *phaser* effect, discussed in the next section.

6.8 THE PHASER

As with flangers, *phase shifting* or *phasing* produces attenuation of several frequency bands. Unlike flangers, this happens through:
- using one or more allpass filters (in place of a delay line)
- the subsequent mixing of the allpass filter's output signal with its input signal.

The **phaser** effect's main differences with respect to the flanger are the following:
- the frequency bands are not necessarily equidistant
- the flanger generally does not allow you to control the bandwidth of the notches, whereas this is possible with the phaser by using the Q parameter of the second-order allpass filter.

• •

INTERACTIVE EXAMPLE 6G.1 • *Different phaser effects*

• •

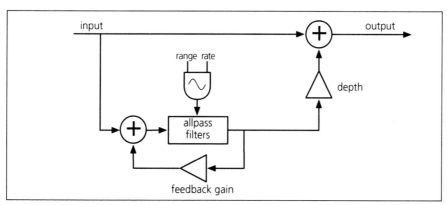

Fig. 6.26 Block diagram for the phase shifting

You can use second-order allpass filters to create a phase shifting algorithm (figure 6.26). These filters, as we have already seen, alter the phase of the frequencies around the user-definable turnover frequency. Remember that the phase of the frequencies is most modified near the *turnover frequency*: the phase at this point is inverted in relation to the phase of the input signal. (see figure 6.23).

As we mentioned in the preceding section, by mixing the original and phase-shifted signals, we can attenuate the frequencies that have a sizable difference in phase (or *phase lag*) with respect to the phase of the same frequency in the input sound. The central frequencies of these attenuated bands are not fixed, but can be varied over time in an oscillating manner using a LFO. What makes the phase shifter distinctive, compared to the flanger (as we also mentioned) is that its central frequencies are not necessarily equally-spaced but rather can be chosen arbitrarily. Since every notch in the spectrum is controlled by a different

221

allpass filter, you can control any number of attenuated bands, as well as their bandwidth, and center frequency.

To attenuate several bands, several allpass filters (one for each band) must be connected in cascade (in series). The phase deviation of the filters is consequently summed together, so when cascading two allpass filters, for example, the phase will make two complete rotations (figure 6.27). The graph in the figure is that of two cascaded allpass filters, both having a turnover frequency equal to 11025 Hz (half the Nyquist frequency considering a sampling rate of 44100 Hz). We can see that the attenuated bands are located a little before and a little after the central frequency (which now ends up being perfectly in phase) – this is due to the fact that the phase rotations of both filters are added together.

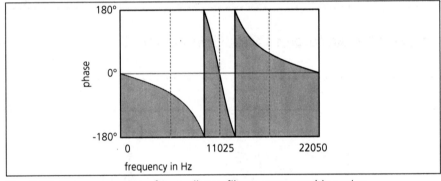

Fig. 6.27 Phase response of two allpass filters connected in series

In phasers, the number of allpass filters (or stages) determines the number of attenuated bands. A phaser with 16 allpass filters, for example, would create 16 notches in the spectrum. In commercial applications of the phaser the term stages is most often used. A phaser with 4 stages is a phaser with two allpass filters (two stages per filter), therefore an n-stage phaser will have n/2 attenuated bands.

By connecting three filters with the same parameters, we obtain this phase response (fig 6.28):

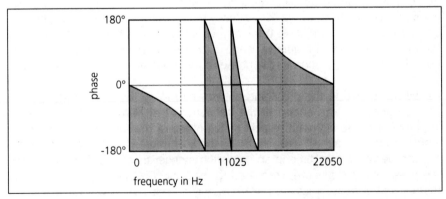

Fig. 6.28 Phase response of three allpass filters connected in series (example I)

Now we have three attenuated bands, the second of which is once again located at 11025 Hz. So, in practice, when using several allpass filters it is not easy to define the frequency that we want to eliminate, because the phase responses of all the filters mutually influence each other. For example, if we set the turnover frequency of one of the three allpass filters to 8000 Hz, the graph (figure 6.29) of the phase response becomes:

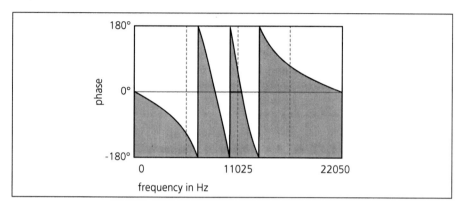

Fig. 6.29 Phase response of three allpass filters connected in series (example II)

As you can see, changing the turnover frequency of just one filter causes the displacement of all three bands.

THE PARAMETERS OF THE PHASER

DEPTH

In the phaser it can be useful to decide the amount of filtered sound to mix with the original. A parameter that controls the balance between wet and dry can therefore be inserted into the algorithm. This is generally called depth in phaser applications. The larger the depth parameter, the greater will be the attenuation of the specified frequency band. In practice, this parameter works as a multiplier for the amplitude of the filtered sound, and is used to control the mix, or balance (figure 6.30).

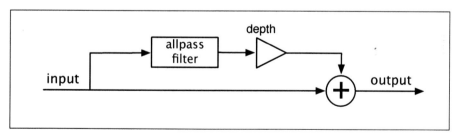

Fig. 6.30 Block diagram showing *depth* in the phaser

INTERACTIVE EXAMPLE 6G.2 • *Different phaser effects with variations in depth*

In the phaser it is useful to be able to decide the amount of filtered sound to mix with the original.

RANGE

Range is the amplitude of the LFO that controls the variations in the turnover frequency (in some software and hardware implementations this is confusingly referred to as *depth* or *sweep depth*, so be careful when you see these terms used).

INTERACTIVE EXAMPLE 6G.3 • *Different phaser effects with variations in range*

FEEDBACK

With the *phaser*, feedback simply amounts to adding the output of the allpass filter back into its input (figure 6.31). Like the *flanger*, the *phaser* can also have a negative feedback gain, in which case the feedback signal will be subtracted from the input (instead of being added to it).

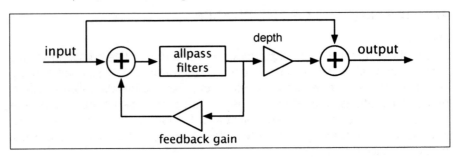

Fig. 6.31 Feedback gain in the phaser

INTERACTIVE EXAMPLE 6G.4 • *Different phaser effects with variations in feedback*

SPEED/RATE

This parameter is the speed with which the LFO makes one cycle of variation: in other words, how many times it oscillates between the minimum and maximum turnover frequency in one second.

Q FACTOR
The Q factor is used to widen or narrow the attenuation band. The smaller the Q value, the larger will be the resulting attenuation band, up until values near 0, which will eliminate the greater part of the signal.

6.9 PITCH SHIFTING, REVERSE AND VARIABLE DELAY

In this section we will learn how to realize **pitch shifting** – a variation in the frequency of a sound via the use of a delay. This allows us to modify the pitch of a signal in real-time, in order to create interesting effects such as a harmonizer, which takes a sound and superimposes the same sound modified in pitch in real-time without changing its duration. The harmonizer lets us create multiple pitches (double, triple, etc.) that can be tuned to user-defined intervals in order to play specific chords.

We have already seen that a delay line is created with a read pointer and a write pointer (see section 6.2), and we have made an analogy between this implementation and an analog tape recording system made up of a record head and a playback head positioned a certain distance from one another. In this scenario the playback head will play the recorded sound with a certain delay dependent on the playback speed of the tape and the distance between the two heads. When the position of the playback head on such an analog delay line is continuously varied (without sudden jumps) it creates a variation in frequency of the recorded sound – in other words a pitch shift – because the relative speed between the tape and the playback head is modified. For this situation there are several possible scenarios:

1) the playback head is stationary – the relative speed is therefore equal to the speed of the tape.
2) the playback head is moving in the opposite direction of the tape (getting closer to the record head) – in this case the relative speed can be given as the sum of the tape speed and the speed of the moving playback head (just like when two cars traveling in opposite directions pass each other while driving down the street), and therefore increases the sounds' frequency.
3) the playback head moves in the same direction as the tape (moving farther away from the record head), but moving slower than it – the two speeds are subtracted and the relative speed therefore decreases causing the sound's frequency to decrease.
4) the playback head moves faster than the tape (but still in the same direction) – this would be the same as if the tape were running in reverse (like when a car overtakes another, from that driver's point of view the other car seems to be receding backwards), and so the sound is played in reverse. In this case we can even control the frequency of the reverse playback. Remember that in general the reverse playback effect implies reading a sound from the last sample in the buffer (or sound file) to the first.
5) the playback head moves at the same speed and in the same direction as the tape – the resulting relative speed is zero (just like two cars driving next to each other at the same speed) and therefore there is no output sound (the frequency goes down to 0 Hertz).

INTERACTIVE EXAMPLE 6H.1 • *Examples of the 5 playback scenarios*

. . . .

In order to calculate the relative speed, we need to *subtract* the speed of the playback head from the speed of the tape. However, we also need to take into consideration that if the head travels in the same direction as the tape, its speed is positive and if it travels in the opposite direction its speed is negative. In the latter case, our subtraction will actually become an addition because subtracting a negative number amounts to adding that same number as a positive value. Lets take a look at some practical examples:

a) beginning with the last scenario (number 5), if the tape speed is v and the speed of the head is also v, we have v-v = 0.
b) if the speed of the head is v/2 (in the same direction as the tape), we have v-v/2 = v/2; in other words the frequency is halved.
c) if the speed of the head is equal to that of the tape, but traveling in the opposite direction, we could say that its speed is -v, so we therefore have v-(-v) = 2v; in other words the frequency is doubled. (This is consistent with the observation that we made above: the frequency increases when the tape and head are going in opposite directions and it decreases when going the same direction.)
d) for reverse playback, we have to move the head faster than the speed of the tape, in the same direction (as stated above), so if the speed of the head were 2v, we would have v - 2v = -v; in other words reverse playback without a change in pitch.

If we wanted to change the frequency of the sound using a precise ratio (2 = one octave higher, 1/2 = one octave lower, etc.) we would need to subtract this ratio from 1 and multiply the result as a multiplier by our speed, v, in order to obtain the speed of the tape head. Here are some examples:

a) if we wanted the pitch to be an octave higher (a ratio of 2) we would have 1 - 2 = -1, so the speed of the head would be -v (that is equal to the tape but in the opposite direction, as shown above).
b) to play the sound an octave lower (a ratio of 1/2) we would calculate 1 - 1/2 = 1/2, thus obtaining a speed of v/2 for the head (half the speed of the tape and in the same direction).
c) for reverse (a ratio of -1) we have 1 - (-1) = 2, or 2v.
d) for reverse an octave higher (a ratio of -2) we have 1 - (-2) = 3, or 3v.
e) if we wanted to raise the pitch a semitone (a ratio of 1.059463, i.e., the twelfth root of 2) we have 1 - 1.059463 = -0.059463 so the speed of the head would be -0.059463v (note that a negative speed value means the head is traveling in the opposite direction to the tape).
f) finally, if we do not want to change the pitch (a ratio of 1), we have 1 - 1 = 0, meaning the head is stationary.

INTERACTIVE EXAMPLE 6H.2 • *Different pitch shifting effects*

· ·

So, how do we translate all of this information into delay times we can use with our delay line? In practice, if the head moves at speed v it means that in one second the delay time is increased by one second, if it moves at a speed of 2v, it means that in one second the delay time is increased by 2 seconds, and if it moves at a speed of -v, the delay time is decremented by one second.

So, let's say we want to lower the pitch by 12 semitones for five seconds, in which case the head needs to move at a speed of v/2. The delay time will initially be set to 0 and will be gradually incremented until it becomes a delay of 5 seconds, 2.5 seconds later.

If we want to raise the pitch by 12 semitones for 5 seconds we need to move the head a speed of -v (i.e., in the opposite direction) and therefore we will begin with a delay of 5 seconds and gradually decrease the delay time to 0 over 5 seconds.

In summary:
- To raise the pitch you start at a given delay time and arrive at 0.
- To lower the pitch or reverse the sound, you start from 0 and arrive at a given delay time.
- The starting and ending delay times depend on the desired duration multiplied by the speed of the head. For example, to lower the pitch by 12 semitones (half speed) for 5 seconds, we need to start from 0 and increase to a delay of 2.5 seconds (5 · 1/2).

All of this works only if the speed of the head is constant (in other words it does not accelerate). In cases where the speed is variable, with accelerations and/or decelerations, we will obtain glissandi.

VARIABLE DELAY WITHOUT TRANSPOSITION

It is also possible to vary the speed of motion of the playback head, allowing it to accelerate and decelerate without causing any pitch transposition to the sound. This can be done by using one or more cross-fades between one delay and the next. Practically this means that instead of progressively varying the playback speed to change the playback location (resulting in glissandi), we will cross-fade the output of two (or more) delay lines with different delay times. This technique can be used to create a **variable delay without transposition**.

6.10 THE KARPLUS-STRONG ALGORITHM

In this section we will talk about a synthesis technique based on delay lines created by Alex Karplus and Kevin Strong. This technique (the **Karplus-Strong algorithm**) is used to simulate both plucked string (i.e., pizzicato) and percussive sounds.

"The basic idea, in 1983, was to begin with noise and recursively filter it until it becomes a sound with a very simple spectrum – nearly sinusoidal. Since Karplus and Strong were trying to perfect an algorithm that could be easily implemented in hardware (specifically on the microcomputers of the 1980s), they had to limit the maximum number of operations. They therefore thought up the idea of starting with a table filled with random values, and reading it cyclically, averaging the current and previous samples with each read cycle." (Bianchini, R., Cipriani, A., 2003, pp. 343-344)

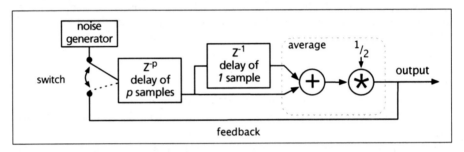

Fig. 6.32 Karplus-Strong algorithm

In practice, this table is a delay line that is repeatedly read (in a **circular buffer**) using a technique similar to the one we used to create loops, explained in section 6.3. When creating loops, the length of our delay line was in the range of one or more seconds, but for the Karplus-Strong algorithm, much shorter delay lines need to be used; the length corresponds to the period of the pitch we want to produce. The switch shown in figure 6.32 connects the table to the noise generator,[18] which is thereby used to fill a circular buffer (a delay line with feedback) with random values, but only when starting a new note. Once the table has been filled the switch turns off and the signal begins to circulate in the buffer.

"The repeated passage through the delay line causes it to create a periodic waveform, whose period is equal to the duration of the entire loop cycle. ... The length of the delay line determines the pitch, and a fractional delay line may be used in order to have precise control over it." (Uncini, 2006, p. 547)

If we disregard the idea of using a fractional delay for the moment, we can see that it is precisely because of the recursive nature of the algorithm that the

---

[18] For information on pseudo-random generators, see section 3.7.

input signal, made up of random values, immediately becomes a sound with a definite pitch, right from the sound's attack. The output sound of the algorithm, when simulating plucked strings, is bright and metallic during its attack, and then slowly loses energy in the high frequency range, eventually becoming quasi-sinusoidal. The frequency of the resulting sound naturally depends on the sampling rate, in addition to the length of the table.

· ·

INTERACTIVE EXAMPLE 6J.1 • *Simulating Plucked Strings with K&S*

· ·

As already mentioned, the table is initially filled with random values, after which the first value in the table is sent to two places: in addition to going to the output, it is also sent into a one-sample delay, after which it becomes summed with the subsequent sample. This way, each current sample gets added to the previous sample, and this sum is divided by two (see figure 6.32) in order to obtain an average of the two samples. The resulting average is re-written into the table, creating feedback in the main delay line. (i.e., not the one-sample delay). Once all the samples have been read, we return again to the start of the table where we now find the previously-stored averaged values, and continue the process of reading and averaging, as before. With this averaging process, the signal attenuates over time, first losing high harmonics and then vanishing altogether.

Looking at this process in more detail, one sample of sound can be calculated using the following formula:

$$y(n) = \frac{x(n) + x(n-1)}{2}$$

where x(n) is the current sample and x(n-1) is the previous sample. This operation creates an average, which is simply a first-order lowpass filter in audio terminology. Nevertheless, we should be aware that the sample y(n) which is calculated using this formula is rewritten into the delay line in order to be used as an input value during the next cycle through the values. There is one other aspect to this algorithm that we should be careful not to overlook: normally, a lowpass filter is applied to a "new" input signal, but in the case of the Karplus-Strong algorithm, the lowpass filter repeatedly processes the previously-filtered output signal. Once the table is filled with random values, the switch shown in figure 6.32 is closed, so no new values can enter the filter. Thus, the formula can now be written:

$$y(n) = \frac{x(n-p) + y(n-p-1)}{2}$$

In this case, **p** is defined as the length of the delay line in samples (therefore representing the period of the pitched note we will create), so this formula tells us that, in order to calculate the current output sample, we use the two adjacent samples that were calculated **p** samples previously. Note that in the right hand part of the formula we no longer use new **x** samples in the input, as we do in the previous formula, but instead exclusively use the **y** (output) samples which had been rewritten into the delay line. Let's demonstrate this with an example. In order to simplify the example, let's suppose that we have a table with only 16 values (obviously in reality we use more), and instead of using random values for this example (as we normally would do for this algorithm), let's take simple values in order to better help us follow how the algorithm works. The table (whose length is 16 samples, so therefore **p** is equal to 16) initially contains the following series of values:

```
0
0.25
0.5
0.75
1
0.75
0.5
0.25
0
-0.25
-0.5
-0.75
-1
-0.75
-0.5
-0.25
```

Applying this formula will give us:

(sample **x(n)**	+	sample **x(n**-1)	/2	=	output value
0	+	0)	/2	=	0
(0.25	+	0)	/2	=	0.125
(0.5	+	0.25)	/2	=	0.375
(0.75	+	0.5)	/2	=	0.625
(1	+	0.75)	/2	=	0.875
(0.75	+	1)	/2	=	0.875
(0.5	+	.75)	/2	=	0.625
(0.25	+	0.5)	/2	=	0.375
(0	+	0.25)	/2	=	0.125
(-0.25	+	0)	/2	=	-0.125
(-0.5	+	-0.25)	/2	=	-0.375
(-0.75	+	-0.5)	/2	=	-0.625
(-1	+	-0.75)	/2	=	-0.875
(-0.75	+	-1)	/2	=	-0.875
(-0.5	+	-0.75)	/2	=	-0.625
(-0.25	+	-0.5)	/2	=	-0.375

and from this point onward:

(sample $x(n-p)$	+	sample $y(n-p-1)$)	/2	=	output value
(0	+	-0.25)	/2	=	-0.125
(0.125	+	0)	/2	=	0.0625
(0.375	+	0.125)	/2	=	0.25
(0.625	+	0.375)	/2	=	0.5

The second group of values will therefore be:

0
0.125
0.375
0.625
0.875
0.875
0.625
0.375
0.125
-0.125
-0.375
-0.625
-0.875
-0.875
-0.625
-0.375

The table that follows hereafter shows a series of output amplitude values of different initial series (though for the sake of brevity we only show the first part). As the calculation progresses, you will notice that the absolute value of the output amplitudes continually decreases until it arrives at zero after a (theoretically) infinite number of cycles.[19]

0	1	2	3	2	1	0	-1	-2	-3	-2	-1
0	0,5	1,5	2,5	2,5	1,5	0,5	-0,5	-1,5	-2,5	-2,5	-1,5
-0,5	0,25	1	2	2,5	2	1	0	-1	-2	-2,5	-2
-1	-0,125	0,625	1,5	2,25	2,25	1,5	0,5	-0,5	-1,5	-2,25	-2,25
-1,5	-0,5625	0,25	1,0625	1,875	2,25	1,875	1	0	-1	-1,875	-2,25
-1,875	-1,0313	-0,1563	0,6563	1,4688	2,0625	2,0625	1,4375	0,5	-0,5	-1,4375	-2,0625
-2,0625	-1,4531	-0,5938	0,25	1,0625	1,7656	2,0625	1,75	0,9688	0,	-0,9688	-1,75
-2,0625	-1,7578	-1,0234	-0,1719	0,6563	1,4141	1,9141	1,9063	1,3594	0,4844	-0,4844	-1,3594
-1,9063	-1,9102	-1,3906	-0,5977	0,2422	1,0352	1,6641	1,9102	1,6328	0,9219	0	-0,9219
-1,6328	-1,9082	-1,6504	-0,9941	-0,1777	0,6387	1,3496	1,7871	1,7715	1,2773	0,4609	-0,4609

---

[19] In reality, the sound will never completely get to zero, and often it can actually create a DC offset that accumulates after many repetitions; a highpass filter with a low cutoff frequency can be used to eliminate it (see section 6.1).

-1,2773	-1,7705	-1,7793	-1,3223	-0,5859	0,2305	0,9941	1,5684	1,7793	1,5244	0,8691	0
-0,8691	-1,5239	-1,7749	-1,5508	-0,9541	-0,1777	0,6123	1,2813	1,6738	1,6519	1,1968	0,4346
-0,4346	-1,1965	-1,6494	-1,6628	-1,2524	-0,5659	0,2173	0,9468	1,4775	1,6628	1,4243	0,8157
0	-0,8156	-1,423	-1,6561	-1,4576	-0,9092	-0,1743	0,582	1,2122	1,5702	1,5436	1,12
0,4078	-0,4078	-1,1193	-1,5396	-1,5569	-1,1834	-0,5417	0,2039	0,8971	1,3912	1,5569	1,3318
0,7639	0	-0,7635	-1,3294	-1,5482	-1,3701	-0,8626	-0,1689	0,5505	1,1441	1,474	1,4443
1,0479	0,382	-0,3817	-1,0465	-1,4388	-1,4592	-1,1164	-0,5158	0,1908	0,8473	1,3091	1,4592
1,2461	0,7149	0,0001	-0,7141	-1,2426	-1,449	-1,2878	-0,8161	-0,1625	0,519	1,0782	1,3841
1,3526	0,9805	0,3575	-0,357	-0,9784	-1,3458	-1,3684	-1,0519	-0,4893	0,1783	0,7986	1,2312
1,3684	1,1666	0,669	0,0003	-0,6677	-1,1621	-1,3571	-1,2102	-0,7706	-0,1555	0,4884	1,0149

What we have been using is actually a first-order lowpass filter with a cutoff frequency equal to half the Nyquist frequency (see section 3.4). This filter outputs a mean value between the current and preceding samples, resulting in a 1/2-sample delay. In order to tune this sound precisely, we need to be able to use a delay capable of delaying the signal a fraction of a sample (in other words, a fractional delay), otherwise the available pitches would be determined by the number of samples in the table plus one half sample. Dodge and Jerse (1997) state that one way to create a fractional delay line is to insert an allpass filter into the system. As we have already seen, allpass filters can be used to change the phase of a sound. By using the phase offset generated by an allpass filter, we can create a delay line which is not necessarily a whole number multiple of the sampling period. In this case the fundamental of the output sound will be determined by the number of samples in the table, plus half a sample, plus a phase shift component provided by the allpass, that we can freely control. Some programming languages include a built-in option to set a fractional delay time – in other words, within the algorithm that manages the delay line, they already contain an allpass filter with a system that calculates the correct parameters which allow it to obtain a desired frequency.

The simulation of a plucked string with this algorithm is fairly realistic, and the calculation time is minimal. To achieve a more accurate effect, Roads (1996) recommends filling the table with different random values for each note, in order to give a slightly different timbre to each note event. Simulating the sound of an acoustic instrument often requires a lot of comparison and reasoning, before obtaining a realistic result. For example, let's take a look at the duration of the sound. In addition to the fundamental frequency, the decay time of sounds produced by the Karplus Strong algorithm is directly proportional to the length of the table. We can therefore deduce that high notes will have a shorter delay than low notes, which is also exactly how plucked strings behave. The difference between the decay of the high and low notes in our algorithm, however, is a little too pronounced. Jaffe and Smith (1983) have therefore proposed adding a damping factor to the decay in order to shorten the decay time when necessary. This technique consists of scaling the signal in the feedback loop, essentially by multiplying it by a number between 0 and 1. This way, with every cycle, the sound will become attenuated and as a result will decay more rapidly. Naturally, this technique should be applied only to notes on the lower end of the spectrum.

TESTING • QUESTIONS WITH SHORT ANSWERS (max. 30 words)

1) What is the perceptual difference between a sound delayed with a delay time greater than the Haas zone and a sound delayed with a delay time less than it? Is this perception also dependent on the sound's envelope?
2) What would happen to a delayed signal if the feedback gain of the delay were set to 98%? Why should we never use a feedback gain of 100%?
3) If we are writing to and reading from a circular buffer, and using a sampling rate of 48000 Hz, and we want to create a delay of 25 hundredths of a second, what is the distance, in samples, that we need to use between the write pointer and read pointer?
4) What are the main differences between a flanger and a phaser?
5) How do you create a loop using a delay line, technically speaking?
6) How do you create detuning between the dry and wet signals in a chorus effect? How do we control the amplitude and frequency of this detuning?
7) How can we control the parameters of a comb filter so that it passes from a comb filter into a delay effect?
8) What is the difference between a Schroeder allpass filter and a second-order allpass filter?
9) In a delay line used for pitch shifting, how do we calculate the relative speed between the "tape" and "playback head"?
10) In the Karplus-Strong algorithm why is it more effective to fill the table with different random values for each note?

. . . .

TESTING • LISTENING AND ANALYSIS ACTIVITIES

• Is the effect in sound example AA6.1 that of a flanger or chorus?
• Is the effect in sound example AA6.2 that of a flanger or a phaser?
• Is the effect in sound example AA6.3 that of a phaser or a chorus?
• Is the effect in sound example AA6.4 that of an echo or a loop?
• In sound example AA6.5, the value of which phaser parameter is being increased?
• In sound example AA6.6, is the effect of the comb filter that of equally-spaced notches or a delay?
• In sound example AA6.7, which parameter of the Karplus-Strong algorithm is being modified?
• In sound example AA6.8, which parameter of the Karplus-Strong algorithm is being modified?
• In sound example AA6.9, which parameter of the Karplus-Strong algorithm is being modified?

abc FUNDAMENTAL CONCEPTS

1) In order to simulate effects such as echo, flanger, chorus, loop, pitch shifting or reverse, we need an algorithm (more or less complex) that contains a delay which receives an audio signal at its input and duplicates it at its output after a certain pre-determined time known as the delay time. This delay time can be range from a few milliseconds to several seconds, or varied over time (i.e., modulated) via a low frequency oscillator (LFO). The delayed sound can be added to the original sound (or not), depending on the effect we intend to create. In most cases this delay is implemented via an IIR comb filter.

2) As Rocchesso (2003) states, "the terminology used for audio effects is not consistent, as terms such as *flanger*, *chorus*, and *phaser* are often associated with a large variety of effects that can be quite different from each other." When constructing algorithms, we therefore need to be aware of the parameters for each effect, and know how to relate the terms in common use (like depth, width, etc.) and the scientific terms used in signal processing.

3) To create a phase shifting algorithm you can use second-order allpass filters, composed of just two samples of delay. These filters have the ability to change the phase of the frequencies located around a user-definable turnover frequency. The central frequencies of the attenuated bands are not fixed, but vary over time via the use of an LFO. In the phaser, this oscillation is generally implemented non-linearly.

4) The Karplus-Strong synthesis technique is based on a system of delay lines. This technique can be used to simulate the sound of a plucked string (i.e., pizzicato). The algorithm is based on a generator, active only at the start of a note, which fills a circular buffer with a series of random values. Each time the table is read, the current and previous values are averaged (through the use of a one-sample delay). This intermediate value becomes the new value sent to the circular buffer.

GLOSSARY

Allpass Filter
A filter, based around a delay, which allows sounds to pass through unaltered in amplitude and frequency, but which alters their phase with respect to the input signal.

Balance
A parameter used to control the proportion of wet and dry sound. This is also the term used for the left/right channel ratio in a stereo system.

Chorus
An effect born out of the idea of imitating the voices of a chorus singing in unison, with relative variations in amplitude, frequency and attack time for each voice.

Circular buffer
A circular buffer is simply memory that, after having been completely filled with sample values using a write pointer, is rewritten again from the first memory location.

Comb Filter
A filter whose name is derived from its characteristic output spectrum, emphasizing certain frequencies at equally-spaced distances from one another.

Delay time
Given a sound A, the delay time is the time after which sound A takes place.

Dry
An audio signal that has not had any processing applied to it.

Echo
The echo effect is the repetition of a sound after a sufficient amount of time that it is perceived to be a separate sound from the original. If there are several copies of the sound, we obtain a multiple echo.

Feedback
The mechanism by which a delayed and scaled input signal is sent back to the input to be summed with the input signal.

Feedforward
The mechanism by which a signal and a delayed and scaled version of that signal are summed to create an output signal.

Flanger
A dynamic filtering effect built using a delay with a constantly-changing oscillating delay time.

Haas Zone
The time zone where the repetition of a sound begins to be perceived as fused with the original sound.

Loop
Cyclical repetitions of a single sound fragment.

Loop Time
The parameter of a filter with feedback that indicates the time it takes for a signal to make one complete cycle of the loop (from input to output and back to input).

Multiple Loops
Different simultaneous feedback loops that can be turned on or off at will. For example, turning-on the input to one loop thereby creating a

235

new loop, while other loops continue to repeat other sound fragments.

Multitap delay
A multi-delay effect which is created using several independent delays with user-definable amplitudes and delay times, arranged in parallel along a single delay line. The effect can also be created using several such independently-controllable delays arranged in series.

Phase lag
The difference in phase between two sounds, measured in degrees.

Phase shifting
An effect constructed with allpass filters that causes some frequency bands to be eliminated in a continually oscillating manner.

Ping-pong delay
A stereo delay based on the idea of "bouncing," where the sound alternates between the left and right channels.

Pitch shift
Variation in the playback frequency of a sound.

Read pointer
A pointer to the location in memory from where samples, previously written by a write pointer, will be read.

Reverse
Reading a sound from the last sample in the buffer (or file) to the first.

Slapback delay
A type of echo, generally without feedback and therefore with only one repetition, that creates a sense of doubling or rebounding of the original sound.

Turnover Frequency
In an allpass system this is the point along the frequency axis where the phase deviation is at its maximum offset of 180 degrees.

Wet
A processed audio signal.

Write pointer
A pointer to the location where input samples will be written to memory.

DISCOGRAPHY

(**Karplus-Strong**) **David A. Jaffe** "Silicon Valley Breakdown" in "Dinosaur Music" CD Wergo (WER 2016-50) 1982
(**flanger**) **The Beatles** "Tomorrow Never Knows" in Revolver Parlophone 1966
(**phase shifting**) **Jimi Hendrix** "Machine Gun" in Band of Gypsies Polidor 1960

• •

6P

DELAY LINES: ECHOES, LOOPING, FLANGER, CHORUS, COMB AND ALLPASS FILTERS, PHASER, PITCH SHIFTING, REVERSE, KARPLUS-STRONG ALGORITHM

PREREQUISITES FOR THIS CHAPTER
- THE CONTENTS OF VOLUME 1, AS WELL AS CHAPTER 5 (THEORY AND PRACTICE), INTERLUDE C AND 6T

OBJECTIVES
ABILITIES
- TO BE ABLE TO DISTINGUISH AND CONTROL DIFFERENT TYPES OF DELAY LINES
- TO KNOW HOW TO BUILD DELAY LINE EFFECTS SUCH AS ECHO, ECHO WITH FEEDBACK, TAPE DELAY SIMULATION, SLAPBACK DELAY, PING-PONG DELAY, MULTITAP DELAY, MULTIBAND-MULTITAP DELAY
- TO KNOW HOW TO BUILD AND CONTROL LOOPS USING DELAY LINES
- TO KNOW HOW TO BUILD FLANGER AND CHORUS ALGORITHMS
- TO KNOW HOW TO PROGRAM AND USE DIFFERENT TYPES OF COMB AND ALLPASS FILTER ALGO-RITHMS, AND TO CONSTRUCT HARMONIC RESONATORS AND PHASER EFFECTS.
- TO KNOW HOW TO BUILD DELAYS THAT CONTROL PITCH SHIFTING, REVERSE AND VARIABLE DELAY EFFECTS INCLUDING GLISSANDI AND CHANGES OF DELAY TIME WITHOUT TRANSPOSITION
- TO KNOW HOW TO PROGRAM THE KARPLUS-STRONG ALGORITHM TO SIMULATE THE SOUND OF PLUCKED STRINGS AND OTHER SOUNDS
- TO KNOW HOW TO USE DELAY LINES FOR MAX MESSAGES

SKILLS
- TO BE ABLE TO CREATE A BRIEF COMPOSITION BASED ON THE USE OF SAMPLED SOUNDS, USING LOOPS, REVERSE, DIFFERENT TYPES OF DELAY LINES WITH VARIOUS MODIFICATIONS.

ACTIVITIES
- BUILDING AND MODIFYING ALGORITHMS

TESTING
- ACTIVITIES AT THE COMPUTER

SUPPORTING MATERIALS
- LIST OF MAX OBJECTS - LIST OF ATTRIBUTES, MESSAGES AND ARGUMENTS FOR SPECIFIC MAX OBJECTS

6.1 DELAY TIME: FROM FILTERS TO ECHOES

To create a delay line with Max we can use the **delay~** object, which delays a signal a certain number of samples, as we have already seen in section 3.6P of the first volume. Rebuild the patch shown in figure 6.1.

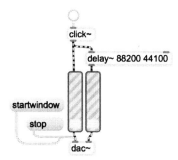

Fig. 6.1 The **delay~** object

The signal output by the **click~** object is delayed by 44100 samples on the right channel[1]; if the sampling rate of your audio interface is 44100 Hz, the delay would be equal to one second.

It is easy to understand that specifying the delay time like this – in samples – is rather inconvenient if we need to express a delay in seconds, since the number of samples representing one second could change depending on the sampling rate being used, and thus we could never be sure that the delay time would be the same in every situation. Generally, the **delay~** object is used in cases where we need to delay a signal by a specific number of samples (as we did for the filters in section 3.6P). Nonetheless, it is always possible to express the delay time in other formats by using the appropriate syntax for the different time units that we learned in section IC.1. Modify the previous patch as shown in figure 6.2.

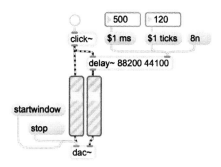

Fig. 6.2 Specifying the delay time with different time formats

---

[1] Remember that the two arguments to the object represent the amount of memory reserved for the delay (in other words the maximum possible obtainable delay) and the delay actually created by the object, respectively. Both values are expressed in samples by default.

The figure shows how to specify the delay time for the **delay~** object in three different formats: milliseconds, ticks and note value. The desired value should be sent to the second inlet of the object, thereby replacing the argument 44100. Please refer to section IC.1 (subsection "Time Values") for the complete list of available formats[2].

Later in this chapter, we will often be using delay times that vary over time. In this case, in order to avoid discontinuities, the delay time will be sent as a signal, not as a Max message. It is possible to vary the delay time of the **delay~** object using a signal, but this can only be used to define a time expressed in samples, bringing us right back to the "inconvenient" situation we found ourselves in, above.

If we need a continuously variable delay it is always preferable to use the pair of objects called **tapin~** and **tapout~**, which respectively write and read a signal (with a pre-defined delay) into a given allocated memory location. The delay time for these objects is expressed in milliseconds, and can be modified using a signal, or via Max messages. Furthermore, with a **tapin~** and **tapout~** pair, it is possible to create a feedback loop in the delay line. In other words, it is possible to send the delayed sound back into the input of the delay line – something that is not possible with the **delay~** object. One limitation inherent in a **tapin~** and **tapout~** pair is that you cannot create a delay time less than the Signal Vector Size (see section 5.1P), whereas with the **delay~** object, as we already have seen, we can even create a delay as small as one sample. The **tapin~** and **tapout~** objects will be very useful throughout the next sections, so you should be sure to understand and learn how to use them well. Reconstruct the patch shown in figure 6.3.

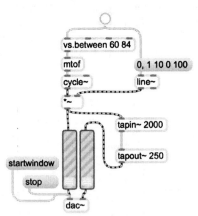

Fig. 6.3 The **tapin~** and **tapout~** objects

In the upper part of the patch we have a simple algorithm that creates a brief sound with a random frequency with each successive bang. This sound is

---

[2] Another possibility is to convert a value expressed in milliseconds into a value in samples using the **mstosamps~** object which we have already seen in section 2.4P of the first volume.

immediately sent to the left channel, and delayed with a **tapin~/tapout~** pair on the right channel. Let's take a closer look at how these objects work.

The **tapin~** object takes one argument which defines the maximum possible delay time in milliseconds (not samples). This object actually "takes over" (allocates) a chunk of memory whose length in samples is determined by dividing the argument by 1000 (to convert the duration to seconds) and then multiplied by the sampling rate. In the case shown here, the argument is 2000 (milliseconds), which equals 2 seconds when divided by 1000, so if the sampling rate is 44100 the amount of memory allocated by the object would be 88200 samples. This memory is used by **tapin~** to write (i.e., record) the signal it receives. Each time it arrives at the end of the allocated memory (after 2 seconds, in our case) it begins again from the memory's starting location, overwriting what had been recorded previously. Technically speaking, this is known as a circular buffer (see section 6.2 in the theory part of this chapter), which we could imagine as a loop of magnetic tape running past a record head (represented by **tapin~**). The **tapout~** object, on the other hand, functions as a playback head, and reads the same circular buffer at a certain distance (given by the argument) with respect to the record head of the **tapin~** object it is connected to, thereby creating a delay of the desired length. In the case of figure 6.3, the circular buffer is 2 seconds long (2000 milliseconds), as indicated by the argument to **tapin~**, and the current delay time is 250 milliseconds, as indicated by the argument to **tapout~**. We will see how to vary these arguments in the next section.

We would also like to point out that the cable connecting **tapin~** and **tapout~**, as you can see, is not an audio cable (since it is a plain grey line), but a connection that allows **tapin~** and **tapout~** to both share the same circular buffer. If we connect a **print** object to the outlet of **tapin~** and click on the "startwindow" message box, we can see the "tapconnect" message printed in the Max window. The **tapin~** object sends this message to the **tapout~** object each time the DSP engine is activated, and is used to allow both objects to share the same pre-allocated memory zone.

In order to create two read locations along one delay line, it is possible to connect several **tapout~** objects to one single **tapin~**. Alternatively, you could provide **tapout~** with multiple arguments, each one corresponding to a read location (in milliseconds).

6.2 ECHOES

To create an echo effect using the **tapin~** and **tapout~** objects, rebuild the patch illustrated in fig. 6.4.

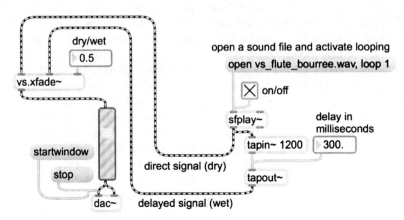

Fig. 6.4 The Echo effect

Note that the message box on the right has two messages separated by a comma: the first opens the sound file, whereas the second sets the loop mode for **sfplay~**. As we already know, the sound file vs_flute_bouree.wav is contained in the Virtual Sound library and Max should be able to find it without your needing to specify the entire file path, presuming you have installed this library correctly. If you want to load a different sound, you will need to send **sfplay~** the "open" message, which will open up a system dialog allowing you to select the sound file you want to use. If you want to test out the effect using an instrument or your voice, you will need to connect a microphone to your audio interface and replace the **sfplay~** object with **adc~**. You can do this the majority of the patches that we will talk about in this chapter, but just be careful not to create feedback between the speaker(s) and microphone! When starting out, we suggest using headphones, until you are confident about using the effects in a live situation.

The **vs.xfade~** object (which we already covered in section 3.5P of the first volume) located on the left lets you mix the direct (dry) signal coming from **sfplay~** with the delayed (wet) signal coming from **tapout~**. Remember that the number sent to the third inlet is used to adjust the proportion between the signals connected to the first two inlets, in other words it controls the *balance*: a value of 0 means only the first signal will be output, a value of 1 means only the second will be output, a value of 0.5 indicates an equal mix of both, and so forth.

We can set the delay time by sending a numerical message to **tapout~**. Click on the **toggle** connected to the **sfplay~** object and try changing the delay time to hear the different possible resulting echo effects. Remember that in order to hear a distinct repetition of the sound, the delay time has to be above the Haas zone, which is in the range of 25-35 milliseconds. Using the sound file shown in the figure (that of a flute with a fairly soft attack) you really only sense a clear doubling of the sound when the delay is above 50 milliseconds. Since the bourée in the sound file is played at 100 bpm, try setting the delay time to 300 milliseconds (corresponding to a delay of an eighth note, or quaver) and multiples of it. Using the **tapin~/tapout~** pair you can also introduce feedback in order to create multiple echoes (something that is impossible to do with **delay~**). Modify the patch as shown in figure 6.5.

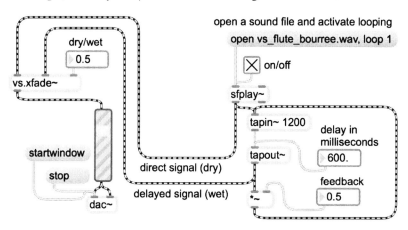

Fig. 6.5 Echo with Feedback

Here, the signal coming from **tapout~** is scaled using a signal multiply object controlled by a floating-point number box (under the label "feedback"). The scaled signal is sent back to the input of **tapin~**, where it is added to the new signal coming from **sfplay~**.

But be careful! In order to avoid distortion, you should set limits on the values output by the floating point number box that controls the feedback. To do this, open the object's inspector, go to the Value category and set the "Minimum" and "Maximum" attributes to 0 and 0.99, respectively. These attributes limit the range of values that can be output by the number box, so you can easily avoid setting a feedback value greater or equal to 1, and therefore be sure that the repetitions of the echo will gradually die out.

As we mentioned earlier, feedback can be created using a **tapin~/tapout~** object pair, but not with **delay~**. In fact, MSP does not actually allow *feedback loops*[3] within the flow of its signal chain.

---

[3] Creating a feedback loop, which causes an error in MSP, should not be confused with looping an audio file, which we discussed in Chapter 5..

By carefully observing the two loops shown in figure 6.6, we can immediately see the difference between a loop made with the **delay~** object (which will stop the DSP engine) and one made with **tapin~** and **tapout~**: on the left side, the audio signal flow is connected in a completely closed loop (all of the connections are made with yellow and black audio cables), whereas on the right the audio loop remains open, because the connection between **tapin~** and **tapout~** is not made with an audio cable.[4]

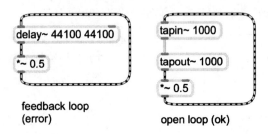

feedback loop
(error)

open loop (ok)

Fig. 6.6 A feedback loop

. . . .

ACTIVITY

In order to avoid the accumulation of DC offset in the patch shown in figure 6.5, insert a first-order highpass filter (see section 3.4P in the first volume) between the **sfplay~** and the delay algorithm. The cutoff frequency should be set lower than the audible bandwidth (for example 10 Hz) in order not to eliminate any meaningful components present in the input signal.

. . . .

---

[4] As already stated, with this connection, the **tapin~** object sends the "tapconnect" message to the **tapout~** object, allowing both objects to share the same circular buffer without an explicit audio connection.

SIMULATION OF TAPE DELAY

In order to simulate Tape Delay we need to insert a lowpass filter after the output of **tapout~** (see figure 6.7).

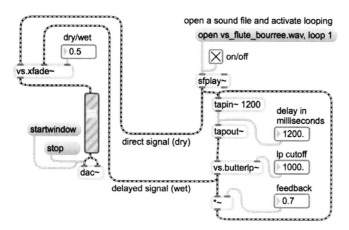

Fig. 6.7 "Tape Delay" with lowpass filter and feedback

Here, we used a Butterworth filter (**vs.butterlp~**, see chapter 3) to do this. Try to rebuild this patch by adding the parameters shown in the figure. You will hear that every copy of the delayed sound is slightly darker in timbre than the previous one. To hear just the filtering effect by itself, click on the "on/off" **toggle** to start the sound file and then, after about a second, click again to stop it.

To avoid continually accumulating low frequencies, as well as to help make the repetitions themselves clearer, we can also add a highpass filter such as **vs.butterhp~** (figure 6.8). As a welcome side effect, this filter also eliminates the accumulation of any DC offset that the input signal might possibly contain.

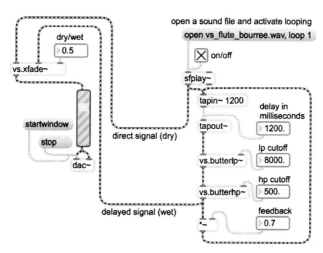

Fig. 6.8 Adding a highpass filter to the tape delay

247

Try using different cutoff frequencies; using a relatively steep cutoff for both filters in the medium high frequencies (4000 Hz for the lowpass and 1000 Hz for the highpass) lets you create a "telephone" sound effect, for example.

· ·

 ACTIVITY

Starting with the patch in figure 6.7, use different types of filters, such as the bandpass filter **vs.butterbp~** or a filterbank using **fffb~** (see section 3.7P), in order to modify the spectral content of the delayed signal. In all cases, be very careful of the Q values you use! They should definitely not go under 0, nor be to high, for that matter. Always start using a feedback value of 0, and then raise it slowly and cautiously.

· ·

SLAPBACK DELAY

As already discussed in the theory part of this chapter, *slapback delay* lets us spatialize a monophonic sound in the stereo field by sending the direct signal to one channel and a slightly delayed copy to the other channel. Considering that this effect does not need to have its delay time modulated, nor does it use feedback, we can always create it using the **delay~** object. Rebuild the patch shown in figure 6.9.

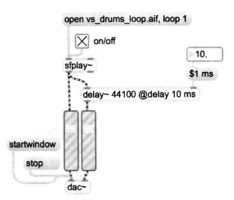

Fig. 6.9 Slapback delay

As you can see, it is always possible to define the delay time for the **delay~** object in formats other than samples using the @delay attribute, or by sending a value followed by the name of the time unit we want to use.

Let's now return to the *slapback delay* effect itself, experimenting with different delay times, and using the sound file vs_drums_loop.aif, found in the Virtual Sound library, or another sound with sharp, clean attacks.

It may be useful to listen to this particular effect with headphones. Even when using a 1 millisecond delay, the sound seems to be predominantly panned to the left – that is: in the channel which has the direct signal. This is due to the Haas effect, also known as the precedence effect, where a sound arriving at the ears (normally one that is reflecting off the walls of a room, and therefore arriving to the ear several times in very rapid succession) appears to be positioned in the direction it initially comes from.[5] This effect becomes more accentuated as we increase the delay time to around 20 milliseconds. If we continue to increase the delay time from this point, we increasingly begin to hear the effect as the typical doubling created by a *slapback delay*. The most effective values to use with the vs_drums_loop.aif sound file are between 30 and 50 milliseconds. Little by little, as we get nearer 100 milliseconds, the sounds on the two channels become more and more separated, and over 100 milliseconds the rebound effect begins to disappear entirely, creating simply an accent displacement in the delayed channel and thereby disrupting our clear perception of the drum loop rhythm.

• •

ACTIVITIES

• Apply *slapback delay* to the patch IC_06_poly_step_seq3.maxpat which we saw in section IC.3 of interlude C (you will need to add the delay to the output of the **poly~** object). Listen to how this effect affects short and long notes differently.

• A variation of the preceding activity: insert the *slapback delay* into the polyphonic patch p.sawtones~.maxpat and control the delay time via the "Extra 1" parameter in the **live.step** object. Note that the polyphonic instance is muted when the note is finished – in other words as soon as the envelope is over. In order to avoid clicks, you will need to make it stay active until the end of the delayed signal. One possibility, among others, would be to lengthen the envelope in the main patch by adding a silent segment (in other words a segment starting at 0 and ending at 0), whose duration is equal to the delay time, to the end of the list output by the **function** object.

• •

MULTITAP DELAY

For this effect, let's return to using the **tapin~/tapout~** object pair.

The **tapout~** object, as we mentioned in section 6.1, can have several "playback heads," each with its own delay time, allowing us to create a multi-tap

---
[5] We will look at this and other phenomena related to spatialization more deeply in the third volume.

delay. To create multiple "taps" on our circular buffer, we just need to provide `tapout~` with as many arguments as the number of outlets we want to create; reconstruct the patch in figure 6.10.

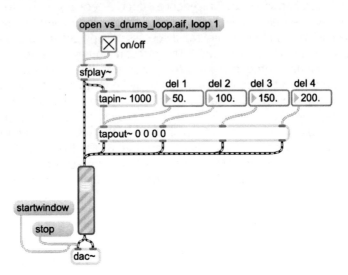

Fig. 6.10 Multiple delays

In this (still relatively simple) patch we have provided `tapout~` with 4 numerical arguments. These arguments all have a value of 0 because we are using them only to create 4 different user-definable delays, consequently the `tapout~` object now has 4 inlets (used to set the delay time for each of the 4 delays) and 4 outlets, one for each of the delayed singals. When listening to this patch, remember you can also optionally use an `adc~` instead of the `sfplay~`, in case you want to try it out with a microphone.

The delay times can also be sent to `tapout~` as a list, which makes it very convenient to control a large number of delays (for example 16) with a graphical object like `multislider`.

Open the file **06_01_multitap.maxpat** (figure 6.11).

Here, a series of brief sinusoidal sounds is sent to a 16-output `tapin~/tapout~` setup whose delay times are defined with a 16-element list output by a `multislider`. We have modified the `multislider` settings so it will create a list of 16 values between 1 and 1000 (the maximum delay time we have given as an argument to `tapin~`). Try the different presets and notice how the delayed sounds are superimposed on each successive direct sound when the metronome's beat is less than 1000 milliseconds. Create and store several new presets.

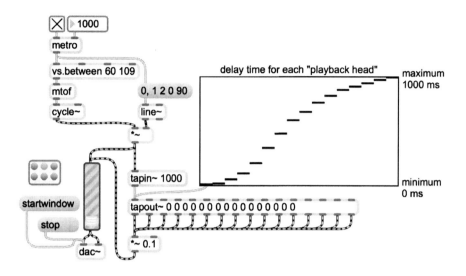

Fig. 6.11 The file **06_01_multitap.maxpat**

In the next patch, we will use the **vs.explist** object to create a sense of speeding up or slowing down via the delay times set in the multitap delay. We already learned the **vs.explist** object in section 2.4P of the first volume: it is an object that generates a list of values with an exponential or logarithmic profile.

Open the file **06_02_multitap2.maxpat** (figure 6.12).

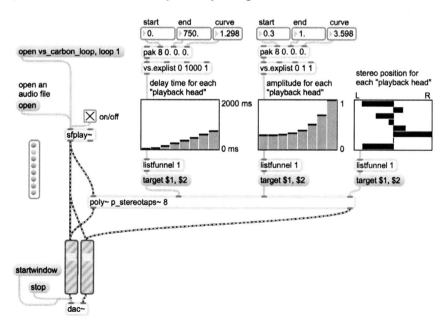

Fig. 6.12 The file **06_02_multitap2.maxpat**

As you can see, the patch has two **vs.explist** objects, each of which generates an 8-element list (displayed in the two **multisliders** below them). The values of these lists set the delay time and amplitude parameters for each "playback head". It is also possible to define the stereo position (panning) of each individual delay using the **multislider** on the right side of the patch. First listen to the presets, paying careful attention to the parameters sent to the **vs.explist** objects.

In this patch we used the **poly~** object to manage the different delays. The p_stereotaps polyphonic patch contains a **delay~** object, therefore we are not using a circular buffer shared by multiple playback heads, but rather creating as many individual buffers as there are polyphonic instances of the patch. The result of the effect is exactly the same, but we are using use more memory to create it (this should not pose a problem, however, given the quantity of memory currently available in the average computer).[6]

Note also that the signal output by **sfplay~** is sent to the first inlet of **poly~**; as we learned in section IC.3, any signal that is input to **poly~** is sent to all instances of the polyphonic patch.

The list values output by the **multisliders** and the **vs.explist** objects are sent to the various polyphonic instances using the **listfunnel** object.[7] Let's now analyze the file **p_stereotaps~.maxpat** which has been loaded into the **poly~** object (figure 6.13).

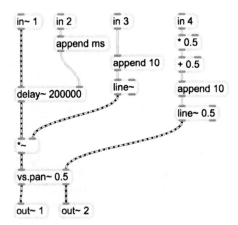

Fig. 6.13 The file **p_stereotaps~.maxpat**

This is a very simple patch: the first inlet sends the audio signal, the second sends the delay time, the third the amplitude and the fourth the stereo position (panning). Because the **vs.pan~** object uses values between 0 and 1 to define the stereo position of a sound, but our **multislider** in the main patch sends values between -1 and 1, we need to convert the value range using a multiplication and an addition. Once again, listen to all of the presets and try creating some new ones.[8]

Let's take a look at a variation on the preceding patch; load the file **06_03_multitap3.maxpat** (figure 6.14).

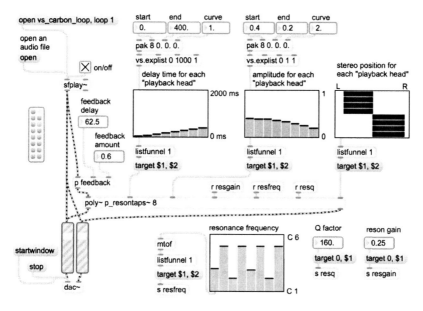

Fig. 6.14 The file **06_03_multitap3.maxpat**

In this patch a resonant filter has been added to each delay, in addition to an independent delay with a feedback loop before the **poly~** object. First listen to all the presets; those in the first column do not use feedback, while those in the second column do.

The parameters for the resonant filters are located in the lower part of the patch. The resonant frequency for each of the instances inside the **poly~** object is set using a **multislider**, whereas the Q and feedback gain are globally set for all instances. The resonant frequencies are defined with MIDI note values from C1 to C6 (you can see this by opening the **multislider**'s inspector), which are converted to frequencies in Hertz using the **mtof** object. The filter parameters are all sent to **poly~** using a **send-receive** object pair.

---

[8] There is a Max for Live (M4L) device similar to this patch, though somewhat more complex. It is called "MaxDelayTaps", and if you have M4L you can compare the two algorithms. We will talk more about M4L in Interlude E of this volume.

As we already mentioned, the feedback loop located in the [p feedback] sub-patch is independent from the delays handled inside the **poly~** object. Figure 6.15 shows the contents of this subpatch.

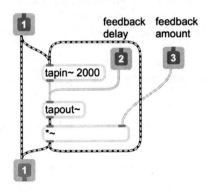

Fig. 6.15 The subpatch [p feedback]

As you can see in the figure, the feedback loop has been created using a **tapin~** and **tapout~** object pair. The audio signal arrives in the first inlet, and the second and third inlets are used to set the delay time (labeled "feedback delay") and the multiplier used for the feedback loop ("feedback amount"), respectively. Both the direct signal and the signal from the feed-back loop are sent to the outlet.

Now let's look at the contents of the file **p_resontaps~.maxpat** that has been loaded inside the **poly~** object (figure 6.16). We will leave analysis of this patch to the reader; however, be sure to note that, as before, we have automatically modified the filter gain to be directly proportional to Q.

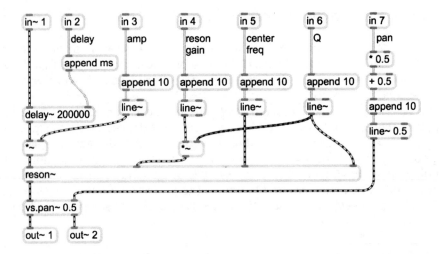

Fig. 6.16 The file **p_resontaps~.maxpat**

ACTIVITY

Create a polyphonic patch that contains a `tapin~`/`tapout~` pair with feedback, a bandpass filter and stereo panning. Then, create a main patch with a **poly~** object that can handle 6 instances of the polyphonic patch; each instance will therefore have its own feedback loop. The various parameters – delay time, feedback, center frequency for the filter, Q and panning – should each have their own `multislider`.

· ·

MULTIBAND-MULTITAP DELAY

If we separate the input signal into different frequency bands and apply a different delay to each band we can create some very interesting effects. To separate a signal into different bands we will use the **cross~** object which was designed specifically for this purpose. This object contains two third-order filters (consequently having an 18dB per octave drop-off): a lowpass and a highpass. These filters both have the same cutoff frequency, so it can therefore be referred to as the crossover frequency. Rebuild the simple patch shown in figure 6.17.

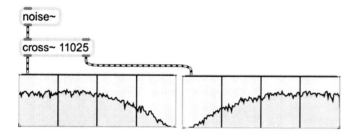

Fig. 6.17 The **cross~** object

This object has two outlets which output the signal whose frequency band is lower than the crossover frequency and the signal whose frequency is above it, respectively. The crossover frequency can be given as an argument, or sent to the object's right inlet as a message. In figure 6.17 we can see the two frequency bands resulting from using a crossover frequency of 11025 Hz.

Let's look at one possible application of the crossover filter; reconstruct the patch in figure 6.18.

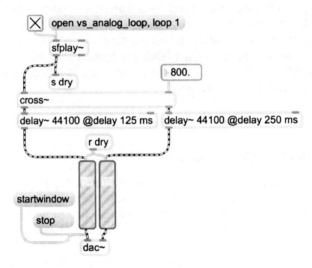

Fig. 6.18 Delays segregated by frequency band

In this patch, a drum loop is sent to the two audio output channels (using a **send/ receive** pair with the argument "dry"), and is additionally sent to a crossover filter which divides the signal into two frequency bands. The lower of the two bands (from 0 to 800 Hz) is delayed 125 milliseconds and sent to the left channel, while the higher band (from 800 Hz to the Nyquist frequency) is delayed 250 milliseconds and sent to the right channel. Try changing the delay times (adding a number box for each of the **delay~** objects) as well as the crossover frequency.

To split the signal up into three or more frequency bands we need to use several crossover filters in cascade, as illustrated in figure 6.19.

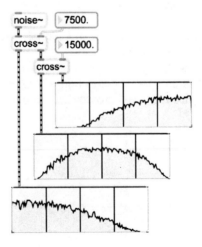

Fig. 6.19 Two cascaded crossover filters dividing the signal into three bands

In this figure, the white noise in the input is separated into three frequency bands, between 0 and 7500 Hz, 7500 Hz and 15000 Hz and 15000 Hz to 22050 Hz (assuming we are using a 44100 Hz sampling rate), respectively. Let's look at a slightly more complex example; open the file **06_04_multiband_tap. maxpat** (figure 6.20).

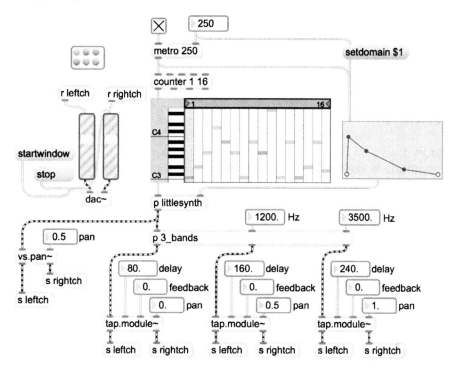

Fig. 6.20 The file **06_04_multiband_tap.maxpat**

This patch has a small subtractive synthesizer (inside the [p littlesynth] sub-patch) which is controlled by a step sequencer and a **function** object, used to determine the envelope. The sound produced by the synthesizer is sent to the following two places:
- to a **vs.pan~** (on the left), whose output is then sent to the audio outputs (using a **send/receive** pair)
- to the [p 3_bands] subpatch which contains two cascaded **cross~** filters, dividing the signal into three frequency bands
Notice that the second and third inlets of the [p 3_bands] subpatch are used to set the two crossover frequencies that are used to define the three frequency bands.

The sound output by the [p 3_bands] subpatch is sent to three instances of the `tap.module~` abstraction, which is located in the same folder as the main patch itself[9] (Chapter 06 Patches) and contains a delay with feedback and adjustable stereo position (panning).

Try the various presets provided, carefully study their different parameters, and analyze and describe the algorithm in the patch. You should also open and analyze the [p littlesynth] and [p 3_bands] subpatches, as well as the `tap.module~` abstraction.

· ·

ACTIVITIES

Modify the patch in figure 6.20 in the following ways:
• dynamically vary the crossover frequency using a pair of LFOs

• dynamically vary the stereo position of the direct and delayed signals using LFOs

• create 4 frequency bands

• use a sampled sound as input.

· ·

---

[9] This abstraction is consequently only visible to patches that have been saved in the same folder as it. If, on the other hand, the abstraction were located in Max's search path, it would be visible to any patch. For details, please refer to section IA.4 in the first volume.

PING-PONG DELAY

Implementing a ping-pong delay is relatively simple: you just need to create two delay lines and send the feedback of the first delay into the input of the second, and vice-versa. Open the file **06_05_pingpong_delay.maxpat** (figure 6.21).

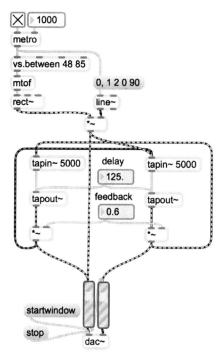

Fig. 6.21 The file **06_05_pingpong_delay.maxpat**

In the patch shown in the figure, the direct signal is sent both to the left channel and to the delay line that is connected to the right channel. The same delay time and feedback parameters are used to control both delay lines.

· ·

ACTIVITIES

Create the following variations on the patch illustrated in figure 6.21:
- add a highpass filter and a lowpass filter, as we did for the tape delay effect

- use two different sound sources: one for the left delay line and one for the right

- use different delay times for each of the delay lines

- on each channel, add a direct feedback loop with its own delay time, independent of the one used for the "crossed" feedback (you will need to provide two arguments for each of the two **tapout~** objects)

259

6.3 LOOPING USING DELAY LINES

To create a loop with a delay line, we will use a **tapin~/tapout~** object pair with an automatic system to turn on and off the volume for both audio input and feedback. Load the file **06_06_delay_loop.maxpat** (figure 6.22).

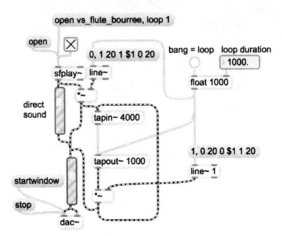

Fig. 6.22 The file **06_06_ delay_loop.maxpat**

This algorithm uses two **line~** objects to create a cross-fade between the input sound and the feedback multiplier. Initially, the input sound, on the upper left, is closed (because it is multiplied by the output of **line~** which, by default, is 0), whereas the feedback, in the lower part of the patch, is open (because it is multiplied by the out of a **line~** whose argument is 1, and therefore outputting a stream of samples with a value of 1). Clicking on the bang on the right causes the value stored in the **float** object (set to 1000 in the figure) to be sent to two message boxes connected to the two **line~** objects, as well as to the **tapout~**. The message box connected to **line~** that controls the audio input creates an envelope that opens the input for a length of time equal to that provided in the **float** object that we previously mentioned, in addition to a 20 millisecond attack and a 20 millisecond release, which are used to avoid clicks. At the same time, the other **line~** object closes the feedback for exactly the same amount of time. Therefore, every time you send a bang, the delay line records a portion of the input signal and then re-opens the feedback when recording is finished. The delay line then circles around continuously, creating a loop, until a new bang causes the feedback to close and open again. It is possible to modify the duration of the new loop by changing the value in the number box connected to the **float** object. Since this **float** is also connected to the **tapout~** the value it stores will also change the delay time, and therefore the duration of the loop.[10]

---

[10] This patch is still not entirely devoid of possible clicks – we actually also need to delay the Max message that modifies the delay time by 20 milliseconds, so that the change happens when the amplitude of the delayed signal is 0. To do this we would need to use an object capable of delaying messages instead of signals. This will be covered later, in section 6.11.

ACTIVITIES

- Add a `metro` object to vary the loop at regular intervals, creating four loops for each bang of the `metro`

- Randomly vary the number of repetitions of the loop in the previous exercise

- Create a system with several loops that can be turned on and off independently of one another, each having its own, different, beat rate. The loop algorithms should be contained within instances of a polyphonic patch loaded by `poly~`.

- Create a chain of effects by connecting the loops generated by the previous exercise to another delay-based algorithm, such as a slapback delay or ping-pong delay.

· ·

6.4 FLANGER

In order to be able to set the minimal delay times that characterize this effect, you should be sure to check that the Signal Vector Size in the Audio Status window is sufficiently small.[11] The minimum delay that can be created using `tapin~` and `tapout~` is equal to the length of the Signal Vector Size, so setting this value to 16 samples, for example, allows us to have a minimum delay of 0.36 milliseconds (at a sampling rate of 44100 Hz), which is sufficient for our purposes. You should set the Signal Vector Size to 16 samples, since we will need to use this setting throughout the rest of this chapter.

The flanger effect consists of modulating the delay time with an LFO (Low Frequency Oscillator), which is usually a unipolar oscillator whose two extremes, both positive, represent the minimum and maximum delay times of the delay line. Therefore, if we want to use the `cycle~` object as an LFO we first need to transform it into a unipolar oscillator (as shown in figure 6.23).

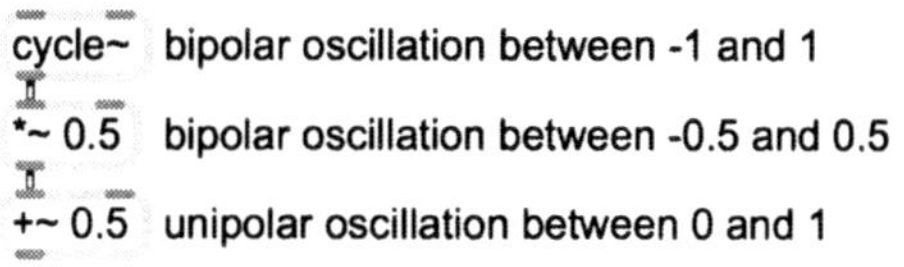

cycle~   bipolar oscillation between -1 and 1

*~ 0.5   bipolar oscillation between -0.5 and 0.5

+~ 0.5   unipolar oscillation between 0 and 1

Fig. 6.23: From bipolar to unipolar oscillation

---

[11] Remember that we already extensively discussed the Audio Status window and its parameters in section 5.1P.

First, we reduced the amplitude by half, and then added a DC offset of 0.5. This way, the oscillator's values will now vary between 0 and 1. The amplitude (corresponding to the range) can be varied using other multiplications, and the minimum value output by the LFO can be set using other additions. The maximum value will naturally correspond to the minimum value plus the amplitude (figure 6.24).

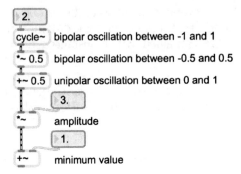

Fig. 6.24 LFO with *range*

The example in the figure shows a sinusoidal LFO that oscillates at a frequency of 2 Hz, with an amplitude of 3 (this is the width parameter defined in the theory section) and a minimum value equal to 1 (in the theory section we mentioned that this parameter is inappropriately called delay in many commercial flanger applications). The maximum value therefore will be equal to 3 + 1 = 4.[12] We should take care to remember that the minimum and maximum values represent the delay time in milliseconds, so if we connect this oscillator to a **tapout~** object, we can make the playback head oscillate between two positions that correspond to a 1 millisecond and 4 millisecond delay. The oscillation itself takes place at a rate (frequency) of 2 Hz, meaning that each second there are two cycles which go back and forth between the two positions. This is the parameter referred to as speed or rate in the theory part of this chapter. Reconstruct the patch shown in figure 6.25, which shows a preliminary flanger implementation.

---

[12] Those who are skilled in mathematics will have probably realized that we could save on using two MSP operators by multiplying the bipolar oscillator by half of the desired amplitude and adding a DC offset equal to half the amplitude plus the minimum value, but we preferred to illustrate the procedure step-by-step in order to explanation the logic clearly.

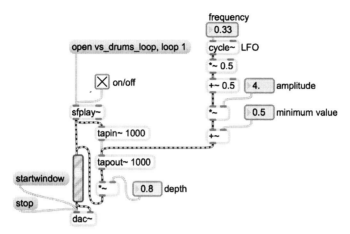

Fig. 6.25 The *flanger* effect

We have added a multiplier to the output of the delayed sound to be able to control the quantity of delayed sound to mix with the original. This parameter is referred to "depth" in the theory section. Try some different parameter settings, modifying the parameters' values within the given ranges:

LFO frequency: between 0.1 and 1 Hz
amplitude: between 1 and 10
minimum value: between 0.4 and 3
depth: between 0.75 and 1

The results of this effect are usually more evident when applied to a full-spectrum sound, such as a drum loop.

If you try incrementing the LFO frequency above 1 Hz you will probably realize that the pitch change effect produced by the flanger increases with the frequency of the unipolar oscillator. To better hear this, try using the sound file **vs_flute_bouree.wav** with the following parameters:

LFO frequency: 0.1 Hz
amplitude: 5
minimum value: 1
depth: 1

The effect is very delicate and sometimes hardly perceptible, but of you increase the LFO frequency to 2 Hz, you will obtain a vibrato effect that becomes continually more obvious as the frequency increases. From around 30 Hz it transforms into an actual modulation effect (which we will cover in chapter 10).

What is the reason for this change in effect? It is due to the fact that, as the frequency of the LFO controlling the location of the **tapout~** "playback head" increases, it moves more and more quickly along the delay line, thereby more noticeably detuning the original sound.

263

If we wanted to change the LFO frequency without increasing the detuning effect, we would need to make the frequency and amplitude of the unipolar oscillator inversely proportional, in other words as we increase the frequency, we reduce the amplitude proportionally (if the frequency doubles, the amplitude is halved, and so forth). To obtain this result, we need to use the frequency as a dividing factor for the amplitude, which consequently ceases to be an amplitude but becomes a "pitch deviation" parameter. Modify the patch as shown in figure 6.26.

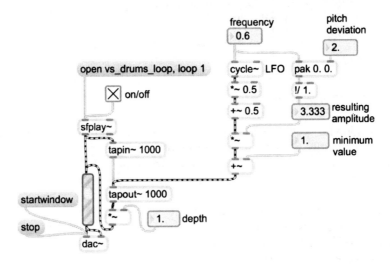

Fig. 6.26 The *flanger* effect, version 2

As you can see, we have connected the LFO frequency and the "pitch deviation" parameters to a division operator which calculates a "resulting amplitude." In the example shown in the figure, using a frequency equal to 0.6 and a pitch deviation equal to 2 results in an amplitude value of 3.333. Since the minimum value is 1, this means that the maximum is 4.333 (1+ 3.333). In other words, the delay time oscillates sinusoidally between 1 and 4.333 milliseconds at a frequency of 0.6 Hz. Start with the parameters illustrated in the figure, and then gradually increase the LFO frequency: you will notice that the oscillation gets increasingly faster, but the pitch deviation remains constant.

In summary, using this configuration we no longer have an adjustable amplitude value for the LFO, but instead a pitch deviation parameter; the amplitude will vary in relation to this parameter and the LFO frequency. Let's now take a look at the same algorithm with the addition of feedback. Open the file **06_07_flanger.maxpat** (figure 6.27).

In this patch you can choose from among several audio files, whose names have been added to a **umenu** object in the upper-left part of the patch. Explain what happens from the output of the **umenu** to the **sfplay~** object. Try out the presets provided, and create some new ones.

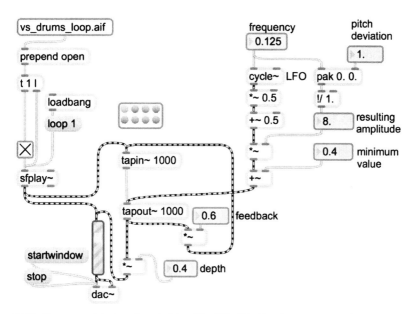

Fig. 6.27 *flanger* with feedback (the file **06_07_flanger.maxpat**)

Note that if you try to modify the number box labeled "resulting amplitude" you can't change it – the number box seems to be "jammed." This happens because we enabled the "Ignore Click" attribute in the inspector, which inhibits the object from being able to be selected or modified with the mouse when the patch is in performance mode. Enabling this attribute is useful when we are using the object to display some particular bit of information that we do not want the user to be able to modify (as in this case).

To avoid saturating the loop, the values in the float number box control-ling the feedback gain have been limited between -0.999 and 0.999 (using the inspector). It is possible to heighten the flanger effect by increasing the feedback, thereby obtaining an accentuated resonance that oscillates at a frequency corresponding to the delay time – in other words between 1/mini-mum_delay Hz and 1/maximum_delay Hz. With the settings shown in figure 6.27, where the minimum delay is 0.4 milliseconds and the maximum is 8.4 milliseconds, the resonance will oscillate between 1/0.0004 = 2500 Hz and 1/0.0084 = 119.5 Hz.[13] When the feedback value is negative (e.g., -0.6) the resonant frequency will be halved (lowered one octave), because the delayed signal in the feedback loop is inverted with each repetition. This inverts the phase of the waveform with each cycle, meaning that we perceive two con-secutive cycles (with opposite phase) as one, resulting in the sound being lowered by one octave (try it!).

---

[13] Remember that in order to get the frequency in Hertz corresponding to one period, you need to express the period in seconds, not milliseconds. The times shown in figure 6.31 (0.4 and 8.4 milliseconds) are therefore expressed as 0.0004 and 0.0084 seconds.

🖱 **ACTIVITIES**

- Add a lowpass or highpass filter to the feedback loop. Do not use resonant filters, because they can easily saturate the loop; instead use the Butterworth filters: **vs.butterlp~** and **vs.butterhp~**.

- Starting with the previous exercise, use the **selector~** object (see section 1.6) within the feedback loop to be able to choose the lowpass, highpass or original unfiltered signal (the argument given to **selector~** should therefore be 3).

- Apply the flanger to one of the synthesizers we used in Interlude C.

- Change the LFO waveform. For example, you might try using the **vs.triangle~** (bandlimited triangle wave) oscillator, or the noise generators **rand~** or **vs.rand3~**.

- In section 6.4T we mentioned that flanger implementations often have a fixed delay applied to the dry sound so that the wet sound does not always lag behind it, but can sometimes come ahead of it (when the variable delay time of the wet sound is less than the fixed delay time of the dry sound). Add this kind of mechanism to the patch **06_07_flanger.maxpat**, in such a way that the dry sound is always at the center of the oscillation of the wet sound. In other words, if the LFO causes the wet sound to oscillate between 0 and 10 milliseconds, the dry sound should have a delay time of 5 milliseconds. The fixed delay time for the dry sound should be calculated automatically by the patch – based on the LFO amplitude – and not set by hand!

· ·

6.5 CHORUS

The chorus algorithm is essentially the same as that of the flanger: a delay with variable delay time. The most important differences are: the choice of parameters (delay times for the chorus effect are generally longer), the type of LFO used (usually a random generator is used), the absence of feedback, and the use of several delay lines simultaneously. Taking things in order, let's first look at a simple version of this effect (figure 6.28).

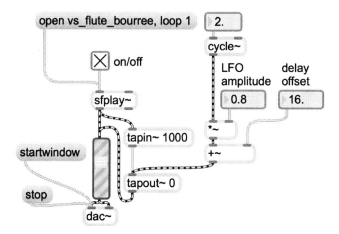

Fig. 6.28 The *chorus* effect

Compared to our flanger, we have slightly modified the LFO control. Here, we use a central delay time (delay offset) that becomes shortened and lengthened by a bipolar oscillator. In accordance with what we learned in the theory section, it would be enough to take the patch that implements a flanger without feedback and modify the parameters appropriately in order to obtain the chorus effect. However, we decided to show a different (and, in our opinion, easier) method that helps us control the parameters for this effect more efficiently. Furthermore, this system allows us to save on the use of two MSP operators for each LFO. In the case of the patch shown in the figure, the delay time effectively varies between 16 + 0.8 = 16.8 milliseconds and 16 - 0.8 = 15.2 milliseconds.

Try rebuilding the patch and using it with a melodic sound such as the file **vs_flute_bouree.wav**, as shown in the figure. The typical filtering effect inherent in the flanger is no longer there because the direct and delayed sound are never so close as to cause cancellation or emphasis of common frequency components. Nonetheless, there is a continuous detuning effect of the delayed voice, which, when summed with the original signal, gives the sense of "thickening" the sound.

Let's add a second voice to increase the effect (figure 6.29).

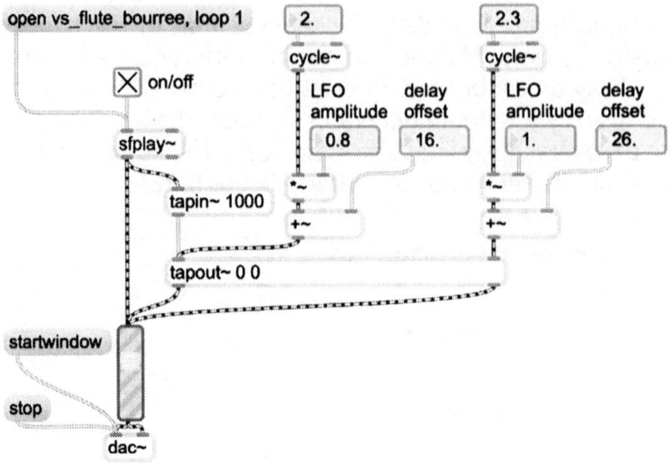

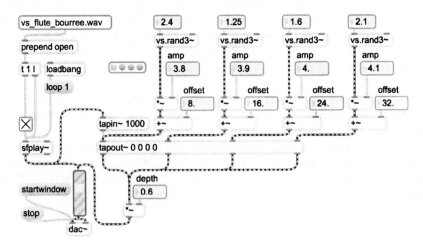

Fig. 6.29 The *chorus* effect, version 2

Note that the frequencies of the two LFOs are different (in order to help mask the effect of the periodic oscillation of the intonation that was present in the previous patch) and the delay times are distant enough that we can avoid having them cross paths as they oscillate (which could cause flanging). Change the parameters and experiment with the different possible sonorities of the chorus. You can also try to use "extreme" values, such as delays over 200 milliseconds or LFO frequencies of 100 Hz or more, in order to get results that have little relationship to the original effect that we started off with.

Let's take another step forward by modifying the patch so it uses random LFOs, increasing the number of voices and inserting a "depth" parameter (as shown in figure 6.30: the **file 06_08_chorus.maxpat**).

Fig. 6.30 The *chorus* effect, version 3 (the file **06_08_chorus.maxpat**)

Now that we have 4 voices in our chorus, the depth control for the effect becomes all the more important because the volume of the four delay lines summed together is much greater than that of the original sound.

This patch allows us to create a chorus effect that is more than acceptable. It uses the **vs.rand3~** generator discussed in chapter 3, allowing us to eliminate the periodic feeling caused by **cycle~**. It should be mentioned that we need to use a greater amplitude for this random generator than we would need to use for a sinusoidal modulator. This is because, unlike a sine wave which oscillates evenly between -1 and 1 with each cycle, the random generator wanders within oscillation band, rarely approaching the extremes, and therefore covering a narrower range during its cycle.

To create a stereo chorus we can use a single LFO to control two delay lines, inverting the LFO waveform for one of the two delay lines (figure 6.31).

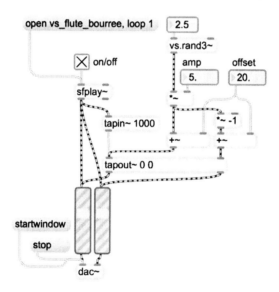

Fig. 6.31 Stereo *chorus*

By multiplying the output signal of the LFO by -1 we can invert its waveform, so each time the delay increases in one channel it will decrease in the other and vice-versa. This lets us create stereo depth using a monophonic sound source.

- Create stereo chorus patches with two and four voices per channel (your patch should therefore have two or four LFOs whose waveforms are inverted in one of the channels).

- Apply a stereo chorus to one of the synthesizers we use in Interlude C.

- Modify the chorus shown in figure 6.28, substituting the sinusoidal LFO with the **vs.rand3~** random generator and adding a feedback loop to the delay line. Create several presets with this new configuration.

- Create a stereo flanger by adapting the same technique used in the chorus shown in figure 6.31. To efficiently implement feedback in both channels, we recommend using two independent **tapin~/tapout~** object pairs.

· ·

6.6 COMB FILTERS

MSP comes with the standard comb filter object called **comb~**, which implements a delay with both feedback and feedforward (figure 6.32).

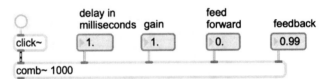

Fig. 6.32 The comb filter

This object takes 4 parameters in its inlets: delay time, gain (a multiplication factor for the input signal), feedforward (a multiplier for the delayed sound without feedback) and feedback (a multiplier for the sound being fed back into the delay). If we set the feedback parameter to 0 we create a FIR comb filter, otherwise we create an IIR filter when this parameter is non-zero (see section 6.6T). The object can also have 5 arguments which respectively indicate: the maximum delay time (defining the amount of memory the object will reserve for its delay line), initial delay, gain, feedforward and feedback. In the figure, we only provided one argument to set the maximum delay, whereas the other parameters have been set with messages sent via number boxes connected to the parameters' respective inlets.

Figure 6.33 shows a block diagram representing the signal flow inside the object. This has already been discussed sufficiently in the theory section (6.6T). The only difference between that description and the Max implementation is that here the delay time is expressed in milliseconds instead of samples.

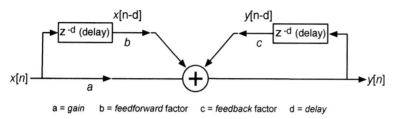

a = *gain*   b = *feedforward* factor   c = *feedback* factor   d = *delay*

Fig. 6.33 Block diagram showing the signal flow of the **comb~** object

You may be asking yourself why we have been using a **tapin~/tapout~** pair for the effect examples up to now, if a single comb filter object already exists in the Max environment, and implements the same signal processing algorithm in less space. Our reply would be that, using **comb~**, it is not possible to insert additional signal processing within the feedback loop, and therefore not possible to create all of the effects we have discussed thus far (one example would be the tape delay). Furthermore, with **comb~** it is not possible to have multiple "playback heads" associated with a single "record head" and its circular buffer (as it is with **tapin~/tapout~**), so for multi-tap effects we would need to use as many **comb~** objects as the number of "playback heads" we wanted, resulting in a greater use of memory as well as being less efficient.

We could also pose the opposite question: why do we need a **comb~** object if **tapin~** and **tapout~** let us do the same things much more flexibly? Quite simply, the **comb~** object allows us to have delays smaller than the Signal Vector Size (see section 6.2) and is likely more efficient than an equivalent comb filter designed with a **tapin~/tapout~** pair, as long as it is not used in a multi-tap situation (but this could depend on the version of Max you have on your computer). At the very least, **comb~** takes up a lot less space on your computer screen!

Try rebuilding the patch shown in figure 6.34 (be careful of the feedback! – its value should not exceed 1). Each impulse output by the **click~** object causes a harmonic resonance with a 1000 Hz fundamental to be created (presuming the delay time is set to 1 millisecond), resulting in a spectrum which looks like the teeth of a comb.

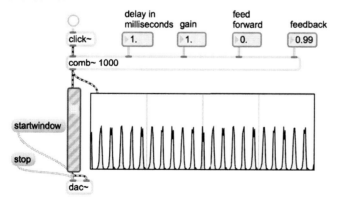

Fig. 6.34 Frequency response of the comb filter

271

However, if we want to use **comb~** to create resonators tuned to arbitrary frequencies, we first need to transform the frequency values into time intervals expressed in milliseconds (see figure 6.35).

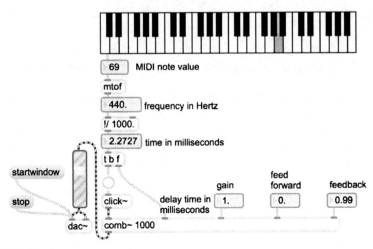

Fig. 6.35 Comb resonator

Generally, when we create a comb resonator it is useful to be able to set a resonance time instead of a feedback coefficient. We have already learned how to calculate the resonance time in the theory section, but it is not necessary to redesign this algorithm from scratch – instead we can use the **vs.comb~** object (figure 6.36).

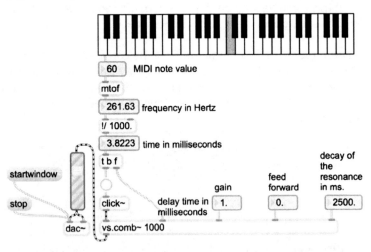

Fig. 6.36 The **vs.comb~** object

This object is very similar to **comb~** – the sole difference being that in place of the feedback coefficient we can set the desired decay time of the resonance; the calculation that transforms decay time into a feedback coefficient has already been implemented inside the object itself.

Comb filters can naturally be applied to any kind of signal, such as a sound file. Let's look at one possible application in a patch that implements a bank of comb resonators with the **poly~** object. Load the file **06_09_comb_resona-tors.maxpat** (figure 6.37).

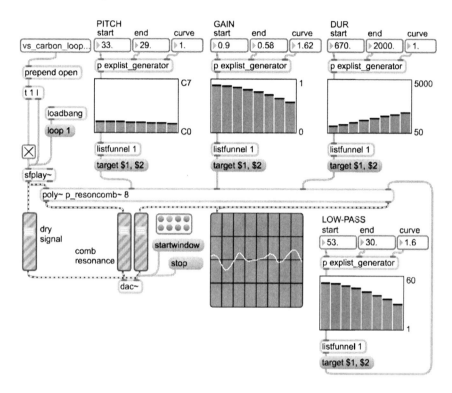

Fig. 6.37 The file **06_09_comb_resonators.maxpat**

First, listen to all of the presets. You will notice that in this patch the volume of the dry (unprocessed) signal can be controlled independently of the volume of the comb resonators (using the **gain~** sliders on the lower left). The eight resonances are distributed across the stereo field and if you listen carefully for a long enough time, you will notice that they very slowly move, in a random manner (we will see how this was done in a moment).

The **poly~** object contains the polyphonic patch p_resoncomb~ (which we will also analyze shortly), which creates a bank of comb filters. Each of the parameters for this filter bank is generated by a **vs.explist** object, using a technique similar to the one already shown in the multitap patches.[14]

As you can see the parameters used are: resonant frequency (expressed as a MIDI note from C0 to C7), gain, duration (in milliseconds) and cutoff frequency

---

[14] To save space, the **pak** and **vs.explist** objects have been put inside a subpatch.

for the lowpass filter. The cutoff frequency is not expressed in Hertz, but rather as a multiplication factor of the resonant frequency: this way the ratio between the resonant frequency and the filter's cutoff frequency always remains constant. To give an example, if the resonance of a given comb filter is 220 Hertz and the multiplication factor for the associated cutoff frequency is 20, the actual resulting cutoff frequency will be equal to 220 · 20 = 4400 Hertz.

Let's now take a closer look at the contents of p_resoncomb~ (figure 6.38).

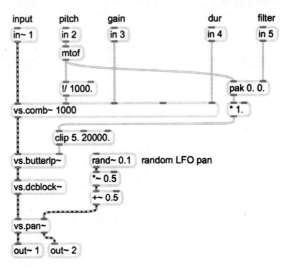

Fig. 6.38 The polyphonic patch p resoncomb~

You can see that our MIDI pitch is converted into a frequency value using the **mtof** object and then into a delay time using the division object. On the upper right side of the patch there is the multiplication factor (for the cutoff frequency of the filter), which is multiplied by the resonant frequency. Under the comb filter itself we have the lowpass filter and the **vs.dcblock~** object used to eliminate any eventual DC offset (you can double-click on this object to open it and see that it is implemented with a highpass filter). Finally, as we previously mentioned, each comb resonator is slowly moved in the stereo field using a random LFO whose frequency is 0.1 Hz.

. . . .

ACTIVITIES

- Inside the polyphonic patch p_resoncomb~, add the ability to set the frequency of the random generator that controls the stereo panning of the resonances.

- Add a second random LFO to be able to vary the resonant frequency by some small percentage (for example between 0% and 10%) which can be defined by the user. The frequency used for this LFO will be the same as for the LFO that controls the sound's stereo position.

6.7 ALLPASS FILTERS

In MSP there is also an `allpass~` object which implements a two-delay Schroeder model allpass filter shown in figure 6.39. This has already been described in section 6.7 of the theory part of this chapter.

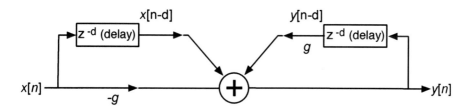

Fig. 6.39 Block diagram showing the signal flow of the `allpass~` object

This object has three inlets, respectively used for the signal, delay time and the gain/feedback (or **g** coefficient). The object additionally takes maximum delay, initial delay and gain as its arguments (figure 6.40).

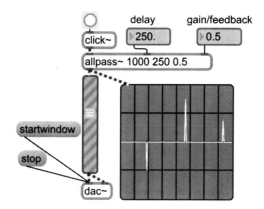

Fig. 6.40 The `allpass~` object

First, rebuild the patch shown in figure 6.40, so we can make a "phenomenological analysis" of this important filter – in other words analyze its impulse response. Beginning with the settings shown in the figure and sending a unit impulse to the filter, you will see that at the filter's output we first get the signal inverted in sign (because of the internal multiplier **-g**) and with half the amplitude (because **g** is 0.5) After 250 milliseconds (the delay time) we have the sum of the unscaled original signal (feedforward) and the feedback signal multiplied by **g**. Since this signal had previously been multiplied by **-g**, its amplitude is now $g \cdot (-g) = -g^2$ which, when added to the feedforward signal (not scaled and therefore with an amplitude of 1), gives us a total amplitude of **1-g²**. The subsequent repetitions of the feedback signal will be continuously scaled by **g**, yielding the following series of amplitudes: **g · (1-g²), g² · (1-g²), g³ · (1-g^2),** etc.

275

As we increase the value of **g** (being careful that it does not exceed 1) we will obtain a progressively lengthier series of impulses, but also more attenuated because, if **g** is very close to 1, the shared multiplier for all of the repetitions of the feedback loop, **1-g^2** will obviously be very close to 0.

To test this out, try setting **g** equal to 0.99. This will create a long series of impulses at a very low amplitude level. If **g** is set to 1, the feedback will be eliminated altogether because **1-g^2** is equal to 0.

There is also a version of this allpass filter in the Virtual Sound library (**vs.allpass~**) which allows us to define the feedback duration instead of directly setting the coefficient g (figure 6.41).

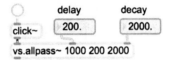

Fig. 6.41 The **vs.allpass~** object

This object, together with **vs.comb~** will be useful for constructing reverberation algorithms in the next volume.

6.8 THE PHASER

To create a phaser we need to use a second-order allpass filter, as we learned in the theory part of this chapter. The Virtual Sound library includes the **vs.allpass2~** object, which is precisely a second-order allpass filter created by connecting a **filtercoeff~** to a **biquad~** (as we already saw in chapter 3P). This object lets us set a center frequency and Q factor. Since this filter lets all frequencies pass without modifying their amplitude, we can only hear the effect of the filter by adding it to the unfiltered signal. Rebuild the patch shown in figure 6.42.

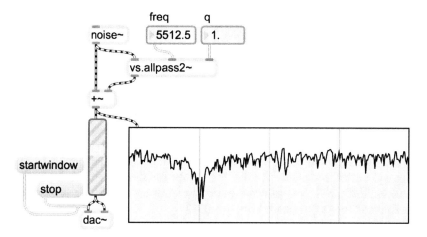

Fig. 6.42 A second-order allpass filter

This patch uses white noise as a source signal because it will allow us to assess the effect of the filter for audible frequencies, due to its flat spectrum. Note first of all that the filtering effect (which we can see in the **spectroscope~**) is that of the sum of the original and filtered signals; the filtered signal on its own would simply have a flat spectrum, just like the original input signal.

The effect seems to be that of a notch (bandstop) filter, which attenuates frequencies around a center frequency. In reality, as we have already learned, this attenuation happens because we are adding frequencies with different or opposite phases (see section 6.8 in the theory section). By changing the Q factor we can widen or narrow the attenuation band; Q values very close to 0 will eliminate most of the signal.

Let's now examine the effect of two cascaded filters with identical parameters (figure 6.43).

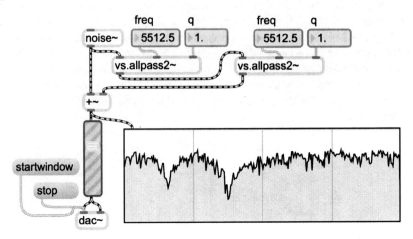

Fig. 6.43: Two cascaded allpass filters

Now the two attenuation bands are symmetrically equidistant from the center frequency, which is consistent with the phase response that we have already seen in section 6.8T. We are now ready to create a first, simple version of the phaser. Reconstruct the patch in figure 6.44.

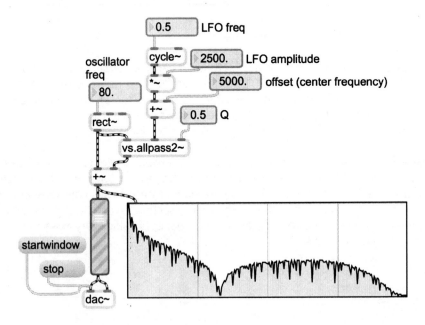

Fig. 6.44 The phaser effect

As a source sound we are using a bandlimited oscillator: `rect~` (a square wave generator). The effect we obtain is that of a single allpass filter whose center frequency is modulated by a sinusoidal LFO.

The parameters of the LFO are: the oscillation frequency (described as speed or rate in section 6.8T), the amplitude (range) and an offset that can be used to displace the central point around which the sinusoid LFO oscillates. The figure shows an offset of 5000 and an amplitude of 2500 – this means that the LFO will oscillate between the values 2500 (5000 - 2500) and 7500 (5000 + 2500). The Q factor is equal to 0.5, which provides us with a wide attenuation band. Since the source is an 80 Hz square wave, the effect affects the upper harmonics of the sound.

Try changing the LFO offset and amplitude, as well as the Q factor, in order to obtain different sonorities. As you can see, the effect is rather subtle, so let's add another allpass filter and make a few changes to the LFO (figure 6.45).

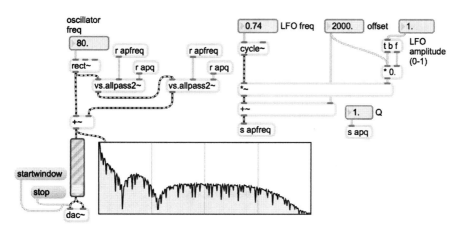

Fig. 6.45 The phaser, version 2

Just one LFO is used to modify the central frequency of both allpass filters (it is connected to both of them using **send** and **receive**). Note that the amplitude is not expressed in terms of absolute values, but rather as a multiplication factor of the offset. This means that when the amplitude is 1 (as in the figure) the sinusoid will oscillate between 0 and twice the offset (in the case of the figure, this means between 0 and 4000). Meaningful amplitude values are therefore between 0 (no oscillation) and 1 (maximum oscillation). Try replacing the sinusoidal LFO with another generator such as a non-bandlimited triangle wave (see the **triangle~** object shown in section 1.2) or a random generator like **rand~** or **vs.rand3~**. Then, try using a sound file as a source (the effect will be most effective when using a sound which is rich in partials, such as a recording of a drum set or other percussion or even an electric guitar).

Finally, let's see a more complex example of a phaser – open the file **06_10_ste-reo_phaser.maxpat** (figure 6.46).

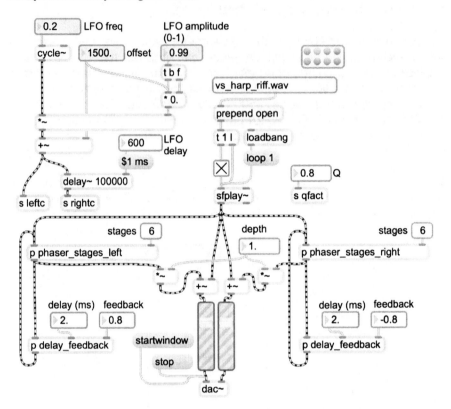

Fig. 6.46 The file **06_10_stereo_phaser.maxpat**

This patch implements a stereo phaser with 8 stages (or 4 allpass filters) for each channel. Each channel also has a delay with feedback, used to vary the effect.[15]

In the upper left part of the patch there is the LFO module that sends its control signal to two **send** objects: [s leftc] and [s rightc] (this latter has a user-definable delay so you can easily distinguish the effect on the two channels); we will soon look at the corresponding **receive** objects. On the right, there is a float number box connected to the [s qfact] object. This value represents the Q factor of the allpass filters contained in the phaser (we will also discuss this in more detail shortly).

---

[15] The delay with feedback inevitably adds comb filtering, but when used within certain limits this does not really interfere with the phaser. The delay time should be very low – in the order of a few milliseconds – or else it will create a sort of reverb that blurs the effect. Remember that, because the delay is created with a `tapin~`/`tapout~` pair, this delay time can never be less than the Signal Vector Size. Note also the difference between a flanger and a phaser: in a flanger the delay time is modulated, whereas in the phaser it is the center frequency of the allpass filters which is modulated.

The audio signal is sent to two subpatches [p phaser_stages_left] and [p phaser_stages_right]. The output of these subpatches (the wet sound) is summed with the unprocessed signal (dry sound). Furthermore, the wet sound is multiplied by the depth parameter (adjustable between 0 and 1) before being mixed with the dry sound; this controls the intensity of the effect. The right input of the [p phaser_stages_left] and [p phaser_stages_right] subpatches is used to set the number of stages in the phaser, and the object connected to it is not a number box but a **umenu** containing even numbers from 0 to 8. In figure 6.47 we can see the contents of the subpatch on the left (the one on the right is similar).

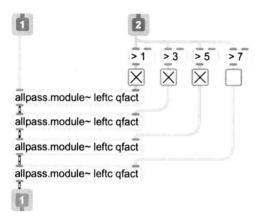

Fig. 6.47 The contents of [p phaser_stages_left]

There are 4 cascaded copies of the abstraction called **allpass.module~**.[16] The right input of this abstraction is used to activate and deactivate the module. In the figure, we can see that the first three modules are active and the fourth is has been deactivated, therefore constituting a 6-stage configuration built from 3 cascaded allpass filters (see also figure 6.46). To activate and deactivate the modules we use the relational operator >. In this case, the value 6 has arrived in the right inlet of the [p phaser_stages_left] subpatch, and since it is greater than 1 3 and 5, but less than 7, the **toggles** connected to the first three operators have become active, whereas the last has been deactivated. The **allpass.module~** abstraction can accept two arguments, so internally it evidently contains two replaceable arguments (i.e., the symbols #1 and #2 – refer to section IC.4 in this volume). The two arguments are leftc and qfact. If you look once again at figure 6.46 you will realize that these arguments are the names of the **send** objects which send the LFO control signal and Q factor to the allpass filters.

---

[16] This abstraction is also "local" – in other words it has been saved in the same folder as the main patch.

Let's therefore take a look at the contents of the original file for the **allpass. module~** abstraction (figure 6.48).

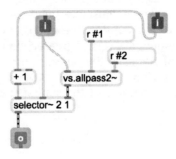

Fig. 6.48 The file **allpass.module~.maxpat**

We see that the first argument (#1), i.e., the control signal for the LFO, is used as the center frequency for the allpass filter, whereas the second argument (#2) is used to set the filter's Q factor. We will leave it to the reader to analyze the rest of this simple abstraction.

Returning to the main patch, the subpatch containing the allpass filters is connected to another subpatch ([**p** delay_feedback]) which contains a delay module. This is also a very simple subpatch whose analysis we will leave to the reader.

Listen attentively to all the presets that we have saved, paying careful attention to the different parameters before saving some presets of your own.

· ·

ACTIVITIES

Modify the patch in the file **06_10_stereo_phaser.maxpat** in the following ways:
• Change the oscillator used by the LFO

• Add other phase shifting stages

• Allow a different amplitude and offset to be set for each of the phase shifting stages

• Allow a different waveform and LFO frequency to be used for the left and right channels

• Change the sound source by replacing the **sfplay~** with one of the synthesizers we used in Interlude C.

· ·

6.9 PITCH SHIFTING, REVERSE AND VARIABLE DELAY
PITCH SHIFTING AND REVERSE

As we already learned in section 6.9 of the theory chapter, in order to modify the frequency of a sound using a delay line, we can dynamically vary the delay time. In Max we can do this using an object such as `line~`. Rebuild the patch shown in figure 6.49.

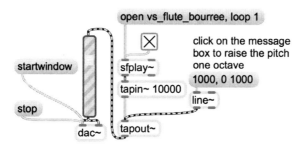

Fig. 6.49 Transposition using a delay line

In this example a sampled sound is raised one octave in pitch for one second. The `line~` object continually changes the delay time from 1000 milliseconds to 0 over the course of 1 second (1000 milliseconds), so the speed of the "playback head" on the delay line is therefore equal to -v (since it moves in the opposite direction of the "tape" that has been recorded with the "record head" – see theory section 6.9). To lower the sound by an octave, try connecting a message box with the message [0, 500 1000]. Here, the delay time changes from 0 to 500 over one second, thus having a speed of v/2 in the same direction as the tape.[17]

Now, insert the following values in message boxes into your patch, connect them to `line~`, and listen to how each of them changes the pitch of the sound (be sure to use a sound file with a definite pitch, such as the sound of a piano, flute or other pitched instrument).

2000, 0 1000 - the sound is raised one octave and a fifth for one second
0, 1500 2000 - the sound is lowered two octaves for 2 seconds
0, 3000 2000 - the sound is played in reverse and lowered one octave for 2 seconds
0, 500 500 - the sound stops (is silenced) for half a second

As you can see, working directly with delay times is not very intuitive; it would be much better if we could set the frequency ratio and duration that we want and let Max calculate the proper values for `line~`. In the theory section we saw that in order to calculate an appropriate playback speed, we need to subtract a given frequency ratio from a value of 1.

---

[17] As in the theory section, we are using positive values to indicate an increase in delay and negative values to indicate a decrease.

So, if we wanted to lower the pitch of a sound by 2 octaves (a ratio of 1/4 or 0.25) we need to set the playback head's velocity to 1 - 0.25 = 0.75v. When this value is positive (as it is here) we need to start from a delay time of 0 and increment it, because we are moving in the same direction as the tape. If we wanted this pitch change to last 2 seconds, we would need to increase the delay to 1.5 seconds over 2 seconds of time (see the second example, above). In practice, as we learned in the theory section, we just need to multiply the desired duration by the speed of the head in order to get the correct delay value for `line~`. Try modifying the patch from figure 6.49 so it looks like the one shown in figure 6.50.

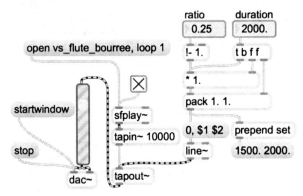

Fig. 6.50 Transposition using ratio and duration

Here we can set any ratio less than 1 (in other words, to lower the frequency or reverse the sound) and a duration in milliseconds. Note that we use the `!-` object to subtract the ratio from 1 and then multiply it by the desired duration. The result is grouped together with the duration into a 2-element list (using the **pack** object) which is sent to the message box [0, $1 $2], where the two elements take the place of the variables $1 and $2.

Each time we change the duration or the ratio, the pitch of the audio file will be modified. To repeat the prior transposition, you can simply click on the message box connected to `line~`; the message box on the lower right is just used to display the two values (delay and duration).

As we already stated, this structure only works for ratios less than 1, for ratios greater than 1 we need to use the configuration shown in figure 6.51.

Here, the ratio is still subtracted from 1, but because ratios greater than or equal to 1 produce negative values we need to transform them into positive values using the **abs** object (don't forget to give the object a floating-point argument or it will only output integer values).[18]

---

[18] Actually, since our ratios are greater than 1 we could just replace [!- 1.] with [- 1.], without needing to add the **abs** object, but we prefer to do this explicitly for the sake of clarity.

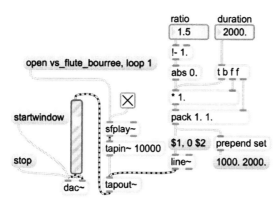

Fig. 6.51 Algorithm for upward transpositions

The resulting value, multiplied by the duration, represents the starting delay time – not the ending point – which means that the message box connected to **line~** now becomes [$1, 0 $2].

To see how to create a patch that handles any ratio, whether or not it is less than or greater than 1, open the file **06_11_pitch_shift.maxpat** (figure 6.52).

In this patch, the number box that sets the ratio (located more or less in the center of the patch) is sent to the **vs.split** object. This object has one argument that determines the "split" point of the input numbers: numbers less than this argument are sent out the left outlet, and numbers greater than or equal to it are sent out the right. This way, we can send ratio values less than 1 and greater than 1 to their respective algorithms.

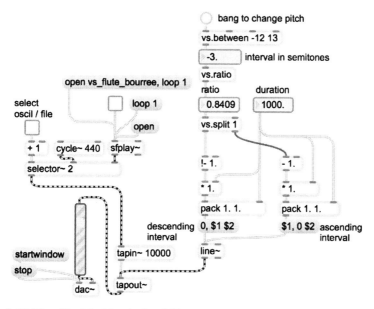

Fig. 6.52 The file **06_11_pitch_shift.maxpat**

Since it is much easier to transpose sounds using a musical interval, we can use the **vs.ratio** object (see section 5.4P) to convert an interval in semitones (ascending or descending) into the appropriate ratio. Each click on the button connected to **vs.between** will create a different transposition interval in semitones. If you are using the oscillator **cycle~** as a sound source, you should be able to clearly hear the equal-tempered transposition interval.

REAL-TIME PITCH SHIFTING

The pitch shifting technique that was just shown contains a noticeable delay of the input signal, and thus does not seem to be well adapted to the task of real-time transposition. However, if we use a very small delay (for example 1/10 of a second), the delay would be acceptable, even though the fragment of transposed sound would be too short. This apparent problem can actually be solved using a series of regular line segments produced by **phasor~** in place of the single segment output by **line~**. The easiest way to understand how this works would be to see it in action by reconstructing the patch shown in figure 6.53.

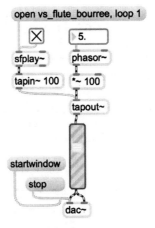

Fig. 6.53 Real-time pitch shifting, version 1

This patch, in addition to producing a considerable number of clicks that we will deal with later, transposes an input sound one octave lower. Let's take a look at how it works. The **phasor~** and the multiplier are used to generate 5 ramps going from 0 to 100 each second; this series of ramps is sent to **tapout~**. The duration of each ramp is 200 milliseconds (the period corresponding to 5 Hz.), and the delay time value goes from 0 to 100 milliseconds, meaning that the "playback head" is moving at a speed of v/2 in the same direction as the "tape." As we know from what we have already learned in the theory part of this chapter, this results in lowering the pitch of the input sound by one octave.

What does the tape speed *v* correspond to in this algorithm? The answer may not be immediately clear, so we should throw some light on the subject, to see how it relates to the frequency of the **phasor~**. We have already stated that the system outputs ramps that go from 0 to 100, therefore covering the entire range of the 100 millisecond delay line. This means that the entire "tape," moving at speed *v*, will "run" over 100 milliseconds of time, in other words over 1/10 of a second, which implies a frequency of 10 Hz. If we also set the frequency of the **phasor~** to 10 Hz, we would hear nothing because the "playback head" would be moving at the same speed in the same direction as the "tape," and would therefore be stationary with respect to it (try it and you will only hear clicks).

So, if we wanted to lower the sound by 2 octaves, what frequency do we need to give **phasor~**? Given that a two-octave downward transposition is equal to a ratio of 1/4 (0.25), the speed of the playback head should be 1 - 0.25 = 0.75v. Since we already know that *v* equals 10 Hz (in this patch), 0.75 would be equal to 7.5 Hz – try it out!

Now, let's raise the pitch of the sound by one octave: the ratio is 2, so the speed is equal to 1 - 2 = -1v. The frequency of the **phasor~** should therefore be -10 Hz (also try this out for yourself).

In this case, you will notice that using a negative frequency value works perfectly to transpose the sound upward, because the ramp generated by the **phasor~** and the multiplier now goes from 100 to 0 (and not from 0 to 100 as it would for positive frequencies). The "playback head" therefore moves contrary to the direction of the "tape", conforming to what we have already learned in the theory part of this chapter.

Generally, to obtain the correct frequency in Hz for the **phasor~**, we subtract a given transposition ratio from 1, as we would normally do, and multiply it by 10 [19]. Now, modify the patch as illustrated in figure 6.54.

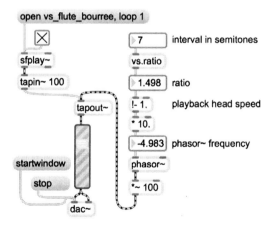

Fig. 6.54 Real-time pitch shifting, version 2

_____

[19] We should reiterate this concept because it is important: we are multiplying by 10 here because this value was obtained from the length of our "tape", which is 100 ms. (1/10 of a second). If its length were 200 ms. (1/5 of a second) we would have needed to multiply by 5, instead (and naturally also multiply the ramp output by **phasor~** by 200, not 100).

In this patch we set a transposition interval in semitones, convert it into a ratio using the **vs.ratio object**, and continue the rest of the frequency calculation for the **phasor~** as previously explained.

Let's now take a look at how we can get rid of the annoying clicks created by the algorithm. These clicks are created when the playback head, controlled by **phasor~** and the multiplier, jumps suddenly from 100 back to 0 (or from 0 to 100 if the **phasor~** frequency is negative), creating a discontinuity in the output signal. In order to eliminate it, we need to use an envelope that takes the volume to 0 at the point where the jump in the ramp happens. To do this, we have chosen a sinusoidal envelope, created by making the (co)sine wave output by **cycle~** into a unipolar signal. Modify the patch as shown in figure 6.55.

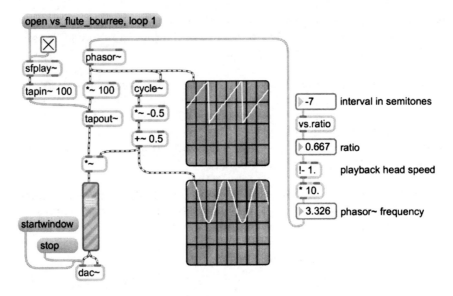

Fig. 6.55 Real-time pitch shifting, version 3

Note that the **phasor~** object sends its signal to the right input of **cycle~**, therefore continually modifying its phase.[20] In order to be able to be used as an envelope for the output of **tapout~**, the sinusoid generated by **cycle~** is first reduced in amplitude by half and simultaneously phase-inverted using the [*~ -0.5] object, then converted into a unipolar signal with the [+~ 0.5] object. Comparing the two oscilloscopes, we can see that whenever **phasor~** produces a discontinuity (the upper oscilloscope), and therefore a click, the envelope (lower oscilloscope) is at 0 and so the click will be inaudible.

We have succeeded in removing the clicks by applying this envelope, but we have also caused the amplitude of the output sound to continually oscillate.

---

[20] We have already discussed the use of the right inlet of **cycle~** in detail in section 2.1P of the first volume (in the section dedicated to phase).

We can solve this problem by adding a second playback head that is controlled by a series of ramps that are a half a cycle out of phase from the ramps used for the first head. This way, when the amplitude of the first envelope is at 0, the amplitude of the second envelope will be at 1 and vice-versa. To see a complete implementation of this, open the file **06_12_rt_pitch_shift.maxpat** (figure 6.56).

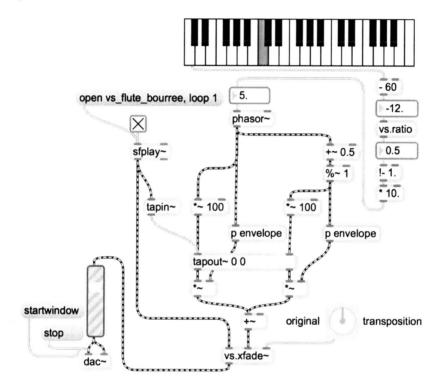

Fig. 6.56 The file **06_12_rt_pitch_shift.maxpat**

As you can see, the **tapout~** object here has two "playback heads" both controlled by a single **phasor~**. You will notice that the second of these has had its phase offset by half a cycle, using an addition and an modulo operator.[21] Inside the [p envelope] subpatch we can find the algorithm that creates the sinusoidal envelopes (identical to that shown in figure 6.55). The **kslider** keyboard at the top of the patch lets us transpose the sound up to 2 octaves lower and one octave higher. The **dial** object in the lower part of the patch can be used to mix the original sound with the transposed one (i.e., wet/dry balance).

---

[21] Describe the de-phasing algorithm for yourself. We have already seen a similar strategy in the section about Shepard Tones in section IB.9 of the first volume.

This algorithm works fairly well with melodic sounds that have a soft attack (like the flute), and less well for percussive sounds. Furthermore, when the transposition is too great (and especially when transposing upward), the amplitude modulation caused by the rapidly alternating sinusoidal envelopes becomes clearly audible (we will discuss this effect more in Volume 3). In the third volume we will also take a look at other techniques that can be used to transpose sounds.

. . . .

ACTIVITIES

- Using the patch in figure 6.56, control the transposition factor using an LFO connected to a **snapshot~**. You could use a noise generator to slightly vary the intonation of the sound, or a sine wave oscillator to create cyclic glissandi above and below the original pitch.

- Add a feedback loop to the patch shown in figure 6.56, making sure the feedback multiplier does not exceed the interval between -1 and 1. Note that each time the signal is sent back to the delay line it will be transposed again. You should also add a highpass filter (or the **vs.dcblock~** object) to make sure that you do not accumulate DC offset in the feedback loop.

- Add other pitch shifters with different transposition factors to the patch in order to create a "harmonizer" effect for the input signal. To save space, you could put the pitch shifting algorithms into subpatches.

. . . .

GLISSANDO

As we have already learned, if we want to create a glissando using a delay, we can't just simply move the playback head along the delay line at a constant speed, but need to move it with an acceleration or deceleration. In other words the change in delay time should not follow a straight line, but rather a curve.

The **line~** object that we have been using only outputs line segments, but we have already seen in section 1.3P that there exists a similar object called **curve~** which can create curves using a syntax similar to that of **line~**. As we have seen, this object needs to be given a third parameter for each breakpoint, so, in addition to the value and time, we need to add a "curve factor" that varies from -1 to 1. Positive values indicate exponential curves, with different slopes, and negative values represent logarithmic curves.

To hear the effect created by using **curve~** with a delay line, open the file **06_13_delay_gliss.maxpat** (figure 6.57).

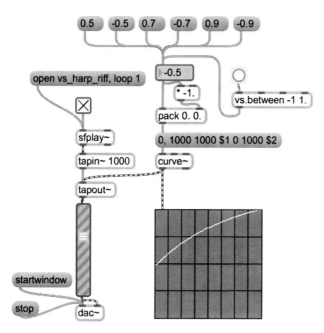

Fig. 6.57 The file **06_13_delay_gliss.maxpat**

The delay time varies from 0 to 1000 milliseconds and then returns to 0 over a total duration of 2000 milliseconds. The ascending and descending curve factors have the opposite sign. It is possible to choose between a selection of predetermined curve factors using the message boxes at the top of the patch, or to generate a random curve factor using the **vs.between** object.

• •

ACTIVITY

Starting with the patch in figure 6.57, modify the message box to create different glissandi.

• •

VARIABLE DELAY WITHOUT TRANSPOSITION

The **delay~** object allows us to create a variable delay without transposing the sound. When its delay time is changed, the **delay~** object does not move the "playback head," but instead creates a crossfade between the previous delay and the new one (using two alternating internal "playback heads"). It is possible to define the length of the crossfade (which is 50 milliseconds by default) using the "ramp" message.

When the delay is continuously modified (when using the **line** object, for example), the **delay~** object internally creates a series of crossfades between the rapid succession of static delay times. Because of this behavior, it is possible to modify the duration of an input sound without modifying its pitch. Rebuild the patch in figure 6.58.

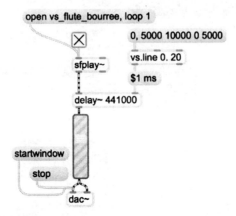

Fig. 6.58 Variable delay

A note of caution about the argument to **delay~**: it is set here to 441,000 samples, which implies a maximum delay time of 10 seconds at a sampling rate of 44100 Hz. If the sampling rate of your system is different, you will need to modify this argument.

Activate the patch and, after waiting a few seconds to let the delay line fill up with sound, click on the message box connected to the **vs.line** object: the length of the flute sound will be reduced by half for 10 seconds, and then doubled for 5 seconds, without changing its pitch. If we had used a **tapin~/tapout~** pair with these same parameters (and using a signal to modify the delay time), we would have transposed the sound down by one octave for 10 seconds, then up one octave for 5 seconds, corresponding to the halving and doubling of the playback speed.

Needless to say, we can also use **tapin~** and **tapout~** to create such a variable delay without transposition, however to do this we need to build our own cross-fading mechanism between a pair of playback heads.

Why would we need to implement this algorithm with **tapin~/tapout~** if the feature already exists in **delay~**? If we wanted add a feedback loop to our variable delay or allocate a circular buffer (create a delay line) whose length is expressed in milliseconds instead of samples, we would need to use a **tapin~/tapout~** pair. Furthermore, the cross-fading technique can be put to good use in other situations where parameter changes might create unwanted clicks.

There are several ways to implement such a cross-fade mechanism.[22]

---

22 Here we are using an algorithm proposed by Richard Dudas.

Rebuild the patch shown in figure 6.58b.

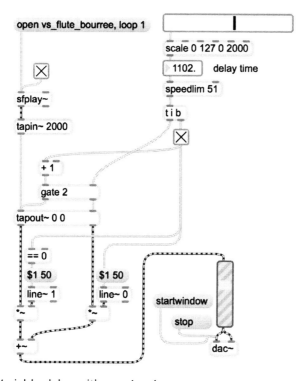

Fig. 6.58b Variable delay with `tapin~/tapout~`

To create a click-free series of delay time changes, we recommend turning on the Scheduler in Overdrive and In Audio Interrupt options in the Audio Status window (see section 5.1P).

We can change the delay time using the **slider** in the upper right part of the patch. New delay values are sent to the **speedlim** object. This object, as its name suggests, limits the speed of incoming messages, only outputting messages as fast, or slower than, the interval which is provided as an argument (in this case 51 milliseconds). The values received by **speedlim** are sent to the [**t** i b] object which first sends a bang to the **toggle** underneath. With each bang, the **toggle** alternates between 1 and 0; these values are used to open one of the two **gate** objects connected to the two **tapout~** objects (the two "playback heads"). The numerical value that is then sent out the left outlet of [**t** i b] will be used to update the delay time for one of the two playback heads (the one which is not currently being output). Returning to the **toggle**, we can see that its value is also being used to create 50 millisecond ramps (using two **line~** objects) which alternately ramp up and ramp down the amplitude of the output signal of the two **tapout~** objects. Therefore, the "playback head" that receives the new delay value will be faded in while the "playback head" with the old delay value will be faded out, thereby creating a cross-fade between the two **tapout~** objects.

293

6.10 THE KARPLUS-STRONG ALGORITHM

In order to simulate a plucked string with the Karplus-Strong algorithm we need to use a noise generator to fill a memory buffer, which in turn will be played in a loop and lowpass filtered with each repetition. The length of the buffer determines the frequency of the resulting sound, while the filter makes the components in the sound progressively lose energy.

We can use a `tapin~/tapout~` pair with feedback to create a circular buffer. The delay time determines the length of the buffer and consequently also the frequency of the output sound. To play a note we need to inject a burst of white noise (i.e., a random sequence of sample values) into the delay line; the length of this noise burst should be the same as the length of the delay line itself. To open and close the noise generator, we can simply use an envelope controlled by the `line~` object. In figure 6.59 we can see a basic implementation of this algorithm.

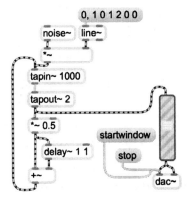

Fig. 6.59 The Karplus-Strong algorithm

First of all, make sure that the Signal Vector Size in the Audio Status window is set to a sufficiently low value (16 samples, for instance), otherwise it will not be possible to create high-pitched sounds. A rectangular envelope (i.e., with an immediate attack and release) has been applied to the noise generator; the envelope has been set to 2 milliseconds, which is the same as the delay time, which therefore produces a 500 Hz sound (since 1/0.002 = 500). The feedback loop includes a first-order lowpass filter, previously discussed in section 6.10 of the theory section, which has ben realized using a `delay~` and a multiplier. In reality, the frequency will not be exactly 500 Hz, because the filter, as we previously learned, creates a half-sample delay. Therefore, if our sampling rate is 44100 Hz, the resulting frequency will be precisely 44100 / (88+0.5) = 498.3 Hz. Note how this value was calculated: the two-millisecond delay corresponds to 88.2 samples, but since our delay must be a whole number of samples, the value has been rounded to 88, to which we have added the half-sample delay caused by the lowpass filter. The ratio of this value to the sampling rate gives us the exact frequency of the sound generated by the algorithm.

Generating a frequency of exactly 500 Hz therefore does not seem to be possible, because of the two-tenths of a sample which had to be rounded off from the delay length. Nonetheless, as we know from studying the theory section of this chapter, we can create precise intonation using an allpass filter which lets us create a fractional delay. Creating this kind of very precise allpass filter is not very easy, but there is good news: the **tapout~** algorithm contains a built-in interpolation system that allows fractional delay times, so it is not necessary to add an allpass into the feedback loop for the purposes of tuning.

To produce a sound with a precise arbitrary frequency, we therefore need to first convert the frequency in samples, subtract 0.5, convert it back into milliseconds, and use it as the delay time. Additionally, because of delays inherent in the interpolation algorithm, the fractional delay ends up being one sample longer than the actual delay time we specify, so we also have to subtract an extra sample to compensate for this when making the calculation. Figure 6.60 shows the complete algorithm.

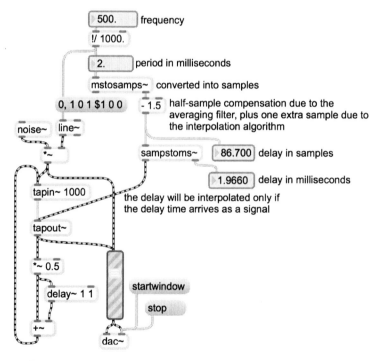

Fig. 6.60 The Karplus-Strong algorithm, version 2

First, notice that in this implementation the signal output by **noise~** and its envelope has also been connected to the output. This is because the output of **tapout~** has one period of delay, which can be noticeable for very low-pitched sounds. Notice also that the delay time is not sent to **tapout~** as a signal (from the left outlet of **sampstoms~**) because this object does not interpolate values if the delay time is provided as a numerical Max value.

Now let's look at how we could improve this algorithm. First, you may have already noticed that low notes are longer than high ones. Although this does correspond to what actually happens with real plucked strings, the difference is much more pronounced, even excessive. Fortunately, we can add an attenuation factor into the feedback loop to help shorten the low notes, as suggested by Jaffe and Smith.[23] Additionally, because the delay line could produce an accumulation of DC offset, we should also add a highpass filter before the audio output in order to eliminate it.

Finally, there is the problem of the minimum delay time inherent in the **tapin~/ tapout~** pair, which corresponds to the Signal Vector Size we are using. This value corresponds to the highest note we can create using the Karplus-Strong algorithm. Suppose, for example, we are using a Signal Vector Size of 16 samples and our sampling rate is 44100 Hz. The minimum possible delay would be equal to 16/44100 = 0.000363 seconds, corresponding to about 2765 Hz. If we wanted to generate a sound with a higher pitch, we would need to decrease the Signal Vector Size, but, as we have already learned in section 5.1P, this would increase the amount of CPU used by MSP to run the patch (in other words it would be less efficient). There is, however, a way to reduce the signal vector size for only part of the patch, using a **poly~** object. Using the "vs" argument, this object lets us define a different Signal Vector Size than that of the main patch, which will be used for the abstraction loaded by the **poly~** object itself. Therefore all we need to do is put the feedback loop into a **poly~** object (with just one voice) and set the **poly~** object's signal vector size very low – for example down to 4 samples.

Load the file **06_14_karplus_string.maxpat** which includes the corrections and improvements we have been discussing (figure 6.61).

On the left, under the keyboard, we calculate an attenuation factor (which is none other than a multiplier for the feedback) that will be used to slightly reduce the length of all notes whose frequency is less than 440 Hz. Here, we used the **zmap** object, which is similar to **scale** (see section IB.8), except that input values which lie outside the given input range are constrained (clipped) within the limits of the output range. What this means in this context is that any input values greater than 440 Hz will create an attenuation factor equal to 1 and any values less than 0 Hz will create an attenuation factor equal to 0.99.[24] As you can see, the attenuation factor is always very close to 1 (which itself implies no attenuation). These values were chosen empirically and consequently might now cause very low notes to have a resonance that is too short; try modifying the parameters in order to make it sound more natural (remembering that the attenuation factor should never be greater than 1!).

---

[23] See section 6.10T.

[24] If we had use the **scale** object here, an input value of 880 Hz would have generated an attenuation factor of 1.01, which would have caused the delay line to continually get louder and eventually "explode."

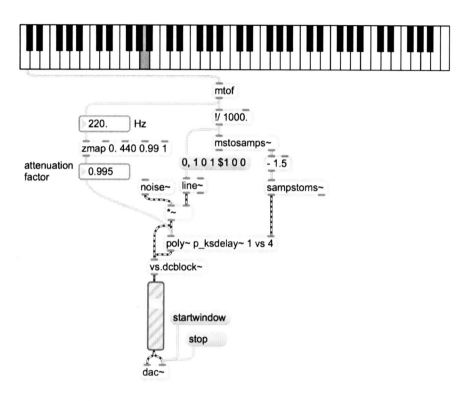

Fig. 6.61 The file **06_14_karplus_strong.maxpat**

Our delay line is located inside the **poly~** object. Note that the "vs" argument is used to set the Signal vector Size inside **poly~**: in this case it has been set to 4 samples. As you can see, we are not using the **poly~** object here to take advantage of its polyphonic capabilities (it has only been provided with one single voice), but rather to be able to have a sufficiently low Signal Vector Size without excessively affecting the CPU usage. The **poly~** object, in fact, has a wide range of uses that goes above and beyond what its name suggests. For example, it also has the arguments "up" and "down" that can be used, respectively, to increase or lower the sampling rate inside the abstraction loaded by the object, so "up 4" would signify that the sampling rate inside **poly~** would be quadrupled with respect to the sampling rate of the system.

In figure 6.62 we can see the contents of the abstraction **p_ksdelay~.maxpat** used inside `poly~`.

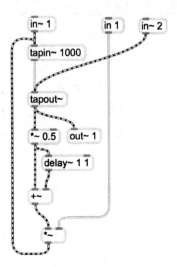

Fig. 6.62 The abstraction **p_ksdelay~.maxpat**

At the bottom of the patch we have added a multiplier for the attenuation factor inside the Karplus-Strong algorithm's feedback loop. Note also that at the top of the patch there are two objects, `in~` and `in`, which both have the argument 1. This has been done so that the **poly~** object's first inlet can receive both signals and Max messages; signals are passed to the abstraction via the `in~` object and messages via `in`. We will leave the reader to analyze the rest of the main patch.

. . . .

ACTIVITIES

Make the following modifications to the patch from figure 6.61:

- Normally a very forcefully plucked string will have a brighter spectrum than one plucked delicately. You can create this effect by reducing or increasing the bandwidth of the noise generator. Therefore, add a lowpass filter to the output of **noise~**, using a lower cutoff frequency when playing quieter notes on the string (you will have to find the optimum values for yourself). Control everything with the **keyslider**, associating the frequency to the MIDI note that it outputs, and the lowpass cutoff frequency to the MIDI velocity value (you will probably need to use **scale** or **zmap**).
- Control the note generation using a step sequencer.
- Add a slapback delay to the plucked string sound.
- Replace the slapback delay with a tape delay.
- Replace it with the multitap delay used in the patch **06_02_multitap2.maxpat** (figure 6.12)

- Replace it with the multiband delay shown in the patch **06_04_multiband_tap.maxpat** (figure 6.20)
- Apply a flanger to the patch.
- Replace the flanger with a chorus.
- Replace it with a phaser.

· ·

6.11 DELAY LINES FOR MAX MESSAGES

In addition to delaying audio signals, it is also possible to delay Max messages, using the appropriate objects. The first object that we will look at is called **delay** (without tilde) and is used to delay a bang message sent to its inlet (figure 6.63).

Fig. 6.63 The **delay** object

This object takes an argument that represents the delay time in milliseconds, or in one of the time values we covered in section IC.1 (in which case it should be set using the @delaytime attribute). Alternatively, it is also possible to send the delay time to the object's right inlet.

When the **delay** object receives a bang in its left inlet, it will "wait" the amount of time indicated and then output the bang via its outlet. In figure 6.64 we can see an example that will generate a series of clicks a half second apart. Rebuild the patch and analyze how it works.

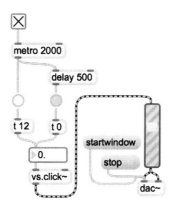

Fig. 6.64 A click generator

The object can only delay one bang at a time. If it receives a new bang before the delay time has elapsed, the previous bang will be cancelled (and therefore not sent out the outlet), and the new bang will be delayed, instead. Needless to say, if a third bang arrives before the delay time has elapsed, the second bang will be cancelled, and so forth. To give an example, in the patch shown in figure 6.65, the **delay** object will only send a bang if the **metro** is turned off, because as long as the delay time is greater than the tempo of the metronome, each new bang output by the **metro** will cancel the previous one held in the delay (try it!).

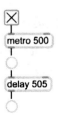

Fig. 6.65 A constantly postponed bang

If we send a numeric value to the left inlet of **delay**, the object will wait the corresponding amount of time and then output a bang, in addition to setting the delay time used to delay subsequent bangs.

In order to delay numerical values we can use the **pipe** object. This object can have a variable number of synchronized inlets and outlets, depending on the number of arguments given. Rebuild the patch in figure 6.66

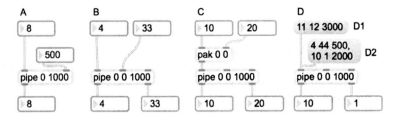

Fig. 6.66 The **pipe** object

Example A shows a **pipe** object with two arguments. The final argument is always used to set the delay time, whereas the preceding arguments determine the number of elements that will be delayed (in this case just one). A numerical value sent to the rightmost inlet can be used to change the delay time. The big difference with delay is that **pipe** can store more than one delayed element; try sending a series of numbers by rapidly changing the value in number box connected to the left inlet with the mouse.

Example B shows how to delay two numerical values. Remember that only the left inlet of **pipe** is a hot inlet, so in order to generate two delayed output values we have to send a value to the first inlet.

It is also possible to send numerical values as a list (shown in example C). By using the **pak** object, we can also make the second inlet a hot inlet (as we have already learned). If the list has one element more than the number of values that **pipe** can delay, this element is used as a new delay time (as shown in example D1). Different lists can also have different delay times, and **pipe** is capable of managing them all independently (example D2).

Like the **delay** object, **pipe** can also work with the time values we discussed in section IC.1 (using the @delaytime attribute).

Now let's take a look at one possible application of **pipe**; open the file **06_15_delay_max.maxpat** (figure 6.67).

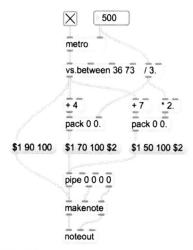

Fig. 6.67 The file **06_15_delay_max.maxpat**

This patch creates a stream of random notes using the **vs.between** object. With each note you hear an arpeggiated major triad with decreasing MIDI velocity. If the randomly generated note were a middle C, we would hear the following notes in succession:

Note	Velocity
C3 (60)	90
E3 (64)	70
G3 (67)	50

If the random note were a D3, we would hear the following notes in succession:

Note	Velocity
D3 (62)	90
F#3 (66)	70
A3 (69)	50

...and so on. As you can see, there are three message boxes in the patch. The leftmost message box is directly connected to the **makenote** object, and sends a list containing the random note value generated by **vs.between** ($1), the value 90 (used by **makenote** as a velocity value), and the value 100 (used for the duration of the note). The second message box is connected to the **pipe** object. It sends a list whose first element is the random note value plus 4 ($1), the second element is 70, the third is 100 and the fourth (which will be used as the delay time) is 1/3 of the metronome's tempo ($2). The third message also sends a list to the **pipe** object. This list's first element is the random note value plus 7 ($1), the second element is 50, the third is 100 and the fourth (used as a delay time) is 2/3 the tempo of the **metro** ($2).

· ·

ACTIVITIES

- Analyze the patch in figure 6.67 and explain how it works.

- Add a fourth note, a minor seventh (10 semitones) from the random note, to the arpeggio. For each bang of the **metro** you should therefore play 4 notes (instead of 3) at regularly-spaced intervals in time.

· ·

Using the **pipe** object it is also possible to create a feedback effect. Open the file **06_16_feedback_max.maxpat** (figure 6.68).

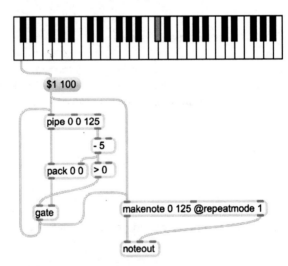

Fig. 6.68 The file **06_16_feedback_max.maxpat**

With each mouse click, the **kslider** object sends a note value to the message box, which creates the list [$1 100]. This list is sent directly to the **makenote**, which creates a MIDI note to send to **noteout**, using the note value from kslider, a velocity of 100 and a duration of 125. The same list is sent to the **pipe** object which delays it by 125 milliseconds. At the output of the **pipe**, the velocity is reduced by 5; if the result is greater than 0, the note with the reduced velocity goes through the gate, is played, and once again sent to the **pipe** where the feedback loop starts over. After a certain number of repetitions, the velocity will no longer be greater than 0, so the gate will be closed and the feedback loop broken.

Note the "repeatmode 1" attribute that has been given to the **makenote** object. This attribute is used to define the behavior of the object when multiple notes of the same pitch are superimposed. By default ("repeatmode 0") the object will create a regular note off for each note, even when the same note is played twice, sounding at the same time. This means that if we have two or more C3 notes superimposed, the first note off that arrives would shut off the most recently played C3, or possibly all of the C3 notes that are playing. When "repeatmode" is set to 1, each time that a new note-on whose pitch is the same as one of the notes currently playing is received, **makenote** will first send a note-off for the old note, and then send a note-on for the new one. In other words, this ensures that two of the same note will never be allowed to play simultaneously, since it shuts off older instances of the same note as necessary. There is also a "repeatmode 2" which causes **makenote** to send only one note-off for the final note of any superimposed notes of the same pitch, suppressing the output of any preceding note-off messages for that pitch. In the inspector, these three attribute modes are called "Poly", "Re-Trigger" and "Stop Last".

. . . .

ACTIVITIES

Make the following variations on the patch shown in figure 6.68:

• in addition to the velocity, lower the pitch of the note by one semitone with each repetition.

• randomly vary the pitch of the note, within 3 semitones of the original note, for each repetition.

• with each repetition, make the velocity value increase (instead of decrease), starting around 30 and stopping when the value exceeds 127 (the maximum possible velocity).

• make the duration of the note decrease with each repetition (changing from legato to staccato)

• modify the time interval between repetitions so it decreases (creating an accelerando)

• modify the time interval randomly between repetitions

LIST OF MAX OBJECTS

allpass~
An allpass filter whose feedforward and feedback are implemented with two separate delay lines.

biquad~
Allows any kind of second order filter to be created. However, instead of using the usual filter control parameters, such as cutoff frequency and Q factor, this object takes 5 coefficients which can be generated by objects like **filtercoeff~** and **filtergraph~**.

comb~
A comb filter that implements a delay with feedback, also incorporating a feedforward stage.

cross~
A third order filter used to separate a signal into two frequency bands, also known as a crossover filter.

delay
An object used to delay a single bang message sent to its input. The delay time, expressed in milliseconds, can be provided as an argument or sent to the right inlet.

delay~
A basic audio delay unit. It takes two arguments, both expressed in samples: the first is the maximum possible delay time and the second is the actual delay time used.

pipe
An object used to concurrently delay multiple numeric messages. It can have a variable number of inlets and outlets (depending on the number of arguments provided).

tapin~
This object functions like a "record head" for a delay line. The object allocates (i.e., it "owns") a portion of memory where it can write, or record the signal it receives. Each time it reaches the end of its allocated memory, it returns to the beginning, overwriting what had been previously written. Technically speaking, this is known as a circular buffer.

tapout~
This object is used in conjunction with **tapin~** (above), and functions like a "playback head," reading the same circular buffer as the **tapin~** it is associated with, at a given distance with respect to the latter object's record head, thereby creating a specified delay.

vs.allpass2~
A second order allpass filter

vs.comb~
A comb filter implementing a delay with feedback, also incorporating a feedforward stage. The difference between this filter and **comb~** is that it uses a decay time parameter for the resonance, instead of a feedback coefficient. The object internally transforms the decay time into an appropriate feedback coefficient.

vs.dcblock~
A highpass filter used to eliminate DC offset.

vs.explist
This object generates a list of numbers in a numerical series. The number of elements, minimum and maximum values and direction of this series can be defined using the object's 4 inlets.

vs.pan~
This object implements a panning algorithm, taking an input sound and placing it in a stereo field according to a control signal sent to its right inlet.

vs.split
This object has one argument that determines the "split" point of numbers sent to its inlet. Numbers less than the argument will be output from its left outlet, whereas numbers greater than (or equal to) the argument are output out the right.

zmap
Converts one range of input values into a different range of output values, rescaling each value into the new range, and outputting the converted value. Input values outside the range are constrained (clipped) within the given output range.

LIST OF ATTRIBUTES, MESSAGES AND ARGUMENTS FOR SPECIFIC MAX OBJECTS

delay~
-Ramp (message)
This is used to determine the length of the crossfade between two "playback heads" internal to the object, when changing the delay time.

flonum
-Minimum and Maximum (attributes)
These attributes limit the range of values that a floating point number box can output. These attributes are also available for integer number boxes.

makenote
-Repeat Mode (attribute)
Determines the management (and thus the ordering) of note-off messages when simultaneously playing several notes with the same pitch.

poly~
-Vs (argument)
This can be used to define a different Signal Vector Size for the abstraction loaded by the **poly~** object than is used by the main patch

-Up and Down (arguments)
These can be used to raise or lower the sampling rate inside the **poly~** object, with respect to the sampling rate of the system.

tapin~ and tapout~
-Tapconnect (message) .
This message (output automatically when the DSP engine is turned on) allows the **tapin~** and **tapout~** objects to share the same circular buffer.

various objects
-Ignore Click (attribute)
This prevents the object from being selected or modified using the mouse when the patch is in performance mode.

7T
DYNAMICS PROCESSORS

PREREQUISITES FOR THE CHAPTER
• THE CONTENTS OF VOLUME 1, CHAPTERS 5 AND 6 (THEORY AND PRACTICE) AND INTERLUDE C

OBJECTIVES
KNOWLEDGE
• TO KNOW THE DIFFERENT TYPES OF DYNAMIC PROCESSORS
• TO KNOW THE POSSIBLE USES FOR ENVELOPE FOLLOWERS
• TO KNOW THE USES AND PARAMETERS OF COMPRESSORS, DE-ESSERS AND LIMITERS
• TO KNOW THE USE AND PARAMETERS OF EXPANDERS AND (NOISE-)GATES
• TO KNOW THE USES AND DIFFERENCE BETWEEN:
  DOWNWARD COMPRESSION, DOWNWARD EXPANSION
  UPWARD COMPRESSION, UPWARD EXPANSION, PARALLEL COMPRESSION
  MULTI-ZONE COMPRESSORS, MULTI-BAND COMPRESSORS
  COMPRESSORS WITH EXTERNAL TIME THRESHOLD, SIDE CHAIN AND DUCKING,
  ADAPTIVE GATE AND DUCKER, TRIGGERING GATES, GATE SEQUENCERS
  FEEDBACK WITH CONTROLLED DYNAMICS

CONTENTS
• ENVELOPE FOLLOWERS
• COMPRESSORS AND LIMITERS
• EXPANDERS AND GATES
• DOWNWARD, UPWARD AND PARALLEL COMPRESSION
• DOWNWARD AND UPWARD EXPANSION
• SIDE CHAIN AND DUCKING
• TECHNICAL AND CREATIVE USES OF DYNAMICS PROCESSORS

ACTIVITIES
• SOUND EXAMPLES

TESTING
• TEST WITH SHORT ANSWERS
• LISTENING AND ANALYSIS TEST

SUPPORTING MATERIALS
• FUNDAMENTAL CONCEPTS – GLOSSARY – DISCOGRAPHY

In Section 5.1 we spoke of the dynamic range as being the ratio between the maximum and minimum amplitudes that can be represented by a given piece of hardware, software or storage medium. This is a purely technical description, based on the number of bits used. Within this range, defined by the number of bits, we can make technical and expressive choices that could be different for each piece or each sound. Although we may be working with a system that technically has a dynamic range of 90 dB, we could decide to compose a work for television, whose dynamic range would therefore be reduced, say, to 15 dB. In this context, the use of dynamics processors does not have anything to do with the number of bits available (this is predetermined by the working environment settings when creating a new project and thus cannot be changed) but rather on technical and expressive choices that can be used within a given system in order to change the dynamic range of a sound or piece.

Dynamics Processors are devices that process a sound (or a series of sounds or even an entire piece) by transforming its dynamic range for a wide variety of purposes, either technical or creative. Remember that dynamic range is expressed as a ratio, or difference, between maximum and minimum amplitude, and is therefore a very different concept from absolute amplitude. For example, you could have a piece of music whose dynamic range is 20 dB with a maximum amplitude of 0 dB, and another with the same dynamic range whose maximum amplitude is -3 dB. We will soon see how to work with both of these parameters, but for the moment it is important just to remember that the main purpose of dynamics processors is to transform the dynamic range in different ways.

In this chapter we will look specifically at envelope followers / envelope shapers, different types of compressors and expanders, limiters and gates.

7.1 ENVELOPE FOLLOWER

The **envelope follower** (sometimes called a peak amplitude follower or envelope detector) performs the function of extracting the envelope of a sound by measuring the amplitude of its waveform's positive-valued peaks. The envelope follower produces a control signal based on a series of amplitude values extracted from a given sound A. This control envelope can then be imposed upon another sound B (by simply multiplying it by the extracted envelope), or used to control the center frequency of a filter or other effect parameters. There are an endless number of possible applications: percussive envelopes can be applied to continuous sounds, or the envelope of a recording of the waves of the sea could be applied to the sound of a chorus, as will be demonstrated in the examples that follow.

You could even remove the envelope from a sound by dividing the sound's signal by its own envelope. Doing this actually cancels out the sound's envelope by giving it a constant value of 1.[1] The resulting sound will thus have no

---

[1] Any number divided by itself is equal to 1.

changes in dynamics. This is useful, because once its dynamics have been flattened out, the amplitude envelope of an entirely different sound can be effectively applied to it, by multiplying the sound and envelope together.

You could also invert a sound's envelope, so that when the original sound is at its maximum peak amplitude, the inverted sound will be at its minimum. These types of operations are sometimes referred to as envelope shaping.

Another function we will look at is often called *balance* in some audio programming languages[2] (not to be confused with the same term which is commonly used to indicate control of stereo spatialization). This technique is used in cases where a filtered sound, for example, is significantly weaker (or louder) than the original, unfiltered sound. A typical example would be when the center frequency of a bandpass filter is not present or has a very low amplitude in the original sound. Using the balance algorithm, the envelope of the original sound can be applied to the resulting filtered sound.

. . . .

SOUND EXAMPLE 7A.1

     a) Envelope of a piano imposed on the sound of a flute
     b) Envelope of a snare drum applied to a trumpet
     c) Excerpt from Cipriani, A., *Aqua Sapientiae/Angelus Domini*: envelope of
        sounds of ocean waves applied to contrapuntal voices.

. . . .

An envelope can be measured using different types of systems: one of these, described by Dodge and Jerse, uses a technique called *rectification*, which amounts to transforming the amplitude values of the samples that make up a sound into absolute values (i.e., without a + or - sign). This way all negative sample values will become positive. The "rectified" signal is then sent to a lowpass filter (with a sub-audio cutoff frequency) which is used to round out the sharp edges of the waveform. If the filtering is too excessive, the resulting curve will be too far from the original, but if the filtering is too light you will notice some bumps and a general "edginess" to the envelope. Therefore, it is important to know what kind of lowpass filter should be applied, based on both the complexity of the envelope in sound A, and the eventual use the envelope will be put to as a control signal. Nonetheless, it is always good to have higher definition when extracting complex envelopes.

Another system is based on calculating the average of the absolute values of the of the samples' amplitudes. In this case, the degree of definition of the envelope will be due to the number of samples uses to calculate the average: the more samples that are used, the less accurate will be the envelope's profile.

---

[2] Cfr. Dodge and Jerse 1997, p. 181

The control signal generated by an envelope follower can also be applied to filter parameters, as we mentioned earlier. For example, you could decide that the control signal from an amplitude follower (with appropriately scaled values) could be used to control the center frequency of a bandpass filter or the cutoff frequency of a lowpass filter. These filters can affect a second sound, or be used to modify the original sound itself. (Be careful not to confuse the rounding function of the first lowpass filter, which helps create the control signal output by the envelope follower, with the second lowpass filter that is itself controlled by the envelope follower's output, in order to affect another sound.) Using this system you can also obtain a result similar to that of a VCF of an analog synthesizer (described in Section 3.5T), in which the frequency of a filter depends on the amplitude envelope, following its profile, and resulting in a more brilliant sound when the amplitude is at its maximum and a darker sound as the amplitude decreases. This actually corresponds to the behavior of a wide range of acoustic instruments.

• •

SOUND EXAMPLE 7A.2

   a) Envelope follower controlling the filtering of a second sound (bandpass)
   b) Envelope follower used to control the filtering of a second sound (lowpass)
   c) Envelope follower used to control the filtering of the same sound whose envelope was extracted (bandpass)
   d) Envelope follower controlling the filtering the sound whose envelope was extracted (lowpass).

• •

7.2 COMPRESSORS AND DOWNWARD COMPRESSION

THE COMPRESSOR

A **compressor**[3] is a dynamics processor used to reduce the dynamic range of a sound. There are many uses for compressors – both technical and creative – so this remains an important device in the electroacoustic sound-processing chain. Before going into the many possible uses for this device, let's try to describe something similar to what happens inside a simple compressor. Imagine we have an amplifier with a single volume knob, and an input sound that varies in unpredictable ways. We want this sound to always maintain a

---

[3] Warning! The word compression can be ambiguous, since it is used both for data reduction (as we discussed in section 5.3) and compression intended to reduce the dynamic range of a sound (which is being covered in this section). For this reason, in Chapter 5 we referred to the reduction of data specifically as "data compression," leaving the simple term "compression" to indicate a reduction in dynamic range.

high output sound pressure level, but not above a certain intensity. How do we do this? As soon as we realize the sound has gone above a certain threshold, we can immediately reduce the gain (in other words, lower the volume), and when the sound goes below the threshold we can bring the gain back to its original position.

- What is the threshold above which we lower the volume?
- How much should we lower it?
- How fast should we turn the knob to lower the volume?
- How fast should we return the knob to its original position?

By answering these questions we get closer to understanding some of the basic concepts of compressor parameters:
Threshold: over what threshold in dB does a compressor begin to take effect?
Compression ratio (or slope): how is the amplitude scaled when it is above the threshold?
Attack time: for each increase in amplitude, how much time, starting from the moment when the input signal exceeds the threshold, does it take the compressor to reach the determined ratio via a reduction in gain?
Release time: for every decrease in amplitude, how much time does it take the compressor to reach the determined ratio via an increase in gain?

It is also important to mention here that a lot of literature on the subject insists on the false notion that the release happens only when the sound drops again below the threshold or that the attack happens only when it goes above the threshold. In reality, the release happens with every decrease in amplitude, even when the sound remains above the threshold. Only the final release that takes place will actually correspond to the return of the sound's amplitude to the level below the threshold.[4] In the same way, as long as the sound is above the threshold, an attack will happen each time there is an increase in amplitude.

Some of the possible uses for a compressor are:
- **to make the voice of a speaker more easily understandable.** In the case of something like a documentary film, there might be a section with both music and ambient sound where we additionally might want to superimpose the voice of a speaker without reducing the level of the other two signals very much, but be able to keep the voice clearly comprehensible. In such a scenario there could be some phonemes pronounced by the speaker that could be easily masked by the music, while others remained clear (i.e., having the right intensity). A compressor could be used to attenuate only the loudest parts, without affecting the soft parts, so that, once leveled-out, the entire signal could be globally increased to be able to be understood above the music.

---

[4] For more information, see Izhaki, R., 2012, pp. 280-1

- **to create musical effects:** the very heavily compressed sound of an electric guitar is well-known in the rock world – this practically makes the attack of each note disappear, eliminating the characteristic sound of the plucked string. Also, strong compression on a voice will compress vocal peaks, allowing all the less evident vocal sounds like breath and sounds produced by moisture in the mouth to come to the fore..

- to compress the dynamic range in order **to be able to increase the overall level of the signal**. If a given piece of music has some peaks at 0 dB but the vast majority of the sounds in the piece have a much lower intensity, it is impossible to increase the amplitude of the entire signal because the peaks, which are already at the maximum amplitude 0 dB, will become distorted. Therefore, if we apply a compressor to reduce all the peaks to -3 dB, but leaving the low intensity sounds untouched, we can then increase the overall level of the compressed signal by 3 dB, bringing the peaks back to 0 dB, but also increasing the level of all the other sounds present in the signal. If this function is applied to an entire audio file (for example to an entire piece of music during the mastering process) as well as to a sound or series of sounds, using a limiter (which we will talk about later in this chapter) is generally preferred.

- **to level-out unequal sound pressure of selected instruments:** for example with wind instruments which tend to produce greater intensity for high frequencies than they do for lower ones. In this case, as we will see, we could use a multi-band compressor.

- **to reduce sibilance in vocal sounds**. This is possible using a special combination of a lowpass filter and a compressor. For this purpose there exists a special compressor called a de-esser (useful when a speaker or singer has S sounds that are too sibilant), which we will discuss at the end of this section.

• •

SOUND EXAMPLE 7B.1 • Examples of Compression
(examples before and after compression)

a) Voice of a speaker rendered more understandable using compression
b) Compression as a means to change timbre (electric guitar example)
c) Use of compression to increase the overall level of a signal
d) Use of compression to level the unequal sound pressure of some instruments
e) Use of a de-esser to reduce sibilance of a voice.

• •

COMPRESSOR PARAMETERS AND DOWNWARD COMPRESSION

There are two distinct types of compression: **downward compression**, which attenuates peaks above a threshold (this is the kind of compression we have been discussing up to now), and **upward compression**, which increases the level of low intensity zones (which we will discuss later).

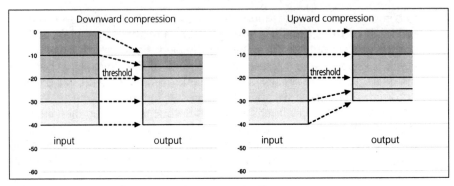

Fig. 7.1 Downward and upward compression[5]

We can't provide you with any hard and fast rules for regulating all the parameters of dynamics processors, because one situation can be vastly different from another, and there are often many different strategies to achieve the same results. Therefore, we will simply provide you with some rudimentary information along with a little bit of advice. In this section we will take a look at the various parameters of a compressor in detail and analyze them from the point of view of *downward compression* (i.e., attenuating peaks above a threshold). Remember that the parameters we are dealing with are:

- **Threshold** in dB. This is the level above which compression is activated. How can we set an appropriate threshold? With *downward compression* a very low threshold can flatten the general level of a sound because in this case not only the peak zones are attenuated, but also sounds with medium intensity. On the other hand, a very high threshold will only reduce the most extreme peaks, leaving most of the sound as it originally was (there are situations where this can be useful). The advice Bob Katz gives in his text "Mastering Audio" (Katz, 2003) is to begin by identifying a threshold between the parts that we do and do not want to compress, keeping a very high compression ratio and short release time setting during the listening process. By listening to the sound and adjusting the threshold, we can decide which sounds will be compressed and which will remain as they are, after which we can lower the ratio and release time to proper values. Let's now take a look at what the *ratio* is:

- **Ratio (compression ratio)**. This is also sometimes called slope, particularly if there is a complex ratio. For the ratio, the denominator is usually set to 1 and

---

[5] Image adapted from Izhaki, R., 2012, pag. 263

the numerator defines the compression ratio with respect to the original signal. For example, if the ratio is 3:1, the part of the signal above the threshold will be reduced by 1/3 the original value, so a sound that is 6 dB above the threshold therefore will be reduced to 2 dB above the threshold after compression.

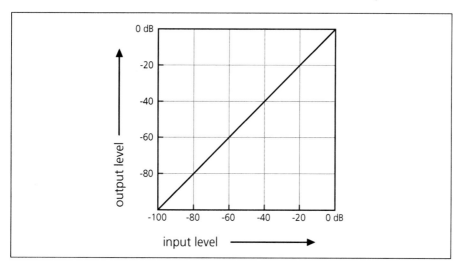

Fig. 7.2 Uncompressed signal level

In figure 7.2 we can see a graph representing input/output amplitude (expressed in dB). The x-axis represents the input amplitude of the sound and the y-axis represents its output amplitude. Given that the function in the graph is a perfectly straight diagonal line, the input value will correspond directly to the output value: -60 dB on the x axis will correspond to -60 dB on the y-axis, -20 dB on the x axis will correspond to -20 dB on the y-axis, etc. The diagonal therefore represents the level of an uncompressed signal.

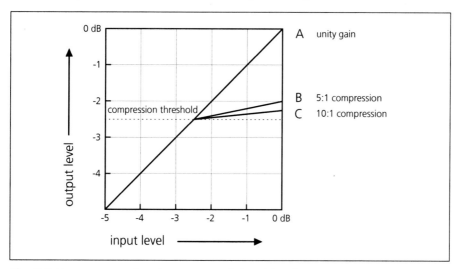

Fig. 7.3 Uncompressed and compressed signal levels

In figure 7.3 line A represents the same thing as the graph in the previous figure – this state is generally referred to with the term *unity gain*, where a value of 1 (i.e., unity) on input corresponds to 1 on output. Line B represents a 5:1 compression ratio applied, as usual, only above the threshold of compression, so the values under the threshold on the x-axis will correspond to unity gain and therefore not be compressed. Input values above the threshold will be compressed, however, so a value that is +5 dB above the threshold will correspond to +1 dB above the threshold on the y-axis, etc. Line C represents a greater compression ratio of 10:1. As before, below the threshold the signal will stay as it is, but above the threshold there will be a much sharper compression compared to B, so for example a value that is +5 dB above the threshold will correspond to +0.5 dB above the threshold on output (i.e., along the y-axis). It is also possible to represent the ratio as a percentage.

The bent line that we see in this graph does not always necessarily have just one breakpoint where the angle changes – there could be more than one point to provide some kind of curvature to the graph. To determine the actual compression ratio we also need to take into consideration the following sub-parameter of the ratio: the *knee*.

KNEE (or curvature)
A compression graph can change angle at one or more points (therefore changing the slope or compression ratio). This point of change is known as a knee, due to its resemblance to an articulated joint. When we have a single breakpoint and two segments (unity gain and a ratio segment) we have what is known as a *hard knee* (an angled graph, with a sharp, rigid joint), but we could also introduce a soft curve in place of the angle, known as a *soft knee*, as shown in figure 7.4.

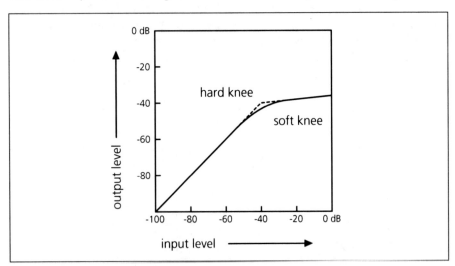

Fig. 7.4 Hard knee and soft knee

In this figure we have a very low threshold (-40 dB) and a very high compression ratio (10:1). Compared to the graphs shown in figure 7.3, the soft knee allows a smoother transition in the border zone between uncompressed and compressed sounds. This "less steep step," even when using a very high compression ratio, means that the curvature (and therefore heaviness of the intervening compression) will increase with the intensity of the sound. If the compression ratio is 3:1, when we have a soft knee this ratio will increase gradually from unity gain (1:1) to 3:1 across a transition zone ranging from below to above the threshold. The range of this transition zone is measured in relation to the dB scale of the input sound. At the center of this transition zone is the threshold (for example -6 dB). If the transition zone is 4 dB (2 dB below and 2 dB above the threshold), the curvature of the soft knee (and therefore the activation of the compressor) will begin from -8 dB (we will call this value the lower knee threshold) and will arrive at the specified ratio when the input sound reaches -4 dB (we will call this value the higher knee threshold). Obviously a transition zone of 0 dB will yield a hard knee.

THE RELATIONSHIP BETWEEN THRESHOLD AND RATIO
Let's take a sound of a voice that is fairly regular around -6 dB, with two brief peaks to 0 dB and a drop in amplitude to -12 dB, and imagine two different compression scenarios:

1) restraining the peaks
2) general reduction of the dynamic range for the entire sound

If we are interested in simply restraining the peaks we could set the threshold to -5 dB (just above the middle level of the sound) and use a high ratio, such as 9:1. On the other hand, if we wanted to greatly reduce the dynamic range of the sound, we could put the threshold a -11 dB and apply a much more restrained compression ratio, such as 1.5: 1.

We can therefore deduce that by lowering the threshold, the compression effect will be greater because we are compressing larger portions of the sound. However, if the ratio is not sufficiently high, we may not be able to hear the resulting effect.

• •

SOUND EXAMPLE 7B.2 • Examples of Compression

   a) uncompressed file
   b) compressed file (with contained peaks)
   c) compressed file (general reduction of the dynamic range for the entire sound)

• •

ATTACK (in milliseconds)

Once the sound has gone above the threshold, the attack is the time it takes for the compressor to go from being completely inactive to completely active, in other words the time it takes the compression to reach the specified ratio. If the sound is already above the threshold and increases in amplitude, the attack is the lag time between the moment the sound changes amplitude and when it arrives at its new level.

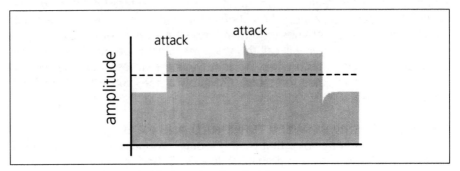

Fig. 7.5 Attack above and below the threshold

If we have an impulse-like sound with a percussive attack, we can choose to make the compressor react immediately within the very first part of the sound's attack, by setting the attack lower than 10 milliseconds. This can "round out" the attack, since having less of a sharp impulse at the very beginning of the attack will make it softer. On the other hand, if we wanted to keep the percussive nature of the sound unchanged, we would need to work with attack times greater than 10 milliseconds. Typical attack times vary between 50 and 250 ms. When working with attack times under 50 ms. (and all the more so when they are less than 10 ms.) you will need to pay careful attention to low-pitched sounds, whose period could have a greater duration than the compressor's attack time. In this case you need to be cautious because the compressor could create a sharp change in amplitude reduction during the first cycle of the low sound, thereby creating audible distortion of the waveform. This kind of alteration of the waveform can be used creatively (as we will learn in the section on non-linear distortion in the next volume), but this kind of tampering, even if perfectly legal to do, to some extent "betrays" the intended purpose of dynamics processors, which should ideally process a sound's dynamics with minimal alteration of its waveform. Nonetheless, there are some kinds of music which use simple compressors to distort the final master. In this case, compressors are being used for creative purposes, which confirms what we have already stated: compressors can be used in many, many ways. What we are hoping to provide you is the basic knowledge to use these devices, thoroughly understanding what you are doing, even when trying to discover new ways to use dynamics processors.

RELEASE (in milliseconds)
When the amplitude of the sound is above the threshold, the release is the time it takes the compressor to reach the new compression level after each reduction in amplitude. When the reduction in amplitude is such that the level of the sound goes below the threshold, the release corresponds to the lag time between the moment it crosses under the threshold to the moment in which the signal arrives once again at unity gain.

The problem with fast attacks and low-pitched sounds, which cause distortion of the waveform or an unnatural quick change in dynamics, is equally applicable to the release time, so it is always good to pay close attention to low sounds when using very short release times. Typical release times range from 50 to 500 ms., but you could always decide to resort to shorter or longer times. Some compressors have an auto-smoothing function that attenuates the effects of distortion on the waveform that are caused by very quick attacks or releases. Some high-quality compressors also have two types of release (fast and slow). By placing a delimiter at 75 ms, for example, you can "teach" the compressor to consider transients less than 75 ms. as fast, and those longer as slow. The compressor will consequently apply a shorter release for sounds with fast transients, and a longer release for sounds with slow transients, creating a more natural feeling that is more coherent with the sound.

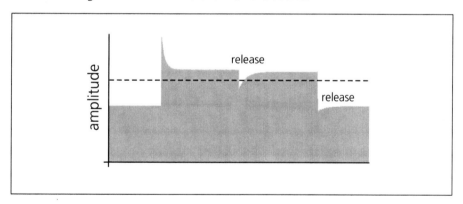

Fig. 7.6 Release above and below the threshold

· ·

SOUND EXAMPLE 7B.3 • Attack and Release in the compressor

Different configurations of attack and release.

· ·

GAIN REDUCTION METER

Otherwise more simply known as a **reduction meter**, it is an instantaneous level reduction meter in dB (in compressors these are always values under 0 dB) that is used to monitor the moment-by-moment dB reduction level of the sound affected by the compressor (that is, when it is above the threshold at any given instant).

OUTPUT GAIN or GAIN MAKEUP

It is always possible to regulate the output gain (in dB) of the compressed sound. Adjusting the output level after compression can be very useful to increase (or reduce) the output intensity level in order to compensate for the effects of compression on a general level.

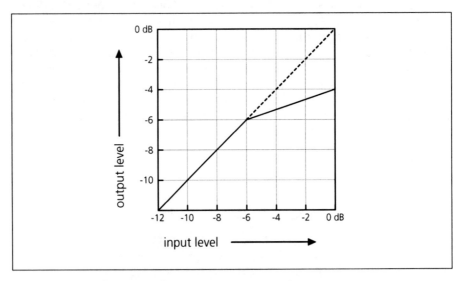

Fig. 7.7 Downward compression without gain makeup

Figure 7.7 shows downward compression with a threshold of -6 dB. By following the dotted line representing unity gain, you will notice that the peaks of the sound whose amplitude is 0 dB will be compressed by 4 dB. In this case it would be useful to set the makeup gain to +4 dB. This is a typical operation (when not using automatic gain control) to increase the general intensity of a sound after it has been compressed in the downward direction. We can see in figure 7.8 how the graph changes after increasing the output gain: input sounds which were at -12 dB become -8 dB on output, those which were at -6 dB become -2 dB, and so forth. We therefore obtain a sound whose absolute amplitude is at 0 dB, just like the original, but with greater RMS amplitude (the RMS amplitude corresponds to the mean square of the samples' amplitude values, and is a good indicator of perceptual volume).[6]

---

[6] To calculate the RMS amplitude the input samples are squared (and therefore all become positive), then averaged, and finally the square root of the average is taken.

It is also possible to have automatic gain control in addition to manual adjustment.[7]

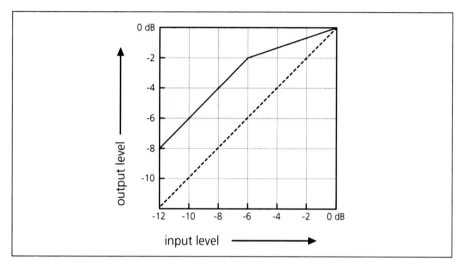

Fig. 7.8 Downward compression with gain makeup

SIDE-CHAIN

The term side-chain has two meanings: the first (used only by technicians) refers to the parallel path of the signal whose envelope is being measured and compressed, as it passes through various stages of processing which will be described shortly. It is considered a side-chain in the sense that it does not actually influence the audio until its output is eventually multiplied by the signal itself. The second meaning of the term is much more well-known by musicians and refers to external side-chain processing. This is a kind of processing that happens when the side-chain is activated based on an external signal (called a *key input*), instead of being based on the same signal that is being compressed. In this case, the side-chain becomes external with respect to the sound being compressed. We will talk about this more in section 7.7.

---

[7] Regarding this adjustment, in most compressors when you lower the threshold you also lower the output signal because there is a general level reduction. This option is called Low level reference mode or Lo Ref. In this case, if the output level is too low after adjusting the threshold, we can affect the output intensity level by manually controlling the output gain. If, in spite of changing the threshold of intervention for the compressor, we wanted to be assured an output level similar to that before the change, we could use the Peak level reference mode or Peak Ref. Actually, in this case when we lower the threshold we simultaneously raise the output gain in order to compensate for the greater reduction and therefore cause the output level to be more or less the same as it had previously been.

THE STRUCTURE OF A COMPRESSOR

The structure of a compressor can be highly variable, but let's take a look at a basic layout in order to help us be able to identify the different internal modules and their functions. As we can see in figure 7.9, the input signal is routed in two different directions. The first is to the internal side chain where the sound's envelope is scaled and transformed in various ways, while the other is simply the signal which will be multiplied by the output of the side chain, resulting in the compressed output sound. Let's first take a look at the side chain, which is the more complex part of the algorithm. As we already mentioned, the signal input into the side-chain can either be the same one that goes to the output, or an entirely different signal. In both cases it can sometimes be useful to filter this signal, in cases where you might want to use only a part of the input signal (for example to attenuate low frequencies).[8]

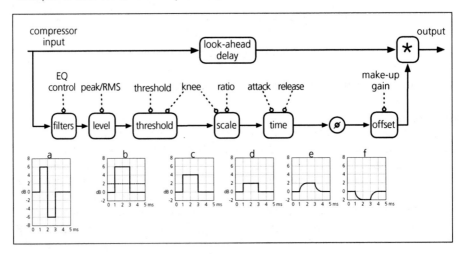

Fig. 7.9 Structure of a compressor [9]

The signal is then measured using an envelope follower. Here you can choose either the peak mode, which follows the profile of amplitude peaks in the signal, or the RMS mode, which follows the RMS amplitude of the signal. The latter is often used for vocal compression. Once we get the envelope of the input signal,

---

[8] As Izhaki (ibid., p.307) states, low frequencies tend to activate compressors more easily than high frequencies for two principal reasons. The first is that, because low frequencies have a longer period, they tend to stay above the threshold for a longer amount of time than high frequencies. The second is that low frequencies need to have a larger amplitude in order to attain the same perceptual intensity as higher frequencies (see section 1.2T for a discussion of isophonic curves). To make sure that a compressor is not excessively activated by bass frequencies, thus producing unnecessary compression for the high frequencies present, a highpass filter can be used before the input to the side-chain. Such a filter can also be used to avoid having a different compression for low frequencies with respect to high ones, for instance when compressing the voice. Naturally, this filtering can be controlled in different ways, or combined with other kinds of processing, depending on the sound used and the compressing objectives, before entering the side-chain.

[9] Image adapted from Izhaki, R., 2012 - pp. 272 e 283

based on a given number of samples, we are able to measure the *overshoot*, which is the excess in dB with respect to the given threshold. The amplitude is then scaled by the given compression *ratio*. This scaling is not necessarily linear, but rather based on a curve specified by the *knee* parameter – a dB value defining a transition zone between a lower threshold (where the knee effectively starts) and an upper one. For example, if the value of the knee parameter is 0 dB it will create a *hard knee*, where compression starts immediately once the threshold is exceeded. On the other hand, if the parameter's value is 6 dB, the *soft knee* curve will begin 3 dB under the threshold and finish 3 dB above it. The scaling values thus obtained are not simply reached immediately when scaling the amplitude of the signal, but rather smoothed-out by a given set of attack and release times (for example 30 ms. and 100 ms.). At this point, the general progression of these positive-signed amplitude values defines an actual envelope, so in order to be used as a gain that can be applied to control the intensity of an audio signal, its sign needs to be inverted (see figure 7.9 e and f). Remember that the input audio signal also needs to be slightly delayed to compensate for the latency inherent in the signal coming from the side-chain. Note that before rescaling the input signal, a make-up gain value can be added to the envelope in order to compensate for the global reduction in amplitude due to compression. This is basically just a volume dial that affects both the part of the signal that has been compressed, and that which has not.

PARALLEL COMPRESSION

An interesting solution to obtain a high RMS amplitude and not simultaneously squash peaks in the piece is to use **parallel compression**. This method comprises mixing two signals, the original (uncompressed) signal and the compressed signal. Since compressed sounds are generally delayed 5 to 10 samples with respect to the original sound, mixing them together could cause problems with destructive interference (see section 2.1T) so we therefore need to delay the original sound by several samples to be able to synchronize the two waveforms in order to eliminate these kinds of problems.

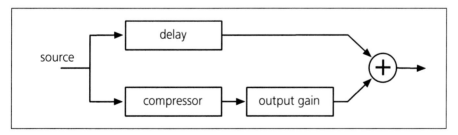

Fig. 7.10 Mixing the original and compressed signals in parallel compression

By keeping the intensity of the compressed sound very low with respect to the original and pushing only low intensity sounds to the fore, we can obtain an increase in RMS amplitude, better definition of sounds under the threshold and a more natural feeling to the sound, due to the fact that the peaks in the high zone are not compressed even though the general sensation of volume is increased. On the contrary, reducing amplitude peaks, and consequently smoothing out attacks, will tend to be more readily noticed than increasing the intensity of low dynamic levels in a sound, so in many cases this is preferred over using a simple downward compression.

As Bob Katz[10] states, one way to create parallel compression is to use downward compression with a very low threshold on the sound being compressed. This way, all sounds above this low threshold will be ultra-compressed, leaving only the low intensity sounds uncompressed and therefore allowing them to come to the fore with respect to the others. Using such a configuration by itself would give quite poor results, but when using it within the context of parallel compression it can be very effective. Let's take a look at how this works. The compressed sound is mixed (at a low volume level) with the original signal, which is thus audibly more predominant. When there are peaks in the music, as listeners we are not at all aware of the presence of the compressed sound, because the ratio between the original peaks and the compressed ones is skewed in favor of those in the original sound. However, when the overall intensity of the sound drops, the sound that has been processed with downward compression will emerge (though quite discreetly).

The ratio between the original and compressed sound will cause an increase in RMS amplitude and a greater definition of low intensity sounds. In order to create this kind of parallel compression, we advise using: a threshold between -30 and -40dBFS[11], a ratio between 4:1 and 10:1 (depending on the sound file that is being compressed[12]), the shortest attack time possible (in order to retain the natural attacks in the sound, as well as immediately compress those in the compressed file), a release time somewhere between 250 and 500 milliseconds (determined empirically), an output gain between -5 and -15dB for the compressed sound and a dry (i.e., unprocessed) sound level a little lower than 0dB so as to leave some space for the increase in intensity resulting from adding the compressed signal. In section 7.6 we will take a look at another type of parallel compression which in some cases can be more efficient than the model we have just described.

---

[10] This method was pioneered by Richard Hulse and Bob Katz, and described in B. Katz (2003).

[11] dBFS = deciBel Full Scale, that is -50dB considering that 0dB is the maximum level before distortion.

[12] Bob Katz advises lower thresholds (around -50dBFS) and ratios between 2:1 and 5:1. Obviously, when using thresholds this low, the ratio must consequently be smaller. In any event, be careful when setting the threshold for the part of the sound you want to emphasize, as there is often only background noise or reverberation under -50dBFS, or else other sounds will be brought to the fore. It goes without saying that you should always set the threshold based on carefully listening to the signal.

SOUND EXAMPLE 7B.4 • Parallel compression

- dry sound
- sound compressed with downward compression
- sound processed with parallel compression

• •

MULTI-BAND COMPRESSOR

Until now we have been talking about dynamics processors while considering the signal as a whole. However some of the most effective uses of dynamics processors actually are those that subdivide the signal into different amplitude zones[13], frequency zones or tempo-based zones[14] which are processed differently.

In this section we will deal with multi-band compressors. They are widely used, as they allow the input signal to be split into different frequency zones, each of which can be compressed in a different way. So, in a certain sense this tool is a hybrid based on both the concepts of equalization and compression. In some cases, where the input signal is not very complex, you could choose to use the sound in one band as a key for the compression of other frequency zones, or create special kinds of equalization where the amplitude modification in a certain frequency zone is not linear but depends on the amplitude of the input signal in that zone.

• •

SOUND EXAMPLE 7B.5 • Multi-band compression

- dry sound
- different types of multi-band compression

• •

---

[13] Multi-zone compressors (or expanders) divide the input signal into multiple amplitude zones, applying a different compression (or expansion) preset for each of the zones. Thus, you could choose to compress the zone between 0 and –6dB one way, while compressing the zone between -6 and -12dB in an entirely different way.

[14] In this case the subdivision of zones in the input signal is based on the duration of the transients present in the sound. In this case, you could have the compressor apply a longer release time to input sounds whose attack is not very quick, and very short release times to sounds that have a very short attack. This system is based on envelope extraction, essentially estimating the instantaneous amplitude of the peaks in the input waveform, so their attack or decay can be changed by modifying the parameters of the compressor according to whether the attack or decay of a sound falls within or outside of a given temporal threshold. The difference between using this system compared to using a normal compressor is that the specific attack or decay of each input sound is additionally taken into account when the sound is modified.

THE DE-ESSER

A close relative of the multi-band compressor is the de-esser, which is used to attenuate sibilant sounds. Sometimes when recording or processing signals, sibilant sounds can become pronounced, especially when using downward compression on the voice. This happens because the "s" sounds fall into an amplitude zone under the compression threshold, and because sibilant sounds fall into a frequency range where the human ear is particularly sensitive (between 2.5 and 9 kHz), they thus tend to stand out. In cases where sibilance is particularly strong, you can use a special type of fast-reacting compressor with a narrow band, known as a de-esser (or sibilance controller). You could also use a multi-band compressor to only compress the band where the sibilant sounds are located, as we will see in section 7.2P.

• •

 SOUND EXAMPLE 7B.6 • De-esser

- dry sound
- sound compressed with downward compression
- sound processed with parallel compression

• •

7.3 LIMITERS AND LIVE NORMALIZER
THE LIMITER

As with downward compression, a ***limiter*** can be used to reduce the dynamic range of an input signal.
Limiters are most commonly used during the mastering stage of a piece, soundtrack or other audio project. This stage takes place after mixing, when the various choices regarding the sound content of a piece (including reverberation, equalization, compression, etc.) have already been set in the sound file. The role of the limiter is to increase the average level of the signal in a file without introducing audible side effects. Therefore, whereas compressors, in principle, are used to modify the "feeling" (and ultimately the timbre) of a given sound, the limiter tends to have a certain transparency when comparing their final result with the sound at their input. Consequently, limiters are generally used for purely technical purposes.

Generally, the threshold of a limiter (called the ***ceiling***) is set to 0dBFS (with a ratio of ∞:1), but you could always design limiters with lower thresholds, for example in the mastering process the final level is often limited to -0.2dBFS in order to avoid possible small amounts of distortion added to the signal during analog-to-digital conversion. Usually a limiter's attack is immediate (i.e., set to 0 milliseconds) and it also uses a ***look-ahead*** function that allows it to know the general progression of the sound in advance. This is possible due to a delay mechanism in-between the sound being processed and the envelope detected by the peak follower within the limiter. This look-ahead time (given in milliseconds) allows the limiter to start to react when the sound is still under the threshold, creating a soft knee which softens the impact of the hard knee which takes effect when the level exceeds the ceiling. Obviously, it is also possible to use a limiter creatively. By excessively lowering a limiter's threshold, you can "squash" or otherwise flatten a sound's amplitude until its timbre is noticeably changed. Nevertheless, as we have already mentioned, the most typical uses for limiters are purely technical. Not surprisingly, in most limiters you cannot adjust the attack, ratio or other parameters, as they are usually set to predetermined values.[15] Let's take a look at how limiters can be used:

- *To increase the RMS amplitude of a sound or mix*: in this case limiting is used to reduce the amplitude of all the peaks, leaving all low intensity sounds unmodified. Each limiter has an output gain to bring the limited signal back to the maximum level.

- *To prevent potential overloads in live recordings*: because musicians on stage can sometimes produce sudden unforeseen bursts of excessive intensity, a limiter (typically an analog one) can be inserted into the signal path just before it enters the recording system.

- *To reduce the dynamic range of a musical piece*: this is done when the piece needs to be broadcast on TV or radio, both of which are incapable of providing a suitably large dynamic range.

At this point we should make it clear that for the most part, pop music, techno, house, etc., generally do not make use of the entire available dynamic range, even to a small degree. Compressors and limiters are used not only to provide a specific sound quality, but also to give a greater sense of volume, and to fall within the limited dynamic range used by radio and television, or the homogeneous dynamics used in environments with high background noise, such as supermarkets, department stores, cars, airplanes, etc. If there is significant background noise, any music with a lot of dynamic fluctuation will only be able to be heard when it exceeds a certain intensity, since the low intensity parts of the music will be masked by the noise. However, the general tendency to compress sounds more intensely in order to obtain increasingly higher and more homogenous volume levels leads to flattened waveforms, extremely restricted changes in dynamics, etc. Regarding our perception of volume, we also should realize that, ideally, we need to additionally take some psychoacoustic and cognitive elements into consideration. For example, a sound with very high intensity

---

[15] Often there is a Program Dependent Release mechanism which allows "intelligent" control of the release in order to allow the processed sound to seem more natural and closer to the input sound, in spite of its reduction in dynamic range. Furthermore, we can also use compressors (which also sometimes include a PDR) to exaggerate operations on the attack and release at will, so to speak, ranging from a natural-sounding intervention to one which "reinvents" the original sound.

is perceived as being even more "powerful" if it is preceded by sounds with low intensity. This interplay of extreme dynamics can be very effective for both cinematographic sound and classical music. The tendency to crush and flatten the dynamics of commercial music (in addition to other kinds) ends up additionally "compressing" the dynamic freedom of those who are making the music. By adhering to volume standards, we are constricted within a highly limited dynamic area, even if the medium where the music is finally stored allows us a much wider range of dynamic freedom. When compression is used excessively, even the depth and fullness of the stereo image become degraded and flattened. Therefore, as always, the means used can influence some musical styles, favoring some kinds of creative behavior over others. As you can see, the topic of compression is not really secondary in music, so we need to adopt different strategies for using dynamics processors, depending on the type of work or music we are creating.

In spite of the above statements, which portray limiters as having a purely technical purpose, not a creative one, it is worth remembering that we can "bend" any algorithm to our needs in order to invent "improper" and creative uses of it. This can happen in two ways:

1) by modifying the algorithm so that its basic function changes (we will see some examples of this is section 7.8)

2) by using the algorithm as-is, and simply altering its parameter values to obtain special effects

A striking example of the latter is the use of a limiter with a very low ceiling in the final section of Luigi Ceccarelli's piece "Exsultet"[16], where aspects of the voice and breath of the singer which are normally hidden become greatly emphasized.

. . . .

SOUND EXAMPLE 7C.1

Excerpt from "Exsultet" by L. Ceccarelli (RAI TRADE/DUCALE)

. . . .

This example comes from an "improper" use of a dynamics processor normally used to limit the intensity of a sound while maintaining as much fidelity as possible to the original sound. To do this, the ceiling value was simply changed to use this processor in a new way without changing the algorithm itself.

---

[16] This is an electroacoustic piece based on Gregorian chant which received Honorary Mention at the 1997 Prix Ars Electronica in Linz, Austria.

THE LIVE NORMALIZER

By modifying the limiter algorithm we can create a special kind of dynamics processor that we will call a *live normalizer* – not to be confused with the normalizer that is found in practically all hard disk recording software, and which increases a sound's amplitude by bringing its peak amplitude value to 0 dB, proportionally increasing the amplitude of all other samples. With the **live normalizer**, both signals that are above as well as those that are below the threshold will be brought to 0dB; in other words, it sets the mean amplitude of the signal to 0dB, (or to any other desired level).

The difference between it and a limiter is that it uses a minimum threshold (for example -120dB), so the entire sound could therefore potentially have its dynamics altered, and not only the part that exceeds 0dB, as in a limiter. This means that any signal above -120dB will be brought to 0 dB – i.e., amplified if it is less than 0dB or attenuated if it is greater. As you can probably imagine, the live normalizer algorithm can be easily used for creative purposes.

· ·

SOUND EXAMPLE 7C.2 • Live normalizer

   - dry sound
   - sound compressed using a live normalizer

· ·

7.4 EXPANDERS AND DOWNWARD EXPANSION

THE EXPANDER

The expander increases the dynamic range of a sound. It can use either downward expansion or upward expansion (we will look at the latter case in section 7.6). With downward expansion the gain of sounds under the threshold is reduced, thereby making their intensity even less. The amount of reduction in intensity will depend on the undershoot – the signal that exceeds the threshold in a downward direction. This reduces the intensity of weak sounds, but consequently expands the dynamic range (the difference between the low and high dynamic zones in a sound). In some cases this type of expansion can be used to attenuate undesired low-intensity sounds. Normally we use a gate for this kind of operation (see section 7.5), but sometimes it can be important to just attenuate these sounds with downward expansion because, unlike a gate, the attenuation can be controlled according to the ratio and in proportion to the undershoot. This type of expansion is therefore useful when you want to attenuate these kinds of sounds in a smooth and controllable way.

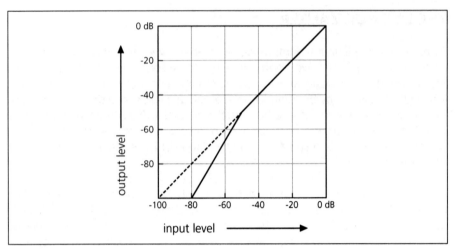

Fig. 7.11 Downward expansion

PARAMETERS OF THE EXPANDER

Most of the parameters used by the expander can be intuitively deduced based on the similar information we have already learned about compressors. Let's now look at these parameters as they apply to downward expansion.

THRESHOLD
With downward expansion the threshold is the point *below* which the sound will be reduced in intensity.

RATIO
The expansion ratio should always be given as a value between 0 and 1, since the input is always less than the output, from the point of view of dynamic range. For example, an expansion ratio of 1:2 means that if the input sound passes below the threshold by -1dB, the sound will be expanded to -2dB and sent to the output.

KNEE
For expanders, the concept of a *knee* is identical to that which we have already seen for compressors, however with the soft knee, the higher knee threshold obviously will correspond to the point where there is no more expansion (unity gain), and the lower knee threshold to the point where the specified ratio is reached.

ATTACK
Once the level of the sound goes below the threshold, the attack is the time it takes for a completely inactive expander to become completely active – in other words, the time it takes for the expander to reach the desired ratio. If the sound is already below the threshold and there is a decrease in amplitude, the attack is the amount of time that elapses from the moment that the sound changes amplitude to the moment at which the expansion reaches the new level..

RELEASE

When a sound's amplitude is below the threshold, the release is the time in which the expander reaches the new expansion level, after each increase in amplitude. When the increase in amplitude is enough that the sound returns above the threshold, the release corresponds to the time that elapses between the moment it exceeds the threshold and the moment where the signal returns to unity gain. The attack and release features of the expander are quite naturally different from the analogous parts of the compressor. For example, the attack of a compressor happens each time that the sound has an accent (such as a drumbeat), whereas for the expander this will trigger the release. This means that if we want to shape an existing accent, using a compressor will affect its attack, whereas an expander will affect its release. It is worth noting that a slow release in an expander may cause too much attenuation, or even "swallow up" the accent that triggered it.

GAIN REDUCTION METER

The concept of a gain reduction meter is the inverse of that which is used for downward compression. It is a level meter that monitors the moment-by-moment reduction level in dB of the sounds to which the expander is being applied (i.e., those that are under the threshold at that moment).

OUTPUT GAIN (or gain makeup)

The concept of output gain is the same as that used for compression. As a matter of fact, the intensity of the sound is reduced for both downward compression and downward expansion, so in either case we can apply gain makeup to once again increase the overall amplitude level.

SIDE-CHAIN

The side chain is the same as for a compressor, but with different values and uses. If you want, you can also use an external side chain with an expander.

• •

SOUND EXAMPLE 7D.1 • Downward expansion

   a) dry sound
   b) sound compressed using *downward expansion*

• •

7.5 GATES

The noise gate acts like a special kind of extreme downward expansion that reduces sounds under a certain threshold, until they are completely silenced. The term *noise gate* is often abbreviated using just the word *gate*.[17] This makes sense, because this dynamics processors is not only used to suppress noise, but can have a wide variety of uses, such as eliminating live feedback problems, or shortening percussive sounds. In *gates*, the signal above the threshold will pass through unaltered, but when the amplitude level of the signal falls below this threshold the sound is completely silenced (or heavily attenuated, as we will soon see). This all happens over a length of time determined by the *release* parameter, which starts as soon as the level falls below the threshold.[18] If the release is slow the sound will die out gradually, and if it is short, the sound will be cut off quickly and cleanly. The resulting signal at this point will be eliminated entirely until the input signal once again rises above the threshold. At that moment the gate opens up again, over a period of time determined by the attack. In practical applications a gate is usually designed with two thresholds: one used for opening the gate (attack) and another for closing it (release). The term **hysteresis** is used to define the distance in dB between the two thresholds. If we look at figure 7.12, we can see that when the signal crosses above the opening threshold, the gate opens, thereby letting the sound pass. When the gate descends below the closing threshold (which you can see is lower than the opening threshold), the gate closes, canceling (or heavily attenuating) the sound.

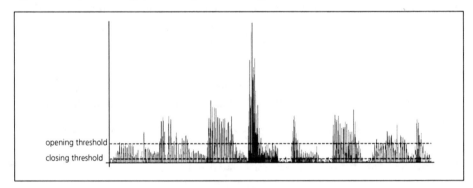

Fig. 7.12 Opening and closing thresholds in a gate

---

[17] This abbreviation may cause some confusion, since the word *gate* is used within synthesizers as a synonym for *voltage trigger* or simply as a way of referring to the activation of a note from a keyboard. Nonetheless, throughout this text the term gate will be used as an abbreviation referring to the dynamics processor called a *noise gate*.

[18] Note that for gates, the attack and release will work oppositely of those in a *downward expansion*. For example, the release is the time from the moment the sound crosses the threshold downward to the moment the predetermined sound processing takes place. For downward expansion, on the other hand, the attack has this function.

So, why is it advantageous to have two thresholds? This is done to eliminate a possible negative effect known as **chattering** – a kind of distortion to the signal that happens when there is just one threshold. This happens when the gate opens and closes repeatedly over a short space of time.

As we already mentioned, a gate can be useful to reduce noise in a signal, especially when this noise is noticeable only during pauses. Another common use is to use a gate with a short release on percussion sounds in order to accentuate the speed of the sound's decay, causing them to seem even more percussive. Gates can also be used with live signals in order to reduce unwanted feedback that can happen when a microphone picks up the sound from a speaker, causing a certain frequency to loudly and piercingly increase in volume. In this case, if you have an instrumental sound with a long release, and are also adding reverberation to it, you could use a gate to prevent the initiation of feedback, and setting the reverb level in such a way that the resulting sound does not appear noticeably "cut off."

A common parameter used in gates is called **floor**, which is the destination level of the sound when the gate is in operation. Usually this is set to the minimum value, in other words −∞ dB, but floors between -80 and -100 dB are also often used. In some cases (such as when reducing feedback in a live microphone situation), the floor can be set to a low level, rather than completely eliminating the low-intensity sounds, so as to "soften" the effect of closing the gate on the signal. In this case, you might think that the effect is more of a downward expansion than an actual gate, since the sound is just attenuated, and not completely canceled. However there is one major difference between the two: the amount of attenuation in gates (often defined by the term *range*) is pre-defined by the user, whereas in downward expanders, the amount of attenuation additionally depends on the intensity of the signal itself, in other words on the *undershoot*. It is precisely because of the various possible floor values and the independence of the attenuation from the undershoot, that the control is not based on a ratio but on a range (i.e., a quantity of attenuation).

• •

SOUND EXAMPLE 7D.2 • Gate

  a) dry piano or percussion sound
  b) the same sounds using a gate with different attack and release times
  c) the same sounds using a gate with different floor values

• •

7.6 UPWARD COMPRESSION AND UPWARD EXPANSION

UPWARD EXPANSION

The intensity of sounds above a certain threshold may be increased using **upward expansion**. This can be useful in cases where you want to put back some vitality or impact into sounds whose peaks have been too heavily compressed. While downward compression reduces peaks and increases the intensity of sounds under the peaks (by increasing the output gain after compression), upward expansion restores a certain amount of dynamics to the peaks. Often after using this type of expansion the output gain level is reduced in order to avoid distorting any peaks in the expanded sound.

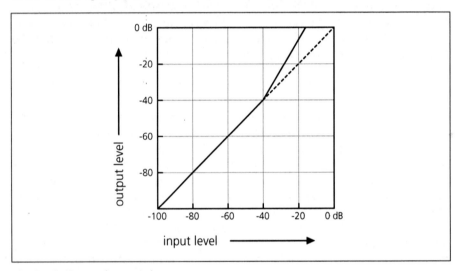

Fig. 7.13 Upward expansion

In upward expansion the threshold is the point above which the sound is expanded.

An expansion ratio of 1:2 means that if the sound exceeds the threshold by 1 dB, the sound is expanded to 2 dB. Generally when upward expansion is used to reduce the dynamics of peaks in the sound, only a light expansion ratio – usually not greater than 1:1.2 – is used. In any event, the ratio used will always be between 0 and 1, since the dynamic range of the input will always be less than that of the output.

Increasing the release used with upward expansion can also help to give a longer sustain to the expansion, even immediately after the attack. To put back a little bit of vigor into sounds that are too flat, you could always set a very short attack time (even as low as a handful of milliseconds); if the resulting attacks in this scenario are excessively quick, you can increase the time up to around 150-300 ms. If the attacks are still unnaturally fast at this point, it probably means that *upward expansion* is not the effect that you are looking for.

UPWARD COMPRESSION

Often, when people imagine upward compression, they make the mistake of believing that an increase in intensity such as this (i.e., an increase in the level of low-intensity sounds) does not correspond to compression. However, do not forget that compression and expansion do not refer to the intensity of a sound but to the sound's dynamic range. When we talk about the dynamic range of a group of sounds, we are not referring to their peak amplitude (in this case an amplitude which could be increased), but rather the ratio between the sounds' low and high intensities. Therefore, even if the low intensity sounds within the group are increased in amplitude by the compressor, we will still obtain a reduction in the difference between the high and the low intensity sounds, effectively compressing the dynamic range of the original audio signal.

Remember that, since upward compression implies an increase in gain under a given threshold, the intensity of the sounds in the lower part of the dynamic range will be increased, leaving those above the threshold unchanged (see figure 7.14).

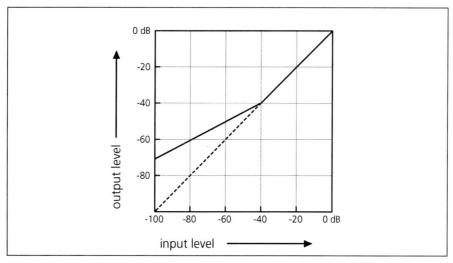

Fig. 7.14 Upward compression

In reality, there are not many commercial compressors that directly include upward compression. As we have already seen, this kind of compression can be created using parallel compression, or, as in the figure, by using an expander "backwards", by giving it a ratio greater than 1:1. Using downward expansion, we were able to extend the dynamics of sounds under the threshold (for example using a ratio of 1:2), but of we used an expansion greater than 1 (such as 1: 0.5) we could compress the sounds under the threshold in a upward direction.

OPERATIONS AND DYNAMICS PROCESSORS
To sum up what we have learned, we need to know how to distinguish between the operation that we want to perform and the dynamics processor that we will

need to use in order to achieve it. In table 7A we can see the different kinds of dynamics processors available to us:

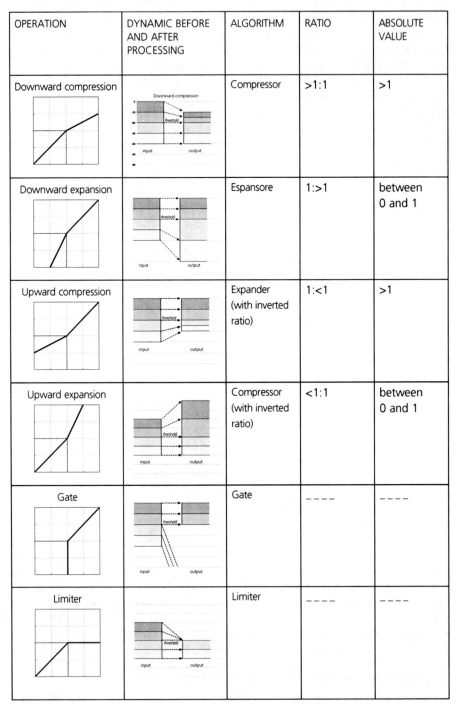

OPERATION	DYNAMIC BEFORE AND AFTER PROCESSING	ALGORITHM	RATIO	ABSOLUTE VALUE
Downward compression		Compressor	>1:1	>1
Downward expansion		Espansore	1:>1	between 0 and 1
Upward compression		Expander (with inverted ratio)	1:<1	>1
Upward expansion		Compressor (with inverted ratio)	<1:1	between 0 and 1
Gate		Gate	– – – –	– – – –
Limiter		Limiter	– – – –	– – – –

Table 7A

UPWARD PARALLEL COMPRESSION

As we have already seen in section 7.2, parallel compression is made up of mixing two signals: the original signal (uncompressed and slightly delayed) and the compressed signal. Let's now take a look at a slightly different and lesser-known model of parallel compression that uses upward compression instead of downward compression for the compressed signal.[19] In this scenario, the compressed sound will not undergo limiting of its peaks, but will be a signal in which sounds under a certain threshold (set to a low level like -30 dB or -40 dB) are increased in intensity (with a ratio between 1:3 and 1:5). This compressed sound will be mixed with the original (which has been delayed several samples in order to avoid destructive interference). The compressed (i.e., wet) signal should be set to about 5-10% of the amplitude of the dry signal, and it is precisely this prevalence of the dry signal that distinguishes *upward parallel compression* from a simple *upward compression*. The majority of the sound that we can hear will thus not have been processed by the compressor, so the sound will benefit from this in terms of "naturalness". Obviously, the values of the various settings will depend both on the contents of the sound file being compressed and the intended purpose for using parallel compression in the first place. One of the most common uses is within the final stage of mastering – in other words when finalizing the definitive levels of a master for a piece of music or sound design. Remember that, before being compressed, a sound should be set to a level lower than 0 dB, so that when the original and compressed sounds are added the overall intensity will not increase. Often the intensity is kept in the range of -3 to -4 dB, so that the intensity of the compressed sound can be varied in the mix without running the risk of distortion.

Compared to downward parallel compression (explained in section 7.2), upward parallel compression has the advantage of not compressing peaks and consequently leading to more "natural" sounding results.

7.7 EXTERNAL SIDE CHAIN AND DUCKING

Normally a compressor starts to work each time that the input signal (which we will refer to as A) exceeds the threshold. When the external side-chain is activated, the compressor will compress sound A each time that it is activated by another signal (which we will refer to as B), generally referred-to as the key input, external key input, or simply key). The entire side-chain therefore becomes "external" (with respect to the sound being compressed) since it is activated by a completely different sound.

---

[19] The details of this technique were shown by Prof. Marco Massimi in a series of lectures held in 2009 at the Electronic Music School of the Frosinone Conservatory of Music and at the Masters of Sound Engineering program of the Electronic Engineering Faculty of the University of Rome, Tor Vergata.

Creative uses of external side chain processing can often be found in mixes and in compositions in the techno, house and similar genres.

In the commercial realm (either among musicians or in manuals for plug-ins) this technique is referred-to using the abbreviated term: side-chain.

This technique consists of using a sound such as a bass drum for the key signal and the rest of the music (or a part of it) as signal A, so that with each beat of the drum the rest of the music (or part thereof) is compressed for a brief moment in order to allow the drum beat to be perceived clearly. This way, the sound of the drum itself becomes more clearly defined, while allowing a higher general level. When the drum is not present, signal A can therefore be kept at a higher level than it could if sound A and sound B were simply being super-imposed without side-chain compression. Similarly, the dynamic of the drum is also better able to stand out in the mix with less masking.

Obviously, this kind of technique influences both musical thinking and taste, thus inevitably prompting DSP effect programmers to continue to invent new techniques along similar lines.

Another very well-known technique is **ducking**, which is used widely in radio commercials, where, as soon as the voice-over enters the intensity of the music is reduced so that it will maintain the maximum global intensity without dis-tortion, and without allowing the music to mask the voice, which could lead to it being incomprehensible. As soon as the voice-over is finished the music automatically returns to its maximum intensity. In this case the key signal that triggers the compressor is the voice (signal B) and the compressed signal is the music. What is special about the ducker algorithm, is not so much that it uses a different key signal than the one being compressed (it is also possible to create a ducker in which the input sound and the sound being compressed are one and the same, as we will see in section 7.8), but that, unlike a compressor, it is not dependent on the *overshoot* level. The amount of reduction in intensity is actually fixed and this reduction is activated each time the sound exceeds the threshold (regardless of how much) and remains active while the input sound remains above the threshold.

7.8 OTHER CREATIVE USES OF DYNAMICS PROCESSORS

In the section dedicated to the *limiter*, we have already seen a creative use based on a simple modification of the parameter values used for an algo-rithm. In this section, however, we will take a look at three specific algorithms designed explicitly for creative uses of dynamics processors: the adaptive gate/ducker, the gate-trigger and the gate-sequencer (or live slicer).

ADAPTIVE GATE

It is possible to design a gate that, instead of closing when the sound's intensity goes below the threshold, closes each time the sound decreases in intensity (thus silencing the sound) and opens when the sound increases in intensity (letting it pass through unchanged), irrespective of a predetermined threshold. This kind of gate is called "adaptive", since its behavior continually varies based on the changes of amplitude in the sound. In order to detect dynamic accents in the sound independently of its RMS amplitude, it is necessary to construct a system based on two envelope followers. The first envelope follower only uses a small number of preceding samples, so it will therefore be relatively fast to follow and describe the sound's variations in intensity. The second uses a large number of samples to calculate the envelope, so it will be slower than the other one in its description of the sounds variations in intensity. The *adaptive gate* will let the sound pass through once the intensity of the fast envelope follower becomes greater than that of the slow one, and will close again in the opposite scenario. Naturally, we need to calibrate the number of samples that are taken into consideration for both the fast and slow envelope followers, according to the kind of effect that we want to obtain. The attack and release parameters are very important, since in this case they simply define the attack and release of the output sound that we will hear. Using a fast release we can practically make the closing of the sound coincide with the moment where the slow envelope follower goes above the fast one, thereby shortening the original sound events (see sound example 7.E.1). You can also slow down attacks in the sound (see sound example 7.E.2) by slowing the time between the moment the slow follower passes the fast one and the actual opening of the *adaptive gate*.

• •

SOUND EXAMPLE 7E.1

   a) original sound (drum sequence)
   b) sound processed with an adaptive gate with a fast release
   c) sound processed with an adaptive gate with a slow release

SOUND EXAMPLE 7E.2

   a) original sound (drum sequence)
   b) sound processed with an adaptive gate with a fast attack
   c) sound processed with an adaptive gate with a slow attack

• •

ADAPTIVE DUCKER

As we previously mentioned, a ducker can be constructed using a single sound, instead of using an external key input. This might initially seem to be useless, but if we use an *adaptive gate* in the opposite way (i.e., closing the gate when the fast envelope follower becomes greater than the slow one and opening it up again when the slow one becomes greater than the fast one) we obtain an *adaptive ducker*. (Remember that a ducker is simply a gate that works backwards.) The possible effects using an adaptive ducker are somewhat special, since the sound appears every time the intensity drops, and it disappears every time the intensity increases. Nonetheless, for both the adaptive gate and the adaptive ducker you can set the floor to a low level, instead of completely eliminating the sound, in order to "smooth out" the effect of "shutting off" the signal.

SOUND EXAMPLE 7E.3

a) original sound
b) sound processed with an adaptive ducker

TRIGGERING GATE

Normally, when the input sound goes above the threshold, a gate opens to let the sound through. What if something different were to happen once the threshold was passed? For example, if it activated an envelope, filtering, delay, displacement in the stereo field, or triggered the same sound played in reverse? In these scenarios the gate's function would be similar to that of an event trigger – in other words something that activated a specific process – with the difference being that the activation, unlike that of a normal trigger, would depend on crossing the threshold.[20]

SOUND EXAMPLE 7E.4

a) original sound
b) different kinds of processing associated with a triggering gate

GATE-SEQUENCER (LIVE SLICING)

In section 5.4T we described the *live slicer*, sometimes called a *gate sequencer*, which uses a sound processing technique in which the input signal to the live slicer is subjected to regular rhythmic envelopes in real-time. By applying different processes (even synchronized ones) to individual fragments, we can create rhythmic sequences with pre-determined accents, using variations in intensity, pitch and spatialization, or by using techniques such as filtering, delay, and the like. Actually, in this scenario the rhythmic opening and closing of the gate is not based on a pre-determined threshold, since the algorithm does not include

---

[20] Once again, we should clarify that the terms gate and trigger are used here outside of their nomenclature typically used with synthesizers, where a gate is considered synonymous with voltage trigger. Here we are using the term gate in the context of dynamics processors (i.e., as in noise gate), and trigger as a generic event activator.

an envelope follower, so the term *gate-sequencer* consequently should be understood in the broadest sense, since only the idea of opening and closing the gate based on amplitude has been retained.

In the following sound examples you can hear different kinds of filtering and spatialization based on a rhythmical pulse and its subdivisions (for example half, 1/3, 1/4, 1/5, etc.). In these examples, the values used to control the cutoff frequency and spatialization are generated randomly based on a user-defined range, and vary on the basis of these rhythms. In the practical section we will take a look at one way to realize this kind of *gate-sequencer*.

• •

SOUND EXAMPLE 7E.5

- different examples of a live slicer

• •

FEEDBACK WITH CONTROLLED DYNAMICS

In section 6.2 we spoke about feedback in delay lines, and we saw how the attenuation coefficient in the feedback signal can never have a value equal to 1 (100% feedback), let alone greater than 1, which would increase the amplitude of the signal indefinitely.

On the other hand, feedback of this type can produce musically interesting sounds and timbres if its amplitude is carefully controlled. In order to be able to easily do this, we can use a limiter inside our delay with feedback algorithm, so that the resulting sound never exceeds 0 dBFS. This way, we can be free to experiment with different multiplication factors greater than 1 for the feedback without causing the signal's amplitude increase indefinitely, and therefore be able to listen to different timbral modifications resulting from this unusual use of feedback. For example, if we used several independent delay lines whose delay times were modulated using an LFO, we could create interesting distortion and resonant effects, using such controlled dynamics within our feedback system.

• •

SOUND EXAMPLE 7E.6

a) original sound
b) sound processed using a delay with feedback limited in dynamics

• •

TESTING • TEST WITH SHORT ANSWERS (MAXIMUM 30 WORDS)

1) Based on the following image:

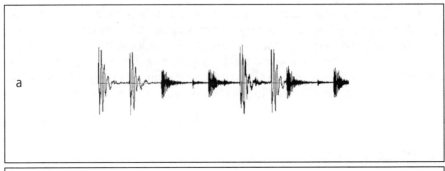

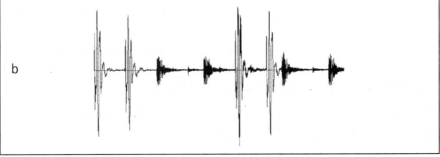

what type of dynamics processing has been used? (multiple choice question)

    a) upward compression
    b) upward expansion
    c) downward compression
    d) downward expansion
    e) gating
    f) limiting
    g) parallel compression
    h) multi-zone compression
    i) multi-band compression

2) Based on the following images:

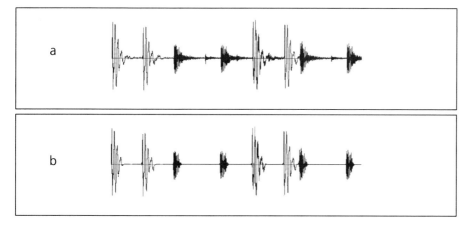

what type of dynamics processing has been used? (multiple choice question)

    a) upward compression
    b) upward expansion
    c) downward compression
    d) downward expansion
    e) gating
    f) limiting
    g) parallel compression
    h) multi-zone compression
    i) multi-band compression

3) If we needed to give more dynamics to a piece of music that we only have in a version whose peaks have been compressed too much, what type of dynamics processor would we need to use, and how? (max. 30 words)

4) If we want to increase the RMS level of a musical piece without attenuating the peaks using downward compression, what type of dynamics processor would we need to use and how? (max. 30 words)

5) If we were processing a sound of an instrument in real-time and its output produced audible background noise only when the instrument was not playing (since the noise is masked when the instrument is being played), what type of dynamics processing could we use in order to eliminate the background noise at moments when there is a rest in the music? (max. 30 words)

6) If we wanted to create a live ducking effect, which dynamics processor would we use and how? Also, what kind of key input should we use? (max. 30 words)

LISTENING AND ANALYSIS ACTIVITIES

1) In the two sounds presented in sound example 8, which one has had downward compression applied to it?

2) In the ducking effect in example number 9, which one of the two signals is the key input?

. . . .

FUNDAMENTAL CONCEPTS

1) Dynamics processors are devices that transform the dynamic range of a sound (or series of sounds, or an entire piece, etc.), for many different purposes, either technical or creative.

2) Envelope followers can be useful in sound processing, in particular to shape a sound by applying an envelope from another sound to it. The recognizability of a particular sound depends heavily on the sound's attack, therefore it is possible to render a sound completely unrecognizable not by altering its waveform, but by altering only its envelope. Envelope followers are at the basis of side chains in dynamics processors such as compressors or expanders.

3) In principle, the use of a compressor can help to change the "feel" (and ultimately the timbre) of the sound being processed, while the use of a limiter tends to maintain a certain degree of "transparency" when comparing the final result with the original sound. Limiters are generally used for technical purposes – to limit peaks in the sound so they are not so apparent – while compressors can be used for many different objectives, including creative processing of sounds. Similarly, gates are generally also used for technical goals, while expanders can be used in various ways, including both technical and creative applications. Nonetheless, limiters and gates could also be used for creative purposes, by modifying their parameter values from those normally used, or inserting them within a more complex sound processing algorithm.

4) Compressors and limiters are very often used to provide a greater sense of volume, to conform the sound to the limited dynamic ranges used in radio or television, or to provide the necessary dynamic uniformity for music used in situations where it needs to be heard over other sounds, such as noise pollution, for example. The tendency to keep compressing sounds more and more to obtain an increasingly more uniform volume level can result in flattened waveforms, very limited changes in dynamics, and so forth. When compression is used excessively it also affects the depth and amplitude of the stereo image, which becomes degraded and "squashed," although such uses could be the result of artistic choices. It is nevertheless always important to consider the final goals and broadcast or diffusion format of the work at hand, in order to be able to decide on an appropriate dynamic range to use. When used judiciously, dynamics processors can help achieve a good compromise between dynamic variation and the requirements of different technical standards.

GLOSSARY

Adaptive Ducker
A type of ducker that closes every time the sound increases in intensity and opens when the sound decreases in intensity, independently of a predetermined threshold.

Adaptive Gates
A type of gate that closes every time the sound reduces in intensity and opens when the sound increases in intensity, independently of a predetermined threshold.

Attack
The time in which a completely inactive dynamics processor becomes completely active. In gates, the attack is the time in which the sound goes from the floor level to its original intensity after crossing the given threshold.

Ceiling (in limiters)
A term used to identify the threshold of a limiter.

Chattering (in gates)
Distortion of a signal that happens when a gate with only one threshold opens and closes many times in rapid succession.

Compressor
A dynamics processor used to reduce the dynamic range of a sound.

Compressors/Expanders with a time threshold
Dynamics processors that analyze the envelope of a signal and set threshold based on the transient times in the input sound; the sound's content can then be processed in different ways via compression or expansion.

De-esser
A special kind of compression that attenuates sibilance of "s" sounds in the voice or other sibilant sounds. Also sometimes called a sibilance controller, this narrow band compressor acts very fast and compresses only the band containing the sibilant sound.

Downward compression
A type of compression where amplitude peaks above a given threshold are attenuated.

Downward expansion
Decreasing the amplitude of sounds below a given threshold, thereby further reducing their intensity.

Dynamic Range
The ratio between the maximum and minimum amplitudes that can be represented within a given piece of hardware, software or storage medium.

Dynamics Processor
A device that modifies the dynamic range of a sound.

Envelope follower
Also known as a *peak amplitude follower*, it extracts a sound's envelope by measuring the positive peak amplitudes in a waveform. The envelope follower produces a control signal based on this series of amplitude values extracted from the sound. The control signal may then be imposed upon another sound in order to control its envelope, or used in various other ways.

Envelope shaper
Envelope shaping is another way to indicate the function of an envelope

follower when it is used to redesign a sound's envelope using a control signal extracted from another sound.

Expander
A dynamics processor used to increase the dynamic range of a sound.

Feedback with Controlled Dynamics
A feedback loop controlled by a limiter or other dynamics processor, which is designed to keep the sound from exceeding 0dBFS when the feedback attenuation percentage is 100% or greater.

Floor
The minimum level of a sound that is reached when a gate is in operation. In gates the floor is oftentimes set to the minimum value (i.e., $-\infty$).

Gain expansion Meter
A level indicator that is used to monitor the moment by moment expansion level in dB of a sound that is actively being expanded (i.e., when it is over the threshold).

Gain Reduction
A parameter used in dynamics processors to lower a sound's output gain.

Gain Reduction Meter
A level indicator that is used to monitor the moment by moment reduction level in dB of a sound that is actively being compressed (i.e., when it is above the threshold).

Gate (or Noise Gate)
A dynamics processor that attenuates sounds under a certain threshold (and able to silence them completely when the floor is equal to $-\infty$). Sounds above the threshold remain unchanged.

Gate-sequencer
An algorithm in which the input signal is subjected to regular rhythmic envelopes in real-time. By applying different (synchronized) processes to individual sound fragments, rhythmic sequences with predefined accents can be created by using variations in intensity, filtering, pitch, spatialization, delays, etc. Because the opening and closing of the gate is not based on a threshold, the algorithm does not contain an envelope follower.

Hysteresis
Distance in dB between the closing threshold and the opening threshold in a gate or other system.

Key Input or External Key Input
A signal that activates a dynamics processor which is used to modify an entirely different signal. The key input is used when the external side chain function is activated. In this case, all of the side chain is "external" in relation to the sound being compressed, since it is activated by a totally different sound.

Knee
Curvature of the compression ratio. This could be a *soft knee*, when the curve has a gentle slope, or a *hard knee*, when the curve changes abruptly.

Limiter
A dynamics processor used to keep the input signal from going above a given threshold, called a ceiling.

Live Slicer
see Gate-sequencer

Multi-band Compressors/Expanders
Dynamics processors that use equalization functions in addition to

347

dynamics processing. These permit the signal to be subdivided into different frequency zones, each of which can be processed in different ways, using compression or expansion.

Multi-zone Compressors/Expanders
Dynamics processors that subdivide the signal into different amplitude zones and process them in different ways, using compression or expansion.

Output gain or Gain makeup
A parameter used in dynamics processors to regulate a sound's output gain.

Parallel compression
A compression method made up of mixing two signals, the original (uncompressed) one and the compressed one, so as to increase the sound's RMS level without compressing its peaks.

Ratio
Compression (or expansion) ratio of signals whose level is beyond a given threshold, with respect to the signal's original intensity. It can be expressed as a ratio or a percentage.

Release
The time in which a completely active compressor (or expander) becomes completely inactive – this is the time between the moment where the sound once again returns below the threshold and the moment in which the signal returns to its normal unity gain. In gates, the release is the time it takes for the sound to reach the floor from its original intensity.

Side-chain
This term has two meanings: the first of which refers to the side processing chain inside a dynamics processor. The second (also called *external side-chain processing*) refers to the operational mode of a dynamics processor where its activation is decoupled from its own input signal, allowing it to be activated by an external control signal (*key input*).

Slope
Another way of indicating the compression ratio, based on the slope of the curve used for the compression.

Threshold
A given level beyond which dynamics processing is activated.

Triggering gate
A gate whose function is similar to an event trigger (in other words something that activates a process). This is different from a normal trigger in that the activation depends on exceeding a threshold.

Upward compression
A type of compression where the amplitude of low intensity sounds is increased.

Upward expansion
Increasing the amplitude of sounds above a given threshold.

DISCOGRAPHY

Luigi Ceccarelli "Exsultet", Rai Trade, CD RTC006
Alessandro Cipriani "Aqua Sapientiae/Angelus Domini" in Al Nur, CNI, CD CNDL 13172

· ·

7P
DYNAMICS PROCESSORS

PREREQUISITES FOR THE CHAPTER
• THE CONTENTS OF VOLUME 1, CHAPTERS 5 AND 6 (THEORY AND PRACTICE), INTERLUDE C AND CHAPTER 7T

OBJECTIVES
ABILITIES
• TO BE ABLE TO APPLY THE ENVELOPE OF ONE SOUND TO ANOTHER SOUND OR OTHER PARAMETERS
• TO BE ABLE TO CONSTRUCT ALGORITHMS FOR ENVELOPE FOLLOWERS, DOWNWARD AND UPWARD COMPRESSION, PARALLEL COMPRESSION, DE-ESSER, LIMITERS AND LIVE NORMALIZERS
• TO BE ABLE TO APPLY APPROPRIATE PARAMETER VALUES TO ANY KIND OF DYNAMICS PROCESSOR.
• TO BE ABLE TO BUILD ALGORITHMS FOR GATES, DOWNWARD OR UPWARD EXPANDERS, SIDE CHAIN AND DUCKING
• TO UNDERSTAND HOW TO USE DYNAMICS PROCESSORS FOR BOTH TECHNICAL AND CREATIVE PURPOSES

CONTENTS
• ENVELOPE FOLLOWERS
• COMPRESSORS, LIMITERS, LIVE NORMALIZERS AND DE-ESSERS
• EXPANDERS AND GATES
• CREATING DOWNWARD AND UPWARD COMPRESSION AND EXPANSION
• CREATING PARALLEL COMPRESSION
• CREATING EXTERNAL SIDE CHAINS AND DUCKING
• CREATING ADAPTIVE GATES AND DUCKERS, TRIGGERING GATES, GATE-SEQUENCERS AND FEED-BACK WITH CONTROLLED DYNAMICS

ACTIVITIES
• BUILDING AND MODIFYING ALGORITHMS

SUPPORTING MATERIALS
• LIST OF MAX OBJECTS - LIST OF COMMANDS, ATTRIBUTES, AND PARAMETERS FOR SPECIFIC MAX OBJECTS

7.1 ENVELOPE FOLLOWERS

There are different ways to create an envelope follower in Max. As we will discover, each of these methods has its own qualities that make it more or less useful for different possible applications. We will analyze the different ways an envelope follower can be designed, and consider the most effective uses for each of them.

The first object that we will learn is **average~**. Rebuild the simple patch shown in figure 7.1.

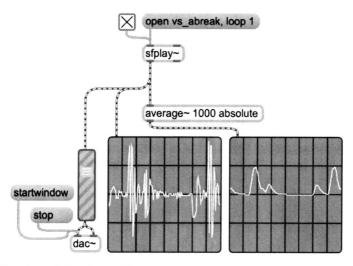

Fig. 7.1 Envelope following with **average~**

This object creates a signal representing an average of the input sample values. As you can see in the figure, its output signal follows the dynamic profile – i.e., the envelope – of the input signal. The first argument to **average~** indicates the number of input samples that will be taken into consideration when calculating the mean value, or average (this is 1000 in the figure). The second argument ("absolute" in the figure) specifies the mode that will be used to calculate the average. The three possible modes are:

1) *bipolar* (the default mode): this mode simply calculates the average of the input samples. More specifically, the sample values are summed and the result is divided by the number of samples used for the sum. For audio signals this average tends to be near zero, especially when using a large number of samples (at least as many as there are in one cycle of an input waveform), because the equivalent quantities of positive and negative values in a bipolar signal tend to cancel each other out.

2) *absolute*: here, the average is calculated using the absolute value of the input samples (i.e., they are always positive values). This is the mode shown in the figure.

353

3) *rms (root mean square)*. In this mode, the input samples are first squared (consequently becoming all positive) before being averaged. The square root of this average is then calculated. Although this method is more expensive in terms of CPU usage, it provides the most accurate results. Nonetheless, the absolute mode is generally sufficient in many situations.

You can change the operational mode by sending the messages "bipolar," "absolute" or "rms" to the **average~** object, and additionally change the number of samples it uses to calculate the average by sending it an integer value. Note that this value cannot be greater than the numerical argument you provided.

So, just how many samples do we need to use in order to obtain adequate envelope following? Unfortunately, it is impossible to define a good value that would work in all situations. Nonetheless, you should be aware that as the number of samples increases, any accents in the input sound will tend to be smoothed-out in the resulting envelope-followed signal. Conversely, as the number of samples decreases, the envelope will begin to more and more faithfully follow the amplitude peaks in the original signal, until the point where one sample is used for the "average," thereby just reproducing the instantaneous sample values of the input waveform.

We can now apply the envelope obtained from **average~** to a signal with a constant amplitude. Modify the patch as shown in figure 7.2.

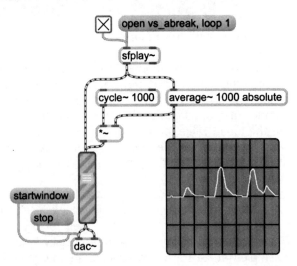

Fig. 7.2 Envelope applied to an oscillator

In this example, the envelope from a drum loop sound is applied to a sinusoidal oscillator at 1000 Hz. When you activate the patch you will probably notice that the envelope applied to the oscillator seems to be delayed with respect to the direct drum sound. This happens because each sample output by **average~**

results from averaging the preceding 1000 samples. A simple solution to correct this would be to delay the direct signal (the one going from **sfplay~** to the **gain~** object) until the two sounds seem to be in sync. Try this out by inserting a 200-300 sample delay.

Now, try modifying the number of samples that **average~** uses to calculate the mean by connecting a number box to the object. What happens when you use 1000 samples? What about with 10 samples? Or with just 1?

We can also use the envelope obtained from the envelope followed to control some sound processing parameters. Modify the patch as shown in figure 7.3.

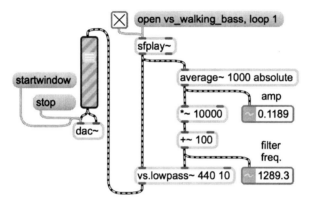

Fig. 7.3 Envelope controlling a filter

Here, the sound vs_walking_bass.wav has been loaded, and the envelope calculated by the average~ object is used to control the lowpass filter that is applied to this sound file. As you can see, the frequency of the filter follows the dynamic profile of the sound. The amplitude of the envelope is multiplied by 10000 and then the value 100 is added to it and the result is used as a cutoff frequency. Actually, in this example the signal generated by the envelope follower will rarely exceed 0.1, so the maximum cutoff frequency will be around 1100 Hz (10000 · 0.1 + 100). Try changing the values of the multiplier, addition, Q factor (second argument to the filter) and the filter type (for example, try using a highpass filter).

Let's now take a look at how we can control different parameters using the envelope follower; open the patch **07_01_envfollow.maxpat** (figure 7.4).

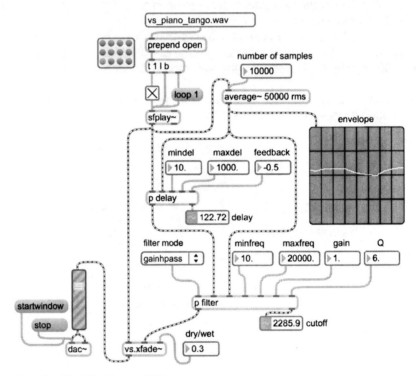

Fig. 7.4 The file **07_01_envfollow.maxpat**

In this patch, the envelope follower is used to control both the delay time and the cutoff frequency of a filter simultaneously. The signal output by **sfplay~** is sent to an **average~** object that creates the envelope (in rms mode) and sends it to two subpatches. The first subpatch, [p delay], takes the envelope in its second inlet and uses it to control the delay time of the sound sent to its left inlet. The delay time can vary between the given minimum and maximum values (via the two **flonum** objects labeled "mindel" and "maxdel"), and could optionally include feedback. The delayed signal is sent out the left outlet of the subpatch, while its right outlet outputs the actual delay time (displayed in the **number~** object). The contents of the subpatch are fairly simple (figure 7.5).

The signal outptut by **average~** ("env" inlet) is sent to a **scale~** object that modifies the 0-1 range of the envelope into the mindel-maxdel range set in the main patch.[1] The delay time is sent to the **tapin~/tapout~** object pair with feedback on the left side of the subpatch.

---

[1] Note that it is very unlikely that the envelope values output by **average~** will ever get close to the maximum value of 1, and therefore also unlikely that you will ever reach the maximum delay time. Therefore, this should be taken into account when setting the "maxdel" parameter.

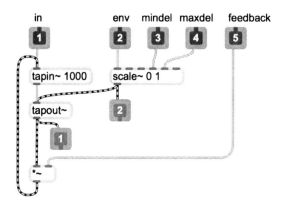

Fig. 7.5 The [p delay] subpatch

Next, the delayed signal in the main patch is sent to the [p filter] subpatch, which uses the envelope to modulate the cutoff frequency of a filter. The parameter here is also scaled between a minimum and maximum range ("minfreq" and "maxfreq"), and it is additionally possible to control the filtered signal's amplitude ("gain") and Q factor.

You can always change the filter type using the **umenu** object labeled "filter mode". There are three available filters: gainlpass, gainhpass and gainbpass – more specifically a lowpass filter, a highpass filter and a bandpass filter, all of which have optional gain control. Let's now take a look at the contents of this subpatch (figure 7.6).

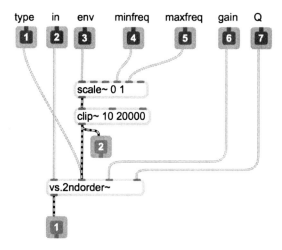

Fig. 7.6 The [p filter] subpatch

This subpatch also uses a **scale~** object to modify the 0-1 range of the envelope into the frequency range that has been set in the main patch (using "minfreq" and "maxfreq"). In the lower part of this patch you can see the filter

vs.2ndorder~, which is made up of a second order filter whose behavior can be freely modified by sending the desired filter type (highpass, bandpass, etc.) to the second inlet. Actually, this object is has been created using the standard **filtercoeff~** and **biquad~** objects.[2] You can see the different types of possible filters that can be used inside the object's help patch (they are the same as those used by the **filtercoeff~** object).

Now return to the main patch and listen to all the example presets, after which you can try to create some new ones. Notice that the different presets also change the number of samples used by **average~** to calculate the envelope signal, in on order to make the output envelope more or less reactive with respect to the input signal. Also, be sure to notice the "dry/wet" parameter at the bottom of the patch, which can be used to control the ratio between the direct signal and the processed sound.

If you take a moment to think about it carefully, the **average~** object can actually be categorized as a filter, since the values it produces simply result from the sum of a certain number of preceding input samples multiplied by a given coefficient. Therefore, it is actually a special type of FIR filter (a lowpass one to be precise) that multiplies the last n values in its input by the coefficient 1/n and sums the result. For example, when the average is computed using only two samples (in bipolar mode) the resulting audio signal is identical to that output by the lowpass filter we discussed in section 3.6[3] – in both instances the filter equation is in fact: **y(n) = 1/2 x(n) + 1/2 x(n-1)** (figure 7.7).

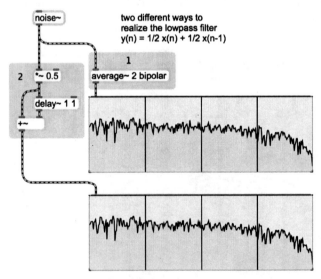

Fig. 7.7 Comparing the **average~** object and a lowpass filter

---

[2] These objects have already been presented in chapter 3P.
[3] This is actually the same filter used for the Karplus-Strong algorithm (section 6.10), which takes the average between the current input sample value and the preceding output sample value.

Since the **average~** object is just a lowpass filter, couldn't we also use a "normal" lowpass filter to create an envelope follower? We certainly can, although we first need to transform the negative values of the input bipolar waveform into positive values, and then use a very low cutoff frequency (as shown in figure 7.8).

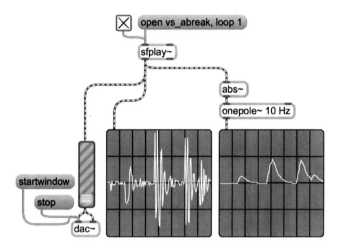

Fig. 7.8 Envelope following using a lowpass filter

In the figure, we used the **onepole~** object, which implements a first-order IIR lowpass filter, with a cutoff frequency of 10 Hz.

. . . .

ACTIVITY

In the patch **07_01_envfollow.maxpat** (figure 7.4), replace the **average~** object with the **abs~/onepole~** object pair. The number of samples used by the **average~** object in the various presets should be transformed into an appropriate cutoff frequency for **onepole~**. What kind of operation could be used to achieve this? Note that with this new patch you will not be able to get the exact same results that were produced by the original.

. . . .

Now let's take a look at two other objects in Max that we can use to create an envelope follower: **rampsmooth~** and **slide~**. Rebuild the patch shown in figure 7.9.

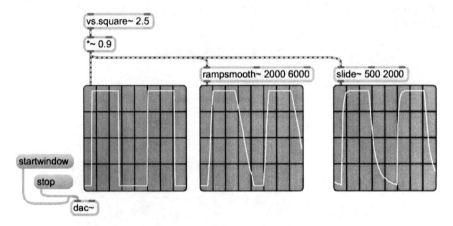

Fig. 7.9 The **rampsmooth~** and **slide~** objects

These objects can be used to "smooth out" the input signal, or more precisely to interpolate the jumps between one sample and the next using a linear ramp (**rampsmooth~**) or a logarithmic one (**slide~**). In figure 7.9 there is a square wave that oscillates between the values -0.9 and 0.9 at a frequency of 2.5 Hz. It is displayed in the first oscilloscope. The **rampsmooth~** and **slide~** objects, as you can see other two oscilloscopes, modify the waveform by making the sudden jump between the two values less abrupt. For both objects, the ascending ramp can have a different duration than the descending ramp, since both use two numerical arguments (or values in their second and third inlets) to determine the interpolation time of the two ramps. For the **rampsmooth~** object, the two arguments (called "ramp up" and "ramp down") represent the number of samples used to passed from one value to the next. In the figure this is set to a linear interpolation of 200 samples when the value goes from -0.9 to 0.9 (ascending ramp) and 6000 samples when it goes from 0.9 to -0.9 (descending ramp).

The **slide~** object is slightly more complex. Its two arguments (called "slide up" and "slide down") actually represent a "slide factor" for increasing and decreasing values. If we call the slide factor **sl**, the current input sample **x(n)**, the current output sample **y(n)** and the previous output sample **y(n-1)**, we can obtain the following formula:

y(n) = y(n-1) + ((x(n) - y(n-1))/sl)

In the figure the slide factor is set to 500 for increasing values ("slide up"), and 2000 for decreasing values ("slide down").

Using these two objects we can create envelope followers with separate reaction times for the attack and release of a sound, which, as we will soon see, is extremely useful for designing different kinds of dynamics processors.

Normally, in a dynamics processor such as a compressor, the reaction time for a sound's attack and release are expressed in seconds (or in milliseconds). To transform the attack and release parameters into values which can be used with **rampsmooth~**, you can use an object that converts milliseconds into samples, such as **mstosamps~** or **translate**[4] (figure 7.10).

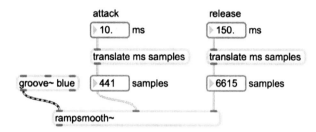

Fig. 7.10 Attack and release times for **rampsmooth~**

Using attack and release times with the **slide~** object is slightly more difficult. The logarithmic interpolation shown above actually works in such a way that the new sample is in theory only reached after an infinite amount of time. However, in reality the new sample value is reached in a finite amount of time, albeit still too long for our purposes, due to the inherent limitations of numerical precision within a digital system (which was discussed in chapter 5).

One practical solution is to calculate the time it takes to cover 99% of the value range. The corresponding slide factor (or at least a good approximation of it) can be obtained by converting the time into samples and dividing the result by 4.6 (as shown in figure 7.11).

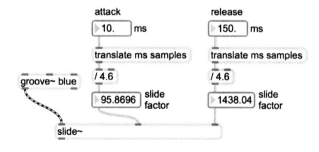

Fig. 7.11 Attack and release times for **slide~**

---

[4] We have already encountered this object in section IC.2.

Hence, by using this calculation, we are able to determine the approximate amount of time that `slide~` needs to output a signal which covers 99% of the distance between two values.

By setting the attack time to 0, we obtain an envelope follower that instantly registers peak values found in the input sound, so it therefore does not present the kinds of delay problems that we encountered in the patch in figure 7.2. Try modifying that patch as shown in figure 7.12.

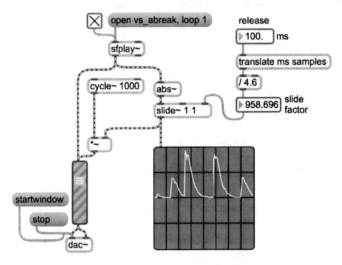

Fig. 7.12 Peak follower

In this patch, the `slide~` object has a slide factor equal to 1 for increasing values ("slide up"), meaning that it will not actually perform any interpolation[5], meaning that it will not actually perform any interpolation [5], whereas it has a variable slide factor for decreasing values ("slide down"). Note that before being input into the `slide~` object, the signal is turned into a unipolar signal by the `abs~` object.

Using an envelope follower we can also "flatten" the envelope of a sound, making its average amplitude equal to 1. To do this, we simply need to divide an audio signal by its own envelope, as output by the envelope follower, as we learned in chapter 7.1T. Reconstruct the patch in figure 7.13 (it is a variation of the preceding patch), based on this system.
This is actually the inverse operation of applying an envelope to a sound. As we learned in the very first chapter: in order to provide an envelope to a sound which doesn't have one (such as the signal produced by an oscillator), we need to multiply the sound by a signal that represents the evolution in time of

---

[5] Indeed, if we insert a value of 1 for sl in our equation $y(n) = y(n-1) + ((x(n) - y(n-1))/sl)$, we obtain $y(n) = y(n-1) + ((x(n) - y(n-1))/1) = y(n-1) + x(n) - y(n-1) = x(n)$. In other words, the output sample $y(n)$ is equal to the input sample $x(n)$.

the envelope itself. Therefore, if we can apply an envelope using multiplication, we can remove an envelope using division.

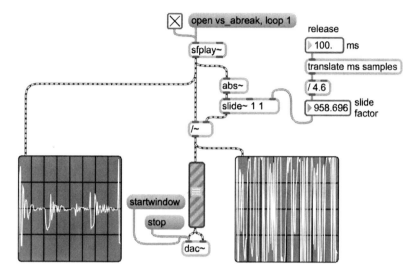

Fig. 7.13 How to remove a sound's envelope

Now load the file **07_12_balance.maxpat** (figure 7.14).

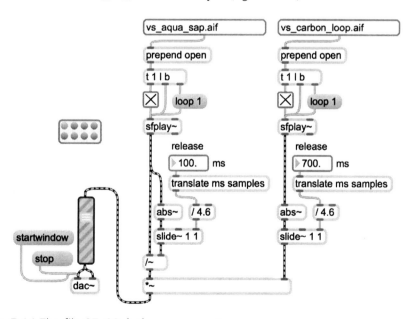

Fig. 7.14 The file **07_02_balance.maxpat**

In this patch, a sound file loaded into the **sfplay~** object on the left has its envelope removed using the method which has just been illustrated. The sound without an envelope is the multiplied by the envelope obtained from another

363

sound (coming from the **sfplay~** object on the right). Notice how the effect changes when the release parameters of the two envelope generators are modified.

Test out the different presets (which change the two release parameters), before making some presets of your own.

Apart from imposing the amplitude envelope of one sound onto another, this technique is also useful to create a balance function (already described in section 7.1T). In the Virtual Sound Macros library there are two objects, **vs.balance~** and **vs.balance2~** which implement this. The first object uses a lowpass filter as an envelope follower, and the second uses a **slide~** object (basically containing the algorithm shown in the patch in figure 7.14).

Let's now take a look at an example in figure 7.15.

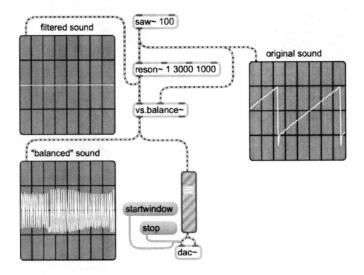

Fig. 7.15 the **vs.balance~** object

The **vs.balance~** object applies the amplitude of the signal that it receives in its second inlet and applies it to the signal sent to its first inlet. The third inlet is used to define the cutoff frequency of the lowpass filter used for envelope following (by default this frequency is 10 Hz).

In the figure there is a sawtooth waveform at 100 Hz that is filtered by a band-pass filter with a center frequency of 3000 Hz (in practice this should be the 30th harmonic of the input sound) and a Q factor equal to 1000. As you can see in the oscilloscope on the left, the amplitude of the filtered sound is near zero. This sound is sent to the first inlet of the **vs.balance~** object, while the original, unfiltered, sound is sent to the second inlet. The **vs.balance~** object outputs the filtered sound with the envelope of the unfiltered sound applied to it.

7.2 COMPRESSORS AND DOWNWARD COMPRESSION

The standard Max distribution already contains some ready-to-use dynamics processors:

`omx.comp~` upward/downward compressor
`omx.4band~` 4-band multi-band compressor
`omx.5band~` 5-band multi-band compressor
`omx.peaklim~` limiter

However, in this chapter we will not deal with these objects for the following reasons:

1) Not all the dynamics processors are present – for example, objects used specifically for the purposes of gating and ducking are missing. Furthermore, the compressor is simultaneously an upward and downward compressor; it is not possible to separate these two functions.

2) Some parameters of the **omx** objects are controlled using seemingly arbitrary value ranges which are difficult to comprehend.

3) These objects are "black boxes" whose exact internal operation is not necessarily known. What interests us, on the other hand, is to assemble dynamics processors starting from basic building blocks in order to better understand the details of their behavior.

4) Building dynamics processors "from scratch" (that is, starting from zero) actually allows us to master new and interesting techniques for signal manipulation within Max.

So, let's now look at how we can build our own compressor.
First of all, let's deal with the part of the algorithm that calculates the attenuation in intensity of the input signal. As we know, this algorithm should identify the part of the signal that goes above a predetermined threshold and should calculate how much this part of the signal should be attenuated, in order to be compressed to the extent specified by the ratio.

To give a hypothetical example, imagine we have a threshold equal to -20 dB and a ratio equal to 4. If at a given moment the signal reaches an intensity of -4 dB, it has exceeded the threshold by 16 dB (in other words the amount of overshoot is 16 dB). Dividing this amount by the ratio we get 16/4 = 4, so the signal should only exceed the threshold by 4 dB after compression (not by 16). This means that at this point the signal needs to be attenuated by 16-4 = 12 dB.

Note that there is a linear relationship between the amount of overshoot and the attenuation of the signal in dB. Therefore, if **os** denotes the amount of overshoot, **rt** represents the ratio and **at** the attenuation, we obtain:
at = os - os/rt

Specifically, when the intensity of the signal in the preceding example varies between -20 and 0 dB (consequently meaning the amount of overshoot will vary between 0 and 20 dB), the attenuation will vary between 0 and 15 dB (20 - 20/4 = 15).

In figure 7.16 we can see how to transform these simple calculations into a patch.

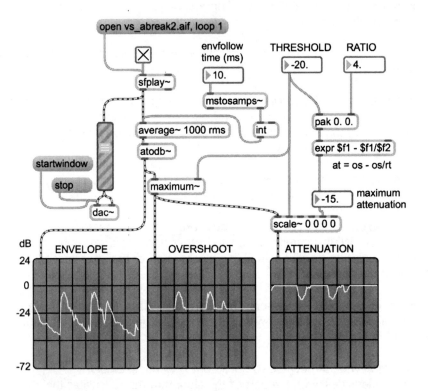

Fig. 7.16 Calculating the attenuation of a signal

First, we obtain the envelope from the input signal using the **average~** object. The amount of signal that is taken into consideration is set in milliseconds and subsequently converted into samples[6].

The signal output by the envelope follower is subsequently converted into dB, because our compressor works with intensities expressed in decibels. For this reason, the three oscilloscopes at the bottom of the patch have had their Display Range set between -72 and 24 dB, via the object inspector.

---

[6] Note how the **int** object has been added in order to convert the floating-point number output by **mstosamps~** into an integer; the **average~** object only actually accepts integer values.

Using the **maximum~** object (which compares the values received in its left and right inlets and outputs the higher of the two)[7] we can isolate the part of the signal that exceeds the threshold: the second oscilloscope shows the overshoot in relation to the threshold. The signal processed this way is then sent to the **scale~** object which transforms it from decibel values ranging between -20 dB (the threshold) and 0 (maximum possible intensity) into attenuation values between 0 (no attenuation) and -15 (maximum attenuation). The trajectory of the attenuation factor is visible in the third oscilloscope. The maximum attenuation, obtained using the formula we discussed above, is calculated with the **expr** object, which lets us construct mathematical expressions using combinations of operators and functions (we have already covered this in Interlude B, section IB.8).

As we have already learned, a compressor does not follow the instantaneous attenuation curve thus calculated, but rather a version of it whose response has been slowed down using the attack and release parameters. To be precise, the attack time influences increasing attenuation values and the release influences decreasing values. As you can see in figure 7.17, we can use the **slide~** object to control these parameters.

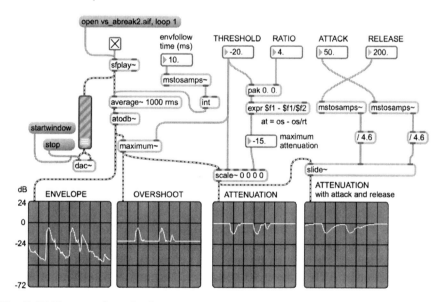

Fig. 7.17 The attack and release parameters

Note that the attack and release parameters are interchanged before being sent to the **slide~** object. This is because our attenuation is actually a negative value, so increasing it causes a succession of decreasing values ("slide down"), while reducing it causes successively increasing values ("slide up"). Before we

---

[7] This is the MSP equivalent to the [maximum] object that we previously used in section 5.3P, figure 5.21

look at an example of a complete compressor, let's look at how we can graphi-cally create a compression curve – having this kind of visual feedback actually helps us understand how a signal's dynamics will be modified by our compressor.

Recreate the patch shown in figure 7.18. The graphical display object on the right is a multislider whose "range" parameters have been set to [-100, 0] in the inspector.

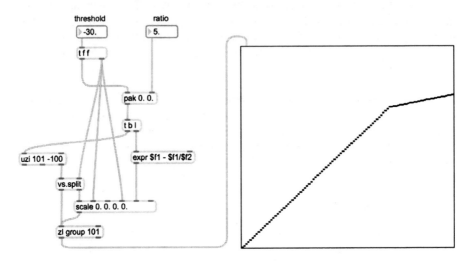

Fig. 7.18 Compression curve.

This patch contains an algorithm similar to the one that is used to calculate the attenuation for the signal being compressed. The two number boxes can be used to set the threshold and ratio. These two values are used to transform the value range between the threshold and 0 into a range between the threshold and (threshold - (threshold/ratio)), using the **scale** object. For example, in the figure the range between -30 and 0 is mapped to a new range going from -30 to -24.

Each time that either the threshold or the ratio is modified, the **uzi** object receives a bang, causing a sequence of values between -100 and 0 to be out-put. These are sent to the **vs.split** object, which we encountered earlier, in section 6.9P. This object compares the number it receives in its left inlet with its argument (or with a number that it has previously received in its right inlet, as in this example). If the number is less than the argument it is sent out the object's left outlet, and if it is greater than or equal to the argument it is sent out the right outlet. Therefore, in our example, all values less than the threshold -30) will be sent out the left (and consequently not modified), while values greater than or equal to the threshold will be sent to the **scale** object via the right outlet (and transformed as previously explained). Both the modi-fied and the unmodified values are sent to the [**zl** group 101] object, which assembles them into a list consisting of 101 elements, which is then sent to the **multislider** object.

At this point, we can now examine the complete compressor; open the file **07_03_compressor.maxpat** (shown in figure 7.19).

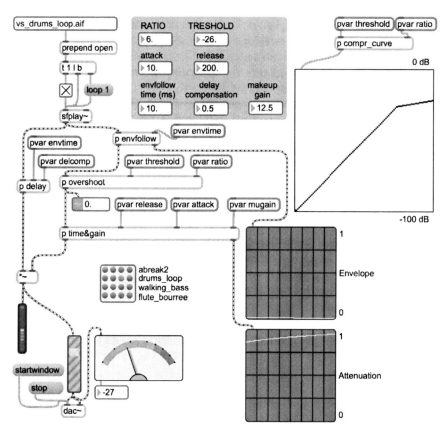

Fig. 7.19 The file **07_03_compressor.maxpat**

In this patch we are making use of the **pvar** object to allow us to separate the user interface from our computational algorithm. We have already learned how to use this object for precisely this purpose in the context of the subtractive synthesizer (see section 3.5P and IC.2). All of the number boxes visible in the rectangular panel have been given a scripting name corresponding to a **pvar** object in the patch (you can double-check the scripting name by opening the inspector for each of the number boxes).

In addition to the algorithms show in the three preceding figures, we have added makeup gain, in order to increase the intensity of the sound after compression, and delay compensation, which is applied to the signal being compressed in order to compensate for the delay introduced by the amplitude follower. Note that the delay compensation parameter is not expressed in absolute values, but rather is proportional to the envfollow time parameter – when the delay compensation is 1, the delay is equal to the value of the envfollow time, when it is 0.5, the delay is equal to half, and so forth.

369

Let's look at how the compressor works. The signal output by the **sfplay~** object is sent to the compression algorithm (on the right) which we have already seen in figure 7.16 and 7.17. The algorithm has been subdivided into three subpatches. The first, [p envfollow], contains an **average~** object used as an envelope follower (its envelope can be seen in the first oscilloscope on the right hand side of the main patch). The envelope is sent to the [p overshoot] subpatch, which calculates the attenuation factor for values above the threshold. The [p time&gain] subpatch receives this attenuation factor and applies the attack and release parameters to it, via the **slide~** object. The result is displayed in the second oscilloscope on the right-hand side of the main patch. Continuing with the inner-workings of the [p time&gain] subpatch, the makeup gain factor is added to the signal output by **slide~**, converted to linear amplitude (using **dbtoa~**) and then output to the main patch where it is multiplied with the input signal being compressed.

As we have already mentioned, before compression, the audio signal needs to be slightly delayed in order to compensate for the delay that is introduced by the envelope follower. In our patch this happens in the [p delay] subpatch visible on the left side of the patch. This delay compensation parameter is a multiplicative factor of the amount of the input signal that is used for envelope following (given by the envfollow time parameter) – in the example shown in the figure, this delay time is 5 milliseconds (10 · 0.5).

Listen to the different presets for this patch. The first preset in each row contains the uncompressed sound, while the others use different compression factors.

Warning: this is not a text about mixing and mastering, but rather about creative uses of synthesis and sound processing. The presets that have been provided for our compressor (as well as those for the subsequent dynamics processors) are therefore purposefully exaggerated in order to show how you can completely transform the characteristics of a sound by manipulating its dynamics.

Note that we have used a very fast envelope follower for the sound file **vs_walking_bass.wav** with respect to its frequency content. This can lead to compression of the waveform itself, resulting in distortion (listen, for example, to the fourth preset in the third row) – although it is a side-effect of the compressor, it can nonetheless be interesting and useful for creative sound manipulation. Also listen carefully to the last preset of the flute sound (the fourth one in the fourth row) and compare it with the original sound (the first preset in the fourth row): using the compressor we are able to make the phrasing more legato than it is in the original.

Take care to study all of the parameter values in the presets and try changing them, one at a time, in order to change the resulting output sound. Finally, try creating some new presets that you can use with other sound files.

ACTIVITY

Replace the `slide~` object in the [p time&gain] subpatch with `rampsmooth~`, so the attack and release will be linear instead of logarithmic. Note that you will also need to modify the part that converts the time values into samples (see figure 7.10). Listen once again to the presets: can you hear the difference?

• •

Now let's see how we can implement a soft knee that can be added to our compression algorithm. As you know, a soft knee is a function that creates a gradual transition between the uncompressed sound below the threshold and the compressed sound above it (i.e., a curve instead of an abrupt change). The soft knee has width in dB that is centered on the threshold level itself, so, if the threshold is -10dB and the soft knee has a width of 12 dB, the curve begin at -16dB (known as the lower knee threshold) and will end at -4dB (the higher knee threshold). Obviously, for intensities under -16dB the ratio will be 1:1 (i.e., no compression) and dynamics above -4dB will be fully compressed. So, what kind of compression takes place within the soft knee range? Let's suppose that the compression ratio is 4:1. The curve of the knee needs to define a gradually changing value between an initial ratio of 1:1 (unity gain) and our final compression ratio of 4:1 without an abrupt change at the threshold. Actually, the threshold that should be used for this calculation is not the actual threshold but the lower knee threshold (see figure 7.20).

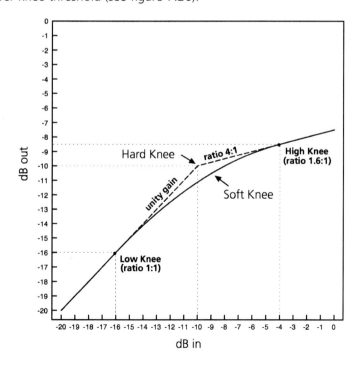

Fig. 7.20 Soft-knee

How is the actual ratio of the soft knee calculated? Let's first think about how the equivalent algorithm would be implemented for a hard knee. For half the distance (from -16 to -10 dB) the intensity would not be reduced because it would have a 1:1 ratio, and for the remaining part (from -10 dB to -4dB) it would be reduced by 1/4 (a ratio of 1:4). The intensity at the end of a soft knee must therefore also be (1+1/4)/2 = 5/8 = 0.625 with respect to the intensity of the input signal, meaning a ratio of 1.6:1. In other words, the soft knee will start from a 1:1 ratio and gradually and smoothly change into a 1.6:1 ratio as it goes from at -16dB to -4dB.

So, using the above values (threshold = -10dB, ratio = 4:1), an input signal with a –4dB intensity will be compressed using the following formula (in a hard knee scenario).

threshold + overshoot/ratio
-10 db   + 6/4 dB   = -8.5 dB

This means that when the input signal has an intensity of -4dB, the compressor will lower that intensity to -8.5dB.
If we use a soft knee with a -12dB width (and consequently a lower knee threshold equal to -16dB) we have:

threshold + overshoot/soft_knee_ratio
-16 dB   + 12/1.6   = -8.5 dB

In this case, an input signal intensity of -4dB will also correspond to an output intensity of -8.5dB. The two points therefore exactly coincide and the soft knee curve will join perfectly at the point where there is a compression ratio of 4:1.

Now let's see how this soft knee can be implemented within a compressor. Open the file **07_04_soft_knee_stereo_compressor.maxpat** (figure 7.21).

In addition to defining a soft knee (third parameter in the boxed section at the top), this patch also contains a highpass filter (sixth parameter) that is used to attenuate low frequencies in the signal that is used for envelope following (see the [p filter_envfollow] subpatch). As was previously discussed, this filter keeps low frequencies from causing excessive compression. Note that the two parameters "loknee" and "hiknee" in the upper right part of the patch are not manually set, but instead calculated by the [p kneecalc] subpatch each time that the threshold or soft knee parameter values are changed. (We suggest that you look at and analyze this subpatch for yourself.)

This patch implements a stereo compressor, so an envelope follower is applied to both channels. Both of the resulting envelopes are continuously compared, sample by sample, and the one with the maximum value is sent to the compression algorithm.

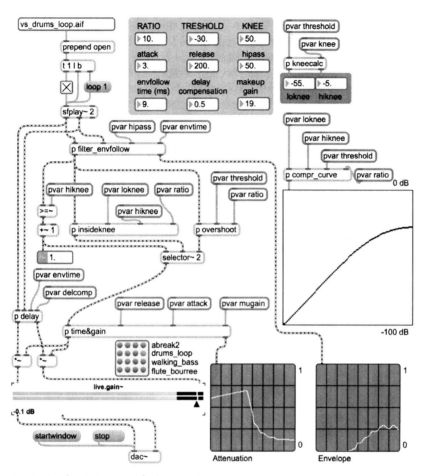

Fig. 7.21 The file **07_04_soft_knee_stereo_compressor.maxpat**

In figure 7.22 we can see the [p filter_envfollow] subpatch that contains the highpass filtering and control system for the stereo envelope.

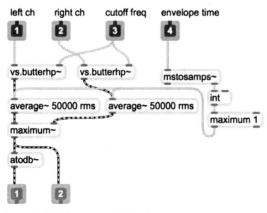

Fig. 7.22 The subpatch [p filter_envfollow]

373

Notice that there is a new object in the bottom part of the main patch: the live.gain~ object. This object is part of the Max for Live library (but is also available for those who do not own a Max for Live license), and is used to replace the gain~ object. We are using it here because it allows us to manage a stereo signal in a visually compact way, and additionally graphically displays both the signal level and numerical gain reduction in dB. To raise the gain of the live.gain~ object, you should move the triangular cursor (located in the lower part of the object) to the right.

Now let's analyze the algorithm that controls the soft knee. Note that in addition to the [p overshoot] subpatch also present in the previous compressor patch, there is also a [p insideknee] subpatch that is used to apply the compression over the soft knee range. Both of these patches are sent to a **selector~** object which lets the signal calculated by the [p insideknee] subpatch pass through it when the input signal is less than the higher knee threshold, and lets the signal calculated by the [p overshoot] subpatch pass when the input signal is greater than or equal to the higher knee threshold. Are you able to describe how this selection mechanism works?

Now open the subpatch [p insideknee] (figure 7.23).

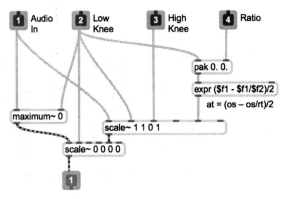

Fig. 7.23 The subpatch [p insideknee]

There are two **scale~** objects inside this patch: the object at the bottom is used to calculate the attenuation for the input signal, as we have already seen in figure 7.16.

The **scale~** object at the top of the subpatch is used to calculate the ratio inside the soft knee. As with the preceding patch, we can calculate the attenuation to apply to the input signal using the following formula:

at = os – os/rt

Here, the overshoot *os* is calculated based on the lower knee threshold level and not the actual threshold. As we already stated, this formula is applied to the **scale~** object in the upper part of figure 7.22, and the result is divided by 2, for reasons explained above. Note that when the intensity of the input signal is less than or equal to the lower knee threshold, the attenuation is equal to 0, and that when the intensity of the input signal is at the higher knee threshold point, the attenuation is equal to (os - os/rt)/2. When the signal is in-between the lower knee threshold and the higher knee threshold the attenuation will be an intermediary value between 0 and (os - os/rt)/2.

Now listen to all the presets and try changing the soft knee and cutoff frequency of the highpass filter for each of them. Listen carefully to how these parameters affect the resulting output sound, and then try creating some new presets of your own.

• •

ACTIVITY

Replace the `slide~` object in the [p time&gain] subpatch with a `rampsmooth~` object, as you did in the previous activity, in order to be able to have a linear, instead of logarithmic, attack and release. You will also need to modify the part of the patch that converts the time into samples (see figure 7.10). Now listen to your new presets – can you hear the difference?

• •

PARALLEL COMPRESSION

A parallel compressor can be made by adding the uncompressed (dry) signal to the compressed one. As explained in the theoretical part of this chapter, the latter signal needs to be delayed by the same amount of time as the compressed signal in order to avoid unwanted phase cancellation when the two signals are summed. The compression algorithm is basically the same as the previous one. You can see in the patch **07_05_parallel_compressor.maxpat** that we have added an additional control for adjusting the intensity of the dry signal (figure .24).

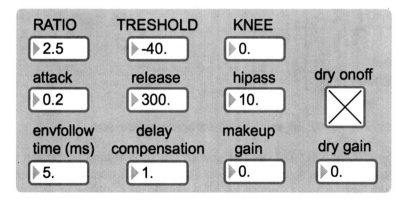

Fig. 7.24 The control panel for the patch **07_05_parallel_compressor.maxpat**

Notice the [p mix] subpatch on the lower left hand side of the main patch, which is used to mix the dry and wet signals. Open and analyze its (simple) inner-workings.

Listen to all the presets. You will notice that the attack time is always very short, because we want to immediately compress the signal above the threshold in order to increase the volume of the softer parts of the signal.

MULTI-BAND COMPRESSION

If we want to create a multi-band compressor we simply need to divide the input signal into different frequency bands using filters, compress each band with a different compressor, and sum the resulting compressed signals together to once again obtain the complete full-spectrum sound.

In the patch **07_06_multiband_compressor.maxpat** (figure 7.25) we can see a realization of a three-band compressor.

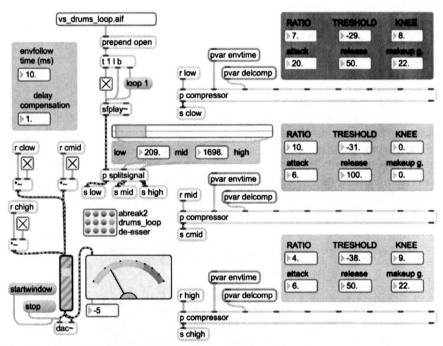

Fig. 7.25 The file **07_06_multiband_compressor.maxpat**

The signal output by **sfplay~** is sent to the [p splitsignal] subpatch which divides it into three frequency bands. This subpatch contains two cascaded crossover filters (**cross~** which we have already encountered in section 6.2P) – open up the subpatch to see how this was done.

The interface object located immediately beneath **sfplay~** is called **rslider**. This is a slider that lets us select a range of values. In the figure, for example, you can see that the range 209-1698 has been selected. The selected range is indicated by a gray band and the two values at the ends of this range are shown in the two float number boxes just under the object.[8] These two values represent the crossover frequencies of the two **cross~** filters. This implies that the first of our three bands will go from 0 to 209 Hz, the second will go from 209 to 1698 Hz and the third from 1698 to 22050 Hz.

The three frequency bands generated by [p splitsignal] are sent to the three [p compressor] subpatches at the right of the main patch using **send** and **receive** objects. Each of the compressors has its own set of parameters, although they all share the same envelope follower and delay time parameters, located on the left side of the patch. Each compressor sends its compressed signal to the **gain~** object on the left, using additional **send** and **receive** objects. Each frequency band can be activated or deactivated using the toggles located on the left – this can be very useful while setting up the parameters for an individual band and listening to the result produced. Listen to the presets and notice how this sole patch takes on the function of both compressor and equalizer, and lets us even modify the input sound quite heavily.

The last row of presets simulates a de-esser using compression only on the high frequency band. The first preset in this row uses a recording of a voice with strongly present sibilant sounds; the subsequent presets in the row attenuate the sibilant sounds with different parameters.

Try creating some additional presets.

• •

ACTIVITY

Make a stereo version of the multi-band compressor.

• •

7.3 LIMITERS AND LIVE NORMALIZER

A limiter, as we have already learned, is used to prevent an input sound from exceeding the 0dB threshold (or any other threshold we define). Consequently we need to use a peak follower (see figure 7.12) to let us know immediately when the threshold has been exceeded (i.e., without any delay). For limiters, this is defined as the ceiling, and any part of the signal that goes above this

_____
[8] The value range of this rslider has been set in the inspector to a minimum of 50 and a maximum of 4000.

threshold is brought back down below it. This means that if an input signal goes above the threshold by 6 dB, the limiter should attenuate the signal by -6 dB. Let's now take a look at a simple implementation of this algorithm, shown in figure 7.26.

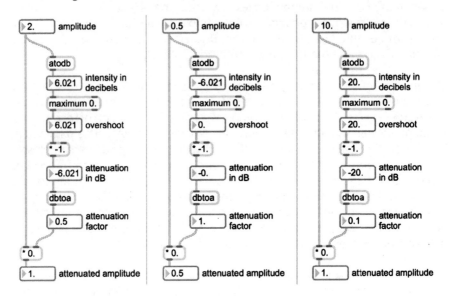

Fig. 7.26 A limiting algorithm

The patch is repeated three times with three different amplitude values. In the patch on the left, let's imagine we have received an amplitude value (output by a hypothetical peak follower) equal to 2, and therefore about 6 dB. The [maximum 0.] object is used to let any intensities above the ceiling pass through it (in other words, the overshoot). The overshoot is then changed in sign to convert it to a negative value (−6dB) and transformed into amplitude using the **dbtoa** object, the result of which can be used to reduce the amplitude from 2 to 1 (i.e., from 6 dB to 0 dB).

In the middle patch the input amplitude, 0.5, does not exceed the ceiling, so consequently there is no overshoot and the attenuation factor is therefore equal to 1 (no attenuation). As you can see, in this case the output amplitude is equal to the input amplitude.

The patch on the right has an input amplitude equal to 10, so the overshoot is 20 dB. Consequently, the attenuation factor is 0.1 and the output amplitude is therefore equal to 1 (i.e., 0dB), as it was for the first of the three.
In the event that the ceiling is set to a value less than 0dB, we would need to amplify the input amplitude value so that the ceiling would once again be located at 0dB. For example, if the ceiling were set to -3dB, we would need to increase the intensity of the envelope by 3dB. Let's look at a practical application of this in figure 7.27.

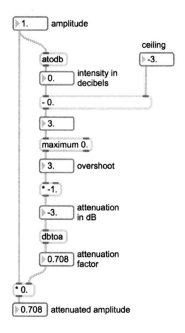

Fig. 7.27 Limiting with ceiling

Since the ceiling is a negative value, that value will be subtracted (not added) in order to amplify the intensity of input signal. As you can see in the figure, an amplitude equal to 1 (i.e., 0 dB) has an overshoot of 3 dB – in other words it exceeds the ceiling (which in this case is -3 dB) by 3 dB. Therefore the attenuation factor is 0.708, which corresponds to -3 dB.

Now load the patch **07_07_limiter.maxpat** (figure 7.28).

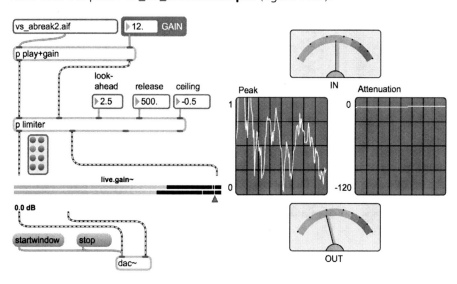

Fig. 7.28 The file **07_07_limiter.maxpat**

In this patch we are simulating a sound whose amplitude is greater than 0 dB by amplifying the sound of an audio file (inside the [p play&gain] subpatch). In the figure we can see that the sound file **vs_abreak2.aif** is being amplified 12 dB via the floating-point number box labeled "GAIN".

The [p limiter] subpatch contains our limiter's algorithm, but before analyzing how it works, let's look at the parameters that are sent to the object. The first parameter is the look-ahead, which is the time (in milliseconds) that the limiter is given in order to know the sound's trajectory in advance. In reality this is used to delay the sound being processed with respect to the envelope detected by the peak follower.
The second parameter is the release of the peak follower (also in milliseconds); the attack is, naturally, set to 0. The third parameter is the ceiling (in dB). In figure 7.29 we can see the contents of the [p limiter] subpatch.

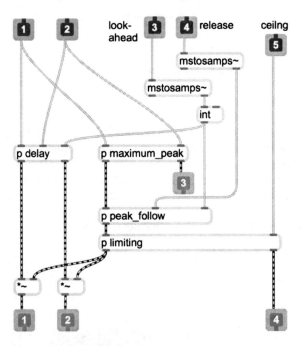

Fig. 7.29 The contents of the [p limiter] subpatch

This subpatch itself contains four subpatches: the first ([p delay]) delays the sound being processed with respect to the peak follower, as already mentioned. The second subpatch ([p maximum_peak]) compares the left and right channels of the input sound and outputs the maximum peak amplitude of the two. These two subpatches are simple enough that we will leave it to the reader to analyze their contents.

The third subpatch implements the peak follower; its contents are shown in figure 7.30.

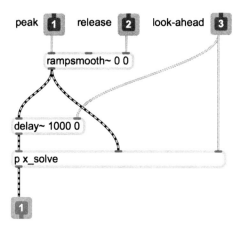

Fig. 7.30 The contents of the [p peak_follow] subpatch

The peak follower has been realized with the **rampsmooth~** object and not with the **slide~** object that we previously used for compressors, because the linear release of **rampsmooth~** will less perceptibly alter the dynamics of the input sound[9].

The envelope output by **rampsmooth~** is delayed by the look-ahead parameter and sent, alongside a non-delayed version of the same envelope to yet another subpatch: [p x_solve]. Why, exactly do we need two different versions of the same envelope? The non-delayed version is used to "predict" the arrival of an overshoot (i.e., when the intensity exceeds the threshold) so that the limiter can react in advance. The delayed version (which is also in synch with the delayed audio signal, see above) is used to hold the attenuation when the threshold has been passed. In practice, the limiter should follow the trajectory of the envelope that is producing the largest values, at any given moment.

---

[9] The limiter's task is actually not to modify the dynamic profile of the sound, but rather to ensure that it does not exceed a certain threshold.

Now let's look inside the [p x_solve] subpatch (figure 7.31).

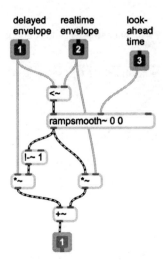

Fig. 7.31 The contents of the [p x_solve] subpatch

This patch compares the delayed and non-delayed (realtime) envelopes. When the first is less than the second, the <~ object will output 1, otherwise it will output 0. Disregarding the **rampsmooth~** object for the moment, you will notice that when the <~ object outputs a 1 (when the realtime envelope is greater than the delayed one), the realtime envelope is multiplied by 1, and is therefore allowed to pass, while the delayed envelope is multiplied by 0 (because of the [!-~ 1] object) and therefore zeroed out. The opposite happens when the <~ object outputs a 0. Therefore at any given instant we always have the envelope whose value is greater being output by the [p x_solve] subpatch.

The **rampsmooth~** object is used so that when the <~ outputs a 1 (when the realtime envelope is greater than the delayed one), the transition between the two envelopes takes place gradually, using a cross-fade whose length is that of the look-ahead time. This technique is used in order to avoid any discontinuities in the attenuation, which could cause clicks. However, when changing from the realtime to the delayed envelope, the transition should be immediate or else the input signal would exceed the ceiling value. In this case the possibility of a click occurring is infinitesimal because the realtime envelope is in its release stage which, unlike the attack stage, is not immediate. The combination of the two envelopes is sent to the [p limiting] subpatch that contains the attenuation algorithm discussed above (see figures 7.26 and 7.27).

Listen to the different presets. Note that the limiter will also work if you increase the input signal volume to 120 dB (in other words increasing it 1,000,000 times)!

In order to avoid altering the dynamic profile of the sound, an appropriate release time should be used. Using a release that is too short will result in a dynamic compression of the sound, while using one that is too long may attenuate the intensity of a sound for too much time after an overshoot. Appropriate release times will vary between 500 milliseconds and 5 seconds, depending on the input material. Presets 7 and 8 use extremely short release times, and the resulting sound is heavily distorted (this could possibly be useful if you wanted to obtain precisely that kind of distortion effect). In preset number 8 in particular, you can hear the enormously amplified sound of the flautist taking breaths.

Try creating some new presets.

. . . .

ACTIVITIES

- Create a patch that puts the stereo compressor with soft knee that we analyzed above and the limiter together in series, and create some presets where the compressor goes above the 0 dB threshold and the limiter takes the dynamics back down to a range under 0 dB.

- Make another patch, similar to the one above, that uses your stereo version of the multi-band compressor in place of the soft knee compressor.

. . . .

LIVE NORMALIZER

With just a small modification to our limiter algorithm, we can create a dynamics processor that brings either signals above the threshold or those below it to 0dB, as explained in the theory section. To do this all we need to do is lower the argument to the **maximum~** object inside the [p limiting] subpatch (figure 7.32).

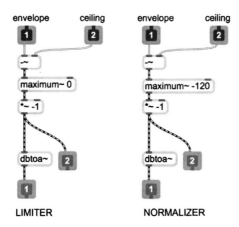

Fig. 7.32 From limiter to normalizer

The patch **07_07b_normalizer.maxpat** (almost identical to the preceding one) shows the effect of this algorithm. There are four pairs of presets: the first preset in each pair lets you listen to the original sound, while the second lets you listen to the normalized sound (we have also added a bypass button to let you switch quickly from one to the other). The first pair of presets lets us hear the normalization effect applied to a sound file that progressively attenuates 20 dB; with normalization this attenuation disappears. Additionally, by using a very short release value, we can obtain heavy distortion even if the amplitude of the original file is under 0dB (see presets 6 and 8).

7.4 EXPANDERS AND DOWNWARD EXPANSION

The expander algorithm is very similar to that of the compressor that was shown in the previous section. As we learned in section 7.4T, the biggest difference between downward compression and downward expansion is that with downward expansion the signal above the threshold is not attenuated, but rather the signal below it.

Open the patch **07_08_soft_knee_stereo_expander.maxpat** (figure 7.33).

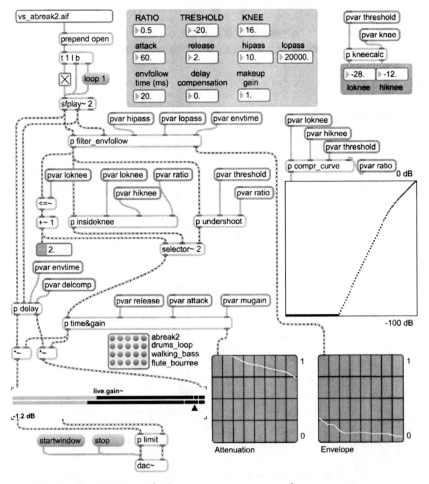

Fig. 7.33 The file **07_08_soft_knee_stereo_expander.maxpat**

As you can see, this patch is very similar to the compressor shown in figure 7.21. Let's analyze the differences:

- The relational operator >=~, visible on the left side of the compressor, has been substituted with the <=~ operator. This allows us to check if the amplitude of the signal goes under the level of the lower knee threshold. When the amplitude is less than the lower knee threshold the attenuation calculated by the [p undershoot] subpatch is used; this subpatch is identical to [p overshoot] used in the compressor. When the amplitude is greater than this threshold, the attenuation output by the [p insideknee] subpatch is used, instead.

- In the [p insideknee] subpatch, the function of the higher knee threshold and lower knee threshold has been reversed: the attenuation factor is equal to 1:1 when the signal reaches the higher knee threshold, and equal to (1 + ratio)/2 when the signal reaches the lower knee threshold level – in the compressor this worked the opposite way.

- A lowpass filter has been added to the envelope follower (in addition to the highpass filter). By adjusting the cutoff frequency of the two filters, we can modify the dynamics of sounds in interesting ways.

- A limiter has been added just before the output (in the [p limiter] subpatch). This subpatch contains the limiter that we analyzed in the previous section, and is used to make sure that the output signal does not go above the 0dB threshold (which could happen if you set the makeup gain level and then change the threshold afterward).

Listen to the presets and try creating some new ones. As we already learned in section 7.4T, the ratio should be set within the 0 to 1 range and not between 1 and some value greater than 1, as it is for compressors and limiters. Also note that if you want to avoid a sound's attack being "eaten up" by the attenuation brought about by an earlier low level signal, you should set a low release time. Finally, pay close attention to the use of the filters in the last two presets of each row.

7.5 GATES

The gate works very similarly to the downward expander in that it reduces the intensity of sounds under a certain threshold. The difference, as we learned in section 7.5T, is that the amount of attenuation of the gate is fixed, whereas with the downward expander it depends on the intensity of the signal.

Let's look at a patch implementing this algorithm; load the file **07_11_gate.maxpat** (figure 7.34).

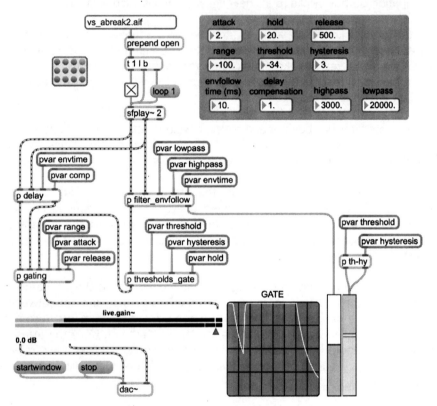

Fig. 7.34 The file **07_11_gate.maxpat**

The parameters of this gate are as follows:

attack:	opening time of the gate
hold:	time in which the gate remains open after the signal has gone below the threshold
release:	closing time of the gate
range:	the amount of attenuation of the signal under the threshold (in dB)
threshold:	threshold for the opening of the gate
hysteresis:	distance (in dB) between the closing threshold and the opening threshold

envfollow time (ms): the length of signal taken into consideration for the RMS envelope follower

delay compensation: compensation factor for the delay produced by the envelope follower

highpass: cutoff frequency for the highpass filter applied to the envelope follower

lowpass: cutoff frequency for the lowpass filter applied to the envelope follower

Some of these parameters are identical to those that have already been used for the compressor and expander. Let's listen to the various presets and observe how the parameters have been set (note how the filters have been used!). Pay special attention to the first preset in the third row: in this case the gate is used to eliminate the flautist's breaths in the sound file **vs_flute_q2.aif**.

Now let's analyze how the patch works. The contents of the two subpatches [p delay] and [p filter_envfollow] are identical to the similarly named subpatches we already saw in the expander (figure 7.33) and compressor (figure 7.21), so we do not need to analyze them again. Nonetheless, we should simply remind you that in the [p filter_envfollow] subpatch the signal is filtered before being used for envelope following, while in the [p delay] subpatch input signal is delayed to compensate for the delay introduced by the envelope follower.
The signal produced by the envelope follower is sent to the [p thresholds_gate] subpatch, which takes care of opening and closing the gate based on the level reached by the envelope (figure 7.35).

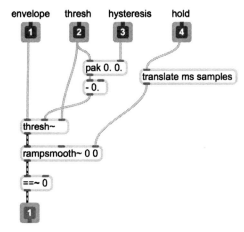

Fig. 7.35 The contents of the [p thresholds_gate] subpatch

We will analyze this patch shortly, but first notice that it employs a new object **thresh~**. This object checks to see if the input signal is above or below two thresholds either specified as arguments or sent to its second and third inlets. Specifically, the object will output a signal value of 0 when the input signal goes below the first threshold and will output a value of 1 when it goes above the second.

Rebuild the patch shown in figure 7.36.

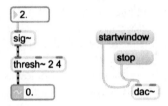

Fig. 7.36 The **thresh~** object

Remember that you need to start the DSP engine by clicking on the "startwindow" message in order for the patch to work.

By moving the value in the number box, you can see for yourself that the **thresh~** object will output 1 when its input signal becomes greater than or equal to 4. When you lower this value under 4, the **thresh~** object will continue to output 1 until the input signal reaches a value of 2 or less, at which point it will output 0. By increasing the number once again above 2, the **thresh~** object will continue to output 0 until the input signal reaches a value of 4 or greater.

This object is thererfore perfect for controlling a threshold with a hysteresis. Returning to the [p thresholds_gate] subpatch (figure 7.35), we can see that the first level of **thresh~** has been set to a value equal to threshold – hysteresis (which we will call the closing threshold of the gate), while the second level is set to the threshold value itself (the opening threshold of the gate). When the envelope goes above the opening threshold, the **thresh~** object will output 1, and when it goes below the closing threshold, it will output 0.

The **rampsmooth~** object connected to **thresh~** is used to control the hold phase of the gate. When using this object, the transition from 0 to 1 (when the envelope goes above the opening threshold) is instantaneous, but the transition from 1 to 0 (when the envelope goes below the closing threshold) takes place over the amount of time specified by the hold parameter, using a descending ramp that gradually takes it from 1 to 0. Underneath **rampsmooth~**, the [==~ 0] object checks to see if the input signal is equal to 0, and performs a kind of value inversion: when its input signal is zero it outputs 1 (corresponding to closing the gate, as we will see when we analyze the next subpatch) and when the input signal is non-zero (either when it is 1 or another ramp value generated by **rampsmooth~**) it outputs 0 (corresponding to opening the gate).

To sum up what has happened so far, the [p thresholds_gate] subpatch receives the envelope produced by the envelope follower and when the envelope goes above the opening threshold, the subpatch outputs a signal of 0. This value continues to be output until the envelope goes below the closing threshold and stays below it for a given period of time, determined by the hold parameter, at which point the subpatch's output signal changes from 0 to 1. Once the envelope returns above the opening threshold, the signal output by the sub-patch will switch from 1 to 0 again and the cycle starts over once more.

The signal output by the [p thresholds_gate] subpatch is sent to the [p gating] subpatch, shown in figure 7.37.

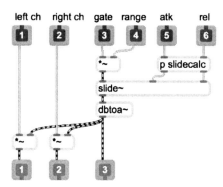

Fig. 7.37 The contents of the [p gating] subpatch

As you can see in the figure, the two channels of the signal being processed arrive in the first two inlets of the subpatch. The third inlet receives the opening and closing signal for the gate that was output by the [p thresholds_gate] subpatch, and the fourth inlet receives the range, or attenuation in dB that corresponds to the closing level of the gate. The gate and range values are multiplied together, and the result is the attenuation in dB that will be applied to the input audio signal.

For example, imagine we have a range value equal to -110 dB. The open gate corresponds to a value of 0 which, when multiplied by the range value (-110 dB), will yield 0 dB, in other words no attenuation. A closed gate, on the other hand corresponds to a value of 1 which, when multiplied by the range value (-110 dB) will yield -110 dB, our desired attenuation. The values produced by this multiplication are sent to the **slide~** object which smooths out the abrupt transition between the opening and closing of the gate (using the attack and release parameters).

To conclude our analysis of this algorithm, we will demonstrate an interesting technique you can use to design "complex" graphical objects. To the right of the **scope~** object there are two level indicators which visually display the opening and closing of the gate. The first shows the trajectory of the sound's envelope, and the second shows the two thresholds used for opening and closing the gate. In both cases, the **multislider** object has been used. The second indicator was made by superimposing two **multisliders** – one for the opening threshold (in red) and one for the closing threshold (in yellow). In order to make both superimposed objects visible at the same time, we have given a transparent background to the object on the upper level, so it does not obscure the other one. This object was created last, so it is graphically placed on top of the other, but be aware that you can also modify an object's level in relation to another by selecting Bring to Front or Send to Back in the Arrange menu. These options do exactly what they say: they bring a selected object (or group of objects) to the highest or lowest levels. You can alternately use Bring Forward or Send Backward to move a selected object just one level from where it is.

Returning to the object that we are making transparent, the parameter that we have set is the background color "**Opacity**." After opening the `multislider` inspector, select the "**Background Color**" attribute (under the "Color" tab) and click on the zone located to the right of the attribute name. A color selection window will appear and in the lower part of this window you will see the "Opacity" parameter, which you can set to 0%. The result can be seen in figure 7.38.

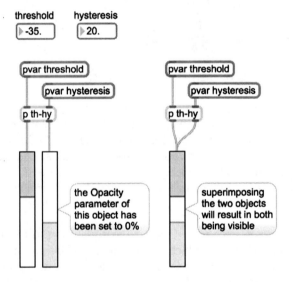

Fig. 7.38 Using the "Opacity" parameter

The [**p** th-hy] subpatch is very simple; we suggest you analyze it on your own.

Listen once again to all the presets in the patch and try to create some new ones.

7.6 UPWARD COMPRESSION AND UPWARD EXPANSION

In section 7.2 we saw how the algorithms for downward compression and downward expansion work. By simply modifying ratio in these two algorithms we can obtain, respectively, upward expansion and upward compression, as shown in the table in section 7.6T.

More specifically, by using a ratio between 0 and 1 with the downward compression algorithm, we can create upward expansion, and using a ratio greater than 1 with out downward expansion algorithm, we can create upward compression. The patch **07_09_upward_stereo_compressor.maxpat** and **07_10_upward_stereo_expander.maxpat** contain these modifications to the preceding patches along with some example presets.

The parallel upward compressor, on the other hand, is demonstrated in the patch **07_09b_upward_parallel_compressor.maxpat**. As with the "classic" parallel compressor, this was also created using a simple modification of one of the previous patches: we simply added the dry signal to the upward compressor.

There is not much more to say about these two patches from the point of view of the algorithms they use; just try out the various presets and make some new ones. Note that the upward expander will generate a considerable increase in the overall volume when the ratio is low, so it is necessary to attenuate the intensity of the signal with negative makeup gain values.

7.7 EXTERNAL SIDE-CHAIN AND DUCKING

Transforming our stereo compressor into a compressor with an external side chain is fairly easy. We simply need to send one sound into the algorithm that calculates the attenuation and apply this attenuation to a different sound. Open the file **07_12_side_chain_compressor.maxpat** (figure 7.39).

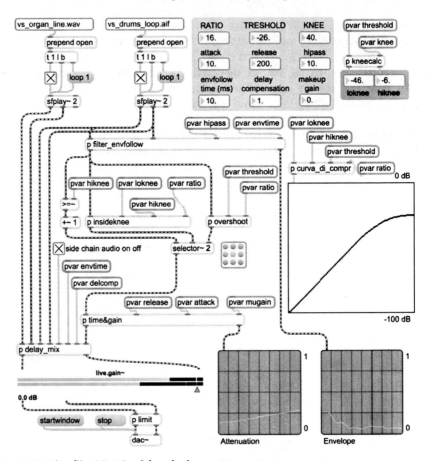

Fig. 7.39 The file **07_12_side_chain_compressor.maxpat**

Compared to the patches for the previous compressor, we have added a new **sfplay~** object in the upper left part of the patch in order to play the sound that will be compressed. This sound and the sound that is used for the side-chain (key input) are both sent to the [p delay_mix] subpatch on the lower left, which mixes the two sounds and applies the compensation delay. Using the **toggle** connected to this subpatch, we can choose to exclude the audio of the sound used for the external side-chain and only listen to the sound being compressed. Listen to the various presets. In each row, the first preset lets you listen to both sounds without compression, the second activates the compression, letting you also hear the key input sound, and the third lets you only listen to the compressed sound. As always, try creating some new presets.

ACTIVITY

Explain how the [p delay_mix] subpatch works.

. . . .

As we already learned in the theory chapter, a gate can also be used with an external side-chain, allowing us to create some rather interesting effects. Open the file **07_13_key_input_gate.maxpat** (figure 7.40).

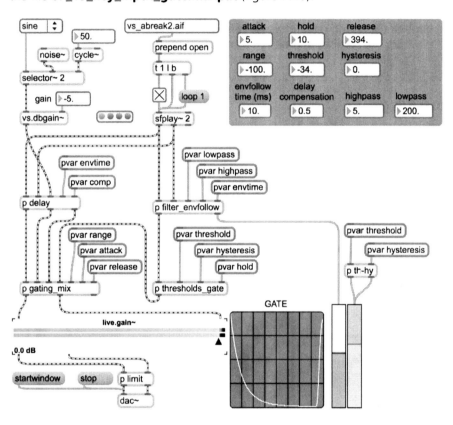

Fig. 7.40 The file **07_13_key_input_gate.maxpat**

Also in this example we have two different input signals: the sound used for the key input is an audio file, whereas the sound that passes through the gate can be either white noise or a sine wave (you can select one or the other using the **umenu** connected to the **selector~** in the upper left part of the patch). The amplitude of the sound that is being gated is modified by the **vs.dbgain~** object (under the **selector** object), which controls the intensity of the input sound using a value in dB.

There are four presets: in the first a low sound (sub-bass) has been added to the bass drum sound of a drum loop, in the second white noise has been added to each hit on the snare, in the third a high sound corresponding to accents, and in the fourth white noise has once again been added to the snare. Listen carefully and observe how the filters have been used, then try creating some new presets.

....

ACTIVITIES

- Analyze how the [p delay] and [p gating_mix] subpatches work.

- Replace the sound generators **noise~** and **cycle~** with a second audio file playback mechanism and design some other presets.

....

DUCKING

A ducker can be easily created starting from a gate with a key input and reversing its behavior. To do this you need to attenuate the input sound when the key input signal passes above the threshold, and return to the original amplitude when the key input signal goes below the threshold. Open the file **07_14_ducker.maxpat** (figure 7.41).

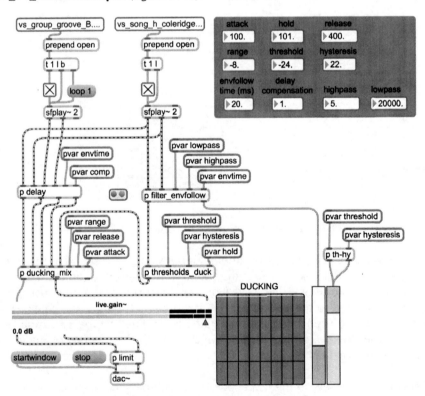

Fig. 7.41 The file **07_14_ducker.maxpat**

As you can see, this patch is very similar to the previous one (07_13_key_input_ gate.maxpat), and its parameters are practically the same. However, in the case of a ducker, the *range* parameter represents the attenuation in dB that will be applied to the input sound when the key signal goes above the threshold.

First listen to the two presets – in both cases we have a speaking voice (which also acts as a key input signal) accompanied by a musical background. In the first preset, the ducking has not been activated (its range is equal to 0dB) and the musical background renders the speaking voice only somewhat intelligible. The second preset, on the other hand, has a range of -8 dB, so each time the speaking voice goes above -24dB, the musical background is attenuated 8 dB. There are two differences between this algorithm and the one used for the gate. The first of these differences is found in the [p thresholds_duck] subpatch shown in figure 7.42.

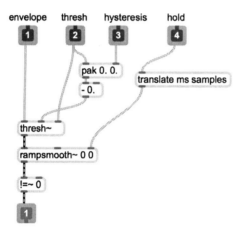

Fig. 7.42 The contents of the [p thresholds_duck] subpatch

This subpatch is the equivalent of [p thresholds_gate] in the gate patch (see figure 7.35), and its function is the identical: to open and close the gate by outputting a 0 to open it and a 1 to close it. However, note that the relational operator [==~ 0] at the bottom of the subpatch used for the gate has here been replaced with the operator [!=~ 0][10], which works in the contrary sense. This object will output a 1 when the value output by **rampsmooth** is non-zero (when the key input signal goes above the threshold), and it will output 0 when the value output by **rampsmooth** is equal to 0 (when the key input signal goes below the threshold and has remained there for an amount of time equal to the hold parameter). As we can probably guess, this means that the gate is closed when the key signal goes above the threshold and it is opened when the key signal goes below the threshold. The second difference between the ducker and gate patches can be seen in the last two inputs to the [p ducking_mix] subpatch located on the lower left side of the main patch. The attack and release parameters (which are

---

[10] Remember that != means "not equal to."

sent to the **slide~** object inside the subpatch) have been interchanged. This is because, for a ducker, the attack corresponds to an attenuation ("slide down"), and the release corresponds to a return to the original amplitude ("slide up").

. . . .

ACTIVITY

Listen once again to the presets in the patch 06_03_multitap3.maxpat (from chapter 6P). Notice how in some cases the direct sound is covered by the delayed sounds of the multitap. Add a ducker to this patch, and use the direct sound as the key input in order to attenuate the sounds output by the multitap. This is a technique that is often used in cases where sound processing creates a mass of sounds that can potentially "submerge" the dry sound. Another possible use is its application to reverberation, which we will cover in the next volume.

7.8 OTHER CREATIVE USES OF DYNAMICS PROCESSORS

As we have already seen in the previous sections, modifying the dynamic profile of a sound does not necessarily need to be linked to the issues of mixing and mastering, but can also be used for creative purposes. In this chapter's final section we will see several other possible applications, although we cannot at all profess to having exhausted this vast subject.

ADAPTIVE GATE/DUCKER

If we create two envelope followers using the **average~** object – a "fast" one (that takes only a few of the previous samples into consideration) and a "slow" one (that uses a large number of the previous samples) – we can create a gate that opens when the value of the fast envelope follower is greater than that of the slow one and close the gate in the converse situation. This gate has the ability to bring out the dynamic accents in a sound, independently of its absolute amplitude, so we can therefore define it as "adaptive" since its behavior will vary with the variations in the amplitude of the sound itself. If we reverse the behavior of this gate – closing it when the fast envelope follower goes above the slow one – we obtain an adaptive ducker. (See also section 7.8T.)
Load the patch **07_15_adaptive_gate.maxpat** (figure 7.43).

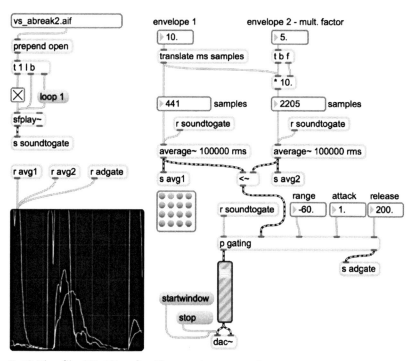

Fig. 7.43 The file **07_15_adaptive_gate.maxpat**

The two number boxes at the top of the patch are used, respectively, to set the signal length (expressed in milliseconds) used by the first **average~** to create

397

a fast envelope follower, and a multiplication factor to apply to this length in order to obtain the length used by the second **average~** to create a slow envelope follower. The **<~** object compares the output of the two envelope followers and opens (0) and closes (1) the gate according to whether or not the value of the first envelope is above or below the second. The value of the gate is sent to the [p gating] subpatch (not very different from the similarly-named subpatch in 07_11_gate.maxpat) which applies the variation in dynamics to the sound. Remember that the attack is activated when the gate is opened, and the release when it is closed.

On the lower left hand side of the patch, we can graphically see the trajectory of the two envelopes (the yellow and blue curves) and the gate (orange curve). This graphic display was created by superimposing three **scope~** objects, two of which have transparent backgrounds (this is the same technique that we used in the patch 07_11_gate.maxpat).

First, listen to the first row of presets. These were all created using a drum loop and demonstrate micro-movements in the sound's dynamics which would otherwise be impossible to obtain using a normal gate.

The second row uses an excerpt from a percussion solo that has a wide dynamic range. Note that the last preset in this row uses a multiplication factor less than 1 for the second envelope so it is therefore faster than the first. This transforms the effect into an adaptive ducker and the resulting sound is reminiscent of a tape played in reverse.

In the third row, the processor is applied to non-percussive sounds, as it also is with the fourth row where the effect is used as a ducker, since the second envelope is faster than the first.

· ·

ACTIVITIES

- Make a stereo version of the adaptive gate

- Add the *hold* parameter.

- Use a sound as a key input and send the output of a sinusoid oscillator or white noise to the gate (as in the patch 07_13_key_input_gate.maxpat).

- Replace the oscillator and noise generator in the previous activity with a second sound file.

· ·

TRIGGERING GATE

The term triggering gate is used to mean an algorithm that triggers the start of some sort of process when a certain amplitude threshold is exceeded. The process could be something such as an amplitude envelope, filtering, moving a sound in the stereo field, etc. (see chapter 7.8T). However, before beginning we need to introduce two new objects, the first of which is called **edge~** (shown in figure 7.44)

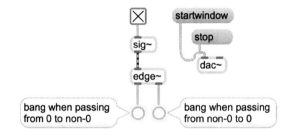

Fig. 7.44 The **edge~** object

This object receives a signal and outputs a bang out its left outlet when that signal changes from 0 to a non-zero value; it sends a bang out its right outlet when the input changes from a non-zero value to 0. If you reconstruct the patch shown in the figure and turn the **toggle** above the **edge~** object on and off, it will alternate sending bangs out its left and right outlets. We will use this object to activate different processes when the signal output by the envelope follower goes above a certain threshold.

Note that all the dynamics processing algorithms we have seen up to now work at audio rate – in other words all of the processing has been done by MSP. The **edge~** object, on the other hand, converts a signal (in the MSP environment) into a bang (in the Max environment). This will result in less temporal precision for the events, but in exchange the management of different sound processing algorithms becomes somewhat easier. This compromise is completely accept-able since we are working in the realm of "creative" applications (which will be discussed in detail shortly), so we do not need the same kind of temporal preci-sion that is required by "classic" processors such as the compressor and limiter. Furthermore, if we set the *Signal Vector Size* to 16 samples or less, and enable the *Scheduler in Overdrive* and in *Audio Interrupt* in the *Audio Status* window (see section 5.1P), the maximum delay that we could possibly have with respect to the audio signal would be equal to 16 samples.

The second new object is **vs.speedlim** (shown in figure 7.45).

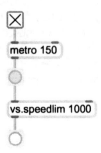

Fig. 7.45 The **vs.speedlim** object

This object limits the speed of messages sent to its input. The argument defines the minimum time that should pass between one message and the next. Messages received before the minimum time has elapsed after the object outputs are discarded. If you rebuild the patch shown in the figure, you will notice how the bangs output by **vs.speedlim** are much slower than those sent by the **metro**.[11]

At this point, you can open the patch **07_16_triggering_gate.maxpat** (figure 7.46).

In this patch, a bang (displayed by the button object halfway down the patch next to the label "gatebang") will be output each time the envelope follower exceeds the given threshold. This bang will activate the trajectories (or envelopes) visible in the two **function** objects on the right side of the patch, which respectively control the stereo position of a sound file and the cutoff frequency of a bandpass filter applied to it.

The parameters of this processor are (apart from the trajectories): threshold, hysteresis, minimum time between one bang and the next (min time), the amount of signal used by the envelope follower (in milliseconds) and the delay compensation. Listen to all of the presets, paying careful attention to the different parameter settings.

---

[11] There also exists a standard **speedlim** object that does almost the same thing. The difference is that when the time limit is over, **speedlim** sends the last message it received during that time, whereas **vs.speedlim** will discard all the messages that arrive before the time limit has elapsed. As you can see, this difference is essential for our patch to function properly, because we will be using **vs.speedlim** to arrange processes that are activated by passing a threshold.

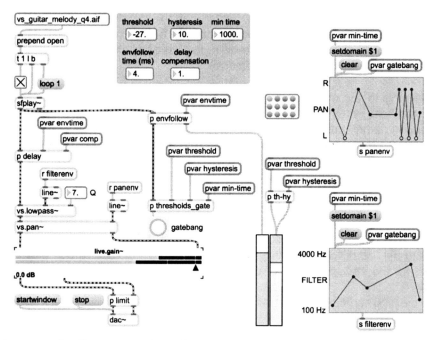

Fig. 7.46 The file **07_16_triggering_gate.maxpat**

Now let's analyze the patch. The signal produced by the **sfplay~** object is sent to the [p envfollow] subpatch, which is very similar to analogous envelope followers that we have already seen in other processors. The output envelope is sent to the [p threshold_gate] subpatch (figure 7.47).

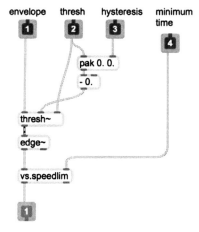

Fig. 7.47 The contents of the [p threshold_gate] subpatch

When the input envelope goes above the threshold, the **thresh~** object outputs a signal whose value is 1, and this change from a value of 0 to a non-zero value causes the **edge~** object to output a bang out its left outlet. The **vs.speedlim** object lets the bang pass through only if its temporal distance

401

from the previously output bang is greater than the given minimum time. (Note that if we used the standard **speedlim** object a bang received too early would be output once this time limit was over, regardless of whether or not the threshold had been exceeded at that moment.)

Returning to the main patch, we can see the bang that is produced by the [p threshold_gate] subpatch is sent to a **button**, which has been given the scripting name "gatebang" (via the inspector). Consequently, every bang that this object receives is transmitted to two [**pvar** gatebang] objects connected to the two **function** objects visible on the right side of the patch. The lists output by the two **function** objects are sent, via two **send/receive** object pairs, to the two **line~** objects on the left, which are connected to the lowpass filter cutoff frequency and the sound file stereo position. Note that the "min time" parameter (the third number box at the top of the patch) is used to determine the length of the breakpoint trajectories in the two **function** objects (using the "setdomain" command), in addition to being used as the minimum time for the **vs.speedlim** object.

Try creating some new presets.

The triggering gate can be used to activate a wide variety of effects. Let's take a look at one example patch that plays the sound in reverse each time that it exceeds a certain threshold. Open the file **07_17_gate_reverse.maxpat** (figure 7.48).

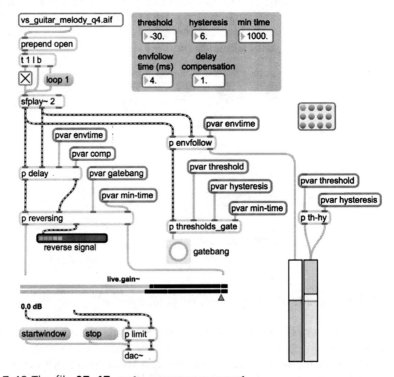

Fig. 7.48 The file **07_17_gate_reverse.maxpat**

If you compare this patch to the previous one, you will notice that the low-pass filter and the **vs.pan~** object have been replaced with the [p reversing] subpatch, which causes the input sound to be played in reverse (for a duration equal to the min time) every time that it exceeds the threshold (figure 7.49).

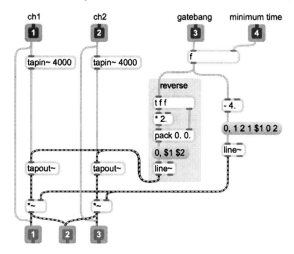

Fig. 7.49 The contents of the [p reversing] subpatch

The first two inlets of this subpatch receive the incoming stereo audio channels which are sent to a pair of delay lines (using **tapin~/tapout~**). The last inlet receives the min time parameter and sends it to the cold inlet of a **float** object. Each time the threshold is crossed in an upward direction, the associated bang is sent via the third inlet to the left inlet of the **float** object, which sends the min time value to two different places. The section on the right outputs an envelope with a very quick attack and release that opens and closes the output volume of the delay line. The section on the left uses the delay time to play the sound in reverse. Are you able to mentally reconstruct this delay-based reverse mechanism? If not, please refer to sections 6.9T and 6.9P.

Note that the two audio channels are additionally sent directly to the output of the subpatch, and therefore summed together with the reversed sounds. Listen once again to all the presets (paying careful attention to the parameters, as usual) and try designing some new ones.

· ·

ACTIVITIES

- Use the triggering gate to change the cutoff frequency of a resonant filter applied to the input sound, in order to obtain a simple sample and hold effect controlled by the envelope follower.

- Make a variation on the patch in figure 7.48 where the sound is sent to a delay with feedback each time that the threshold is exceeded.

- Using the previous activity as a starting point, add a random variation to the delay time each time that the threshold is exceeded.

- Apply the adaptive gate algorithm (figure 7.43) to all the triggering gate patches you have made thus far.

GATE SEQUENCER (LIVE SLICING)

Before we learn how to build a gate sequencer, we need to present a new object: **vs.divmetro**. Open the patch **07_18_divmetro.maxpat** (figure 7.50).

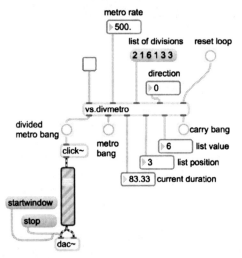

Fig. 7.50 The file **07_18_divmetro.maxpat**

This object is similar to the **metro** object, in that it sends a sequence of bangs at regular intervals. However, with **vs.divmetro** you can additionally subdivide this interval into equal parts by sending a list of divisions to the object. For example, if you send the list "2 4 5" and the beat of the metronome is 500 milliseconds, the **vs.divmetro** object will produce 2 bangs spaced 250 milliseconds apart (500/2), followed by four bangs 125 milliseconds apart (500/4), and finally 5 bangs 100 milliseconds apart (500/5). The fourth inlet determines the reading direction for the input list: 0 means it will be read in the normal sense, 1 means it will be read backwards, and 2 means it will alternate forward and backward. In all three cases the list is repeated cyclically (i.e., it is "played" in a loop). A bang sent to the last inlet acts as a "reset button," causing the list playback to start once again from the first element on the following beat.

The left outlet outputs bangs according to the rhythm set by the list of divisions, while the second outlet outputs the non-subdivided beat (just like the standard **metro** object). The third outlet reports the current interval between one bang and the next (in milliseconds), the fourth reports the position of the current element in the list of divisions, the fifth reports the current list element itself and the last outputs a bang each time playback has reached the end of the loop. Let's now see how this objet can be used in our gate sequencer: load the file **07_19_gate_sequencer.maxpat** (figure 7.51).

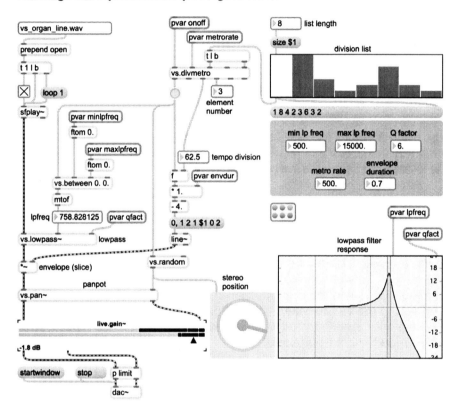

Fig. 7.51 The file **07_19_gate_sequencer.maxpat**

The sound file (played by the **sfplay~** on the upper left) is sent through a low-pass filter, an envelope that "slices" the sound, and then through the **vs.pan~** object that sends each slice to a different position in the stereo field. On the upper right side of the patch there is a **multislider** that can be used to set the list of divisions used by the **vs.divmetro** object visible in the center of the upper part of the patch. The rhythm output by **vs.divmetro** will determine the beat of each slice of sound.

Under the **multisider** there is a control panel where you can set the minimum and maximum cutoff frequency for the lowpass filter, as well as the Q factor, metronome rate and the envelope duration for each slice of sound, with respect to the length of the subdivisions output by **vs.divmetro** (1 = the entire subdivision time, 0.5 = half the subdivision time, etc.). Listen to the various presets, paying close attention to the settings used for the list of beat divisions, and other parameters.

Let's now analyze this patch. The list output by **multislider** is sent to the third inlet of **vs.divmetro** together with a bang to the fifth inlet to reset the playback position of the list to the first element. The metronome rate is sent to the **vs.divmetro** object via the [**pvar** metrorate] linked to the number box "metro rate" in the control panel. The **vs.divmetro** object is activated by the [**pvar** onoff] object that is linked to the **toggle** that starts the **sfplay~** object (in addition to being connected to the **sfplay~**, this **toggle** has been assigned the scripting name "onoff").

The bang output by **vs.divmetro** is first sent to a **float** object (located just under **vs.divmetro**) in which the current beat duration in milliseconds (previously output also by **vs.divmetro**) has been stored. This value is multiplied by the envelope duration factor (equal to 0.7 in the figure) and then sent to the **line~** object using a message box, in order to generate a trapezoidal envelope with a very fast attack and release.[12] Finally, the envelope is sent to the multiplier located just below the lowpass filter.

Returning to the bang output by **vs.divmetro**, its second destination is the **vs.random** object, which outputs random values between 0 and 1. These values are used by the **vs.pan~** object to pan each slice of sound to a different stereo position. The final destination of the bang output by **vs.divmetro** is the **vs.between** object which, in this patch, outputs a cutoff frequency for the lowpass filter, between the given minimum and maximum values. Notice that the frequencies set in the control panel are converted into MIDI values before being sent to the **vs.between** object. The random MIDI values output by the object are once again transformed into frequency values for the lowpass filter. What do you think the purpose of this is?

Finally, notice the use of the **dial** and **filtergraph~** objects on the lower right: both objects are simply here to provide visual feedback for the sound processing that is applied to each slice.

Try creating some new presets.

. . . .

ACTIVITIES

- Add a system to the patch shown in figure 7.51 which bypasses the lowpass filter for a certain percentage of slices. The user should be able to set this percentage in the control panel. You should use a **selector~** object to switch between the dry and filtered signals. The technique to activate events based on a percentage has already been shown in section IB.4 in the first volume (see "A Probabilistic Metronome").

---

[12] Are you able to explain why we subtract 4 from the result of multiplying the division length by the envelope duration factor?

- Using the same technique as in the previous activity, add a delay with feedback that is activated only for a certain percentage of slices.

- Make the delay time in the previous activity change with each slice.

- Add an algorithm that allows the patch to play a certain percentage of the slices backwards.

· ·

FEEDBACK WITH CONTROLLED DYNAMICS

We will now put gating aside in order to do something completely different: using a dynamics processor within a feedback loop. As we already saw in section 7.8T, we can insert a limiter into a delay with feedback, allowing us use feedback multipliers greater than 1 without causing the signal to increase in volume indefinitely. If the delay time in this kind of system were varied using an LFO, and there were several such delay lines running independently, you could create some interesting distortion and resonance effects. Let's now look at an example based on a modified version of the chorus algorithm that we saw in chapter 6.5P: open the patch **07_20_limited_feedback.maxpat** (figure 7.52).

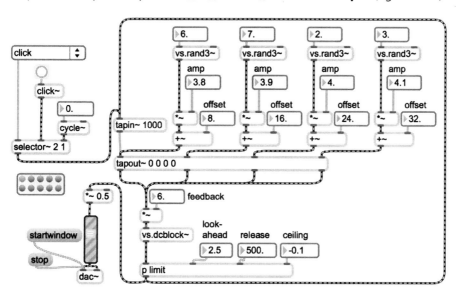

Fig. 7.52 The file **07_20_limited_feedback.maxpat**

First and foremost: be sure to set your audio system to a very low volume level, since the sounds produced by this patch can be extremely piercing! We have already taken the precaution of lowering the amplitude of the signal by half, but we recommend keeping your volume level low, and suggest that, above all, you do not listen to this patch with headphones.

In this patch, we have taken the chorus algorithm from the file 06_08_chorus. maxpat, and given it feedback. In each of the feedback loops we have inserted a limiter and the **vs.dcblock~** object that will eliminate the accumulation of DC offset. The sound sources are a simple click and a sine wave. This system actually feeds on itself, so only one initial impulse is actually necessary to trigger the feedback. The sine wave can be used to provide the patch with a steady constant frequency that will be altered by the variations in the delay time. The sonic result could be categorized into a "noise" aesthetic: modulated distortion that often leads to somewhat "colored" noise.

Listen to the different presets provided; the first row uses the click as a source, while the second uses the sine tone. As always, pay careful attention to the various parameters: the frequency and amplitude of the LFO, the delay offset, and feedback factor. Above all, pay attention to how the look-ahead and release parameters of the limiter affect the final result. Try creating some new presets.

. . . .

ACTIVITIES

- Add a lowpass and a highpass filter in series to the feedback loop.

- Use a compressor in place of a limiter. Since some compressor settings (for example a low ratio) could cause the feedback signal to increase indefinitely, add a limiter before the output (but outside the feedback loop).

- Use a multi-band compressor, taking into consideration the same precautions as in the previous activity.

- Replace the chorus with a phaser (but use a random LFO in place of the sine wave).

. . . .

LIST OF MAX OBJECTS

average~
Outputs a signal that represents the average of the input sample values

edge~
Sends a bang out its left outlet when the input signal goes from 0 to non-zero and a bang out the right when the signal goes from non-zero to 0.

live.gain~
Similar to **gain~**, this object is part of the Max for Live object library but can also be used within normal Max patches.

maximum~
Compares the signal values sent to the left and right inlets and outputs the higher of the two.

rampsmooth~
This object "smooths out" the incoming signal by interpolating jumps between one sample and the next using a linear ramp.

rslider
A slider that allows the user to select a range of values.

scale~
Transforms signal values between a given minimum and maximum value into another range of values defined by the user.

slide~
This object "smooths out" the incoming signal by interpolating jumps between one sample and the next using a logarithmic ramp.

thresh~
This object checks to see if the value of the input signal is above or below two thresholds that are either specified by the user as arguments, or sent to the second and third inlets. This object outputs 0 when the input signal goes below the first threshold, and outputs 1 when the signal goes above the second threshold.

vs.2ndorder~
A second order filter whose behavior can be modified at any time by sending the filter type to its second inlet.

vs.balance~
Takes a signal in its first inlet and applies the amplitude of the signal sent to its second inlet to it. The third inlet is used to define the frequency of the lowpass filter used for envelope following.

vs.balance2~
Similar to **vs.balance~**, but uses a **slide~** object for the envelope following instead of a lowpass filter.

vs.dbgain~
Controls the intensity of an input sound using a value in dB.

vs.divmetro
Similar to **metro**, but is additionally able to subdivide the regular rate of bangs into equal parts, using a list of integer values sent to its third inlet.

LIST OF ATTRIBUTES, MESSAGES AND ARGUMENTS FOR SPECIFIC MAX OBJECTS

average~
-Bipolar (argument)
(default mode) with this argument, the object to simply calculate the average of the input samples.

-Absolute (argument)
with this argument, the average is calculated using the absolute value of the input samples (i.e., they are always positive values)

-Rms (Root Mean Square) (argument)
with this argument, the input samples are squared (and thus all become positive values), averaged, and the square root of this average is taken

slide~
-Slide Up (argument)
slide factor for increasing values

-Slide Down (argument)
slide factor for decreasing values

All Objects
- Background Color (attribute)
attribute in the inspector (located in the "Color" tab) that allows the object's background color to be modified

- Opacity (parameter)
(this option is present in the color selector)
This can allow the selected color to have more or less transparency.

Interlude D
ADVANCED PRESET MANAGEMENT, BPATCHER, VARIABLE ARGUMENTS, DATA AND SCORE MANAGEMENT

PREREQUISITES FOR THE CHAPTER
• The contents of Volume 1, chapters 5, 6 and 7 (theory and practice) and Interlude C

OBJECTIVES
ABILITIES
• To know how to manage complex data storage systems
• To know how to control the partial or total visualization of abstractions and subpatches inside a patch
• To know how to use variable and local arguments in abstractions and subpatches
• To know how to manage data sets and create algorithms for controlling "scores"

CONTENTS
• Advanced systems for managing presets and interpolating between them
• Systems for visualizing abstractions and subpatches inside a patch
• Data management in Max

SUPPORTING MATERIALS
• List of Max objects - List of attributes, arguments, messages and commands for specific Max objects - Glossary

ID.1 ADVANCED PRESET MANAGEMENT

Up until now we have been using the **preset** object to control the parameters present in a patch. This allows us to quickly and easily store and recall the values contained in interface objects such as number boxes or multisliders. Figure ID.1 shows a brief résumé of this object's features.

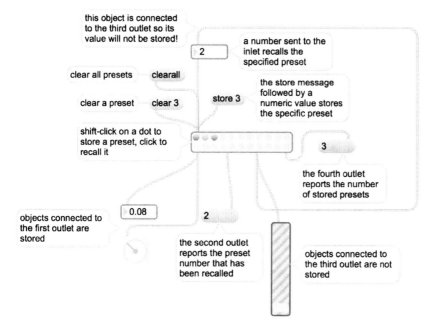

this object is connected to the third outlet so its value will not be stored!

a number sent to the inlet recalls the specified preset

clear all presets   clearall

clear a preset   clear 3   store 3

the store message followed by a numeric value stores the specific preset

shift-click on a dot to store a preset, click to recall it

the fourth outlet reports the number of stored presets

objects connected to the first outlet are stored

the second outlet reports the preset number that has been recalled

objects connected to the third outlet are not stored

Fig. ID.1 The **preset** object

It is possible to include or exclude specific objects from the preset storage using the first and third outlets. Let's take a look at how this works.

- When no objects are connected to the **preset** object's first and third outlets, it will store the values of all the interface objects present in the patch

- When one or more objects are connected to the first outlet, only the values of those objects will be stored, and all others will be ignored

- When one or more objects are connected to the third outlet (but nothing connected to the first), the values of these objects will be ignored and the others will be stored (we have often used the third outlet to exclude storing the values of objects used to control audio output volume, such as **gain~** or **live.gain~**, because the settings for these are dependent on the listening setup being used).

- If there are objects connected to both the first and third outlets, these object will be stored or ignored, respectively, and any other objects in the patch (which are not connected to the **preset** object) will be ignored.

413

As we previously learned, in order to store a preset you just need to shift-click on one of the **preset** object's dots with the mouse. A simple click is used to recall one of the stored presets. You can also recall a preset by sending an integer value to the **preset** object's inlet – a value of 1 corresponds to the first dot, 2 to the second, and so on. To save a preset you can also send the "store" message to the inlet followed by a preset number. The "clear" message, followed by a number, can be used to delete a specific preset and the "clearall" message to delete all stored presets.

Whenever a preset is recalled, the corresponding number is sent out the second outlet, and when a preset is stored, the number is sent out the fourth outlet. Note that in the patch shown in the figure, the number box connected to the inlet has been excluded from preset memorization – can you figure out why?

Although simple and functional, **preset** is fairly limited where parameter management is concerned. For example, it cannot store the state of interface objects contained in subpatches, nor can it interpolate values between two presets. In the next section we will take a look at a more refined (though, needless to say, more complex) system for preset control and management.

THE PATTR OBJECT

The **pattr** object is a universal data container (that is, it can store numerical values, lists or symbols) which is capable of sharing its contents with Max's interface objects. Furthermore, the object can also be used to help us take our first steps toward a more advanced system for preset management. Let's look at some of the features shown in the patches presented in figure ID.2.

Even though these example patches are very simple, we still recommend that you recreate all six of them shown in the figure, because some features of the **pattr** object work quite differently from the standard Max object behaviour that you have learned so far.

In patch number 1, we can see that a **pattr** object accepts any kind of message (numbers, symbols or lists), and that these messages are immediately passed through to the object's left outlet. A bang can be used to re-send the last message received. It is also possible to "bind" an interface object to a **pattr** by connecting the second outlet of **pattr** to the interface object, as shown in patch number 2. Any value output by the interface object will also be stored in **pattr** and sent to its left outlet. And, as you can see in patch 3, a value sent to **pattr** will be forwarded to the "bound" interface object in addition to being sent out the left outlet.

The first argument to **pattr** defines its *scripting name*. Every **pattr** object is *required* to have its own scripting name, so if no argument is provided, a default scripting name will be assigned by Max (see patch number 4). The second argument to **pattr** specifies the scripting name of an interface object, allowing it to be bound to the pattr without a connection. When you rebuild patch number 5, you will need to assign the scripting name "guitar" to the floating-point number box using the inspector. In order to make sure the object is properly bound to the **pattr**, you will need to first assign its scripting name and then create the [**pattr** blue guitar] object afterward. Note that in this case we now have two scripting names: one for the **pattr** object and one for the **flonum**. It is not possible to assign the same name to both the **pattr** and the **flonum** because each object's scripting name must be unique[1].

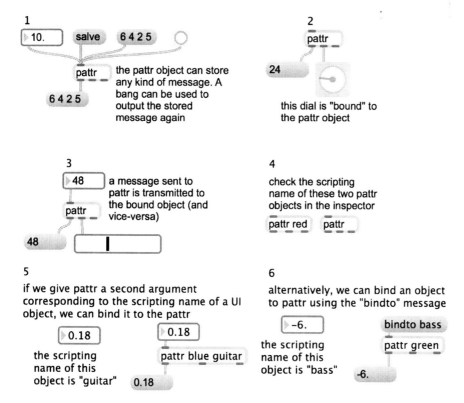

Fig. ID.2 The **pattr** object

We can also bind an interface object to a **pattr** "on the fly" by sending **pattr** the "bindto" message followed by the scripting name of an interface object (shown in patch 6).

When a patch containing **pattr** is saved, the data contained in the object will be saved and recalled each time the patch is opened. The use of this feature can be set with the "autorestore" attribute, which is enabled by default. To

---

[1] We have already learned that some objects, such as **buffer~** and **groove~**, can share the same name. However, in these cases it is not the objects' scripting name that is shared, but rather a named memory space that contains the shared data.

test this out, set the value of the slider in patch 3 to halfway along the slider and then save and reload the patch: the slider's cursor will appear in the same position it was when the patch was saved and not at 0, as it would be for an "unbound" object.

THE PATTRSTORAGE OBJECT

Apart from the autorestore function, the `pattr` object doesn't yet seem to offer any particularly new features that we couldn't also make ourselves using a pair of `send` and `receive` objects and the `pvar` object. However, by using the `pattr` object together with the `pattrstorage` object we can do some new and interesting things. Open the patch **ID_01_pattrstorage.maxpat** (figure ID.3).

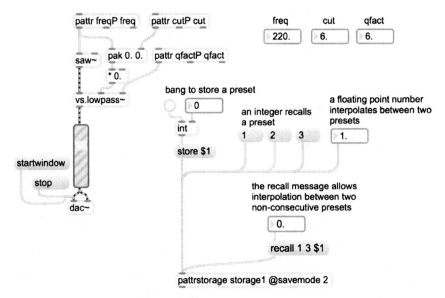

Fig. ID.3 The file **ID_01_pattrstorage.maxpat**

The `pattrstorage` object is the heart of this built-in preset management system, since it lets us save and recall the values contained in all `pattr` objects.

The three **flonum** objects at the top of the patch have been given the scripting names "freq", "cut", and "qfact", and are consequently bound to the three `pattr` objects visible to their left. Note that each of the three `pattr` objects has been given two arguments: the first is the scripting name of the `pattr` itself, and the second is the scripting name of one of the three number boxes to the right. Activate the DSP engine and click on the three message boxes with the values 1, 2 and 3 at the center of the patch – each of these can be used to select one the three presets saved in the `pattrstorage` object.

If we now send floating-point values using the floating point number box connected to `pattrstorage`, we can interpolate between two consecutive

416

presets. For example, the value 1.5 will recall parameters halfway between those contained in the first and second presets. It is also possible to interpolate between two non-consecutive presets using the "recall" message followed by any two (non-consecutive) preset numbers and a floating-point value between 0 and 1, which is used to determine the interpolation between the two given presets. For example, if we send the message "recall 1 3 0.5", the parameter values will be halfway between the values stored in the first and third presets.

A new preset can be stored using the "store" message, followed by a preset number. Now, double-click on the `pattrstorage` object in order to open the window shown in figure ID.4.

Name	Priority	Interp	Data
✔ freqP	0	⇕ linear	360.
✔ cutP	0	⇕ linear	4.
✔ qfactP	0	⇕ linear	4.05

Client Objects [storage1]

Fig. ID.4 The `pattrstorage` client window

This window is called the *client window* – it shows the values stored in the `pattr` objects. As you can see, the "Name" column contains the scripting name of the `pattr` objects (not those of the number boxes!) and the "Data" column (the last one) shows the current values. The first column contains checkboxes that let us select and de-select parameters: deselected parameters are not updated when presets are recalled. The "Priority" column lets us define the order in which parameter updates will be sent (lower values have greater priority over higher ones), which can be quite useful when managing parameters in very complex patches). The "Interp" column lets us define the type of interpolation that will be used when recalling fractional preset values. For the moment we will hold off on discussing the different types of interpolation that are available, but just be aware that linear interpolation has been selected for all three parameters.

As you can see, the `pattrstorage` object is able to "look at" and store the contents of `pattr` objects, ignoring all the other objects in the patch (at least for the time being). The collection of presets is not saved with the patch, but instead in a separate file which, by default, uses the name of the `pattrstorage` object (its first argument) followed by the ".json" extension. In this case of the patch we are currently looking at, the file is called "storage1.json"[2]. This file is saved in the same folder as the patch itself. The "@savemode 2" attribute[3] that has

---

[2] We will soon see how it is possible to save a file with any name; there is no obligatory relationship between the name of the pattrstorage object and the name of the ".json" file.

[3] Remember that when an attribute is written inside an object, it needs to be preceded by the "@" character. Therefore, in reality, the name of this attribute is simply "savemode.".

been typed into the **pattrstorage** object defines the saving mode for the presets, in this case, the file will be automatically saved each time the patch is saved. There are four saving modes associated with the "savemode" attribute, numbered from 0 to 3. Mode 0: no saving, 1: saving with a file name dialog, 2: automatic saving when the patch is saved, 3: automatic saving when the patch is closed.

It is also possible to bind interface objects to **pattr** objects located in sub-patches. To see how this works, open the file **ID_02_pattrstorage2.maxpat** (figure ID.5).

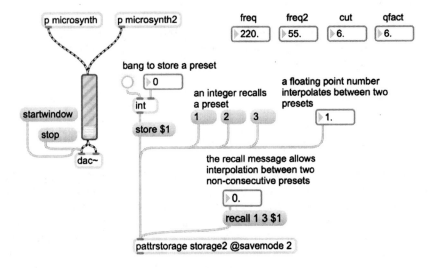

Fig. ID.5 The file **ID_02_pattrstorage2.maxpat**

Here the two subpatches on the upper left each contain the same sound generator used in the preceding patch. The two generators each have their own frequency, but share the filter cutoff and Q factor. In figure ID.6 we can see the contents of the first subpatch.

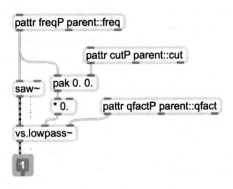

Fig. ID.6 The contents of the [p microsynth] subpatch

Note that the second argument of each **pattr** object begins with the prefix "parent::" – this indicates that the interface object bound to it is located in the patch one level higher (i.e., in the patch containing the subpatch). The second subpatch is identical to this one except that **pattr** on top is bound to the number box "freq2" (the second of the four number boxes in the upper right of the main patch). Try out the three presets and then double-click on the **pattrstorage** object to open its client window (figure ID.7).

⊖ ○ ○ Client Objects [storage2]			
Name	**Priority**	**Interp**	**Data**
☑ ms1		↕	
☑ freqP	0	↕ linear	220.
☑ cutP	0	↕ linear	6.
☑ qfactP	0	↕ linear	6.
☑ ms2		↕	
☑ freqP	0	↕ linear	55.
☑ cutP	0	↕ linear	6.
☑ qfactP	0	↕ linear	6.

Fig. ID.7 Client window with the subpatches' parameters

The names "ms1" and "ms2" displayed in the "Name" column are the scripting names given to the two subpatches. The scripting names of the **pattr** objects contained in each of the subpatches is shown underneath these names. You will notice that the **pattr** names are slightly offset to the right (indented) to indicate that they are located one level lower in the patch hierarchy with respect to the main patch where the **pattrstorage** object is located.

THE AUTOPATTR OBJECT

The **autopattr** object can be used to simplify preset management. When this object is placed in a patch, the **pattrstorage** object is able to directly "see" all interface objects which have been given a scripting name, without needing to connect them to a **pattr** object. We can therefore think of the **autopattr** object as a kind of "super pattr" that automatically binds all named interface objects to it.

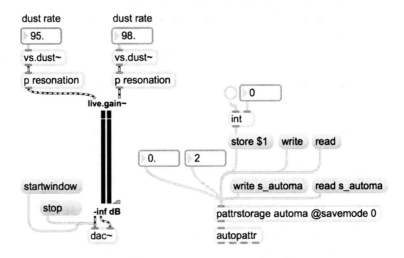

Fig. ID.8 The file **ID_03_autopattr.maxpat**

First, notice that nothing is connected to the **autopattr** object in the lower part of the patch. This is because its mere presence in the patch means that all interface objects that have been given a scripting name will be able to be "seen" by **pattrstorage**. In figure ID.9 we can see the contents of the [p resonation] subpatch.

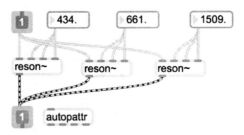

Fig. ID.9 The contents of the [p resonation] subpatch

Notice that there is also an **autopattr** in this subpatch, in addition to three number boxes which have been given scripting names. Listen to the presets that have been stored, and then open the client window by double-clicking on **pattrstorage** (figure ID.10).

Name	Priority	Interp	Data
✔ dustrate	0	⇕ linear	95.
✔ dustrate[1]	0	⇕ linear	98.
☐ live.gain~	0	⇕ linear	-70.
✔ resonation		⇕	
✔ resonfreq	0	⇕ linear	219.
✔ resonfreq[1]	0	⇕ linear	234.
✔ resonfreq[2]	0	⇕ linear	272.
✔ resonation[1]		⇕	
✔ resonfreq	0	⇕ linear	121.
✔ resonfreq[1]	0	⇕ linear	186.
✔ resonfreq[2]	0	⇕ linear	156.

Client Objects [automa]

Fig. ID.10 Client window

The first two names belong to the two number boxes in the main patch which are connected to the two **vs.dust~** objects.
Notice that the name of the second number box is "dustrate[1]". Since this object was created by duplicating the first number box, its scripting name was also copied; when any object that has been given a scripting name is copied, the new object inherits its scripting name, too. However, since two objects with the same scripting name can never exist in the same patch, an incrementing number in square brackets is automatically added to the name. As you can see, the same thing has happened to two of the three number boxes located in the subpatches.

Finally, notice that the client window also contains the name of the **live.gain~** object, although it has been manually deselected. All interface objects in the "Max for Live" library are assigned a scripting name by default, but since we do not want to store the output volume in the preset, we have excluded this object in the client window. We could have also excluded the object by connecting the second outlet of **autopattr** to it. On the other hand, to store the values of certain objects and exclude all others, we could have connected the first outlet of **autopattr** to them. The first and second outlets of this object therefore work just like the first and third outlets of the **preset** object.
Like **pattr**, the **autopattr** object is also provided with an "autorestore" attribute which is enabled by default. This means that all interface objects managed by **autopattr** will be reset to the values they had when the patch was saved (you probably already noticed that a set of values different from the three stored presets is automatically recalled when the patch **ID_03_autopattr.maxpat** is opened).

By using the "autoname" attribute with the **autopattr** object, it is possible to further simplify parameter management in a patch. If we set this attribute to 1 (either using the inspector or by typing it directly into the object) **autopattr** will automatically generate a scripting name for each interface object present in the patch. This means that **pattrstorage** will be able to see and store the values of all these objects. Of course, when you do this it is not possible to give meaningful names to all of the different objects, and this could consequently be a disadvantage for very complex patches. Additionally, since **pattrstorage** can automatically see all interface objects in the patch, you will need to manually exclude those which you would like to ignore. To try this out, type the attribute "@autoname 1" inside the **autopattr** object in figure ID.8, and you will see that the three number boxes used to store and recall presets will be given scripting names so **pattrstorage** will be able to see them. You can verify this by opening the **pattrstorage** object's client window. Note that in figure ID.8, the "@savemode 0" attribute has also been given to the **pattrstorage** object in order to keep the presets from being automatically saved. The presets we are using have been saved in a file named s_automa. json[4], and any modifications to these presets will need to be manually saved to disk by sending the "write" message to **pattrstorage**. The "write" message can optionally be followed by the name of the file you want to save, and thus several sets of presets could be saved to different files with different file names.

To read a preset file we simply need to send the "read" message to **pattrstorage**. When a patch is opened, **pattrstorage** will try to read the last preset file that had been previously loaded before the patch was saved. If for whatever reason the file s_automa.json is not automatically loaded, just click on the [read s_automa] message box.

PRESET AND PATTRSTORAGE

It is possible to graphically control the presets stored in **pattrstorage** using a **preset** object. The **preset** object actually contains a "pattrstorage" attribute which can be assigned a name. When this attribute has been given the name of a **pattrstorage** object located in the same patch, the **preset** object will become an interface for that **pattrstorage**.

Load the patch **ID_03b_graphic_preset.maxpat**. This patch is identical to the preceding one, except that it contains a **preset** object whose "pattrstorage" attribute has been assigned the name "automa" (via the inspector); this is the same name that has been given to the **pattrstorage** object present in the patch. Try storing some new presets using the **preset** object and save them to disk by clicking on the [write s_automa] message box connected to **pattrstorage**. Note that if we were using only the **preset** object (without **pattrstorage**), it would be impossible to store the values of the number boxes located inside the subpatches, nor interpolate between the different presets.

· ·

ACTIVITY

Apply a preset storing system to the patch 06_03_multitap3.maxpat, using the **pattrstorage** and **autopattr** objects. Use this system to create and save some presets to disk. Use a **preset** object to be able to graphically control the presets saved by **pattrstorage**.

---

[4] Note that this is an arbitrary name, different from the object name; it should be reiterated that the names of the preset file and pattrstorage do not need to be in any way related.

ID.2 BPATCHER, VARIABLE ARGUMENTS AND LOCAL ARGUMENTS

In this section we will delve deeper into some important aspects of abstractions and subpatches in order to be able to program more flexibly in Max.

THE BPATCHER OBJECT

Let's start by taking a look at the **bpatcher** object, which lets us load an abstraction or subpatch and display all or part of it in the main patch. Open the patch **ID_04_bpatcher.maxpat** (figure ID.11).

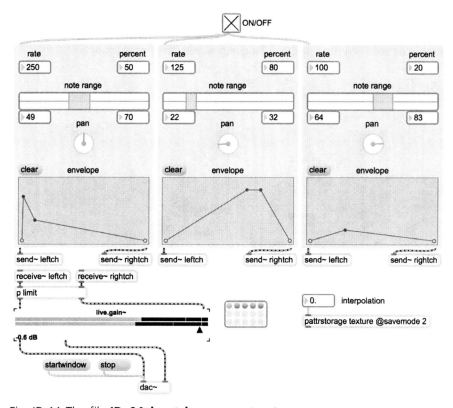

Fig. ID.11 The file **ID_04_bpatcher.maxpat**

In order to listen to the presets we first need to click on the `toggle` labeled "on/off" in the upper part of the patch, as well as raise the volume of the `live.gain~` object, below. The "pattrstorage" attribute of the `preset` object in this patch has been given the name "texture" (the name of the `pattrstorage` object next to it), so it can be used to control the `pattrstorage`. You can click on the `preset` object to recall the stored presets, as well as use the floating point number box connected to `pattrstorage` to interpolate between adjacent presets.

423

The three control panels that take up the top half of the patch are all **bpatcher** objects in which the abstraction **texture.generator.maxpat** has been loaded. Each panel controls a stream of sounds defined by parameters controlling the beat rate, percentage of sounds actually generated, a range of random patch values, as well as the envelope and stereo position of the sound.

In order to see the contents of the original abstraction, switch the patch over to edit mode and click on one of the three bpatchers with the right mouse button (Windows) or Control-click on one of them (Mac). A contextual menu will appear allowing you to select the "Object/Open Original texture.generator.maxpat" item which will cause the original abstraction to be opened in a new window. The patch opens in presentation mode because the "Open in Presentation" attribute for this patch has been enabled in the Patcher Inspector. [5] Click on the "blackboard" icon in the toolbar at the bottom of the patch in order to leave Presentation mode and be able to see the entire patch in Patching Mode (shown in figure ID.12).

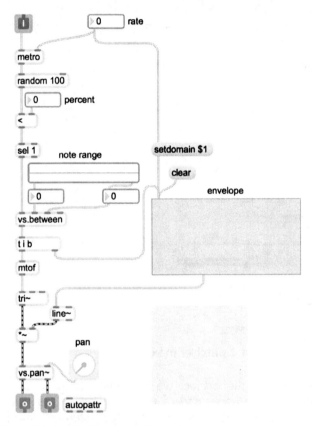

Fig. ID.12 The patch **texture.generator.maxpat**

---

[5] We already talked about the Patcher Inspector in chapter 1.3 P. Remember that you can access it by selecting it from the View menu or by right-clicking on the patcher window itself, when in the patch is in edit mode.

Note the **autopattr** object inside this abstraction, which allows its parameters to be stored in the **pattrstorage** object located in the main patch. We will leave the analysis of this simple subpatch to the reader.

To place an abstraction inside a **bpatcher** you need to assign its file path to the **bpatcher**'s "Patcher File" attribute, using the inspector. Try this out by creating a new **bpatcher** in an empty patch and load the file texture.genera-tor.maxpat or any other patch inside it. By default the upper-left part of the patch will be shown in the **bpatcher**. If you enlarge the **bpatcher** by drag-ging its lower right corner, you will be able to display the entire abstraction.

It is possible to change the part of the abstraction that is displayed in the **bpatcher** by holding down the Shift-Control keys (Windows) or Shift-Command keys (Mac) while clicking and dragging the mouse cursor inside the **bpatcher**.

You can additionally put a subpatch (in other words a max patch that is saved with the main patch and not in a separate file) inside the **bpatcher** object. Open the patch **ID_05_bpatcher_subpatch.maxpat** (shown in figure ID.13).

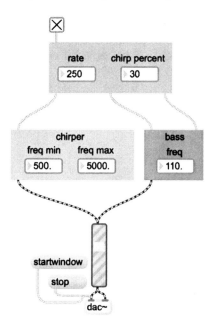

Fig. ID.13 The file **ID_05_bpatcher_subpatch.maxpat**

Each of the three colored panels in the patch is actually a **bpatcher** contain-ing a subpatch. If you switch over into edit mode and right-click (Windows) or control-click (Mac) inside the **bpatcher** at the top, the usual contextual menu will open up. Select the "Object/New View of <none>" item at the bottom of the menu to open up the subpatch in its own window. Note that, unlike the preceding patch, there is no file name present, but instead the string <none>,

425

which is the default name assigned to a subpatch created inside a **bpatcher**. If you deactivate presentation mode you will see that there is an [autopattr @ autoname 1] object that has been used to automatically assign names to all interface objects in the patch (in this case just the two number boxes). Open up the other two subpatches in the same way and analyze how their algorithms work.

To create a subpatch inside a **bpatcher** you first need to enable the "Embed Patcher in Parent" attribute in the inspector. After doing this, you can open the subpatch window via the contextual menu. Since the patch in figure ID.13 has no **preset** object or **pattrstorage**, can you explain why values are automatically set in the number boxes when the patch is opened?

VARIABLE AND LOCAL ARGUMENTS

As we already learned in section IC.4, arguments can be provided for abstractions using the # character followed by a number from 1 to 9 (e.g., #1, #2, etc.) inside the subpatch itself. These symbols (called *replaceable arguments*) are "placeholders" for arguments that will eventually be passed to the object.

You can also use replaceable arguments with the **bpatcher** object. Using the object inspector, you can define a list of elements for the "Argument(s)" attribute. When you then load a patch containing the symbols #1, #2, etc. inside the **bpatcher**, these symbols will be replaced by the elements in the list you provided.

One of many possible uses for replaceable arguments is to give a name to a **send/receive** pair inside an abstraction. Imagine that we have an abstraction like the one shown in figure ID.14a.

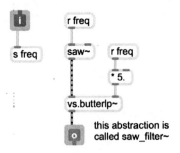

Fig. ID.14a Abstraction containing **send/receive**

If we create a patch that uses several copies of this abstraction, it would be impossible to change the frequency of one of them without also affecting the frequency of all the others, because the [s freq] object will communicate with all of the [r freq] objects, even if they are located in other copies of the abstraction. However, if we replaced the name "freq" with #1 (as shown in figure ID.14b) we could solve the problem.

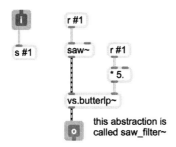

Fig. ID.14b Use of replaceable arguments (#) in send/receive objects contained in an abstraction

This way, we can distinguish between the different **send/receive** pairs by providing a different argument to each copy of the abstraction: the first could be called [saw.filter~ freq1], the second [saw.filter~ freq2], the third [saw.filter~ freq3], etc. If we needed two or more **send/receive** pairs inside a given abstraction we could always use two or more arguments, but this system would soon become inconvenient, since we might quickly discover that we have too many arguments to easily manage. Fortunately, we can take advantage of another feature of replaceable arguments: the ability to append text to the argument itself. Open the patch **ID_06_arguments.maxpat** (figure ID.15). In this simple patch there are three copies of the saw.filter~ abstraction, each one provided with a different argument.

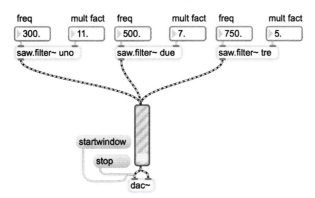

Fig. ID.15 The *patch* **ID_06_arguments.maxpat**

If you open the original file[6] you will see that the replaceable argument #1 is followed (without space) by two different suffixes ("_freq" and "_fact") which are used for two different **send/receive** pairs.[7]

---

[6] Remember that in order to open an abstraction's original file, you can simply double-click on the object to open its patcher window, and then click on the first icon in the toolbar at the bottom of the patch (labeled "Modify Read Only"). The icon, which initially looks like a pencil, will then transform into the familiar lock icon that can be used to switch the patch over to edit mode.

[7] The replaceable argument always needs to come first in the name we want to create. In other words, it will not work if you write freq_#1.

If you open the first copy of the abstraction in the patch by double-clicking on it, you will see that the replaceable argument #1 has been used to create two different names: "uno_freq" and "uno_fact" (Figure ID.16 a and b). With this system, it is possible to use a single argument to create several different (unique) names that can be applied to different **send/receive** object pairs, as shown in this example.

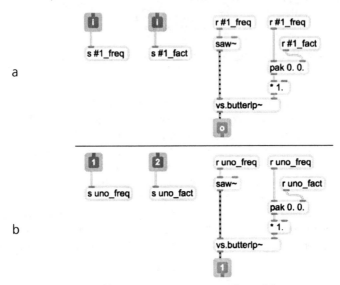

Fig. ID.16 Creating different names using replaceable arguments

We can also optionally save ourselves the trouble of always needing to think up different argument names for each copy of subpatches that we use. To do this, the symbol #0 can be used as a replaceable argument. Unlike #1, #2, etc., this symbol is not substituted by an argument, but rather by a unique identifier value automatically generated by Max. This identifier is different for each copy of the abstraction. To see an example, open the patch **ID_07_unique_identifiers. maxpat** (figure ID.17).

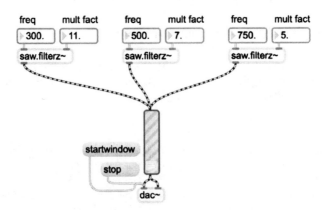

Fig. ID.17 The file **ID_07_unique_identifiers.maxpat**

This patch is very similar to the preceding one. It contains three copies of a new abstraction **saw.filterz~**, without arguments. Let's compare the contents of one of them with the original file (figure ID.18).

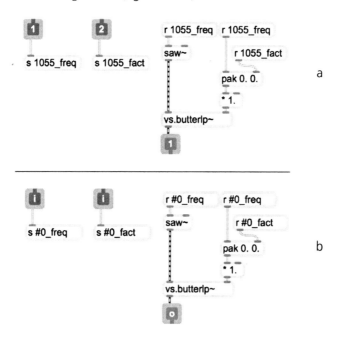

Fig. ID.18 Using the symbol #0

In figure 18a (the original file) we can see that the **send/receive** object pairs have been given an argument that begins with the symbol #0. In figure 18b (the contents of the abstraction), this symbol has been replaced by Max with the unique identifier 1055. It is highly probably that the identifier present in your abstraction will be a different numerical value. Now, open all three abstractions and notice how each one has a different identifier – this means that the **send/ receive** pairs will not transmit messages from one abstraction to another.

ARGUMENTS AND ATTRIBUTES INSIDE ABSTRACTIONS AND SUBPATCHES

As we have already learned, in addition to providing standard Max objects with arguments, it is also possible to set attributes (variables whose value defines the object's behavior). Attributes can either be set in the object's inspector or directly into the object itself, by typing the @ symbol followed by the attribute name and the value we want to assign to it. For example, in the object [**autopattr** @autoname 1] the value 1 has been assigned to the "autoname" attribute.

Now let's take a look at how it is possible to manage attributes and arguments inside abstractions and subpatches using the **patcherargs** object.

Before we talk about **patcherargs**, we first need to introduce another extremely important object that will also be useful in subsequent chapters: the **route** object. Rebuild the patch shown in figure ID.19.

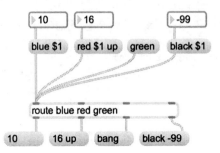

Fig. ID.19 The **route** object

The **route** object[8] is fairly similar to the **select** object, in that it compares the input message with its arguments. If the input message is a list whose first element corresponds to one of the object's arguments, **route** will send the rest of the list to the outlet whose position corresponds to the position of that argument (the first outlet corresponds to the first argument, the second to the second, and so on). If the input message is not a list but a single element corresponding to one of the arguments, a bang will be sent out the outlet in question (in this scenario **route** functions just like **select**). If the first element of the input message does not correspond to any of the arguments the entire message is sent out the object's last (rightmost) outlet.

Let's look at a simple example of how to use route. Open the file **ID_08_route.maxpat** (figure ID.20).

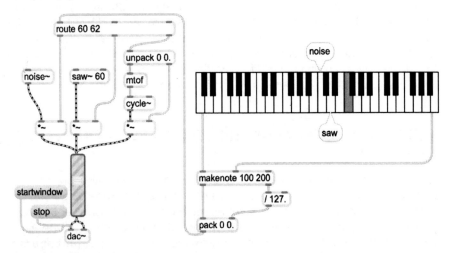

Fig. ID.20 The file **ID_08_route.maxpat**

---

[8] Not to be confused with the **router** object that was presented in section IC.2.

Each time you click on the notes C3 and D3 of the `kslider` in this patch, you will obtain white noise and a 60 Hz sawtooth waveform, respectively. All other notes will play a sine tone corresponding to the key's frequency. The patch is relatively simple to analyze. First, the MIDI velocity value is transformed into an amplitude value by simply dividing it by 127, and then the note-amplitude pair is grouped into a list of two values and sent to the [`route` 60 62] object. If the first element of the list is 60 (C3), the corresponding amplitude is routed to the first outlet of the `route` object and sent to the multiplier for the white noise; if the first element of the list is 62 (D3), the amplitude is routed to the second outlet and sent to the multiplier for the sawtooth oscillator. For all other notes, the note-amplitude list is sent out the third outlet of route where both values are used to play a sine tone.

Now let's go on to the **patcherargs** object. First, open the Max window and then load the file **ID_09_patcherargs.maxpat** (figure ID.21).

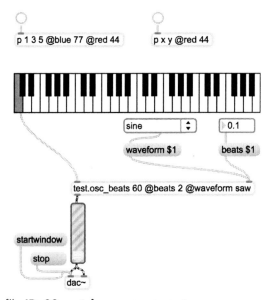

Fig. ID.21 The file **ID_09_patcherargs.maxpat**

In the upper part of the patch there are two subpatches that have been given arguments and attributes (the latter are preceded by the @ symbol). Let's open up the first subpatch, shown in figure ID.22.

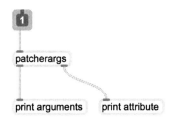

Fig. ID.22 A subpatch containing the **patcherargs** object

431

The contents of this subpatch are very simple: there is a **patcherargs** object connected to two **print** objects which post the messages they receive to the Max window. When the main patch is opened, the contents of the **p** (patcher) object are sent as a list to the left outlet of **patcherargs**, while the attributes are sent out its right outlet, one at a time and without the @ prefix. When all the arguments and attributes have been sent, the object sends the message "done" out its right outlet. When you open the patch, you will notice that several lines of text are printed in the Max window:

arguments: 1 3 5
attribute: blue 77
attribute: red 44
attribute: done
argumentsB: x y c d
attributeB: red 44
attributeB: blue 666
attributeB: done

The first four lines were printed by the subpatch on the left and the last four by the subpatch on the right. You have probably already noticed that the subpatch on the left printed exactly the same number of arguments and attributes that were typed into the **p** (patcher) object, but the subpatch on the right printed more. This is because the **patcherargs** object inside the subpatch on the right contains default values (figure ID.23), which eventually get replaced by any typed arguments present in the **patcher** object that contains **patcherargs**.

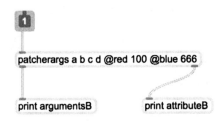

Fig. ID.23 A subpatch containing the **patcherargs** object with default values

Let's now take a look at a "real" example using the **test.osc_beats** abstraction at the bottom of the patch (located in the same folder as our main patch). This abstraction creates beating with different kinds of waveforms that can be selected using the **umenu** object. Note that we have given the abstraction an argument (60) and two attributes ("@beats 2" and "@waveform saw"). Try playing some notes with the **kslider** in the main patch, using the **umenu** to select from among the different kinds of waveforms. Also try changing the number of beats using the float number box connected to the [beats $1] message box.

Afterwards, open the abstraction by double-clicking on the **test.osc_beats** object (figure ID.24).

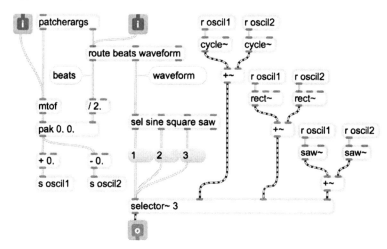

Fig. ID.24 The contents of the **test.osc_beats** object

As we have already said, when the patch is loaded the `patcherargs` object will send the values of the arguments and attributes that have been given to the abstraction to the objects connected to it. At this point, the algorithm inside the abstraction should be simple and clear enough for you to analyze by yourself. Nonetheless, note the group of objects on the left that is used to calculate the frequencies for the beating oscillators: this is the same calculation we used in section 2.2P in the first volume. Be sure to pay close attention to how the `route` and `sel` objects have been used to `route` the messages that are sent as attributes.

It is also possible to use the `patcherargs` object inside a `bpatcher`. In this case, the attributes should come after the arguments and the attribute names should be preceded by the @ symbol when typing them into the "Argument(s)" attribute in the inspector, as was already mentioned in the "Variable and Local Arguments" section of this chapter.

ID.3 MANAGING DATA AND SCORES WITH MAX

Up to this point we have been using objects capable of manipulating lists, such as the message box or `zl` object, in order to manage and store data. In this section we will learn the kinds of resources that are available to us in the Max environment when we need to manage much larger data sets.

THE TABLE OBJECT

We will start with the **table** object, which lets us manage and store an array of integers. An array is a kind of multiple variable, which contains a given number of elements all of the same type (e.g., integers, floating point numbers, symbols, …), each of which can be accessed using an index number. Let's take a look at several of the object's features, shown in figure ID.25.

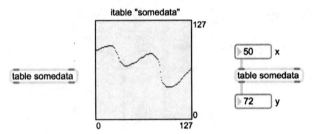

Fig. ID.25 The **table** and **itable** objects

The **table** object can take an argument to define its name; this way, two **table** objects can share the same data. By double-clicking on the object (in performance mode), the object will open up a window that displays and lets you edit its values graphically.

The graphical element in the center of the figure is the **itable** object, which is basically a version of **table** where the graphical display is shown in the patch itself, without needing to open a second window to view it. A name can also be given to the **itable** object using the inspector (using the "Table Name" attribute in the "Table" category). In the figure, we have given the **itable** object the same name ("somedata") as the two **table** objects on either side of it. Graphically changing the contents of the **itable** will also cause the data of the two **table** objects to be modified, and vice-versa.

By default, a **table** object contains 128 integer values between 0 and 127, and the indices of these 128 values also range from 0 to 127. In the graphical representation of the data the indices run along the x-axis and the corresponding value for each index is displayed on the y-axis. Sending an index number to the left inlet causes the corresponding value to be output (see the **table** object on the right in the figure).

To set the values in the table without relying on the graphical interface, it is always possible to send index-value pairs as a list to the first inlet, or to send a value in to the table's right inlet followed by an index to the left inlet (figure ID.26).

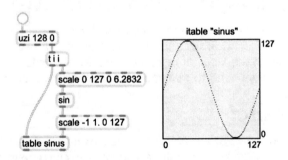

Fig. ID.26 An algorithm for the **table** object

In this patch, which we also suggest you rebuild for yourself, we are generating one cycle of a sinusoid waveform, and storing it in a **table** object. To save the contents of a table together with the patch, you need to turn on the "Save Data With Patcher" attribute in the inspector in the "Table" tab. The other attributes in this category also let you change the range of values displayed by the table ("Table Range"), as well as the dimensions of the table ("Table Size").

The values stored inside a table can also be saved to a separate file, by sending the "write" message to the **table** object, and subsequently reloaded into the object using the "read" message. When a patch containing a named **table** object is opened, Max will first search the disk for a file with this name, and load its contents into the object, if such a file exists.

Let's now take a look at an example that uses the **table** object to store different scales. Open up the file **ID_10_scales.maxpat** (figure ID.27).

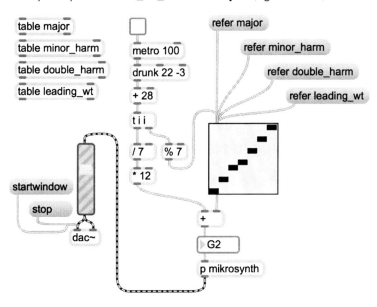

Fig. ID.27 The file **ID_10_scales.maxpat**

This patch takes advantage of the "refer" message, which enables table and itable objects to reference the contents of other tables. In the upper left part of the patch there are 4 tables, each containing the semitone intervals (pitch classes) that make up the following scales: major, harmonic minor, double harmonic scale (C Db E F G Ab B) and whole-tone scale with leading tone (C, D, E, F#, G#, A#, B).
The four message boxes to the right contain the "refer" message followed by the name of one of the tables, thus allowing the **itable** object to reference the data stored in any of these tables. The random note selection is created using the **drunk** object, which we learned in section IA.5 in the previous volume. Here, values between 0 and 21 are randomly generated, with a step

435

no larger than 2 between one value and the next, and without any repeated consecutive values (because a negative value has been provided for the step argument).

The random note generation in this patch takes into consideration that we are using 7 note scales and not 12 semitones. Therefore the value 28 that is added to the random value output by **drunk** represents an increase of 4 octaves (7 · 4 = 28). The resulting value then undergoes a modulo operation by 7 in order to obtain the scale degree that will be played, and is also divided by 7 (integer value division) to acquire to octave where that scale degree will be played. The value output by the modulo operator is sent to the **itable**, which retrieves the scale degree in semitones (pitch class), and this is added to the octave value multiplied by 12 (the number of semitones in an octave). This sum is then sent to the [p mikrosynth] subpatch that contains a filtered sawtooth oscillator.

THE COLL OBJECT

The **coll** object lets us store indexed sets of any kind of data (lists, numbers or symbols). Open the patch **ID_11_coll.maxpat**, shown in figure ID.28).

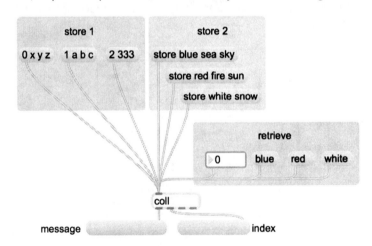

Fig. ID.28 The patch **ID_11_coll.maxpat**

Begin by clicking on the three message boxes inside the rectangle labeled "store 1", and then double-click on the **coll** object itself. This will open an editor window containing the following text:

0, x y z;
1, a b c;
2, 333;

As you can see, this is basically the information from the lists in the three message boxes that you just clicked. Notice, however, that the first element of each list is now separated from the rest of the list by a comma. The first element in the messages we sent is actually the index, followed by the rest of the stored data (numbers, symbols or lists). Unlike the **table** object, the index used for a stored item in the **coll** object does not have to be an integer. Close the **coll** window, click on the three message boxes inside the rectangle labeled "store 2", and then re-open the **coll** window. You will notice that there are now three new lines corresponding to the three messages you just sent. Note that when you are using non-numerical indices, you need to add the "store" message to the head of the list.

Each time the **coll** object receives an index (either numerical or a symbol) that is the same as that of a previously stored list, it will send the list (without the index) out its first outlet and the index out its second outlet (naturally, it outputs these right to left, so the index is sent before the data). Try sending the index values 0, 1 and 2, as well as the symbol indices, using the number box and message boxes inside the rectangle labeled "retrieve." The corresponding data will be displayed in the first message box underneath, and the index will be displayed in the second message box. Note that when the data stored in a **coll** is not a list or numerical value, but a single word (or symbol), it will be preceded by the "symbol" message. The same thing happens for indices: when you click on the "white" message **coll** will output the messages "symbol snow" and "symbol white."

If you want to, you can always manually add other data directly to the **coll** object by editing the data in its window. However, be sure to adhere to the data format! You must add a comma after the index and add a semi-colon at the end of every line. Once you have added the new data, you can close the **coll** window and a dialog, asking you if you would like to store the changes you made, will appear. To store the changes, click on the "Save" button.

Presuming you wrote the new data correctly, it will now be stored inside the **coll** object. If you made a mistake, such as forgetting a comma or semi-colon, something fairly annoying will happen: Max will delete the line with the error as well as any subsequent lines, without an "Undo" option! In versions of Max before 6.0.7, there is not even a warning before this happens, but fortunately as of version 6.0.7 Max is somewhat more "lenient" towards our mistakes, and now warns us that we are about to do something potentially disastrous, and giving us the option to cancel closing the window, so we can go back and correct the error.

Let's now look at a practical example using `coll`. The frequency ratios for the seven degrees of the natural scale (which we spoke about in section 1.4T of the first volume) have been stored in a coll; we will use them to create note sequences based upon this natural intonation. Open the patch **ID_12_natural_scale.maxpat**, shown in figure ID.29.

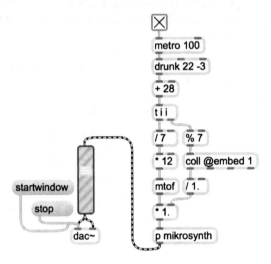

Fig. ID.29 The patch **ID_12_natural_scale.maxpat**

Open up the `coll` editor window by double-clicking on the object; you will notice that it contains the frequency ratios of the natural scale. As you can see, each line contains two numeric values corresponding to the numerator and denominator of the fraction representing the frequency ratio. You will also notice that the "@embed 1" attribute has been used so that the `coll` object will save its contents together with the patch.[9]

This patch is somewhat similar to ID_10_scales.maxpat – it creates a series of random values using `drunk`, and for each step in the scale the `coll` object will provide the two values that represent the frequency ratio. These values are divided by one another and the result is used as a frequency multiplier for the base frequency (which serves as the "tonic" degree of the scale). The base frequency has been derived from the octave value for each note, calculated, as before, by dividing by 7 and multiplying by 12. The result is sent to the [p mikrosynth] subpatch.

---

[9] Note that "embed" is the actual name of the attribute, whereas "Save Data With Patcher" is its descriptive name as used in the inspector; the same attribute is available for the table object.

Now let's take a look at how we can use the coll object to store the timbre characteristics of a sound. Open the patch **ID_13_gongs.maxpat** (figure ID.30).

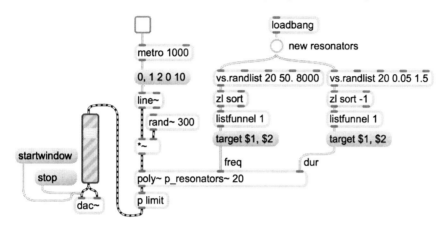

Fig. ID.30 The patch **ID_13_gongs.maxpat**

This patch uses a variation of the "resonant bodies" algorithm that was presented in the final part of section IC.3 (if you do not remember the details of this, you should re-read that section).

Let's first discuss the **vs.randlist** object, which outputs a list of random values each time that it receives a bang in its left inlet. It takes three arguments that represent the list length, as well as the minimum and maximum values for the random number choice, respectively. The first of the two **vs.randlist** objects in this patch generates a list of frequencies between 50 and 8000 Hz, whereas the second creates a list of random durations between 0.05 and 1.5 seconds. The [**zl** sort] object is used to sort the elements of the frequency list in an ascending order (from low to high), and similarly the [**zl** sort -1] object is used to sort the durations in a descending order (due to the argument –1), so they go from longest to shortest. This means that lower frequencies will be associated with longer durations. The **listfunnel** object and subsequent message box are used to distribute the different values among the voices in the **poly~** object – you have already seen this technique in the patch IC_07_ resonant_filters.maxpat. The polyphonic patch p_resonators~ is the same that was used with the patch IC_08_bouncing_bodies.maxpat. Each time a bang is sent to the two **vs.randlist** objects a new resonator configuration is created.

Turning on the **metro** on the left produces a series of short impulses using the **rand~** noise generator with a frequency of 300 Hz. These sounds are sent to the **poly~** object which creates the resonance. In contrast to the click that was used in section IC.3, the impulse sound being used here produces less energy in the high frequency range, thereby bringing out low frequencies in the resulting sound. Try playing the patch by turning on the **metro** and clicking on the button labeled "new resonators" from time to time. You will notice that each random resonator configuration you create replaces the previous one, although it would be nice to be able to save a series of resonator configurations and use them to simulate a "gong orchestra." The **coll** object can be used to do precisely this.

Before we do this, however, we should take a closer look at some features of coll. Open up the file **ID_14_coll_sorting.maxpat** (figure ID.31).

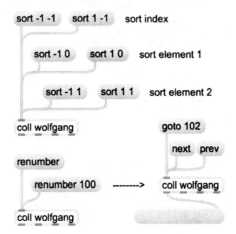

Fig. ID.31 The file **ID_14_coll_sorting.maxpat**

In this patch there are three **coll** objects which all share the name "wolfgang": as with the **table** object, two or more colls sharing the same name will share the same data content. Furthermore, when a patch with a named **coll** object is loaded, Max will search the disk for a file with this name[10] and load it into the object. In this case, there is a file called wolfgang.txt inside the "Interlude D Patches" folder which should have been loaded by **coll**. Double-click the **coll** to open its window and you should see the following data:

620, Die Zauberflöte;
492, Nozze di figaro;
621, Clemenza di tito;
588, Così fan tutte;
527, Don giovanni;

As you can see, the index numbers are not consecutive and they are in neither ascending nor descending order.[11]

---

[10] Max will always first search for the file in the same folder as the patch itself, and then search in the search patch that has been specified in the "File Preferences" window (in the Options menu).
[11] Be aware that this does not necessarily constitute a problem: if you sent the number 620 to the coll, you would still get the output "Die Zauberflöte" in return.

Now close the `coll` window, click on the first message box at the top of the patch ("sort -1 -1) and re-open the window. You will see that the index numbers now appear in ascending order. Click on the second message box, close and reopen the `coll` window, and you will notice that the indices are now in descending order (from 621 to 492). The "sort" message, as its name suggests, sorts the data contained in the `coll`. The two values that follow the message respectively indicate the sorting direction (-1 = ascending, 1 = descending)[12] and the element that will be used to sort the items (-1 represents the index, 0 the first element in the list, 1 the second element, and so on). Click on the other message boxes containing the "sort" message and notice that the sorting will be based on the corresponding list element. In the case of symbols and strings, the sorting will naturally be done in alphabetical order.

It is also possible to renumber all of the indices using the "renumber" message. This message causes `coll` to replace all the indices with increasing integer values starting from 0. An additional argument to this message can be used to supply the starting index number. Try clicking on the [renumber] and [renumber 100] message boxes on the lower left side of the patch and carefully observe how the index numbers are changed.

After clicking on the [renumber 100] message box, try clicking several times on the "next" and "prev" messages on the lower right side of the patch – you will notice that these messages tell `coll` to continuously cycle trough its stored data. The "next" message goes through the lists successively; each time that this message is sent `coll` retrieves the list after the one previously output. The "prev" message, on the other hand, runs through the data in reverse order: each time you click on it, it will cause `coll` to retrieve the item that is located just before the one which was last output. The "goto" message will position the `coll` at a predetermined index, but without outputting the corresponding data. If you then send a "next" or "prev" message, `coll` will output the item determined by the "goto" message, not the previous or next one. Try this out.

---

[12] Note that this syntax is the reverse of that used for [zl sort], where an argument of –1 means descending order.

There are actually dozens of other messages you can send to `coll` – it is a very complex object – but for the time being, the above information should be sufficient for the task at hand. Now open the patch **ID_15_gamelan.maxpat** (figure ID.32).

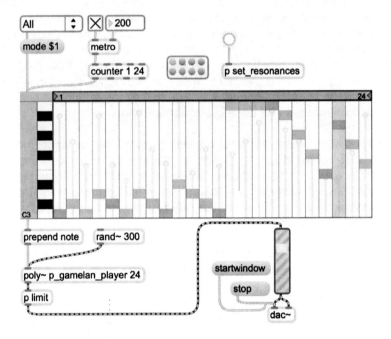

Fig. ID.32 The patch **ID_15_gamelan.maxpat**

In this patch, the resonant frequencies and durations for 12 different "gongs" have been stored, using the same parameters as those in the ID_13_gongs.max-pat patch. The **live.step** object is used to play sequences with this "gong orchestra." The 12 timbres have been assigned to the note range C3 (60) – B3 (71). The **preset** object has been used to save several different sequences in the **live.step** object; try listening to them all. Note that the sound is velocity sensitive; you can see the velocity values stored inside **live.step** using the **umenu** on the upper left.

Each time that you click on the button connected to the [p set_resonances] subpatch, 12 new gong timbres will be created. While you are listening to the sequences, try clicking on this button and notice how it changes all of the timbres at once.

442

Now let's take a closer look at how this patch actually works. The [p set_reso-nances] subpatch contains the algorithm that creates and stores the timbres in a coll. Double-click on it to open its window (shown in figure ID.33).

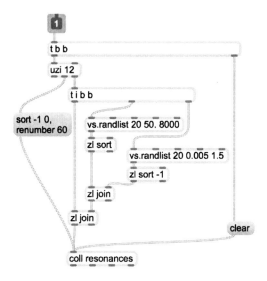

Fig. ID.33 The contents of the [p set_resonances] subpatch

When this subpatch receives a bang, the first thing that happens is that the "clear" message is sent to the [coll resonances] object, deleting any data that may be stored inside.

A bang is then sent to the [uzi 12] object which sends a series of numbers from 1 to 12 out its right outlet, which is connected to a **trigger**. For each of the 12 values output by **uzi**, a list of 20 frequencies in ascending order will be generated, in addition to a list of 20 durations in descending order. These lists are both joined along with the current value in the series and sent to the **coll** object. After outputting the series of numbers, the **uzi** object will output a bang via its middle outlet and send it to a message box containing two messages. The first message, "sort -1 0", sorts the collection of lists inside **coll**, putting them in ascending order based on the first element of the list (the lowest resonant frequency). The second message, "renumber 60", renumbers all of the indices starting at 60 (corresponding to MIDI note C3) and ending at 71 (B3). This means that the 12 resulting timbres will be, by and large, ordered by pitch in an ascending direction. Of course, we already know from Chapter 2.1T in the first volume that the sensation of "pitch" of an inharmonic spectrum does not so much depend on its lowest frequency component but rather on the amplitude and general distribution of all its components. Double-click on the **coll** to open its window and see the twelve 40-element lists sorted in ascending order based on the first element in the list.

The "gongs" are played by the [**poly~** p_gamelan_player 24] object. This object receives the list output by **live.step**, which is made up of the step number,

443

MIDI note and velocity. Notice that the signal output by the noise generator [rand~ 300] (the same that was used for ID_13_gongs.maxpat) is also sent to the poly~ object. Let's now take a look at the contents of the polyphonic patch (figure ID.34).

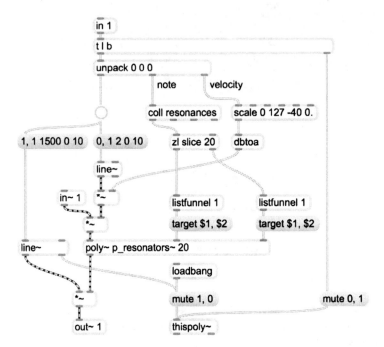

Fig. ID.34 The polyphonic patch p_gamelan_player

A list of three elements arrives from **live.step** in the main patch: the step number, note and velocity. The list is sent to a **trigger** object that deactivates the muting of the polyphonic patch instance and renders it busy; it thereafter sends the list to **unpack**. The MIDI velocity value is converted to dB and then to an amplitude multiplier in the same manner as in previous patches. This value is used as a multiplier for the brief envelope output by the **line~** object in the middle of the patch.

The note value (from 60 to 71) is used as an index number for [**coll** resonances] whose contents have been filled by the [**p** set_resonances] subpatch we analyzed, above. The frequency and duration values for the resonators are sent to the [**poly~** p_resonators 20] object, just like they were in ID_13_gongs.maxpat.

444

The envelope output by the **line~** object is scaled in amplitude by the value calculated from the velocity, and this is applied to the signal that is connected to the first inlet of the **poly~** object, via the [**in~** 1] object. [13] As we have already discussed, this signal is the noise produced by the [**rand~** 300] object in the main patch.

A second **line~** on the right is used to make a rapid fade out after 1.5 seconds (the maximum duration possible for any of our resonances), after which a bang will mute the instance and free it from being in the "busy" state. Listen once again to the various presets and try creating some new ones.

· ·

ACTIVITY

Try modifying the parameters used to generate the resonator settings in the [**p** set_resonance] subpatch, in order to create a different set of "gongs." Try creating very high-pitched, or very low-pitched gongs, gongs with long or short durations, or gongs with fewer or more frequency components. You may need to make some changes to the related parameters inside the poly-phonic patch.

· ·

CREATING SCORES WITH COLL

We are using the term "score" here not in relation to musical notation, but rather to mean a series of instructions distributed in time which activate and set parameters for synthesis algorithms and sound processing. With this definition, the term "score" has the same meaning as it does in Csound. However, whereas the Csound software requires the use of such a score, and therefore has a well-defined score format, Max does not have any predefined score format. Consequently Max has no object specifically designed for the purposes of score management. Therefore, what we need to do, in practice, is borrow the notion of a score from Csound and see how it could be implemented in Max.

For the following examples we will use the coll object, since it seems to be one of the more suitable objects for such a task. Needless to say, there are also other ways to obtain the same results, as is often the case when using Max.[14]

---

[13] As was already mentioned in section IC.3, it is possible to have both an **in** and an **in~** object with the same number. When we do this **poly~** will have a single inlet shared by both objects. The Max messages that are sent to this "double" inlet are sent to the in object, while the signals are sent to the **in~** object.

[14] Another object that is well suited for score management is the **qlist** object (although it will not be introduced here). We generally prefer **coll** because of its greater flexibility.

Open the patch **ID_16_score1.maxpat**, shown in figure ID.35.

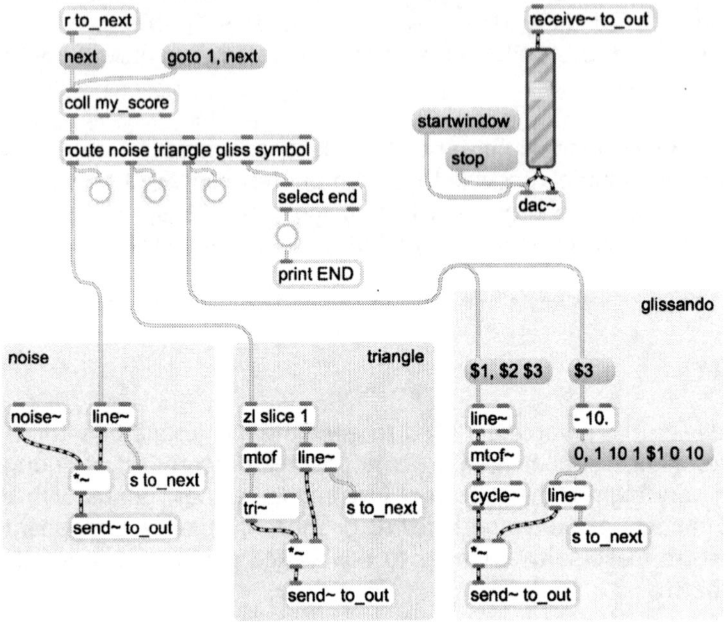

Fig. ID.35 The patch **ID_16_score1.maxpat**

First, turn on the patch and click on the [goto 1, next] message box that is connected to the [`coll` myscore] object. You should hear a series of sounds while the **button** objects connected to the **route** object "flash." Listen to this series of sounds several times before continuing further.

This patch contains three small instruments: a noise generator, a triangular oscillator and a sweeping sine wave glissando generator. The noise generator receives just the values for the envelope created by the **line~** object, the triangle wave oscillator receives a MIDI note value followed by the envelope values, and the glissando generator receives the starting note value, the destination note value and the duration of the glissando. The **coll** contains the following lines:

1, triangle 35 0 0 1 50 1 200 0 100;
2, triangle 84 0 0 1 2 0 350;
3, noise 0 0 0.2 1000 0.5 100 0 500;
4, gliss 48 52 1000;
5, gliss 80 24 500;
6, noise 0 0 1 10 0 250;
7, end;

Let's take a closer look at how this patch works. When we click on the [goto 1, next] message box, two messages are sent to the **coll** object. The first message "goto 1" positions the **coll** object's internal pointer to index number 1, but without causing the list at that index to be output. The second message, "next", causes coll to output the list at the index indicated by the "goto" message (if you do not remember how the coll object's "next", "prev" and "goto" messages work, please refer back to the ID_14_coll_sorting.maxpat which we analyzed, above).

The message output by coll is "triangle 35 0 0 1 50 1 200 0 100", which the route object routes to the instrument in the middle (albeit without the symbol "triangle" at the start of the message). We will not take the time to analyze this extremely simple instrument, but do take note that the right outlet of line~ is connected to a [s to_next] object, and the corresponding [r to_next] object is connected to the "next" message that is, in turn, connected to coll. This means that when the line~ object finishes its envelope it will send a bang to the "next" message causing coll to output its next list.

The other two instruments also similarly send a bang to the "next" message when their envelopes are finished. Therefore, each time a sound reaches its end, the next sound in the "score" is triggered. Take some time to analyze how the three instruments work, and carefully check the syntax of the lists that are sent by coll.

Note the last line contained in the coll object: "7, end;". As we have already learned, when a message consists of a single symbol, the coll object will precede it with the message name "symbol" when it is output. It is precisely for this reason that the last argument to the route object is "symbol" and the corresponding outlet is connected to the [select end] object which will output a bang when it receives this "end" message.

· ·

ACTIVITIES

• Add other lines to the score contained inside the coll, making sure that the resulting sounds were exactly what you expected to hear.

• Add a fourth instrument called "filtered_saw": a sawtooth oscillator with a lowpass filter. The instrument should be able to receive the filter cutoff frequency (expressed as a multiplier of the fundamental frequency) and Q factor, in addition to the note and envelope.

· ·

Naturally, this simple first implementation of a score in Max has some shortcomings. The first is that every sound is always played immediately after the previous one, so it is not possible to have a rest between notes (unless you create an envelope with silence at the end), nor is it possible to superimpose two sounds. The second inadequacy is not due to mechanism itself, but rather in how we are using it – defining every parameter in such a precise way for each note means that we will need to write considerably large scores even for short pieces of music. A third problem with this preliminary implementation is that it is very difficult to easily control the temporal placement of the events in the score.

Before we learn how these problems can be corrected, we will present a new object: **forward**. Rebuild the patch shown in figure ID.36.

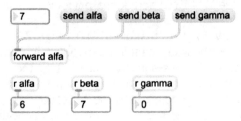

Fig. ID.36 The **forward** object

This object is a "variable send". In fact, just like the **send** object, it will also remotely send messages to the **receive** object(s) with the same name. However, the **forward** object is able to change its destination using the "send" message followed by the name of a **receive** object. Try this out by clicking on the "send beta" message box connected to **forward** and then send some numerical values using the number box. The values should arrive to the number box connected to the [**r** beta] object.

Now let's take a look at a new score management patch. Load the file **ID_17_score2.maxpat** (figure ID.37).

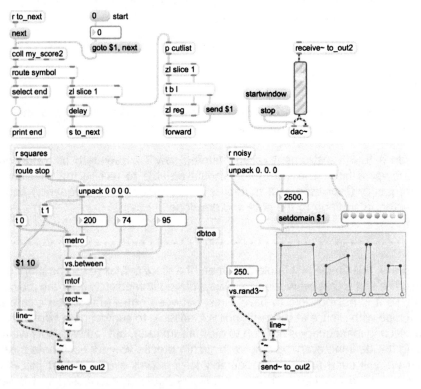

Fig. ID.37 The file **ID_17_score2.maxpat**

First, listen to the score by clicking on the [0] message box at the top of the patch. In this patch, there are two instruments: the first generates a series of random notes using a square wave oscillator, and the second generates noise with variable frequency using a choice of 8 envelopes stored in a **preset**.

Now open up the **coll** window and you should see the following score:

1, 2000 squares 125 48 73 -6;
2, 1000 noisy 2000 500 1 : squares 100 60 67 -12;
3, 1000 noisy 4000 1000 3 : squares 60 24 32 -12;
4, 1000 noisy 5000 3000 4 : squares stop;
5, 2000 squares 200 74 95 -18;
6, 0 noisy 250 2500 7 : squares stop;
7, end;

First, let's clarify some terminology. We will be using the term "event" to mean the contents of one line in the score; our score therefore has 7 events. Playback of the score can be started from any event by setting the event number in the number box connected to the [goto $1, next] message box at the top of the patch.

Note that we have also changed the syntax. The first value of each list is now the duration between events (in milliseconds), in other words, the amount of time it takes to go from one event to the next. After the duration we have the name of one of the **receive** objects connected to the instruments ("squares" or "noisy"), followed by its associated parameters. It is possible for an event to have multiple messages sent to multiple instruments, by separating them with the symbol ":" (colon).

The "squares" instrument needs to receive a list containing the tempo (or beat) of the random notes, the minimum and maximum values between which notes will be chosen, and the intensity in dB. To subsequently stop the random note playback, the instrument needs to receive the "stop" message (see line 4 and line 6 in the score).

The "noisy" instrument needs to receive a list containing the frequency of the noise generator, the duration of the envelope and the envelope preset number.

Because we have change the syntax of the score, the messages output by **coll** need to be processed in a slightly different way, compared with the previous patch. Here the messages are first sent to the **route** and **select** objects to intercept the "end" message that signals the end of the score. If the message is not "end", it must be a message that begins with a timing duration. This message is sent to the [**z1** slice 1] object that separates the duration (sent out the left outlet) from the rest of the message (sent out the right). This message is then sent to the [**p** cutlist] subpatch which subdivides it into multiple messages based on the position of the ":" symbol.

Let's see how this subpatch works (figure ID.38).

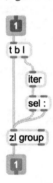

Fig. ID.38 The contents of the [p cutlist] subpatch

First, however, let's learn a new feature of the [zl group] object that we haven't talked about until now. We have already learned that this object groups the messages it receives into lists whose length is determined either by an argument or by a number sent to its right inlet. However, it is also possible to create lists with of a variable length using the bang message: each time the object receives a bang it will group together all of the elements that it has received and output them as a list. Notice that we have not specified a list length as an argument because the list length will be determined by the bangs that the object receives[15].

When this subpatch receives a list, it first sends it (via the right outlet of [t b l]) to the iter object which brakes it down into single elements (i.e., it iterates the list). The [sel :] object below then lets all elements except the ":" symbol pass through its right outlet; the colon, on the other hand will cause a bang to be sent out the left outlet, and this bang causes the [zl group] object to output a list made up of all the preceding elements. Because the list sent to the [p cutlist] subpach does not end with a colon (":"), we need to send an additional bang to output the final list. This bang comes from the left outlet of the [t b l] object at the top of the patch, after all the elements in the input list have already been sent to [zl group].

Returning to the main patch, the lists that are output by the [p cutlist] subpatch are made up of the name of a **receive** object and a series of parameters, as we previously mentioned. The name is used to set the destination of the **forward** object, and the parameters are then sent to that destination. Analyze the part of the patch underneath [p cutlist] and explain how it works.

Let's go back to the [zl slice 1] object connected to the right outlet of the **route** object. The duration value that comes out the left outlet of this object

---

15 If we do not send a bang, the object will output a list when it reaches the maximum possible list length (which is 256 by default).

is sent to the **delay** object which, as we already learned in section 6.11P, is a kind of "delay line" for the bang message. When this object receives a numerical value in its left inlet, it waits the corresponding time (in milliseconds) and then outputs a bang, which triggers the "next" message, telling coll to output its next list.

· ·

ACTIVITY

Analyze and describe how the two instruments in the patch ID_17_score2. maxpat work.

· ·

In this patch we have separated the event timing from the actual duration of the events themselves, as well as added the ability to send parameters to different instruments within a single event. We have also created some "macro-controls" for the instruments so that we do not need to define every single note or every single envelope breakpoint in the score.

Note that the starting point of each event depends on the sum of all the preceding durations. If a new event is added in the middle of a score, all the subsequent events will be displaced by an amount of time equal to the duration of that event (so they will happen later), unless, of course, we compensate for the new event by modifying the previous or later events in the score. Consequently, we need to try out a slightly different approach, creating an algorithm where the starting point of each event is independent of the preceding or following events.

Before continuing, we should take a look at a new object: timepoint. Reconstruct the patch shown in figure ID.39.

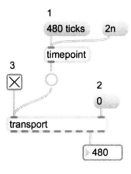

Fig. ID.39 The **timepoint** object

The **timepoint** object outputs a bang when the master clock that is controlled by the **transport** object reaches a predetermined point in time. This predefined position to be reached can be expressed in any of Max's time values and sent to **timepoint**'s inlet, or else be provided as an argument.[16]

In the patch shown in figure ID.39, click on the [480 ticks] message box, and then on the [0] message box in order to reset the master clock to start counting time from the beginning, and then turn on the **toggle**. After half a second[17] the **timepoint** object should output a bang and the number of ticks that have elapsed should be visible in the number box connected to the outlet of the **transport** object that reports the current time in ticks. Now, click on the [2n] message box and once again on the [0] message box – after one second, the number of ticks displayed should be 960. Try this out with other time values, not forgetting to reset the master clock to the beginning by clicking on the [0] message box.

It is because of this object that we are able to create our third score management patch. Open the file **ID_18_score3.maxpat** (figure ID.40).

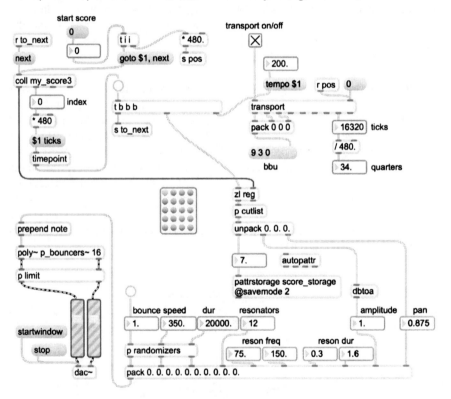

Fig. ID.40 The file **ID_18_score3.maxpat**

---

[16] See section IC.1 for more information about the time values in Max. If you do not remember the details of time management in Max, it might be a good idea to re-read the entire section.
[17] This duration was calculated based on the default metronome time of 120 bpm.

Here is the score contained in the [coll my_score3] object:

```
0, 1 -6 0.5;
2, 2 -3 0.75;
4, 3 -3 0.1 : 4 -3 0.9;
7, 4 -3 0.5;
8, 5 -3 0.25 : 6 0 0.5 : 7 -3 0.75;
11, 17 -6 0.5;
13, 17 -6 0.5;
14, 17 -6 0.5;
15, 17 -6 0.5;
16, 17 -6 0.5;
18, 16 -9 0.5;
21, 16.25 -9 0.5;
24, 16.5 -9 0.5;
27, 16.75 -12 0.5;
30, 17 -6 0.5 : 11 -6 0.1 : 11 -6 0.9;
34, 8 0 0 : 8 0 0.5 : 8 0 1 : 7 0 0.125 : 7 0 0.875;
```

First, listen to the patch by clicking on the [0] message box at the top.

There is just one instrument that creates bouncing resonant body sounds; the algorithm for this has been taken from the IC_10_poly_bouncing_bodies.max-pat patch. We have limited ourselves to using just one instrument in order to focus our attention on the time management aspects of this patch. The patch has 20 presets, each of which uses **pattrstorage** to store the first 8 parameters for the instrument. The amplitude and stereo position, on the other hand, are defined in the score. Each sound is therefore defined by a preset number, an amplitude value (in dB) and a position in the stereo field (a value between 0 and 1). The index number represents the starting time of the event expressed in quarter notes. Notice that the **transport** object on the right hand side of the patch has been set to a tempo of 200 bpm (equal to a metronome mark of 200).

Let's see how the patch works. After clicking on the message box at the top of the patch, the value 0 is sent to the right inlet of the **transport** (via the [s pos] and [r pos] objects). As we have already discussed, this resets the master clock to its starting point. The "goto 0" message followed by "next" is then sent to the **coll** object, which consequently outputs the index number via its second outlet followed by the list defining the event out its left outlet. The index number, which represents the starting time of the event expressed in quarter notes, as mentioned earlier, is transformed into ticks and sent to the **timepoint** object, while the list defining the event is stored in the [z1 reg] object.

As soon as the master clock reaches the point in time corresponding to the index value, the **timepoint** object will output a bang and send it to a **trigger** object. This **trigger** outputs three bangs: the first is connected to the

453

transport object and is used to display the current time, the second is sent to the [z1 reg] object which sends the list defining the event to the [p cutlist] subpatch (identical to the one in the previous example). From this subpatch, the three instrument parameters (preset, amplitude in dB and stereo position) are sent to an unpack object that sends the values to their associated number box. The third bang output by trigger is sent to the "next" message in the upper-left-hand corner of the patch, telling coll to output the next event.

Note that parameters labeled "bounce speed" (initial and final rebound frequency) and "dur" (duration of the series of rebounds) in the lower part of the patch are sent to the [p randomizers] subpatch that randomly varies the parameters by 10%. This is used to make sure that two sounds played at the same time by a single preset are not exactly the same, otherwise they would be perceived as a single resonant body. Open the [p randomizers] subpatch and take a moment to reverse-engineer how it works.

Let's return to the score listing for a moment. You should have noticed that events 21, 24 and 27 have a fractional preset value. This takes advantage of the pattrstorage object's ability to interpolate between two adjacent presets. Concerning this interpolation, if you open up the pattrstorage client window you will see that the interpolation for the "min_freq" and "max_freq" parameters (defining the minimum and maximum resonant frequency) as well as "min_speed" and "max_speed" (minimum and maximum speed, or frequency, for the rebounds) has been set to exponential, and not linear (as it is by default). Since these parameters relate to frequency, using exponential interpolation gives a more natural perception when interpolating.

Also, you should notice that the priority assigned to the "min_speed" parameter here in the client window has a higher value (6) than the priority of the other parameters (0). As we already discussed in section ID.1, lower values have priority over higher ones, meaning that in this case we can be assured that the "min_speed" parameter will be sent last. This is necessary because this parameter is sent to the "hot" inlet of the pack object and should therefore arrive after the other parameters have already been set.

Finally, it goes without saying that the fact that we have defined our tempo in quarter notes is completely arbitrary. We could always transform quarter notes into eighth notes by multiplying the value output via the second outlet of coll by 240 instead of 480, or by multiplying it by 120 to obtain sixteenth notes – try it!

ACTIVITIES

- Add other instruments to the patch ID_18_score3.maxpat and use the **forward** object to send the parameters to the different instruments.

- It is possible to use any kind of time value with the **timepoint** object, as has already been stated. For example, we could use a time in bbu (which is format-ted as a character string such as 01.03.120; see section IC.1). In the score, try to replace the single numerical values we used as an index with values in bbu format. You will obviously need to make other changes to the patch, accord-ingly.

- Remember that when the index is not a numerical value but a string (or symbol), the **coll** object will output it preceded by the message "symbol". Because it has two decimal point characters, the bbu format is not considered a numerical value, but rather a symbol so you will need to use the **route** object to filter out the message name "symbol".

• •

LIST OF MAX OBJECTS

autopattr
allows the **pattrstorage** object to "see" the named interface objects in a patch.

bpatcher
an object that can load an abstraction or subpatch and display all or part of it inside its parent patch.

coll
an object that allows data sets (lists, numbers, or symbols) to be indexed and stored.

forward
similar to the **send** object, but capable of changing its sending destination

patcherargs
allows argument and attribute management inside a subpatch or abstraction.

pattr
a universal data container (that can store numerical values, lists or symbols) which is able to share its contents with Max interface objects.

pattrstorage
allows saving presets and offers advanced control over them. It saves the values contained in **pattr** objects and, when an **autopattr** object is present, also inside named interface objects.

route
compares the initial element of an input list with its own arguments. If the element is the same as one of the arguments, the object will send the rest of the list out the outlet corresponding to the position of the argument.

table
stores and manages an array of integers

timepoint
outputs a bang when the master clock reaches a predefined point in time.

vs.randlist
outputs a list of random values

LIST OF ATTRIBUTES, ARGUMENTS AND MESSAGES AND COMMANDS FOR SPECIFIC MAX OBJECTS

autopattr
- autoname (attribute)
When this attribute is enabled, the **autopattr** object will automatically assign a scripting name to every interface object present in the patch.

-autorestore (attribute)
When a patch containing **autopattr** is saved, this attribute allows the data contained in the object to be recalled each time the patch is opened.

bpatcher
- Argument(s) (attribute)
Using this attribute, it is possible to provide a list of arguments and attributes to the abstraction loaded by **bpatcher**.

- Embed Patcher in Parent or embed (attribute)
By enabling this attribute, it is possible to create a subpatch inside a **bpatcher**.

- Patcher File (attribute)
Contains the file patch of the abstraction that will be loaded by **bpatcher**.

coll
- embed (attribute)
Allows the contents of a coll to be saved together with a patch.

- goto (message)
Positions the **coll** at a given index

- next (message)
Runs through the lists stored in a **coll** in a forward direction

- prev (message)
Runs through the lists stored in a **coll** in a backward direction

- renumber (message)
Renumbers the indices of a **coll** using consecutive increasing values

- sort (message)
Re-orders the contents of a **coll** either alphabetically or numerically.

forward
- send (message)
Lets you change the destination of messages sent to the **forward** object.

pattr
- autorestore (attribute)
This attribute tells the **pattr** object to save its current values when a patch containing it is saved. This data is recalled each time that the saved patch is opened.

- bindto (attribute)
Establishes a link (or binding) between a **pattr** and an interface object that has been given a scripting name

- parent::
A possible prefix for the second argument of all **pattr** objects. This prefix indicates that the interface object bound to it is located one level up in the patch hierarchy – in other words in the patch which contains the subpatch.

- scripting name (attribute)
The first argument to **pattr** becomes its scripting name. If no scripting name is provided, one is automatically assigned by Max.

pattrstorage
- read (message)
this message lets you read a saved preset file

- recall (message)
lets you interpolate between two non-consecutive presets

- savemode (attribute)
Attribute indicating the saving mode of the presets

- write (message)
this message lets you save a group of presets to disk in a .json file
The "write" message can be optionally followed by a file name, and you can always save several different sets of presets in different .json files.

preset
- clear (message)
Command, followed by a preset number, which can be sent to the **preset** object's inlet. This is used to delete a preset.

- clearall (message)
Command that can be sent to the **preset** object's inlet to delete all presets.

- pattrstorage (attribute)
This attribute can be used to give a name to a **pattrstorage** object. In this way, both **preset** and **pattrstorage** can share the same data.

- store (message)
Command sent to the **preset** object's inlet that can be used to store a preset.

table
- refer (message)
Allows the table to point to (access) the contents of another table.

- Save Data With Patcher (attribute)
Allows the contents of a table to be saved together with the patch.

- Table Range (attribute)
Sets the range of values displayed by the table

- Table Size (attribute)
Sets the size of the table (i.e., the number of elements it contains).

LIST OF IMPORTANT COMMANDS

Change the part of the abstraction displayed in the bpatcher
Drag the cursor inside the **bpatcher** while holding down the Control-shift (Windows) or Command-Shift (Mac) keys.

Display the contents of the original abstraction in a bpatcher
Right-click (Windows) or Control-click (Mac) on a **bpatcher** in edit mode causes a contextual menu to appear; select the "Object/Open Original..." item at the bottom of this menu.

GLOSSARY

Client window
The window that shows the preset values stored in the **pattrstorage** object.

File ".json"
The file where the entire group of presets from a **pattrstorage** object is saved. By default it uses the name of the **pattrstorage** object (its first argument) followed by the ".json" suffix.

8T
THE ART OF ORGANIZING SOUND: MOTION PROCESSES

PREREQUISITES FOR THE CHAPTER
- THE CONTENTS OF VOLUME 1, CHAPTERS 5, 6 AND 7 (THEORY AND PRACTICE), INTERLUDE C AND D

OBJECTIVES
Knowledge
- TO KNOW THE VARIOUS POSSIBLE MODALITIES OF SOUND MOTION
- TO KNOW THE INTER-RELATIONSHIP BETWEEN DIFFERENT TYPES OF MOTION
- TO KNOW THE TYPES OF MOTION THAT CAN BRING OUT A PERCEPTUAL TRANSITION BETWEEN ONE PARAMETER AND ANOTHER
- TO KNOW SOME DIFFERENT POSSIBILITIES FOR MOTION INSIDE TIMBRE
- TO KNOW THE LIMITS AND AMBIGUITIES CONCERNING THE CATEGORIZATION OF MOTION

CONTENTS
- SIMPLE, COMPLEX AND COMPOUND MOTION
- MOTION SEQUENCES
- TYPES OF MOTION WITHIN A TIMBRE

ACTIVITIES
- SOUND EXAMPLES AND INTERACTIVE EXAMPLES

TESTING
- LISTENING AND ANALYSIS TEST WITH SHORT ANSWERS (MAXIMUM 30 WORDS)

SUPPORTING MATERIALS
- FUNDAMENTAL CONCEPTS - GLOSSARY

The domain where music takes form is a heavily spatialized temporality. But to be clear: music does not thereby become visual; it exists and persists wholly within the ear. Nonetheless, its organization and logic-based connections come into our minds via the visual world – the world of space. [...] We thus find ourselves confronting the very breath of matter itself.
(Salvatore Sciarrino, 1998)

Our principal metaphor for musical composition must change from one of architecture to one of chemistry. [...] This shift in emphasis is as radical as possible – from a finite set of carefully chosen archetypal properties governed by traditional "architectural" principles, to a continuum of unique sound events and the possibility to stretch, mould and transform this continuum in any way we choose, to build new worlds of musical connectedness.
(Trevor Wishart, 2004)

– to compose no longer with notes but with sounds;
– to no longer compose only sounds but the differences that distinguish them from one another;
– to act on these differences – namely, to control the evolution (or the non-evolution) of the sound and the speed of this evolution;
(Gerard Grisey, 2001)

8.1 WHAT ARE MOTION PROCESSES?

INTRODUCTION
Up until now we have been creating single sounds or even sequences of sounds without any particular inclination to explore how they can be artfully organized into larger forms. From this point onward we will begin to work on the sounds' various possible articulations, as well as their motion. This chapter (alongside the corresponding practice chapter) is designed to further enhance the theoretical knowledge and practical skills you have learned thus far (both in terms of sound analysis and listening as well as in terms of programming), and to bring out your creativity and capacity to build motion processes. As already mentioned in the introduction to this volume, we will limit ourselves to sound articulations under one minute in duration, exploring an intermediate area between the micro-form inherent in individual sounds, and the macro-form of an entire sound composition.[1] In this chapter we will therefore discuss the motion processes of sound independently of a more extensive formal scope and context, namely that of an actual sound composition. This does not necessarily mean that your creative process needs to follow this sequence (from the creation of individual sounds, to motion processes followed by the construction

---

[1] The term "composition" is being used here to mean an activity and experience that goes beyond just musical composition in the literal sense, but also encompasses works of sound art, sound design, audio-visual works, soundtracks, soundscapes, etc.

of an overall compositional form), but nonetheless this progressive order works well from a purely pedagogical perspective.

In practice, every sound artist follows his or her own way of building a sonic form in time and/or space, whether that means starting from the project as a whole, working on the detailed specification of its sound components at a later stage, working at all structural levels simultaneously or actually entrusting the computer to make some of the formal choices.

For the creation of interactive installations (even those that exist online), the compositional forms used may not take on specific predetermined shapes, so the purpose of the composer/artist in such a context is to design an interactive environment where the form is constantly recalculated, based on the choices of users inside that environment.

Finally, a sound designer who wants to create sounds destined for moving image, interactive games, and the like, will have to make formal decisions that relate to environments created by others, or developed by third parties.

All of the topics covered in this chapter should be beneficial for any type of creative sound work regardless of its eventual intended purpose. When composing, constructing and processing timbres right down to the minutest detail, it is actually very important to know how to create and manage the various structural levels (from the micro to the macro) relative to the goals of the creative project at hand. Therefore it is also important to know how to listen to and evaluate the results, by "zooming" in and out from one level to another. Horacio Vaggione speaks of this as "an action/perception feedback loop".[2] "As a painter who works directly on a canvas must step back some distance to perceive the result of his or her action, validating it in a variety of spatial perspectives, so must the composer dealing with different time scales.[3] This being so, a new category must be added to the action/perception feedback loop, a kind of 'shifting hearing' allowing the results of operations to be checked at many different time scales. Some of these time scales are not audible directly and need to be validated perceptually by their effects over other (higher) time scales."[4]

One such shift in hearing is going from listening to individual sounds as independent units, to listening to the motion inherent in the sounds themselves. By listening in this way, we are able to notice the effects of sounds by "observing"

---

[2] *"The meaning of any compositional technique, or any chunk of musical knowledge, arises from its function in support of a specific musical action, which in turn has a strong bearing on the question of how this action is perceived. Action and perception lie at the heart of musical processes, as these musical processes are created by successive operations of concretization having as a tuning tool – as a principle of reality – an action/perception feedback loop."* (Vaggione, 2001, p.61)
[3] We could also extend this idea further by adding: "and in space."
[4] *(Vaggione, 2001, p.60)*

them from a slightly higher structural level, but not so high that we "look at" them in the context of an entire creative work. We will confront some higher formal and temporal levels in the next volume, and begin to define ideas and/ or projects in terms of their form. Nonetheless, both the theory and practice sections of this chapter are designed to help you develop a "mobile" sense of listening and the ability to set an action/perception feedback loop into motion within the context of your own knowledge, skills and creativity.

MOTION PROCESSES

Motion Processes are evolutions within sound that happen via variations in spectrum or space or which can occur through interactions between these and other parameters.[5]

There can be multiple types of motion (even contrasting or ambiguous ones) within a single sound sequence, so it is very important for anyone working with sound to learn how to control and create complex motion sequences that evolve from an organic combination of simple types of motion, and lead to the creation of rich sonic environments. In this chapter (and in the corresponding practice chapter) we will offer the reader some different technical approaches that may be taken in order to create the kinds of sounds exemplified by the types of motion being described.

---

[5] This term was adapted from an article by Denis Smalley (Smalley 1986), and is fundamental to understanding the compositional process in electronic (and other kinds of) music. For Smalley, motion processes are processes of evolution within sound that can happen through variations in spectrum or space, or by the interaction of these and other parameters. The point of view from which Smalley observes motion in sound is not a technological one – he does not even touch upon electroacoustic processes and techniques used for the production of music. His emphasis focuses on concentrated listening and the aspects of sound that emerge from such listening. The terminology that Smalley uses to describe the different types of sonic motion can also be useful to help us better understand and listen to pieces of electroacoustic music with greater awareness, even though they may not have a printed score. (Naturally this also applies to composing such music, for those who have the skill and desire to do so.) However, there is one important difference between Smalley's notion and ours: from our perspective, motion processes are not merely considered from a listening point of view, but also from a technical-creative one. The upshot of this is that the idea of something like unidirectional motion, from our standpoint, does not simply represent an audibly recognizable increase or decrease in frequency, for example, but rather a general increase from lower to higher values (or vice-versa) in different perceptually relevant domains, such as frequency, duration, amplitude, etc. In this way, unidirectional motion can be understood in the broadest possible terms: transversal movement in relation to its parameters. The task of separating all the parameters in a sound, although extremely useful when listening to a piece analytically, must give way to expectations of complexity and interrelationships of sounds within the field of sound creation; these ideas will be developed further in the chapter dedicated to sound creation in the next volume. The technical and compositional purposes of this book lead us to work within an essentially different process than that of Smalley's concept of "spectromorphology". Therefore, our purpose in listening to sounds is not to arrive at a definition of their characteristics and possible evolution in time, but rather to begin with definitions and listening in tandem with one another, in order to work toward the creation of sonic motion.

Nonetheless, you should be aware that you may find yourself confronted with examples whose motion may have a very different sense when defined from a technical perspective than it would when observed from a perceptual standpoint. This should not actually pose any problems, per se, but rather offer an opportunity to contemplate how one is constantly in contact with contradictions and ambiguities while in the act of organizing sound[6], and that getting to know and accepting these elements will provide richness and multiple levels of meaning to your work.

However, our aim here is not to build a regular and coherent theory, but to take an open, interactive educational approach (even sometimes a problematic one) where the reader can genuinely and practically begin to take his/her first steps and eventually venture out to make his/her own choices and discoveries.

Naturally, it is important to understand that, from a creative perspective, our goals, methods and ways of looking at the parameters and properties of sound are also sometimes very different from those when dealing with sound from a physical point of view.

For example, during the process of creating a musical work we are able to pass from the time domain to the frequency domain with ease. Furthermore, where perception is concerned (and hence also where music is concerned), we tend to mix parameters of highly differing natures, passing through different notions of time and space and exploring the boundaries between one property of sound and another. Therefore, in order to be able to talk about the art of organizing sound, we need to mix different approaches in a way that would be irreconcilable for a scientist (because the necessary leaps in logic could neither be formulated nor verified by any kind of scientific method) so we will need to review some of the concepts that we have learned in previous chapters from a broader perspective (or at least less rigorously from a technical stance), but one which is closer to the approach which needs to be taken by composers, sound artists and sound designers. In particular, we will consider frequency, amplitude and duration to be basic parameters whose organization in time gives way to other, more complex sound properties such as timbre, rhythm and spatialization. Often, we will find ourselves moving from one to the other smoothly without a break, since this chapter has been designed to provide an experiential path to be followed. Even the categories that will be introduced here should only serve as points of reference to help you better understand their limits and boundaries.

---

[6] This is the broadest term we can use to describe creating and giving structure to sound using new technologies. It was coined by Leigh Landy in his influential book (Landy 2007), and also relates to the concept of "organized sound" proposed by Edgar Varèse.

MOTION CATEGORIES

We have chosen to use just a few categories, organized in increasing order of complexity:

Simple Motion
 - motion resulting from changes in the values of just one parameter of one sound

Complex Motion (which contains simple motions)
 - motion resulting from changes in the values of several of a sound's parameters

Compound Motion (which could also contain simple and/or complex motions)
 - motion characterized by changes in the values of the parameters of several sounds

Motion Sequences (which could contain any type of motion)
 - a series of motions which relate to one another

These categories are not absolute and unconditional – they are simply based on conventions which we have adopted, and many "gray-zones" exist in-between them. Let's take a look at a couple of examples of these kinds of ambiguous areas.

1) **Ambiguity arising from the distinction between motion in one sound (simple and complex motion)** and motion in several sounds (compound motion). What, precisely, is a single sound? This entirely depends on our perception of that sound – some sounds (the sound of the sea, for example) can either be considered a single sonic element or a composite sound made up of several simultaneous autonomous units (such as the sound of waves). The intentions of the person working with the sound should also be taken into consideration: a sound with many components can move as a single object, or the parameters controlling its various components can be moved separately.

A sound recorded to an audio file or originating from an algorithm could also contain compound motion but if we deal with the sound as a single unit, such as changing its overall intensity, this motion could be considered to be simple because it acts on just one of the sound's parameters. On the other hand, if we separately affect the various individual sounds that make up the composite sound, we would be creating compound motion.[7]

2) **Ambiguity between simple and complex motion within a system that it is in and of itself complex.** Let's take the use of filters as an example. If we add a filter with an upward-moving cutoff frequency to a sound, the movement of this filter is an example of simple motion, since just one parameter is being changed. Obviously, when the user creates this kind of simple motion, what goes on *inside* the filter is something much more complex.

---

[7] The concept of the "objet sonore" (sound object), theorized by Pierre Schaeffer, could also give rise to this same ambiguity, so we prefer not to introduce this concept at the present time.

The same thing happens in a stereo spatialization system: the motion from one extreme to the other, using a panning parameter from 0 to 1 is simple in that we use just one simple line segment to move the sound from one side to the other. However, it is simple *only* if we do not take into consideration what is happening inside the panner, which is actually a double control over the intensities of the left and right channels, inversely proportional to one another. For practical and logical reasons these motions are included in the first category.

Vaggione observes that "some types of representation that are valid on one level cannot always retain their pertinence when transposed to another level. Thus, multi-level operations do not exclude fractures, distortions, and mismatches between the levels. To face these mismatches, a multi-syntactical strategy is 'composed.'"[8]

For this reason, paradoxically, we have divided the types of motion into categories in order to be able to highlight the gray-zones – the areas of overlap – that we run into every step of the way when learning and practicing electronic music and sound design. The notions that follow should therefore not be taken as law, nor are they intended to be exhaustive (something virtually impossible in the field of sound research). They are simply intended to provide a journey into sound and its different kinds of motion in order to help you acquire a deeper awareness of them – this is a prerequisite for those who want to venture into the art of sound organization.

Now that we have briefly described the most thorny aspects and limitations relating to the formalization of the structural levels, we can finally begin to describe the various motion processes themselves.

8.2 SIMPLE MOTION

Simple motion refers to the evolution within a sound that results from modifying the values of just one parameter.

SIMPLE UNIDIRECTIONAL MOTION

Simple **unidirectional** motion is a result of parameter values being changed in one direction, such as going from lower values to higher values, or from higher to lower. Let's take a look at some examples:

UNIDIRECTIONAL MOTION – FREQUENCY
Here we will examine ascending (or descending) frequential motion within a harmonic sound making a glissando from 200 to 2000 Hz (or vice-versa). This kind of motion can result from using a line segment or an exponential, logarithmic, or other type of curve, depending on the kind of shape we want to impose on the motion itself. The motion could even take place in steps, using

---

[8] Vaggione, 2001.

a discrete system (i.e., a non-continuous one), such as one that makes use of a sample and hold mechanism to sample the ascending ramp at regular intervals.

It is also possible to create ascending (or descending) motion via an increase (or decrease) in frequency band, such as when white noise is filtered with a band-pass filter with an ascending (or descending) center frequency and high Q value.

• •

SOUND EXAMPLE 8A.1 • *Simple Unidirectional Motion – Frequency*

  - A harmonic (synth) sound whose frequency increases in steps

• •

UNIDIRECTIONAL MOTION – DURATION AND RHYTHM
Seen from a broader perspective, unidirectional motion can also be used to affect other parameters of a sound, in addition to frequency. Using Stockhausen's idea of a continuum between formal durations (i.e., the structures defining musical form, ranging from 15 minutes down to 8 seconds), rhythmic durations (from 8 seconds to 1/16 of a second) and oscillations (i.e., waveform periods rang-ing from 1/16 of a second to a 4200th of a second and beyond)[9], we can thus interpret the raising or lowering of pitch not simply as an increase or decrease in the number of cycles per second, but rather as the speeding up or slowing down of a rhythm. There is one fundamental difference between the parameter for duration and the parameters for frequency and amplitude. Durations are not variable in time if the sound itself is not repeated – a long sound followed by a shorter sound, for instance – whereas frequency and amplitude can both change over time within a single sound. Duration, being the most complex parameter of rhythm, which itself can be defined as the organization of the durations of sounds and silences in time, can nonetheless be variable in time when applied to a group of homogenous sounds, and not just a single sound. From this point of view, motion that lengthens and shortens sounds' durations, as well as that which accelerates and decelerates rhythms will be considered as simple motion.

It should also be noted that the idea of rhythm is being used here not only in the classic sense, where it generally associated with one or more regular pulses and an overall meter. Our definition of rhythm can obviously also include poly-rhythms (different rhythms which are superimposed on one another), regular rhythms with internal irregularities and even completely irregular rhythms, in addition to regular rhythms. Such a broad definition lets us explore rhythm along a continuum ranging from extreme regularity on one end to extreme irregularity "in which the organization of durations is independent of any

---

[9] These ideas (with slight variations in the numbers used) are described in the (Stockhausen, 1976) article.

reference to a pulse (and thus considered to have an 'indefinite tempo' or 'free rhythm')" (Giannattasio, 1992, p.108), on the other. Therefore, when talking about rhythm, we need to define it in a very broad and all-inclusive way. One such interesting definition has been provided by Meyer and Cooper: "Rhythm is defined as our ability to mentally group or ungroup events that are close or far from each other in terms of pitch, time, timbre, space, etc." (Meyer and Cooper, 1960).

Of course there are limits to these definitions. For instance, there exist some rhythmic constructions whose temporal grid is so large (one pulse every 30 seconds, for example) or so constricted (such as pulsations 10 thousandths of a second apart) that it becomes impossible to mentally group the events together. In these cases, the perception of rhythm is lost entirely and we consequently enter into the domains of other sound properties or parameters.

In music which has "free rhythm" (as is the case with a lot of electroacoustic music), the organization of durations, even when organized according to a given temporal musical logic, is effectively released from actual (regular) rhythmic influences (Giannattasio, 1992, pp.108-109).

Let's now take a look at some examples of unidirectional motion in rhythm.

If we cause the frequency of sounds being generated to smoothly glide upward (or downward) via a line segment (or exponential or other type of curve) we can create an increasing rhythmic motion (an accelerando) or a decreasing one (rallentando). When creating increasing rhythmic motion, we could end up superimposing some events when their individual durations are greater than the beats of the rhythmic pulse itself. Where irregular or free rhythms are concerned, any increase (or decrease) in motion could be defined by an increase or decrease in the overall density of events.

Another increase or decrease in rhythm could be implemented using multiple delays on a click sound, where the delay time progressively increases (or decreases) between one delay and the next. From a technical perspective, this kind of realization would require setting the delay times beforehand, so it does not actually consist of varying a parameter in time. Nonetheless, from a perceptual point of view, it still allows us to obtain an increase or decrease in rhythm.

One other possibility would be to use a loop on a small section of a longer sound, and gradually shorten (or lengthen) the loop little by little, so the number of repetitions per second of the fragment progressively changes as it loops.[10] (See sound example 8A.2.)

Let's now take a look at some examples of unidirectional motion of durations.

---

[10] See also chapter 5.4, interactive example 5I - PRESET 6 – from blocks to grains.

If we repeatedly generate a sound every 250 milliseconds and decrease its duration from 250 milliseconds down to 1 millisecond while keeping its rhythm steady, thereby increasing the duration of the rests, the sound will become transformed into a click. Conversely, we could increase the sound's duration, thereby obtaining superimposed sounds.

. . . .

SOUND EXAMPLE 8A.2 • Rhythmic accelerando or rallentando

a) The attack of an electric bass sound with multiple slowing-down delays (rallentando)
b) Using a progressively shortening loop to increase the number of repetitions per second

. . . .

PLANAR MOTION AT THE BEGINNING OR END OF UNIDIRECTIONAL MOTION
As an extension of this idea, unidirectional motion could also include motion where an increase in frequency or amplitude ends (or begins) with planar motion (i.e., where the values are more or less static), or else where decreasing motion ends with planar motion. An example of this kind of frequency portamento can be found in a passage from *Glissandi* by Ligeti.[11]

. . . .

SOUND EXAMPLE 8A.3 • Planar motion at the beginning or end of
unidirectional motion
a) Portamento: a glissando ending with planar motion
b) Rhythmic portamento: bass sounds with an initially stable rhythm; after several seconds the number of attacks per second decreases

. . . .

COMPLEXITY WITHIN SIMPLE UNIDIRECTIONAL MOTION

Simple unidirectional motion could at first seem rather banal. However, from a listening perspective the result of this basic motion can often be somewhat more interesting. Nonetheless, even when only one parameter is modified from a technical perspective, it could result in a sensation of motion within other parameters, or even the transformation of one parameter into another. Let's look at some examples.

---

[11] See Ligeti, G., CD Wergo 60161-50, from 1'58" to 2'02".

FROM RHYTHM TO TIMBRE

By listening to a 1 second sound file in a loop, and playing each repetition of the loop with a shorter and shorter duration, we can create an increase in rhythm. However, when the duration of the loop goes down to the zone between 80 and 50 milliseconds, any perception of rhythm is lost, due to the loop's extreme speed, and we enter into a perceptual dimension where the repetitions become an attribute of timbre, exhibiting aspects of roughness.

• •

SOUND EXAMPLE 8A.4 • Progressively increasing rhythm, with a perceptual transformation from the rhythm domain to the timbre domain[12]

-   Shortening a loop of a vocal sound from 24 ms. to 0.5 ms.

• •

Similarly, a looped sound file whose playback speed becomes increasingly faster can also used for such a perceptual transformation. Even though we are only modifying the values of one parameter unidirectionally from a technical point of view, the perceptual result is much more complex. So what, precisely, do we hear? The result is an audible modification of two parameters: an increase in frequency and an accelerando in rhythm. As the rhythm slowly speeds up, little by little, the perception of the accelerating rhythm passes from the rhythm domain to an ambiguous area between rhythm and the timbre of a continuous sound finally arriving at a pure timbre.

• •

SOUND EXAMPLE 8A.5 • Progressively increasing the playback speed of a sound file

a) Looped vocal sound with constantly increasing frequency (ratio from 1 to 16)
b) Looped rhythmical fragment played back with increasing frequency (ratio from 1 to 80)

• •

Regarding these two examples, the source sound is that of a voice, and the output sound has been transformed. Note that there are several different stages relating to the recognizability of the initial sound and the final transformed sound: at first, the modified sound is recognizable, and at the end of the transformation

---

[12] In the last part of the sound, you may notice that a random interplay of the final fragments has been added in order to improve the sound quality. However, the essential part of the sound demonstrating the passage from rhythm to timbre has been left unmodified.

it is totally unrecognizable. In this regard, Alain Savouret [13] makes a distinction between a "transformation based on the source" and a "transformation based on a process." In the former, an output sound has a strong connection with its source sound, thus a relationship can be perceived between the two. However, in the latter type of transformation, the output sound is dictated more by the process applied to it than the content of the source, resulting in no perceptible relationship between them. Nonetheless, we should consider these to be the two extremes of a continuum, and therefore numerous other possibilities exist in-between; even when listening to these two examples we can perceive these intermediate zones. On the other hand, if we only listen to the initial and final parts of the sounds, there seems to be an enormous distance between them, and hence there is no recognizable relationship between them. When creating, composing and designing sounds, you should also take into consideration that even when the transformation of a sound is based on the process, intermediate sounds may also be used in order to help the listener mentally reconstruct the path that goes from a recognizable sound, such as the voice, for instance, to a totally abstract sound like a heavily processed vocal sound.

FROM RHYTHM TO PITCH

If we create an impulse or click (i.e., a single sample with an amplitude value of 1) every tenth of a second, we perceive a regular rhythm. However, when we increase the frequency of impulse generation, we will lose any sensation of single clicks once we enter the audible frequency range (from 20 Hz upward), and will begin to perceive a single low pitch with a continuously upward glissando.

· ·

SOUND EXAMPLE 8A.6 • Planar motion followed by a progressively
increasing rhythm created by an impulse

- Single sample with amplitude of 1 repeated with an increasingly faster rhythm, and with decreasing rests until it becomes a single long, continuous sound.

· ·

---

[13] Cited in Wishart, 1994, p.24.

FROM PITCH TO TIMBRE
If we ramp the frequency of a sine wave from 20000 Hz to 20 Hz over the span of 10 milliseconds we get an inharmonic impulse. This can also be done in an ascending direction.

· ·

SOUND EXAMPLE 8A.7 • Fast unidirectional frequency motion

- Five descending glissandos with durations of 10, 20, 30, 40 and 80 ms.

· ·

FROM THE RHYTHM OF OSCILLATORY MOTION IN INTENSITY TO PITCH
If we create two harmonic sounds of equal frequency and very slowly ramp up the frequency of one of them by a few Hertz, as the difference between the two frequencies slowly increases, the rhythm of the beating caused by this minuscule difference also increases.[14] In this case, by altering just one parameter (frequency) with simple unidirectional motion, the changes in this parameter can only be perceived via the rhythms resulting from the oscillatory movement of another parameter (amplitude/intensity).

As we have already learned (see section 2.2T and P), once a certain distance between the frequencies has been exceeded, we are no longer capable of perceiving individual beats and their rhythm, but only sense the interference between the two waves, perceiving a general "roughness" in the sound – something quite complex to define from a perceptual perspective – since both a sense of pitch and timbre are involved. Further increasing the difference allows us to finally perceive the two sounds separately. Considering the starting and ending points of the unidirectional motion from a perceptual point of view, the sound goes from an increase in rhythm resulting from an oscillation in amplitude, to an increase in frequency difference between two sounds.
The three examples above help us to understand that there are actually many intermediate zones between one parameter and another and that an in-depth study of motion in sound can help us overcome the rigidity that often results from only studying this subject from a technical standpoint.

SIMPLE RECIPROCAL MOTION

Similarly to Smalley's definition of the same term, we consider **simple reciprocal motion** to mean unidirectional motion that is balanced by a return motion. This kind of motion can be either symmetric or asymmetric.

---

[14] In this case the perceived frequency changes. On the other hand, if the two (initially equal) frequencies moved symmetrically in opposite directions, the perceived frequency would remain the same while beating takes place, and therefore the only parameter that would seem to change would be the rhythm of the beating itself.

ASYMMETRIC RECIPROCAL MOTION
If we listen to the sound of individual waves of the sea, and try to mentally separate the individual parameters that the waves are composed of, we can determine a relatively quick expansion of the sound (until the wave breaks) and then slower reductions in the spectral band. This is an example of asymmetric reciprocal motion. Since we naturally recognize the source as the sound of the sea, our perception tends to associate the two stages of the sound – the more energetic sound and its subsidence – so we are consequently also able to distinguish the different waves from one another.

To simulate this sound, we could simply start with white noise that is filtered by a lowpass filter, creating a glissando in the cutoff frequency, first ascending and then descending back to its starting point, being careful to design non-symmetrical attack and release times. We could even apply this filtering envelope to other types of sounds such as the sound of a motorcycle engine, for example. Finally, we could also extract the envelope from an actual ocean wave sound using an envelope follower and apply it to a harmonic sound such as that of a choir or guitar arpeggio. Naturally, the characteristic asymmetry of waves could be reversed and we would lose any sense of imitating the sound of the sea, while still retaining an overall sense of undulation. We could also take the envelope from a note played on the piano and apply it to these sounds; this would still be an example of asymmetric reciprocal motion.

SYMMETRIC RECIPROCAL MOTION
If we used an ascending exponential ramp immediately followed by a descending exponential ramp with the same parameters (length and curvature), we would get a symmetric reciprocal signal which could be used as an envelope for frequency or any other parameter of a sound. For example, we could modify example 8A.7 and make it reciprocal by using a descending-ascending glissando with slightly longer times.

• •

SOUND EXAMPLE 8B.1 • Symmetrical reciprocal motion

• •

SIMPLE OSCILLATORY MOTION

Simple oscillatory motion is when there is an oscillation in the values of a single parameter of a sound. Basically, from a technical point of view this means that instead of using a line segment or exponential (or other) ramp to change the parameter, a low frequency oscillator (LFO) with various waveforms is used in its place. Therefore, oscillatory motion could also have its own shape, which could be symmetrical when using a sine or triangle waveform, asymmetrical when using a sawtooth waveform, or irregular when using a pseudo-random LFO. Obviously, these waveform shapes only affect the way the parameter is changed and should not be confused with the waveform of the sound that we hear during the motion itself. For example, we could take a random waveform such as white noise, and control its amplitude with a square wave LFO; in this case the oscillatory motion would be regular, even if the waveform itself is irregular.

It is important to remember that any oscillation used for the motion of a sound should be at sub-audio frequencies or else it might produce frequency modulation (if we are applying oscillatory motion to the frequency parameter) or ring modulation (if we are applying oscillatory motion to the sound's amplitude) where the sound will contain pairs of side-by side frequencies. The details of this will be explained in the third volume in the chapter dedicated to nonlinear synthesis. Let's now take a look at a series of examples demonstrating simple oscillatory motion applied to frequency.

· ·

SOUND EXAMPLE 8C.1 • Simple oscillatory motion in frequency

· ·

You can also create oscillatory motion in amplitude. Sinusoidal oscillatory motion in amplitude has the same perceptual result as beating. However, in this case the amplitude oscillation is a result of its being controlled by an LFO, instead of the difference between two closely spaced frequencies.

There are a wide variety of other possible examples, such as applying oscillatory motion to rhythm, to the playback frequency of a sound file, to stereo spatialization, or any other parameter. Up to now we have used only classic waveforms for the oscillatory motion of parameters, but you could also use a system that extracted the envelope of a sampled sound to create the shape of the motion. For example the envelope of the sounds of different ocean waves could be extracted using an envelope follower, repeated in a loop, and applied as an envelope to unrelated sounds, such as the sound of a choir or an arpeggio played on a guitar, or else used as a motion profile for the cutoff frequency of a lowpass filter and applied to white noise. In the case of the former, the profile of a natural sound is imposed on another sound to change its character; in the latter its purpose is to imitate a natural sound using oscillatory motion with a synthetic sound.

· ·

SOUND EXAMPLE 8C.2 • Asymmetrical oscillatory motion

a) Envelope extracted from the sound of ocean waves applied to the sound of a choir and a guitar arpeggio
b) The same envelope applied to the cutoff frequency of a lowpass filter

· ·

LISTENING AND ANALYSIS ACTIVITIES

In sound example AA8.1, is the reciprocal motion symmetric or asymmetric?

In sound example AA8.2 do you perceive beats or two separate superimposed sounds?

When perceiving the transition from one parameter to another in sound example AA8.3, what is the first parameter and what is the second?

What type of portamento can be found in sound example AA8.4?

· ·

FUNDAMENTAL CONCEPTS

1) We have divided the types of motion into 4 typologies: simple motion, complex motion, compound motion and motion sequences.

2) The profiles of these types of motion can be based on programming or extracted from existing sounds and imposed upon other sounds.

3) Simple motion includes unidirectional, reciprocal and oscillatory motion of a single parameter of a sound, and this motion can be linear, exponential, logarithmic, and either continuous or discontinuous.

4) Reciprocal motion can be either symmetric or asymmetric.

5) Oscillatory motion can be symmetric, asymmetric or pseudo-random.

6) Complex motion in a sound is made up of several kinds of simple motion, or even built from other types of complex motion.

7) These categories are only conventions; in reality, knowing the ambiguous zones between them is an integral part of a deep knowledge of their inter-relationships and the multiform quality of sound and its motion.

SIMPLE PLANAR MOTION: STATIC TIME?

Planar motion refers to sound structures where no parameter moves in an obvious manner.

· ·

SOUND EXAMPLE 8C.3 • Planar Motion

- Static band

· ·

In these cases, should we think about the absence of motion? Or should we call it non-directional motion? Here we begin to observe that there is a double sense of time, something that Jonathan D. Kramer defines in the following way: "music is a series of events, events that exist not only in absolute time [(clock time)] but also contain subjective time and shape it. [...] The difference between absolute time and musical time is the difference between the time that a piece of music occupies and the time that the piece presents or evokes." (Kramer, 2001)

Essentially, when we listen to a 3 minute piece that is divided into 6 equal sections of 30 seconds, exactly three minutes pass in the realm of absolute time, but, depending on the sound content of the piece, we could have the impression of different overall durations – either greater or lesser – and actually have the impression that the 30 second sections have different lengths from one another.

Here, planar motion in the above sound example occupies a certain number of seconds of time and therefore from a certain point of view can still be considered motion because it "leads" the listener from one point in absolute time to another, even though the interior of the sound itself does not contain any (perceptible) motion. However, if we observe the musical time that the sound evokes, we immediately notice a total stasis in the sound, which alludes to time being "frozen", static, non-directional, or even entirely obliterated. If we only concentrate on clock time, a sound in a static tempo would be impossible, but the power of organized sound lies in the possibility of being able to reshape absolute time, to re-think each instant as alluding to and creating different kinds of time. In this situation, the absence of changes in a sound's properties could offer interesting implications, including being able to experience motion without direction: the suspension of time.

"OTHER" KINDS OF TIME

Marta Grabócz speaks about three new structural ideas invented for electroacoustic music: alongside extra-musical models and articulations that follow graphs and diagrams are those structures which have a static character. It is actually possible to build not only individual motion processes but also entire pieces whose form is characterized by stability with extremely slow or imperceptible transformations of the sound material itself. Grabócz talks about pieces which "manifest a clear preference for fluid masses, states of tension, elongated forms, without having a normal resolution, and leaving an available option for indeterminacy" (Grabócz, 1997).

Pieces such as John Chowning's composition, *Stria*, are cited as examples of this type of form. Naturally these types of electronic pieces, characterized by extremely slow motion or static structures, suspended or "frozen" in time, have even influenced musical compositions for instruments and voices since the 1950s, such as in works by composers like Ligeti and the French spectralists. One good example of the latter would be the opening of the piece *Partiels* by Grisey, in which the orchestration is based on the evolution of sonic components in the low E of a trombone, analyzed via spectrograms and transcribed for an instrumental ensemble, with some necessary changes. In this case, an extremely short amount of time (that of the trombone E and its internal spectral evolution) is expanded and reproduced within a time frame that allows listeners to perceptually appreciate its evolution in detail. Grisey spoke about such stretched time as being "whale time", in contrast to normal "human time" and compressed "insect time". Before him, Messiaen had meticulously transcribed the fast evolution of pitches in birdsong, and after him Luigi Ceccarelli created a stretched version of fast birdsong, in his composition *Birds*, in order to highlight its similarity with the sounds of a bass clarinet. In any event, the procedure being used here falls within the realm of sound processing, not transcription or imitation. It can be defined as a "zooming" into the time stream of a natural sound, in order to create a musical sound by decontextualizing it and modifying it in time. Electroacoustic music is therefore also able to directly mold and shape absolute time, not only metaphorically but also literally, by operating directly on a sound itself.

Other types of time modification can take place within our perception. This does not only happen while we are listening to a piece of music, but can also take place after listening. For example, when we know a piece that we have already listened to, we can instantly recall a global memory of the entire piece, and immediately have a mental image of it. This does not only happen when listening, but also can happen while composing a piece, even if the piece is still incomplete – the memory of its individual parts can be mentally recalled in an instant. It is precisely this ability to compress time that allows us to develop the necessary connections not only for the "mobile listening" that Vaggione mentions (see section 8.1), but also for "mobile memory" – allowing us to evaluate different time frames and the results of operations performed on them, compressing and expanding time, according to the given time frame we may be thinking about. For example, we could imagine a section of a piece and slow it down in our memory, or instantly recall a mental image of one minute of music. A loop of a piece or part of a piece, could even remain "in our head" for hours, even while sleeping. This ability to contract, lengthen or repeat time allows us to realize that we do not simply listen to music or compose it in time, but instead often experience and listen to times other than absolute time while perceiving sound.

Messiaen, in his *Traité* (Messiaen, 1994, I, p.11) speaks of two basic rules for the perception of time, attributed to philosopher Armand Cuvillier:

1) In the present, the more that time is filled with events, the shorter it will seem; the more it is devoid of events, the longer it will seem.
2) In the past, the more that time was filled with events, the longer it will seem to have been, the more empty it was, the shorter it will seem to have been.

· ·

SOUND EXAMPLE 8C.4 • Changing absolute time

- An excerpt from Ceccarelli, L. – *Birds*

· ·

8.3 COMPLEX MOTION

Complex motion is constructed from simple motion on several parameters of a sound. Complex motion can even contain other kinds of complex motion. Complex motion involves at least two parameters but can also involve more. In his text *On Sonic Art*, Trevor Wishart uses the term "dynamic morphology" to refer to a specific case of complex motion, in which all (or at least the vast majority) of a sound object's properties (e.g., timbre, temporal evolution, pitch, intensity, etc.) are in motion.

Motion in sound is a unique form of motion and our experience of it thus allows us to appreciate its properties globally, regardless of whether we are in the act of creating or listening. Our ability to compartmentalize all types of motion by observing the individual parameters that define it can be used, didactically, to promote a better understanding of the inner workings of sound itself. Nonetheless, in an advanced stage of learning, you should eventually have the ability to see motion in sound as an indivisible whole, while simultaneously being able to analyze its properties.

Multiple types of motion can be arranged in parallel (where a different type of motion is applied to each parameter in the sound) or in series (where one type of motion, such as unidirectional motion, is applied to another type of motion, such as oscillatory, which, in turn, is applied to one of a sound's parameters). It is naturally also possible to have complex motion arranged in parallel or in series. We will now provide some examples, although it would obviously be impossible to provide an exhaustive demonstration of all of the possible combinations.

RHYTHM AND DURATION
Where regular rhythms are concerned, you can always make the general assumption that durations will shorten little by little as the beat rate increases, and vice versa. This way you could choose to always have legato sounds (where

the beginning of one sound corresponds to the end of the previous one), by not allowing them to overlap them as the rhythm accelerates. On the other hand, you could also choose to control the durations in such a way that there is always a pause between one sound and the next.

UNIDIRECTIONAL RHYTHMIC MOTION WITH OSCILLATORY FREQUENCY MOTION

By using a square wave LFO to control and alternate the pitch of a sound, we can create a unidirectional motion in rhythm, such as an accelerando, by ramping the LFO frequency value upward (for example from 0.1 Hz to 7 Hz). This creates an intensification in the rhythm of the cyclically alternating frequency.

• •

SOUND EXAMPLE 8D.1 • Increasing the rate of oscillation between frequencies

- A sound whose frequency is controlled by a square wave LFO with amplitude of 200 Hz, DC offset of 300 Hz and frequency ramping from 0.125 Hz to 16 Hz.

• •

INCREASING RHYTHM AND FREQUENCY

At this point there is nothing preventing us from creating a combination of two motion processes by simultaneously increasing both the pitch and rhythm of oscillation. All we need to do is ramp both the LFO's frequency and its DC offset.

INCREASING THE SPEED OF MOTION IN THE STEREO FIELD

A sawtooth waveform can also be used with an LFO to control a sound's spatial positioning in the stereo field. This LFO could also be triangular and would thereby create an oscillating effect, constantly moving the sound faster and faster from left to right and vice versa.

INCREASING RHYTHM AND POSITION IN THE STEREO FIELD

The same LFO whose frequency is making an upward glissando could also be used to create not only a rhythm of alternating (low/high) frequencies, but could also be applied to a second LFO (and even synchronized with it if so desired), and used to control the spatial position of the sound in the stereo field. The same LFO could even be used in the event that we wanted to use the same waveform (such as a square wave) for both. Otherwise, the LFO used to control the spatial position could be a triangle wave and therefore create an accelerating left-right oscillation in the stereo space. In both cases, you could imagine that when the frequency is in the highest part of its range, the sound will be panned completely right, and when it is at the lowest part of its range the sound will be panned completely left. On the other hand, you could also imagine starting from a central position and increasing the amplitude of the LFO little by little in order to end up with increasingly farther panning positions.

481

Hypothetically, we could also increase a rhythm simultaneously with an accelerating oscillation in the stereo field while increasing both intensity and frequency. This would begin to come close to Wishart's concept of "dynamic morphology", where the vast majority of a sound object's properties are in motion.

. . . .

SOUND EXAMPLE 8D.2 • Frequency, rhythm, acceleration of left-right oscillation and increase in intensity

- A sound file whose amplitude is controlled by a line segment with increasing values, controlled in frequency by a square wave LFO whose amplitude and DC offset increase proportionally and a triangle wave LFO, whose frequency ramps from 0.1 to 16 Hz, used to control the sound's spatial position in the stereo field.

. . . .

A SPIRAL: OSCILLATORY MOTION OF RHYTHM AND SPATIALIZATION WITH UNIDIRECTIONAL FREQUENCY MOTION

If we use a sinusoidal LFO with a frequency of 0.5 Hz to control the rate of generation of a series of short sampled sounds (for example from 8 to 18 Hz), and simultaneously synchronize a triangular LFO to it (with a frequency between 2 and 4.5 Hz – a quarter of the first LFO's frequency) in order to control the overall motion of short sampled sounds in the stereo space, we can exponentially glide the frequency of a high-pass filter being applied to these sounds upwards (from 70 to 7000 Hz, for example) to create a sound whose characteristics seem to define an ascending spiral. Obviously, when we speak of motion in space, we need to consider that there are some parameters which are related to the actual listening space, others which are connected to virtual spaces, and still others which are not globally shared. One example of the first type would be panning in the horizontal plane, which influences our perception of the location of the sound in the actual listening space via a balance of intensity between channels. An example of the second type would be the depth of the virtual space (which can be simulated using a combination of equalization, intensity, reverb, etc.). An example of the third type (which we used to try to achieve something resembling the physical notion of a spiral) would be vertical displacement, which we attempted to create without actually having speakers above and below us by using unidirectional motion in frequency, and by supposing that in an ideal space we associate higher pitched sounds with higher physical locations than lower ones. Even though many people may share this perception of vertical frequency localization, this premise could be easily questioned; a pianist thinking of the piano keyboard might mentally associate high pitches with the right and low pitches with the left, or a cellist could localize higher pitched sounds downward and lower pitched ones upward, for instance. Spatial relationships can be particularly complex and the motion shapes that we are talking about should not be taken as actual concrete relationships, but rather as suggestions that can help to give meaning to some kinds of phenomena.

SOUND EXAMPLE 8E.1 • Ascending Spiral

· ·

A SPIRAL: DECREASING OSCILLATORY MOTION OF RHYTHM AND SPATIALIZATION WITH DECREASING UNIDIRECTIONAL FREQUENCY MOTION

We could also imagine a descending spiral where the source sounds are filtered white noise with an exponentially descending glissando in the filter's central frequency (from 7000 to 70 Hz.). A sinusoidal LFO with a frequency of 0.5 Hz is also used here to control a second LFO which modifies its own DC offset in a linearly descending direction so that the rhythm of sound generation and spatial stereophonic motion (a quarter of the frequency, as in the previous example) initially oscillate between 12 and 18 Hz and end up oscillating at 2/8 Hz. This way, the rhythmic motion and spatialization are not simply subjected to a simple oscillation (as in the previous example), but also to a descending motion of this oscillation.

· ·

SOUND EXAMPLE 8E.2 • Descending Spiral

· ·

PARALLEL MOTION IN FREQUENCY[15]

A harmonizer (an effect which doubles or triples the frequencies of a sound via real-time pitch shifting) can be used and applied to oscillatory or unidirectional frequency motion.

· ·

SOUND EXAMPLE 8E.3 • Parallel Motion

· ·

---

[15] Warning! Here parallel motion implies that the frequencies of the various components are transposed in pitch while constantly maintaining the same ratio to the original frequency (such as 2/1 for an octave, and so forth). This kind of parallelism in frequency is different from the concept of parallel structure that we discussed at the beginning of this chapter. Even though these are two entirely different concepts, we could nonetheless say that a harmonizer has a parallel structure and can thus be used to create parallel frequency motion.

OPPOSING UNIDIRECTIONAL MOTION

INCREASING RHYTHM AND DECREASING AMPLITUDE AND BANDWIDTH OF THE SPECTRUM

Imagine a ping-pong ball that is dropped from above and allowed to rebound on a marble table. This creates a combination of a progressive increase in rhythm and a simultaneous progressive decrease in amplitude and reduction in amplitude of the higher components of the timbre.

. . . .

SOUND EXAMPLE 8E.4 • Progressive increase in rhythm with a simultaneous decrease in the amplitude and frequency of a lowpass filter

. . . .

Playing the sound in reverse creates a slowing down rhythm with increasing amplitude.

If we want to obtain the same effect using the actual sound of a single bounce of the ping-pong ball, we could apply a multitap delay with increasingly slower delay times and increasing amplitude values.

If we also add oscillatory motion for stereo spatialization, we could synchronize the global decrease in amplitude with a decrease in amplitude of the LFO used to control the width of the left-right spatialization so that the spatial positioning is extreme when the amplitude is at its maximum, and arrives at a central panning position as the sound disappears.

. . . .

SOUND EXAMPLE 8E.5 • Progressive decrease in rhythm with a simultaneous progressive increase in amplitude and decrease in the width of stereo spatialization

- A multi-tap delay applied to a single sound.

. . . .

Even though at this point we will avoid getting into a more complex discussion concerning structural functions, it is nonetheless interesting to note the difference between sound example 8D.5 and sound examples 8E.3, 8E.4 and 8E.5, in terms of perceptual tension. In example 8D.5 the tension of the sonic gesture (created using a simultaneous increase in the rhythm of the frequency oscillation, an acceleration in the left-right panning oscillation and an increase in intensity) becomes progressively higher and alludes to a climax in the sound, whereas in the others the opposing parameter motion creates a gesture which can be interpreted in different ways. In the process of creating a sound, you could always decide to avoid such clear motion, as illustrated in example 8D.5, in order to concentrate on other types of motion. Nonetheless, it can also be important to understand how a simultaneous "coherent" increase in several parameters, like those which we have described, can result in specific effects in the perceptual realm, and how modifying just one of the parameters could be enough to create radically different sound gestures, as demonstrated in the following example.

Decreasing Rhythm and Increasing Frequency

- -

SOUND EXAMPLE 8E.6 • Progressive decrease in rhythm with a **simultaneous progressive increase in frequency**

   - Excerpt from Cipriani, A. – Al Nur (La Luce)

- -

A SPIRAL WITH OPPOSING MOTION: DECREASING OSCILLATORY MOTION OF RHYTHM AND SPATIALIZATION WITH INCREASING UNIDIRECTIONAL FREQUENCY MOTION
One could also imagine creating an ascending spiral figure using opposing parameters. The source sounds are filtered white noise where the filter's center frequency makes an exponential upward glissando (from 70 to 7000 Hz). At the same time, the LFO is used to modify its own DC offset linearly in a downward direction so that the rate of sound generation and the motion in the stereo space (always one fourth of the frequency as in the previous example) begin with an oscillation between 12 and 18 Hz and end up oscillating at 2/8 Hz.

- -

SOUND EXAMPLE 8E.7 • Ascending Spiral with Descending Rhythm

- -

ASPECTS OF RANDOMNESS IN MOTION

We will now propose a somewhat more abstract notion, where the idea of motion is less strongly linked to a specific parameter, by introducing an element of irregularity that can be applied to the motion of different parameters. This could be used to allow us to shift between a sinusoidal vibrato to one with a random shape over time, for example. It should be noted that such forms internal to motion, like the use of random, sample and hold, exponential settings, and so forth, can be applied to all continuous parameters and should thus be considered as qualitative elements which operate laterally to the parameters themselves.

INCREASING THE AMOUNT OF RANDOMIZATION IN RHYTHM

First, we will introduce a random element to rhythm, using the values 0 and 1 to represent a degree of random variation between nothing and completely random, respectively. In the case of a regular rhythm, the degree of randomness is 0, and as the rhythmic irregularity increases, it goes toward the maximum degree of variability (in other words, a degree of 1). To create this kind of unidirectional motion, which characterized by an increase in randomness in the LFO waveform, we can simply cross-fade between a square wave and a random waveform.

. . . .

SOUND EXAMPLE 8F.1 • Degree of Variation in Rhythm

- A triangle wave controlled in frequency by an LFO with a square wave having an amplitude of 200 Hz and a DC offset of 300 Hz. The LFO waveform is variable, using a cross-fade between a square wave and a random waveform.

. . . .

RANDOMIZING THE PARAMETERS OF READING BLOCKS

In section 5.4T and P we saw a variety of ways to create random variation in duration, in the rate of block generation, or the increment/decrement of cues when dealing with blocks. One could also imagine using various types of synchronization and relationships between the three types of random (for example, when the duration increases with respect its central value, the rate of block generation could also be made to increase by the same amount).

. . . .

SOUND EXAMPLE 8F.2 • Randomizing the Parameters of Reading Blocks

. . . .

UNSTABLE MORPHOLOGY AND DYNAMIC UNSTABLE MORPHOLOGY

Wishart defines "unstable morphology" as the condition where the sound motion is expressed by sudden and fast changes in a zig-zag fashion. This type of motion could be easily applied to a group of several parameters, in order to obtain a type of "unstable dynamic morphology" where all or nearly all parameters are moving in an erratic unstable way.

. . . .

SOUND EXAMPLE 8F.3 • Randomizing the Parameters of Motion Control

a) Example of unstable morphology on a single parameter: frequency
b) Example of unstable morphology on nearly all parameters

At this point we could propose another lateral parameter, namely one that marks the speed of changes in a sound over time, where planar motion would be at one end of the continuum and unstable dynamic morphology would be at the other. With regards to this, Michel Chion (1997) has talked about the idea of slow sound and fast sound within the context of some reflections on audiovisual media (and naturally also on slow images and fast images). We will return to this topic again in the next volume.

TRANSITIONS FROM ONE SOUND PROPERTY TO ANOTHER

FROM PITCH TO RHYTHM TO PLANAR MOTION

One particularly interesting example comes from one of the most important electronic music works of the 1950s, Karlheinz Stockhausen's *Kontakte*.[16] Here, Stockhausen takes the idea of transitioning from the domain of frequency to that of rhythm, and puts it into practice by using impulses to create a sound which glides from high to low frequency. As the sound reaches low fundamental frequencies which render the pitch of the sound barely discernible, the sound makes a transition from a decrease in frequency to a decrease in rhythm. This means that the impulses which were initially tightly spaced and continuous become separated by larger and larger pauses, and subsequently become increased in duration until they arrive at what Smalley would probably refer to as planar motion – that is to say: a single elongated sound with stable frequency, but in this case also with stable timbre and amplitude. The use of reverb at this final stage is of particular interest, since it further increases the sensation of the progressive reduction in tension created by the decreasing frequency and rhythm, in addition to terminating the directivity of the musical line via a transition from this reduction to planar motion.[17]

SOUND EXAMPLE 8F.4 • Progressive Decrease in Rhythm with a
Simultaneous Progressive Decrease in Pitch

- Excerpt from Stockhausen, K. – *Kontakte*

---

[16] From 17'00" to 18'30", "K. Stockhausen, CD3", Stockhausen Verlag
[17] For an in-depth analysis of *Kontakte*, see Cipriani, 1995a and 1998.

8.4 EXPLORING MOTION WITHIN TIMBRE

FROM INTERVALLIC PITCH TO NOISE

Electronic music possesses one specific and unique trait: the creation and transformation of timbre. We have already previously alluded to the notion that timbre, as a parameter, is dependent on many variables and cannot be reduced to simple numbers like other parameters like amplitude and frequency. The idea of organizing timbre into scales and hierarchies, as proposed by Lerdahl (1987), cannot be easily and consistently applied to our models of motion processes, precisely due to the inherently nonlinear nature of a complex parameter such as timbre.

On the other hand, the timbre of a sound is characterized by its components' amplitudes and frequencies and their evolution over time. Therefore we can begin taking a look at some aspects of timbre using additive synthesis, subtractive synthesis and vector synthesis.

THE IMPORTANCE OF ATTACK ON THE PERCEPTION OF TIMBRE

The attack portion of a sound usually contains an immense amount of information that can be used to recognize and distinguish various timbres. Let's take a look at some of these properties.

First, let's look at extremely brief sounds – those which seem to be made up of only an attack, such as the sound of a wood block, a rim shot played on the edge of a snare with the drumstick, or even two stones striking each other.

Wishart[18] proposes three types of envelopes that can be used to characterize these sorts of brief sounds:

The first type of envelope, shown in figure 8.1a, can be applied to sounds to obtain the characteristic quality of struck objects.

The second type (figure 8.1b) has a much more gradual attack which, depending on the sound being used, can result in a sound similar to that created by rubbed objects.

The third type (figure 8.1c) can be used to create sounds that seem to have been put into motion by an external object such as a violin bow or a saw, etc.

Naturally, to obtain any of these effects, the envelopes should be tested out on different types of sounds. For instance, one possibility would be to apply these envelopes to the blocks technique, using different envelopes for each block in order to obtain widely varying qualities for each one.

---

[18] in Wishart, 1994, p. 45

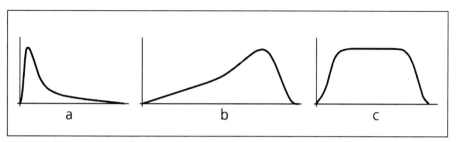

Fig. 8.1 Three types of envelopes

· ·

Sound Example 8G.1 • Various types of envelopes applied to short sounds

· ·

It is naturally also possible to impose a different timbral quality upon sounds of longer duration by altering the components in their attack. For precisely this reason, Wishart has created a technique called *octave stacking*, which can be useful in cases where we want to imbue a sound with additional brilliance. **Octave stacking** uses higher-pitched versions of the attack portion of the sound itself (created using faster playback speed, such as double speed for an octave transposition) which are mixed together with the sound's original attack, immediately disappearing thereafter, leaving only the original sound. The same technique, albeit with transpositions lower in pitch than the original, can also be used to give a sense of depth to the sound.

· ·

SOUND EXAMPLE 8G.2 • Various types of octave stacking

TIMBRAL MOTION USING RESONANT FILTERS
If we apply four resonant filters, each with a different fixed frequency, to the sound of a spoken or singing voice, and in parallel also process the voice using a harmonizer with 4 transpositions making a glissando, when the outputs of both effects are added together, we obtain a change in timbre. However this resulting timbre has some ambiguity between our perception of the pitch of the harmonized sounds (which tend to be perceived as chords), and the pitch of the filters, where the emphasized frequencies are perceived as internal components of the sound itself. This happens because the four resonant filters accentuate some of the fixed frequencies inherent in the sound, while the harmonizers work in relation to the voice's changes in frequency.

· ·

SOUND EXAMPLE 8G.3 • Various types of timbral motion using resonant filters

· ·

INCREASING SPECTRAL COMPLEXITY

In section 8.2 we already spoke about increasing a sound's overall intensity or frequency, but now we will take a look at how we can apply an increase in intensity to a sound's individual components.

Some sounds occupy a very small range of the space occupied by the entire audible spectrum, while other sounds completely fill it. The continuum from the first typology to the second can be controlled using an increase in intensity of a sound's components, starting from zero. As each of the sound's components become successively more intense, one by one, we begin to become aware of its increasing spectral complexity.

Another way to create an increase in spectral complexity is to use frequential motion for a sound's components, starting from a single frequency (and therefore creating the impression of a single sound), and creating glissandi with different curves to different pitches (but maintaining the lowest component at a fixed frequency). Yet another way would be to start with a harmonic sound (which is therefore perceived as a single sound) and allow its components to make a glissando towards inharmonic ratios with respect to the lower components which remain fixed, thereby creating a greater sense of spectral richness.

. . . .

🖱 **SOUND EXAMPLE 8G.4 • Progressively saturating spectral space**

a) Increasing the saturation of the spectral space using additive synthesis with a 20-component variable spectrum. Here, each successive component becomes perceptible as its intensity becomes increased.

b) Increasing the saturation of the spectral space using additive synthesis with a 20-component variable spectrum. Here, all components begin at the same frequency (100 Hz) and, one by one, they each make a different glissando to another frequency.

c) Increasing the saturation of the spectral space using additive synthesis with a 20-component variable spectrum. Here each component starts from a frequency having a whole number ratio to the fundamental (100 Hz) and gradually makes a glissando to a different frequency, even sometimes lower than 100 Hz.

. . . .

In these three sound examples we go from the dimension that Smalley calls "intervallic pitch" – i.e., notes with a recognizable determinate pitch – to relative pitch – i.e., those notes which we perceive as an inharmonic spectrum whose frequency spacing is not easily and readily identifiable. "The bell and metallic resonances are the usual examples of inharmonicity, and they suitably represent the inharmonic dilemma because inharmonic spectra can be ambiguous in that they can include some intervallic pitches. To be regarded as properly authentic, an inharmonic spectrum cannot be resolved as a single note, and its pitch-components need to be considered relative, not intervallic." (Smalley, 2006, p. 100).

Smalley also defines a continuum which has *intervallic pitch* at one end and *saturate noise* (i.e., where all areas of the spectral space are completely filled) at the other. At this latter end of the continuum, it is impossible to recognize any kind of pitch whatsoever, as is the case with the sound of the sea, for example. In between these two extremes are inharmonic spectra which contain relative pitch. However, there are many additional ambiguities to be found along this continuum. For instance, there are many instrumental sounds which can be considered intervallic pitches even though their attack contains noise components (for example the hammer sound of the piano), and there are also saturate noise sounds which have a recognizable note or pitch within them (for instance when the sound of the sea has been filtered with a very narrow bandpass filter).

Let's now take a look at this very example: we will begin with an audio recording of the sound of the sea, filter it with a 6th order bandpass filter with an extremely narrow bandwidth (such as 1 Hz), then, gradually increase the filter's bandwidth. At first, we can only hear a single pitch, similar to a sine wave. Once we increase the bandwidth a little bit we begin to hear a little noise, even though the sound still has the same definite pitch as before. As the bandwidth continues to increase, we become less and less able to distinguish the pitched component which initially had been so clear, and instead begin to hear how the spectral space becomes gradually occupied with noise having a increasingly wider frequency band. It should be noted that saturate noise can even include noise sounds with a narrow frequency band, as long as they have no clearly distinguishable pitch. One example would be if we exaggeratedly prolong the "s" sound when we pronounce a word such as "salt": the area of the spectrum that this sound occupies is actually quite confined, but at the same time that small area is completely saturated with noise, and has no definite pitch. On the other hand, if we similarly prolong the "z" sound in a word like "zap" (or if we imitate the sound of a mosquito!), a recognizable pitch component becomes added to the noise sound. If you switch back and forth between one sound and the other, you will notice that the saturate noise of the "s" sound also remains inside the "z" sound, even though it is slightly masked by harmonic components.

· ·

SOUND EXAMPLE 8G.5 • Progressively saturating spectral space

- White noise filtered by a bandpass filter whose bandwidth starts at 1 Hz and gradually increases

· ·

PROGRESSIVE SATURATION IN SPECTRAL COMPLEXITY WITH AN ASCENDING AND DESCENDING GLISSANDO

The continuum that goes from one very small region of the spectral space to a large area filling the entire spectral space can also be combined with an overall increase on the frequency scale. By modifying sound example 8G.4 we can create the sensation of an increase in spectral complexity, and at the same time cause the sound to make a glissando, either upward or downward. Note that if the glissando is very quick, our perception of the sound will be focused more on its global motion, rather than on its internal motion. On the other hand, by making a very slow glissando, we can find a balance between the perception of the overall glissando and the motion internal to the sound itself.

• •

SOUND EXAMPLE 8G.6 • Progressively saturating spectral space with a light but slightly more pronounced glissando

- All three examples from 8G.4 have been recorded to sound files which are read with a gradually increasing (or decreasing) playback speed, creating an overall ascent (or descent) in frequency at the same time as the phenomenon of progressive saturation of spectral space.

• •

INCREASING THE AMOUNT OF RANDOMIZATION IN A WAVEFORM

Another example of an increase in variability is the progressive filling of the spectral space using vector synthesis. This can be done by starting from a complex periodic waveform and cross-fading to a sound file containing a sum of 30 other periodic waveforms whose fundamental frequencies do not have a harmonic relationship, then finally cross-fading once again to a random waveform. In this scenario we first perceive a single note, to which inharmonic components progressively become added until the sound transforms entirely into white noise.

• •

SOUND EXAMPLE 8H.1 • Degrees of variability for waveforms

- A sawtooth waveform is cross-faded to a pre-recorded sound that contains a mix of 30 periodic waveforms whose fundamentals have a non-harmonic relationship to each other. This is then cross-faded to a random waveform.

• •

DISTRIBUTION CURVES FOR SPECTRAL COMPONENTS

Until now, we have been describing inharmonic sounds in a rather general way, by simply stating that their components' frequencies do not have a whole number ratio to the fundamental. Nonetheless, in our discussion of periodic and non-periodic sounds in chapter 2.1 we already mentioned some situations where a periodic waveform could sound inharmonic, as well as situations where a non-periodic waveform could produce a sensation of pitch.

One example of this would be harmonic beating (which was already discussed in sections 2.2T and 2.2P), which can be created by summing several harmonically complex waveforms whose frequencies are only a short distance apart (for example only 0.07 Hz apart, like the frequencies: 109.86 Hz, 109.93 Hz, 110 Hz, 110.07 Hz, 110.14 Hz etc.). The frequencies therefore do not have a harmonic relationship to one another, but to an extremely low fundamental 0.07 Hz!), but are close enough to each other that they produce a perceptibly harmonic sound, as demonstrated in our next sound example (8H.2).

• •

SOUND EXAMPLE 8H.2 • Harmonic Beating

• •

When listening to this example, we perceive a harmonic sound around 110 Hz with a large degree of timbral variation due to the complex rhythm of beating which continually emphasizes different harmonics of the various waveforms over time.

Together with the previous examples that demonstrate transitions from one parameter to another, this last example is particularly interesting because it helps us understand that within our categorization of parameters there are zones which intersect one another: "gray areas" where something is what it is, but where it is also something else at the same time. This is not at all a bad thing, or something which should be avoided, but rather an area of extremely rich sonic territory that can be explored.

Even when subjected to the most detailed analysis, music (and art in general) is not something that can always be accurately defined or described, but something that can be interpreted in a multitude of ways, and can even be used to make allusions to other things. Sound, moreover, is no exception. However, the harmonic beating example tells us something else entirely: that it is possible for inharmonic structures to be something other than seemingly random, and that they can be carefully designed to create a particular type of sound.

DISTRIBUTION OF COMPONENTS IN WHITE AND PINK NOISE
Although white and pink noise have already been described in the section on subtractive synthesis in section 3.1 of the first volume, it may be useful to take a closer look at these two types of noise from the standpoint of the spectral distribution of their components.

Let's begin with white noise. The spectral distribution of its components' intensities is uniform and therefore constant for all frequencies. This means that within a given range of positive maximum and negative minimum values, any given value will occur with the same probability as any other value in the range. However, if we measure the intensity of white noise by octave frequency bands, we discover that there is a 3dB increase in overall amplitude for each octave as we go higher and higher in the spectrum. So, even though white noise has a uniform distribution, its intensity is not constant when measured octave by octave.

Pink noise, on the other hand, has a spectral distribution with constantly decreasing intensity as the frequency increases (a 3 dB per octave decrease, to be precise). This means that it will produce a uniform amplitude level when its intensity is measured by octave bands.

FROM NOISE TO NOTE
If we create a series of impulses, each made up of just one sample value of 1 every tenth of a second, and we filter it using 30 filters in parallel using 30 different closely spaced inharmonic frequencies which slowly and continually move apart from one another, we can create a transition from a saturate inharmonic sound to an inharmonic sound in which some components can be distinguished from one another, and then to an inharmonic sound made up of 30 distinct frequency components. If the filter frequencies are then gradually arranged so they have a harmonic relationship to the lowest filter frequency (i.e., with whole number frequency ratios to it), we can create a transition from a relative pitch to an intervallic pitch, or note.

. . . .

SOUND EXAMPLE 8H.3 • From Noise to Note

-   From clicks to colored noise to a relative pitch to a note, or intervallic pitch

. . . .

We suggest you listen again carefully to all of the above examples, and try to describe them, either mentally, or in writing. These same examples will be used in the practice chapter, as the starting point for programming activities and the creation of motion in sound.

8.5 COMPOUND MOTION

Compound motion can be defined as motion between different sounds. This type of motion could be synchronized or not, and it could additionally contain simple motion, complex motion or even other types of compound motion within it. Let's take a look at some examples.

COMPOUND CENTRIFUGAL OR CENTRIPETAL FREQUENTIAL AND SPATIAL MOTION

Let's now try to imagine a type of motion that simultaneously implies both an increase and a decrease – in other words two or more unidirectional motions that start from a central frequency zone (an arbitrary one of our choosing) and move away from this point of reference in opposing directions (or vice versa: starting away from it and moving toward it).

For instance, we could create 5 ascending glissandi and balance them with 5 descending glissandi, all of which start from the same base frequency and move to 10 different destination frequencies over the same duration. We could also synchronize this centrifugal frequency motion with a similar centrifugal motion in space, by initially locating all 10 sounds at a central panning location and moving them to different, and more extreme spatial locations (see sound example 8I.1). Naturally this outward centrifugal motion could also be constructed in the opposite direction to create inward or centripetal motion.

• •

SOUND EXAMPLE 8I.1 • Centrifugal or Centripetal Frequential and Spatial Motion

• •

SYNCHRONIZED CENTRIFUGAL/CENTRIPETAL OSCILLATORY MOTION

Another possibility would be to create centrifugal (or centripetal) motion where the various glissandi do not just move to their upward or downward destination in a straightforward manner, but oscillate in their trajectories, as if they are "uncertain" about their final destination. For example, you could add oscillatory motion to 4 harmonic sounds that all start from a narrow frequency range and gradually move to a larger one. Although the oscillatory motion may cause them to temporarily return toward the boundaries of the center range, they nonetheless expand outward toward a wider range after each subsequent return. As we previously explained, such ascending and descending motion could be made either smoothly or in steps – i.e., controlled by a sample and hold mechanism or a random walk (both of which we have already encountered in section IA.5 of the first volume).

SOUND EXAMPLE 8I.2 • Synchronized Centrifugal/Centripetal Oscillatory Motion

· ·

The types of motion that have just been described (whether continuous or discontinuous) can naturally be synchronized or else have different durations. In the first example we used a mechanism to create an overall repetition in the compound motion at the end of each return toward the center range. Let's now look a different way of doing it.

OPPOSING MOTION: CONTINUOUS INCREASE AND DECREASE IN PITCH USING SHEPARD TONES

A Shepard tone[19], as we have already learned (see sections 2.3T and IB.9), is a sound which seems to make an infinite glissando without ever reaching point of arrival. Although this is not an example of simple motion from a technical perspective, from a perceptive point of view it nonetheless creates the illusion of never-ending unidirectional motion, and simultaneously creates the illusion of the suspension of time, in a somewhat different manner than planar motion. That having been said, we cannot truly consider the motion of a Shepard tone to be non-directional, because it clearly sounds like it is ascending or descending. Nonetheless, just as with planar motion, we get the paradoxical impression that the sound is continually moving but that it remains static at the same time. Although planar motion evokes the idea of stasis during the passing of time (absolute time to be precise), Shepard tones, on the other hand, give us the illusion that time is in circular motion. To make a parallel with our visual perception, it would be as if a large wheel were continually turning clockwise by itself, but we could only see a quarter of it, such as the only upper left hand quadrant, at any given time. Returning to the domain of sound, we know that such motion can be achieved by continually cross-fading sounds making a glissando that are arranged in parallel octaves, and slightly offset in time from one another.

· ·

SOUND EXAMPLE 8I.3 • Opposing Motion: Ascending and Descending Shepard Tones

· ·

---

[19] See Shepard, R. N., 1964.

Let's now listen to another kind of opposing motion made up of two superimposed Shepard tones: one ascending and one descending. Although you might initially think that this would result in a double glissando – one infinitely ascending and the other infinitely descending – it actually, and paradoxically, dispels the illusion! This is because the sensation produced by the superimposed opposing motion helps put limits on the two oscillations, and indeed even additionally creates a slow oscillating feeling within the glissando itself (it first sounds like it is ascending, then descending, ascending again and so on).

• •

SOUND EXAMPLE 8I.4 • Opposing Motion: Two Opposing Shepard Tones

• •

OSCILLATORY MOTION OF A BANDPASS FILTER APPLIED TO CENTRIFUGAL MOTION
If we take a random LFO with a frequency of 1 Hz and use it to control the center frequency of a bandpass filter between 100 Hz and 10100 Hz, and then apply it to the sound from example 8I.1, it creates a sound that highlights different frequency bands across its centrifugal motion.

• •

SOUND EXAMPLE 8I.5 • Synchronous Oscillatory Motion: Random LFO **controlling the center frequency of a filter applied to sounds moving in opposing centrifugal motion**

a) Sounds filtered by 3 bandpass filters controlled by 3 random LFOs with frequencies of 1 Hz, 2 Hz and 3 Hz (thus having a least common multiple of 1 second)
b) Sounds using 2 random LFOs at .7 Hz and .5 Hz (LCM at 10 seconds)

• •

When listening carefully to the last sound example, you will notice that it takes a mechanism that we have often seen applied to the micro-form of individual sounds – the oscillatory motion of components within an individual sound – and expands it over a larger amount of time so it becomes easily discernible. In this example, the composite rhythmic cycle repeats itself only when it reaches the least common multiple between the durations. So, in the first example this means that the least common multiple is 1 second, since that is the point when the rhythm of all three durations (333.333 ms., 500 ms. and 1 second) becomes synchronized. Within this fairly short time frame we are able to perceive the synchronicity between the three repeating rhythms.

In the second example, the least common multiple is 10 seconds, so the synchronization and rhythmic ratio of the 2 LFOs becomes more complex, since the entire rhythmic cycle takes 10 seconds to repeat.

If the ratio between the durations were irrational, there would be a continuous global motion without any repetition whatsoever, since there would be no least common multiple between the durations. If the LCM between the durations were so long that it could not be recognized, the perceptual result would be similar to the scenario where the durations have an irrational relationship. The following shows an example of this:

· ·

SOUND EXAMPLE 8I.6 • Asynchronous Oscillatory Motion

- using 2 random LFOs with frequencies at .77 Hz and .97 Hz

· ·

The examples presented here bring to mind a similar idea concerning the periodicity or aperiodicity of a waveform. Here, however, due to the longer durations being used, we no longer hear the waveform's components in the frequency domain, but rather enter the realm of rhythm. It is interesting to note that, depending on the choices you make, it is possible to distinguish forms within the sounds' microstructures which correspond to the macro-structure – i.e., the overall form of an entire piece – from a logic-based perspective, or even intermediary forms such as those which we are studying in this section. Of course, it is not necessarily a given that listeners will be able to actually perceive these relationships between micro- and macro-structure. Often, the motivation behind trying to create some kind of close-knit relationship or structural similarity between the macro-form and micro-form (internal to the sound itself), is purely for the sake of creating conceptual coherence, or to devise some kind of logical or mathematical sense within the overall organization of a piece. It goes without saying that this is just one possibility among millions, and we will continue to more deeply investigate these issues in the chapter about the organization of sound in the next volume.

"SKIDDING" CENTRIFUGAL OR CENTRIPETAL MOTION: RANDOM WALK APPLIED TO FREQUENCY

One other possibility would be to use a random walk to create an irregular "skidding" effect. More precisely, this would consist of applying a random walk procedure to the 16 frequencies in opposing motion, so that as the random values are chosen, one after the other, any given value could not be more distant from the previous one than the value of the step parameter.

· ·

SOUND EXAMPLE 8I.7 • Random Walk Applied to Frequency

"SKIDDING" COMPOUND MOTION: IRREGULAR BUT SYNCHRONIZED RHYTHM, PITCH AND SPATIALIZATION

You could also synchronize the random walk's rate of change with that of another random walk used to control the sound's stereo spatialization, in order to provide it with a stronger sense of "skidding". To further increase this effect, it would also be possible to apply yet another a random walk to the frequency that is used to control the rate of generation of the others. This would create an irregular, although still synchronized, rhythm for both pitch and spatialization.

· ·

SOUND EXAMPLE 8I.8 • Irregular but Synchronized rhythm, pitch and spatialization.

· ·

CENTRIFUGAL AND CENTRIPETAL COMPOUND MOTION: SPACE AND PITCH

If we use hundreds of very short sounds (each around 20 milliseconds in length) that are generated at an extremely high rhythmic rate and initially position all of them at the center of the stereo field, we can make them move outward (centrifugal motion) and back inward (centripetal motion). That same motion could simultaneously also involve other centrifugal or centripetal processes to control the sounds' frequencies.

· ·

SOUND EXAMPLE 8I.9 • Impulses moving away from a given frequency and spatial location

· ·

COMPOUND MOTION BASED ON ACCUMULATION AND RAREFACTION
Salvatore Sciarrino describes accumulation processes as "The transition from a lower to a higher density of events" (Sciarrino, 1998, p.28), and proposes the example of raindrops on a balcony where, depending on the amount of wetness, it goes from a sparse state made up of just a few drops, to being completely saturated. If we take the same analogy and apply it to the rain drying, we start from a saturated state and move toward a rarefacted one.

Although we have not yet dealt with the idea of two or three dimensional "spaces" for spatialization, we can still imagine a cartesian graph where the x axis represents stereo panning position and the y axis represents frequency, as shown in the figure.

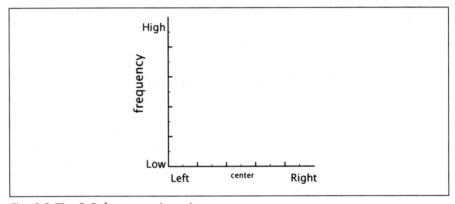

Fig. 8.2 The 2-D frequency/panning space

To fill this space with gradually accumulating sounds, we could use motion characterized by an increase in the rate of sound generation. In order to fill the square virtual "space" where we will be adding the brief sounds (i.e., "raindrops") we will employ 2 random LFOs: one which controls the stereo panning (using values between 0 and 1) along the x-axis, and another which controls the frequency of the sounds (with values between 50 and 10000 Hz for instance). Naturally, the feeling of spatialization is much clearer for high frequencies, which our ears can localize more accurately than low ones.

As the rate of sound generation becomes faster and faster, we tend to perceive a transition from a seeming multitude of individual sounds to that of a single "swarming" sound.

Motion characterized by accumulation and rarefaction can also contain both foreground and background sounds within it. However, since we have not yet delved into the subject of reverberation, for the time being we will need to create a near and far effect by using a lowpass filter to create "far away raindrops" and not filtering sounds that we want to appear to be "close". As we have already learned, each time we filter a sound in a subtractive way, we also decrease its overall amplitude, unless there is some added means of amplitude compensation.

SOUND EXAMPLE 8I.10 • Accumulation using 2 LFOs (space and pitch)

• •

One other example would be the progressive addition of more and more oscillators (say, from 2 to 200), each generating short sounds within a restricted frequency range and controlling their frequencies using a system of individual random walks for each frequency within the same narrow frequency range. This scenario would create a feeling of discrete events when there are only a few oscillators and would produce a saturated, narrow frequency band when there are many.

• •

SOUND EXAMPLE 8I.11 • From 2 to 200 Oscillators within a confined **frequency band**

• •

8.6 ALGORITHMIC CONTROL OF MOTION

We are using the term "algorithmic control" to mean automatically generating events whose parameters are defined using calculations and not decided upon in advance or otherwise precisely predetermined by the sound artist. In a certain sense, all the examples in this chapter that we have been listening to up to now far could be considered algorithmic because some kind of computer-based process has been used to control the sounds' parameters in practically every one. However, the objective in doing this was to obtain a pre-determined type of motion, so the algorithms used consequently have been tailored to that kind of use.

In this section, however, we are going to concentrate on "algorithmic motion" or, put in more simple terms, on processes where the detail present in the resulting sound is a side-effect of the algorithm itself, and not a result of the precise control of the individual parameters on a such a minute level of detail. Nonetheless, when using this type of control, the sound result is usually predetermined, but the internal detail within the motion itself has been left up to the computer instead of being carefully designed by a human.

A classic example of this can be seen in some early compositions by Steve Reich, such as his earliest "tape music" compositions *It's Gonna Rain* and *Come Out*, and also in his later piano duo piece, *Piano Phase*. These pieces are built upon the idea of experimenting with a very slight difference in the playback speed of multiple versions of the same looped sound sequence played simultaneously. Doing this continuously creates a slight phase shift between the sequences, first perceptible as a change in timbre then in rhythm. The sequences constantly go out of phase with each other, and become synchronized again momentarily before once again going out of phase. Reich uses this technique to construct a musical process, but then allows the evolution of the process itself to control the detail of the sonic result.

We could consider these pieces to have some type of oscillatory motion similar to that of beating, but extended over a much broader time frame and thus producing a more complex outcome. This type of motion could even be created using the masking techniques that were discussed in chapter 2.4 T and P, by using 2 or more copies of a looped sound and working with the time/frequency distribution of different kinds of sequences.

. . . .

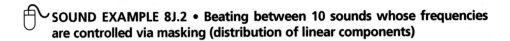

SOUND EXAMPLE 8J.1 • Phase-shifting 2 or more copies of the same loop [20]

    a) 2 copies
    b) 8 copies
    c) 36 linear copies

. . . .

Due to their graphical nature, the masking techniques described in volume 1 can actually be useful to help us visualize or otherwise think about things like centrifugal or centripetal motion, in addition to providing high level control over the motion of individual components.

FROM PITCH TO TIMBRE
By carefully listening to the next example, created using the masking technique and making use of beating, we can perceive how the beats themselves can create not only rhythmic but also granular phenomena. This happens when 10 equidistant sound components (their placement is linear on the frequency scale) are so close that they create beats, but since they are constantly moving farther apart and closer together in a restricted frequency range, they also simultaneously create multiple accelerandi and rallentandi.

. . . .

SOUND EXAMPLE 8J.2 • Beating between 10 sounds whose frequencies are controlled via masking (distribution of linear components)

. . . .

ALGORITHMIC CONTROL OF RHYTHM
A similar type of motion could also be achieved by selecting from among a varied set of rhythms algorithmically (i.e., determining them using a given range), using various possible distributions, such as linear, exponential, logarithmic, etc.

_____
[20] An excerpt from *La danza del tempo* ("The Dance of Time") by Vincenzo Core (2011)

ALGORITHMIC CONTROL OF SPATIALIZATION

We have taken a look at only a few of the many ways of applying a high-level control to parameter values. At this point you may be asking questions like: "In what situations could it be useful to algorithmically control motion processes? What would be lost by not having complete manual control over the individual parameter values? Is this merely an ideological issue, or a practical consideration?"

Needless to say, there are a wide variety of opinions on this subject, but our advice would be to listen carefully to the sound itself – our own sense of perception will help guide us through the act of composing. For example, if we are working on a section of a piece where we want to control 30 different superimposed rhythmic lines, an algorithmic approach could be beneficial. If, in such a situation, we had determined each individual parameter value manually, the listener would probably not be able to tell the difference, but by using high-level algorithmic control, we can more easily try out different scenarios until we obtain the precise effect we are looking to achieve.[21] Of course, if we really need to be very precise about the different values we want to use, it might actually be worth it to carefully program each individual event by hand, as long as this extreme precision is actually perceptually meaningful for the musical result.

Horacio Vaggione (2002) affirms that it is a question of "going beyond the dichotomy between algorithmic processing and direct intervention. [...] A local action of writing can be integrated into an algorithmic process in the same way that, symmetrically, the product of an algorithmic process can be transformed locally by an action of direct writing." Therefore we should not rigidly limit our thinking to one or the other of the two methods, but strive towards their possible integration. Paradoxically, the same Xenakis who used stochastic processes, cellular automata and other generative algorithms in his compositions to determine the length of the events, the number of sound events in a given unit of time, the distribution of pitches, etc., considered "instinct and subjective choice [to be] the only guarantors of a work's value." (Xenakis, 1958/59)

---

[21] Something similar to these sorts of algorithmic processes can also be found in some instrumental compositions in the "aleatoric music" genre that make use of controlled random processes. One example of such music would be the first movement Witold Lutoslawski's Symphony No. 2, where the composer has pre-determined some musical parameters (such as pitch and intensity), but allows each of the performers to freely interpret the music, without constantly needing to think about synchronizing with the others. The upshot of this is that the sonic result is not always exactly the same (even though it always creates a similar musical texture), but this is precisely the composer's intention: such rhythmic precision is not required because the musical organization of the composition is not centered around the aspect of rhythmic accuracy.

8.7 INTRODUCTION TO MOTION SEQUENCES

CONTRASTS

SUPERIMPOSED CONTRASTS

One can also work effectively with contrasts in music – this could mean superimposed motions, or even contrasts which follow one another in time.

Many examples of co-existing contrasting sonic motions appear throughout music history. For example, low and high pitched sounds played simultaneously can be found in countless instrumental works, from the last variation of Beethoven's piano sonata Op. 109 or his bagatelle Op.119 No. 7, to compositions by Ligeti such as *Volumina* and *Lux Aeterna*. Needless to say, there are also numerous examples to be found in works of electroacoustic music, such as *Songes* by Jean-Claude Risset.

In addition to pitch, contrasts can also be created with other musical parameters: rhythmic contrasts (a slow rhythm alongside a fast one), timbre contrasts (extreme harmonicity against sonically saturate inharmonicity), etc.

· ·

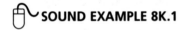 **SOUND EXAMPLE 8K.1**

Co-existing high and low pitched sounds
a) An excerpt from Ligeti, G. – *Volumina*
b) An excerpt from Ligeti, G. – *Lux Aeterna*
c) Co-existing fast and slow rhythms
   An excerpt from Cipriani, A. and Latini, G. – *Rotazione* (an audiovisual opera)
d) Co-existing opposing timbres
   An excerpt from Parmerud, A. – *Les objets obscurs*

· ·

ALTERNATING DYNAMIC CONTRASTS

By the 16th century, alternating between piano and forte had become a fundamental element of musical expression for composers like Giovanni Gabrieli. It is no less important in contemporary works such as *Schattentanz*[22] by Helmut Lachenmann, which uses just two notes that are played with strong contrasts in dynamics (and consequently also in timbre). One very clear example in the electronic music repertoire can be found in György Ligeti's piece *Glissandi* [23], where the same musical gesture is given different meanings depending on whether

---

[22] The last piece from his piano suite *Ein Kinderspiel*.
[23] From 1'16" to 1'23" and from 1'24" to 1'46" (Ligeti, G. CD Wergo 60161-50). These two sections of the piece clearly evoke a "memory" effect, resulting from the repetition of a series of sounds, which initially had strong intensity and clear spectral definition, at a much lower intensity.

it is played with a greater or lesser intensity. Examples of very extreme alternating contrasts can be found in a variety of pieces by Ludger Brümmer (such as *The Gates of H.*), and in Paul Dolden's *Below the Walls of Jericho*.

• •

SOUND EXAMPLE 8K.2 • Alternating compound motion – using sounds **with compound motion at high intensity alongside identical sounds a lower intensities**

    a) An excerpt from Gabrieli, G. – *Sonata Pian e Forte*
    b) An excerpt from Lachenmann, H. – *Schattentanz*
    c) An excerpt from Ligeti, G. – *Glissandi*
    d) An excerpt from Brümmer, L. – *The Gates of H.*
    e) An excerpt from Dolden, P. – *Below the Walls of Jericho*

• •

CONTRASTS LEADING TO FUSION: "LITTLE BANG"
The types of reciprocal motion that we have dealt with up to now (in sections 8.2 and 8.3) have always been associated with a visible or imagined source (such as the sound of the sea). In reality, however, as listeners we tend to create a perceptual association between a more intense and faster sound and a less intense one that arises from it. This perceptual phenomenon takes place even when the sound is not undulating or repetitive (such as a percussive sound and its tail) or even when the vibrations do not come from sources made of the same material (such as when we strike the wooden body of a guitar, and subsequently hear the vibrating strings as a "tail" of the first, percussive, sound event).

A perceptual association between an energetic event and its tail almost always takes place, even when no reference can be made to a known sound source, or even when the two sound events are produced separately and placed one after the other. We will now take a look at the *little bang* phenomenon which Sciarrino has written about in his enlightening text *Le Figure della Musica* (Sciarrino, 1998). His term for this phenomenon was developed as a reference to the *big bang* theory which hypothesizes about the explosion which gave birth to the universe.

When talking about a sequence of two consecutive sound events, Sciarrino states, "A gigantic explosion is not necessary because the two components [24], – the more energetic one and its tail – are related […]. Only one element needs to take a dominant position in order to attract weaker elements […]. Should any events actually be different from one another, their proximity would be enough

---

[24] A word of caution: since Sciarrino's "Le Figure della Musica" is not a technical text, the word "component" is used here not to refer to the individual components within a sound, but rather to two different sounds: an energetic sound, followed by a less energetic consequent sound or "tail".

to associate them. If the first of two events can be characterized either by incisiveness, weight or force, it will assume the role of mother, or generating event: such is the case with the *little bang*, where the lighter element seems to levitate as a result of the heavier one. Our perception continually imposes cause and effect relationships between phenomena. When an unforeseen event occurs within a static musical texture, it will not happen without consequences." (ibid. p. 68)

. . . .

SOUND EXAMPLE 8K.3 • *Little bang*

. . . .

But what, exactly, is an unexpected event in music?

If we create complex unidirectional motion, using an increase in rhythm, intensity or in the occupation of spectral space, we create a directional motion or gesture whose eventual destination at a given peak moment cannot be immediately predicted. Conversely, if we create planar motion or an extremely rarefacted alternation of events with slow attacks at low intensities, if a very intense percussive sound or screaming voice suddenly comes in, followed by a "tail" of quiet rarefacted sounds, the event is unexpected because its presence has not been prepared in advance. In this case, Sciarrino's statement ("When an unforeseen event occurs within a static musical texture, it will not happen without consequences.") raises issues concerning listeners' expectations, which cannot easily be rationalized theoretically.

In general, we can consider these unexpected events (Smalley calls them "gestures") as being similar to questions, in so much as they force us to expect something else. The response could be an immediate or delayed repetition of the same gesture, or a transformed version of it, or it could even be created using an entirely different gesture. Be aware that we are not trying to provide any explicit behavioral rules, since expectation can often be violated purposefully for the sake of art. The important thing to remember is simply that a question has been asked, and thus an anticipation has been created. It is up to the artist and composer to choose to answer it or not, or even to pretend to respond to it or not, using his innate creative skills and logic within the temporal and spectral domains.

Dowling and Harwood describe some of these concepts derived from George Mandler's emotional theory (Mandler, 1984), in which the human cognitive process is seen as working by means of perceptual-motor patterns through which (primarily unconscious) expectation is generated both concerning the occurrence of events and anticipating future behavior. Interrupting a pattern or ongoing plan causes biological stress: a signal that something has gone wrong. This reaction, in turn, provokes "a search for a cognitive interpretation of what happened – a search for meaning. The arousal and the interpretation

join together in producing an emotional experience of a particular quality."
(Dowling, W.J. and Harwood, D., 1986, p.214)

Anticipation, prediction and expectation are all based on the listener's knowledge and familiarity with the given style of music that he is listening to. Nonetheless, many researchers [25], have concluded that there are some general principles, based on Gestalt theory, which group stimuli together using various criteria. These grouping mechanisms are based on the following principles, as described by Giannattasio (ibid. p.267):

"a) the principle of **proximity**, in which we tend to associate contiguous elements together; [...]
b) the principle of **good continuation**, in which we tend to group sonic elements that follow a common rule;
c) the principle of **similarity**, which intervenes when neither good continuity nor common rules can be detected (i.e., for sound sequences which are timbrally related);
d) the principle of **periodicity**, in which we tend to group sound events based on their uniformity; [...]
e) the principle of **symmetry**, in which perceptual precedence is given to symmetrical groupings over asymmetrical ones;
f) the principle of **common fate**, in which various elements are grouped by their mutual relation, so the variation of one element (repetition, transposition, modulation, etc.) can predict how the change will be reflected on the group."

Obviously these are just general principles which can be adapted to different contexts, to different cultures, to different interactions over time, etc. But it is precisely this flexibility that allows us to imagine examples of these principles within the realm of electronic music. Let's take a look at (or rather a listen to) some examples of them:

· ·

SOUND EXAMPLE 8K.4

 a) Proximity
 b) Good Continuation
 c) Similarity
 d) Periodicity
 e) Symmetry
 f) Common Fate

· ·

---
[25] These include Meyer, Imberty, Deutsch, Howell, Cross, West, Dowling and Harwood.

GESTURES AND TEXTURES

We have already mentioned the term "gesture" in several different contexts up to this point, but will now talk about it in a little more detail. Smalley points out that there is a continuum which has gesture at one end and texture at the other. A wide variety of sounds can be categorized on the **gesture** end of this continuum: individual sounds – either long or short – or even entire sections of a sonic creation (provided they are based on a gestural compositional approach). Gestures are characterized by energetic movement in which there is a strong sense of spectral and morphological change, which tends to make the listener wait for the next series of events. "Gesture is concerned with action directed away from a previous goal or towards a new goal; [...] it is synonymous with intervention, growth and progress, and is married to causality. [...] Texture, on the other hand, is concerned with internal behavior patterning, energy directed inwards or re-injected, self-propagating" (Smalley, 1986). "Gestural music, then, is governed by a sense of forward motion, of linearity, of narrativity" (Smalley, 1997). This propensity of gesture can belong either to the motion within a sequence or to a sequence of motions themselves. As we approach the other end of the continuum – towards **texture** – "the slower the directed, gestural impetus, the more the ear seeks to concentrate on inner details [(presuming they exist!)]. A music which is primarily textural, then, concentrates on internal activity at the expense of forward impetus" (ibid.).

When listening to the last few minutes of Rossini's *William Tell* Overture, we are constantly projected forward, searching for an event that will eventually resolve the continuous series of gestures. On the other hand, when listening to the overture to Wagner's *Das Rheingold*, (a continuous river of sound that is paradoxically both always the same and always different – an exploration or orchestral timbre within a frozen E-flat major chord), after a few moments we begin to concentrate on the present rather than on the future, in other words on the inner details of the sound and its internal motion.

· ·

SOUND EXAMPLE 8L.1

a) An excerpt from Rossini, G. – Overture to the opera *William Tell*
b) An excerpt from Wagner, R. – Overture to the opera *Das Rheingold*

· ·

Even a sudden and unexpected silence within a piece can be categorized as a gesture! In such cases, instead of simply functioning as a background within which sounds are placed, silence itself can be thought of as a musical shape, just like sound, and can often be an important or decisive event in a piece of music.

SOUND EXAMPLE 8L.2

- Silence as a gesture
  An excerpt from Cipriani, A. and Latini, G – *Rotazione* (an audiovisual opera).

· ·

Naturally, textures can sometimes also contain gestures (texture-setting) and large gestures can also contain textures (gesture-framing). Music is rarely only gestural or textural. That having been said, one important thing to keep in mind is that these categories can be applied to many types of music, and can even sometimes help us to understand the inner workings of music which might initially seem unintelligible, just as a piece of noise music created only with saturate inharmonic sounds might actually be based on older musical models in the structural design of its motion over time. For example, we immediately recognize the abrupt interruption of the musical texture (with the entry of a voice) at the end of the afore-mentioned Wagner overture. This could be interpreted as a little bang in reverse, similar to a scenario where textural sounds are interrupted by a gesture whose spectromorphology is both sudden and energetic, such as one built from white noise.

Listen once again to the overture, which we provided as an example of texture. As with motion sequences, the important thing to grasp is that our interpretation of it depends on the level of "zoom" that we listen with. If you listen to just a half minute of this overture, you can define it as textural music, in that your attention is focused on motion within the large orchestral sound. Since there is no expectation of any particular gesture, you listen to the "here and now" which in a certain sense means that you are listening "outside" of the passage of time. However, if you take a closer look at (or rather listen to!) the overture as a whole, you will see that it is actually just one very large gesture that begins pianissimo and slowly moves toward a climax in all parameters (intensity, rhythm, expansion of the timbre and pitch range). If we were to classify this overture as a whole, we could say that it falls into the gesture-framing category – in other words an immense gesture containing textures. As with all the other aspects of listening that have been described, knowing how to interpret a gesture or texture also requires some flexibility alongside an ability for "mobile listening" (see section 8.1), and orientation within the various levels of "zoom" that we can use while listening.

· ·

SOUND EXAMPLE 8L.3 • Little Bang and Reversed Little Bang

SOUND EXAMPLE 8L.4 • An Example of Gestural Music

SOUND EXAMPLE 8L.5 • An Example of Textural Music

SOUND EXAMPLE 8L.6 • Examples of Gestures inside a Texture ("Gesture-Framing")
- An excerpt from Cipriani, A. – soundtrack to *The Return of Tuuli* (a documentary by Latini, G., Di Domenico, S., Rovetto, M., Rome: CNI, 2001)

SOUND EXAMPLE 8L.7 • Examples of Textures inside Gestural Music ("Texture-Setting")
- An excerpt from Giri, M. – *Appunti dalla Città Oscura (Notes from the Dark City)*

• •

It goes without saying that the musical content of gestures cannot be fully appreciated when they are isolated outside their original context within a given work, thus rendering them devoid of their intended formal function. Although it is beyond the scope of this chapter to delve any deeper into the subject, it is nonetheless important to understand how the motion processes that we have been describing can actually be used to create motion sequences along the continuum between gesture and texture.

REGULARITY IN RHYTHMIC SEQUENCES AND THEIR FUNCTION

We have already stated that using a gestural strategy tends to lead the listener toward the future, as he tries to predict the next event or goal that will be reached. When a regular rhythm is used, this is often interpreted as a texture, but in this scenario, while listening to the present moment, the listener's attempt at predicting tends to assume a particular character. As Pablo Garcia-Valenzuela states, a regular rhythm has a special effect on our attention that we will call temporal organization – the system that controls our attention and keeps rhythmic information in our short-term memory. If a regular rhythm is repeated this mechanism is used to "predict" the next event – in this way 'listening' is replaced with 'listening for'. (Garcia-Valenzuela, 2009.) It is as if listening could be used to predict what would happen next based on information coming from our short-term memory. It is important to understand these mechanisms in our attention that develop and change while listening to a regular rhythm.

As we will soon see, rhythm is one of the properties of motion in sound whose articulation both determines and qualifies the differences between different types of musical repertoire and their function. Therefore, exploring the topic of rhythm without any preconceived notions or prescriptive rules is of the utmost importance for anyone involved in electronic music and sound art. According to psychologist Nelson Cowan (2005), the amount of information that can persist within our **working memory** (i.e., the type of memory that simultaneously allows us to both store and process data) is limited.[26]

---

[26] Psychological studies have linked our perception of the present precisely to our short term memory, which is generally broken up into temporal spans between 4 and 8 seconds in length. (see Snyder, 2008)

It is fairly unrealistic to think that we can completely fill a single instant with information and expect that our listeners will be able to take in the full range of sound information. Consequently it is essential to be aware that the capacity of any listener's working memory will not allow him to be able to process all the information at once – or at the very least not on the first hearing. Of course, the density of events and the attention that can be paid to details within a piece of music will vary in relation to the proportions of the piece itself. But nonetheless it is interesting to note that in all eras, there has been a general tendency to balance the complexity of musical parameters.[27] Countless musical examples could be cited to show where complexity in one parameter has been balanced with stability or simplicity in others, as if for centuries we have collectively already been aware of the limitations inherent in our attention.[28] In his acousmatic piece, Below the Walls of Jericho, Paul Dolden focuses attention on timbre and spectral density, with little regard to rhythmic motion, while on the other hand Paul Lansky, in his piece Table's Clear, concentrates attention on rhythmic/frequential motion and to a much lesser extent on processing timbre.

The expectation created by a regular rhythm involves the utilization of part of our working memory, so it is possible that our attention to other sound properties, such as timbre, intensity, etc., may consequently be less detailed. This was certainly one of the reasons why the use of a regular rhythm was banished in electronic "art music" (particularly until the end of the 1970's), as though it would automatically generate a response of "distracted listening" for the listener. It was as if a regular rhythm unavoidably signified banality or a return to the past. We will soon see that such matters concerning regular rhythms and distracted listening are not quite as simple as they might initially appear.

With respect to regular rhythms, there are several conditions that can lead our attention elsewhere. Once we have perceived coherence within a regular rhythmic pattern, after a certain amount of time (which can vary depending on both subject and context) it is put into the "background" and we are able to effectively focus our attention on other properties of the sound, as long as the internal structure of that rhythm remains stable or predictable. Generally speaking, our attention to sound and its motion is not linear but highly mobile, multi-faceted and diverse, depending on the person and listening context. For instance, it is possible that there is some kind of internal mechanism which distracts us from the details of a stable rhythm, thereby allowing us to simultaneously listen to other sound properties in detail. This

---

[27] Dahlhaus, for precisely this reason, proposes a sort of unwritten law of compensation: "The technique of composition includes – unintentionally rather than purposefully – a calculation of the aesthetic effect. At all times the tendency to balance complexity in one direction by simplicity in another seems to have prevailed. The simple and customary – invariable meter or limited chord vocabulary – provided the support and foil for complications in rhythmic or motivic details or in harmonic-tonal relationships." (Dahlhaus 1983 p.50)

[28] In some pieces by Stravinsky, for example, the melodic information is not as complex as the rhythmic, whereas quite the opposite is true of Bellini, where the melodic information completely predominates over a none-too-elaborate rhythmic scheme.

is exactly what happens in some pieces of IDM (*Intelligent Dance Music*), where the dominant regular pulsation is supplemented with sub-rhythms that are so fast and complex that they shift the listener's attention onto their timbral quality, instead. Forcing us to put the principal rhythm into the background level of listening so we can concentrate on other parameters can also happen in other kinds of music such as Prelude No. 1 from the *Well-Tempered Clavier* by J. S. Bach, or in a minimalist piece like Steve Reich's *Octet*.

· ·

SOUND EXAMPLE 8M.1

a) An excerpt from Bach, J. S. – Prelude No. 1 from The *Well-Tempered Clavier*
b) An excerpt from Reich, S. – *Octet*
b) An excerpt from Squarepusher – *Greenways Trajectory*

· ·

What would happen if there were other extremely stable or predictable parameters in addition to rhythm? In this case, our general attention level might decrease and a mechanism of distraction would take over. This is what is known as "**distracted listening.**" We shouldn't necessarily consider this kind of listening to be something unequivocally negative or superficial, however, is important to understand the functions of such overly predictable music, which naturally depend on the listening context of the music itself. Giannattasio (ibid. p.210-212) points out three basic functions for music:

1) **Expressive Functions**: music can convey meanings and evoke or represent extra-musical events, emotions, concepts and moods.

2) **Functions for the organization and support of social activities.** Music can be used to represent different forms of identity, including (but not limited to) social, political, generational, class-based, ethnic, national and religious identity. It is becoming increasingly evident that this does not necessarily lead to standardization; participation in a particular musical genre can sometimes be used "to distance oneself from a cultural origin, community or social authority in which one was born" (Keller, 2005, p. 1116-7). To this ends, Keller states that music is "an activity that can be used at the same time to both unite with someone and separate from someone else – anywhere and at any time." (ibid.)

3) **Functions for the induction and coordination of sensory-motor reactions.** These functions actually lie midway between the first two classes, since they refer to:
- specific kinetic schemes connected to a musical event: "participatory" listening, working songs, and dance.
- they way that music interacts with the automatic and voluntary mechanisms of the human body. This can contribute to kinesthesia and emotional reactions

that affect the process of symbolization and can furthermore contribute to the induction into altered states of consciousness. Rouget states that music "is the only language capable of speaking simultaneously [...] to both head and legs" (Giannattasio, p.214).

Giannattasio also informs us that these functions are not exclusive and may be present together.

Let's now take a look at some examples of these, using a variety of pieces that are all highly repetitive in all their parameters, and that have very little musical evolution, within several different possible listening contexts:

1) We are sitting in a concert hall, and therefore carefully listening to the piece at a medium volume level. Initially we are probably listening attentively. After a few minutes, the excessive uniformity of the elements in the music causes us to anxiously desire change. Our minds probably begin to wander and we may possibly become completely distracted from listening, or even annoyed due to boredom, or perhaps both. In this case the distraction can be considered a negative element caused by the banality of the music in relation to the expectations of the listener.

2) We are at an *electrohouse* musical event at a discotheque, where the volume of the sound is deafening and we are dancing. The piece has the same characteristics as the one in the first example. We are distracted, and therefore not listening attentively. However, in this case not only is the distraction not at all a negative element, but actually the main goal of the DJ's work. Any structure inherent in the songs being mixed is avoided, although some fragments are exposed for our short-term memory, in order to avoid any obvious structure, narrative or meaning which could force the listener to concentrate, or otherwise listen analytically or attentively. The point of this is to weaken the shape of the individual pieces being played. The music is therefore being used in this context precisely to induce a loss of attention, individual pleasure and/ or collective oblivion, alternating with a few moments of awakened attention. This function of repetitive and regular rhythm can be used in various ways and have completely different meanings, but is nonetheless employed in a lot of types of traditional popular music that make use of dance and trance. Here it functions differently than in the first example: hundreds of people are dancing to the same rhythm, and as such they are not only listening more or less passively but interpreting the music through dance, using their own body movements. Any negative judgment of "distracted listening" should therefore be offset by the function the music has in this environment.

We should also note that this distraction, if modulated, can even become functional in cases where this relentless game of loss and rediscovery of attention is precisely what is being is sought. With some types of house music, we can often provoke distraction through the rhythm that is being used to make us move. As we continue to move, but are no longer listening to the rhythm in detail, if not listening to it "in the background" despite the violent intensity of the sound. Paradoxically, the loss and rediscovery of our attention to the rhythm of house music is well calculated, sometimes even happening via the sudden disappearance of the rhythm itself. When the rhythm disappears something happens to the audience: the system that governs our attention manages to keep the rhythmic information for several seconds, so the people dancing are momentarily waiting and "listening for" the return of the sound of the low frequency percussion with its regular rhythm that characterizes the music. The rhythm, which had previously become a background for the mind and a pulsation for synchronizing body movements, serves a new function when it disappears: it is now imagined within the mind and dancing body, which is awaiting its return, so the DJ or producer has some space to create timbral or frequential motion (such as unidirectional motion of saturate noise, created using a set of bandpass filters with ascending central frequencies, often coupled with the melodic profiles of electronic instruments, processed voices or extremely fast drum rolls). When the regular beat in the bass returns, the person dancing is gratified when their synchronized movement "in the dark" coincides with the return of the actual rhythm. At this precise moment, you can observe how people accentuate their movement, often raising their arms in a ritual that is repeated over and over throughout the evening dancing session. For us, what is interesting is being able to observe the shift of attention that takes place when we use a regular rhythm in a variety of different ways. The listening function that has just been described is precisely that of modulated distraction.

3) We are in a session for relaxation techniques, or for certain types of meditation with music. There is a piece playing at low volume, with a very slow regular rhythm, and the music is always more or less the same. In this scenario, losing attention serves to slow down the fast engine of thought, and render it less present. In this case the distraction from "external" listening forces a shift in our concentration on internal listening, where musical listening does not have any importance by itself (in fact, it is characterized by a lack of attention), but is used for the therapeutic relaxation function it helps perform.

From this point of view, we should not lose track of "the ways (albeit not always very clear) that music induces kinesthetic reactions and acts within the emotional domain by interacting with the automatic and voluntary mechanisms of the human body – for example triggering high respiration rates, heart rate, etc. [...] In this context, it should be remembered that sounds, in addition to their purely acoustical (or neuro-sensory) function for musical perception, can also be absorbed directly by the body via skeletal and muscular-cutaneous pathways. It is known that low tones are preferentially localized to dependent parts of our body, and high tones to the head and neck, with possible intermediate sensations" (Postacchini, 1985, p.156, cited in Giannattasio p.217). Even some examples of *ambient music* have similar effects on listening (decrease in listening attention, etc.), even though they are created for a different purpose.

These examples all help us to understand that, regardless of the type of music or sound creation we wish to create, we can learn a lot by knowing the mechanisms behind other types of music which are different from our own. We always need to remember that there is no singular definition of music simply because each culture and each era defines music in its own unique way. Therefore we should remember that when we talk about music, we are actually talking about it in the plural – multiple "musics".

• •

SOUND EXAMPLE 8M.2

> **An example of *electrohouse music***
> An excerpt from *Deadmau5 Slip*
>
> **An example of *Ambient music***
> An excerpt from Eno, B. and Budd, H. – "First Light" from *Ambient 2 The Plateaux of Mirror*

• •

POLYRHYTHMS AND RHYTHMIC IRREGULARITY

It is also possible to superimpose several regular rhythms, for example by overlaying 6 different rhythmic sequences based on a similar additive rhythm. Together these sequences constitute a continuously changing global compound motion that repeats only when it reaches the least common multiple of the 6 durations. Using polyrhythms can be an extremely complex endeavor, and is well beyond the scope of this chapter. Nonetheless, you may find the ninth chapter (titled "Time") of Trevor Wishart's book *Audible Design* to be an interesting read on the subject.

Various different types of polyrhythms and irregular rhythms are presented in the following sound example.

• •

SOUND EXAMPLE 8M.3

> a) **Constantly changing irregular rhythms with interspersed brief regular rhythms**
> An excerpt from Squarepusher - *Greenways Trajectory*
>
> b) **Polyrhythm (with a possible slight feeling of irregularity)**
> An excerpt from Boulez, P. – *Rituel*
>
> c) **Transition from irregular to regular rhythm**
> An excerpt from Lansky, P. – *Table's Chair*

d) **Transition from regular to irregular rhythm**
An excerpt from Giri, M. – *Just in Time*

e) **Completely irregular rhythms**
An excerpt from Harrison, J. – *Unsound Objects*

f) **Absence of rhythm**
An excerpt from Chowning, J. – *Turenas*

• •

THE RELATIONSHIP BETWEEN FIGURE AND GROUND

One topic that we will touch on lightly, but discuss more fully in the third volume, is the relationship between figure and ground. When we speak about figure, we are not using the term in the musical sense (a musical motif used as a basic building block for a composition) but rather taking the concept from the visual world, where it refers to a subject which is placed in relationship to the background and other planes coexisting in a painting, photograph or other image. The evolution of a sonic image, in fact, may include motions which are brought to the fore and highlighted, alongside others which are less prominent. All of this may initially seem rather simple, but actually the relationship between figure and ground incorporates many different sound properties. These include the "relationship modes" and "qualifiers for spectral space", as defined by Smalley, on one hand, and the speed/slowness of sound defined by Chion, as well as the intensity, central or extreme spatial positioning, near or far positioning in the virtual space (i.e., "depth"), on the other. as well as the relationship these all have to the concepts of gesture and texture.

Let's now define these relationship modes. Smalley speaks of two principal relationship modes: dominance/subordination and conflict/coexistence.

1) dominance/subordination: Given two sound motions in which one is slightly more prominent than the other, we can create a perceptual scene where the motion of the dominant sound or sounds also determines that of the subordinate ones.

• •

SOUND EXAMPLE 8N.1 • An Example of Dominance and Subordination

- An excerpt from Truax, B. – *Sequence of Later Heaven*

• •

2) conflict/coexistence: Two sound motions which are equally important can be placed in counterpoint to one another by means of dialogue which could escalate to conflict, via each one's fight to triumph over the other.

One example taken from *Al Nur (La Luce)* for percussion, voice and electronics by Cipriani clearly demonstrates such a dialogue/conflict scenario between the irregular rhythmic motion of the sounds of the zarb (performed by a percussionist) and the processed zarb sounds.

• •

SOUND EXAMPLE 8N.2 • An Example of Conflict/Coexistence between sonic motions

- An excerpt from Cipriani, A. – *Al Nur (La Luce)*

• •

In this example, the two types of sounds are placed in similar spaces at similar intensities (though on opposite sides of the stereo field), but a struggle could also involve a difference in space and intensity, like a lion pitted against a kitten.

To better elucidate these relationship modes, Smalley lists some of these diametrically opposed concepts in groups of two or three, each group representing a continuum and its extremes, and each able to be placed into the dominance/subordination and conflict/coexistence relationship mode categories:

equality – inequality
reaction – interaction – reciprocity
activity– passivity
activity – inactivity
stability – instability

We can provide examples for each of these relationship mode dimensions. Naturally, since they are generic descriptions, each of them may be interpreted in myriad ways, so we will only be able to cover some of them.

The extremes defined by equality-inequality can relate to intensity, position in the virtual space (i.e., the proximity or distance the sound is perceived to have, which obviously depends on a number of parameters including intensity, reverberation and brilliance of the sound), the occupancy of spectral space (with larger or smaller bands), or even the referencing of real-world sounds (from the squeak of a mouse to the trumpeting of an elephant), etc. Remember, however, that these are just the two extremes of the continuum and that the spectromorphological play between them can be extremely varied. For instance, we could take a very present and intense elephant sound alongside that of a very distant and quiet mouse, and progressively create a transition, first obtaining a certain equality between them via parameter motion, then continuing the transition by equalizing the elephant with a bandpass filter to make it sound like it came from a telephone and/or was positioned very far away in the listening space, and increasing the intensity and presence of the mouse squeak in contrast to it. Often, comical effects are created when the perceptual characteristics of sounds are distorted in such a way.

SOUND EXAMPLE 8N.3 • From Inequality to Equality to Opposing Inequality

a) Sounds of an elephant and a mouse with modifications in space and intensity.
b) An excerpt from Giomi, F. – *That's All Folks*

. . . .

The three modes reaction-interaction-reciprocity all refer to a single contrapuntal mechanism. We can think of this type of relationship as being between the motion of sounds in an acousmatic piece (i.e., without a live component), or between the sounds (or body movements) of a performer and live electronics, or even between the different performers in a laptop ensemble (live or networked). Interactive installations or happenings also provide a good example of this relationship since all three modes are continuously triggered back and forth between the user and the system/environment that has been designed by the author of the work.

. . . .

SOUND EXAMPLE 8N.4 • Reaction-Interaction-Reciprocity

- An excerpt from Roads, C. – *Half Life*

. . . .

Activity-passivity, activity-inactivity and stability-instability can all refer to different types of unstable and dynamic morphologies (either alternating or overlapping) on one side of the spectrum, and planar motion and textures with little inner motion on the other.

. . . .

SOUND EXAMPLE 8N.5 • Active-Passive, Active-Inactive, Stable-Unstable

- An excerpt from Hyde, J. – *Zoetrope*

. . . .

TESTING • LISTENING AND ANALYSIS ACTIVITIES

1) Do you recognize the gesture in sound in example AA8.5? At which point in the sound does it take place? What kind of motion is used here?

2) Do you recognize the gesture in sound in example AA8.6? At which point in the sound does it take place? What kind of motion is used here?

3) Do you recognize the texture in sound in example AA8.7? At which point in the sound does it take place? What kind of motion is used here?

4) Do you recognize the texture in sound in example AA8.8? At which point in the sound does it take place? What kind of motion is used here?

5) What kind of intermediate zone can you recognize in the gesture-texture continuum in sound example AA8.9? What kind of motion was used to create it?

6) What kind of intermediate zone can you recognize in the gesture-texture continuum in sound example AA8.10? What kind of motion was used to create it?

7) Was there a little bang in sound example AA8.11? What kind of motion was used to achieve this?

· ·

MULTIPLICATION PROCESSES

Many "fine grained" textures are built from inseparable elements. However, slightly more "coarse grain" textures can often be created out of a tangle of lines or small elements.

This second type of texture comes close to the multiplication processes that Sciarrino defines as "processes which tend towards compact size and should be placed between macro and micro form." These processes are "a complex of combinations made up of two, three, four, five or more superimposed lines" (ibid. p.41). Of course, in this last definition Sciarrino is referring to canons and counterpoint played by acoustic instruments, but we can nonetheless apply this idea to multiple superimposed sound motions, instead of melodic lines.

As an extension of this idea, we could think about creating spatial counterpoint based not on instrumental music models, but rather on extra-musical models inspired by nature.

SOUND EXAMPLE 8N.6 • Two Examples

a) Short Motion (or phrases of short motion) in counterpoint
b) Lowpass-filtered white noise with gliding cutoff frequency in undulatory motion imitating ocean waves. Each wave is placed at a different point in the stereo field in order to reproduce the constantly changing spatial location of a series of waves.

Further expanding this concept of multiplication, Sciarrino points out a process used in the piece *Partiels* by Grisey, where the multiplication is used within timbre, since each musical instrument represents one partial of a more complex sound entity. We could also imagine a similar multiplication process where each new element that enters the sound is part of an additive process built from bands of sound containing planar motion.

SOUND EXAMPLE 8N.7

- An excerpt from Vaggione, H. – *Agon*

Another, completely different, example would be superimposing multiple tiny units of sound. This could be achieved using the blocks technique, for instance, by creating a type of canon by heavily superimposing many very short blocks (around 100 milliseconds) in their original direction and advancing the cue extremely slowly. This scenario would create a multiplication process that could be defined as a "micro-canon", due to its tendency to repeat small sections of the whole as it progressively moves along. Of course, this is quite different from performing "Frère Jacques" with several voices in canon!

Granular synthesis could also be used to achieve a similar multiplication process that would be even thicker, within the range of hundreds of micro-events per second up to the type of density that brings to mind the "kaleidoscope of elementary particles" that Sciarrino talks about. This topic will be covered in the last volume of this series.

GLOSSARY

Complex Motion
Motion involving several of a sound's parameters.

Compound Motion
Motion involving several parameters of several sounds.

Motion Sequences
Sequences made up of several different kinds of motion.

Oscillatory Motion
Motion where one or more of the parameters has values which oscillate over time.

Planar Motion
Motion where all the parameter values are steady.

Portamento
An effect categorized by flat/planar motion at the beginning and end of unidirectional motion.

Reciprocal Motion
Motion where a unidirectional trajectory is balanced by a return motion. These could be either symmetrical or asymmetrical.

Simple Motion
Motion involving only one of a sound's parameters.

Spectromorphology
The ensemble of interaction characteristics between sound spectra and the way in which they evolve over time.

Unidirectional Motion
Motion where the values of one or more parameters change in only one direction.

8P
THE ART OF ORGANIZING SOUND: MOTION PROCESSES

PREREQUISITES FOR THE CHAPTER
• THE CONTENTS OF VOLUME 1, CHAPTERS 5, 6 AND 7 (THEORY AND PRACTICE), INTERLUDE C AND D, AND CHAPTER 8T

OBJECTIVES
ABILITIES
• TO KNOW HOW TO ENVISION AND CREATE DIFFERENT KINDS OF MOTION WITHIN SOUNDS AND DIRECTIONS OF MOTION WITHIN THEIR TIMBRE.
• TO KNOW HOW TO BUILD ALGORITHMS TO INTERRELATE DIFFERENT TYPES OF MOTION AND MOTION SEQUENCES.
• TO KNOW HOW TO APPLY APPROPRIATE PARAMETER VALUES IN ORDER TO CAUSE THE LISTENER TO PERCEIVE A TRANSITION FROM ONE PARAMETER TO ANOTHER WITHIN A PROCESSED SOUND.

CONTENTS
• PRACTICING SIMPLE, COMPLEX AND COMPOUND MOTION PROCESSES
• PRACTICING MOTION PROCESSES WITHIN THE TIMBRE OF A SOUND
• PRACTICING BUILDING MOTION SEQUENCES

ACTIVITIES
• BUILDING AND MODIFYING ALGORITHMS
• REVERSE ENGINEERING ACTIVITIES

SUPPORTING MATERIALS
• LIST OF MAX OBJECTS

8.1 MOTION PROCESSES

Since motion processes have already been described in detail in chapter 8T, this practice chapter will consist mostly of a series of activities alongside some analysis and "reverse engineering" exercises that may be realized in parallel to reading the theory chapter. Note that for our purposes, the aim of reverse engineering sounds is not to faithfully reconstruct them, but rather to be able to redesign the motion that has been applied to the sound.

Naturally, when creating the small electronic music and sound design études proposed throughout this chapter, you may rely on any of the techniques you have learned in the previous chapters. Although this chapter is short, it will nonetheless require a fair amount of work. Let's start off with the first of our various motion typologies.

8.2 SIMPLE MOTION

UNIDIRECTIONAL MOTION – FREQUENCY

Applying simple motion to frequency essentially amounts to creating a glissando. Naturally, the main objects that could be used to achieve this are `line~` and `curve~`. Since we are already well acquainted with a wide variety of techniques making use of these objects, we will not dwell on them here for very long.

Creating simple stepwise motion (in other words non-continuous) can be done in several different ways. Rebuild the patch shown in figure 8.1.

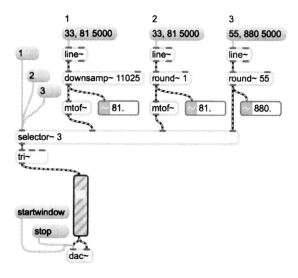

Fig. 8.1 Three different ways to quantize a glissando

All three methods shown in the figure express simple unidirectional motion from A0 to A4. The first "quantized glissando" was created with the **downsamp~** object, which downsamples the input signal using a sample and hold technique. Its argument indicates the sampling period (expressed in samples). Therefore, the object in the figure will sample (and hold) one value every 11025 samples – this amounts to a quarter of a second, presuming we are using a sampling rate of 44100 Hz. The glissando is done with MIDI values, which are converted to frequency values after the sample and hold.

In the second example, the [**round~** 1] object is used to round the signal values to the nearest multiple of a given interval value. The argument indicates the interval that will be used – if it is 1 the signal value will be rounded to the closest whole number value, if it is 2 it will round it to the closest multiple of 2, 3 to the closest multiple of 3, and so on. It is also possible to round values to multiples of floating-point numbers: using an argument of 0.5 would produce output values that are multiples of 0.5. In the example shown in the figure, this quantization produces a series of ascending semitones.

In the third example, a glissando is created using frequency values directly, instead of via MIDI note numbers. Here, the values are rounded to multiples of 55, thereby creating a glissando across the harmonic series based on the note A (55 Hz).

. . . .

ACTIVITIES

• Try to discover at least three other techniques for quantizing a glissando.

• Reverse-engineer sound example 8A.1, using a sampled sound of your choice.

. . . .

UNIDIRECTIONAL MOTION – DURATION AND RHYTHM
To create this type of motion, we can use the technique illustrated in the patch 05_13_blocks_tech_accel.maxpat (see section 5.4P). The **vs.randmetro** object (see section IC.3) could additionally be used in order to introduce a little bit of irregularity into the rhythm.

. . . .

ACTIVITIES

• Reverse-engineer sound example 8A.2, using a sampled sound of your choice.

• Create a unidirectional motion in rhythm that makes a transition from a regular beat to an irregular one.

• Create a rhythmic motion where the sound progressively shortens even though the generation of the rhythm remains fixed.

- Create a series of accelerandi and rallentandi using multiple delays (you can take inspiration from the patch 06_02_multitap2.maxpat) using at least 32 delay taps.

• •

PLANAR MOTION AT THE BEGINNING AND END OF UNIDIRECTIONAL MOTION
This type of motion does not require any new knowledge from a technical point of view. You just need to use a little forethought in order to delay the start of the glissando/accelerando/rallentando (when adding planar motion to the beginning of another kind of motion) or continue the sound after the glissando/accelerando/rallentando (when adding planar motion to the end).

• •

ACTIVITY

Apply planar motion the beginning or end of all the other motion exercises which you created in the previous activities.

• •

FROM RHYTHM TO TIMBRE
This is basically an extreme version of the previous accelerando examples which takes the beat rate right down to the 50-80 millisecond region.

• •

ACTIVITY

Reverse-engineer sound examples 8A.4 and 8A.5, using a sampled sound of your choice.

• •

FROM RHYTHM TO PITCH
In this case the beat rate is brought down into the zone of audible frequencies (i.e., below 50 milliseconds, which is equivalent to 20 Hz).

• •

ACTIVITY

Reverse-engineer sound example 8A.6.

• •

FROM PITCH TO TIMBRE

. . . .

 ACTIVITY

Reverse-engineer sound example 8A.7. Try also creating an ascending glissando, and experiment with other waveforms, even random ones.

. . . .

FROM THE RHYTHM OF OSCILLATORY MOTION IN INTENSITY TO PITCH

. . . .

 ACTIVITY

Take the patch 02_07_beats.maxpat from the first volume and use it to create different kinds of accelerandi in beating, as described in the analogous section in chapter 8.1T.

. . . .

SIMPLE RECIPROCAL MOTION
Also here, `line~` and `curve~` are the principal objects you will need to use in order to create simple reciprocal motion.

. . . .

 ACTIVITY

Reverse-engineer sound example 8B.1, making sure to try out different kinds of waveforms (including random ones).

. . . .

SIMPLE OSCILLATORY MOTION
As was already explained in the Theory chapter, this type of motion can be created using an LFO. Naturally, you should try to free yourself from the "classic" concept of the LFO, and use its oscillatory motion to create interesting dynamically moving sounds. Figure 8.2 shows a patch that creates quantized oscillatory motion and applies it to the frequency of a sound. The result is similar (but not identical) to sound example 8C.1. Rebuild the patch, explain how it works and create some variations on it.

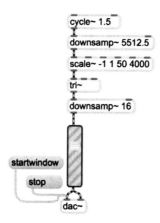

Fig. 8.2 Simple oscillatory motion applied to frequency.

• •

ACTIVITIES

• Use an envelope follower to create asymmetric oscillatory motion (using an appropriate sound, such as a series of slowly-strummed guitar chords or the sound of the sea). Apply this motion to the amplitude of other sampled sounds or noise generators.

• Create asymmetric oscillatory motion as in the previous activity, but instead apply it to the cutoff frequency of a lowpass filter.

• •

SIMPLE PLANAR MOTION: STATIC TIME?

There are various techniques for creating planar motion, but the fundamental thing they all have in common is the subtle and continuous variation of some of a sound's parameters. This creates a sense of immobility that is interesting from a perceptual point of view, because the extremely slow and irregular motion creates variations in the sound that are below the threshold of conscious perception.

Imagine we have a bank of 16 bandpass filters with a randomly chosen center frequency and a Q value between 1 and 3. A random LFO at a very low rate (such as 0.05 Hz) is used to control the center frequency of each filter, and the amplitude of each LFO is equal to 5% of the center frequency of the filter (i.e., if the center frequency is 100 Hz the amplitude of the LFO will be equal to 5 and cause the center frequency of the filter to oscillate between 95 Hz and 105 Hz). If we now play a very static sound through the filter bank (a chord played on an organ, a sustained note played on the contrabass or an inharmonic sound created with additive synthesis) we obtain planar motion – that is to say that the sound does not have any apparent motion, but neither is it perceived as being completely static.

One other possibility would be to apply beating to a sound. Imagine we have created an inharmonic sound with 16 sinusoidal components using additive synthesis. This sound would be totally static, and thus probably seem rather uninteresting. If, however, for each of the components we added 2 or 3 other components whose frequency was randomly chosen within a maximum distance of 0.1 to 0.5 Hz from the frequency of the original component, we would get random beating for each component in the inharmonic sound. When adding the extra components, they should have an amplitude less than the original component itself, so that the resulting interference only slightly modifies the original component's dynamic profile, without ever canceling it completely.

Note that a lot of parameters are modified in the first example in order to obtain relatively static motion, whereas in the second example static motion has been created without varying any parameters at all (each of the frequencies is completely stationary), but rather by taking advantage of the perceptual phenomenon of beating.

. . . .

ACTIVITY

Create patches for the two kinds of planar motion described above.

. . . .

8.3 COMPLEX MOTION

To create complex motion, we will either use several instances of simple motion (such as "glissando" and LFO) in parallel, each one being used to vary a different parameter, or use them cascaded in series, so each type of motion is used to modify the next and the final result used to vary one or more parameters. Naturally, we could even consider using combinations of the two techniques. Rebuild the patch shown in figure 8.3 and describe how it works.

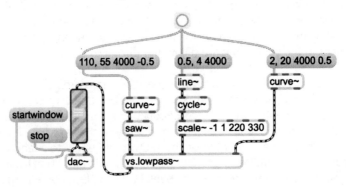

Fig. 8.3 Complex motion

ACTIVITIES

- Reverse-engineer sound example 8D.1, using a sampled sound of your choice.

- Create oscillatory motion in the stereo field on a sampled sound, gradually increasing the rate of oscillation.

- Add pitch variation to the previous example, synchronizing the pitch change of the sound to the stereo motion (when the sound is right it is higher in pitch, when it is left it is lower).

- Reverse-engineer sound example 8D.2, using a sampled sound of your choice.

. . . .

SPIRAL MOTION

. . . .

ACTIVITY

Take the patch IC_09_bouncing_bodies2.maxpat, and use it to sample a bouncing resonant body with `sfrecord~`. Use this sound to reverse-engineer sound examples 8E.1 and 8E.2.

. . . .

PARALLEL MOTION IN FREQUENCY

. . . .

ACTIVITY

Make 4 copies of the real-time pitch shifting algorithm used in the patch 06_12_rt_pitch_shift.maxpat. Use either oscillatory or unidirectional motion to control the frequency of the pitch shifting for each of the 4 copies of the algorithm. Use a band limited oscillator as a sound source.

. . . .

OPPOSING UNIDIRECTIONAL MOTION

. . . .

ACTIVITY

Refer to the description in the analogous section of chapter 8T in order to reverse-engineer sound examples 8E.4, 8E.5 and 8E.7.

ASPECTS OF RANDOMNESS IN MOTION

. . . .

ACTIVITIES

- Reverse-engineer sound examples 8F.1. Use **vs.rand3~** to create a random LFO.

- Take the patch 05_15_rand_blocks.maxpat and add the types of motion corresponding to sound examples 8F.2 a-g.

- Reverse-engineer sound example 8F.3a, using the patch 02_19_masking. maxpat as a basis.

- Use the **groove~** and **vs.pan~** objects with random LFOs in series and parallel to create motion similar to that used in sound example 8F.3b, using a sampled sound of your choice.

. . . .

8.4 EXPLORING MOTION WITHIN TIMBRE

Let's now take a look at how we can create "motion" within the timbre of a sound itself by gradually modifying both an envelope and its duration. Load the file **8_01_morphing_envelope.maxpat** (figure 8.4).

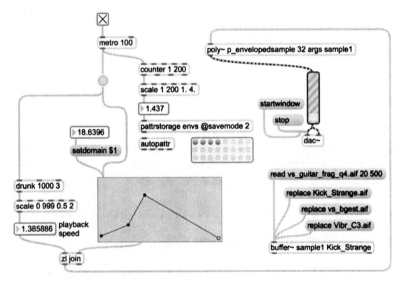

Fig. 8.4 The file **8_01_morphing_envelope.maxpat**

In this patch, both the envelope shape and its duration have been saved into 4 presets, using a **pattrstorage** object. Here, the **metro** object is used to gradually interpolate between one preset and the next, in addition to being used to generate a sound by sending the envelope and a value corresponding to the playback speed of a sound file to the [**poly~** p_envelopedsample] object at the upper right hand side of the patch.

You can analyze this patch and the polyphonic patch loaded inside the **poly~** object[1] by yourself.

Now, open the **function** object's inspector. You will immediately notice that the "Output Mode" attribute has been set to "List" mode. As was already explained in section IC.3, using the patch IC_06_poly_step_seq3.maxpat as an example, when the "Output Mode" is set to "List", the **function** object will send all of its envelope parameters as a single list instead of outputting the initial value by itself, followed by a list representing the rest of its trajectory, as it does by default. Can you explain why we need to send the envelope as a single list in this patch? Try changing the sound file being used by clicking on the message boxes on the lower right. Note that the message in the first message box is slightly different from the others – providing two additional numeric values to the *read* message allows us to select only a certain region of the sound file that will be read. The two values represent the starting point in the sampled sound and the duration that will be read, respectively.

We could also take some inspiration from the live slicer (or gate sequencer) that we previously saw in section 7.8P as the basis for creating a type of "timbre pulverizer" that applies envelopes with random shape and duration to a sound. The mean frequency and density of the enveloped slices should be user-controllable. Even though we are using the idea of a live slicer as a starting point, the final algorithm should nonetheless be quite different, mainly because we need to use random envelopes that are generated without any rhythmic regularity.

Open the patch 8_02_short_envelopes.maxpat and test out the various presets. Note that by using very high frequency values we begin to enter into the realm of granulation and amplitude modulation, both of which will be covered in detail in the next volume.

• •

ACTIVITY

Analyze the patch 8_02_short_envelopes.maxpat and create different kinds of motion by adding a preset management system (using **pattrstorage**) and using it to gradually interpolate between different presets.

• •

---

[1] Polyphony management using the **poly~** object has already been explained in detail in section IC.3.

It is also possible to make some modifications to the patch 8_01_morphing_ envelope.maxpat to create octave stacking. Rebuild the patch shown in figure 8.5, analyze it mentally and be able to explain how it works.

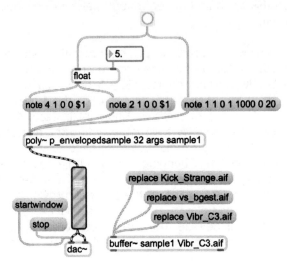

Fig. 8.5 Octave stacking

TIMBRAL MOTION USING RESONANT FILTERS

To create a harmonizer, you can use the real time pitch shifting patch we saw in section 6.9P.

. . . .

ACTIVITY

Reverse engineer sound example 8G.3, using a different sound file.

. . . .

INCREASING SPECTRAL COMPLEXITY

. . . .

ACTIVITIES

• Reverse engineer sound example 8G.4a and 8G4c.

• Analyze the patch 8_03_spectral_complexity.maxpat

• Reverse engineer sound example 8G.5.

. . . .

PROGRESSIVE SATURATION IN SPECTRAL COMPLEXITY WITH AN ASCENDING AND DESCENDING GLISSANDO

· ·

ACTIVITIES

• Reverse engineer sound example 8G.6.

• Add the real time pitch shifting algorithm from the patch 8_03_spectral_ complexity.maxpat and create an upward or downward glissando (with a random interval choice) in parallel to the sound's evolution.

· ·

INCREASING THE AMOUNT OF RANDOMIZATION IN A WAVEFORM

· ·

ACTIVITIES

• Reverse engineer sound example 8H.1.

• Create a second version of the motion in the previous activity where the individual components of the inharmonic waveform are substituted with those of a sawtooth waveform, one by one, at different points in time.

· ·

DISTRIBUTION CURVES FOR SPECTRAL COMPONENTS

· ·

ACTIVITY

Create a new version the patch 02_09_beats_harm_comp.maxpat that uses a polyphonic patch for the individual instances of the **wave~** object. Make sure that both the number of oscillators being used (from 2 to 32), as well as the number of components per oscillator can be defined by the user. The oscillator frequencies should be calculated automatically by the patch using a base frequency and a value representing the spacing in Hz between each of the oscillators' frequencies. For example, if the base value is 110 Hz and the distance is 0.05 Hz, the frequencies calculated for the oscillators will be 110 Hz, 110.05 Hz, 110.1 Hz, 110.15 Hz, etc.

· ·

FROM NOISE TO NOTE

. . . .

**ACTIVITIES**

- Reverse engineer sound example 8H.3

- Analyze the patch 8_04_noise_comb.maxpat and explain how it works.

. . . .

8.5 COMPOUND MOTION

COMPOUND CENTRIFUGAL OR CENTRIPETAL FREQUENTIAL AND SPATIAL MOTION

. . . .

ACTIVITY

Once you have analyzed the patch 8_05_fat_oscillator.maxpat and are able to explain how it works, reverse engineer sound example 8I.1 using the instrument from this patch as the principal sound generator.

. . . .

SYNCHRONIZED CENTRIFUGAL/CENTRIPETAL OSCILLATORY MOTION

. . . .

ACTIVITY

Reverse engineer sound example 8I.2 using the instrument from the patch 8_05_fat_oscillator.maxpat as the principal sound generator.

. . . .

OSCILLATORY MOTION OF A BANDPASS FILTER APPLIED TO CENTRIFUGAL MOTION

. . . .

ACTIVITIES

- Starting with the sound you created in the previous activity, reverse engineer sound examples 8I.5 and 8I.6. Try using interpolated random oscillators (either **rand~** or **vs.rand~**) in addition to regular (periodic) LFO waveforms.

- Create a variation on the previous activity by applying some kind of motion (such as accelerando, rallentando, or a change in DC offset) to the LFOs themselves.

- Create a further variation on the previous activity by also applying motion to the filter's Q factor.

• •

"SKIDDING" COMPOUND MOTION

• •

ACTIVITY

Reverse engineer sound example 8I.8 and 8I.9 starting from the sound you already created in the previous activities.

• •

COMPOUND MOTION BASED ON ACCUMULATION AND RAREFACTION

• •

ACTIVITIES

- Reverse engineer sound example 8I.10 using the instrument in the patch 8_06_little_grains.maxpat.

- Reverse engineer sound example 8I.11 using the **ioscbank~** object.

• •

8.6 ALGORITHMIC CONTROL OF MOTION

Now let's look at an example of an algorithmic process, roughly inspired by the Steve Reich compositions which were discussed in section 8.6T. Open the patch **8_07_algorithmic_motion.maxpat** (shown in figure 8.6).

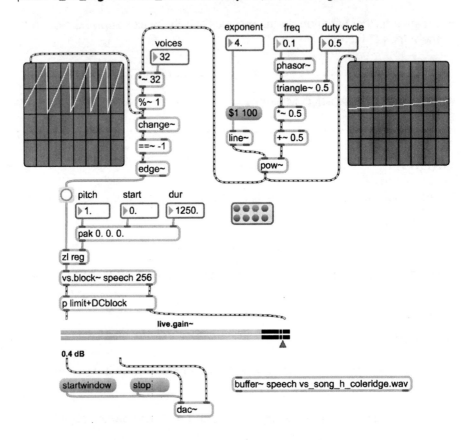

Fig. 8.6 The file **8_07_algorithmic_movement.maxpat**

First, listen to the 8 presets in order. You will hear a repeated spoken fragment that is initially repeated in a regular rhythm, and thereafter with a more and more accentuated oscillation between accelerando and ritardando applied to it. When the sound fragments are compressed into a very short temporal space you will notice that there is change in timbre resulting from the phase cancellation between the various repetitions.

The motion in this patch is generated with a triangular oscillator that has first been rendered unipolar and then from linear to exponential using the **pow~** object (you can see the result of this in the **scope~** on the right).

The signal output by the **pow~** object – having values that oscillate between 0 and 1 – is then multiplied by 32 so its values range between 0 and 32. This signal is then sent to the [% 1] object, which "slices" it into 32 individual ramps with a progressively changing slope, resulting from the exponential shape of the input signal. The series of ramps enters into the **change~** object, which is used to detect changes in the input samples. More precisely, the object will output a 1 if the current input sample is greater than the previous one, a -1 if the current sample is less than the previous, or a 0 if the current and previous input samples are the same. Therefore the [==~ -1] object it is connected to will output a 1 when change outputs a -1 and a 0 in all other cases. In other words, it outputs a 1 at the start of each new ramp. Can you explain why?

The output of the [==~ -1] object it is connected to an **edge~** object[2] that outputs a bang from its left outlet each time that [==~ -1] outputs a 1, which means at the start of each new ramp. This bang is used by **vs.block~** to create a fragment of sampled sound, or a "block."

Listen once again to the presets, paying careful attention to the different parameters, and in particular to the number box labeled "exponent", which determines the slope of the exponential curve.

• •

ACTIVITIES

• Create some additional presets for the patch 8_07_algorithmic_motion. maxpat. Be sure to also change the "voices" value sent to the multiplier in the upper left part of the patch (which determines the number of ramps that will be created with each cycle), as well as the parameters of the blocks being played.

• Use a random generator in place of the triangle wave.

• Modify the block parameters using additional LFOs.

• •

---

[2] The **edge~** object was introduced in section 7.8P. Remember that it outputs a bang from its left outlet when the input signal changes from zero to non-zero, and a bang out its right outlet when the input changes from non-zero to zero.

8.7 INTRODUCTION TO MOTION SEQUENCES

ACTIVITY

After having carefully listened to all of the sound examples listed in section 8.7T, create at least 5 small études between 30 seconds and one minute in length, based on the themes listed, below. You may use any or all of the techniques you have learned up to this point, including the algorithms for score management presented in section ID.3.

1) An étude in contrasts
2) An étude focused on gestures and textures
3) An étude on regular rhythms
4) An étude using irregular rhythms and polyrhythms
5) An étude about figure and ground

LIST OF MAX OBJECTS

change~
Indicates a change in the value of the input samples. The object outputs a 1 if the current input sample is greater than the previous one, a -1 if the current sample is less than the previous, or a 0 if the current and previous input samples are the same.

downsamp~
Downsamples a signal sent to its input using a sample and hold mechanism.

round~
Rounds the input signal according to the interval provided as an argument.

9T
MIDI

PREREQUISITES FOR THE CHAPTER
• THE CONTENTS OF VOLUME 1, CHAPTERS 5, 6, 7 AND 8 (THEORY AND PRACTICE), INTERLUDE C AND D

OBJECTIVES
KNOWLEDGE
• TO KNOW THE MIDI PROTOCOL
• TO KNOW THE STRUCTURE OF AND BE ABLE TO USE CHANNEL AND SYSTEM MESSAGES
• TO KNOW THE BASIC USES OF MIDI CONTROLLERS

CONTENTS
• THE MIDI PROTOCOL: CONNECTIONS AND MESSAGES
• TRANSMITTER AND RECEIVER MODULES: THE FLOW OF MIDI DATA.
• THE STRUCTURE AND USE OF CHANNEL VOICE MESSAGES AND CHANNEL MODE MESSAGES
• THE STRUCTURE AND USE OF SYSTEM REAL TIME MESSAGES
• MIDI CONTROLLERS: FROM QUASI-INSTRUMENTAL INTERFACES TO CONTROL SURFACES
• ADVANCED MIDI CONTROLLERS: FROM USING A MIDI DATA GLOVE TO GESTURE MAPPING

TESTING
• TEST WITH SHORT ANSWERS (MAXIMUM 30 WORDS)

SUSSIDI DIDATTICI
• FUNDAMENTAL CONCEPTS - GLOSSARY

9.1 THE MIDI STANDARD

The exchange of information between electronic musical instruments, controller systems and computers often makes use of the *MIDI protocol*, a standard created in the early 1980s, and still widely in use today. The term MIDI is an acronym for Musical Instrument Digital Interface. The MIDI protocol is used by a large number of applications, often very different from one another. In this chapter we will cover only those parts of MIDI which are essential for our purposes, alongside some important basic information.

There are two types of MIDI devices:
- *controllers*: these are devices that output MIDI messages
- *sound modules*: these are devices that use the MIDI messages they receive to generate or modify sounds.

Furthermore, sound modules themselves can be divided into two categories:
- instruments, such as synthesizers and samplers, which output sound
- sound processors, such as delays, reverberators and other effects, which are used to modify external sound sources.

Sometimes, one device, such as a computer, can behave as either transmitter or receiver, depending on how it is being used. Note that a computer by itself cannot communicate with external devices using MIDI unless it has MIDI interface connected to it (or a built-in MIDI Interface Card). Today, the majority of MIDI instruments being manufactured have a built-in digital connection (such as USB) that can connect directly to a computer, allowing it to receive and transmit MIDI data to the computer without the need for a dedicated MIDI interface. Figure 9.1 shows a generic back panel of a MIDI interface with two MIDI Out ports, two MIDI In ports and a USB port which connects to the computer.

MIDI OUT   MIDI OUT   MIDI IN   MIDI IN   USB COMPUTER

Fig. 9.1 Back panel of a generic MIDI interface

Today MIDI is used in a wide variety of applications, many of which cross over into the realm of professional audio. Furthermore, MIDI is a continually evolving protocol, and is used by computers, the internet, mobile devices (such as mobile phones), complex sound control systems, light boards, multimedia systems, and countless other devices. There exist several other communication protocols which are even faster and more flexible than MIDI (such as OSC, for example), although they are not very commonly found on electronic musical instruments such as keyboards, MIDI guitars, etc. As such, MIDI remains universally utilized due to both its ease of use and strong presence in the realm of commercial musical instrument production.

9.2 MIDI MESSAGES

Before delving into the details of MIDI messages, we feel it is necessary to first point out that MIDI messages themselves do not contain any sound, but instead define the way in which a particular sound, residing elsewhere in memory, will be played. In other words, they simply express what note will be played, when that note will begin and end, what dynamic it will have, and so forth. Therefore, it is very important to differentiate a sound file (containing a sound's waveform, along with its duration, envelope, timbre, frequency, etc.) from a MIDI message, which simply provides information relating to the way a given sound will be played, and not its waveform. The waveform itself is usually stored somewhere in memory (or generated by an algorithm which is stored in memory) in a separate location from the MIDI message. In other words, a keyboard sends MIDI data, and this data is used to trigger the sound-generating module receiving it. This module could have waveforms stored in memory, or could use some other type of sound-generating algorithm, and would produce sound only in reaction to MIDI messages coming from the keyboard. In order to be completely clear: the keyboard only sends instructions to the sound module via MIDI, and the module receiving these instructions outputs the sound via its own audio interface. One reason that there is sometimes confusion about this is that there are two types of MIDI keyboards:

1) a mute keyboard, or *Master Keyboard*, which exclusively performs the function of a transmitter – in other words, a basic *MIDI Keyboard Controller*. This kind of keyboard generates only MIDI data, which can be sent to external MIDI receivers using via its MIDI Out port.

2) a keyboard that works as a sampler or synthesizer – that is, a keyboard which also contains its own internal sound generation module in addition to generating MIDI data. This type of keyboard can act as both transmitter (via MIDI out) and receiver (via MIDI in), just like a computer, but it has an additional internal connection that sends the MIDI messages it transmits to an internal sound generation module. When we play a key on this kind of keyboard, we create MIDI messages that can be sent to either an external module (via MIDI out) or to the internal module that outputs sound from the keyboard's audio outputs (or to both places). Nonetheless, even in this situation the MIDI data itself (either that output by the keyboard or sent to the internal sound module) *does not contain any sound information*: the sound is always generated by an external or built-in sound module.

As we will learn in the next section, MIDI controllers come in all shapes and sizes. In addition to keyboards, there are also MIDI guitars, MIDI string and wind instruments, MIDI percussion and pedals (even Key Pedalboards, usually one or two octaves, and generally used for low-pitched sounds like organ pedals), just to name a few. These are all controllers whose shape and use is similar to that of the acoustic instruments they emulate, but which, as we have said before, are only used to send MIDI messages to a sound module – either external or built-in.

This module could contain sounds that match the interface (such as the sound of a guitar played by a MIDI guitar controller) or not (for example the sound of a flute or automobile horn being activated by a MIDI clarinet).

Now that we have hopefully cleared-up the general concept of MIDI and what types of information are *not* included in MIDI messages, let's move on to learn about the actual information that *can* be contained in them. The most basic use of MIDI is a sound module responding to a message resulting from a key being played (Note On) and the same key being released (Note Off) on a mute keyboard, along with pressure associated with playing that key. This pressure is called Key Velocity, because it is actually measured as the speed with which the key was played (not actually its pressure). It corresponds to the dynamic that note would have if it were played on a piano.

Because everything in MIDI is expressed in terms of numbers, we need to know the convention that has been adopted. This convention (as we learned in section 1.4T) means that each note (or better yet, each key) corresponds to a particular number (Key Number, in MIDI terminology): middle C is equal to 60, C# equal to 61, D to 62, D# to 63, etc.

The possible note values range from 0 to 127, even if the MIDI instruments themselves are not capable of producing every available note. A MIDI keyboard with the same range as the piano would only be able to produce note values between 21 and 108.[1]

Analogously, each dynamic corresponds to a number ranging between 0 and 127. The variation in dynamics within the sound generating module is generally on a logarithmic scale, in order to better match the ear's perception of dynamics and thus make the step between any two values have the same audible change in dynamics.

The MIDI protocol, to a limited extent, also allows the performance of notes outside the tempered tuning system[2], either by using instruments that are set up to handle tunings other than equal temperament (this is heavily dependent on the instrument being used – not all instruments are designed to handle alternate tunings), or by sending MIDI information that determines a variation in pitch for each note (with respect to its "normal" pitch), before the note is played.

---

[1] If you happen to have a controller with fewer octaves than the sounds available in the sound module you are using, you can always change the position of the sound by associating it with the keys an octave higher or lower, so that it falls within the instrument's actual playable range.
[2] See section 1.4T in the first volume for information about tuning systems.

This information is called *Pitch Bend*, and has the same effect as the physical *Pitch Bend Wheel* (or *Pitch Bender*) controller found on practically every MIDI instrument. This controller is generally some kind of wheel or slider that lets you momentarily alter the intonation of the notes being played.

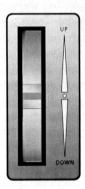

Fig. 9.2 A generic *Pitch Bend Wheel*

Furthermore, it is possible to select between different types of sounds (timbres or programs) stored in the instrument itself. There is a dedicated MIDI message, called *Program Change*, that lets you select a sound from among the different ones available in the instrument.

Let's now take an in-depth look at the two types of MIDI messages:
- Channel Messages
- System Messages

CHANNEL MESSAGES
If one MIDI transmitter (a computer, for example) is connected to several instruments, it is important to be able to establish a way of sending MIDI messages to just one particular instrument, otherwise all the instruments would simultaneously play the same "part." For this reason, each MIDI message is associated with a specific *channel number*, so each instrument can be set to handle only the messages that are relevant to it – in other words, only those messages which have the same channel number that the user has defined for the instrument itself. Channel Messages, are therefore addressed to a specific channel, and can be received and handled only by instruments that are set to receive on that particular channel. There are two types of Channel Messages: Channel Voice Messages, which deal with performance modes and execution times, and Channel Mode Messages which indicate the behavior of the receiving device. Let's begin by taking a look at the main Channel Voice Messages: Note On, After Touch, Polyphonic Key Pressure, Note Off, Program Change, Pitch Bend and Control Change.

NOTE ON
The Note On message corresponds to playing a given key on a MIDI keyboard or otherwise activating a note using one of the previously mentioned MIDI controllers. In addition to the note number (or Key Number) and Key Velocity,

this message also contains the MIDI channel number. In this instance the *Key Velocity* could be more aptly called *Attack Velocity* since it relates to the speed with which the key was played.

Just to give an example, a MIDI message that plays middle C is composed of three pieces of information: 144 60 120. The first number (called the Status Byte) is 144 and this value represents a "Note On" message, indicating a key has been pressed. The second number (called the First Data Byte) is 60, and this represents the note, or Key Number (middle C in this case). The third number (called the Second Data Byte[3]) is 120 and corresponds to the Attack Velocity (the maximum value for which is 127). So, what about the MIDI channel? This information is included in the first number. A Note On can actually be activated using any number between 144 and 159 as the Status Byte. If the first number is 144 (as it is here) the note is sent on MIDI channel 1, if the number were 145 it would be sent on midi channel 2, and so on, until number 159, which indicates transmission on channel 16.

NOTE ON MESSAGE			
	Status Byte	**1st Status Byte**	**2nd Status Byte**
Message Sent	Note ON + MIDI Channel	Note Number	Attack Velocity
Range of Values Transmitted	144 – 159	0 – 127	0 – 127
Message Contents	144 = Note ON MIDI ch. 1 145 = Note ON MIDI ch. 2 etc......... ....up until 159 = Note ON MIDI ch. 16	0 = C, first octave [4] 1 = C#, first octave etc......... ....up until 127= G, last octave	0 = no attack 1 = minimum amplitude etc......... ....up until 127= maximum amplitude

---

[3] You should be aware that sometimes the *Status Byte* is referred to as the 1st byte, the first *Data Byte* as the 2nd byte and the second *Data Byte* as the 3rd byte. Regardless of the terminology used, the content of the three bytes is the same, whether you split them into two groups (Status Byte and Data Bytes), or if the bytes are simply numbered according to the order in which they are sent and received.

[4] According to the MIDI standard, there are different ways of numbering octaves. Here, we are defining the lowest octave that can be represented by MIDI as octave -2, and the highest octave as octave 8. Taking into consideration that the highest octave only goes as high as G because of the 128-note limitation inherent in MIDI, there are a total of 10 and a half octaves from -2 to 8. With this definition, middle C on a piano keyboard falls in the third octave, and can therefore be referred to as C3. The standard 440 Hz A is thus called A3.

CHANNEL PRESSURE (OR CHANNEL AFTER TOUCH)

This equates to pressure variation for the entire keyboard. Some keyboards send a message providing information about whether there is a greater or lesser amount of pressure exerted on the entire keyboard while any of its keys are being held down. These messages provide a constant stream of values defining variations in pressure on the keyboard, until all of the keys are released. The Status Byte indicates that this is a Channel Pressure (After Touch) message, and, just like the Note On message, its status byte also contains information about the MIDI channel on which the message is being sent. The value range for this After Touch status byte ranges from 208 and 223. A value of 208 corresponds to variations in pressure on MIDI channel 1, 209 for channel 2, and so on. The Channel After Touch message has just one data byte indicating the amount of pressure exerted on the keyboard at any given instant. This control is normally used to change some characteristic of the sound while it is being played, such as changing the depth or rate of vibrato, for instance. Remember that this message affects *all* of the notes that are currently sounding, and for this reason the additional data byte that would normally indicate the note number is not present in the message (as can be seen in the following table).

CHANNEL PRESSURE (CHANNEL AFTER TOUCH) MESSAGE		
	Status Byte	**1st Data Byte**
Message Sent	Variations in Channel Pressure + MIDI Channel	Pressure Exerted
Range of Values Transmitted	208 – 223	0 – 127
Message Contents	208 = After Touch MIDI Channel 1 209 = After Touch MIDI Channel 2 etc......... ....up until 223 = After Touch MIDI Channel 16	0 = no pressure 1 = minimum pressure etc......... ....up until 127= maximum pressure

POLYPHONIC KEY PRESSURE (OR POLYPHONIC AFTER TOUCH)

This equates to an independent pressure variation for each key on the keyboard. Some keyboards send a message providing information about whether there is a greater or lesser amount of pressure exerted on each individual key while it is being held down. These messages provide a constant stream of values defining variations in pressure, until the key is released. This kind of *After Touch* naturally also contains the data byte indicating the note number of the key whose pressure is being transmitted.

POLYPHONIC KEY PRESSURE (OR POLYPHONIC AFTERTOUCH)			
	Status Byte	**1st Data Byte**	**2nd Status Byte**
Message Sent	Variations in Pressure for a Single Note + MIDI Channel	Note Number	Pressure Exerted
Range of Values Transmitted	160-175	0 – 127	0 – 127
Message Contents	144 = Note OFF MIDI ch. 1 145 = Note OFF MIDI ch. 2 etc......... ....up until 159 = Note OFF MIDI ch. 16	0 = C, first octave 1 = C#, first octave etc......... ....up until 127 = G, first octave	0 = no pressure 1 = minimum pressure etc......... ....up until 127 = maximum pressure

NOTE OFF

The Note Off message corresponds to the release of a given key on the keyboard when it is finished being played. Be aware that both the note number and its release velocity (speed of the release) are sent together, but the latter is not very often used and generally set to 64.[5]

NOTE OFF MESSAGE			
	Status Byte	**1st Data Byte**	**2nd Status Byte**
Message Sent	Note OFF + MIDI Channel	Note Number	Release Velocity
Range of Values Transmitted	128 – 143	0 – 127	0 – 127 (only in some devices). The RV is usually set to 64.
Message Contents	128 = Note OFF MIDI ch. 1 129 = Note OFF MIDI ch. 2 etc......... ....up until 143 = Note OFF MIDI ch. 16	0 = C, first octave 1 = C#, first octave etc......... ....up until 127 = G, first octave	

---

[5] In reality, most MIDI keyboards simply send a Note ON message with a velocity of 0 instead of using the Note OFF message.

PROGRAM CHANGE

This message is used to change the current program being played on a given MIDI Channel. Basically, this command lets you select a different timbre to be played a sampler or synthesizer, or change the effect being used by an outboard effect unit or other MIDI device.

PROGRAM CHANGE MESSAGE		
	Status Byte	**1st Data Byte**
Message Sent	Program Change + MIDI Channel	Pressure Exerted
Range of Values Transmitted	192 – 207	System-Dependent
Message Contents	192 = Program Change + MIDI Ch.1 193 = Program Change + MIDI Ch.2 etc........ ....up until 207 = Program Change + MIDI Ch. 16	System-Dependent

PITCH BEND

Corresponds to the activation of the Pitch Bend Wheel, which modifies the tuning of all the notes on a given MIDI Channel.

PITCH BEND MESSAGE			
	Status Byte	**1st Data Byte**	**2nd Status Byte**
Message Sent	Pitch Bend + MIDI Channel	LSB[6] (Least Significant Bit)	MSB (Most Significant Bit)
Range of Values Transmitted	224-239	0 – 127	0 – 127
Message Contents	224 = Pitch Bend + MIDI Ch. 1 225 = Pitch Bend + MIDI Ch. 2 .... 239 = Pitch Bend + MIDI Ch. 16	Generally either contains the same values as the second byte or is set to 0.	0 = Lowest Possible Downward Pitch Bend 64 = No Pitch Bend 127= Highest Possible Upward Pitch Bend

---

[6] Because MIDI data values are expressed using a 7-bit number (a byte where only 7 of the 8 bits are available) they can only express values between 0 and 127 (the maximum value a 7-bit number can represent is 1111111 in binary or 127 in decimal numbers). In some cases, however, a larger

Sound Example 1

Use of the pitch bend wheel to raise then lower the pitch of a sound by a semitone

. . . .

CONTROL CHANGE

This message is sent when a MIDI Controller (such as a pedal, slider, wheel, button, dial, joystick, breath controller[7] or other kind of sensor) is moved, used or activated. The message is composed of an ID number indicating the controller being used, followed by a value representing the position of the controller itself.

CONTROL CHANGE MESSAGE			
	Status Byte	1st Data Byte	2nd Status Byte
Message Sent	Control Change + MIDI Channel	Controller ID Number	Value of the Controller referenced in the first byte
Range of Values Transmitted	176-191	0 – 127	0 – 127
Message Contents	176 = Control Change + MIDI Ch. 1 177 = Control Change + MIDI Ch. 2 etc......... ....up until 191 = Control Change + MIDI Ch. 16	Controller Number (see below)	Controller Value (see below)

---

range of values needs to be used to be able more accurately express certain kinds of musical data. In these cases, two bytes are used together to express a 14-bit value ranging from 0 to 16383. In this situation, the rightmost 7 bits of the number are called the *least significant byte* (LSB) and the 7 on the left are called the *most significant byte* (MSB), because of their relative "weight" in the value of the number. (See also the note in section 5.2 concerning LSB and MSB.)

[7] A *breath controller* is used to simulate the emission of sound in wind instruments and sends MIDI messages whose values are proportional to the pressure exerted on the controller by the performer's breath.

Controller	Status Byte (176-191)	1st Data Byte	2nd Data Byte
Bank Number	176-191	0	from 0 to 127
Modulation Wheel	176-191	1	from 0 to 127
Breath Controller	176-191	2	from 0 to 127
Undefined Controller	176-191	3	from 0 to 127
Foot Controller	176-191	4	from 0 to 127
Portamento Time	176-191	5	from 0 to 127
Data Entry Slider (Cursor)	176-191	6	from 0 to 127
Main Volume	176-191	7	from 0 to 127
Balance	176-191	8	from 0 to 127
Undefined Controller	176-191	9	from 0 to 127
Panning	176-191	10	from 0 to 127
Expression Controller	176-191	11	from 0 to 127
Effect Control 1	176-191	12	from 0 to 127
Effect Control 2	176-191	13	from 0 to 127
Undefined Controlles	176-191	14 - 15	from 0 to 127
General Use Controllers n. 1-4	176-191	from 16 to 19	from 0 to 127
Undefined Controllers	176-191	from 20 to 31	from 0 to 127
Least Significant Byte for Controllers 1-31	176-191	from 32 to 63 (32 = LSB for Controller 0 33 = LSB for controller 1 etc.)	from 0 to 127 LSB
Sustain Pedal	176-191	64	from 0 to 63 = off from 64 to 127 = on
Portamento (Pedal)	176-191	65	from 0 to 63 = off from 64 to 127 = on
Sostenuto Pedal	176-191	66	from 0 to 63 = off from 64 to 127 = on
Soft Pedal	176-191	67	from 0 to 63 = off from 64 to 127 = on
Legato Pedal	176-191	68	from 0 to 63 = off from 64 to 127 = on

Hold 2	176-191	69	from 0 to 63 = off from 64 to 127 = on
Sound Controller 1	176-191	70	from 0 to 127
Sound Controller 2	176-191	71	from 0 to 127
Sound Controller 3	176-191	72	from 0 to 127
Sound Controller 4	176-191	73	from 0 to 127
Sound Controller 5	176-191	74	from 0 to 127
Sound Controller 6	176-191	75	from 0 to 127
Sound Controller 7	176-191	76	from 0 to 127
Sound Controller 8	176-191	77	from 0 to 127
Sound Controller 9	176-191	78	from 0 to 127
Sound Controller 10	176-191	79	from 0 to 127
General Use Controllers (No.5-8)	176-191	from 80 to 83	from 0 to 127
Portamento Control	176-191	84	from 0 to 127
Undefined Controllers	176-191	from 85 to 90	
Effects Controller 1	176-191	91	from 0 to 127
Effects Controller 2	176-191	92	from 0 to 127
Effects Controller 3	176-191	93	from 0 to 127
Effects Controller 4	176-191	94	from 0 to 127
Effects Controller 5	176-191	95	from 0 to 127
Data Increment Controller	176-191	96	
Data Decrement Controller	176-191	97	
Unregistered Parameter Number LSB	176-191	98	from 0 to 127
Unregistered Parameter Number MSB	176-191	99	from 0 to 127
Unregistered Parameter Number LSB	176-191	100	from 0 to 127
Unregistered Parameter Number MSB	176-191	101	from 0 to 127
Undefined Controllers	176-191	from 102 to 119	

The Control Change numbers from 120-127 are dedicated to Channel Mode Messages, as you can see in the table below. As we already mentioned, these work differently than the Channel Voice Messages in that they indicate the way that a receiving MIDI device will react to MIDI messages. Even though they are included in the Control Change list, we will cover the various Channel Mode Messages separately because they serve a rather different function, as you will soon discover.

Channel Mode Message	Status Byte (176-191)	1st Data Byte	2nd Data Byte
All Sound Off	176-191	120	0
Reset All Controllers	176-191	121	0
Local Control	176-191	122	0 = off – 127 = on
All Notes Off	176-191	123	0
Omni Mode Off (+ trigger All Notes Off)	176-191	124	0 (ignored)
Omni Mode On (+ trigger All Notes Off)	176-191	125	0 (ignored)
Mono Mode On (deactivate Poly + trigger All Notes Off)	176-191	126	Number of Channels
Poly Mode On (deactivate Poly + trigger All Notes Off	176-191	127	0 (ignored)

The official MIDI specification document has the following to say about Channel Mode Messages:

"Four Mode messages are available for defining the relationship between the sixteen MIDI channels and the instrument's voice assignment. The four modes are determined by the properties Omni (On/Off), Poly and Mono. Poly and Mono are mutually exclusive, i.e., Poly disables Mono, and vice versa. Omni, when on, enables the receiver to receive Voice messages on all voice Channels. When Omni is off, the receiver will accept Voice messages from only selected Voice Channel(s). Mono, when on, restricts the assignment of Voices to just one voice per Voice Channel (Monophonic). When Mono is off (Poly On), a number of voices may be allocated by the Receiver's normal voice assignment (Polyphonic) algorithm."

Therefore, when a receiving device is set to Omni On (first Data Byte = 125), it will recognize and accept all messages regardless of the channel on which they are being transmitted. These messages can be assigned to notes polyphonically (if the device is in Poly mode) or monophonically (meaning that they can only play one voice at a time) if the device is set to Mono mode. When using Omni Off mode (first data byte = 124), the device will only recognize messages that have been transmitted on a particular channel, or channels. Likewise, in this case the messages can be assigned polyphonically on one channel (Omni Off, Poly) or on a number of channels equal to the number of voices (Omni Off, Mono). Furthermore, transmitting devices can also be configured with these settings so that they match those of the receiving device(s). Generally, messages are always sent on a predetermined channel. If the device's channel is set to 6, all of the voices will be sent on channel 6. The only exception is when using an Omni Off, Mono configuration. In this case the messages of the voices will be sent on a number of channels equal to the number of voices. For example, if there are 5 voices being played and the transmitting device is set to channel 6, each individual voice will be sent on a different channel: 6, 7, 8, 9 and 10.

In addition to the above modes, there are four Channel Mode Messages: All Sound Off, All Notes Off, Reset All Controllers and Local Control. The **All Sound Off** message causes all currently sounding notes (whose Note On message has already been received but which have not yet received a corresponding Note Off) to be stopped. When using a non-mute keyboard (such as that on a synthesizer or sampler), this message applies only to those notes that were played in response to messages via its MIDI In port, not the notes being played directly on the keyboard. The **All Notes Off** message is similar to *All Sound Off*. The difference is that *All Sound Off* stops all notes, even if they are being held by the Sustain Pedal, and stops them immediately, independently of whatever kind of release the sound's envelope may have[8]. The *All Notes Off* message, on the other hand, simply sends the necessary Note Off messages, thereby allowing the pedal and release of the note to be taken into consideration. **Reset All Controllers** sets the following controllers to their default values:

- Controls concerning the LSB and MSB parameter numbers (from 98 to 101) are set to a null value:
- Expression is set to 127
- Modulation is set to 0
- The pedal values are set to 0
- Pitch Bend is set to its central value
- After Touch (both Channel Pressure and Polyphonic Key Pressure) is set to 0

Local Control is used to disconnect a keyboard from its sound generator, in order to allow the generator to respond to external MIDI messages arriving via the MIDI In port instead of those coming from the keyboard itself. This can be useful when a non-mute keyboard (i.e., a keyboard that has its own sound generator) is connected to a program (such as a sequencer) which is being used to record events played on the keyboard. In this scenario, if Local Control is not active, the internal sound generator could end up playing each note twice: once when triggered by the sequencer and once by the keyboard itself. The result of this literal note doubling would be clearly audible and could have an undesirable effect on the sound being played.

---

[8] In MIDI terminology, *release* is used to mean the decay time of the note after the *Note Off* message.

SYSTEM MESSAGES

System messages are those which are received by all devices connected to the system, independent of channel. There are three types: System Common Message, System Exclusive Message and System Real Time Message. Given the specific intentions of this book, we will not provide any detailed explanation of System Common Messages, which deal with designation synchronization and tuning between devices, nor System Exclusive Messages (also known as SysEx Messages), which communicate information specific to (and only use-able by) devices made by a given manufacturer. Although the latter type of messages are not universally viable, they can nonetheless become important in setups where there are several MIDI devices of the same brand, since they will all share an exclusive manufacturer-designed message system that allows them communicate information to each other in addition to the standard MIDI messages.

System Real Time Messages have the unique ability of being able to be sent at any given moment, even during the transmission of other messages (in-between Status and Data bytes), which are momentarily suspended, in order to let the System Real Time Messages "pass through." These have priority over other messages precisely because they mainly deal with timing and synchronization between devices and therefore must be sent in real time.

Let's take a look at the main **System Real Time Messages**:

The **MIDI Clock** message (Status Byte 240) is used in order to synchronize a transmitting MIDI device (Master) with a receiver (Slave), such as a Master Sequencer imposing its tempo on a slave sequencer so the two are tightly synchronized. The master device transmits MIDI Clock messages to the other sequencer at regular intervals, based on a given tempo (the tempo defined in the sequence of the master device).[9]

There are 24 *MIDI Clock* messages sent for or every quarter note. This means that if the tempo is set to 60 BPM (i.e., 60 quarter-note beats per minute) the master device will transmit $24 \cdot 60$ (= 1440) MIDI Clock messages per minute. If the tempo were increased to 90 BPM it would send $24 \cdot 90$ (= 2160) MIDI Clock messages every minute, and so on.

The **MIDI Start** message (Status Byte 250) is used to synchronize the start of a sequence present in a slave device with the Start message transmitted by a Master device. When the master sends this signal, the slave device goes to the beginning of its own note sequence and starts from 0, in sync with this signal.

---

[9] The master and slave devices are considered transmitter and receiver, respectively, only where the MIDI Clock is concerned. Even though a slave device is constantly adapting its tempo to that of a master, it can still act as a transmitter for messages to other MIDI devices in the system.

The **MIDI Continue** message (Status Byte 251) is used to synchronize the start of a sequence present in the slave device with the Continue message sent by the master device. The difference between this and the MIDI Start message is that the MIDI Continue message takes the position of the cursor within the slave device's sequence into consideration. For example, if the cursor in the slave device's sequence is set to the second beat, the Continue message will start playback of the sequence from that point, and not from the beginning, like the Start message.

The **MIDI Stop** message (Status Byte 252), as its name suggests, can be transmitted by a master device to stop playback of a sequence present in a slave device.

The **MIDI Active Sensing** message (Status Byte 254) is a message that is transmitted at regular intervals to ensure that the connection between two devices is still active. This is mainly a security measure – imagine a situation where a musician is performing on a MIDI keyboard that is sending MIDI messages to a sound generator (an expander, for example). Beginning at any moment, the expander could receive very long note messages (Note On messages without their corresponding Note Off). In this case, either the performer is holding down a very long chord, or there could potentially be some kind of connection problem. If the connection was interrupted after the expander received the Note On, it would not be able to receive the Note Off and the notes would be sustained indefinitely. This is where the Active Sensing function can be useful. If the expander does not receive an Active Sensing message after 300 milliseconds, it can "recognize" that the keyboard is no longer connected and shut off the sustained sound.

The **MIDI System Reset** message (Status Byte 255) reinitializes the device as if it had just been turned on at that moment; this function is only very rarely used.

9.3 MIDI CONTROLLERS

One of the most interesting uses for MIDI is its application to the real-time control of a sound's parameters. Up until now, we have only dealt with MIDI on the simplest terms: to activate notes using a given, predetermined timbre based on messages that control the notes' duration, amplitude and pitch. Nonetheless, there are many other uses for MIDI within more specific areas of synthesis and sound processing. For example, MIDI messages can be sent in real-time in order to control not only the parameters of a sound's components, but also filter parameters, control oscillator parameters, reverberation parameters and much more. It is also possible to use MIDI as a means of real-time control for processing live sound coming from a microphone.

SIMPLE CONTROLLERS

There is already an astronomical number of controllers that musicians can use to send MIDI messages via the motion of their hands (or other body parts). Let's begin exploring controllers by taking a look at some of the more basic manual controllers commonly found on keyboards. These include sliders, wheels (such as used for pitch bend), dials, buttons, etc., which generally handle just one type of control data at a time. If a given parameter is assigned to the motion of one of these controllers (either real or virtual) its values can be changed with the movement of that controller's physical surface. When such a controller is virtual, this simply means that it is a graphical surface simulating an actual (real-world) controller, and this controller's values can be changed using the mouse.

Other controllers are designed specifically for use with a performer's feet. These include On/Off pedals (Foot Switches), or pedals that can send values between 0 and 127 (Expression Pedals). There are also Breath Controllers whose output values change in accordance with the amount of breath pressure being blown into them. These can be very attractive controllers to use, since the continuous stream of pressure values they output could be applied to After Touch, Pitch Bend or any other sound processing parameter (such as vibrato depth, for example).

The joystick is a common controller whose output values can be manipulated with a single hand. Even though most joysticks were created for use with video game consoles , they are also useable with MIDI (for example, by using the movement along the x axis to control the center frequency of a filter, the movement along the y axis to control the Q factor of the filter, and the button to turn filtering on and off.)

One special tool that is not a MIDI controller per se, but which can be adapted to use with MIDI, is the photoelectric cell, whose output values depend on variations in light intensity. Such devices, among other kinds of sensors, are often used in interactive sound installations, where they can be activated in real time by the movement of those experiencing the installation – either knowingly or unwittingly – and used as on/off switches controlling as many MIDI messages as there are types of sound processing used in the installation. The list of available controllers and their various uses is constantly growing and would be far too long to mention here in any detail. Nonetheless, due to the nature of this text we thought it could be useful just to mention several examples of simple MIDI controllers in order to give you a general idea of how they can potentially be used for musical goals.

CONTROL SURFACES

At some point, using a single mouse, hand or foot controller may no longer be adequate for our purposes, and this is where more complex controllers, requiring the simultaneous use of both hands, come into play. The generic name for these types of controllers is Control Surface. There are various types of control surfaces, but they are all designed to be played as if they were an instrument, and output a stream of MIDI data that can be used for real-time sound processing.

One very common example of such a control surface is the MIDI mixer, which usually has several sliders, each of which can be connected to a different sound processing function. For example, one slider could be used to control the amplitude of the fundamental frequency of a sound, the next to control the amplitude of the second harmonic, the third for the third harmonic, etc. Used this way, the MIDI value of 0 could correspond to the minimum amplitude of the harmonic, and 127 to its maximum amplitude.

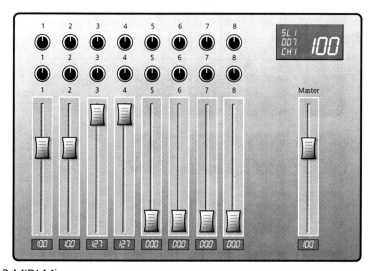

Fig. 9.3 MIDI Mixer

A control surface with a similar level of complexity is the MIDI Foot Controller, which is an entire set of pedals, instead of just one. (This is not to be confused with the MIDI Key Pedalboard, which is more of an instrumental (note-based) controller.) Foot Controllers generally have several pedals, each of which could serve a different function, depending on how the entire controller and MIDI system have been configured. For example, one pedal could act as an on/off switch for an effect, another pedal could act as a continuous controller and send MIDI values between 0 and 127 to control the amplitude of repetitions of a sound, another continuous controller pedal could control the frequency of an oscillator used for vibrato, another to control the panning movement of the sound in the stereo field, etc. These are very common controllers for musicians who need to use their hands to play their instrument, but who have their feet free to control the processing of their instrumental sound in real-time.

Fig. 9.4 MIDI Foot Controller

Another control surface that can be used as a percussion instrument is the MIDI Trigger, which is composed of a series of touch-sensitive pads that respond to both velocity and pressure. These pads can have different levels of sensitivity, depending on whether the control surface is a MIDI Trigger designed to be played with drumsticks, or a Finger Trigger played with the hands, as shown in the accompanying figure.

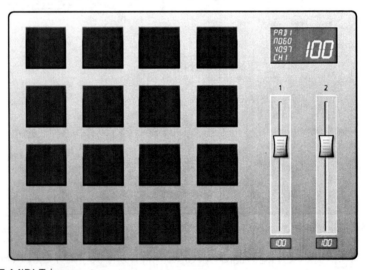

Fig. 9.5 MIDI Trigger

MIDI SENSORS, MIDI DATA GLOVE AND MOTION TRACKING

A MIDI controller configuration can become even more complex if we begin to use motion within a space to control the parameters of a sound. There is a wide variety readily available MIDI sensors that can be used to measure some physical quantity (such as light, pressure or sound) and transform it into a stream of MIDI messages in real time, using an appropriate converter. Some sensors are designed to be attached to different parts of the body, and thus can be easily used by dancers, performers and actors in order to control the parameters of sound, light or images in real time, via MIDI. Naturally, the scope of what can be done with these types of sensors increases dramatically and also offers a springboard for reflection on the theme of possible connections between the arts, and also on the relationship between technology, control, and emotional expression through the use of the body, sound, light, image processing and the like. In addition to sensors which can transform the real time movements of performers into streams of MIDI data, there is also a special multi-sensor glove known as MIDI Data Glove that can be used to control a large number of parameters (depending on the number of sensors built into the glove) in real time using the motion of the hand and each of the fingers in three-dimensional space.

Systems that use the entire body as a controller can be even more complex. One such system is known as Motion Tracking, which allows gestures (such as those coming from a dancer) to be mapped, via the use of one or more video cameras (and sometimes also a system of markers applied to the dancer) together with software that analyzes the silhouette (or skeletal structure) of the person in order to extract their overall movement and use of space. Other software is then used to connect this data to the various parameters that control the sound. Considering that even a single data glove can furnish more than 15 streams of data to control just as many sound parameters, imagine how complex the relationship between body movement and sound must be! The control of such an immense number of parameters requires an in-depth reflection on the relationship between sound, gesture and physical expression, and thus can open up an enormous realm for exploration.

Furthermore, it is possible to apply a pitch tracker – a system which generates MIDI note on and off messages derived from the analysis of audio signals – to the sound of an actual instrument (such as an acoustic guitar).[10]

---

[10] We will cover sound analysis in the third volume

TESTING • TEST WITH SHORT ANSWERS (MAX. 30 WORDS)

1) Describe an example of a MIDI connection setup where the computer is used simultaneously as a transmitter and receiver. Be sure to describe all of the connections in detail.

2) What is the difference between Polyphonic After Touch and Channel After Touch? Apart from keyboards, what other kinds of controllers could use these messages?

3) If we had a MIDI message whose Status Byte was 180, followed by a second bite with the value 2 and a third byte with the value 127, which kind of device is involved, which MIDI channel is it using, what kind of message is it sending, what parameter could be controlled by such a message, and what would be the final result of the message?

4) In an Omni Off configuration, if we had a status byte with a value of 178 followed by a first Data Byte with a value of 126 and a second Data Byte with a value of 3, what result would this give us from the point of view of voices and channels?

. . . .

FUNDAMENTAL CONCEPTS

1)   The MIDI Protocol is used to allow different kinds of instruments to com-
     municate with one another. These instruments can act as transmitters,
     receivers or both. The MIDI IN, OUT and THRU connections can be made
     with traditional MIDI cables, USB connections or more advanced connec-
     tions such as wireless or virtual connections via software.

2)   MIDI messages themselves do not contain any sound, but rather are used
     to determine the way a particular sound, residing in the memory of a sound
     generating device, should be played.

3)   MIDI messages can be divided into two categories: System Messages and
     Channel Messages. Channel Messages can be further divided into Channel
     Voice Messages and Channel Mode Messages, and System Messages can
     be divided into three sub-groups: System Common Messages, System
     Exclusive Messages and System Real Time Messages.

4)   MIDI also provides a means of sending messages in real time in order to
     control parameters relating to a sound's components, filtering, control
     oscillators, reverberation, etc. It is even possible to use MIDI as a means
     of controlling the real time sound processing of live audio input from a
     microphone. These messages can be sent using simple controllers, control
     surfaces, MIDI sensors, MIDI Data Gloves, Motion Tracking systems or other
     devices.

GLOSSARY

All Notes Off
A mode message that is used to stop any note currently playing as the result of a Note On message which has not yet received a Note Off. This message does not cause the sound to be stopped abruptly, but rather takes into account both the release of the note and the position of the sustain pedal.

All Sound Off
A mode message that is used to abruptly stop all notes currently playing, as the result of Note On messages, that have not yet received a corresponding Note Off.

Bank Number
A number that refers to the group of timbres or effects in a sound module.

Breath Controller
A controller whose output values change in proportion to the breath pressure of the performer.

Channel Message
A MIDI message that is sent via a specific channel and only received by devices that respond to that particular channel.

Channel Mode Message
A channel message that is primarily used to indicate the way a receiving device will respond to MIDI messages.

**Channel Pressure
(or Channel After Touch)**
A voice message whose value indicates the variations in pressure on the ensemble of depressed keys of a keyboard or other instrumental controller. It affects the parameters of all notes being played.

Channel Voice Message
A channel message that sends timed musical performance information.

Control Change
A voice message that specifies which controller will be activated and what value it will be given at any given moment.

Control Surface
A multi-purpose controller that is able to control multiple parameters at the same time.

Data Byte
Bytes which follow the Status Byte, and are used to send the actual data of the MIDI message.

Expander
An external sound generator (or processor) without a keyboard or other controller, that usually only works as a receiver in a MIDI system.

Finger Trigger
A control surface made up of a series of velocity and pressure sensitive pads designed to be played with the fingers. This kind of controller can also be used as a percussion instrument.

Foot Controller
A control surface comprised of different kinds of pedals.

Instrumental Controller
A MIDI transmitter made up of control surfaces whose shape and function is similar to that of acoustic instruments, like guitars, string and wind instruments, keyboards, percussion, etc.

Joystick

A controller designed to be manipulated with one hand that outputs multiple parameter values through the use of buttons and a two-dimensional lever.

Key Number

A note number expressed by the conventional MIDI values from 0 to 127.

Key Pedalboard

A one or two octave MIDI pedal board similar to the pedals on an organ.

Local Control

A mode message that is used to decouple a keyboard from its built-in sound generator.

Master Keyboard (or Mute Keyboard)

A special kind of keyboard that only functions as a MIDI transmitter; it does not have a sound module nor can it receive MIDI messages.

MIDI Active Sensing

A real time system message that is used to determine if the connection between two MIDI devices is currently active.

MIDI Channel

A channel number form 1 to 16 over which MIDI messages can be sent.

MIDI Clock

A real time system message that is able to synchronize the sequences played by MIDI devices.

MIDI Data Glove

A multi-sensor MIDI device resembling a glove that can transform data from its sensors into a series of MIDI data streams.

MIDI In, Out Thru

These are the three types of MIDI connections that devices may have and are used for MIDI message input, output and forwarding, respectively.

MIDI Interface

An interface that is used to connect MIDI devices to other devices that are not specifically designed for MIDI (a computer, for example).

MIDI Keyboard

A keyboard, containing its own sound module, capable of sending and receiving MIDI messages.

MIDI Keyboard Controller

A keyboard that works as a MIDI message transmitter.

MIDI Message

A message composed according to the MIDI protocol, which is sent from a transmitter device to a receiver device.

MIDI Mixer

A MIDI control surface with various kinds of sliders and buttons, each of which can be assigned to send a different MIDI message.

MIDI Pad

A surface controller, made in various sizes, composed of rubbery pads which can be played either with the hands or with drum sticks, depending on the type of controller.

MIDI Protocol

Musical Instrument Digital Interface: a communication protocol between electronic musical instruments, and even extending to devices outside the realm of music.

MIDI Sensor

A device capable of transforming a

physical property (such as light, pressure or sound) into a stream of MIDI data values.

MIDI Sound Module
A module that receives MIDI messages from a transmitter and produces sounds on the basis of these messages.

MIDI start, continue, stop
Real time system messages used to synchronize the starting stopping and resuming playback of sequences.

MIDI System Reset
A real time system message used to reinitialize the device as if it has just been turned on.

MIDI Trigger
An instrument falling somewhere in-between control surface and percussion instrument, that is made up of multiple velocity and pressure sensitive pads.

Modulation Wheel
A wheel or lever that sends a MIDI Control Change message indicating the value for variations in modulation (amplitude, frequency or other) applied to the notes being played.

Mono Mode (Poly Off)
A mode message used to limit the voice assignment of notes to one per channel. It is the opposite of Poly mode.

Motion Tracking
A complex system of body movement analysis that uses one or more video cameras alongside sensors that transform the analysis data into a series of MIDI signals.

Note Off
A voice message indicating that a key on a keyboard (or pressure on some other kind of instrumental controller) has been released.

Note On
A voice message indicating that a key on a keyboard has been depressed (or that pressure on some other kind of instrumental controller has been activated).

Omni on/off
A mode message that allows a receiver either to respond to messages on all channels (Onmi On) or to accept voice messages on only one channel (Omni Off).

Photoelectric Cell
An on/off switch that is triggered by variations of light or other parameters in a given environment, which can be used to control the activation and deactivation of different musical parameters.

Pitch Bend Wheel (or Pitch Bender)
A wheel or lever that transmits voice message values indicating a variation in intonation of all the notes being played with respect to their "normal" frequency.

Poly Mode (Mono Off)
A mode messages that is used to enable polyphonic note assignment in a device. It is the opposite of Mono mode.

Polyphonic Key Pressure (or Polyphonic After Touch)
A voice message whose value indicates the variations in pressure exerted on the individual depressed keys of a keyboard or other instrumental controller.

The message affects the parameters of only one specific note being played.

Program Change
A MIDI message used to select a specific timbre or effect preset stored in a device.

Reset All Controllers
A mode message used to set a selection of continuous controllers to their default values.

Sampler
A generic term used to define a sound module (either virtual, with a keyboard, or an expander) that can sample, store and reproduce sounds at different pitch levels in different octaves.

Sequencer
A digital device capable of storing multiple MIDI note sequences sent from another MIDI device, and able to play them back synchronously.

Simple Manual Controllers
These are controllers (even virtual ones) that are able to send MIDI messages based on simple hand movements. These include controllers like faders, dials, sliders and switches, and generally only control one parameter at a time.

Standard MIDI File
This is a file standard for writing MIDI data to disk in order to be able to share it between devices.

Start Bit
A bit that precedes the 8 bits of a MIDI message.

Status Byte
The first byte in a MIDI message, indicating both the message type and the MIDI channel.

Stop Bit
A bit that follows the 8 bits of a MIDI message.

Sustain Pedal
A pedal acting as an on/off switch that transmits a MIDI Control Change message used to sustain the notes that are currently playing.

Synthesizer
A general term used to designate a sound module (either virtual, with a keyboard or an expander) which can synthesize sounds at different pitch levels in different octaves.

System Common Message
System messages that deal with designation synchronization and tuning between devices.

System Exclusive Message (or SysEx Message)
System messages which are used to communicate information that is relevant only for devices made by a particular manufacturer.

System Message
Messages received by all devices connected to the MIDI system, independently of channel.

System Real Time Message
System messages sent in real time that have priority over other messages.

Velocity or Key Velocity
A MIDI parameter containing information about the dynamics associated with the pressure when a key on a keyboard is depressed (or when a component of some other kind of controller is otherwise activated).

9P
MIDI AND REAL-TIME CONTROL

PREREQUISITES FOR THE CHAPTER
• THE CONTENTS OF VOLUME 1, CHAPTERS 5, 6, 7 AND 8 (THEORY AND PRACTICE), INTERLUDE C AND D AND CHAPTER 9T

OBJECTIVES
ABILITIES
• TO BE ABLE TO USE MAX TO MANAGE MIDI DATA FLOW WITHIN A SYSTEM OF INTERCONNECTED VIRTUAL DEVICES.
• TO BE ABLE TO USE MAX TO MANAGE MIDI DATA FLOW (INCLUDING POLYPHONIC DATA) BETWEEN MIDI HARDWARE DEVICES AND SOFTWARE.

CONTENTS
• MIDI OBJECTS IN MAX AND HOW THEY ARE USED TO MANAGE MESSAGES
• ADVANCED MIDI POLYPHONY MANAGEMENT IN BETWEEN MAX AND EXTERNAL MIDI HARDWARE.

SUPPORTING MATERIALS
• LIST OF MAX OBJECTS - LIST OF ATTRIBUTES FOR SPECIFIC MAX OBJECTS

9.1 MIDI AND MAX

Up to now we have only lightly touched on the subject of MIDI in the Practice chapters of this series. In this chapter we will finally delve a little deeper into some aspects of the relationship between Max and MIDI in order to provide some essential information about their combined use.

In addition to note messages, which were already covered in section IB.1, other types of MIDI messages may also be sent and used to modify the parameters of the instrument (or effect) receiving them. Thus far, we have only been using MIDI to communicate with the built-in synthesizer of the computer's operating system, but it is nonetheless also possible to interface with any kind of MIDI device.

In Max's Options menu you can open up the MIDI Setup dialog. This window contains a list of all the MIDI devices – both physical and virtual – which are connected to the computer (see figure 9.1).

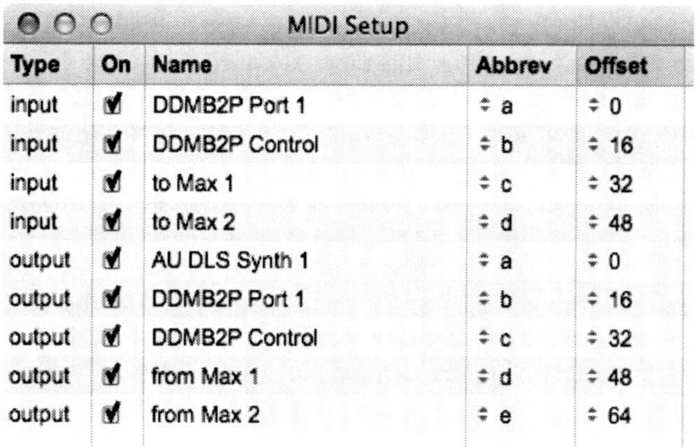

Type	On	Name	Abbrev	Offset
input	☑	DDMB2P Port 1	‡ a	‡ 0
input	☑	DDMB2P Control	‡ b	‡ 16
input	☑	to Max 1	‡ c	‡ 32
input	☑	to Max 2	‡ d	‡ 48
output	☑	AU DLS Synth 1	‡ a	‡ 0
output	☑	DDMB2P Port 1	‡ b	‡ 16
output	☑	DDMB2P Control	‡ c	‡ 32
output	☑	from Max 1	‡ d	‡ 48
output	☑	from Max 2	‡ e	‡ 64

Fig. 9.1 The MIDI Setup window

The window includes both a list of input devices (those that can send MIDI messages to Max) as well as output devices (which can receive MIDI messages from Max). As you can see, some of the devices shown may be used for both input and output. This would be the case for a device such as a physical MIDI interface (not a virtual one) connected to the computer which has ports for both MIDI IN and MIDI OUT connections (like the DDMB2P device in the first line of the list shown in the figure).

Each device can usually handle 16 communication channels of MIDI data. However, one device could actually be able to control several instruments simultaneously, and some of these instruments could even be polytimbral – that is, capable of producing sounds with different timbres simultaneously. In this scenario, different MIDI channels would be used to address the different instruments, or different sections of a polytimbral instrument. For example, if we connect a digital piano, a polytimbral synthesizer and a reverb unit, we could decide to send MIDI messages to the digital piano on channel 1, to the polytimbral syntheziser on channels 2, 3, 4 and 5 (to which we have assigned four different timbres), and to the reverb on channel 6. The **noteout** object, which has been used extensively throughout these first two volumes, has three inlets: the first for the MIDI note value, the second for the velocity and the third for the MIDI channel.

Each device has a name and we can additionally define an abbreviation and a channel offset.[1] using the MIDI Setup window. Each of the MIDI objects in Max can refer to a particular device using one of these parameters (generally given as arguments to the object).

In the MIDI Setup window, any device can be activated or deactivated by clicking on its checkbox (located in the "On" column), as well have its abbreviation or channel offset modified. Note the "AU DLS Synth 1" device which is the virtual synthesizer in Mac OSX (or the analogous device in Windows, which is called Microsoft DirectMusic DLS Synth): this is the synthesizer that we have been using up to now for all the MIDI examples.

Finally, some information about the devices called "to Max 1," "to Max 2," "from Max 1" and "from Max 2": these are virtual connections between Max and other programs running on the same computer, and are only available on Mac OSX. If you launch a program that uses MIDI (such as a sequencer) while Max is running, you will also see these virtual Max devices among the list of interfaces recognized by the program. This way you can send MIDI messages to Max using the "to Max 1" (or 2) port, as well as receive MIDI messages from Max using the "from Max 1" (or 2) port. In order to do the same thing on Windows, you need to use third-party software such as LoopBe1 (http://www.nerds.de) or LoopMIDI (http://www.tobias-erichsen.de).

---

[1] As we have already mentioned, there are 16 MIDI channels numbered from 1 to 16. However, because of the channel offset it is possible to use higher values, since the offset is added to the channel number. For example, you can see in the figure that device b has an offset of 16. This means that its channels (1-16) will be seen by Max as channel 17-32. Therefore when we send (or receive) a note message on channel 17, we are actually sending it to channel 1 on device b. The arguments to the MIDI objects let us specify the name of the device and channel, or only the channel (with a possible offset). In other words, with the settings shown in figure 9.1, the objects [noteout b 2] and [noteout 18] will both send messages to the same device and channel: the second channel on device b.

9.2 MIDI MESSAGE MANAGEMENT

In addition to the **noteout** object, used to send MIDI note messages, there is also a notein object that receives note messages from an external device, such as an actual (hardware) keyboard. Moreover, Max has a variety of other built-in objects capable of handling MIDI messages; some of these are shown in figure 9.2.

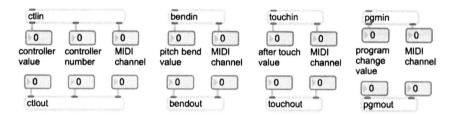

Fig. 9.2 Some other MIDI objects

The **ctlin** and **ctlout** objects receive and send control change messages. These messages are generally sent by controllers capable of transmitting a continuous stream of numerical values, such as the modulation wheel found on countless MIDI keyboards (and often used to control the a sound's vibrato), or pedals, faders, etc. (see chapter 9.3T). There are 128 controllers (numbered from 0 to 127) available on each MIDI channel, and each controller can be used to transmit (or receive) values between 0 and 127. Control change messages are generally used to modify some characteristic of an instrument's sound (such as adding vibrato to a sound, or changing the cutoff frequency of a filter) or some parameter of an effect (such as controlling the amount of distortion applied to the sound of an electric guitar being sent through a distortion effect).

The **bendin** and **bendout** objects receive and send pitch bend messages. These values (between 0 and 127) determine the modification of a note's pitch, used to simulate small glissandi on string instruments such as a guitar or violin, or on winds like clarinet or sax. The control mechanism used for this on MIDI keyboards is generally some kind of wheel.

The **touchin** and **touchout** objects receive and send after touch messages. These messages are output by MIDI keyboards based on the pressure exerted on the entire keyboard while keys are being held down. This is often used to modify some parameter of the sound, such as its volume or the cutoff frequency of a filter, and is therefore used similarly to a control change. Once again, the value range is between 0 and 127. The after touch message is global for the entire keyboard – the same message will be sent regardless of the key or keys that are being played. There is another MIDI message, polyphonic key pressure (not shown in the figure), that can send an independent pressure value for each key that is depressed, however this feature is rarely found on keyboards with the exception of perhaps some of the most expensive ones. That having been said, most keyboards are able to send global after touch messages.

The **pgmin** and **pgmout** objects receive and send program change messages, which are the equivalent of changing presets. Sending a program change message (yet again a value between 0 and 127) to a synthesizer (either real or virtual) tells it to change the timbre that it will be used to play subsequent notes. Note that in the Max environment, program change values are between 1 and 128, and are converted into values between 0 and 127 (the values are simply decremented by 1) before being sent to the device.

MIDI objects in Max can have the name of the device[2], the MIDI channel number or both as arguments (see footnote 1). For objects that receive MIDI messages, if the channel number is given as an argument, the associated outlet will disappear; see figure 9.3.

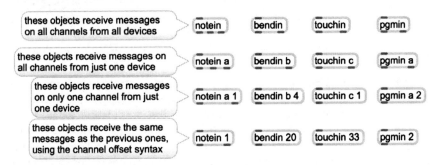

Fig. 9.3 Arguments to objects that receive MIDI messages

This figure provides an example for each possible combination of arguments. Note that the objects in the last two rows have one less outlet – they are missing the outlet corresponding to the MIDI channel, because this has been provided as an argument. Taking into consideration the device abbreviation and channel offset settings shown in the MIDI Setup window in figure 9.1, the objects in the last row will receive the messages on the same channel and from the same device as those in the row just above it.

The **ctlin** and **ctlout** objects deal with arguments in a slightly different way. There are 128 controllers per MIDI channel (numbered 0 to 127), and each of these can send values between 0 and 127. So, if these objects have just one argument, it is considered to be the controller number. This argument can be preceded by the device name, followed by the channel number, or both. If we want to specify a MIDI channel without defining a specific controller, we can use the value -1 as a controller number (see figure 9.4).

---

[2] The device name can be its abbreviation, which consists of a single letter, or the full name of the device as it appears in the "Name" column in the MIDI Setup window. When the full name is made up of several words separated by spaces, the name should be provided in quotes. Referring to the devices shown in figure 9.1, if we wanted to use the first device, we could either type the abbreviation a, or else use the full name "DDMB2P Port 1".

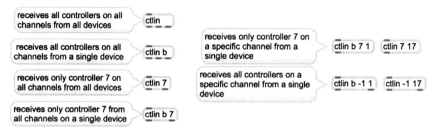

Fig. 9.4 Arguments for the `ctlin` object

The first outlet always corresponds to the value output by the controller. In the event that the object only has two outlets, the second outlet will correspond either to the MIDI channel number, as in the case of [ctlin 7] and [ctlin b 7], or the controller number, as in the case of [ctlin b -1 1] and [ctlin -1 17]. Take a moment to think carefully about this and be able to explain why.

If we double-click on a MIDI object while the patch is in performance mode, a contextual menu will appear, allowing one of the available devices to be selected. The selected device would be used in place of any that may have been provided as an argument to the object.

Now let's take a look at a patch that lets us modify the sound of a software or hardware synthesizer connected to the computer via MIDI. Open the file **09_01_MIDI_synth.maxpat**, shown in figure 9.5.

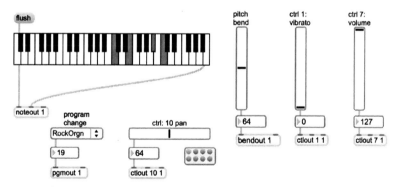

Fig. 9.5 The file **9_01_MIDI_synth.maxpat**

By default, this patch connects to the computer's internal synthesizer, but it is always possible to use another device by changing the settings in the MIDI Setup window. The `kslider` object on the upper left is in "Polyphonic" mode, and therefore capable of sending note on and note off messages.[3] The [flush] message connected to the object is used to send a note off for all of the currently active notes.

---

[3] We have already discussed this mode, which can be set via the inspector, in section IB.1 in the first volume.

In addition to program change and pitch bend, this patch also uses several controllers defined by the General MIDI standard.[4] The second and third sliders on the right allow us to send values for controller 1 (used for the vibrato depth in the sound) and controller 7 (used for volume), respectively. Additionally, there is a horizontal slider (just underneath the **kslider**) that lets us set the value of controller 10 (used for panning). Note the menu connected to the **pgmout** object (the object that sends program change messages) – this menu contains all of the timbres defined in the General MIDI standard so if the receiving MIDI device adheres to this standard, the available timbres should correspond to those listed in the menu. Try out all of the presets and try modifying the different controls in the patch.

· ·

⌖ ACTIVITY

Starting from the patch shown in figure 9.5, create a second group of objects which send the MIDI note, program change, pitch bend, etc., on MIDI channel 2. Select the same program change value on both channels and slightly alter the pitch bend on channel 2, in order to create a chorusing effect when the same note is played on both channels. If you have a MIDI keyboard, use it to control both channels simultaneously.

· ·

The objects we have seen up to now are "specialized" objects, in the sense that each of them receives or transmits a specific type of MIDI message, ignoring all other types of messages. Nonetheless, there also exist two generic MIDI objects in the Max environment, **midiin** and **midiout**. These objects send and receive "raw" MIDI data. Load the patch **09_02_raw_MIDI_data.maxpat** (figure 9.6).

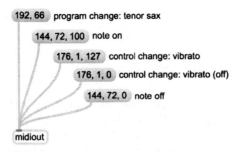

Fig. 9.6 The patch 09_02_raw_MIDI_data.maxpat

---

[4] For more information about the General MIDI standard and the MIDI protocol, you can consult the official site: http://www.midi.org.

This patch also connects to the computer's internal synthesizer by default. By clicking on the message boxes from top to bottom we can send a series of raw-format MIDI messages. The first number in each message box specifies the type of MIDI message being sent, and on which channel (more details about this in a moment). The numbers which follow them are the values associated with the message.

For example, the number 192 in the first message box corresponds to a program change message on channel 1. The next number 66 is the program change value that will be sent – in the General MIDI standard this corresponds to a tenor sax sound. In the second message box, the value 144 corresponds to a note on message on channel 1, 72 is the note value (C4) and 100 is the velocity. Notice that the numbers in all of the message boxes are separated by commas: this is because raw MIDI data must be sent as a series of single values, not in the form of a list.

Technically speaking, the first value in each of the message boxes (the one which indicates the message type) is called the status byte, and the values after it are called data bytes. Furthermore, as we previously mentioned, the status byte also includes the MIDI channel being used. By incrementing the value of the status byte, messages can be sent on higher MIDI channels. For example:

144: note on MIDI channel 1
145: note on MIDI channel 2
146: note on MIDI channel 3
...
159: note on MIDI channel 16

Naturally, this procedure works for all status byte messages.[5]

If you have a physical MIDI controller such as a keyboard, create a **midiin** object and connect it to a **print** object. You will notice that, for each key or controller you activate on the device, the corresponding raw MIDI data will be printed in the Max window.

The **midiin** and **midiout** objects are very useful when different types of MIDI messages need to be dealt with simultaneously. Fortunately, there are three other objects that can help us interpret the MIDI messages more easily: **midiparse**, **midiselect** and **midiformat**.

---

[5] The list of status byte messages can be found at http://www.midi.org, or else they could be constructed using the **midiformat** object, which will be discussed in a moment.

The **midiparse** object can be connected to a **midiin**, in order to recognize and separate the different MIDI messages being received. The various messages are routed to its outlets, each of which is dedicated to a specific message type (see figure 9.7).

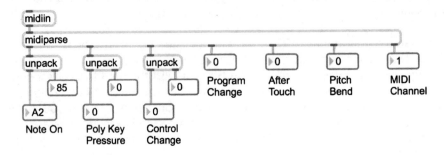

Fig. 9.7 The **midiparse** object

You will notice that the object has 7 outlets which correspond to note, polyphonic key pressure, control change, program change, after touch, pitch bend and MIDI channel, respectively. The first three outlets send lists of two values, because the messages they represent (note, polyphonic key pressure and control change) must be made up of two values (for example, polyphonic key pressure transmits both note number and pressure value). This way, a raw MIDI data stream output by **midiin** can be translated by **midiparse** into more conventional Max messages. In the example shown in the figure, a note on message has been received on channel 1.

Naturally the data that **midiparse** interprets can also be sent by any other object (not just to **midiin**). To test this out, let's try to send a message to control MIDI volume using a message box (figure 9.8):

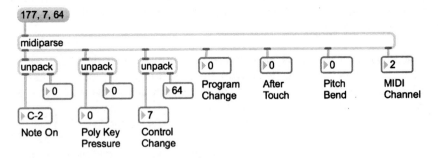

Fig. 9.8 Raw MIDI data in a message box

The values 177, 7 and 64 which are sent using the message box (and separated by commas so they are sent as individual values and not a list of three elements) are interpreted as a control change message on channel 2 – more precisely, a MIDI volume control change message (controller number 7) with a value of 64.

Another object that is similar to **midiparse** is **midiselect**. This object allows us to set which specific MIDI messages will be interpreted by setting its attributes. Any messages which are not interpreted are sent out the object's rightmost outlet in their original raw format. Imagine we are receiving a stream of MIDI data from an external device, and that this data is made up of note messages, control change messages, etc., on several channels. If we only wanted to transpose the notes on channels 2 and 4 up an octave, leaving all other MIDI messages unchanged, we could create a patch to do this, using the **midiselect** object, as shown in the patch in figure 9.9.

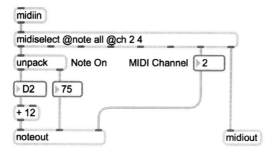

Fig. 9.9 The **midiselect** object

Let's analyze the figure in detail. The first 7 outlets of **midiselect** are exactly the same as the corresponding outlets on the **midiparse** object. However, these outlets are only used if the corresponding attribute for its MIDI message has been enabled, otherwise the raw MIDI data is sent out the object's rightmost outlet. In the figure, the attributes "@note all" and "@ch 2 4" indicate that all of the note values arriving on midi channels 2 and 4 will be intercepted and output via their corresponding outlets, while note messages on other channels, as well as any other type of MIDI messages, will be sent out the last outlet in raw MIDI format. This means that when a note message on channel 2 or 4 is received, it will be sent out the first outlet, transposed up an octave and sent to the **noteout** object, and all other MIDI messages will be sent, unchanged, out the last inlet (in raw format) to the **midiout** object.

The attributes recognized by the **midiselect** object are: note, ctl, (control change), touch (after touch), poly (polyphonic key pressure, bend (pitch bend), pgm (program change) and ch (MIDI channel). For the note, ctl, poly and ch attributes, it is possible to select all values (all), no values (none) or specify which values to output. If we only wanted to transpose the notes C3, E3 and G3 in the example shown in the figure, we could have used the attribute "@note 60 64 67" instead of "@note all".

Unlike the **midiparse** and **midiselect** objects, the **midiformat** object can be used to output a stream of raw MIDI data based on input to its specialized inlets (figure 9.10).

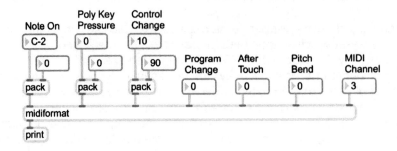

Fig. 9.10 The **midiformat** object

In this example we have sent a control change message to the third inlet. For this message, the controller number is 10, its value is 90, and the channel (the seventh inlet) is 3. This object outputs the corresponding raw MIDI data and sends it to the **print** object which prints the values 178, 10 and 90 in the Max window, each number on a different line. Rebuild the patch for yourself and try it out.

A patch such as the one shown in figure 9.10 can be useful to help us get acquainted with all the status bytes of the different possible MIDI messages. Naturally, the **midiformat** object is generally connected to a **midiout** object.

9.3 MIDI AND POLYPHONY

In this section we will return to discussing the **poly~** object which was presented in section IC.3. If your knowledge of this object is a little "rusty", we strongly suggest that you review that section before continuing.

In the polyphonic patches that we studied in section IC.3, the duration of each note was known in advance, and was therefore always contained in the list of parameters sent to the **poly~** object. However, when an instrument is played from an external device such as a MIDI keyboard, there is no way we can know the duration of each note in advance, because this will obviously depend on when the performer lifts his/her finger off the key.

Consequently, in this situation, when a polyphonic instrument receives a note on it needs to "grab" a free instance (or voice) and play the note. Then, when it receives a note off for a note being played, it needs to once again locate that very same instance and trigger the release of the sound. So, how can we keep track of all the instances being used in a situation where a lot of notes with unknown durations are being played?

The answer is to use the "**midinote**" message. This message has the same basic function as the "note" message which we saw in the patches in section IC.3, in so much that it deals with managing the instances of a polyphonic instrument. However, the first two elements of the list associated with the "midinote" message *must* be the MIDI note and velocity values of the note being played. In other words, the first two elements of the list should be integer values between 0 and 127. When the second element (corresponding to the velocity) is greater than 0, the "midinote" message tells the `poly~` object to find the first free instance in order to play the note, and it also associates that instance with the note value received. When another "midinote" message whose first element is the same as one of the previously activated notes arrives, and the second element of the list is 0 (meaning it is a note off message), the `poly~` object will not look for a free instance, but will send the list to the existing instance that was used to play that note. Obviously, there needs to be some kind of algorithm in the polyphonic patch that is able to "shut off" the note when such a note off message is received.

Even if you do not have a MIDI keyboard handy, you can still use the `kslider` object to output note on and note off messages one after the other. Open the file **09_03_poly_midinote.maxpat** (figure 9.11).

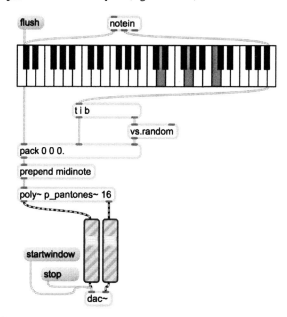

Fig. 9.11 The file **9_03_poly_midinote.maxpat**

If you have a MIDI keyboard connected to your computer, you could play this patch using the `notein` object. Otherwise, you could use the `kslider` object directly, since it has been set to "Polyphonic" mode. As we have already seen in this section and in section IB.1 in the first volume, when using this mode (which can be set in the inspector), the `kslider` object will output a note on when you click on a deselected key, and will output a note off when you click on that key again) This way, it is possible to activate several notes consecutively and deactivate them in any order. The "flush" message (located in the message box connected to `kslider`) will deactivate all of the `kslider` object's active notes by sending corresponding note off messages for them. Note that the `prepend` object just before `poly~` will add the "midinote" message name to the head of the list instead of simply "note." The list itself is made up of three elements: note, velocity and a random (floating point) value between 0 and 1 which will be used to set the stereo position of the sound, as we will shortly see.

Try activating and deactivating several notes, and then open up the **poly~** object (by double-clicking on it) in order to see the contents of the polyphonic patch **p_pantones~.maxpat** (shown in figure 9.12).

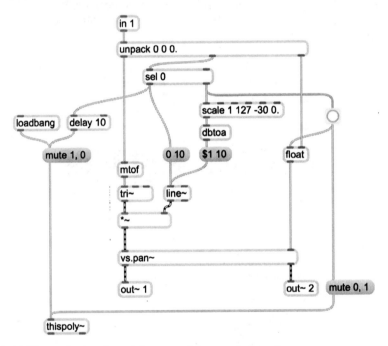

Fig. 9.12 The polyphonic patch **p_pantones~.maxpat**

The three elements of the list that are sent to the inlet of the patch are separated into individual values using **unpack**. The rightmost value (the random number output by **vs.random** in the main patch) is sent to the cold inlet of a `float` object and the middle value (velocity) is sent to the [`sel 0`] object – if the value is not zero (and therefore representing a note on) it is sent out the right outlet of **sel** to a bang button. This button is connected both to a message box used to activate the polyphonic voice (in the usual way) as well as to the hot inlet of the **float** object. As a result, the random value stored there will be sent to the **vs.pan** object where it will determine the stereo position of the sound.

Returning to the right outlet of sel: the MIDI velocity value is converted into an amplitude value using the **scale** and **dbtoa** objects (just as it was in the polyphonic patches shown in section IC.3). Finally, the value on the left, representing the MIDI note, is output to the oscillator.

If the velocity value in the list coming from the main patch is 0 (meaning it is a note off), it will be sent to the instance whose note we want to "shut off." In this case, the [**sel** 0] object will send a bang out its left outlet to a message box connected to the **line~** object in order to ramp its amplitude down to 0. The bang output by sel will also be delayed by 10 milliseconds (by the [**delay** 10] object), and used to free the instance and mute it.

· ·

ACTIVITY

Answer the following questions based on the polyphonic patch p_pantones~.maxpat:

- Why is the third value of the list input to the patch sent to the cold inlet of the **float** object? In other words, why is it not sent directly to **vs.pan~**?

- Why is the bang sent by the **sel** object to the [mute 1, 0] message box (used to free the instance and mute it) delayed by 10 milliseconds?

- Why is the bang output from the right outlet of the **line~** object not used to free the instance, as it was in the polyphonic patches previously shown in section IC.3 (see the patch p_triangletones~.maxpat, for example)?

- What kind of mechanism could we have added to this patch in order to have been able to use the bang output by **line~** to free the instance?

· ·

THE ADSR~ OBJECT

In the previous example we used a crude trapezoidal envelope with its attack and release values both set to 10 milliseconds. However, we could always create a more useful Attack-Decay-Sustain-Release envelope[6] using the **adsr~** object, which was designed precisely to help make polyphonic voice management easier. First, let's see how this object works; rebuild the patch shown in figure 9.13.

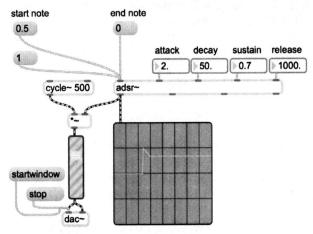

Fig. 9.13 The **adsr~** object

The **adsr~** object takes an amplitude value in its first inlet, while the other four inlets accept the attack, decay, sustain and release parameters. Note that the attack, decay and release values are times in milliseconds, while the sustain parameter is a multiplication factor for the amplitude (generally a value between 0 and 1).

Turn on the patch and alternately click on the two message boxes labeled "start note" and "end note." When **adsr~** receives a value other than 0 in its first inlet, it will output the attack, decay and sustain parts of the envelope, and when it receives a 0 it will output the release segment. During the attack, the envelope goes from 0 to the amplitude that was received in the first inlet, during the decay the envelope will lower until its value is equal to that of the amplitude multiplied by the sustain factor, and finally, during the release the envelope's value will return to 0.

For example, if the amplitude value sent to **adsr~** were 0.5, and the ADSR parameters were those shown in figure 9.13 (2 50, 0.7, 1000), the output signal would go from 0 to 0.5 in 2 milliseconds (attack), then descend over 50 milliseconds (decay) to a value of 0.35 (i.e., 0.7, the sustain multiplication factor, multiplied by the input amplitude, 0.5). This amplitude level would be maintained until an amplitude value of 0 were sent to the **adsr~** object's first inlet, at which point the signal would return to 0 over 1000 milliseconds (release).

---

[6] See section 1.3T in the first volume.

Now lets see how the **adsr~** object is used within the context of a polyphonic patch. Load the patch **09_04_poly_adsr.maxpat** (figure 9.14).

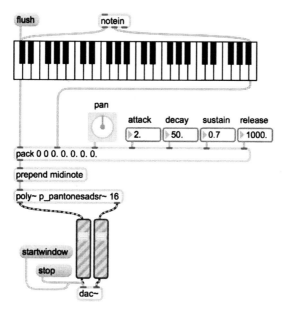

Fig. 9.14 The patch **9_04_poly_adsr.maxpat**

This patch is similar to the preceding one; the only difference is that the stereo panning is now no longer randomly varied and the four ADSR parameters have been added to the list sent to **poly~**. Try modifying the parameters to hear the effect of the envelope on the resulting sound.

Now let's analyze the contents of the polyphonic patch **p_pantonesadsr~. maxpat** (shown in figure 9.15).

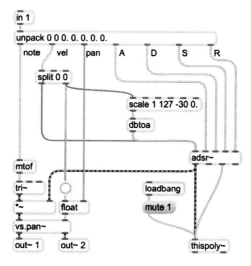

Fig. 9.15 The file **p_pantonesadsr~.maxpat**

Notice that the velocity values are first converted to deciBels then to amplitude values – just as they were in the previous version of this patch – before they are sent to the **adsr~** object. However, here velocity values of 0 (i.e., note off) are separated from the others using the [**split** 0 0] object. This is done because this way the value can be sent directly to the **adsr~** object and used to trigger the release of the note. The standard **split** object is similar to the **vs.split** object (from the Virtual Sound Macros library) that we have already used in section 6.9P. However, with the standard **split** object all of the values located inside the range defined by its two arguments are sent out the left outlet, and all out-of-range values are sent out the right. In the patch shown in the figure, the range for split is "0 0"; this means that only the value 0 will be sent out its left outlet, and all others will be sent out the right.

Notice also that the envelope output by **adsr~** is also sent to **thispoly~**. In our previous polyphonic patches, when we wanted to make a voice busy (by activating its busy state with **thispoly~**), we would send the value 1 to **thispoly~** and when we wanted to free it we would send the value 0. Actually, any value other than 0 will cause the voice to be busy, and a signal can also be used to set the busy state. This means that when we connect the envelope produced by **adsr~** to **thispoly~**, it can be used to make the voice busy for the entire duration of the envelope – once the release stage of the envelope has finished, the value of the envelope will be 0 and the voice will be freed. Furthermore, you have probably also noticed that the third outlet of **adsr~** is additionally connected to **thipoly~**: this outlet actually outputs a "mute 0" message when an envelope starts, and sends a "mute 1" message when the envelope has finished. As we already mentioned, the **adsr~** object was designed to be used for polyphony, and using it together with **thispoly~** saves us the trouble of having to create our own mechanism to activate and deactivate the individual voices when we use **poly~**.

WHEN THERE ARE NOT ENOUGH POLYPHONIC VOICES: THE "STEAL" ATTRIBUTE

Another interesting feature of **adsr~** is its ability to manage polyphonic instances when more voices have been requested than are actually available. Normally, when all the voices in a **poly~** are busy, any new notes sent to the object are ignored. However, when the **poly~** object's "steal" attribute is activated, a new incoming note will "steal" a voice from an active note (usually the note that has been active the longest).[7] Naturally, doing this can cause a discontinuity in the signal – resulting in an audible click – since the note whose voice is being stolen will be interrupted abruptly. The **adsr~** has a mechanism to avoid these unwanted clicks. When a new note is requesting a voice whose envelope is still active, **adsr~** will create an extremely quick release before

---

[7] You will often see this referred to, quite logically, as "voice stealing" in hardware synthesizer terminology.

beginning the new envelope. This is known as *retrigger* in Max jargon and there is even a "retrigger" attribute that can be used to set the duration of the quick release (by default it is 5 milliseconds).

Try modifying the **poly~** object in patch 09_04_poly_adsr.maxpat so it looks like this: [**poly~** p_pantonesadsr~ 2 @steal 1]. By making this modification, the number of voices will be reduced to 2 and the "steal" attribute will be activated. If you now try to play some notes using the patch, you will notice that it is not possible to play more than two notes at a time, and that each new note replaces one of the old ones. In spite of the fact that this patch now uses the retrigger mechanism that we talked about, it is still possible to perceive a discontinuity when a voice is stolen. If you look carefully at the polyphonic patch in figure 9.15, you will realize that the frequency of the new note arrives at the **tri~** object without waiting for the end of the (possible) retrigger stage of the envelope. In principle, the new frequency should actually only be set once the new envelope starts. The **adsr~** object can also come to our rescue in this situation: its second outlet actually outputs a signal whose value is 1 when the envelope is in the attack, decay and sustain stages, and a 0 at all other times – in other words, either during the release or retrigger stages, or when the envelope is not active. So, how can we use this signal? At the end of section 5.2P we learned the **sah~** object which can be used to sample and hold an input signal each time the trigger signal crosses a threshold. If you do not remember precisely how **sah~** works, this may be a good moment to refresh your memory by re-reading the last part of section 5.2P.

We will be using the **sah~** object to hold back the frequency of the new note until the retrigger stage of the **adsr~** is finished. Load the patch 09_05_poly_steal.maxpat. This patch is very similar to the previous one, except that the **poly~** object's polyphony has been reduced to two voices and its "steal" attribute has been activated. The polyphonic patch loaded by the **poly~** object is called **p_pantonessteal~.maxpat**, and is shown in figure 9.16.

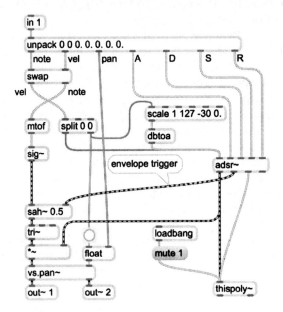

Fig. 9.16 The file **p_pantonessteal~.maxpat**

This shows one of the standard ways of dealing with voice stealing using the **adsr~** object. First of all, observe that the note and velocity values have had their positions swapped using, appropriately enough, the **swap** object[8], so the note value coming from the right outlet will be sent before the velocity. The note value is converted into a frequency (**mtof**), transformed into a signal (**sig~**) and sent to the **sah~** object, which will be outputting the previous value. The second outlet of **adsr~**, which outputs an envelope trigger value (as a signal), is connected to the right inlet of **sah~**. Once a new envelope has started (in the case of a "stolen" voice, this will be after the retrigger stage has finished), the envelope trigger changes from 0 to 1, and causes **sah~** to sample the new frequency and send the value to the **tri~** oscillator.

Why did we use the **swap** object to cause the note value to be output before the velocity? Remember that if the velocity arrives before the note when a voice is not stolen, the envelope trigger would change to 1 immediately, before the frequency arrives, and the **sah~** object would sample the previous frequency value, instead.

---

[8] This object switches the positions of the two numbers it receives in its inlets. It was already discussed in section 5.4P.

ACTIVITY

Add a resonant lowpass filter to the patch p_pantonessteal~, along with the additional parameters for cutoff frequency and Q factor. The cutoff frequency should be proportional to the note being played, and will be modulated by the envelope coming from **adsr~**, using an "env depth" parameter (see the section entitled "Anatomy of a Subtractive Synthesizer" in section 3.5P of the first volume).

· ·

The voice stealing algorithm that we have just seen was designed to work in a polyphonic patch that has an oscillator whose frequency is modified by a signal, since the **sah~** object sends the frequency value (as a signal) at the appropriate time.

However, if our polyphonic patch were a sampler realized with the **groove~** object, each note would be started with a numeric message indicating the point to begin reading the file (see 05_08_groove_commands.maxpat in section 5.3P). In this case we would note be able to use the **sah~** object and we would need to make some modifications to our algorithm. Load the patch **09_05b_samples_steal.maxpat** and try playing some notes. This is also an example of a polyphonic instrument that has just two voices, but is different from the preceding patch in that it reads samples in order to play the sampled vibraphone sound that we have already used several times before. Let's take a look at the modifications that have been made to the polyphonic **subpatch p_samplessteal~.maxpat** (figure 9.16b).

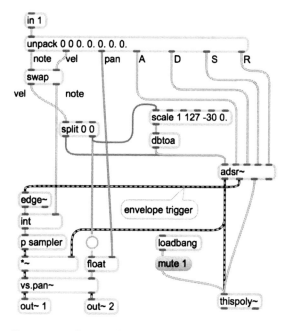

Fig. 9.16b The file **p_samplessteal~.maxpat**

The first thing you will notice is that the **sah~** object has been replaced with **edge~**. This latter object outputs a bang out its left outlet when the input signal goes from 0 to a non-zero value, and outputs a bang out its right outlet when the signal goes from non-zero to 0.

Let's see how it works. The MIDI note value is sent from the **swap** object to the right inlet of the **int** object where it is stored. The envelope trigger signal from the **adsr~** object is sent to the inlet of the **edge~** object. As soon as the envelope trigger value changes from 0 to 1 – in other words, when a new envelope begins (after a possible retrigger stage if the voice was "stolen") – the **edge** object will output a bang from its left outlet, causing the **int** object to output the previously stored note value to the [p sampler] subpatch. This subpatch contains the same sample playback algorithm that we previously saw in the patch 05_10_monosampler.maxpat in section 5.3P. The rest of the algorithm is identical to the previous polyphonic patch.

THE FUNCTION OBJECT AND USING THE SUSTAIN POINTS

Naturally, it would be more interesting to be able to more freely define any kind of envelope using the **function** object. The problem, at least in the way that we have used it up to now, is that the **function** object (combined with **line~**) will output an envelope with a predetermined duration, while (for the purposes of note on and note off) we need an envelope that will remain active for an arbitrary amount of time.

Fortunately, the **function** object actually includes the ability of sustaining an envelope by an arbitrary duration. By Command-clicking (Mac) or Control-clicking (Windows) on the object's interface, it is possible to create a **sustain point**, recognizable by the white ring drawn around the point itself. So, how does a sustain point work? When a bang is sent to the **function** object, it outputs a list of values up to (and including) the sustain point. Sending the "next" message after this causes the remaining part of the **function** to be output. To better understand how this works, reconstruct the patch shown in figure 9.17.

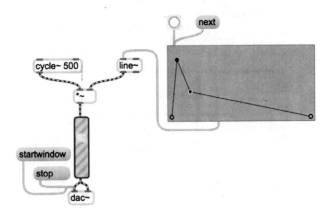

Fig. 9.17 A sustain point

The envelope inside the **function** object has 4 points, the third of which is a sustain point, recognizable by the ring around it. You can alternately activate and deactivate a sustain point by Command-clicking (Mac) or Control-clicking (Windows) on the actual point.

When the **function** object receives a bang, it outputs the first part of the envelope up to the sustain point. When the "next" message is sent, it causes the second part of the envelope (the release) to be output. Note that it is possible to define several sustain points and the "next" message can be used repeatedly to go consecutively from one sustain point to the next until it finally arrives at the release. After the release, another next message will trigger the envelope from the beginning.

So, our problems appear to be solved, right? Think again. Unfortunately, this mechanism works very well for a single voice, but not so well with polyphony. Remember that there should be just one **function** object located in the main patch, so it can be shared by all the polyphonic voices. If the **function** were located inside the **poly~** object (as the **adsr~** was) we would not be able to graphically modify it (similarly to the way that we could change the ADSR parameters in the main patch in the previous examples).

Let's imagine that we are sending data coming from a **function** object containing a sustain point to a polyphonic instrument. For each *note on* we send a bang to the sole **function** object, and for each note off we send a "next" message. At a certain point, two or more notes may end in succession, so we would send two or more consecutive "next" messages. However, when the **function** object receives the second "next" message it would send the part of the envelope from the attack to the sustain, and not the release, and this would knock our polyphonic envelope management system out of phase.

To avoid this problem, we can use a little "trick": when we receive a note off, we can send a bang immediately followed by a "next" message. This kind of system naturally only works when using just one sustain point, but on the other hand, with the simple message system used for MIDI notes, it wouldn't really be feasible to deal with more. Basically, when a note off is received, the initial bang will cause the first part of the envelope to be output. This is immediately discarded, because the subsequent "next" message will cause the second part of the envelope to be output and used, instead.

Rebuild the patch shown in figure 9.18.

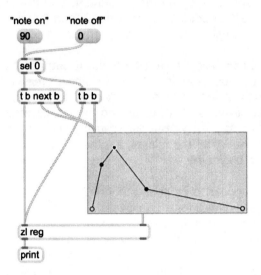

Fig. 9.18 How to use a sustain point

To begin with, this patch has just one **function** object whose breakpoint function represents an envelope with a single sustain point (as we already mentioned, it is important that the envelope has just one sustain point). Open the **function** object's inspector and set the "Output mode" attribute (in the "Value" category) to "List." This attribute is used to specify the format that will be used for messages output by the object's second outlet, and sent to a **line~** object, when it receives a bang. The default mode ("Normal") causes two messages to be output: the first is a single value representing the starting point of the envelope, and the second is a list containing the value/time pairs for all of the remaining points. In other words, this is the same format that we have been using all along to send envelope values to a **line~** object from a message box. In "List" mode, however, **function** sends only a single list, which includes the starting point at time 0. To give an example, if the **function** object outputs the messages "0" and "1 500 0 250" as envelope data in "Normal" mode, it would output only one list with the message "0 0 1 500 0 250" in "List" mode (see also note 18 in section IC.3).

Returning to the patch, you will notice that the two message boxes at the top are used to simulate the velocity values being sent to our algorithm. The value 90 (or any other value between 1 and 127) represents a note on message and 0 the note off. When [**sel** 0] receives the value 90, it sends it to the trigger on the right, which outputs two bangs. The first bang tells the **function** object to output the envelope list up to (and including) the sustain point. This list is stored in the [**zl** reg] object, and the second bang sent to the hot inlet of this object causes the stored list to be sent to the **print** object.

Conversely, when we send the value 0 to the [**sel** 0] object, a bang will be sent to the trigger on the left, causing three messages to be output: bang, next and bang. The first of these bangs (output from trigger's third outlet) is sent to the **function** object, which sends the first part of the list to be stored in [**zl** reg], as before – but not for long! Immediately afterward, the next message is sent to **function** and the second part of the list (from the sustain point to the end) is consequently stored in the [**zl** reg] object, in place of the first part. The final bang output by trigger is sent to the hot inlet of [**zl** reg], which sends its currently stored list (the release of the envelope) to the **print** object.

Try clicking on the two message boxes, and look carefully at the messages that appear in the Max window.

Now, let's look at a practical example using this algorithm. Open the patch **09_06_poly_function.maxpat** (figure 9.19).

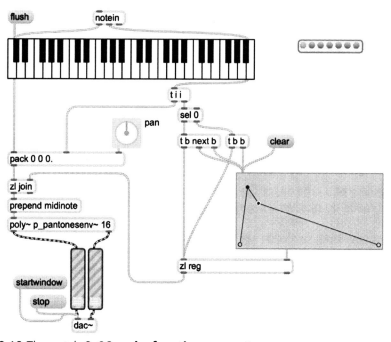

Fig. 9.19 The patch **9_06_poly_function.maxpat**

Each time a new note is played, the velocity value is sent to the algorithm that we just analyzed in the previous patch, in order to output the envelope. Try out the various presets and be sure to hold down the notes long enough so that the envelope reaches the sustain point. Now, create some new presets, taking care to always include a sustain point in the envelope.

Try testing out what happens when you do not include a sustain point. Also try adding more than one sustain point to see how the algorithm reacts. In both of these cases, how and why does the instrument behave incorrectly?

Let's continue by analyzing the contents of the **p_pantonesenv~.maxpat** subpatch (figure 9.20).

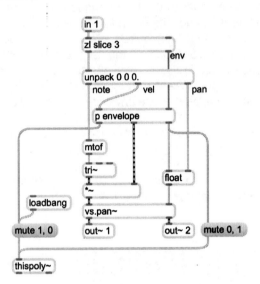

Fig. 9.20 The file **p_pantonesenv~.maxpat**

The [zl slice 3] object separates the three parameters – note, velocity and pan – from the envelope. The note and pan parameters are dealt with in the same way as in the previous polyphonic patches, but the velocity value is sent together with the envelope to the [p envelope] subpatch. Remember that the envelope will be either the first part of the breakpoint function (up to the sustain point) in the case of a note on, or the final part (which we are calling the release, even if it is made up of several segments) in the case of a note off.

The [p envelope] subpatch has three outlets: the central outlet sends the envelope, the right outlet outputs a bang at the start of the envelope and the left sends a bang when the envelope has finished. As for the destination of the two bang messages, you can see that it is no different than in the polyphonic patch p_pantones~.maxpat (figure 9.12). The bang on the right (start of the envelope) un-mutes the voice, makes it busy and causes the pan value to be sent, and the bang on the left (end of the envelope) frees the voice and mutes it again. Let's now take a look at the contents of the [p envelope] subpatch (figure 9.21).

First of all, the list that defines the section of the envelope (from the attack to the sustain in the case of note on, or else the release in the case of note off) is sent from the second inlet (labeled "env") to the **line~** object. After this, the velocity value is sent from the first inlet (labeled "vel") to the [sel 0] object. This way, if a velocity value is between 1 and 127 (therefore representing a note on) the **sel** object sends it out its right outlet to the **trigger** on the right. This **trigger** then sends a bang out the third outlet of the subpatch to signal the start of the envelope, activate the voice and make it busy, as shown in the previous figure. The velocity value is then sent from the **trigger** to the **scale** and **dbtoa** objects to generate an amplitude value which is sent to a multiplier that is used to rescale the envelope output by **line~**. Finally, the **trigger** sends a 0 to close the **gate** object, below.

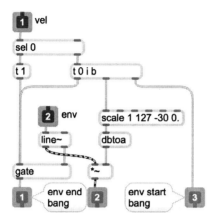

Fig. 9.21 The contents of the [p envelope] subpatch

The **gate** object is used to send the bang output by **line~** to the first outlet of the [p envelope] subpatch, so that the voice can be freed and muted when the envelope is finished (see the preceding figure). However, this should only happen in the note off stage of the envelope, so the gate is therefore closed when the patch receives a note on. If the velocity arriving in the first inlet is 0 (indicating a note off), the [**sel** 0] object will send a bang to the **trigger** connected to its left inlet, causing the gate to be opened. This way, the bang output by **line~** at the end of the release stage of the envelope will be allowed through.

• •

ACTIVITIES

- In one of the activities in section IC.3 we asked you to make the subtractive synthesizer IC_02_subsynth_seq.mapat into a polyphonic synthesizer. Now your task is to take that same patch and implement the polyphonic sustain point technique that has just been shown.

- Take the patch you created in the previous activity, and add a setdomain message that can be used to modify the domain of the **function** object (i.e., its duration) so that the envelope's attack will be shorter when the velocity is higher, and longer when the velocity is lower. Naturally, the domain can be set to its original value for the release stage of the envelope.

• •

ELIMINATING NOTE OFF WITH STRIPNOTE

In some cases, such as when playing certain percussion sounds, we do not need a sustain stage in our envelope because the sound itself evolves independently of the input note's duration. In this case, the note off messages are not at all necessary and can be eliminated. The **stripnote** object was created precisely for this purpose; open the patch **09_07_mallets.maxpat** (figure 9.22).

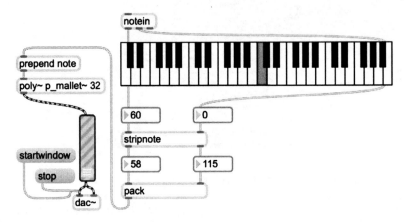

Fig. 9.22 The patch **9_07_mallets.maxpat**

Play the patch using an external keyboard, paying careful attention to the number boxes placed before and after the **stripnote** object. When the velocity value is greater than zero (indicating a note on message) the two input values are passed to the object's output, but when the velocity is 0 (corresponding to note off) the two input values are blocked from being output.

. . . .

🖱 ACTIVITY

Starting with the patch shown in figure 9.5, create a second group of objects that will be used to transmit the MIDI note, program change, pitch bend, etc. on MIDI channel 2. Use the program change message to select the same timbre on both channels, but slightly alter the pitch bend on channel 2 in order to create a chorus effect when the same note is played on both channels. If you have a MIDI keyboard, use it to control the two channels simultaneously.

. . . .

9.4 CONTROLLING A MONOPHONIC SYNTH

Controlling a synthesizer with just one voice in real time is something that is not so trivial as you might initially think. If we use a MIDI keyboard to play a note, which we will call "note A," and, as we continue holding this note, we play "note B," the synthesizer should go from note A to note B without waiting for the note off for note A. When we subsequently lift up the key and stop playing note A, continuing to hold note B, the note off for A should be ignored, and not interrupt note B. On the other hand, if we stop playing note B, and continue playing note A, the synthesizer could be set to either stop playing both notes, or to return from playing note B, back to note A (see figure 9.23).

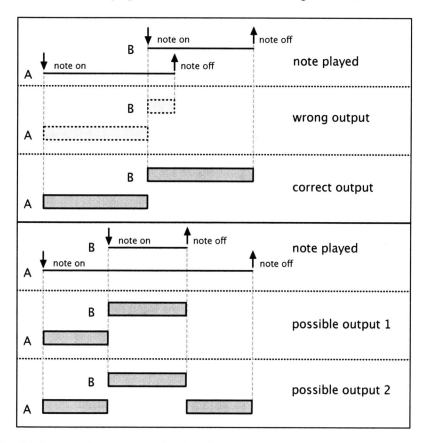

Fig. 9.23 Controlling a monophonic voice

In other words, in the case of two or more held notes, we need to be able to decide which note has priority: the last note played, the lowest, or the highest. Fortunately, these various scenarios can be managed easily by using the **ddg.mono** object, which was designed to filter out undesired notes, keep track of held notes and manage the order of their execution.

Let's now take a look at a practical application of this in the patch **09_08_
mono_synth.maxpat** (figure 9.24)

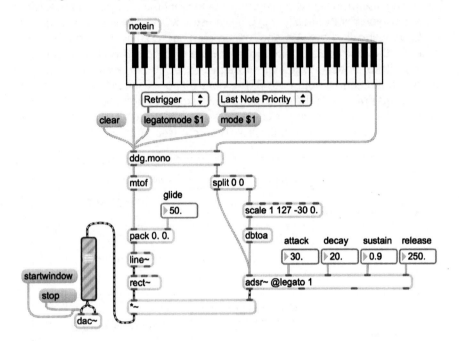

Fig. 9.24 The file **9_08_mono_synth.maxpat**

First, try to play the synthesizer. Ideally you should use an external MIDI keyboard if you have one, but you could also use the **kslider** object.

The **ddg.mono** object has two attributes that are used to define how it beha-
ves: the "mode" attribute sets the priority of the input notes, and the "legatomode" attribute defines how note on and note off will be handled.

The possible values for the "mode" attribute are:
- 0 (Last Note Priority): when several notes are held, the last one received (in
terms of arrival time) will be played.
- 1 (High Note Priority): the highest note will be the one played.
- 2 (Low Note Priority): the lowest note will be the one played.
The possible values for the "legatomode" attribute are:
- 0 (Retrigger): sends a new note for each new note received.
- 1 (Legato): sends a new note only if the new note is different from the previous one.
- 2 (Last Step): sends a note off at the end of the last note played, even if other
notes are being held.

Note the "@legato 1" attribute given to the **adsr~** object: when this attribute
is activated, there is no retrigger stage when a voice is "stolen," but rather the
new attack starts directly from the sustain value of the previous note.

Try deactivating this attribute by sending the message "legato 0" to the **adsr~** object to hear the difference.

The "glide" parameter, which can be controlled by the number box located in the center of the patch, can be used to create a brief portamento between one note and the next – a very typical effect in monophonic synthesizers. Try modifying the parameters of the patch and save some presets.

. . . .

ACTIVITIES

- Add a resonant lowpass filter whose cutoff frequency is proportional to the note being played. Also add the ability to modulate the cutoff frequency using the envelope and an "env depth" parameter (see the section entitled "Anatomy of a Subtractive Synthesizer" in section 3.5P of the first volume).

- Add a second **rect~** oscillator that can be slightly detuned with respect to the first.

- Add an LFO that can be used to control the tremolo and vibrato of the sound (see sections 4.3P and 4.4P in the first volume). Use two external MIDI controllers to modify the amplitude of the tremolo and vibrato (you will need to rescale the controllers' values from the 0 to 127 range to values between 0 and 1).

. . . .

LIST OF MAX OBJECTS

adsr~
Creates an Attack-Decay-Sustain-Release envelope

bendin
Receives pitch bend messages from a MIDI device.

bendout
Sends pitch bend messages to a MIDI device.

ctlin
Receives control change messages from a MIDI device.

ctlout
Sends control change messages to a MIDI device.

ddg.mono
Manages MIDI note messages for virtual monophonic synthesizers

edge~
Sends a bang out its left outlet when the input signal goes from zero to non-zero, and a bang out its right outlet when the input signal goes from non-zero to zero.

midiformat
Outputs a stream of "raw" MIDI data based on values sent to individual inlets.

midiin
Receives "raw" MIDI data (in other words, a stream of individual values representing status and data bytes) from a MIDI device.

midiout
Sends "raw" MIDI data to a MIDI device.

midiparse
Analyzes a "raw" MIDI data stream and routes (or parses) the values to its outlets, each of which represents a particular type of MIDI message.

midiselect
This object can be used to establish which kinds of messages will be understood and output and which will not, via its attribute settings.

pgmin
Receives program change messages from a MIDI device.

pgmout
Sends program change messages to a MIDI device.

split
Sends input values that fall within a specified range to its left outlet; values outside the range are sent out its right outlet.

stripnote
Eliminates note off messages, letting only note on messages pass through.

touchin
Receives after touch messages from a MIDI device.

touchout
Sends after touch messages to a MIDI device.

LIST OF ATTRIBUTES AND MESSAGES FOR SPECIFIC MAX OBJECTS

adsr~
- legato (attribute)
When this attribute is enabled, the envelope will not be re-triggered when a voice is "stolen," but instead will continue from the sustain value of the current note to the attack of the new note.
- *retrigger* (attribute)
Sets the release duration that the object will use when "stealing" a voice, before playing the new note.

ddg.mono
- mode (attribute)
Sets the priority for input notes.
- legatomode (attribute)
Sets the mode for the management of note on and note off messages.

function
- *next* (message)
Causes the remaining part of the breakpoint function after the sustain point to be output.
- *output mode* (attributo)
Sets the mode for the output of messages describing the envelope. Either they are sent as just a list, or as a single value followed by a list (this latter mode is the default setting).
- *sustain point* (graphical element)
In the **function** object, this is a stopping point for the list output by a bang; the next message can be used to output a list representing the remaining part of the breakpoint function (or the part up until the next sustain point). A sustain point is created graphically by Command-clicking (Mac) or Control-clicking (Windows) on the object.

kslider
- flush (message)
When the **kslider** is in polyphonic mode, this messages causes the object to output note off messages for all the currently active notes.

midiselect
- *note, ctl, touch, poly, bend, pgm, ch* (attributes)
These attributes are used to enable outlets associated with values for note, control change, after touch, polyphonic key pressure, pitch bend, program change and MIDI channel, respectively.

poly~
- *steal* (attribute)
When this attribute is enabled, if there are no free voices when a new note arrives, an instance currently playing a previous note will be "stolen" and used to play the new note.

Interlude E
MAX FOR LIVE

PREREQUISITES FOR THE CHAPTER
- The contents of Volume 1, chapters 5, 6, 7, 8 and 9 (theory and practice) and Interludes C and D
- Knowledge of the main functions of the Ableton Live program

OBJECTIVES
Abilities
- To know how to create a Max for Live device
- To know how to control the Live environment using the Live API

CONTENTS
- Building Audio and MIDI devices with Max for Live
- Building virtual instruments with Max for Live
- Using the Live API
- The hierarchical structure of the Live Object Model

ACTIVITIES
- Building and Modifying algorithms

SUPPORTING MATERIALS
- List of Max objects - List of attributes, messages and actions for specific Max objects - Glossary

IE.1 AN INTRODUCTION TO MAX FOR LIVE

In order to be able to follow along with this Interlude, you need to have a user license for both Max for Live and Ableton Live.[1] Since the information contained here is almost exclusively geared toward the use of Max for Live, it will not be a prerequisite for understanding future chapters in this series. Those who do not own both of the licenses mentioned above can therefore skip this Interlude without any negative impact on their understanding of the material presented in later chapters.

WHAT IS ABLETON LIVE?
Ableton Live (or more simply, Live) is a DAW (Digital Audio Workstation) application – in other words software designed for recording, manipulating and playing back audio tracks. In addition to this it can also handle MIDI sequences which can be used to control either external hardware or virtual instruments internal to the application itself. Live's most interesting feature is the ability to handle both audio and MIDI tracks non-linearly. Although the vast majority of DAW systems and sequencers actually put the sequences along a timeline that (needless to say) runs linearly through time, Live is actually able to trigger sequences independently of one another, and therefore create a kind of real-time arrangement of them that can be modified at will during performance.

Since this text is not intended to be a manual for Live, we will assume that you already have some knowledge of the program's main functions. In particular, this implies a general familiarity with the overall structure of the Live set and its sections, including the Help section and Live lessons, the use of audio clips and MIDI in "Session View" and "Arrangement View" modes, the use of standard Live *devices*, the use of the Group function to create *Audio Racks* containing multiple *devices*, the use of different *device* chains within an *Audio Rack*, the use of automation and the use of envelopes inside *clips*.

WHAT IS MAX FOR LIVE?
Max for Live is an extension of Live that allows Max patching language to be used to create new plug-ins (called *devices* in Live jargon)[2] which can be used inside the Live application itself. Max for Live can be used to control different operations in Live, such as changing the volume or panning of a track, stopping or starting a *clip*, or even modifying the parameters of other *devices*.

You do not need a full Max license in order to use Max for Live (henceforth referred to as M4L)[3] – you only need an M4L users' license in addition to your

---

[1] As of Live version 9, Max for Live is included in the packages available with Live Suite.

[2] We already mentioned plug-ins in section 3.8T in the first volume. They are basically software components that are "hosted" inside another program and used to further augment its functionality. Some typical examples of audio plug-ins are effects like compressors, delays and equalizers or virtual instruments such as synthesizers and samplers.

[3] M4L is the abbreviation commonly used for "Max for Live" by its user community.

Live license. Even if you own M4L but not Max itself, you will still be able to use the patches contained in this and the previous volume. However, be aware that in this case Max will not be capable of handling audio and MIDI input and output autonomously. This means that all audio signals and MIDI messages must inevitably be routed through Live.

IE.2 BASICS – CREATING AN AUDIO EFFECT WITH M4L

First of all, we strongly suggest that you read all of the sections of this chapter in order! In other words, even if you just want to use M4L to create an Instrument and not an Audio Effect, you shouldn't skip over that section because it also contains information that is essential to the understanding of subsequent sections.

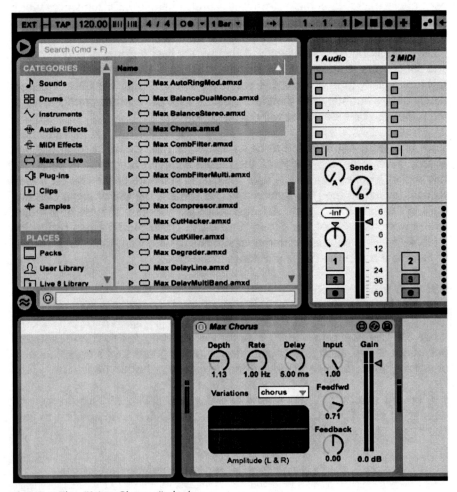

Fig. IE.1 The "Max Chorus" device

Before proceeding any further, make sure that you have installed Max for Live on your computer, in addition to all of the M4L packages available in your account at the www.ableton.com website.

In the first column of the *Live Device Browser* (the area located to the left of the tracks in Live's main window), select the *Max for Live* category. Three folders should then appear in the second column of the *Browser*: *Max Audio Effect*, *Max Instrument* and *Max MIDI Effect*. These three folders are used, respectively, to group together audio effects, virtual instruments and MIDI effects created with M4L. Now, open the Max Audio Effect folder, find the "Max Chorus" device (the list is in alphabetical order) and drag it to an audio track (figure IE.1).

The device, visible in the lower part of the figure, was actually written in Max. To see the associated patch, you will need to click on the first of the three circular icons located on the upper right side of the device's title bar (figure IE.2).

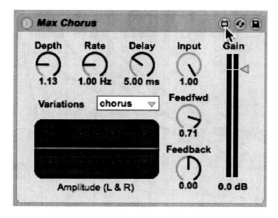

Fig. IE.2 Opening the patch of an M4L device

This will cause the Max application to be launched allowing you to be able to see and modify the patch. The patch initially opens in presentation mode, and by clicking on the familiar icon that enables and disables this mode (the little blackboard in the lower part of the patcher window), the patch can be switched to patching mode.

The patch associated with the "Max Chorus" device is shown in figure IE.3. Since this is a very simple patch, we won't bother to describe it. Note, however the pair of **teeth~** objects in the lower half of the patch – these are simply comb filters whose feed-forward delay and feedback delay times can be adjusted independently (unlike the **comb~** object).

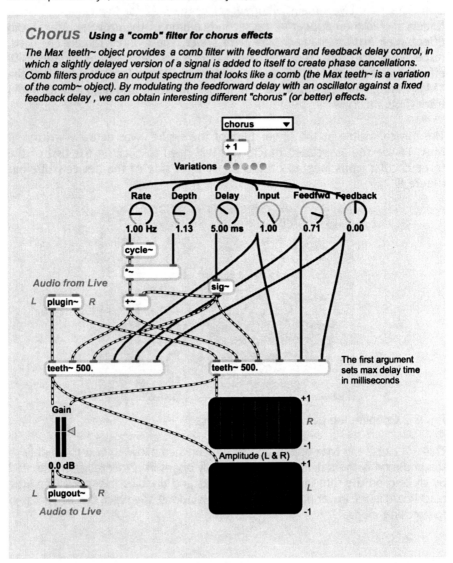

Fig. IE.3 The patch for the "Max Chorus" device

Furthermore, notice the title in the patcher window: "Max Chorus.amxd". The suffix for a patch used as a Live device is .amxd and not .maxpat. Try adding an audio clip to the track to test out the device. You can then try out other M4L audio effect devices, and open their associated patches to see how they work. Have Fun!

Now let's take a look at how to create a new M4L device. To begin with, notice that the first device in the list inside the *Max Audio Effect* folder is simply called "Max Audio Effect" and that it has a different icon from the other devices. This is actually a *template* that we can use as the basis for creating our new device. Drag it to an audio track, or alternatively double-click on its icon, and the default device will appear on the selected track (figure IE.4).

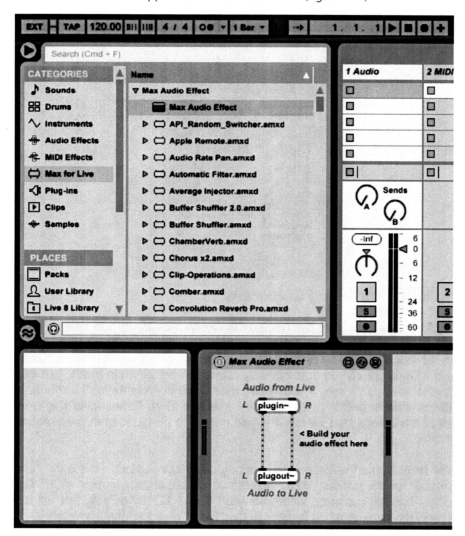

Fig. IE.4 The default device for audio effects

When you open this device you can modify it and save it under a new name. By default, M4L will ask you to save it inside the Max Audio Effect folder located in your "User Library." We suggest that you do not change this path, but rather optionally create a sub-folder where you can collect your own devices.

The default device contains only two objects: **plugin~** and **plugout~**. The former receives audio signals from the track (or from a previous device if there is one) and the latter sends audio to the track's output (or to a subsequent device, if there is one). These two objects basically replace the **adc~** and **dac~** objects used in normal Max patches.

Let's try building a *slapback delay* (see chapter 6.2P). Modify the device as shown in figure IE.5, and save the patch under the name "My Slapback Delay. amxd".

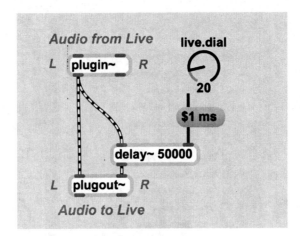

Fig. IE.5 Our first device: a *slapback delay*

Notice that a horizontal line labeled "Device Vertical Limit" will appear when the patch is in edit mode. Only objects located above this line will be visible in the device loaded by Live. As you can see, our device is not in presentation mode; a device can be automatically opened in presentation mode, just as a normal Max patch can, by activating the "Open in Presentation" attribute in the patcher inspector (see Interlude D, section ID.2). Naturally, in this case, all of the objects that we want to use must also be included in presentation mode.

The circular object visible on the upper right is a **live.dial** – this is the "Live version" of the standard **dial** object that we are already familiar with.[4] This object handles numerical values between 0 and 127 by default, but we will shortly see some common features of the "live.*" object set that allow this range to be customized.[5] Load an audio clip into the track and try out the device.

---

[4] This object is located in the Live category in the Object Explorer. If you cannot find it, you can always create it by typing the "l" (lower-case "L") key when the patch is in edit mode. This will cause a generic object box to appear with a text completion menu containing all the names of the objects in the Live category.

[5] We are using the shorthand term "live.*" here to mean any Max object in the Live category whose name begins with the characters "live.".

THE PARAMETERS OF THE "LIVE.*" OBJECTS

Let's pause for a moment here, and look at the `live.dial` object in depth, in order to present some important features common to all of the objects in the "live.*" object set.

As we have already said, the object's default output values are between 0 and 127. Naturally, the object's number format and its value range can be changed. If you open the object's inspector you will notice that there are a series of attributes in the "Parameter" category which are features of the "live.*" objects. Locate the following attributes in the list: "Type", "Range/Enum", "Unit Style" and "Steps" (figure IE.6).

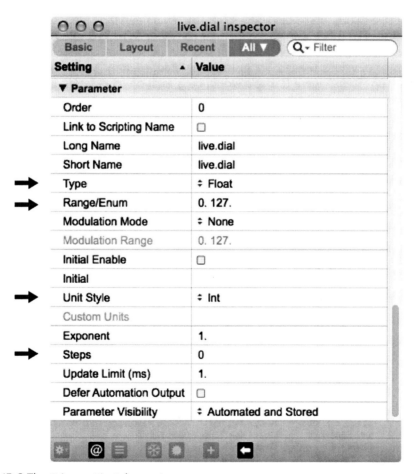

Fig. IE.6 The `live.dial` inspector

The "Type" attribute (set to "Float" by default) establishes the internal value format for the object, which, in the case of `live.dial`, can be either "Float" (32-bit floating-point values), "Int" (8-bit whole number values) or "Enum" (a list of elements to be enumerated, including non-numerical ones).

611

The "Range/Enum" attribute (default value "0. 127.") sets the minimum and maximum value that will be output.

The "Unit Style" attribute (default value "Int") defines how the values will be displayed in the object (although this has no effect on the actual values output). A large number of display formats are available – in addition to "Int" and "Float" there is also "Time", "Hertz" and "deciBel", among others. We will learn some of them in due course.

The "Steps" attribute determines the number of available values between the minimum and maximum that were set in "Range/Enum". For example, if the value of "Range/Enum" were "0 75" and the value of "Steps" were 4, the only available values would be 0, 25, 50 and 75. By default the "Steps" attribute has a value of 0: this is a special value that corresponds to 128 values for floating-point numbers, while for integers it sets the number of useable values to the number of values needed. For example, if "Range/Enum" were "0 75" and the value of "Steps" were 0, there would be a total of 76 different integer values available.

The `live.dial` object has two outlets: the first outputs the values as they are defined by the "Type" and "Range/Enum" attributes, and the second outputs "raw" normalized values between 0 and 1, regardless of the attribute settings. This can all seem rather complicated and might even initially be quite confusing. Therefore, we recommend opening up the patch **IE_01_live_values.maxpat**, which contains several instances of `live.dial` with different settings (figure IE.7).

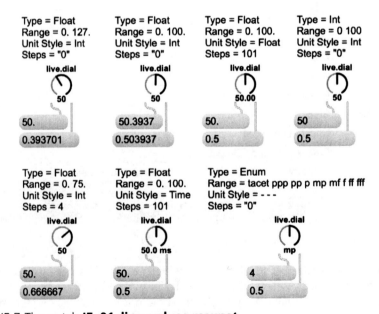

Fig. IE.7 The patch **IE_01_live_values.maxpat**

There are two message boxes connected to each `live.dial`. The first, connected to the left outlet, shows the value corresponding to the range that has been set, whereas the second, connected to the right outlet, shows the raw value, which we have already said is always between 0 and 1, regardless of the range settings. All of the "live.*" objects that output numeric values have a "raw" outlet in addition to the usual one.

Our patch contains seven `live.dial` objects, each with a different setting:

- The first `live.dial` uses the default settings, and the number of steps corresponding to the float format (128) means that all of the whole number values in the 0-127 range will be displayed.

- In the second `live.dial`, the range has been changed to 0-100. Consequently, the 128 steps no longer correspond to whole number values. Notice that, when "Unit Style" is set to "Int," the value displayed inside `live.dial` is an integer (50), even though the actual value sent out its left outlet is 50.3937.

- To avoid this discrepancy, the third `live.dial` has been given an exact number of steps: 101. Note that the "Unit Style" attribute has also been modified so that it shows floating-point values. Here, the value shown is now 50.00.

 - Needless to say, the best thing to do when you need to use integer values is to set the "type" attribute to "Int" (as shown in the fourth `live.dial`). This way, as long as you leave the "steps" attribute set to 0, the number of steps will be equal to the number of integer values in the object's *range*.

- The fifth `live.dial` (in the second row) shows an example of what we talked about earlier: it has only four steps within its 0-75 range. Consequently, the four values it outputs are 0, 20, 50 and 75. Try it out for yourself.

- In the sixth `live.dial` the "Unit Style" has been set to milliseconds. Naturally, this is just for display purposes, since it does not change the value output by the object.

- The seventh and final `live.dial` shows the "Enum" mode used for the "Type" attribute. As we already mentioned, for this mode you do not need to set a range, but rather provide a list of values – which could also include non-numerical items, as is the case here. Our list contains an increasing series of traditional dynamic markings (from *ppp* to *fff*) preceded by the word "tacet," generally used to indicate silence in musical scores. When using the "Enum" mode, the "Unit Style" attribute cannot be set because the elements of the list themselves are displayed inside the object. If the "steps" attribute in "Enum" mode is 0, the number of values is set automatically. Note that the left outlet of this `live.dial` outputs a series of values from 0 to 8, corresponding to the position of the current element in the list.

Try changing the values of all of the `live.dial` objects in this patch, paying close attention to the attribute settings in the inspector. Holding down the Command (Mac) or Control (Windows) key while dragging the mouse lets you have finer control over value changes. For example, in the first `live.dial` dragging the mouse by itself will cause integer values to be output, whereas using the Command/Control key causes it to also output the decimal values in-between. These "fine tuned" values can be seen in the message box connected to the `live.dial` object's left outlet.

. . . .

ACTIVITY

- Modify the `live.dial` contained in our "Slapback Delay" device so that it outputs integer values between 0 and 50. The values should be displayed in milliseconds.

. . . .

CREATING A DEVICE IN PRESENTATION MODE

The time has come to install the devices that were created for this Interlude. In the "Chapter Materials Max Vol 2" folder that you have already downloaded from the support page, there is a folder called "Max for Live Devices" which contains three sub-folders. Copy the "VS Audio Effects" sub-folder into your "User Library" – more precisely into the folder named "Presets/Audio Effects/ Max Audio Effect". To do this you just need to drag it into the Max Audio Effect folder in the Live Device Browser, as shown in figure IE.8.

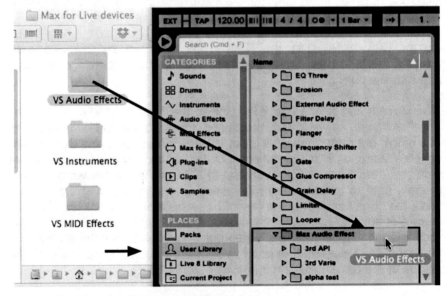

Fig. IE.8 Copying the "VS Audio Effects" folder

After having installed the folder, you will now be able to load the **vs_flanger_1** device into an audio track. This device uses the flanger algorithm that we studied in section 6.4P. The device contains five `live.dial` objects that are used to set the effect's parameters: LFO frequency, pitch deviation, minimum delay time, feedback and depth. (If you do not remember how these parameters work, please refer to section 6.4P.) Underneath the `live.dial` that controls the minimum delay, you will notice a **live.numbox** object (the number box in the "live.*" object set) that is used to display the maximum delay time. This time cannot be set by the user, but is calculated automatically based on the three LFO parameters (refer to section 6.4P for details). If you try changing this number box with the mouse, you will see that it is not possible, because the "Ignore Click" attribute (in the "Behavior" category) has been enabled in order to prevent it from being changed with the mouse, as we also learned in section 6.4P.

Try out this device with an audio clip (for example, a drum loop). Try changing the various parameters in order to alter the effect.

This device is in presentation mode because the "Open in Presentation" attribute has been enabled in the patcher inspector. In figure IE.9 you can see what the patch looks like in patching mode.

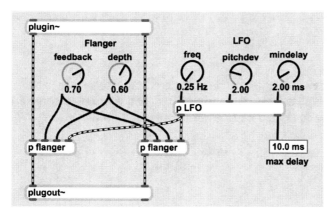

Fig. IE.9 The patch for the **vs_flanger_1** device

We won't bother to analyze how this patch works, because it is very similar to the patch from section 6.4P. However, you will notice that the various parts of the algorithm have been encapsulated and that there are two identical [p flanger] subpatches – one for the left channel and one for the right.

When the device is opened, the `live.dial` objects are already set with values, because of the "Initial Enable" and "Initial" attributes (in the "Parameter" category), which allow all "live.*" objects to be given an initial value. Open each of the objects' inspectors to verify these attribute settings.

You will also notice that each `live.dial` has been given a name that shows its purpose ("feedback", "depth", etc.). This name can be set in the inspector via the "Short Name" attribute (in the "Parameter" category); be sure to also check these settings for yourself in the inspector.[6]

The `live.dial` object, like the other "live.*" objects, uses a linear scale by default. This means that equal value ranges will take up the same amount of space regardless of their position within the set range. It goes without saying that we may sometimes want to use different scales. For example, changing the frequency of an LFO from 0.25 Hz to 0.5 Hz has a more obvious effect than changing it from 9.25 Hz to 9.5 Hz, so lower frequencies should therefore be given a wider range on the `live.dial` than higher frequencies. In other words, it would make more sense to use an exponential scale in this situation. We can modify the scale that "live.*" objects use for their values by changing their "exponent" attribute (in the "Parameter" category): values between 0 and 1 will yield a logarithmic scale and values greater than 1 will yield an exponential scale. Set the `live.dial` object's "Exponent" attribute to 3 and then save the device. Now, you will have a much finer control over the low frequencies than the high ones. Don't forget that you can always have fine control over any parameter by holding down the Command (Mac) or Control (Windows) keys while dragging.

· ·

🖰 ACTIVITY

- Create a device that implements a stereo tape delay (see section 6.2P), containing a lowpass filter, a highpass filter, and a mixer to control the dry-wet mix. The device should be opened in presentation mode.

· ·

---

[6] As you might have guessed, there is also a "Long Name" attribute which we will discover soon.

THE NAMES OF THE "LIVE.*" OBJECTS AND THE PARAMETERS WINDOW

When opening the inspector for a "live.*" object, such as `live.dial`, we can see that it can be given three different names: a *scripting name*, a *short name* and a *long name*.

We are already familiar with the *scripting name*, a feature common to other Max objects as well, which can either be used to create a "wireless" connection with the **pvar** object (see sections 3.5P and IC.2) or to save and recall presets using **pattrstorage** and **autopattr** (section ID.1).

The *short name*, as we have just seen, is used to give a meaningful display name to the `live.dial` object (and other "live.*" objects such as `live.gain~` and `live.slider`). The *long name*, on the other hand, is used to identify the parameters as used in Live: in automations, clip envelopes and MIDI controller assignments (a.k.a. MIDI mapping). In other words, an object's short name is its "public" name, whereas its long name and scripting name are names reserved for internal use. The best thing to do to keep things from getting too complicated, is to give the same name to all three attributes (as has been done in the vs_flanger_1 device). In order to make these naming assignments easier, you can use the "Link to Scripting Name" attribute (in the "Parameter" category), which is used, precisely to make both the scripting name and long name identical.

You can display (and modify) the settings of all of a device's parameters using the **Parameters Window**. In edit mode, right-click (or Control-click on Mac) on the background of the patch in order to call up a contextual menu. From the menu, select the Parameters option to open the Parameters Window, which is divided into columns containing all of the attributes in the "Parameter" category for all of the interface objects present in the patch. Notice that the first column for each parameter has a little letter "p" inside a blue circle. Clicking inside this circle opens up a contextual menu that can be used to locate the associated object in the patch and set its initial value.

Open the patch for the vs_flanger_1 device and try modifying some of the object's attributes using the Parameters Window. You can additionally check to see that these changes have been made to the object itself by using the inspector.

AUTOMATING PARAMETERS IN M4L

Let's now see an example of how Live automation can be used to control our flanger. Open the Live set **IE_02_flanger_automation.als** (figure IE.10).

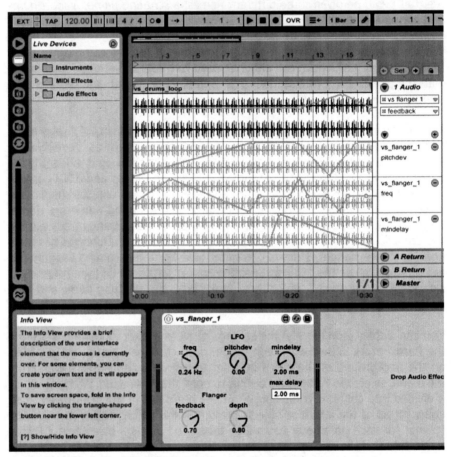

Fig. IE.10 The Live set **IE_02_flanger_automation.als**

In this set we have switched over into "Arrangement View" in Live. Here, the usual drum loop is processed with the vs_flanger_1 device and the parameters of the device are varied continually as the loop is played back. On the right side of the figure you will notice that there are two pop-up menus that let you choose the automation to display. Click on the "Play" button at the top and listen to the sound processing, paying careful attention to the flanger's parameter changes. By using automation, even a simple device such as our flanger can yield interesting results. If you think about it, automating a device's parameters can actually be a very effective means of creating some of the kinds of motion that were discussed in chapter 8.

Nevertheless, it is not always advantageous to be able to automate every parameter in a device. Automating some parameters could cause clicks, end up overloading the computer's CPU, or could even potentially cause conflicts with other parameters. In these situations the "Parameter Visibility" attribute (in the "Parameter" category) can be modified. This attribute can have the following values: "Automated and Stored" (visible for automation and able to be stored in presets), "Stored Only" (able to be stored in presets but invisible to automation), or "Hidden" (invisible for both presets and automation).[7]

Note that the live.numbox which displays the maximum delay of the flanger has been set to "Hidden" mode; modifying this parameter with automation would make no sense, because we have already seen that the maximum delay is derived from other LFO parameters.

MODULATING PARAMETERS IN M4L

It is possible to vary a device's parameters in "session View" mode by using the envelopes for the clips themselves. Open the Live set **IE_02b_flanger_modulation.als** (figure IE.10b).

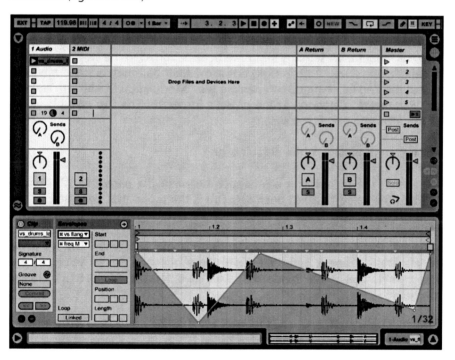

Fig. IE.10b The Live set **IE_02b_flanger_modulation.als**

---

[7] Be aware that we are not talking about Max presets here, but rather device presets, which can be stored by clicking on the third circular icon in the Live device title bar.

To display the envelopes for a clip, you simply need to click on the little circular icon containing the letter "E" in the lower left corner of the Clip Box. In this live set we are modulating the LFO frequency and pitch deviation, which in turn are being used to modify the maximum delay time. Remember that you can select the different parameters' envelopes with the two pop-up menus located in the "Envelopes" panel to the left of the clip's waveform.

Unlike automation, modulation does not define exact values for the parameters, but rather a variation expressed as a percent, according to the mode being used (which we will discuss shortly). Start playing the clip with the drum loop and listen to the effect created by this variation of the parameter. Open the display for the device and look at the movement of the colored part in the circular area of the `live.dial` object labeled "freq" in relation to the variation of the envelope itself. You will see that it varies between the needle on the `live.dial` object (the value that has been set) and the minimum limit of the object. If you change the position of the needle, the range of the variation will change accordingly (try it for yourself).

The circular section of the `live.dial` labeled "pitchdev" is varied, too, but is additionally varied above the needle. This difference in behavior is due to the different modulation settings that have been assigned to the two parameters. By default, the "live.*" objects do not allow their parameters to be modulated, but this can be changed by enabling the "Modulation Mode" attribute (in the "Parameter" category) in the object's inspector. The five possible values for this attribute are as follows:

- None: no modulation (the default value).

- Unipolar: the modulation will happen between the parameter's minimum limit and the value that has been set. This is the mode that was used for the `live.dial` labeled "freq".

- Bipolar: the modulation will happen both above and below the set value. The maximum range is based on the distance between the set value and the closest limit. This is the mode that was used for the `live.dial` labeled "pitchdev".

- Additive: the modulation will happen both above and below the set value, however in this mode the maximum range is the entire range of the parameter, which is added to the given value. This means that, when using this mode, the modulation can often exceed the parameter's limits, in which cases the out-of-range values are clipped.

- Absolute: the modulation will happen between the minimum and maximum defined by the "Modulation Range" attribute, independently of the any value that has been set. In practice, this is similar to automation, even if the variation is expressed as a percentage and not as an absolute value.

In order to better understand the difference between the various modes, we suggest you open the `live.dial` inspector labeled "freq" and try changing the "Modulation Mode" attribute for yourself. Pay close attention to how the movement in the circular section of the object varies differently in each of the modes.

In addition to the modulation we have just seen, it is also possible to use automation within a clip. This works identically to the automation used for the Live set IE_02_flanger_automation.als.

If you open the second pop-up menu in the "Envelopes" panel to the left of the clip's waveform, you can actually see that it contains the names of all the parameters for the device, including the items "freq Modulation" and "pitch-dev Modulation", which are marked by a red box indicating that they already have envelopes in the clip. The parameters "freq" and "pitchdev" are also repeated here, without the use of the term "Modulation."

As a general rule, the menu items that contain the term "Modulation" are used to control parameter modulation; items without the term are used to control parameter automation. Try selecting the automation option named "freq" (without "Modulation") and draw an envelope for it. After you start playback for the clip, watch the `live.dial` that controls the device's LFO frequency. You will see that the needle follows the automation envelope while the colored part of the circular section moves according to the modulation envelope – in other words, the parameter's value at any given moment is the result of the interaction between both the automation and modulation.

By default, pop-up menu in the "Envelopes" panel only displays automation controls. If you want to create modulation envelopes for parameters, you will need to enable their associated controls. To do this right-click (or Control-click on Mac) inside the device on the parameter you want to modulate and select the "Show Modulation" item from the contextual menu. Note that this option can only be selected when the clip is active, not when it is stopped.

SYNCHRONIZING A DEVICE WITH THE LIVE TRANSPORT

In the first section of Interlude C (which you are welcome to re-read if necessary) we saw that Max has a master clock that allows the timing between different objects to be synchronized, by means of the transport object. In a M4L device, the master clock is represented by Live's own transport.[8] When you change the tempo within Live, the objects synchronized to the master clock will be adjusted accordingly.

---

[8] Naturally, it is also possible to create multiple concurrent tempos in M4L, independent from the master clock, by using named transport objects (see section IC.1).

Let's see how we can take advantage of this feature inside a Live device: open the **vs_flanger_2** device inside an audio track. In this version of the flanger, the LFO frequency is no longer expressed in Hertz, but in subdivisions of the beat. In figure IE.11 we can see the associated patch.

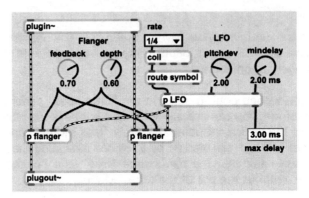

Fig. IE.11 The patch for the **vs_flanger_2** device

The object labeled "rate" is a `live.menu` object, the "live.*" version of the standard `umenu` object. The object contains a list of beat subdivisions expressed as fractions. The corresponding note values (1/4 = 4n, 1/8 = 8n, etc.) are located inside the coll (whose editor you can open by double-clicking on the object.)[9] These values are sent to the [**p LFO**] subpatch. Notice the [**route** symbol] object that is needed to eliminate the word "symbol" which, as we already learned, is appended in front of lone symbols before coll outputs them. In figure IE.12 we can see the contents of the [**p LFO**] subpatch.

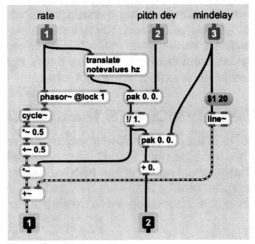

Fig. IE.12 The [p LFO] subpatch

---

[9] For details on the coll object, see section ID.3.

The beat subdivision values expressed in note values enter the subpatch via the first inlet and are sent to a **phasor~** used to control the phase of a **cycle~** (i.e., a sinusoidal LFO). The "lock" attribute, which has been set to 1, is used to make sure that the **phasor~** is always in phase with the live transport, in other words so that each ramp begins precisely at the beginning of each subdivision of the beat. The first inlet is also connected to a **translate** object that is used to convert the subdivision into Hertz. The value in Hertz is used to calculate the amplitude of the LFO.

Load a rhythmic clip inside an audio track and try changing the tempo of the Live metronome itself. You will see how the flanger's LFO changes accordingly, always synchronizing with the given tempo. Try using some automation with it, too.

Let's now see some other possible synchronization techniques. Open the Live set **IE_03_sample_and_hold.als**. The **vs_sampleandhold** device, which, as its name suggests, is an M4L version of the classic rhythmic random filtering effect, has been inserted in the first track. In figure IE.13 we can see the patch for this device.

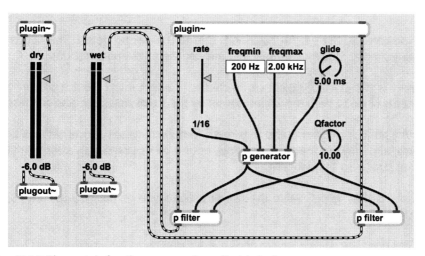

Fig. IE.13 The patch for the vs_sampleandhold device

There are two **live.gain~** objects, one for the dry signal and one for the wet signal. In the center of the patch, under the **plugin~** object, there is a **live.slider** (the "live.*" version of the standard **slider** object), which can be used to select the speed of the random cutoff frequency. The two **live.numbox** objects are used to set the frequency band from which the random frequencies are chosen. You will notice that both these objects use an exponential scale (which you can verify in the inspector). The **live.dial** labeled "glide" is used to set the duration for a brief portamento (glide between notes) between one frequency and the next.

Figure IE.14 shows the [p generator] subpatch used to generate the random frequencies synchronized with the Live transport.

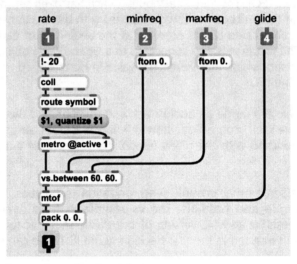

Fig. IE.14 The [p generator] subpatch

As you can see, the synchronization is due to the **metro** object. This subpatch is fairly simple. Study it carefully and answer the following questions:

- Why is the [!- 20] object connected to the first inlet? (Hint: compare the contents of **coll** with the values output by the **live.slider** labeled "rate".)

- Why are the minimum and maximum frequency values converted into MIDI values, and why are the random values output by **vs.between** after that converted back into frequency?

- How is the "glide" value used? (Hint: open one of the two [p filter] subpatches.)

- Why does the **metro** object not have a **toggle** to turn it on and off?

- What is the "quantize $1" message used for? (If you do not remember, refer to section IC.2.)

. . . .

ACTIVITY

- Transform the patch 06_10_stereo_phaser.maxpat into a M4L device. Be sure to synchronize the LFO using the Live transport.

. . . .

USING MAX INTERFACE OBJECTS IN M4L

Up to now all of our devices have been using interface objects from the "live.*" object set (such as `live.dial` or `live.gain~`), instead of the usual Max UI objects (such as `dial` or `gain~`). Sometimes it can be useful to be able to use standard UI objects, such as in cases where an equivalent "live.*" object does not exist.

The Max interface objects can actually be easily used within M4L but, unlike the "live.*" objects, they do not save their default state with the device, nor can they be automated. Nonetheless, it is still possible to give standard objects these properties in one of two ways: either by using a `pattr` object, or by activating the "Parameter Mode Enable" attribute in the object's own inspector.

The first technique is slightly more complicated, but it is the only way to do it in Max 5. However, since there are several devices that take advantage of this, we still advise studying how it is done even if you own a more recent version of Max.

For this technique, any Max object that we might want to use within a device's interface will actually need to be bound to a `pattr` object.[10] In the `pattr` object's inspector, you can enable the "Parameter Mode Enable" attribute, which will cause the various attributes in the "live.*" objects' "Parameter" category ("Long Name," "Short Name," "Initial Enable," etc.) to "magically" appear! The settings for these attributes can then be applied to the interface object that the `pattr` is bound to. Note that it is not possible to use an `autopattr` to enable standard Max objects to be automated; each one needs to be bound to a `pattr`.

Let's quickly look at an example: open the **Live set IE_04_max_parameters.als**. This set contains the **vs_simpletaps** device, whose patch is shown in figure IE.15.

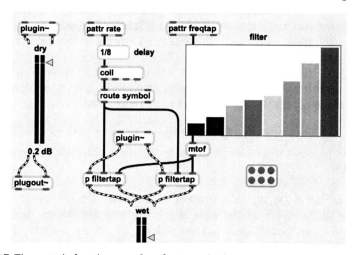

Fig. IE.15 The patch for the **vs_simpletaps** device

---

[10] Regarding the concept of "binding," please refer to section ID.1.

This device uses two Max interface objects, each of which is connected to a `pattr`: a `multislider` (which does not have an equivalent "live.*" object) and a `umenu`. This latter object contains a list of subdivisions expressed as fractions, which are then converted into note values using the contents of a `coll` object (we also used this system in the previous patches).

If you open the inspector for the [`pattr` rate] object you can see that the various "Parameter" category attributes are there. Notice that the "Parameter Mode Enable" attribute has been set in order to make all of the others visible. The "Parameter Visibility" attribute lets us know that this parameter can be used with automation. Pay careful attention to the "Range/Enum" and "Steps" attributes.

Now let's move over to the inspector for the [`pattr` freqtap] object that is connected to the `multislider`. You will notice that the "Type" attribute has been given the setting "Blob". This term is used to indicate that the parameter values are actually lists (as is the case with `multislider`) that can be saved in the device presets, but that they cannot be automated.

Try out the various presets that have already been stored in the `preset` object and then analyze the contents of the [p filtertap] subpatch for yourself.

Fortunately, as of Max 6, most standard interface objects have the "Parameter Mode Enable" attribute allowing all of the attributes in the "Parameter" category to be added to the object itself. This is the second technique that was mentioned earlier, and it makes using the `pattr` object superfluous in most situations.

If you have Max 6 or later, create a new version of the vs_simpletaps device, eliminating the `pattr` object and using the inspector to enable the "Parameter Mode Enable" attribute for both the `multislider` and the `umenu` objects.

Generally, it is better to use the "live.*" interface objects when they are available, only relying on standard Max objects when there is no equivalent "live.*" object available (as is the case with `multislider`, function, etc.).

. . . .

ACTIVITIES

- In the Live set IE_04_max_parameters.als we added the Live device "Limiter" in order to be sure that the sum of the dry and wet signals cannot cause distortion on output. Transform the patch 07_07_limiter.maxpat into an M4L device that can be used to replace the standard limiter.

- Transform the patch 06_09_comb_resonators.maxpat into an M4L device. Be sure to make the `multislider` compatible with M4L using one of the two techniques illustrated above.

SEND AND RECEIVE IN A M4L DEVICE

If we use a pair of **send/receive** objects (or the equivalent **send~/receive~** in MSP) the messages sent by send will be received by all of the **receive** objects with the same name, even of they are located in different devices. Test this out by recreating the simple device shown in figure IE.16 and loading it into an audio track.

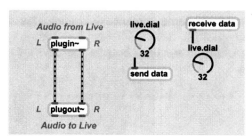

Fig. IE.16 **send/receive** in a device

All the values output by the **live.dial** connected to [send data] will be received by the **live.dial** connected to [**receive** data]. If we now load a second copy of the device, the **live.dial** connected to [**receive** data] in this second device will also receive the same values, even if the device is in a different audio track. Obviously, in most cases this is not at all desirable, so we need a way of making the **send/receive** names unique for each device. In section ID.2 we learned how the #0 symbol can be used to generate a unique name for arguments located inside an abstraction. The equivalent for M4L devices is the symbol --- (three dashes) appended, without any spaces, in front of the argument name. Modify the device as shown in figure IE.17.

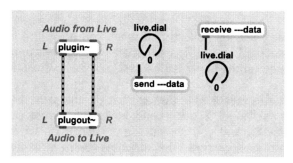

Fig. IE.17 Creating unique arguments in a device

If you now load several copies of this device in an audio track (or tracks), you will see that the --- symbol is substituted with an arbitrary numerical identifier, and each copy of the device contains a different identifier. As you can see, this works in exactly the same way as the #0 symbol within abstractions.

It is very important to understand the hierarchical order of these unique symbols, to better know how and when they should be used:

- the #0 symbol is unique inside an abstraction. This means that when a device contains two identical abstractions that use arguments starting with the #0 symbol, each abstraction will receive a unique numerical identifier. Outside the abstraction, in the device's main patch, or in a subpatch, the #0 symbol will not be replaced by a numerical identifier.

- the --- symbol is unique inside a device. This means that if there are two identical abstractions that use arguments starting with the --- symbol, both abstractions will receive the same numerical identifier. This value is nonetheless different for each copy of the device. Furthermore, the --- symbol will even be substituted outside of an abstraction, both in the device's main patch as well as in its subpatches.

• •

ACTIVITY

- Transform the patch 06_03_multitap3.maxpat into an M4L device. Be sure to make the **multislider** compatibile with M4L using one of the two previously illustrated techniques. Make sure that each of the **send/receive** pairs has a unique argument for each copy of the device.

• •

ANNOTATION AND HINTS

As we begin creating more and more complex devices, it becomes more and more important to describe the function of the different parameters, and sometimes using a simple parameter name is not enough.

You have probably already noticed that when you hover the mouse over the interface of a standard Live device, parameter descriptions appear in the Info View panel located on the lower left hand side of the Live window.

It is also possible to create M4L devices that do the same thing. For example reopen the vs_flanger_2 device and hover the mouse over the various **live.dial** objects, and you should see a description of each parameter appear in the Info View window. The attributes you need to set in order to be able to display this information in Info View are: "Annotation Name", which sets the title of the Info View window, and "Annotation" for the text itself. Both of these attributes are located in the "Description" category. Remember that the "Annotation" attribute is also used to set the descriptive text in the Max Clue Window (see section 1.4P of the first volume). Additionally, the "Hint" attribute, which displays a brief pop-up message (see also section 1.4P), can also be used in M4L devices.

FREEZE DEVICE

Load the **vs_frz_sah** device into an audio track. It is identical in appearance to the vs_sampleandhold device that we have already used, above. However, if you try to open the patch in edit mode, you will realize that it is not possible. This is because the device has been "frozen." This means that it was saved as a "package" containing the files of all the non-standard objects used in the patch (such as objects from the Virtual Sound Macros library, for example), in addition to the file corresponding to the device. This can be useful in case we want to be able to load the device on a computer where the objects and abstractions used to program it are not installed. Freezing also causes any audio files, images, or other necessary external items to be included, rendering the device easily exportable.

To "unfreeze" a device you simply need to click on the second icon in the Toolbar at the bottom (depicting a snowflake). This will create a folder with the name of the device with the word Project appended to it (for example "vs_frz_sah Project") located in the path ~/Documents/Max/Max For Live Devices (for Mac users)[11] or (User Directory)\Documents\Max\Max for Live Devices (for Windows users). The folder that is created will contain all of the elements that are not present in Max's search path. In your case, you will probably only find the file generator.abstraction.maxpat, which was created expressly for this example (and is not located elsewhere in the search path), but if you give this device to someone who does not have the Virtual Sound Macros library, the "vs_frz_sag Project" folder will also contain all of the other VS objects that were used.

The snowflake icon (called the Freeze Button) can, naturally, be used to freeze a device, too. If you want to see the files included in a frozen device, just click on the "Show Containing Project" icon located in the Toolbar at the bottom of the Patcher Window (figure IE.17b), which will open the Project Window for the associated device. (The Project Window and the use of projects in Max will be covered in a future chapter.)

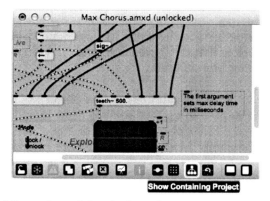

Fig. IE.17b The "Show Containing Project" icon

---

[11] The tilde in Mac path names is used to indicate the Home folder, represented by the house icon.

PRESET AND PATTRSTORAGE IN M4L

Let's now talk a little about presets. Since this term could potentially mean two very different things in Max and in Live, we will use the term "Live preset" to indicate a device preset that was stored by clicking on the last circular icon in the Live device title bar, and we will use the term "Max preset" to mean the preset stored inside a patch using the **preset** and/or **pattrstorage** object(s).

In the vs_simpletaps device that we used earlier, there is a **preset** object that has 6 different presets for the device. These Max presets can be set and saved with the device while the device is being built. Such Max presets can be changed at a later point in time and stored in the **preset** object, exactly as they can when creating and using a normal Max patch. However, if we save a new Live preset after making these modifications and subsequently recall that preset, the contents of the **preset** object will return to their original values, and not our modified ones. In other words, the presets saved in a **preset** object cannot be saved in a Live preset within the Live program; the patch must be opened in Max, new presets stored, and the patch saved once again by Max. This is obviously rather inconvenient.

Fortunately, by using the **pattrstorage** object a group of Max presets can be saved within a single Live preset, without needing to leave Live. This can be very helpful when we need to quickly modify a predetermined set of presets or when we want to interpolate between two Max presets. (If your recollection of preset management using **pattr** and **pattrstorage** has faded, we recommend carefully reading section ID.1 once again.) Here is how this all works:

- First, add a **pattrstorage** object to the device, then enable the "Parameter Mode Enable" attribute in the object's inspector in order to make the attributes in the "Parameter" category visible.

- Keep the **pattrstorage** inspector open, and enable the "Initial Enable" attribute in the "Parameter" category. This instructs the **pattrstorage** object to save all of its presets inside the patch itself, without needing to create an external preset file. Note that the "savemode" and "autorestore" attributes will become disabled when you do this.

- Now you need to allow the **pattrstorage** object to "see" the interface objects used in the device. To do this, you will need to add a named **pattr** object for each standard Max object (but not for any of the "live.*" objects), and enable the "Parameter Mode Enable" attribute for each of the **pattr** objects. For the "live.*" objects you can simply add an **autopattr** to make these objects visible to **pattrstorage**, without needing to connect them to a **pattr**.

Let's now look at a preliminary example – load the **vs_the_enveloper** device (figure IE.18) into an audio track.

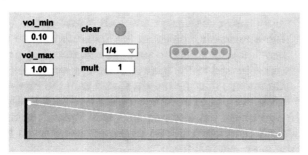

Fig. IE.18 The vs_the_enveloper device

This device imposes a rhythmic envelope on its input audio. It is possible to use the `function` object in the lower part of the device to design the envelope used. The "vol_min" and "vol_max" parameters determine the minimum and maximum amplitude for the envelope. The `live.button`[12] labeled "clear" can be used to delete the envelope. The "rate" and "mult" parameters determine the beat and duration of the envelope. If "rate" is equal to 1/4 and "mult" is equal to 5, for example, the beat rate and resulting envelope duration would be 5/4 – this could be very useful if we want to escape from the "cage" imposed by the standard 4/4 bar.

Try changing the parameters using the sound file vs_organ_line.wav (located in the "sound files" folder of the Virtual Sound Macros library). As you can see, there is a `preset` object on the right hand side of the device, but there are no Max presets stored in it. Try loading the Live preset named the_enveloper_preset (found in the same folder as the device: "VS Audio Effects"), which contains 6 Max presets saved within the Live preset, itself. Listen to the presets and the open up the patch for the device (figure IE.19).

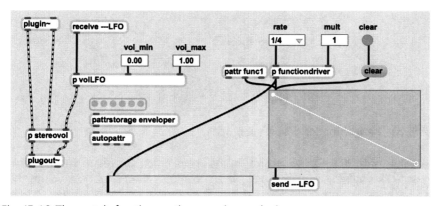

Fig. IE.19 The patch for the vs_the_enveloper device

---

[12] The `live.button` object, needless to say, is the "live.*" version of the standard `button` object.

Notice the **pattr** object connected to the standard Max **function** object: by opening the inspector for this **pattr**, you can check that its "Parameter Mode Enable" attribute has been enabled, allowing the **function** object to be rendered "visible" to the **pattrstorage** and thus allowing it to be saved with the Live preset. The **autopattr** object in the lower part of the patch is used to make the "live.*" objects visible to **pattrstorage**. The **preset** object in the patch has been bound to the [pattrstorage enveloper] object via its "pattrstorage" attribute, so that the presets stored with the **preset** object are actually stored inside the **pattrstorage** object (see section ID.1). Naturally, the **pattrstorage** object has also had its "Initial Enable" attribute enabled, which, as we already mentioned, allows its presets to be saved together with the patch and not in an external file.

Close the patch, return to Live, try creating some new Max presets for the device, and then save a new Live preset. When you thereafter recall this preset, all of the presets that were saved with **preset/pattrstorage** will also be recalled.

Let's now see how the actual enveloping algorithm works. Inside the [p functiondriver] subpatch connected to the **function** object, there is a **phasor~** synchronized with the Live transport (figure IE.20).

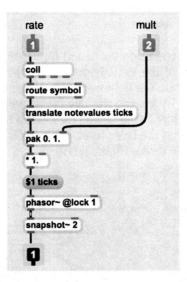

Fig. IE.20 The [p functiondriver] subpatch

The value output by **live.menu** in the main patch arrives in the first inlet ("rate"). This value is sent to **coll**, which contains the list of note values that we have already used in previous devices. The note values are converted to ticks, multiplied by the "mult" value and sent to the **phasor~**. The signal output by the **phasor~** is converted into Max values by the **snapshot~** object.

Returning to the main patch, you will see that the values output by **phasor~ / snapshot~** are sent directly to the **function** object. For once, the **function** object is not being used to send a list to **line~**, but rather simply to output values corresponding to the envelope (in other words, values along the y axis) in response to the continually ramping input values (corresponding to locations along the x axis) sent by **phasor~/snapshot~**. As you can see, to do this we are not using the **function** object's second outlet, as we usually do, but rather its first.

Here we are using the same technique that we used in section 2.4P of the first volume (in the section titled "Using Masking for Control"), particularly the patch 02_19_masking.maxpat, which you should refer to for details. The domain of the **function** object has been set to 1 (which you can verify in the inspector), because the ramp output by **phasor~/snapshot~** goes from 0 to 1.

The values output by **function** are sent to the [p volLFO] subpatch[13]. Here they are scaled to the minimum and maximum volume, and converted into a smoothed signal using a **line~** object (using the same technique that we have seen countless times throughout both the first and second volumes).

In the main patch, notice the rectangular object underneath the **function** – this is actually just a **multislider** object with one slider that is being used to create a vertical line on top of the **function** object to mark time. The input to **multislider** is the same series of output values from **phasor~/snapshot~** that is sent to **function**. In presentation mode, the **multislider** is completely superimposed on the **function** object. But, obviously, the **multislider**'s background has been made transparent by setting its background color's "Opacity" parameter to 0%, so as not to obscure the envelope displayed in the **function** object, (we have already used this technique in chapter 7P, in particular the end of section 7.5P). Furthermore, in order to be able to modify the **function** object itself, the **multislider**'s "Ignore Click" attribute has been enabled, allowing mouse actions to "pass through" the **multislider** to reach the **function** object.[14] If you want to use this kind of technique, you need to make sure the item with the transparent background that you want to appear on top (in our case the **multislider**) is located above the object underneath it. If it isn't, you can always select the first object and select the *Bring to Front* option from the *Arrange* menu, which is designed to bring the object to the frontmost level.[15]

---

[13] Notice the use of the --- symbol for the **send** and **receive** objects.

[14] As of Max version 6.07, the **function** object has been provided with a "cursor" attribute which can be used to display a vertical line superimposed on top of the breakpoint function. Nonetheless, we prefer to use the **multislider** to create this vertical line, both in order to be compatible with older versions of Max, and additionally to illustrate the technique of superimposing graphical objects and using the "ignore click" attribute to allow mouse actions to pass through to the objects located underneath.

[15] Regarding levels in Max, see section 1.7P in the first volume, entitled "The Panel Object and Background Levels"

Let's now take a look at a more complex example: load the **vs_the_BIG_enveloper** device into an audio track (figure IE.21).

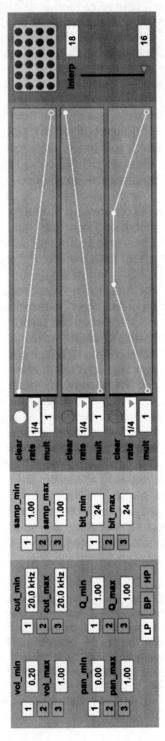

Fig. IE.21: The vs_the_BIG_enveloper device

This device is an extension of the previous one, but in addition to amplitude, we can also give a rhythmical envelope to panning (first colored panel) as well as to the cutoff frequency and Q factor of a filter (second colored panel), and to sound degradation via bit reduction and lowering the sampling frequency (third panel). To refresh you knowledge of "degradation," see section 5.2P.

These 6 parameters can be modulated by one of the three envelopes visible on the right side of the device. The object used to display the three vertical buttons, numbered 1, 2 and 3, to the left of each parameter is called **live.tab**. This object is like a set of pushbuttons made up of a variable number of buttons, arranged in either a row or column, with text displayed in each one. (The text, which also determines the number of buttons the object will have, can be set using the "Range/Enum" attribute). The three buttons at the bottom that can be used to select the filter type are also a **live.tab** object; open the object's inspector to check its settings. This object also has an analogous standard Max object version called **tab**.

In addition to recalling individual presets, this device lets us interpolate between any two presets using the **live.slider** at the far right. Here, also, there is a series of Max presets stored in the Live preset file the_BIG_enveloper_preset. Try using this device with the same audio file as before: vs_organ_line.wav. Even though this patch has been expanded quite a bit, the patch itself should not be too difficult to analyze, so we invite you to open it up and analyze it for yourself.

· ·

ACTIVITIES

- Create a system of Max presets controlled by **pattrstorage** for each of the devices that you have realized up to now.

- Realize the following devices, based on patches presented in chapter 7P: downward compressor, upward compressor, downward expander, upward expander, multiband compressor, live normalizer, parallel (upward and downward) compressor, gate, adaptive gate, triggering gate, reverse triggering gate and gate sequencer. For each of these devices, create a Max preset system using **pattrstorage**.

· ·

IE.3 VIRTUAL INSTRUMENTS WITH M4L

In order to tackle this section, it may be useful to go over chapter 9P once again – in particular sections 9.3P and 9.4P, which deal with creating polyphonic and monophonic instruments that can be controlled by MIDI.

Start by creating a new Live set, and then create an instrument device by double-clicking on the default "Max Instrument" device (located in the folder with the same name in the Max for Live category in the column on the left side of the *Live Device Browser*), as shown in figure IE.22.

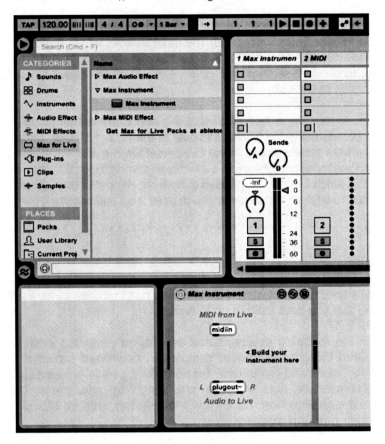

Fig. IE.22 The default device for virtual instruments

Unlike audio effects, instruments have a MIDI input and an audio output. The data coming into the MIDI inlet could be from an external controller, from a MIDI clip in the same track, from a MIDI device (which will be covered later) inserted before the instrument, or from another MIDI track. Let's start by creating a simple synthesizer: modify the default instrument device as shown in figure IE.23 and save it in the "Max Instrument" folder with the name "My Mini Synth.amxd".

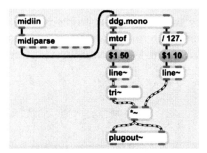

Fig. IE.23 The device "My Mini Synth"

Here, the **midiin** object which, as we have learned, transmits all incoming MIDI messages in "raw" format, is connected to the **midiparse** object which is used to translate and route the various messages to its outlets (for details about these two objects, refer to section 9.2P). The first outlet sends a list corresponding to the note on messages (note and velocity), which are then sent to the **ddg.mono** object. This object, as we saw in section 9.4P is used to manage MIDI note messages for monophonic instruments.

Analyze this simple patch yourself in order to understand how it works. Note the two **line~** objects in the patch: the one on the left is used to create a brief portamento (or glide) between one note and the next, while the one on the right outputs a simple trapezoidal envelope with a 10-millisecond attack and release. The amplitude is derived by simply dividing the velocity value by 127.

Remember that in order to play this instrument with an external MIDI keyboard, you need to set the track's Monitor (in the I/O section located underneath the slot for the clip) to "In," otherwise, if you are using a MIDI clip, it should be set to "Auto."

· ·

ACTIVITIES

- Add a resonant lowpass filter whose cutoff frequency is expressed as a multiplication factor for the oscillator frequency. Use a **dial** to control the frequency multiplier and add a second **dial** for the Q factor. Change the device over to presentation mode.

- Add an envelope using the **adsr~** object, whose parameters are displayed and can be modified in presentation mode. Convert the MIDI velocity first into dB (from -30 to 0) and then to amplitude before sending it to the **adsr~** object.

· ·

At this point you can install the instrument devices found in the "Max Vol. 2 Chapter Materials" folder that you downloaded from the support page, if you haven't already done so. Copy the "VS Instruments" sub-folder from the "Max for Live Devices" folder to the "Max Instrument" folder located inside your User Library.[16] Remember that you just need to drag the folder into the "Max Instrument" folder visible in the Live Device Browser (refer to figure IE.8).

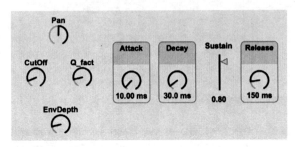

Fig. IE.24 The vs_simple_synth device

You will now be able to load the **vs_simple_synth** device (shown in figure IE.24) into a MIDI track. This device is a polyphonic synthesizer with an ADSR envelope and resonant lowpass filter that can be modulated using the envelope itself (with the EnvDepth parameter on the lower left).
Notice that the `live.dial` objects labeled "Attack," "Decay" and "Release" are in the "Panel" graphic mode, which can be set in the inspector using the "Display Style" attribute in the "Appearance" category.
Try modifying the parameters and playing some notes.

Let's now look at the patch for this device (figure IE.25)

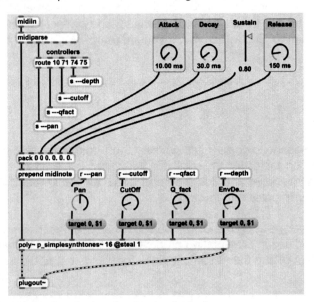

Fig. IE.25 The patch for the vs_simple_synth device

---

[16] The complete path is "User Library/Presets/Instruments/Max Instrument".

Here, too, the MIDI messages coming from **midiin** are translated by the **midiparse** object. In addition to note messages (the first outlet of **midiparse**), we are also using the messages output by four controllers (10, 71, 74 and 75). These controller values are selected by the **route** object and sent to four **live.dial** objects, at the bottom, using a **send/receive** pair.[17] These controller values are sent to the device to modify panning, filter cutoff frequency, Q factor and env depth. Some of the controller numbers used are defined in the General MIDI 2 standard (10 = pan, 71 = resonance, 74 = brightness), but in reality we could have used any other controller number. Naturally, these four parameters can also be modified directly by using the mouse with the appropriate **live.dial**.

Note that, in place of the **midiin/midiparse** pair, we could have used the specialized objects dedicated to individual MIDI messages (in this case, **notein** and **ctlin**). However, we prefer to receive all MIDI messages from a single object, in order to be able to more clearly see which ones are used by the device. Try playing the device with an external keyboard or by using a MIDI clip while varying the different parameters, in order to create a wide range of timbres. Last but not least, let's take a look at the polyphonic patch **p_simplesynthtones~.maxpat** (the actual file is located inside the "VS Instruments" folder), shown in figure IE.26.

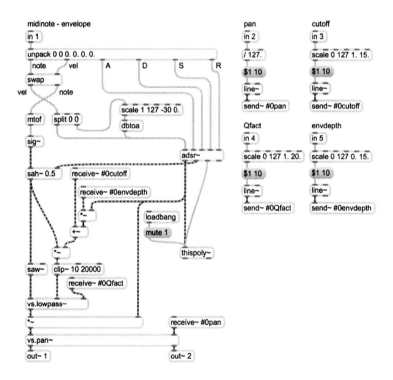

Fig. IE.26 the polyphonic patch p_simplesynthtones~.maxpat

---

[17] Do you remember what the "target 0" message in the message box connected to each **live.dial** is used for?

For the most part, this patch is similar to the p_pantonessteal~.maxpat patch that we used in section 9.3P. Be sure to take note of the "voice stealing" algorithm on the left.

On the right side of this patch there are the inlets for the four parameters: "pan," "cutoff," "Q fact," and "env depth." These parameters all have an input value range between 0 and 127 so they can easily be modified by MIDI controllers. The first thing that happens to each incoming parameter is that its range is modified: from 0 to 1 for pan, from 1 to 15 for cutoff, etc. The stream of values is then smoothed out and transformed into a signal by **line~** and then sent to the main algorithm using **send/receive** object pairs. Notice how the cutoff frequency for the filter is calculated: the *env depth* parameter is multiplied by the envelope, after which it is added to the cutoff parameter and the result is multiplied by the oscillator frequency.

If you want to use this device on another computer, you need to also copy the polyphonic patch, or otherwise you could "freeze" the device prior to copying it.

Now load the Live set **IE_05_simple_synth.als**. Here, the device is used with a MIDI clip that also sends controller values. Notice how the four **live.dial** objects for the parameters "move by themselves" when you play the clip. There is a big difference between the automation that we saw for the Live set IE_02_flanger_automation.als and the controller message that this set uses. In the earlier example, the parameter control happens internally to the Live application and each automation was dedicated to a specific parameter. In the current live set, the MIDI messages can come from any input source and be used to affect any device that is able to receive those messages.

. . . .

ACTIVITIES

- Add a controller for vibrato and one for tremolo, using controller numbers 1 and 92, respectively. Use a MIDI clip to change these parameters.

- Add a second oscillator that can be detuned, with respect to the first, and connect this parameter to controller number 94.

- Add a preset storage system using the **pattrstorage** and **preset** objects. Create and store a series of different timbres.

. . . .

Let's now see how we can load audio files into an instrument – in other words, how we can realize a sampler. Before proceeding, we suggest you reread the section "Building a Sampler" in section 5.3P, paying particular attention to the monophonic sampler patch 05_10_monosampler.maxpat. Afterwards, you can load the **vs_simple_sampler** device (figure IE.27) into a MIDI track.

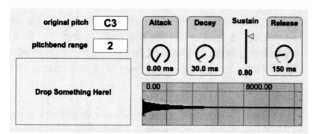

Fig. IE.27 The vs_simple_sampler device

This is a fairly simple polyphonic sampler; it uses a single sampled sound which it transposes to the required pitch. By default, it loads the vibraphone sound that we also used for the monophonic sampler in section 5.3P.

Notice the two **live.numbox** objects on the left: the first is used to set the original pitch of the sampled sound that has been loaded (so it can be correctly transposed), whereas the second is used to define the pitch bend range in semitones[18] (as we will soon see, the device has been programmed to receive pitch bend messages).

Try playing some notes using a MIDI keyboard or from a MIDI clip, changing the envelope parameters. Naturally, you can also try sending pitch bend messages.

To change the sound, you just need to drag an audio file onto the box on the lower left. This object is called **live.drop**, and we will take a look at how to use it in a moment. Now let's look at the patch for this device (figure IE.28).

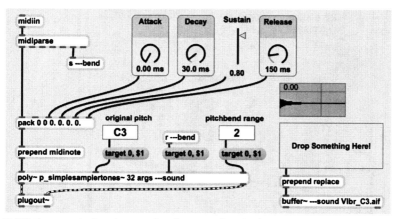

Fig. IE.28 the patch for the vs_simple_sampler device

The **live.drop** object (now located in the lower right corner of the patch), out-puts the path of any file that is dragged onto it – in other words the name of the file

---

[18] Remember that pitch bend is a MIDI message used to dynamically change the pitch of the sound. See sections 9.2T and 9.2P.

preceded by the hierarchy of folders and subfolders where the file itself is located. The "replace" command is added before the path (using the **prepend** object) and the entire message is sent to the **buffer~** object underneath, which loads the specified sound. There is also a Max version of **live.drop**: the **dropfile** object.

The **buffer~** is named "---sound" (notice the --- symbol preceding the name), and by default, as we previously mentioned, loads the sound file Vibr_C3.aif (a vibraphone note). Above the **live.drop** object there is a **waveform~** object that is used to display the contents of the buffer.

The **poly~** object on the left loads 32 instances of the polyphonic patch p_simplesamplertones~, which passes the name of the buffer "---sound" to its instances as an argument. The first inlet of the polyphonic patch itself is sent a list message containing the MIDI note and envelope parameters, the second inlet is sent the original pitch of the sound, the third inlet is sent pitch bend messages and the fourth is sent the pitch bend range. Let's now look at the contents of the polyphonic patch **p_simplesamplertones~.maxpat** (figure IE.29).

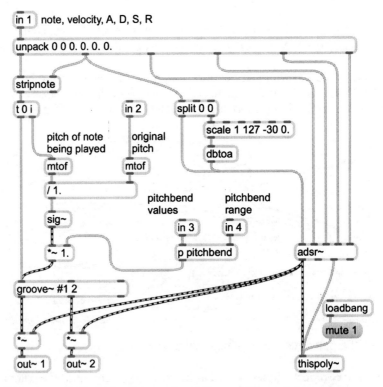

Fig. IE.29 The polyphonic patch **p_simplesamplertones~.maxpat**

On the left side of the patch you will notice the same algorithm that we previously used to calculate playback speed of a sound for the monophonic synthesizer in section 5.3P. For that patch we simply calculated the ratio between the desired pitch and middle C, because the only sampled sound we used with it was precisely this vibraphone middle C sound. Here, however, the ratio is calculated using the base pitch of the sound that was sent to the second inlet of the patch, since any sampled sound may be used with this device.

The third and fourth inlets receive the pitch bend messages and pitch bend range, respectively. This range value denotes the number of semitones that the pitch will be raised or lowered when the pitch bend value is above or below 64. For example, if the range is equal to 2, the note will be raised 2 semitones when the pitch bend is 127 (the maximum) and it will be lowered 2 semitones when the pitch bend is 0 (the minimum). When the pitch bend value is 64, the pitch of the note will not be modified. Naturally, all of the other pitch bend values will result in intermediate changes in pitch. As can be seen in the figure, the value calculated by the [p pitchbend] subpatch is used as a multiplier for the playback speed of **groove~**. Now let's open this subpatch, shown in figure IE.30.

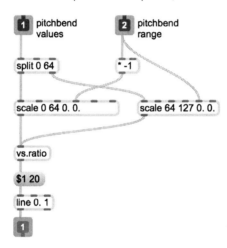

Fig. IE.30 *subpatch* [**p** pitchbend]

As you can see in the figure, the pitch bend values are scaled by the "pitchbend range" in order to convert the original MIDI values (from 0 to 127) to pitch change values in semitones (such as from -2 to 2). This becomes slightly complicated because the central pitch bend value needs to correspond to a change of 0 semitones (i.e., no chance in pitch). If we simply rescale the value range [0, 127] to the [-2, 2] value range, an output value of 0 does not correspond to an input value of 64, but rather 63.5 – a number which does not exist in the MIDI protocol (which deals uniquely with integers). Our solution to this problem consists of separately rescaling the [0, 64] range to [-2, 0], and rescaling the [64, 127] range to [0, 2]. You can see that the **split** object is used to separate the values between 0 and 64 from those between 65 and 127, and the two **scale** objects are used to rescale the two ranges, as just described. The value representing a change in semitones is then converted into a ratio using **vs.ratio**, smoothed out by a **line** object and sent out to the main patch where, as we said, it will be used as a multiplier for the original playback speed of the note.

Returning to our polyphonic patch, the **stripnote** object connected to **unpack**, as we have already learned, is used to filter out the note off messages so they cannot trigger the playback of the sampled sound again from the beginning. Notice the replaceable argument #1 which has been given to the **groove~** object – this will be given the argument that was used to pass the buffer name to the **poly~** object (in this case "---sound").

Remember that if you want to use this device on another computer, you need to additionally copy the polyphonic patch, or else "freeze" the device.

The **live.drop** object internally stores the name of the last file that was loaded, so you could therefore save a Live preset after replacing the vibraphone sound with another one, and each time you recall the preset it will be able to locate the sound that was used with that preset (but only if it is in the same location as it was when you saved the preset).

. . . .

ACTIVITY

- Add a "voice stealing" mechanism to the vs_simple_sampler device. Refer to the polyphonic patch p_samplessteal~.maxpat used in the instrument 9_05b_samples_steal.maxpat that we analyzed in section 9.3P.

. . . .

We have just seen how a simple sampler can be created, but we need to take into consideration that one of the strengths of M4L is not so much that it is able to recreate "normal" instruments (since, anyway, Live already comes with a much more flexible sampler than ours), but rather that it can be used to invent unique and original sound generators and processors. For instance, let's see how we could build a "sound manipulator" that could alter the pitch of a sampled sound differently for each individual MIDI note. Load the vs_sample_manipulator device (figure IE.31) into a MIDI track.

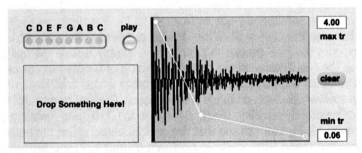

Fig. IE.31 The vs_sample_manipulator device

After having loaded a sampled sound into this device using the **live.drop** object on the left, you can play the sound back, modifying its playback speed (and therefore pitch) using an envelope in a **function** object (on the right, superimposed on the sound's waveform). The minimum and maximum transposition of the sound (expressed in terms of playback speed) can be set using the two **live.numbox** objects at the right, labeled "max tr" and "min tr."

You can listen to the sound by clicking on the circular button labeled "play" and holding down the mouse button. Additionally, 8 different Max presets can be stored via the **preset** object in the upper left; these can be recalled by sending the MIDI notes of the diatonic C Major scale (the white notes on the piano keyboard) between C3 and C4. Sending any other MIDI note causes the last sound to be repeated.

Load the Live preset sample_manipulator_preset and try playing the diatonic notes between C3 and C4. The sound used by default is called **vs_bgest.aif** and is located in the Virtual Sound Macros library. Let's now analyze the patch for this device (figure IE.32), since it has some unique features that should be studied carefully.

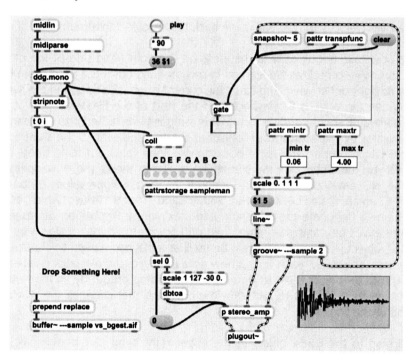

Fig. IE.32 The patch for the vs_sample_manipulator device

The incoming MIDI note from **midiin/midiparse** is sent to the **ddg.mono** object (our instrument is monophonic), and then to the **stripnote** object. The MIDI note value output by **stripnote** is sent to the [t 0 i] object that first sends the value to the **coll** object. Inside **coll** (double-click to open it) there is a list of relations between the diatonic notes from C3 (60) to C4 (72) and the preset numbers that will be recalled: C3 corresponds to preset 1, D3 to

645

preset 2, and so on. The **coll** object's output is therefore sent to the **preset** object which recalls the appropriate preset, but only if the MIDI note is one of the diatonic notes between C3 and C4. The other value output by **trigger** is a 0, which is sent to the **groove~** object to take start playback from the beginning of the sound file each time that a new note is played.

Note that, because the note values come from **stripnote**, all note off messages will be filtered out. Just by looking at the patch, are you able to tell what would happen if the **stripnote** object were not there? (Hint: go back and reread the explanation of the polyphonic patch p_simplesamplertones~. maxpat, used in the previous device).

The velocity output of the **ddg.mono** object is sent to three places: the velocity inlet of **stripnote**, the velocity/dB/amplitude conversion algorithm that we have already used several times, and the first inlet of the **gate** object on the right. The first inlet of the **gate** object, which, as we have already learned, controls the opening and closing of the gate, opens when a new note on arrives (i.e. with a velocity value between 1 and 127) and closes when a note off arrives (velocity 0). We will come back to this object in a moment.

Let's now take a look at what happens on the right hand side of the patch. The **groove~** object, as we learned in section 5.3P, outputs a ramp from 0 to 1 via its right outlet which indicates the current playback position in the sound file (when the value is 0, playback is at the start of the file, when it is at 0.5 it is halfway through, and so forth). This ramp is transformed into a stream of Max values by the **snapshot~** object at the top and sent to the **function** object which outputs the corresponding envelope value out its leftmost outlet. As you remember, we did something similar in the vs_the_enveloper and vs_the_BIG_enveloper devices in section IE.2. The envelope values output by **function** are scaled between the "min tr" and "max tr" values (which, as we mentioned, designate the minimum and maximum transposition represented by the envelope), and then smoothed and transformed into a signal by the **line~** object. The signal can then be used as a playback speed to control the **groove~** object. So, each time a new note is played, the playback position of the **groove~** object is set to 0, restarting the ramp output by its third outlet which, in turn, is used to generate the envelope that changes the playback speed of the sound file.

Returning to the **gate** object in the upper right hand part of the patch, it also receives the ramp values output by **groove~** in its second inlet. The graphical object, underneath, to which the output of the gate is connected, is a **multislider** with just one slider. It has the same function as the one used in the vs_the_enveloper and vs_the_BIG_enveloper devices in section IE.2: to indicate the playback position of the envelope. In presentation mode this object is superimposed on the **function**. The gate closes when a note off arrives, as we already mentioned, in order to make the **multislider** position stop. In reality, the **groove~** object actually continues playing after the note off arrives, even though the amplitude has returned to zero. Without the gate, the slider would continue to the end of the envelope, giving incorrect visual feedback. On the lower right, there is a **waveform~** object that shows the contents of [**buffer~** ---sample] – in presentation mode this object is located exactly underneath the **function** object (whose background has been made transparent) in order to show the precise playback point in the file. Therefore, three objects were employed to make the box on the right side of the device: a **multislider**, a **function** and a **waveform~** object.

The [p stereo_amp] subpatch contains an **adsr~** object that outputs the envelope for the sound: A = 0, D = 0, S = 1, R = 50. The envelope is used simply to provide a brief release when a note off arrives (in order to avoid unwanted clicks), but does not otherwise dynamically change the amplitude of the sound being played.

Finally, notice the button labeled "play" at the top of the patch. This object is called **pictctrl** and can be used to create buttons, switches or dials. By default the **pictctrl** object outputs 1 when you click on it with the mouse and 0 when the mouse button is released. We are taking advantage of this behavior to send a note to **ddg.mono** when it is clicked and a 0 when it is released. The MIDI note being sent is C1 (36), i.e., one of the notes outside the preset range (from 60 to 72).

· ·

ACTIVITY

- Add a second **function** object to the device, connecting the right outlet of the **groove~** object to this object in order to control an envelope for the cutoff frequency of the filter. Additionally, add another **live.tab** object to determine the type of filter being used: lowpass, bandpass, or highpass (refer to the vs_the_BIG_enveloper device).

· ·

IE.4 MAX MIDI EFFECTS

MIDI devices (the third and final category of devices in Live) are essentially used for two purposes: 1) to modify and transform MIDI messages sent to them, and 2) to autonomously generate and output MIDI messages.

Open the default M4L MIDI device by double-clicking on the "Max MIDI Effect" device (located in the folder of the same name in the Max for Live category in the Live Device Browser column on the left), and shown in Figure IE.33.

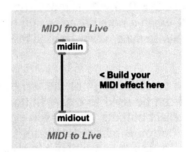

Fig. IE.33 The default device for MIDI effects

This type of device receives and transmits MIDI messages. Let's move on to an example that actually processes its input data: rebuild the device shown in figure IE.34 and save it with the name "My MIDI Transposer.amxd".

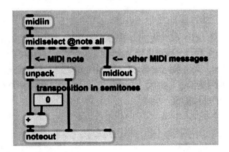

Fig. IE.34 The My MIDI Transposer device

This device transposes the MIDI notes sent to its input. In the example shown in the figure, the transposition is 5 semitones (a perfect fourth). Naturally, in order to be able to hear something, we need to load an instrument after our device.

First, notice that the **midiselect** object has been used to decipher the raw MIDI data coming in. As we already learned in section 9.2P, unlike the **midiparse** object (which we used for virtual instruments) the **midiselect** object will handle only the MIDI messages whose attributes have been enabled, sending all other messages unchanged to its last outlet in raw format. Therefore, in the patch shown in the figure, only MIDI note messages will be handled; the rest will be sent to the **midiout** object. This way, messages not handled by this device will be allowed to pass through it for subsequent use by other devices.

For example, if you load the virtual instrument vs_simple_synth (which we saw in the previous section) after this device, the note messages sent to it will be transposed, but the controller messages used to change the stereo position and filter parameters of the synthesizer will pass through the MIDI device to the virtual instrument unchanged.

However, this simple MIDI device has a problem: if the transposition value were changed while a note is being held, the note off message would have a different transposition than the note on and thus the note played would not be released (try it out for yourself). The solution consists of not simply transposing the note value with an addition operator, but using the **vs.notetransposer** object. This object sends the correct note off message even if the transposition changes while a note is being played. Modify the patch as shown in figure IE.35.

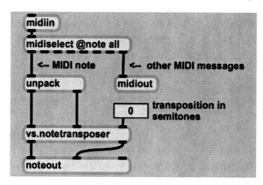

Fig. IE.35 the corrected My MIDI Transposer device

The algorithm used in **vs.notetransposer** was "saved" from an old Max tutorial that is unfortunately no longer a part of the official documentation. (If you are curious to see how this algorithm works, you can always double-click on it to open it.)

If you have not already done so, this would be a good time to install the MIDI devices found in the "Max Vol. 2 Chapter Materials" folder that you down-loaded from the support page. Copy the "VS MIDI Effects" sub folder located in the "Max for Live devices" folder to the "Max MIDI Effect" folder of your User Library.

Let's now take a look at a more complex example – load the **vs_MIDI_feedback** device (located in the "VS MIDI Effects" folder) into a MIDI track. Be sure to also load an instrument that will receive the MIDI data right after this device; you can use the synth or sampler that we looked at in the previous section, or any other Live instrument that has a sound with a fast attack (such as a percussive or plucked string sound). To activate the device, you should turn on the Live transport by pressing the play button.

This device creates a delay with feedback for MIDI note messages and was adapted from the patch 06_16_feedback_max.maxpat that we saw in section

6.11P. Try playing something while modifying the parameters and then open the device's patch (figure IE.36).

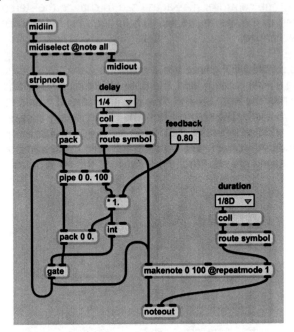

Fig. IE.36 The patch for the vs_MIDI_feedback device

The patch is fairly similar to the one in section 6.11P (which you should refer to for details). Both the delay time and note durations are expressed in note values, while feedback is a multiplication factor of the velocity. Note that the release velocity is scaled using floating-point numbers, since the feedback is a value that varies between 0 and 0.99.

. . . .

ACTIVITIES

Modify the vs_MIDI_feedback device in the following ways:
• in addition to reducing the velocity, also lower the pitch of the note a semi-tone with each repetition

• for each repetition, make the pitch of the note change randomly with respect to the original pitch (no more than 3 semitones higher or lower)

• add the possibility of being able to use a feedback value greater than 1, designing it so that the repetitions stop when the velocity value is greater than 127 (the maximum possible MIDI velocity value).

Change the beats from note values to milliseconds and make the following variations to the patch:

- make the duration of the notes decrease with each repetition (thereby going from legato to staccato)

- reduce the time interval between one repetition and the next to create an accelerando

- make the time interval between one repetition and the next change randomly

• •

The second category of MIDI devices is the generator category. For these devices, MIDI messages are created by the device itself, independently of any input MIDI messages.

A typical example of this type of device is the step sequencer, realized using the **live.step** object which was covered in section IC.2 (if you do not remember it, this would be a good time to review that section). Let's see a very simple implementation in the **vs_step_sequencer** device (figure IE.37).

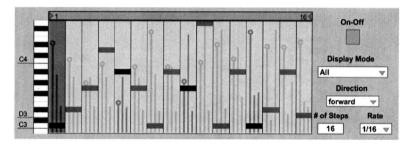

Fig. IE.37 The vs_step_sequencer device

Load the device in a MIDI track and add our vs_simple_synth virtual instrument just after it. In order to start the sequencer you will need to both press the "Play" button on the Live transport as well switch on the "On-Off" switch on the right hand side if the device, if it is not already on. Underneath the "On-Off" switch there is a "Display Mode" menu that can be used to change the display mode of the **live.step** object. If you select the parameters "Extra 1" and "Extra 2" you will see that they are designated "Pan" and "Cutoff" in parentheses, respectively. Controllers 10 and 74 in the vs_simple_synth device have actually been assigned to these parameters which, as you may have already guessed, are used to control the stereo panning and filter cutoff frequency in the device. The menu just underneath can be used to change the playback direction of the step sequencer. The playback options are: forward, backward, back&forth, rotation,[19] or random.

---

[19] Rotation is a variation on back and forth playback, where the first and last steps are repeated. This way, the number of steps is exactly double that of unidirectional playback. Try changing between back&forth and rotation and you should hear the difference.

In the lower part of the device there is a live.numbox that is used to set the number of steps in the sequencer, as well as a menu that can be used to set the beat or rate. Let's now take a look at this device's patch (figure IE.38).

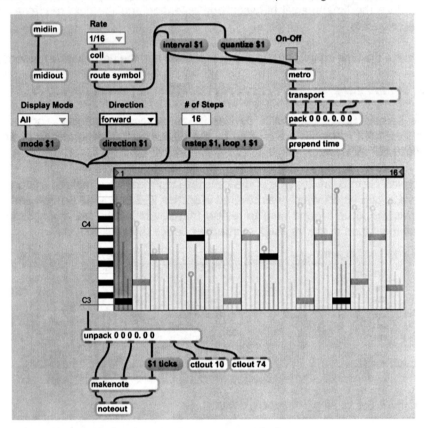

Fig. IE.38 The patch for the vs_step_sequencer device

This patch is very similar to the patch IC_01_step_sequencer.maxpat shown in section IC.2.

First of all, notice the **midiin** and **midiout** objects in the upper left which are connected together: this is done so that the device will echo all the MIDI messages it receives, unmodified.

Next to these two objects there is a **live.menu** object labeled "Rate" which contains subdivisions of the beat expressed as fractions. The values output by **live.menu** are sent to the **coll** object containing the list of note values that has been previously used in other devices. The note values are sent to two message boxes: [interval $1], which sets the duration of each step output by **live.step** as well as the rate of the **metro**, and [quantize $1] which sets the temporal grid used by **metro** (see section IC.2). The **live.step** object receives the relative time values using the "time" message, exactly as per the IC_01_step_sequencer.maxpat patch that we showed in section IC.2. Note that in this case the **transport** object is started by the Live transport "Play" button and not by a **toggle**.

In the upper right there is a **live.toggle** object (the version of **toggle** from the "live.*" object set) that is used to turn on and off the **metro** underneath.

Other messages are also sent to the live.step object in addition to the Display Mode: the "direction" message sets the playback direction for the sequence, the "nstep" message sets the number of steps displayed and the "loop" message is used to indicate the first and last step that will be played. In this case the first step is always set to 1 and the last step is the last step displayed. Also notice the **unpack** underneath the **live.step** object: its last two elements are the parameters "Extra 1" and "Extra 2" which are sent to controllers 10 and 74, respectively.

· ·

ACTIVITIES

- The "Direction" menu in the vs_step_sequencer device has 5 options: analyze and describe how each one determines the beat of the steps.

- Add two live.numbox objects to the vs_step_Sequencer device in order to be able to change the controller number that is linked to the "Extra 1" and "Extra 2" parameters.

- Reread the "Constructing an Arpeggiator" part of section IB.2 in the first volume, and create two MIDI devices by appropriately adapting the patches IB_02_arpeggiator.maxpat and IB_03_random_arpeggiator.maxpat for use as a Live device.

· ·

IE.5 LIVE API AND LIVE OBJECT MODEL (LOM)

In addition to creating audio and MIDI devices, M4L can also be used to control the Live environment itself – this includes tracks, clips, the Live transport, parameters of other devices, etc. This is only possible because the "live.*" objects can access the *Live Application Programming Interface*, or Live API.

The acronym API is used to refer to a collection of procedures, data structures and variables that can be used to perform certain functions in an application. A programmer who wishes to extend the capabilities of an application or otherwise interface with it does not need to start writing code from scratch, but rather can take advantage of the application's own API. For instance, the most widespread computer operating systems have their own dedicated API, and different internet applications like search engines and social networks have API to enable other programs to be run inside them, and so on.

This all may seem rather complicated, but using the Live API via the dedicated objects and abstractions that will be discussed shortly is definitely within the reader's grasp, and furthermore will allow you to take a quantum leap when using M4L!

In order to see just what it is possible to do with the Live API, you should start by loading the Live set designed for the built-in lessons on this subject. To do this, select the "Show all built-in lessons" option in the Live help column (displayed on the right side of the Live window) in order to call up the list of lessons, then choose the "M4L Building Tools" option in the "Live 9 Packs" category to go to the Max for Live lessons page. Select the Max for Live lessons from "Basic Mapping Tools" onwards. These lessons contain an abundance of examples on how to control the different parameters of Live devices using the Live API, and among them are several excellent API devices that are ready to use. In the following section we will learn how to create our own API devices.

DEFINING A PATH

We will begin with a simple example: imagine we want to use a M4L device to access the panning of the first track in a Live set. Two obstacles immediately arise within this scenario: how can we identify the panning used in the first track of a Live set, and how can it be differentiated from the panning used for the second track, for instance? Both of these problems can be resolved by an object called **live.path**. This object takes a path in its inlet specifying the element[20] we are interested in (using a syntax which we will learn in a moment) and returns a unique ID number for that element, allowing it to be differentiated from the others. Once this ID has been obtained, we can use it to find out the state of that element (in other words, to obtain its actual value) or to modify it. The objects that let us manipulate an element are **live.object**, **live.observer** and **live.remote~**, and we will learn how to use them throughout the course of this section.

Let's return to our device that will be used to control the panning of the first track. Create an audio effect as shown in figure IE.39.

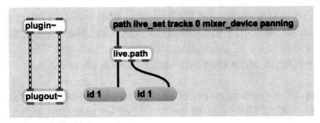

Fig. IE.39 Our first API device

---

[20] A small clarification on our terminology: the official term used for the parts of Live that can be controlled via the Live API is "objects." However we have decided to use the term "element" here in order to avoid confusion with Max "objects."

The `live.path` object receives a path in its inlet, and returns the ID of the device indicated. Let's first analyze the components of the message [path live_set tracks 0 mixer_device panning] that defines the path:

"path" : This message "tells" the `live.path` object that the subsequent list represents a path. More precisely, that it is an absolute path, or one which starts from a *root object*.[21] For the moment, don't worry too much about these terms if they seem complex or ambiguous – we will discuss them in detail later on.

"live_set" : this is the first stage of our path – the element we are looking for is located in the Live set.

"tracks 0" : inside the Live set we will "point" to the tracks and, more precisely, to track number 0, which is the first track in the set. As you can see, the numbering of multiple elements (such as tracks) begins from 0.

"mixer_device" : in the first track we will point to the mixer device, which is the part of the track that contains the controls for volume, panning, sends, and the "mute" button (or track activator).

"panning" : finally, inside the mixer section we can locate the element we are looking for: the panning parameter.

In response to this request, the `live.path` object returns an ID number. In the figure this message is shown as "id 1", but in your case the ID number could possibly be different. The ID numbers are not predefined, but rather are assigned gradually, as needed by requests to the `live.path` object.
Note that the `live.path` object has two outlets that report the ID. The first outlet refers to the element and the second to the path. This means that if the element relating to that path changes, the new ID for that element would be sent out the middle outlet. In our example, if we moved the second track in place of the first and vice-versa, the path would point to a different panning (the one formerly in the second track but now in the first), and `live.path` would send a new ID out its middle outlet, while the first outlet would continue pointing to the panning for the track where the device is located. Naturally if we sent the path to the `live.path` object once again, both outlets would return to pointing to the same element.

So, what happens when an element doesn't exist at the address specified by the path? For instance, what if we tried to access the panning of the third track in a Live set that only has two tracks? In this case, the `live.path` object returns "id 0", which basically translates as: "element not found."

---

[21] Root objects are the point of departure for absolute paths that are given to `live.path`. There are 4 **root** objects: the Live application itself, the Live set, the current device and the control surfaces.

The IDs assigned by the **live.path** object are saved with the Live set. This means that when we recall a Live set in which we had previously created IDs, we would retrieve those IDs assigned to the same elements.

SETTING AND OBSERVING VARIABLES (PROPERTIES)

Now that we have learned how to get an IDs for elements, how can we use them? Let's see how to set the panning value; modify the device as shown in figure IE.40.

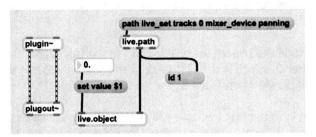

Fig. IE.40 API device, version 2

After clicking on the message box connected to **live.path** at the top of the patch, the ID will be sent to the right inlet of **live.object**. From this moment on, **live.object** will be able to communicate with the panning parameter in the first track. The panning value can now be modified by sending the "set value" message to the object, followed by a numerical value between -1 and 1. Try sending some values (between -1 and 1) using the **flonum** connected to the [set value $1] message and you will see the panning dial in the first track move, as a result.

It is also possible to receive information about the properties of the element whose path was provided. Modify the device as shown in figure IE.41.

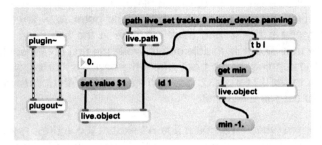

Fig. IE.41 API device, version 3

Don't forget to click on the message box at the top once again after making the changes, so that the ID will be sent to the new objects.

Here, we have added a second **live.object**, to which we send the panning ID and also the "get min" message, which "asks" it to tell us the minimum value that panning is able to receive (which we already know is -1). Obviously, sending the "get max" message can be used to find out the maximum value. The symbols, value, min, and max are called parameter properties (in this case properties of the panning parameter). In general, properties are variables that define the traits of a given element, and are basically the equivalent of attributes for Max objects. Note that the values reported by `live.object` are always preceded by the name of the property (such as "min -1").

In summary: we can get the value of a property by using the *get* message followed by the name of that property. Furthermore, we can use the *set* message followed by the name of a property to set the value of that property. Some properties accept the get command, but not set – for example, it is not possible to modify the minimum and maximum panning values because they are fixed at -1 and 1, respectively.

By adding the "get value" message to our device we can get the current panning value, but subsequent modifications to that value will not be displayed unless we once again send the "get value" message to `live.object`. In cases such as ours, where a property's value might continually change, we could use the **live.observer** object. Modify the device as shown in figure IE.42.

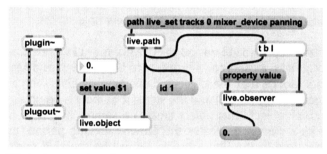

Fig. IE.42 API device, version 4

As usual, after making the modifications, remember to click on the message box at the top so the ID will be sent to the new objects.

In the right hand part of the device you can see the `live.observer` object that has been sent the panning ID and the "property value" message that is used to ask the object to "observe" the element's value. Each time the panning is modified, by directly using the **dial** in the track itself, or using the **flonum** connected to the `live.object` in the left part of the device, the new value is immediately reported by `live.observer`.

MODULATING PARAMETERS WITH LIVE.REMOTE~

Now let's do something a little more interesting: modulating the panning parameter with an LFO. To do this we could use the **cycle~** object with a very low frequency between 0 ad 4 Hz. However, to do this we won't use **live.object**, as you might have thought, but rather the **live.remote~** object. Values modified using **live.object** actually end up being added to

657

the Live application's *Undo History*. Using an LFO with **live.object** would cause hundreds and hundreds of parameter modifications to be recorded in the Undo History in a very short amount of time. In addition to consuming memory and processing power, this could cause problems if we concurrently performed some action that we wanted to undo (such as accidentally deleting a clip). The **live.remote~** object, on the other hand, does not record its actions in Live's *Undo History*. Now modify the device as shown in figure IE.43.

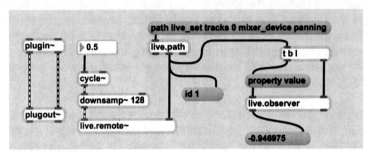

Fig. IE.43 API device, version 5

Did you remember to click on the message box at the top after making the modifications, in order to send the ID to the new objects?

Here, we have replaced **live.object** with the **live.remote~** object. This object can take a value for a property to be modified as a Max message, or as a signal (notice that the object's name actually ends with a tilde). The **cycle~** object acts as an LFO and the signal it outputs is downsampled using the **downsamp~** object. This object creates a sample and hold on its input signal, and its argument indicates the (down)sampling period, expressed in samples. Therefore in the figure the signal will be sampled once every 128 samples. Without this downsampling, using a signal as a control would be too intensive on the CPU – try connecting the **cycle~** directly to **live.remote~** and watch the CPU load measure on the upper right hand part of the Live window. Another way to save CPU would be sending **live.remote~** Max values instead of signals. Indeed, in most cases the receiving element already has a mechanism to smooth potential discontinuities in its input (this is especially true of device or plug-in parameters).

Set the LFO frequency to 0.5 Hz using the flonum connected to **cycle~** and watch the panning dial oscillate back and forth as a result. Note that it is not possible to modify the panning by moving the dial located in the mixer device because the **live.remote~** object has "appropriated" it (something that does not happen when using a **live.object**).

Since the sine wave output by **cycle~** oscillates between -1 and 1, and these values are exactly the extreme limits of the panning values, it was not necessary to rescale the signal. If we wanted to control the volume fader, whose minimum and maximum are 0 and 1, we would need to modify the output range of the LFO accordingly.

A MAP FOR THE LIVE API: THE LIVE OBJECT MODEL (LOM)

At this point you are probably wondering where the information to access the other parameters is located, and how to construct a path to access any element in Live. To get your bearings, you need to take a look at the Live Object Model (or LOM) diagram, shown (partially) in figure IE.44.

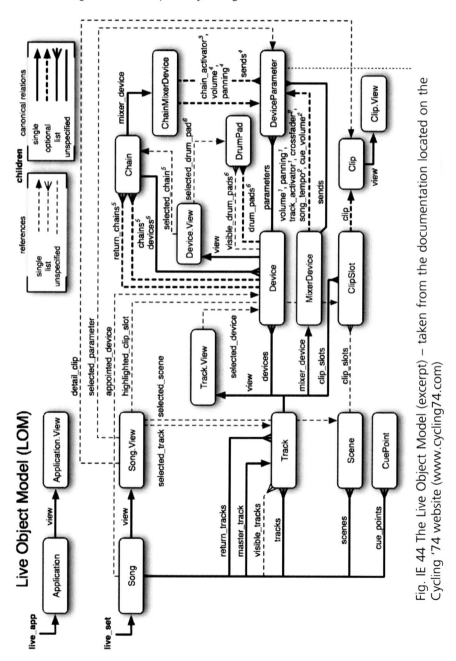

Fig. IE 44 The Live Object Model (excerpt) – taken from the documentation located on the Cycling '74 website (www.cycling74.com)

Do not worry! With a little bit of explanation and some applications, it will not be difficult for you to read this diagram. Once you have learned to orient yourself inside the LOM structure, you will have the key to fully exploit the Live API.

The lines that connect the boxes are the path elements that we provide to the `live.path` object (such as "live_set", "tracks", etc.). The boxes are called classes, and each one represents a Live element, or group of elements: tracks, clips, devices, parameters inside a device, etc. Elements represented by a class are called *instances* of that class.

Classes contain properties and functions that can be accessed using `live.object` (and partially also using `live.observer` and `live.remote~`). The first segment of a path is the so-called *root path*; in figure IE.44 we can see two of them at the left side of the diagram: "live_app", which leads to the Application class (and has the Live application itself as an instance), and "live_set", which leads to the Song class (which has the entire Live set as an instance). There are also two additional root paths (not shown in the figure): "this_device" (which we will talk about shortly) that points to the current device, and "control_surfaces". Each class has one or more paths (called *children* of that class) going from it. These lead to other classes. For example, the Application class has just one child: "view", that leads to the Application. View class. On the other hand, the Track class has 4 children: "view", "devices", "mixer_device" and "clip_slots", which lead to 4 different classes (verify this for yourself on the LOM diagram).

If you look closely at the connections in the figure, you will see that they can be either thick or thin, straight or dashed. The thick connections represent the "canonical path" of connections between one class and another. In figure IE.44 the legend on the upper right labels them as canonical relations. The canonical path is the "main street", so to speak, to reach a given class and each element has its own unique canonical path. Additionally, there are other (non-canonical) connections that allow alternative paths to be made. These paths are represented by thin lines and in the legend in the figure are labeled as references.

Let's make an example path. The canonical "street" to reach the ClipSlot class (in other words the class that manages the rectangular space – or *slot* – that defines where the clip is inserted into a track) passes through the Song and Track classes. Note that you can pass through these three classes using paths represented with thick lines. However, there is also an alternative "street" that goes from the Song class through the Scene class and from here to the ClipSlot class via a non-canonical connection (or reference). If you think about it, the slot for a given clip could actually either be defined vertically, as it appears in a track, or horizontally as it appears in a scene.

Note that some connections end with an arrow, while others have a forked ending with three "prongs." Connections terminating with an arrow represent a single instance inside the class, and those that terminate with a forked ending indicate a multiple instance (provided as a list). For example, the canonical "tracks" connection that goes from the Song class to the Tracks class has a forked ending because there could be more than one track in a Live set. For this reason, you also need to indicate the instance number in addition to the path: "tracks 0", "tracks 1", etc. Conversely, the "master_track" connection that also leads from Song to Track ends in an arrow because there can only be one Master Track in a Live set.

A dotted line represents an optional connection, or a connection from a class that might not exist in certain circumstances. For example, the "clip" connection going from the ClipSlot class to the Clip class is optional because a Live set might not necessarily have any clips in it.

Referring to the path that we used in our API device, let's use the LOM diagram (figure IE.44) to follow the path and the classes along the way:

- "live_set" goes to the Song class (our Live set)
- "tracks 0", a child of Song, brings us to the Track class. Note that we have as many instances as there are tracks in the Live set. In the path we specify that we are referring to the first track (number 0).
- "mixer_device", a child of Track, takes us to the MixerDevice class
- "panning", a child of MixerDevice, brings us to the DeviceParameter class

The DeviceParameter class contains the properties value, min and max which were already mentioned, above. However, these properties are not the only ones available in the DeviceParameter class. How can we find out all of the available properties in a given class? In the Max help (which can be recalled using the Help menu) you can find the page "LOM – The Live Object Model" which, in addition to showing the entire diagram partially reproduced in figure IE.44, lists the properties, functions and children for each class. To call up this list, you simply need to click on the box for any class in the diagram whose details you are interested in seeing. If you can't find the help page, type "LOM" in the search field in the Max help window. The same page can be accessed online in the documentation section of the Cycling '74 website.

From this page we can see that the Track class has other properties, such as *arm*, which can be used to enable or disable the track for recording. We could therefore create a device that takes advantage of this property for a specified track (figure IE.45).

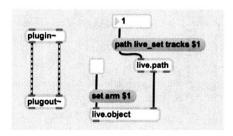

Fig. IE.45 How to "arm" a track

If you compare this with the previous device, you will notice that the path has been shortened, because we are now accessing the Tracks class, and that track being referred to can be variable, due to the use of the variable argument $1 (in the message box at the top). The example shown in the figure lets us enable and disable recording for a second track (remember that numbering starts from 0).

DETERMINING THE CURRENT TRACK

Note that the track being "armed" is independent from the track where the device has been inserted – this naturally brings up the question: "how can we automatically refer to the track where the device has been loaded, regardless of what track it is?" This can be done because all classes have a special child not shown on the LOM diagram, called the "canonical_parent". So, what exactly can this be used for? It determines the parent of the class itself – in other words the class which is one level above it. Since we have already mentioned there is a root path called "this_device" which points to the current device (i.e., to the one whose path is being retrieved), a path like [path this_device canonical_parent] will take us to the device's parent, in other words, to the track that contains it. Modify the previous device as shown in figure IE.46.

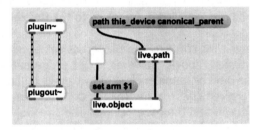

Fig. IE.46 How to determine the current track.

If we load this device in any track and click on the message box at the top, that track (the one containing the device) will be "armed" for recording. In order to simplify our lives a little, couldn't we simply connect a **loadbang** to the message box so it automatically sends the message to **live.path** each time the device is loaded? Of course we could do this, but within API devices it is actually more "correct" to use the **live.thisdevice** object, which is the "live.*" object equivalent of **loadbang** (figure IE.47).

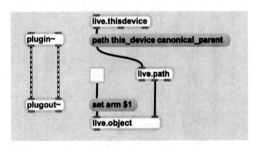

Fig. IE.47 Sending a bang each time a device is loaded

Each time the device in figure IE.47 is opened and finish being initialized, the `live.thisdevice` object sends a bang to the message box underneath which, in turn, provides the path to `live.path`.

Note that up to now we have been using audio effects to create our API device, but there is no reason we couldn't also start with a MIDI effect or instrument and use this technique – for example to arm a MIDI track. Programming with the Live API works across all the possible types of devices.

· ·

ACTIVITY

- Modify the device that modulates the panning of the first track with an LFO so that it always references the track where it has been loaded.

· ·

CLASS FUNCTIONS

We have already learned what class properties are; namely, values that in some cases can be modified by changing the properties of an element. In addition to properties, a class can also have *functions*, which are used to perform specific actions on an instance of a class.

Taking a look at the help page of the Live Object Model, we can discover, for instance, that the Clip class has the functions *fire* and *stop*. The first is used to start the clip (the same as clicking on the play button located to the left of the clip), and the second to stop it (equivalent to clicking on the stop clip button located at the bottom of the clip slot column in the track).

The Song class also has functions to start and stop the Live transport. Let's now see how these functions can be used: rebuild the patch shown in figure IE.48.

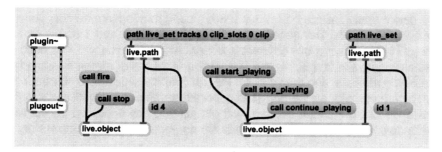

Fig. IE.48 Using *functions* in the Live API

This device contains two paths, the first (on the left) leads to the clip contained in the first clip slot of the first track, and the second goes to the Live set. The message boxes connected to the left inlet of the two `live.object` objects are used to *call the functions* – this is programming terminology that means causing the functions to be executed. As you can see, these functions are called using, appropriately enough, the "call" message (remember that the "set" and "get" messages are used, on the other hand, to access properties).

Load a sound file into the first clip slot of the first track, click on the message box connected to the `live.path` at the top left of the patch, and then click on the [call fire] message box connected to the first `live.object`: if the path was set correctly the first clip should play back. To stop playback, just click on the [call stop] message box.

The second path points to the Live set. The three functions start_playing, stop_playing and continue_playing are used, respectively, to start the Live transport, stop it, and restart from the stopping point. Let's now see how we could use functions to do something more interesting. Modify the device as shown in figure IE.49.

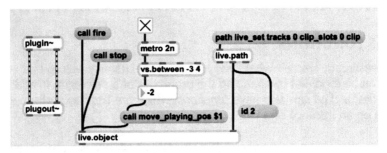

Fig. IE.49 Randomly varying the playback point of a clip

The move_playing_pos function in the Clip class can be used to move the playback position inside a clip (verify this for yourself on the Live Object Model help page). It requires a numerical parameter indicating the number of beats the playback position will be displaced, either forward (using positive values) or backward (negative values).

This device uses a `metro` object that sends a bang to a random number generator every two beats. This generates a number between -3 and 3 that is sent to the [call move_playing_pos $1] message box. Also here, you will first need to load a clip into the first slot of the first track and then click on the message box containing the path, and then click on the [call fire] message box to play back the clip, before you click on the `toggle` connected to the `metro`. Notice that in this device we can use `live.object` without causing any undesired effects with the Undo command, since function calls are not recorded in the Undo History.

ADDRESSING AN ELEMENT WITH THE MOUSE

You have probably realized by now that the technique of using message boxes to define a canonical path is rather inflexible (not to mention inconvenient), especially when creating API devices that need to access different parameters each time. Fortunately, there is a path that allows a parameter to be chosen "on the fly" simply by selecting it with the mouse. Reconstruct the patch shown in figure IE.50.

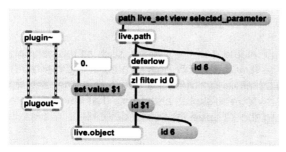

Fig. IE.50 How to select a parameter with the mouse

First of all, let's analyze the address contained in the message box at the top, referring to LOM help page. From the "live_set" root path via the "view" canonical relation we arrive at the Song.View class. From here, we reach the DeviceParameter class via the "selected_parameter" *reference* (or non-canonical connection). The "selected_parameter" reference identifies the parameter that is being selected using the mouse.

If you click on the message box at the top of the device and then select some parameter in the Live set with the mouse (such as the panning or volume in a track, or a parameter in another device, etc.) you will see that the **live.path** object creates a new ID. This ID can be sent to a **live.object** and the parameter can then be modified using a "set value" message, but we need to take a few precautions when doing this.

First and foremost, the **deferlow** object needs to be added after the output of **live.path** (as we learned in section 5.5P, this object assigns low priority to the messages it receives). This is necessary because the message sent by **live.path** is not output by an internal action (like sending a new path), but by an action that is external to the device. In this case **live.path** has received a *notification* from Live telling it a new parameter has been selected. Notifications cannot be used to change the state of an element in a Live set, unless they have been placed at the tail end of the pending processes using the **deferlow** object.

Next, when the mouse is used to select some element that is not a Live parameter, the **live.path** object outputs an ID of 0, which we already know means "no element". This disconnects **live.object** from whatever parameter had previously been selected. As a matter of fact, as soon as we move the **flonum** inside the device to change the selected parameter value, the **live.path** object will actually output an ID of 0 (displayed in the message box connected directly to the center outlet of the object), because the **flonum** is not a Live parameter. Therefore, we need to filter all "id 0" messages to keep them from reaching **live.object**. To do this we are using the [**zl** filter id 0] object, which is used, precisely, to filter out some elements from a list sent to its input.

The elements being filtered are the arguments "id" and "0", so that when the "id 0" message arrives, nothing is output. When any other ID number arrives, only the string "id" is filtered out, but not the number. The subsequent [id $1] message box puts "id" back in front of the number and the complete message can be sent to `live.object`.

Try selecting some element in the Live set, such as the panning or volume in a track, and change it with the `flonum` located in the device. Then, try loading some other device (either an M4L or a native Live one) and select its different parameters – here, too you should also notice that any parameter you select can be modified using the `flonum` inside our device.

If you select a clip you will see that an ID of 0 is output – this is because a clip is not a parameter. So, is there a way automatically obtain the ID for a selected clip? Yes, of course, although there are a few small differences between doing this and selecting parameters. Rebuild the device in figure IE.51 (you can use the device in figure IE.49 as a starting point).

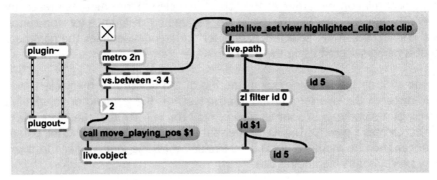

Fig. IE.51 How to address a clip

The beginning of the path is the same as it was for the previous device. However, this time we are using the "highlighted_clip_slot" reference, that points to the clip slot highlighted in the Live set (for instance if it was selected by clicking on it with the mouse). Nonetheless, instead of stopping here, we need to go from the clip slot to the actual clip (possibly) contained in the clip slot, via the "clip" path. The ID output by `live.path` is therefore now that of the clip itself, and not the clip slot. Unlike the previous path, the `live.path` object does not automatically output a new ID when a new clip slot is highlighted, so we need to send the bang coming from the `metro` every half beat to the `live.path` object in order to output any eventual new ID.

Now, in an audio track, load 2 or more clips into as many clip slots as necessary, activate the `toggle` inside the device, and start playing back a clip. The new playback position in the clip will randomly move every half beat as it did in the device in figure IE.49, but if you start another clip, its associated ID will be sent and cause the playback position in the new clip to be randomly displaced.

Note that in this example we have removed the **deferlow** object after the output of **live.path**, since the new ID is actually obtained by an event internal to the device (the bang coming from the **metro**), and therefore does not need to be placed at the end of the message queue.

OBTAINING INFORMATION VIA LIVE.OBJECT AND LIVE.OBSERVER

We have already seen how to get the values of the properties in a class from **live.object** using the get message. This message also lets us obtain information about the canonical relationships and references for a class. Furthermore, the getinfo message can be used to request a set of information about the classes that can be used to build flexible API devices. Let's now take a closer look at these topics.

Returning to the patch shown in figure IE.50, we can see that the selected parameters do not always have the same value range – for example, the panning values for a track go from -1 to 1, but those for the volume or sends go from 0 to 1. The parameters of other devices could have even more widely varying ranges, but fortunately we can use the "get min" and "get max" messages to find out the range limits for any given selected parameter. Let's see an example of how to do this. In the "VS Audio Effects" folder (that you should have already installed, see section IE.2) there is a sub folder called "VS API". Open this and load the **vs_API_set_param** device into an audio track (figure IE.52).

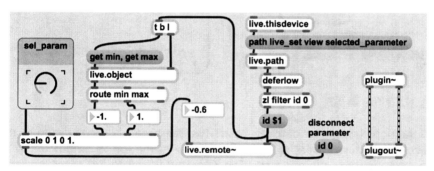

Fig. IE.52 The vs_API_set_param device

The **live.path** object in this device is used to report the ID of the last parameter selected (just like the device in figure IE.50). This ID and the "get min" and "get max" messages are then sent to **live.object** which outputs the property name and its corresponding value (for example "min -1" and "max 1"). The two values are routed to the third and fourth inlets of the **scale** object which is used to scale values from the [0, 1] range into the range reported by **live.object**. This way, the values between 0 and 1 output by the **live.dial** object on the left are scaled accordingly into the appropriate range. The rescaled values are sent to the **live.remote~** object which controls the selected parameter. Try loading several Live devices and select different parameters in each of them to see how the min and max properties output by

667

`live.object` change for each parameter. If you want to "let go" of a select-ed parameter without selecting another, you can click on the [id 0] message box connected to `live.remote~` on the lower right. As we already learned, an ID of 0 corresponds to "no element", so the `live.remote~` object will therefore be disconnected.

If you now open the corresponding patch for this device and take a look at the `live.dial` inspector you will see that the "Parameter Visibility" attribute has been set to "Hidden" – can you explain why? (Hint: try setting this attribute to "Automated and Stored".)

Sending the getinfo message to `live.object` causes it to report all of the information available for the current element. This information is sent as a series of messages following one another, each beginning with the "info" string. The first message is "info id nn" (where nn is the element's ID number), and the last message is "info done". The total number of info messages sent is variable, and depends on the current element's class. Let's now see how this works and how the information can be gathered into a **umenu**. Load the **vs_API_info** device (figure IE.53).

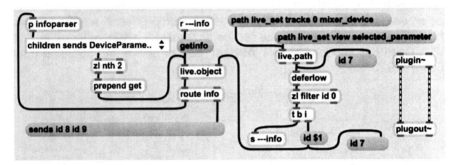

Fig. IE.53 The vs_API_info device

On the right side of the patch there are two message boxes connected to the `live.path` object. Click on the message box at the top to output the ID of the mixer device in the first track. The ID output is sent to the `live.object` at the center of the patch and then a bang is sent to the [getinfo] message box connected to `live.object`, using a **send/receive** object pair. The `live.object` then responds by sending information about the mixer device out its outlet as a series of different messages each beginning with the symbol "info." The [route info] object lets these messages pass out its first outlet, sending them to the [p infoparser] subpatch, which we will analyze shortly. The job of this subpatch is to fill the **umenu** underneath with the information output by `live.object`. Click on the **umenu** to check that the information has been gathered correctly: the first item in the menu should be "id nn", the second "type MixerDevice", the third containing a description of the element, and so on. The last item should simply be "done".

Let's now take a closer look at the format of the messages that were output. The first message reports the ID number, the second the element type, or the class it belongs to, and the third a brief description of the class. The messages that follow represent the canonical relations and references (children or child depending on whether they are multiple or single) that lead to other classes, followed by the name of the class being reached. For example, "child panning DeviceParameter" is a canonical relation of the MixerDevice class that leads to the DeviceParameter class (verify this for yourself in the LOM). After this come the properties and their value types, such as "property value float" which corresponds to the value property in the DeviceParameter class, followed by the functions, such as "function fire" corresponding to the fire function in the Clip class.

If you select an item in the **umenu** which begins with "children", "child" or "property", you can acquire additional information with the get message. The **umenu** shown in the figure has been used to select the item corresponding to the sends of the mixer device. The [z1 nth 2] object underneath selects the second element of the item (the string "sends") and passes it to the [prepend get] object in order to create the "get sends" message This message is sent to **live.object**, which responds by sending the ID numbers of the sends, displayed in the message box connected to the **route** object.

It is important to note that a new ID for the sends will be generated when the get message is sent to **live.object**, if it had not already been previously generated. The same thing would happen, obviously, for any other child of the current class. This means that IDs can be created not only with **live.path**, but also using **live.object** – something particularly useful for creating multiple IDs. For example, if we send the "live_set" ID to **live.object** and then send the "get tracks" message, IDs will be created for all the tracks in the Live set.

Now click on the second message box connected to **live.path** (on the right side of the device); the ID generated will now be the one for the parameter that we select with the mouse. Try selecting the panning in the first track and see how the contents of the **umenu** changes accordingly.
Now let's analyze the [p infoparser] subpatch (figure IE.54).

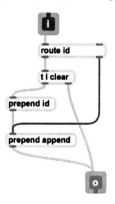

Fig. IE.54 The contents of the [p infoparser] subpatch

Items can be added to the **umenu** by sending the append message followed by the contents of the item. The clear message, obviously is used to completely clear the contents of the **umenu**.

The information output by **live.object** in response to a getinfo message comes in the inlet of the subpatch, albeit without its initial "info" string, which is removed by the [**route** info] object in the main patch.

As we already stated, the first message output by **live.object** is "id nn". The [**route** id] object in the subpatch outputs this ID value out its first outlet, from where it is sent to a trigger that first sends the clear message to the **umenu** in the main patch, thereby erasing any contents that might have previously been there, followed by two prepend messages used to create the message "append id nn" which is also sent to the **umenu**. The subsequent messages from **live.object** are routed to the second outlet of route and sent to the [**prepend** append] object that adds the "append" symbol to each message before being output to the **umenu** in the main patch. When the final message ("done") message is output by **live.object** the **umenu**'s contents are complete.

. . . .

ACTIVITIES

- Add some new paths to the vs_API_info device to get information about the Song, Track, ClipSlot and Clip classes.

- (This one will require a little bit of extra effort....) Use the ID numbers of the child of a class to get information about the destination class. In other words, the child's ID number should be sent once again to live.object, followed by the "getinfo" message. Hint: add [zl slice 1] and [route id] objects after the second outlet of the [route info] object. Think carefully about how the output of [zl slice 1] will be used! You can actually use this algorithm to navigate between classes, via the "canonical_parent" child.

. . . .

We have already seen that when the get message is used to request information about a group of children (i.e., about a relation that leads to multiple instances like tracks in a Live set, or clip slots in a track), **live.object** responds with a list of IDs for all the instances. For example, if we request information about the devices in a track, we can get IDs for all the devices loaded in that track. Rebuild the device shown in figure IE.55 and load it into an audio track.

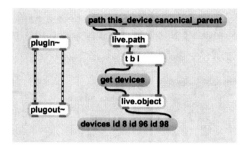

Fig. IE.55 How to obtain the IDs for all of the devices in a track.

The path (the message box at the top) points to the track that contains our device. Once the ID for this track has been obtained, the "get devices" message is sent to `live.object` to get the IDs for all the devices loaded in that track. There are three devices in the track shown in the figure, one of which is the device requesting the information. If we add another device (or take away one of the ones already there), `live.object` will not update the list until the "get devices" message is sent again. If we want to constantly update the list of devices present in the track, we can use the `live.observer` object, which we discussed earlier. Now modify the device as shown in figure IE.56.

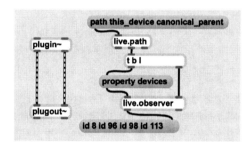

Fig. IE.56 how to "observe" the IDs for all of the devices in a track.

There are two differences between this patch and the previous one. First, the message being sent is "property devices" and not "get devices" – note that the property message needs to be used here even though we are actually dealing with children and not properties. Secondly, the output is not preceded by the word "devices": only the ID numbers themselves are reported. Now if we add or take away a device in the track, our list will update automatically.

We have already said that the list of all the properties, children and functions in a class can be found on the help page for the LOM. For properties and children the possible access types – get set and observe – are clearly indicated. Naturally, the get and set access types are available for `live.object`, while observe indicates that `live.observer` can be used to access a class. For the devices in the Track class, the possible access types are get and observe, but not set.

Once we have obtained IDs for all the devices, we can use this information to know the device names: one property of the Device class, is appropriately enough, name, which can be used to get the device name, or better yet, the name shown in the device's title bar. Modify the patch from figure IE.55 to resemble the one shown in figure IE.57.

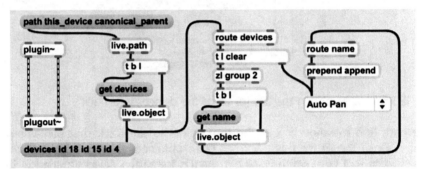

Fig. IE.57 Obtaining the device names in a track.

The device IDs are sent, via **route**, to the [**t** I clear] object which erases the contents of the **umenu** on the right and send the list of IDs to the **zl** object which, in turn, separates them and sends them to **live.object** together with the "get name" message. Consequently, what we get are the names of all the devices present, which are added to the contents of the umenu.

. . . .

ACTIVITY

(This one requires a little bit of skill.) The Device class contains the "parameters" relation which represents the list of all the parameters in the device. Modify the device from figure IE.57 so that each time the name of a device in the **umenu** is selected a second **umenu** will be filled with the names of all the parameters in the selected device. Hint: you will need to create a mechanism that will store all the device IDs in a **coll**, one per row, and recall them when a device name is selected in the first **umenu**. The device ID sent to **coll** should be sent to an algorithm similar to the one that has already been shown, so you can simply duplicate the part of the patch from the [**route** devices] object to the **umenu** (obviously also modifying the argument to **route**).

. . . .

M4L ABSTRACTIONS AND OTHER RESOURCES

By this point we have already learned enough about the Live API and LOM to be able to create useful API devices. The last activities in the previous section were even capable of letting us navigate between classes.

It is also probably fairly obvious at this point that it takes quite a bit of dedication to create devices which take complete advantage of the Live API. Fortunately, we can save a little bit of time and energy by using a series of abstractions and interfaces (bpatchers) created and made available by the developers of M4L–moreover we can "borrow" some parts of the code from the useful devices in the API folder of the M4L Building Tools package as well as from the M4L lessons within Live help.

Let's begin with the abstractions. First, though, where are they located? There is a useful function within the Max environment that we have not yet talked about (but perhaps after practicing Max for 9 chapters and 5 interludes, some of you may have already discovered it for yourself): the ability to grab ready-to-use patch "clippings" from a special folder.

As you already know, when you right-click (or control click on Mac) on an empty part of patcher window in edit mode, a contextual menu will appear. The last item in this menu, "Paste From", is a contextual sub-menu containing other items. Select "audio_output" from this sub-menu, for instance, and a patch clipping containing two **gain~** objects and one **dac~**, along with some other objects and message boxes used for the audio output part of a patch, should appear at the point where you clicked the mouse. By selecting other items in the "Paste From" sub-menu, you can add other useful clippings dedicated to specific tasks to your patch. As you can see, this is a very useful function to have when you continually use the same groups of objects together in your patches (such as the audio output part of a patch, for example). To add a clipping of your own, you just need to save it (as a normal max patch) inside the patches/clippings sub folder located in the same folder as the Max application.

The "Paste From" menu itself has two sub-menus containing abstractions pertaining to the creation of Live devices: "LiveApi Abstractions" and "LiveApi Choosers." The "LiveApi Abstractions" sub-menu contains abstractions that perform fairly complex functions that are not present in the basic functions of the Live API itself, such as selecting the previous or next track from the currently selected one, or retrieving the total number of scenes present in a Live set. Naturally, these functions have been created by combining the standard functions in the Live API, just as the abstractions in the Virtual Sound Macros library were created by combining standard Max objects. Try putting some of these abstractions in a patch and opening them to see how they were made. Let's take a look at an example that uses some of these abstractions: load two or more sound files in as many clips as necessary in an audio track, and then load the **vs_API_sel_scene** device (figure IE.58).

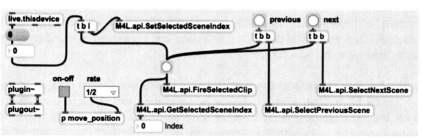

Fig. IE.58 The vs_API_sel_scene device

Let's begin with the part in the upper left corner. The **live.thisdevice** object outputs a bang when the device is loaded. The value 0 in the message box underneath is sent through a number box to the [t b i] object that first sends it to the M4L.api.SetSelectedSceneIndex abstraction. This abstraction selects the scene whose index number (in this case 0) is provided, inside the Live set. A word of caution: this number is the index number *not* the ID! This abstraction actually carries out a rather elaborate operation: first it assigns an ID to the scenes that do not already have one, and then associates an index number to each subsequent scene – 0 for the first scene (the most upper one), 1 for the second, and so on. When the abstraction receives an index number, it selects the corresponding scene using its associated ID.

So, why is it necessary to create and use an index number? Couldn't we just use the ID directly? Unfortunately, no, because the scene IDs could be different each time (depending on the number of IDs already being used during the session), and it is not even a given that they will be progressive values (this depends on the order that they were assigned to the scenes). The index numbers, however, will always be the same and always be progressive values; thus by sending a 0 to the abstraction, we are certain that the first scene will be selected. You can take a look at the index number assigning algorithm by double-clicking on the M4L.api.SetSelectedSceneIndex abstraction.

Returning to the [t b i] object, the second message sent is a bang that goes to a button connected to the M4L.api.FireSelectedClip and M4L.api. GetSelectedSceneIndex abstractions. The former starts playback of the selected clip and the second reports the index number of the selected scene.

Which clip has been selected? The one at the junction between the current track (the one containing the device) and the selected scene. For example, if you loaded (and are displaying) the device in the first track, the selected clip will be the first clip in the first track. Changing the value in the number box on the left allows you to select other scenes and consequently play other clips. In the lower left part of the device you will see the **live.toggle** and **live.menu** objects, both of which are connected to the [p move position] subpatch. This subpatch contains the algorithm that randomly moves the playback position for the current clip, which we saw in figure IE.49.

On the right side of the device there are two abstractions: M4L.api. SelectPreviousScene and M4L.api.SelectNextScene. Naturally, these are used to select the previous and next scenes, respectively. Try clicking on the buttons connected to these abstractions; the selection will be moved upward or down-ward, depending on which one you click on.

As you can see, because of these abstractions we were able to create a device that would have been fairly complicated to make from scratch. Double-click on all the abstractions to open them and see how they were created. We couldn't possibly begin to talk about all of the abstractions found in the "LiveApi Abstractions" sub-menu, but you can have a lot of fun pasting them into a device to discover how they work. Naturally, each abstraction can be opened and inside you will see a detailed explanation of how it works. Nonetheless, be aware that there is not necessarily an abstraction to deal with every possible situation you might be confronted with, and very often the fastest way to solve a given problem is to build a dedicated algorithm by yourself (this will become more and more the case as your experience with the Live API increases).

The second useful sub-menu in "Paste From" is called "LiveAPI Choosers." Here, there are a series of bpatchers that let us navigate between the elements in a Live set. Create a new device and try selecting the "BrowseDeviceParameters" item from this sub-menu, this will open the patch clipping shown in figure IE.59.

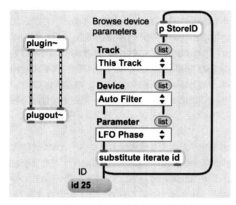

Fig. IE 59 Using **bpatchers** to navigate through the parameters in a device

Here, there are three **bpatchers** connected in series, each one of them containing a **umenu**. The first is used to select a track, the second a device belonging to the selected track, and the third a parameter belonging to the selected device. In other words, this set of **bpatchers** does the same thing we tried to do in the activity at the end of the previous section, but in a much more flexible way, since it can be used to select any track in the Live set, not just the current one. Click on the button labeled "list" located above the first **umenu** in order to update the list of tracks; you will probably need to do this immediately after you load the patch clipping for the first time.

If you have already taken a look at the Live lessons about M4L devices that take advantage of the Live API, you will have realized that they used the exact same group of **bpatchers** to select the elements being controlled.

Each of the three **bpatchers** contains the same abstraction: **M4L.Chooser.maxpat**, the only difference being the arguments which are provided to each abstraction in its inspector. If you open the inspector for the three **bpatchers**, you can see that "Argument(s)" attribute[22] contains

---

[22] We discussed this attribute in section ID.2

a different character string for each of them: "track", "device", and "parameter", respectively. This **bpatcher** is therefore able to browse inside different classes depending on the argument that has been provided to it.[23]

Each time an element is selected in the **umenu**, the left outlet of the **bpatcher** outputs the "iterate" message followed by the ID number of the selected element. This message is sent to the **bpatcher** underneath it, which in response creates a menu with all the elements in the class specified by the "Argument(s)" attribute. At the output of the final **bpatcher**, the "iterate" symbol is substituted with "id", using the **substitute** object[24], in order to get the ID of the element selected in the **umenu**.

If you open the M4L.Chooser.maxpat abstraction[25] used in the **bpatchers**, you will notice that it does not contain the "live.*" objects that we have been using so far, but instead uses the **js** object. This object loads and runs a Javascript program (in this case a specific program called M4L.Chooser.js).[26] It is actually also possible to use the Live API within Javascript, however we won't delve deeper into this because programming in Javascript is outside the scope of this book, but nonetheless we will still use ready-made abstractions that employ it.

As an aside, where is the M4L.Chooser.maxpat abstraction actually located? It can be found in the patches/m4l-patches/LiveAPI recourses/tools sub-folder in the folder containing the Max application itself. In this folder, and in the other sub-folders of patches/m4l-patches/LiveAPI resources, there are a variety of useful abstractions.

Let's now take a look at a device that uses the M4L.Chooser.maxpat abstraction alongside other "borrowed" ready-made material: load the **vs_API_rand_LFO** device inside an audio track (figure IE.60).

---

[23] In the "LiveAPI Choosers" sub-menu there are several different versions of the M4L.Chooser. maxpat abstraction, each with a different argument. The possible arguments are: none, chain, clip, clipaudio, clipmidi, clipslot, cuepoint, device, parameter, fparam, mixerparam, scene, send, track, trackaudio, trackmidi and trackreturn.

[24] The **substitute** object, as its name implies, can be used to substitute a given symbol in its input message with another symbol. The symbol being substituted and the one replacing it are provided as the first and second arguments to the object, respectively.

[25] Remember that in order to see the content of an abstraction contained inside a **bpatcher**, you need to right-click (Windows) or control-click (Mac) on one of the three **bpatcher** while in edit mode and select the "Object/Open Original M4L.Chooser.maxpat" item at the bottom of the contextual menu.

[26] As we already mentioned in the first volume, Max is able to run Javascript programs using dedicated objects like **js** or **jsui**.

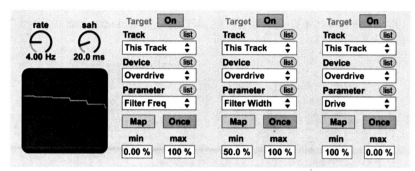

Fig. IE.60 The **vs_API_rand_LFO** device

This device lets us control up to three parameters with a random LFO whose rate and "sampling period" can be set using the **live.dial** objects labeled "rate" and "sah", respectively.

There are three groups of **bpatchers** in the device – one for each parameter that can be selected. The "On" button at the top is used to turn the control on and off. Underneath the **umenu** used for parameter selection, there is a "Map" button used to select the parameter with a simple mouse click, and the "Once" button which, if turned on, causes the "Map" button to deactivate once a parameter has been selected, in order to keep another parameter from being selected accidentally. Underneath these buttons there are two **live.numbox** objects that can be used to set the range of the LFO that will be applied to its associated parameter. Minimum and maximum values of 0% and 100% mean that the LFO will cover the entire parameter range, whereas values such as 50% (for "min") and 100% (for "max") will move the parameter only in the upper range of its values. It is also possible to invert the course of the LFO for the parameter values by setting a "min" value greater then the "max", for example "min" 100% and "max" 0%.

Load some Live or M4L audio devices and try controlling their parameters. One interesting feature of **live.object** is that it can store the ID of an element when the Live set it is contained in is saved, or when it is inserted into a Rack (using the Group command in Live) which is subsequently saved as a Live pre-set. This means that we can create multi-devices by grouping groups of Live or M4L devices together with the API device used to control them. To see an example, load the multi-device **vs_pan_freqshifter** (located in the "VS API" sub-folder). In this group, the vs_API_rand_LFO device controls the "Auto Pan" and "Frequency Shifter" Live devices. Try using this multi-device with an instrumental sound such as vs_guitar_melody_q4.aif.

Let's now see how the patch for the vs_API_rand_LFO device was realized (figure IE.61).

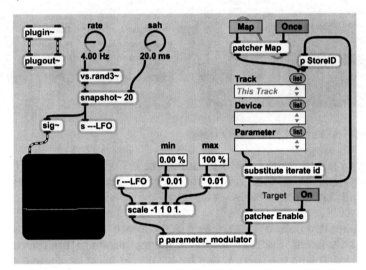

Fig. IE.61 The patch for the vs_API_rand_LFO device

The image for the device is only partially shown in the figure – it only shows the LFO and controls for one parameter, since the two other parameters are, naturally, identical to the first.

As far as the LFO is concerned, the random waveform itself is generated by **vs.rand3~**, and the **snapshot~** object is used to control the sampling period. Note that the "Map" and "Once" buttons at the top which are connected to the [**patcher** Map] subpatch: this section was copied from the API devices located in the API folder inside the M4L Building Tools package. The same goes for the "on" button and the [**patcher** Enable] subpatch at the bottom. Double-click on these two subpatches to open them and see how they were made – they should not be too difficult for you to analyze for yourself.

The [**p** parameter_modulator] subpatch receives the values output by the LFO (rescaled to the value range defined by the "min and "max" **live.numbox** objects) in its left inlet, and also receives the ID for the parameter being controlled in its right inlet. This subpatch is equally easy to analyze, so we suggest you do it for yourself.

. . . .

ACTIVITIES

- Add the possibility of being able to select the LFO waveform used in the vs_ API_rand_LFO device, via a **live.menu** object. The selection of waveforms should be sine, sawtooth, triangular, random with linear interpolation, and random with cubic interpolation.

- Create an API device similar to vs_API_rand_LFO, but which uses an envelope follower in place of the LFO.

- Create an API device similar to vs_API_rand_LFO, using the rhythmic envelope from the vs_the_enveloper audio device instead of the LFO.

- Use the API devices from the previous activities to create at least 3 multi-devices that can be used to control Live and M4L devices.

AUTOMATICALLY CONTROLLING ALL THE PARAMETERS IN A DEVICE

Among the devices present in the Max Audio Effect/Tools/API folder there are some that have been designed to randomly modify a device's parameter values. In particular, the "Max Api DeviceDecimator" device uses a different LFO with a random waveform to control each of the device's parameters. This and the other random devices are used in the Live lesson "Parameter Randomizers." You should open and test out the Live set for this lesson.

Let's now see how we can build a device that modifies all the parameters of a device using random LFOs. Naturally, our device will have different features than the "Max Api DeviceDecimator" device. First, each LFO will be able to have its own (randomly chosen) amplitude and frequency. Furthermore, it will be possible to set a probability deciding whether each parameter will be controlled or not. For example, if the probability is set to 50%, each parameter will have a 50% chance of being controlled, so about half of the parameters (selected randomly) will be controlled by our device, leaving the remaining parameters "free." Finally, it will be possible to activate a metronome whose output bangs can be used to assign new random values to each LFO as well as select which parameters will be controlled (when the probability is less than 100%).

Load the **vs_API_autorand** device (figure IE.62) into an audio track.

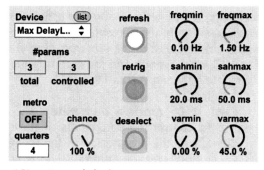

Fig. IE.62 The vs_API_autorand device

On the upper-left there is the famous menu from the M4L.Chooser.maxpat abstraction which can be used to select one of the devices present in the same

679

track where the vs_API_autorand device has been loaded. In the figure the "Max DelayLine" device has been selected (this is one of the basic devices from the M4L Building Tools package. It is located in the Building Blocks subfolder).

Directly underneath the menu, there are two `live.numbox` objects that display the total number of parameters of the device and the actual number of parameters being controlled. As we already stated, the user can actually determine the percentage of devices, selected at random, that will be controlled using the `live.dial` labeled "chance" located under the two `live.numbox` objects. In the figure the percentage has been set to 100%, meaning that all the parameters will be controlled.

On the lower left there is a metronome that, when turned on, reassigns the LFO values with each successive bang. The metronome's tempo is expressed in quarter notes.

From top to bottom, the three buttons at the center of the device are used to refresh the menu, to reassign the LFO values (retrig) and to deselect all parameters of the device being controlled, respectively.

The `live.dial` on the right is used to determine the type of LFO assigned to the various parameters. Each parameter being controlled will have its own LFO with a random frequency chosen between the "freqmin" and "freqmax" values, a sampling period chosen between "sahmin" and "sahmax", and a certain amount of variation applied to the parameter itself chosen in-between the "varmin" and "varmax" values.

Referring to the values shown in the figure, each bang from the metronome or click on the "retrig" button will cause the frequency of all the LFOs to be randomly chosen between 0.1 and 1.5 Hz, their sampling period will be randomly chosen between 20 and 50 milliseconds, and the variation applied to the parameter will be chosen between 0% and 45% of the parameter's range.

To clarify how the variation percentage works, the current value of the all device's parameters being controlled are stored and the LFO oscillates above and below this value according to the percentage that has been provided. For example, if a given parameter has a range that goes from 0 to 1 and the LFO variation is equal to 10% of the range and the current value is 0.3, the value will consequently oscillate between 0.2 and 0.4.

Now load the Live set **IE_06_random_parameters.als** which uses our vs_API_autorand device to control the parameters of the "Max DelayLine" device. Pay careful attention to the progression of the parameters controlled by the random LFOs. Try modifying the control values (the six `live.dial` objects on the right side of vs_API_autorand), selecting both very small and very big values to see how the parameters being controlled change as a result. Try turning on the metronome or clicking on the "retrig" button to reassign the control values.

Let's now analyze the patch for the vs_API_autorand device (figure IE.63).

Fig. IE.63 The patch for the vs_API_autorand device

First, take a deep breath before continuing to read this! Even if the individual elements of the patch do not pose any great difficulty, understanding how they all work together requires a little bit of perseverance.

We will start with a general look at the patch following its overall data flow. The group of objects on the left is used to select a device and obtain the ID for all of its parameters. The central part contains the [p id_parser] subpatch that is used to select the parameters according to the percentage given. Finally, on the lower right there is a **poly~** object whose instances contain the variation algorithm for each parameter.

Let's begin with the part on the left. At the top the **live.path** object recovers the ID for the track where the device is located. The **substitute** object replaces the symbol "id" with "iterate" and sends the resulting message to the **bpatcher** containing the M4L.Chooser.maxpat abstraction. The **umenu** in the abstraction displays the resulting list of devices loaded into the track. If you open the **bpatcher** inspector you will see that, in addition to the "device" argument used to obtain the device list, the "Argument(s)" attribute also contains the "@mixer 0" attribute. This is used to exclude the mixer device (volume, panning, etc.) from the list of devices so it will not be inserted into the **umenu**.

The IDs for the devices being controlled are sent to the M4L.api. GetAllDeviceParameterIds abstraction[27] which returns a list of all the parameter IDs for the device. Each ID number in the list is preceded by the symbol "id", so the [**z1** filter id] object is used to remove the symbol "id" and return an entirely

This abstraction can be found inside the patches/m4l-patches/LiveAPI resources/abstractions subfolder of the folder that contains the Max application.

numeric list. This list is sent to the [t b l] object, which first stores the list of numbers in the [zl reg] object, then sends a bang to the "retrig" button, which sends its bang to another trigger ([t b b b]). The three bangs output by the second trigger are sent in the following order:

- to the [p mute_all] subpatch on the lower right, via the [s ---reset] object. This subpatch is used to mute all of the instances of the polyphonic object [poly~ p_param_var] that contains the LFO that will be used to control the device's parameters. The same bang is also sent to a message box which sets the live.numbox labeled "controlled" (displaying the number of controlled parameters) to 0.

- to the middle inlet of the [p id_parser] subpatch, which we will deal with in a moment

- to the hot inlet of [zl reg] which consequently sends the list of previously stored IDs to the [p id_parser] subpatch.

Now let's look at the [p id_parser] subpatch, which itself contains two subpatches (figure IE.64)

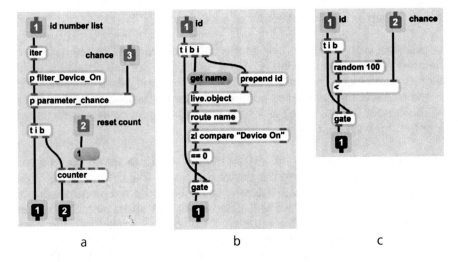

a   b   c

Fig. IE.64 a, b and c The subpatches [p id_parser], [p filter_Device_On], [p parameter_chance]

The third inlet of the [p id_parser] subpatch (labeled "chance") receives a value representing the percentage of parameters that will be controlled. The second inlet ("reset count") receives a bang used to reset a counter that will be discussed shortly, and the first inlet ("id number list") receives the list of IDs. This list is broken into a series of single elements, using the iter object, and these are sent to the [p filter_Device_On] subpatch. One of a device's parameters is actually its on/off switch, located in the upper-left corner of the device window, and since we do not want to randomly control this parameter, it has been eliminated from the list of IDs. To do this, the [p filter_Device_On] subpatch gets the names of all the device parameters and compares them with the name "Device On", using the [zl compare] object. If the parameter name is "Device On" the gate at the bottom of the patch is closed, otherwise it is opened, since the [zl compare] object outputs a 1 if the input list is the same as its argument, and outputs 0 when it is not. The rest of the [p filter_Device_On] subpatch should not be too difficult to analyze, so this will be left up to the reader to do.

The next subpatch, [p parameter_chance], lets only a certain percentage of parameter IDs pass through it. Here we are using a similar algorithm to the one found in the "probabilistic metronome" that we saw in section IB.4 of the first volume. This subpatch is also easy enough for you to analyze on your own.

The ID numbers that are output by the [p parameter_chance] subpatch are sent to the [t i b] trigger object in the [p id_parser] subpatch. The first message output by **trigger** is a bang which increments the **counter**; the value it outputs is then sent to the second outlet. The second message output by **trigger** is the ID number which is sent to the first outlet.

Returning to the main patch (figure IE.63), we can see that the **counter** value coming from the second outlet of [p id_parser] is sent in the following places:

- to the [p mute_all subpatch (on the lower left) that uses the value to determine how many instances to mute when the request arrives

- to the [target $1, mute $1 0] message box, which sends the message to the **poly~** object underneath it and turns on the necessary voices (we will discuss this in detail later)

- to the **live.numbox** object that displays the number of parameters actually being controlled by LFOs

For each value output by the **counter**, the first outlet of [p id_parser] sends the ID number of one of the parameters that will be controlled.

To summarize everything that has just been covered: after selecting a device from the **umenu** at the left, the **poly~** object at the bottom receives the list of parameter IDs that have been allowed to pass through the filtering operation in the [p id_parser] subpatch.

The [p LFOparameters] subpatch sends the range of values used to determine the behavior of all the LFOs to all instances of the **poly~** object. This subpatch is simple enough to analyze for yourself.

The [p mute_all] subpatch is used to mute all the active instances inside the **poly~** object – this happens when you click on the "deselect" button (used to "free" all the parameters) or on the "retrig" button. In this latter case, muting all the instances before reactivating them is necessary because the probability that any given parameter will be controlled might be less than 100%, so for each "retrig" there is no way of knowing how many parameters will actually be chosen to be controlled. This subpatch is also very simple so you should analyze it by yourself.

The live.numbox labeled "total," visible in the central part of the main patch, shows the total number of parameters present in the device being controlled. It is connected to the [z1 len] object that returns the length of the list composed of all the parameter IDs. Note that 1 is subtracted from this value because the Device On parameter has been excluded from the list.

Finally, we come to the polyphonic patch contained in [**poly~** p_param_var] (figure IE.65).

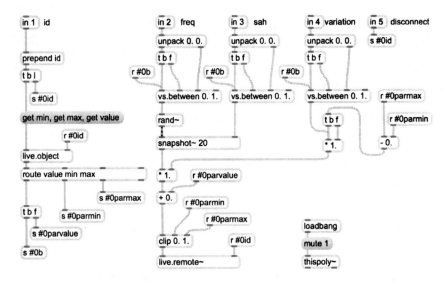

Fig. IE.65 The polyphonic patch contained in [**poly~** p_param_var]

At the heart of the patch is a **rand~** object that acts as an LFO. The signal it outputs is scaled and sent to the **live.remote~** object in order to control one of the parameters of the device chosen in the **umenu** in the main patch. We will discuss how in a moment.

Now let's analyze the polyphonic patch in detail, starting with its inputs, from right to left. The fifth inlet, [in 5] (labeled "disconnect"), receives the messages produced by the [p mute_all] subpatch located in the main patch. As we already mentioned, this subpatch mutes all the instances inside **poly~** and sends the "id 0" message, which is received by both the **live.remote~** object at the bottom and **live.object** at the left side of the patch.

The [in 4] ("variation") inlet receives the values determining the minimum and maximum variation of the LFO. These are first sent to a **vs.between** object and then to a multiplication object, which is used to scale the amplitude of the LFO. We will deal with this in more detail shortly.

The [in 3] ("sah") inlet receives the minimum and maximum values determining the sampling period (i.e. for the sample and hold). These are sent to a **vs.between** object and the resulting value is sent to the right inlet of **snapshot~** which periodically samples the signal output by the LFO to get a series of floating point values.

The [in 2] ("freq") inlet receives the minimum and maximum frequency values for the LFO. Here, too, the **vs.between** object is used to generate the actual frequency used by the instance. By now you will have noticed that each instance generates a different amplitude, sampling period and frequency for its LFO.

The [in 1] ("id") inlet receives the number of parameter IDs that the instance will control. This is first sent to a **trigger** and from there to the **live.object** underneath and to the **live.remote~** at the bottom of the patch. Thereafter the **trigger** sends a bang to a message box which sends the "get min", "get max", and "get value" messages to **live.object**. The min and max parameters are then sent to a subtraction operator on the right side of the patch, in order to calculate the difference and use it as a multiplier for the amount of variation that will be applied to the parameter. The result is used to rescale the amplitude of the LFO (using the * object underneath **snapshot~**). The min and max values for the parameter are also sent to the **clip** object immediately above **live.remote~** – this is done as a precaution just to make sure values outside the parameter's range will not be sent.

Returning to the **live.object** on the left, the "get value" message is used to obtain the current parameter value. This value is sent to the + object (inbetween the * and clip objects) at the center of the patch, and used as an offset for the LFO. The LFO will therefore oscillate above and below the current parameter value, with an amplitude equal to the random variation calculated by the **vs.between** connected to the fourth inlet.

Returning once again to the left hand side of the patch, immediately after the current value is sent, a bang is sent to the three **vs.between** objects to cause them to output new random values for the LFO frequency, sampling period and amplitude variation. Note that each **vs.between** object will output a new random value whenever it receives a pair of minimum and maximum values for frequency ("freq"), period ("sah") or amplitude ("variation") via the respective inlets.

At this point, we hope you have "survived" reading through this long analysis and, above all, have managed to follow this entire section! If not, do not worry – this is probably one of the most complex max patches in this entire volume. Just continue to practice using Max and M4L for your personal musical projects and when you return to this section in several weeks you will probably find it a lot easier to understand.

As we already saw, this device can be used to control only a portion of the parameters by setting the probability (i.e., the "chance" parameter) to a value under 100%. However, it is not possible to manually select which parameters will be excluded. For example, it would be a lot more convenient to be able to keep the dry/wet ratio or output volume of a device from being modified. One possible solution would be to insert the device into a Rack and assign the parameters you want to control to macros and simply control the Rack macros instead of the controlling the device directly. An example of this is shown in the Live set **IE_06b_partial_parameters.als** (figure IE.66).

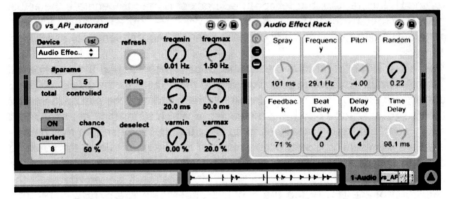

Fig. IE.66 The devices in the first track of the live set IE_06b_partial_parameters.als

In this Live set, we have enclosed the "Grain Delay" device in an Audio Rack, and then assigned the Rack's 8 control macros to 8 device parameters, excluding DryWet and Beat Swing. Additionally, the probability that a parameter will be controlled has been set to 50%, so with each bang from the metronome, the parameters being controlled will also change. Notice also that the total number of parameters reported by the **live.number** on the left side of vs_API_autorand is 9, even though there are only eight dials for the macros. This is because there is actually one extra parameter in the Audio Rack: the Chain Selector. To see this parameter, you need to activate the Chain List by clicking on the third circular icon displayed along the left side of the Audio Rack window. By turning on this "Chain" button, the Chain Select Editor will appear above the Chain List, as shown in figure IE.67.

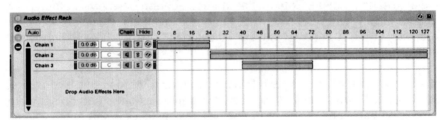

Fig. IE.67 The Chain Select Editor

The Chain Selector is the orange vertical line located in the upper part of the Chain Select Editor. Its value – in other words its position along the horizontal axis – can vary between 0 and 127. The rectangular regions displayed under the Chain Selector are called Zones. Without going into too much detail, the active zones are those located at the Chain selector's current position. So, in the case of figure IE.67, "Chain 2" and "Chain 3" are active because the Chain Selector is in the area that they cover, but "Chain 1" is not active so it will not output sound. By default, a chain will only occupy position 0 of the Chain Selector, but since this parameter can be moved to all positions when it is being controlled by the vs_API_autorand device, the zones need to be extended to 127 (by clicking and dragging one side with the mouse). If you display the Chain Select Editor in the Live set IE_06b_partial_parameters.als, you can check that the zone has been extended from position 0 to position 127.

By using the Rack macro controls, it is also possible to control more than one device at a time. In the Live set IE_06c_two_devices.als, for example, we have inserted the Live devices "Ping Pong Delay" and "Erosion" into an Audio Rack and assigned different parameters from the two devices to macro controls which are then controlled by the vs_API_autorand device.

· ·

ACTIVITIES

- Create at least three Audio Racks, each containing one or more devices, assign some device parameters to the macro controls and control these using the vs_API_autorand device. Do not forget to extend the Chain Select Editor zone! Note that nothing is preventing you from assigning more than one parameter to each macro control.

- What modifications would we need to make to our device in order to not need to extend the Chain Select Editor zone each time that we want to control a Rack? You should both answer this question and make the necessary modifications to the device itself.

· ·

Let's now take a look at an API device that controls all the parameters of all the devices present in a track – this is actually just a variation of the previous device. Load one or more devices of your choosing into an audio track, and then load the **vs_API_totalrand** device: all the devices present will now be controlled by it.

If you add a new device into the track, click on the "refresh" button in the vs_API_totalrand device to include the newly added device. As we already mentioned, this device is very similar to the previous one, but let's look at the differences, shown in figure IE.68.

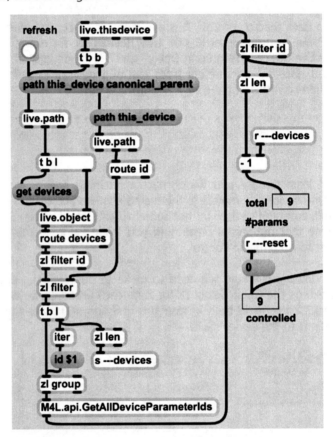

Fig. IE.68 Partial image of the vs_API_totalrand device

The bang output by `live.thisdevice` at the top is first sent to the [path this_device] message box which is used to be able to store the ID for the vs_API_totalrand device in the right inlet of the [`zl` filter] object. This is used to prevent the device from also controlling itself. Another bang is then sent to the [path this_device canonical_parent] message box, which is used to obtain a list of IDs for all the devices present in the track where the vs_API_total-rand is loaded, eliminating the ID for the API device with [`zl` filter], using an algorithm that you should be able to analyze for yourself. The id symbol is then added in front of each number in the list and everything is sent to the

M4L.api.GetAllDeviceParameterIds abstraction that we already used in the previous device. This abstraction returns the IDs for all the parameters of all the devices when it receives a list of device IDs. From this point onward the algorithm is identical to that used in vs_API_autorand.

Note that the number of devices present is subtracted from the total number of parameters shown in the **live.numbox** labeled "total", because the DeviceOn parameter is removed from the list of controllable parameters. If we add the vs_API_totalrand device inside a Rack, only the devices located in the same chain inside the Rack will be controlled, because our device's parent is not the track in this case, but the chain containing the rack (which, in turn, is the parent of the parent, or the "grandfather", while the track itself is the "great-grandfather").

• •

ACTIVITIES

- Add the ability to select the type of LFO (sine, sawtooth, triangular or random) to the vs_API_autorand and vs_API_totalrand devices.

- Make a second version of each of the devices that randomly chooses the LFO type. Each parameter should be able to be controlled by one of the four LFO waveforms.

• •

LIST OF MAX OBJECTS

live.dial
The "live" version of the **dial** object.

live.drop
A graphical object that reports the path of any file dropped onto it. This is the "live" version of the standard **dropfile** object.

live.menu
The "live" version of the **umenu** object.

live.numbox
The "live" version of the number box.

live.object
Allows access to a Live element (object) that has been given an ID number.

live.observer
Reports the value of a Live element (object) that has been given an ID number.

live.path
Assigns an ID number to a Live element (object), which returns its path.

live.remote~
Changes the value of a Live element (object) that has been given an ID number.

live.slider
The "live" version of the **slider** object.

live.tab
Interface object that simulates a set of push-buttons.

live.toggle
The "live" version of the **toggle** object.

pictctrl
A graphical object that can be used to create buttons, switches and dials.

plugin~
Receives audio signals into an audio device.

plugout~
Sends audio signals out from an audio device.

substitute
Substitutes a given symbol with another symbol for all messages that are input to it. The symbol to be substituted and the symbol being used to replace it are given as the first and second arguments, respectively.

teeth~
A comb filter whose feedforward and feedback delay times can be controlled independently on one another.

LIST OF ATTRIBUTES, MESSAGES AND ACTIONS FOR SPECIFIC MAX OBJECTS

"live.*" objects
Annotation (attribute)
Displays informative text in the *Info View* window when the mouse hovers over the object.

Annotation Name (attribute)
Displays text in the *Info View* window's title bar when the mouse hovers over the object.

Exponent (attribute)
Determines the type of scale used for numerical values output by the object: logarithmic, linear or exponential.

Initial (attribute)
Sets the initial value for the object when the device is opened. This value is only output if the "Initial Enable" attribute has been enabled. (see also: Initial Enable)

Initial Enable (attribute)
Allows an initial value to be given to the object when a device using it is opened.

Link to Scripting Name (attribute)
Used to make the *scripting name* and the long name identical. (see also: scripting name, long name)

Long Name (attribute)
A name used to identify the parameters in Live. This is used for automation, clip envelopes and MIDI controller assignments (MIDI mapping).

Modulation Mode (attribute)
Determines the type of parameter modulation that can be done using clip envelopes.

Parameter Visibility (attribute)
Determines whether or not the parameter can be automated and/or stored in Live presets.

Range/Enum (attribute)
Sets the minimum and maximum output values.

Short Name (attribute)
Sets the name displayed on many of the "live.*" objects, such **live.dial**.

Steps (attribute)
Determines the number of values available between the minimum and maximum values set with "Range/Enum" (see also: Range/Enum)

Type (attribute)
Sets the internal format for values output by the object.

Unit Style (attribute)
Specifies the values' display mode.

<Max: command-clic> <Win: control-clic> (action)
Allows fine-tuning of the object's numeric output.

live.dial
Display Style (attribute)
Allows the object's graphic display style to be changed.

live.step
Direction (message)
Sets the playback direction for the steps.

pattrstorage
Initial Enable (attribute)
Allows the **pattrstorage** object to save its presets within the patch itself, without relying on an external file. This is used when Max presets need to be saved within a Live preset.

phasor~
lock (attribute)
Keeps the phasor synchronized with the transport.

various Max objects
Parameter Mode Enable (attribute)
Allows attributes to be used to control M4L parameters, even for objects other than "live.*" objects.

GLOSSARY

Absolute Path (Live API)
The path that identifies a Live element, starting from a root object.

Canonical Path (Live API)
The main path used to reach a given Class as defined by the Live Object Model graph. (see also: Class, Model)

Canonical Relation (Live API)
The main connection between two adjacent Classes. This is indicated by a thick line in the Live Object Model graph. A Canonical Path is made up of a series of Canonical Relations. (see also: Live Object Model)

Child (Live API)
A connection that goes from one Class to another according to the hierarchy illustrated in the Live Object Model (see also: Live Object Model)

Class (Live API)
A model that represents a group of Live elements (objects). For instance, the "Track" class represents (and allows access to) all of the tracks in a Live set.

Freeze Button
A button located in the Toolbar of the window containing the patch for a device which can be used to "freeze" a device. This creates a "package" containing the files of all the non-standard objects in the patch, in addition to the file corresponding to the device itself. "Freezing" a device also causes it to include any sound files, images, etc., thus rendering the device easily exportable to other computers.

Functions (Live API)
Processes used to perform specific actions on an instance of a Class. (see also: Class)

Instance (Live API)
An element represented by a given class. (see also: Class)

Live API
A collection of processes allowing control over the Live application as well as the tracks, clips, devices, and plug-ins contained in a Live set. The "live.*" object that take advantage of these processes are: `live.path`, `live.object`, `live.observer` and `live.remote~`.

Live Object Model (Live API)
A hierarchical representation of Live elements (objects).

LOM
See Live Object Model.

Notification (Live API)
Information sent from Live to an API device in response to a change having taken place in a Live set, such as the selection of a new parameter, for example. In order to be able to use the messages output by a notification inside a device, they need to be put at the tail of the priority queue using the `deferlow` object.

Parameters Window
The window, divided into columns, which contains all of the "Parameter" attributes for the interface objects present in a patch.

Property (Live API)
Variables defining an element's characteristics.

Reference (Live API)
A secondary connection between two Classes (i.e., non-canonical). In the Live Object Model graph this is indicated by a thin line. A path which contains one or more references is not a canonical path. (see also: Live Object Model)

Root Objects (Live API)
The main starting points for paths used to identify Live elements. There are 4 root objects: the Live application, the Live set, the current device, and the control surfaces.

REFERENCES

The decision was made to limit the bibliography in this book to a list of only the most absolutely essential reference works, including the books and articles cited in the text. A more comprehensive bibliography is available online.

Bergson, H. 2001. *Time and Free Will: An Essay on the Immediate Data of Consciousness*. New York: Dover Publications.

Bianchini, R. and Cipriani, A. 2000, 2008[2]. *Virtual Sound*. (second edition). Roma: ConTempoNet.

Bianchini, R. and Cipriani, A. 2003. *Il Suono Virtuale*. (second edition). Roma: ConTempoNet

Boulanger, R. (ed.). 1999. *The Csound Book. Perspectives in Software Synthesis, Sound Design, Signal Processing and Programming*. Cambridge, MA: MIT Press.

Casati, R. and Dokic, J. 1994, *La Philosophie du Son*, Nîmes: Chambon

Chion, M. 1994, *Audio-Vision*. (ed.Claudia Gorbman). New York: Columbia University Press.

Cipriani A. 1995. "Towards an electroacoustic tradition?" *in Proceedings of the International Computer Music Conference*. Banff, Canada: International Computer Music Association, pp. 5-8.

Cipriani A. 1995. "Problems of methodology: the analysis of Kontakte" in Atti del X Colloquio di Informatica Musicale, pp. 41-44 Bologna: Associazione Italiana Musica Informatica AIMI.

Cipriani A., 1998 "*Kontakte* (Elektronische Musik) di K.Stockhausen: genesi, metodi, forma" in *Bollettino G.A.T.M.* anno V, n.1 Bologna: GATM, LIM.

Cipriani A. and Giri M. 2006. "Integrated System for Cross-Platform/Cross-Application Education on Sound Synthesis and Signal Processing" in *Proceedings of the International Computer Music Conference 2006*. New Orleans, LA: ICMA.

Cipriani A. "Editorial" in *Organised Sound* 13/2. Cambridge: Cambridge University Press, 2008.

Cipriani, A. and Giri, M. 2010, 2013[2]. *Electronic Music and Sound Design Vol. 1* (second edition). Roma: ConTempoNet

Cook, P. R. 1999. *Music, Cognition, and Computerized Sound*. Cambridge, MA: MIT Press.

Cowan, N. 2005. "On the capacity of attention: Its estimation and its role in working memory and cognitive aptitudes" *in Cognitive Psychology*, vol. 51, Issue 1, August 2005, pp. 42-100.

Dahlhaus, C. 1983. *Analysis and Value Judgment* New York, Pendragon Press.

Davies, H. 1996. "A History of Sampling" in *Organised Sound* 1(1): 3–11 Cambridge University Press.

Dodge, C. e Jerse, T.A. 2001. *Computer Music: Synthesis, Composition, and Performance*. 2nd Ed. New York, NY: Schirmer.

Dowling, W.J. and Harwood, D. 1986. *Music Cognition*. Orlando, Florida: Academic Press Inc.

Dutilleux, P. and Zolzer, U. 2002. "Delays" in *DAFX Digital Audio Effect*. New York: J.Wiley&Sons.

Ehreshman, D. and Wessel, D. 1978. *Perception of Timbral Analogies*. Paris: IRCAM.

Emmerson, S. 1986. "The Relation of Language to Materials" in Emmerson, S. (Ed.) *The Language of Electroacoustic Music*. London: Macmillan, pp.17-39.

Garcia-Valenzuela, P. 2006 *Temporal Forces in Electroacoustic Music*. Electroacoustic Music Studies Network Proceedings, Beijing.

Garcia-Valenzuela, P. 2009. *Aesthetic in Temporal Forces and Electroacoustic Composition*. Saabrücken, Germany: VDM Verlag

Giannattasio, F. 1992. *Il Concetto di Musica*. Roma: La Nuova Italia Scientifica.

Grabócz, M. 1997. "Survival or Renewal? Structural Imagination in Recent Electroacoustic and Computer Music," in *Organised sound*, 2. Cambridge: Cambridge University Press, pp.83-95.

Grey, J. 1975. *An exploration of Musical Timbre*. Doctoral dissertation. Stanford, CA: Stanford University.

Izhaki, R. 2012. *Mixing Audio*. Oxford, UK: Elsevier, Focal Press.

Jaffe, D. and Smith, J. 1983. "Extensions of the Karplus-Strong plucked string algorithm" *Computer Music Journal* 13(2). Cambridge, MA: MIT Press, pp.48-55.

Karplus, K. and Strong, A. 1983. "Digital Synthesis of Plucked-String and Drum Timbres", *Computer Music Journal*, 7(2). Cambridge, MA: MIT Press, pp.43-45.

Katz, B. 2003. *Mastering Audio*. Oxford, UK: Focal Press.

Keller, M. S. 2005. "La rappresentazione e l'affermazione dell'identità nelle musiche tradizionali e le musiche occidentali" in J. J. Nattiez (ed.) *Enciclopedia della musica, vol.8, L'unità della musica*. Torino: Einaudi, pp.1116-39.

Landone, C. 2006. "I supporti informatici per l'audio cinematografico" in *Atti del convegno Audio Engineering Society*. Roma: Università La Sapienza.

Landy, L. 2007. *Understanding the Art of Sound Organization*, London, MIT Press.

Lerdahl, F. 1987. "Timbral Hierarchies" in *Contemporary Music Review* (2) 1. London: Taylor and Francis, pp.135-160 .

Lomax, A. 1968. *Folksong, Style and Culture*. Washington: American Association for the Advancement of Sciences, p.15.

Mandler, G. 1984. *Mind and body: Psychology of emotion and stress*. New York: Norton.

Meyer, L. and Cooper, G. 1960. *The rhythmic structure of music*. Chicago: University of Chicago.

Postacchini, P.L. 1985. "La psicologia della musica per la terapia", in G. Stefani e F.Ferrari (a cura di), *La psicologia della musica in Europa e in Italia, Atti del primo Colloquio*. Bologna: CLUEB, pp.149-73.

Puckette, M., 1997. *Theory and Techniques of Electronic Music*. Singapore: World Scientific Publishing

Risset, J.C. 1986. "Pitch and rhythm paradoxes: Comments on 'Auditory paradox based on fractal waveform'", *The journal of the Acoustical Society of America*. 80(3), pp.961-962.

Roads, C. 1996. *Computer Music Tutorial*. Cambridge, MA: MIT Press.

Rocchesso, D. 2004. *Introduction to Sound Processing*. Firenze: Mondo Estremo.

Sciarrino, S. 1998. *Le Figure della Musica*. Milano: Ricordi.

Shepard, R. 1964. "Circularity in Judgements of Relative Pitch", *The journal of the Acoustical Society of America*. 36(12), pp.2346-2353.

Smalley, D. 1997. *Spectromorphology: Explaining Sound-Shapes* in Organised Sound, 2(2), pp.107-126, Cambridge University Press.

Smalley, D. 1986. "Spectro-morphology and Structuring Processes" in *The Language of Electroacoustic Music*. London: Macmillan, pp. 61-93.

Snyder, B. 2008. "Memory for Music" in *The Oxford Handbook of Music Psychology* Edited by Susan Hallam, Ian Cross, and Michael Thaut, Oxford University Press

Stockhausen, K. 1962. "The Concept of Unity in Electronic Music (Die Einheit der musikalischen Zeit)". Translated by Elaine Barkin. *Perspectives of New Music* 1, no. 1 (Autumn), pp. 39–48.

Stockhausen,K. 1963. "Wie die Zeit Vergeht" in *Zeugnisse*. Frankfurt: Europäische Verlagsanstalt

Truax, B. 1999. *Handbook for Acoustic Ecology* CD-ROM. Edition. Cambridge Street Publishing.

Uncini, A. 2006. *Audio Digitale*. Milano, McGraw-Hill.

Vaggione, H. 2001. "Some Ontological Remarks about Music Composition Processes" in *Computer Music Journal*, Volume 25, Number 1, Spring 2001, pp. 54-61.

Vaggione, H. 2002. "La composizione musicale e i mezzi informatici: problematiche di approccio" in *Musica e tecnologia domani. Convegno internazionale sulla musica elettroacustica*. Teatro alla Scala 20-21 novembre 1999 a cura di Roberto Favaro. Bologna: LIM.

Varèse, E. 1967. "New Instruments and New Music", in E. Schwartz and B. Childs (eds.) *Contemporary Composers on Contemporary Music*. New York: Norton.

Wessel, D. 1978. *Low Dimensional Control of Musical Timbre*, Paris: IRCAM.

Wishart, T. 1994. *Audible design*. York: Orpheus the Pantomime Ltd.

Xenakis, I. 1958/59. "Le trois paraboles", Stockholm: Nutida Musik, Sveriges Radio

Young, J. 2010. "Forming Form". In *En el límite: Escritos sobre arte, ciencia y tecnología*. Buenos Aires: Departamento de Humanidades y Artes, Universidad Nacional de Lanús

Young, J. 2002. "The Interaction of Sound Identities in Electroacoustic Music". *Proceedings of the 2002 International Computer Music Conference*. Göteborg/San Francisco: ICMA, pp. 342–348

MIDI 1.0 Detailed Specification (Document Version 4.2, rev. Sept. 1995) in www.midi.org/tecspecs/midispec.php

INDEX

v1: volume 1 - v2: volume 2

Lightning Source UK Ltd.
Milton Keynes UK
UKOW02f1158160314

228152UK00006B/103/P